The Archaeologist's Laboratory

The Analysis of Archaeological Data

INTERDISCIPLINARY CONTRIBUTIONS TO ARCHAEOLOGY

Series Editor: Michael A. Jochim, *University of California at Santa Barbara*
Founding Editor: Roy S. Dickens, Jr., *Late of University of North Carolina, Chapel Hill*

Current Volumes in This Series:

THE ARCHAEOLOGIST'S LABORATORY
The Analysis of Archaeological Data
E. B. Banning

AURIGNACIAN LITHIC ECONOMY
Ecological Perspectives from Southwestern France
Brooke S. Blades

CASE STUDIES IN ENVIRONMENTAL ARCHAEOLOGY
Edited by Elizabeth J. Reitz, Lee A. Newsom, and Sylvia J. Scudder

DARWINIAN ARCHAEOLOGIES
Edited by Herbert Donald Graham Maschner

EARLIEST ITALY
An Overview of the Italian Paleolithic and Mesolithic
Margherita Mussi

FAUNAL EXTINCTION IN AN ISLAND SOCIETY
Pygmy Hippopotamus Hunters of Cyprus
Alan H. Simmons and Associates

HUMANS AT THE END OF THE ICE AGE
The Archaeology of the Pleistocene–Holocene Transition
Edited by Lawrence Guy Straus, Berit Valentin Eriksen, Jon M. Erlandson,
and David R. Yesner

A HUNTER–GATHERER LANDSCAPE
Southwest Germany in the Late Paleolithic and Mesolithic
Michael A. Jochim

HUNTERS BETWEEN EAST AND WEST
The Paleolithic of Moravia
Jiří Svoboda, Vojen Ložek, and Emanuel Vlček

MISSISSIPPIAN POLITICAL ECONOMY
Jon Muller

PROJECTILE TECHNOLOGY
Edited by Heidi Knecht

STATISTICS FOR ARCHAEOLOGISTS
A Commonsense Approach
Robert D. Drennan

VILLAGERS OF THE MAROS
A Portrait of an Early Bronze Age Society
John M. O'Shea

A Chronological Listing of Volumes in this series appears at the back of this volume.

A Continuation Order Plan is available for this series. A continuation order will bring delivery of each new volume immediately upon publication. Volumes are billed only upon actual shipment. For further information please contact the publisher.

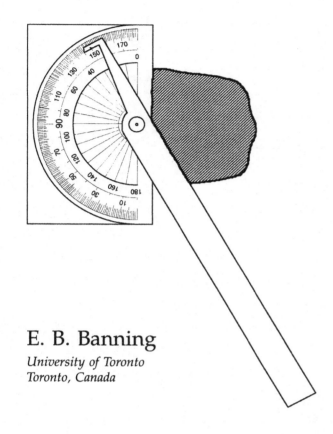

The Archaeologist's Laboratory

The Analysis of Archaeological Data

E. B. Banning

University of Toronto
Toronto, Canada

KLUWER ACADEMIC / PLENUM PUBLISHERS
New York, Boston, Dordrecht, London, Moscow

ISBN 0-306-46369-5

©2000 Kluwer Academic / Plenum Publishers, New York
233 Spring Street, New York, N.Y. 10013

http://www.wkap.nl

10 9 8 7 6 5 4 3

A C.I.P. record for this book is available from the Library of Congress.

Printed in the United States of America

For Cindy

Preface

The purpose of this book is to introduce students to basic laboratory and analytical techniques in archaeology. It is not a text on statistics or archaeometry, although it does contain some statistics and is applicable to archaeometric problems. Although it will familiarize students with a wide range of analytical techniques, the details of most of them are beyond its scope. Only methods that we could reasonably expect undergraduate students to carry out in class are considered in detail. Some more advanced methods are only mentioned for the sake of completeness or to familiarize students with terms they will encounter elsewhere.

I decided to write this book after years of trying to find a reference that students can use to learn how to analyse archaeological data. Some books cover excavation methods, others statistics, classification, faunal analysis, palaeoethnobotany, or archaeometry, while still others deal with spatial analysis or computer applications, but none with the common threads that tie all these things to a core of archaelogical practice. In addition, there is often a gulf between method and theory, when, in fact, no method is useful unless it is informed by theory. This is not an encyclopedic manual for any of these subjects, but an attempt to pull together the common threads of archaeological analytical concepts. Rather than provide a statistics text with archaeological examples, my purpose is to emphasize how archaeological data are formed and recorded, how they are classified or grouped together for analysis, and some relatively simple but important ways these data can be manipulated, compared, examined, or presented to extract information from them and to communicate it to an audience. Whether readers intend to specialize in stratigraphy, phytolith analysis, lithics, archaeozoology, or archaeological architecture, I hope that they can find something of value in this book.

This book is primarily intended for third- or fourth-year undergraduates who already have some background in archaeology, such as an introductory course in world prehistory or a course in field methods. Students will also find it helpful to have had at least a basic course in statistics, although any statistical concepts used here are briefly reviewed. Some good introductions to statistics for archaeologists include Drennan (1996), Fletcher and Lock (1991), Orton (1980), and Shennan (1988), each with its own emphases. Sections of this book that are a little more advanced may be considered optional, and will be identified as such in the first paragraph. It is not a manual to teach how to carry out statistical tests, which we would now do with computers rather than manually. Where I provide a practical example, however, I recommend that readers try to work their way through it, simply to have a better understanding of how or why something works. Although I have written the book with undergraduates in mind, graduate students may also find it useful as a reference, particularly the bibliographies and the introductions to measurement theory, use of graphs, database design, and sampling. For most of the remainder, such as lithics analysis and the like, graduate students will find it more useful to consult the more specialized literature cited here.

Since I wrote the first draft of this book, Sutton and Arkush (1998) published *Archaeological Laboratory Methods*. Their book introduces the analyses of materials such as lithics, pottery, animal bones, and plant remains, generally at a less advanced level than here, and includes some topics, such as glass, textiles, and historical artifacts, that are not specifically treated here. It may be appropriate for first- or second-year archaeological students who are not yet prepared to tackle some of the readings in this book. It is also more focussed on American archaeology and does not cover the more theoretical or quantitative topics.

A few words are in order about my own interests, influences and theoretical perspective, which, although I do try to present alternative views, clearly guide the direction of this book. My early archaeological training shaped me into some version of a "processual" archaeologist, with the view that archaeology could benefit from the methods of science. My early interest in archaeometry also contributed to this view. At the same time, my university training bridged the Anthropology and Near Eastern Studies departments at University of Toronto, and I was also influenced by classicists and historians. Consequently, I had a greater appreciation than many processual archaeologists at the time for the methodology of history, and I knew that history was not the unsophisticated chronicling of events that some processual archaeologists suggested it was. Historians had also long been aware that our interpretation of the past was colored by our own experiences and culture, as well as those of texts' authors, a view that did not have wide currency in anthropological archaeology until the 1980s. This background made me receptive to aspects of the "post-processual" program. I still felt that plausible archaeological analysis and interpretation should have some scientific rigor, in the sense that arguments should be logical and consistent both internally and with our observations, but I found that post-processual relativism was not diametrically opposed to science (cf. VanPool and VanPool 1999). Indeed, philosophers of science, even a century ago, were aware that scientific observations were affected by the preconceptions — the theoretical baggage — of the scientist. Furthermore, even the most vocal post-processualists make use of measurements and data — see, for example, Shanks and Tilley's (1987) analysis of attributes of beer cans — and are particularly concerned with *meaning* in data. I agree with Orton (1988) that measurement and quantitative methods

are not unique to processual archaeology. I emphasize the point that we as archaeologists *create* the measures, categories, and concepts that we use to observe, organize, and interpret the evidence of the past. That does not mean that these creations are not valid or that one set of concepts is as good as any other. What it does mean is that the concepts appropriate for one program of research may not be as useful for another, and that we should think very carefully about the concepts we use when we are designing our research, rather than simply copying the categories and measures of someone else's research uncritically. Another point I make throughout is that it is very easy to mislead others, and ourselves, about the significance of our results if we do not take into account that the observations we make are prone to various kinds of errors and are usually on imperfect samples rather than on the whole in which we are interested. Finally, I stress that the set of concepts we use makes an integrated whole, so that it does not make sense to segregate archaeological theory into zooarchaeological theory, lithics theory, and so on. All analysis in archaeology, even though there are some unique problems, shares a large number of basic theoretical and methodological concerns.

My writing has had other major influences as well. My way of viewing probability, inferential statistics, and research design has been influenced by Bayesian analysis, and particularly the work of Buck, Cavanagh, and Litton (1996). Their work and that of others who have applied Bayesian analysis to archaeological problems especially influenced chapters 4 and 15. Although most of the statistics presented here are not particularly Bayesian, I consider it essential that students are at least aware of this important approach. My views on systematics are most heavily influenced by the work of Dunnell (1971; 1986), as is fairly obvious in chapter 3, but I have found that I agree with many views of Adams and Adams (1991), even though our use of terminology differs and I, like Dunnell, make the distinction between classification and grouping. Another major influence on my views on archaeological data and analysis is Clive Orton, and especially his papers on quantification cited in chapter 5.

Although I have aimed at a reasonable balance of views in the book, it is clear that these influences have had a strong effect on the outcome, and that I feel strongly about some issues, such as measurement error and the futility of complete "objectivity" in analysis. While I do not expect all archaeologists to agree with my own use of terminology or presentation of concepts, I believe it is important for all archaeologists to be clear what they mean by the terms and concepts they use. While I agree with Adams and Adams (1991) that archaeological practice often does not consciously adhere to some theoretical program, that there has been a large gap between practice and theory, and that much everyday work is largely intuitive, I still believe that it is useful to be able to recognize the types of concepts and tools that archaeologists are using, whether intuitively or consciously. Some parts of this book are an attempt to make students and others aware of the conceptual structure that lies behind everyday archaeological laboratory practice.

The Organization of the Book

The various aspects of archaeological research are so interrelated that it is difficult to discuss one without reference to the others. Consequently, some topics, such as sampling, are delayed until after the reader has covered some basic concepts in the definition and recording of data, and some of the more challenging aspects of data compilations are left for the end of chapter 3. Although the book is designed as a course text, with chapters often building on concepts presented in previous ones, readers and instructors may want to reorder the chapters to suit themselves or use only parts of chapters. For example, some instructors may want to cover databases (chapter 3) with lithics (chapter 8), quantification (chapter 5) in the context of osteology (chapter 10), or systematics (chapter 3) along with pottery (chapter 9). I consciously decided not to omit more difficult material, partly to avoid "talking down" to students and partly so that it would be available for future reference. Instuctors may suggest that students skip the equations or more difficult passages if they might prove an impediment.

In addition to general theoretical and methodological issues, the text provides basic introductions to some common kinds of archaeological analyses by focussing on lithics, pottery, animal bones, and plant remains, as well as other laboratory skills, such as illustration and conservation. I make no claim to be an expert in any of these specializations, although as an archaeologist who runs a lab in Toronto and a field project in Jordan I must deal with them at some level on a regular basis. It is important to remember that these chapters are not exhaustive treatments, but only introductions to what is, after all, a vast literature on these subjects. To keep the volume from getting unwieldy, I also had to make the painful decision to omit some topics, such as human remains, spatial analysis, and microrefuse.

In general, the chapters begin with concepts, terms, and a selection of basic measurements commonly found in some kinds of current research, followed by brief discussion of several kinds of laboratory research involving those materials, such as stylistic analysis of lithics or inferring seasonality from faunal remains. These are not intended to instruct students how to do stylistic analysis or measure growth increments on shell, for example, but only to familiarize them with the range of research in that field and some of the measurement and analytical problems they entail.

Throughout the book, words shown in bold refer to significant concepts and terms. My own definitions for these, which may differ from others' definitions, appear in the glossary and usually also when they are first mentioned in the text.

My web site provides sample laboratory exercises that include suggestions as to how an instructor may implement them. They are based on my own experiences of teaching laboratory methods to third- and fourth-year undergraduates at University of Toronto over a period of seven years, and are intended to illustrate specific concepts in the book, such as the effect of sample size on standard error, as well as to expose students to different kinds of archaeological materials. I fully expect that instructors who choose to use the book as a text would want to modify the exercises (and I have sometimes suggested directions such modifications might take), to add others and to make omissions and substitutions. Some instructors, I know, already have long-standing courses in laboratory methods and their own time-tested sets of exercises. The manual is a guide that will, I hope, help those instructors who need some ideas about how to turn some of the book's concepts into a hands-on experience for students. Its URL is: http://www.chass.utoronto.ca/~banning/manual

This book has benefitted from the comments of many colleagues and students in its several iterations over the last five or six years. Many thanks to the anonymous reviewers as well as James Barrett, Roelph Beukens, Mark Blackham, Bill Cavanagh, Michael Chazan, James Conolly, Max Friesen, Andrew Garrard, Alicia Hawkins, David Lasby, Bob Laxton, Susan Maltby, Louise Martin, Steve Monckton, Clive Orton, Larry Pavlish, Rula Shafiq, Cindy Shobbrook, Julian Siggers, Joe Stewart, Karen Wright, and several classes of students for corrections and helpful suggestions on various parts of this book. Barb Leskovec and Jacqueline Stagen helped with the index. Of course I take responsibility for the remaining errors. Thanks also to Eliot Werner for his interest in the project.

> E. B. Banning
>
> Toronto, Canada

References Cited

Adams, W. Y., and E. W. Adams, 1991, *Archaeological Typology and Practical Reality, A Dialectical Approach to Artifact Classification and Sorting*. Cambridge University Press, Cambridge.

Buck, C. E., Cavanagh, W. G., and Litton, C. D., 1996, *Bayesian Approach to Interpreting Archaeological Data*. John Wiley & Sons, New York.

Drennan, R. D., 1996, *Statistics for Archaeologists. A Commonsense Approach*. Plenum Press, New York.

Dunnell, R. C., 1971, *Systematics in Prehistory*. New York: Free Press.

— 1986, Methodological issues in Americanist artifact classification. *Advances in Archaeological Method and Theory* 9:149-207.

Fletcher, M., and Lock, G. R., 1991, *Digging Numbers: Elementary Statistics for Archaeologists*. Oxford: Oxford University Committee for Archaeology.

Orton, C., 1980, *Mathematics in Archaeology*. Cambridge University Press, Cambridge.

— 1988, Review of *Quantitative Research in Archaeology* (ed. M. S. Aldenderfer 1987). *Antiquity* 62:597-98.

Shanks, M., and Tilley, C., 1987, *Re-Constructing Archaeology: Theory and Practice*. Cambridge University Press, Cambridge.

Shennan, S., 1988, *Quantifying Archaeology*. Edinburgh University Press, Edinburgh.

Sutton, M. Q., and Arkush, B. S., 1998, *Archaeological Laboratory Methods: An Introduction*. Kendall/Hunt, Dubuque, IO.

Thomas, D. H., 1986, *Refiguring Anthropology: First Principles of Probability and Statistics*. Waveland Press, Prospect Heights, IL.

VanPool, C. S., and VanPool, T. L., 1999, The scientific nature of postprocessualism. *American Antiquity* 64:33-53.

Credits

Thanks are due to the following for permission to reproduce illustrations or quotations.

Academic Press, J. Dean, M. A. Hardin, and J. Stein for figures 9.28, 12.5, 15. 2; *Antiquity* and J. S. Holladay for figures 16.9, 16.10, 16.11, 16.12; Mark Blackham for figure 14.5; Don R. Brothwell for figure 10.7; Butterworth Heinemann for figures 12.8 and 12.9; Cambridge University Press for figures 2.15, 9.29, 12.1, 12.12; Carnegie Institution for figure 9.27; Harper-Collins Publishers for the quotation from *Zen and the Art of Motorcycle Maintenance* by Robert Pirsig, pp. 274-5; IsoTrace Laboratories and Roelph Beukens for figure 15.6; David Newlands, Claus Breede and McGraw-Hill for figures 9.1, 16.7, 16.8, 16.15 (right), 16.16, 16.17, 16.18; Oxford University Press for figure 9.5; F. A. Lone, M. Khan and G. M. Buth, Srinagar, Kashmir, India, for figure 11.14; Reed-Elsevier for figures 9.13 and 9.14; The Royal Ontario Museum for figures 9.12, 16.15 (left), 16.19; Robert Smith and College of Wooster for figure 3.12; The Smithsonian Institution for figure 9.20; Taraxacum and Owen Rye for figures 9.8, 9.9, 9.10, 9.11, 9.15, 9.16, 9.17, 9.18, 9.19, 9.21, 9.26; and John Wiley & Sons for figures 13.1, 15.8, and 15.9. Figures 16.4, 16.5, 16.6 are from L. Addington's *Lithic Illustration* in the Prehistoric Archeology and Ecology Series, edited by K. Butzer and L. Freeman, used by permisssion of University of Chicago Press (© 1986 by The University of Chicago).

Table of Contents

1 Introduction

Many books introduce and develop the concepts and methods archaeologists use in their fieldwork, and especially in excavation. The subject matter of this book, by contrast, is the set of activities, concepts and intellectual products that follow these excavations and archaeological surveys, with emphasis on the concepts and methods archaeologists use to describe and analyse their observations. It is important to point out that fieldwork and analysis are inextricably linked — we return to this point in discussion of research design in chapter 4 — but the former tends to receive much more attention than the latter. Here I attempt to redress some of this imbalance.

I begin with an overview of what archaeologists actually do. Jean-Claude Gardin (1980) distinguishes between several very broad categories of archaeological activities or intellectual processes. These processes are linked to form a chain from the basic acquisition of data, through constructions of propositions or theories, to publication, and the chain folds back on itself to link up with data acquisition again. This happens because our collection of data is never random or "objective"; it is always directed by our theories, past experience, and preconceptions. Many North American, and especially processual, archaeologists have likened this chain or cycle to the hypothetico-deductive form of reasoning — we will return to this point in chapters 4 and 6 — but similar phenomena occur in **post-processual** or interpretive archaeologies, and especially those that make reference to **hermeneutics**. Gardin's three basic processes in this chain are data acquisition, analysis (from archaeological remains to publication), and observation strategies. Each of these processes he subdivides to consider the details of how archaeologists work.

Analysis and observation strategies are the focus of most of this book. Observation strategies have to do with how we conceive of and perceive phenomena, and how we select the phenomena, or "data," to observe. Chapters 2, 4, and 6 deal with aspects of observation strategies. Gardin (1980) suggests that archaeological analysis includes such basic activities as cataloguing and describing archaeological evidence, such as artifacts. But usually archaeologists are not content with mere inventories or catalogues, and one of the activities that makes important demands on their time involves ordering the evidence into some kind of structure: groups, classifications, and typologies. We tend to think of these structures as applying to portable artifacts, but they are just as applicable to sites, chronologies, phytoliths, economic systems, or "cultures." The methods that we use to create such structures, or systematics, form an important part of this book (chapter 3). Systematics are a prerequisite for more interesting kinds of analysis, and Gardin (1980) describes these as "pattern recognition" and "historical inference." Groups, categories, classes, or types of phenomena form the building-blocks of our analyses. Then we can begin to compare them, to look for interesting interrelationships or contrasts between types or variables, unusual groupings in space or time, or other patterns. The patterns, in turn, allow us either to make inferences or to test hypotheses about changes in human behavior over time, about similarities and differences between groups of people in the past, about the factors that influence human behaviors, or about ways our predecessors have contributed to modern people's ways of life. What Gardin (1980) calls "historical inference" is, in essence, explanation of events, changes, functions, and differences in past human cultures.

Coombs (1964:5) describes analysis as the detection of relations, order, and structure in data. For example, we might detect a relationship between settlement pattern and food-production strategy or between resource scarcity and intensity of lithic reduction.

Processes should have products, and Gardin (1980) classifies the products of archaeological processes as either "compilations" or "explanations." The former involves simply collecting and presenting data. The latter involves work meant to draw out information about technology, symbols, social organization, and other aspects of culture that are not inherent in the "raw" data or the artifacts themselves.

Compilations

Compilations are arguably the most visible result of archaeological work. Gardin (1980: 28) defines a compilation as a systematized set of interrelated propositions that describe material remains to facilitate the study of ancient people. Compilations are often symbolic constructions, with a system or language of representation: computer coding, technical drawings, maps, and digitized representations, for example, are all symbolic representations, and simplifications, of reality. To make compilations useful, we usually resort to something other than natural language to describe and organize the data, an "Information Language." This simply supplies the symbols used to describe such elements as artifacts and attributes, and the rules used to describe their interrelationships. We will discuss information languages in more detail in chapter 3. Information language requires a systematic way of describing or measuring elements and their associations. We will deal with these aspects in the first part of chapter 2.

One of the advantages of information language is that it allows us to manage huge volumes of data with computers. We will discuss the design of archaeological databases in chapter 3 and outline some of the basic processes involved in electronically manipulating data.

One kind of information language that most archaeologists do not typically recognize as a language at all is graphic. The technical draw-ings and maps that archaeologists use to publish archaeological results or illustrate compilations are rarely realistic depictions of artifacts or sites. In fact, they are coded representations designed to convey particular kinds of information to other archaeologists, while omitting details that might obscure the point that an archaeological author is trying to make. We will deal briefly with the language of archaeological technical drawings in chapter 2, and return to it in chapter 16.

Commonly, archaeological materials make life difficult for archaeologists in that they are fragmentary or their quantity does not have an obvious meaning. Before we can create meaningful compilations of pottery or faunal remains, for example, we need to decide what unit or units of analysis we will use. Will we simply count potsherds or bone fragments, or try to estimate the number of pots or animals? Will we instead try to estimate how much food the pots contained or how much meat the animals provided? Are we interested in the absolute number of pots or animals, or only in the proportion of pots or animals in a particular category? These are questions that go beyond basic measurement theory to problems of quantification that are sometimes unique to archaeology. We will deal with these problems in chapter 5.

Some kinds of compilations, especially when cost constrains publication, summarize data rather than describing each element (artifact, site, etc.) in detail. In chapter 2 we will deal in some detail with graphic methods for summarizing data, and briefly review descriptive statistics. The former, when used properly, allow us to visualize patterns in large quantitites of data — to see the forest rather than the trees — and in that sense can be highly effective tools of analysis. The latter allow us to reduce a whole table of observations to a few numerical summaries that can prove useful later on in our attempts to explain patterns in the data.

Explanations

According to Gardin (1980), an archaeological explanation is meant to reconstruct past events or ways of life through the properties of material evidence and any other information available.

Most archaeologists would consider Gardin's definition too narrow, and would consider archaeological explanations to include accounting for long-term processes of change and stability, such as evolution and adaptation, for similarities and differences between groups of people in the past, and the reasons for those people adopting the strategies they did for surviving, interacting with others, and satisfying their physical and psychological needs, among other goals. The important thing about explanatory constructions, as opposed to mere compilations, is that they go beyond the intrinsic properties of the artifacts, "ecofacts," and other items of evidence that archaeologists employ to reconstruct or find the causes of phenomena that are not directly observable. We can describe the chemical composition of an artifact and offer no explanation; the chemical data would form part of a compilation. By contrast, we can use that chemical composition in combination with other data to infer the source of the artifact's raw material, the place where the artifact was made, the technology used to make it, or interregional trade routes. These would all be explanatory constructions. Many of these explanations are ones a philosopher would describe as "ampliative." That is, the final proposition contains information that is not inherent in the initial premises (Salmon, 1982:33). We will return to this property of certain explanations when we discuss inference and deduction in chapter 6.

Explanation or understanding is the goal of analysis. Much of the book consequently deals with approaches to pattern recognition, hypothesis testing, and analysis that allow us to construct and evaluate explanations. Some, but not all, of these are statistical methods. As Gardin suggests, these methods involve the interplay between data that are intrinsic to the artifacts and sites in our compilations and "extrinsic" data (context) that typically concern space, time, function, and what we might call social and psychological contexts. The classes of extrinsic information that particular archaeologists choose as their focus depend on their theoretical perspectives: materialist, idealist, functionalist, structuralist, evolutionary, engendered, Marxist, and so on. I will try in what follows to draw examples of explanations from at least a few of these perspectives.

Analytical Strategies

In many sciences, research designs are based on experiment. The experiment may attempt to hold several factors constant, and vary one, to see what, if any, effect that factor may have on some variable of interest. Most archaeological analyis cannot proceed in this fashion because we cannot control or manipulate things that happened in the past. Only in experimental archaeology, which typically involves attempting to replicate or simulate some past process, such as flint-knapping or use wear on tool edges, can we impose and vary experimental controls. For example, if we hope to discover the factors that cause variations in the microscopic polish and scratches on tool edges during use, we may make a number of chert flakes from identical material and with closely similar edges, and use them to incise or carve identical wood material, holding as best we can all factors constant except motion of use. Once we appear to have isolated the variations in edge wear that are associated with motion of use, we may hold this constant also, but vary the contact material, substituting bone, hide, and other things for wood, thus determining the effect of contact material on the use wear.

Most archaeological analysis, however, consists of the examination and explication of phenomena that resulted from "experiments" over which we had no control, and which took place centuries ago. Archaeologists are not alone in having to deal with this problem. Epidemiologists, for example, often must try to discover the causes of a disease or determine the effectiveness of a medical treatment by analysing case histories in a "retrospective" manner (Streiner and Norman, 1996). Clearly it would be unethical for these researchers to design experiments that intentionally exposed some individuals to a potentially dangerous pathogen, or that withheld a life-saving drug from some individuals, just to serve as experimental controls. Instead they may simply have to search for patterns in the relationship between prevalence of a disease and various factors to which people both with and without the disease were exposed in the past, or between mortality rate and use of competing treatments.

As a substitute for controlling key factors, retrospective analysis, including archaeology, may involve selecting a sample from a population thought to be fairly homogeneous in many respects, but varying in at least one respect that we think may be an important influence on some variable of interest. For example, McGhee (1977) hypothesizes that Thule people in the Canadian arctic associated ivory and the sea with women and winter, but antler and the land with men and summer. He sees this as a set of ideological constructs in Thule culture. We cannot take a Thule site and vary its seasonality from summer to winter and back again, or tweak the proportion of women among its inhabitants up or down to see how seasonality or gender might affect the relative abundance of antler or ivory artifacts. However, we can divide the population of Thule sites into two groups, inland sites and coastal sites, and then see how the evidence for seasonality and the ratio of antler to ivory may vary between these two groups.

Unfortunately, there may be other factors correlated with seasonality or location that may confound any association we might see. For example, maybe the activities that Thule people carried out inland or in summer were functionally very different from those they carried out at coastal winter sites, and required tools made from different materials, or perhaps some materials were simply more easily available inland than at coastal locations. For McGhee's hypothesis to succeed, he has to demonstrate that these competing, functional hypotheses do not account for the patterns he recognizes in his analysis of the data. As it happens, they do not, so his preferred hypothesis remains more plausible. Comparing competing hypotheses with respect to their ability to account for the variations we see is an important aspect of analysis.

Much archaeological research depends on the analysis of comparisons of different types of sites, of sites in different types of location or occupied in different seasons, of assemblages involved in different kinds of economy or formed at different points in time. As discussed in chapter 3, such analysis depends on the meaningful grouping of sites or assemblages, or their classification into "types." We may then try to identify the variables that differ meaningfully among these types. By this we mean that there should be some plausible theory to account for the inter-type differences; without such a theory, it is possible that the differences are just coincidental or due to random variations.

Yet because archaeology has the advantage of being able to recognize changes that occurred over very long periods of time, much archaeological analysis focusses instead on relationships between variables over time. Again, we usually cannot design an experiment that tracks changes over time in one variable as we increase or decrease another. Instead, we retrospectively search for relationships between the variables across sets of well-dated assemblages. Consequently, archaeological analysis typically devotes considerable attention to chronology. Unlike a physicist or epidemiologist, we cannot just use a clock or calendar to track these relationships, so we have to use less certain tools to date our observations. Chapters 13, 14 and 15 deal with the use of some of these dating instruments and interpretation of their results.

As with the comparisons of assemblages or types, we should also have a theory to account for any relationships we see. Even though our inability to come up with a convincing theory does not rule out the possibility that someone may find one eventually, we must keep in mind that, if we search any body of data long enough, we can always find relationships, some of which make no sense at all. For example, there is a correlation between changes in the diameter of the stems of smoking pipes in the United States (Heighton and Deagan, 1971) and the price of wheat in Münich (Kellenbenz et al., 1977:218) over the period from 1688 to 1775 (correlation coefficient, $r = 0.85$, figure 1.1). Surely there is no causal relationship between these two variables, and we would describe it as a "spurious correlation." Nor should we expect a causal relationship between the pipestem figures and the percentage of silver in Japanese *chogin* coins (JCDA, 1975) of the same date, even though the correlation coefficient is -0.75.

Making meaningful comparisons or identifying change over time also requires valid scales of measurement and some way to account for errors in the measures, in the instruments used to make measurements, and in our selection of things to compare. These are topics that the following chapter will consider in some detail.

References Cited

Coombs, C. H., 1964, *A Theory of Data*. John Wiley, New York.

Gardin, J.-C, 1980, *Archaeological Constructs. An Aspect of Theoretical Archaeology.* Cambridge University Press, Cambridge.

Gibbon, G., 1984, *Anthropological Archaeology*, Columbia University Press, New York.

Heighton, R. F., and Deagan, K. A., 1971, A new formula for dating kaolin pipestems. *The Conference on Historic Site Arogy Papers* 6:220-229.

JCDA, 1975, *Coin Types and Modern Paper Money of Japan, Korea, and Manchukuo, and old Asian Gold and Silver Coin Types.* Japanese Coin Dealers' Association, Tokyo.

Kellenbenz, H., Schawacht, J., Schneider, J., and Peters, L., 1977, Germany. In *An Introduction to the Sources of European Economic History*, edited by C. Wilson and G. Parker, pp. 190-222. Cornell University Press, Ithaca, New York.

McGhee, R., 1977, Ivory for the sea woman: The symbolic attributes of a prehistoric technology. *Canadian Journal of Archaeology* 1: 141-149.

Streiner, D. L., and Norman, G. R., 1996. *PDQ Epidemiology*, second edition. Mosby, St. Louis.

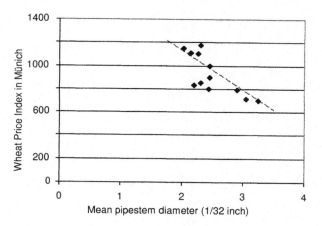

Figure 1.1. A spurious correlation between mean pipestem diameter and the price of wheat in Münich from 1688 to 1775 (data from Heighton and Deagan, 1971; Kellenbenz et al., 1977:218). Although there appears to be a relationship between these two measurements, it is simply coincidental (wheat prices happened to rise while pipestem diameters declined).

2 What Are Data?
Archaeological Measurements

This chapter will consider what constitutes archaeological data and how they are measured and presented. Here we will use "measurement" in a very broad sense of the term, including any kind of observation that an archaeologist can make. The description of color, for example, is a measurement and archaeologists often use a standardized scale to measure it. Measurement theory provides a way of describing things and making them comparable to one another. Later parts of the chapter will deal with summarizing and displaying data.

From the initial collection of data through their analysis and publication, there is always a *selection* of data from a theoretically infinite number of possible observations (Coombs, 1964). Although some archaeologists try to argue that you can collect "objectively," as in all sciences, we only see something if we are prepared to see it.

The novel, *Zen and the Art of Motorcycle Maintenance* makes this point quite well:

According to the doctrine of 'objectivity,' .... We should keep our mind a blank tablet which nature fills for us, and then reason disinterestedly from the facts we observe.

But when we stop and think about it disinterestedly, ... Where *are* those facts? What are we going to observe disinterestedly? ... The right facts, the ones we really need, are not only passive, they are damned *elusive*, and we're not going to just sit back and "observe" them. We're going to have to be in there *looking* for them… (Pirsig, 1974:274-75).

Data are not objects, such as projectile points or potsherds (cf. Sullivan, 1978:189; Thomas, 1976:7). They are observations and **measurements** you make on these objects and on their contexts. In some sense, we do not even merely select facts from an infinite sea of data, but *construct* them by deciding how we will "see" them, and how we will categorize them. Data are theory-laden.

Data in archaeology can include the name or category of an artifact (e.g., "Clovis point"), the density of potsherds on the surface of a site (10 sherds per square meter), the average distance between a site and its nearest contemporary neighbouring site, the invasiveness of retouch on a stone tool, the order of design motifs on a pot, or the date of a wooden artifact in years B.C. It can include the spatial provenience of a flake on XYZ coordinates or the stratigraphic context of a sherd (layer 6 in square 4). It can also include practical or methodological information, such as the mesh size of screens used in excavation, the volume of earth excavated, the number of person-hours per hectare of fields surveyed by walking crews (survey intensity), or evidence of such processes as erosion and deposition on a site. All these measures are ones dicatated by the questions archaeologists are trying to answer, such as, "what is the age of this site?" "who were the people who lived here?" or "what is the social meaning of this design?"

But how do we decide whether or not to measure these things? Some people argue that our perceptive abilities, our interests, our social, economic, and cultural backgrounds, and our unique historical contexts so pervade our choice of questions, and our ways of obtaining answers, that no two archaeologists will ever form the same interpretations of archaeological phenomena. Instead, each archaeologist's interpretation simply makes a target for other archaeologists to reevaluate and perhaps reject. Over time we may come closer to ones that many people, but not all, find broadly acceptable, but the reevaluation process will also encourage the search for new kinds of data that no one considered before. In some cases this will lead to radically new kinds of data and new ways to interpret them.

At the same time, even though we as individuals may not perceive the world in exactly the same way, we as archaeologists operate within a community of archaeologists who can agree about some things at some times. Whether Lewis Binford tells me that a particular pipe stem has a diameter of 3 mm, or Ian Hodder tells me that a particular bone was found in the ditch of a Bronze Age hillfort, I am inclined to accept such information with a rather high level of confidence, or low uncertainty, and with a small margin for error. There are other kinds of reported observations that I am inclined to accept as perfectly reasonable observations, but with somewhat more uncertainty. There are still others I am sure I would have seen differently. I do not have to assume that I would have perceived the evidence in exactly the same way as Dr. Binford or Dr. Hodder to accept them as plausible measurements. This chapter and chapter 4 present some ways we can evaluate these plausibilities.

Some authors suggest an opposition between a "scientific" archaeology that gives primacy to facts and measurements, which are supposed to be neutral or objective (e.g., Shanks, 1992: 26), and other archaeologies in which we suppose facts and measurements to have little or no

place. This is a false dichotomy. Even in "hard" sciences, such as physics, data are theory-laden and the kinds of data collected are influenced by the kinds of instruments available. And even in **post-processual** or "interpretive" archaeology, data provide the basis for interpretations, for discerning meaning in "facts" ranging from the order and orientation of incised chevron bands on pottery (Shanks and Tilley, 1987: 160) to the spatial organization of houses and settlements (Hodder, 1990).

Having decided what kinds of "facts" we want, *how* do we measure them? At what level of detail do we stop measuring? We are always sampling and deciding what kinds of data to collect or ignore. We have to make a conscious decision what kinds of data are important for our purposes or those purposes we can reasonably expect our colleagues and successors to have. Whether or not your research strategy specifically outlines the search for particular kinds of data, it is important to stress that all data are "filtered" through the investigator's senses and instruments. We have to "measure" data with our eyes, measuring tapes, calipers, transits, Munsell soil charts, artifact typologies and other instruments.

Measurement consists of *comparison*. You make an observation by comparing an archaeological object or feature with a scale — whether measuring tape, Munsell chart or some classification or typology. Measurement is a process whereby we assign an abstract symbol — a number, colour, name, icon — to represent the object or the value or magnitude of one of its attributes, or qualities. And we can make this assignment by reference to one of several different kinds of scales of measurement.

SCALES OF MEASUREMENT

Measurement scales can be characterized in a number of ways. A common distinction is between *qualitative* scales, with which we can assign observations to categories, and *quantitative* ones, which represent magnitudes. One scale of scales that is quite useful employs four main categories. These are the nominal, ordinal, interval and ratio scales of measurement.

A **nominal scale** consists simply of categories, such as kinds of pottery decoration, that are unordered and of equal weight. The simplest kind of nominal scale is the **dichotomous scale**, with only two categories, such as male and female, or present and absent. Nominal scales are important in archaeology because archaeologists make so much use of classification and typology (see chapter 3), which employ nominal scales. It is possible to count observations in each category of a nominal scale, but it is inappropriate to apply most mathematical operations to such a scale. Consequently the kinds of statistical methods that we can apply to nominal data are limited.

One of the most common types of analysis is to count how many objects we assign to each class in a nominal scale. This is a process called **enumeration**. For example, for a particular archaeological feature, such as a pit, we might count how many sherds are decorated and how many plain, or how many charred seeds are attributable to maize, chenopods, fleshy fruit, and so on. Enumeration is the first step for several other kinds of measures, and particularly for measuring proportions or percentages.

An **ordinal scale** consists of categories that are ordered. Ordinal scales allow you to make the deduction, for example, that if class A is greater than class B and class B is greater than class C, then class A is greater than class C. Archaeologists frequently use ordinal scales to characterize artifacts or sites by their sizes (large, medium and small), for example, but the most common use of ordinal scales in archaeology is in chronology. Archaeological time periods, such as "Archaic," "Middle Woodland," "Neolithic," or "Early Bronze Age," are all categories on ordinal scales. Stratigraphic units also belong to ordinal scales, and archaeological seriation is a method used to create ranked ordinal scales. A rank scale is a special case of an ordinal scale in which each class contains only one member (except in the case of exact ties), and each observation normally has its own class, as opposed to other ordinal scales that have a small number of classes, each containing many observations. An example of the former would be a ranking of all sites in a region from smallest to largest, while

an example of the latter would be characterization of all the sites as small, medium or large, or as camps, hamlets, villages and towns.

Some people would consider both nominal and ordinal scales to be, simply, "qualitative" scales of measurement because, even if we assign numbers to represent each class, these numbers are only labels and it is not appropriate to apply most arithmetic functions to them. For example, on a ranked scale, we could say that the site ranked 6 was larger than the one ranked 5, but it would be incorrect to conclude that the site ranked 6 was twice as large as the site ranked 3. Furthermore, it would be wrong to conclude that the difference in size between the sites ranked 6 and 5 was the same as that between sites ranked 3 and 2. Ordinal scales contain no information about the magnitude of such differences in ways that we would normally express in units (e.g., meters, hectares, or degrees). Another characteristic of these scales is that, if they have been constructed properly, no observation could possibly belong to two categories of the same scale simultaneously. This property of being unambiguous is necessary. It would create problems if an artifact were red and black simultaneously, or an artifact belonged to both layer 5 and layer 6. As we will see in chapter 3, which deals with the construction of nominal scales ("classification"), there are unambiguous ways to deal with artifacts that are black over one part of their surface and red over another.

The **interval** and **ratio** scales are ones that many would describe as "quantitative." While interval scales, like ordinal ones, contain an inherent order, there are also consistent intervals between points on the scale. That is to say, it is possible to infer that the distance between 3 and 5 is identical to the distance between 6 and 8 or 7 and 9. This makes the operations of addition and subtraction possible, but is insufficient to allow multiplication or division. Ratio scales contain all the characteristics of the interval scale but, in addition, have zero points that are non-arbitrary and represent an absolute *absence* of some quantity. The Celsius scale of temperature is an interval scale because it is possible to say that the difference between 0° and 10° is the same as that between 30° and 40° but, because the zero is arbitrary (the freezing point of water) and does not represent an absence of temperature, it makes no sense to say that 40° is twice as hot as 20°. Consequently it is not a ratio scale. The length of a flint blade, by contrast, can be measured on a ratio scale, and we could appropriately say that, within measurement errors, one blade was twice as long as another, so it is appropriate to apply multiplication and division to this kind of measurement.

Measurement Errors and Uncertainty

Nominal and ordinal scales are always discontinuous, or **discrete**, scales because there are theoretically no "grey areas" between categories where you may make observations (as we will see in chapter 3, this can be a problem for typology). Interval and ratio scales, by contrast, frequently are **continuous**. This means that between any two numbers on the scale you can always find other numbers. In fact, you can find an infinity of them. The practical consequence of this property is that you can never have absolute accuracy on a continuous scale. Even if you measure the length of a projectile point to the nearest 0.00001 mm, you have to accept that the "true" length of the projectile point lies somewhere within 0.00001 mm of your measurement, but is not exactly *equal* to your measurement. It is possible, however, to have discrete measures on the interval and ratio scales as well. Integers make a discrete ratio scale that is appropriate for counting objects and other situations where a fractional observation would not make sense. A flint flake might show scars from one, two, or three previous flake removals, for example, but it will never have 2.3 or 1.6 scars because rake is a discrete event (see chapter 8).

Because our senses and instruments are never perfect, measurements always have errors. Furthermore, as we have seen, even a "perfect" instrument could never have absolute accuracy on a continuous scale, because it is always theoretically possible to "magnify" the observation and record it more precisely. Since some degree of error is inevitable, it is important to know the magnitude of error in the measurements. Consequently, in reporting our research, we should always do our best to estimate the size of these errors and report them to our colleagues. If we

do not, we make it extremely difficult for others to evaluate the precision and accuracy of our observations or to compare observations. If the measure of the proportion of deer bones at one site is different from that at another, for example, it is impossible for us to tell if the difference is meaningful — are the bone assemblages really different? — unless those reporting on the faunal remains from the sites provide estimates of error in those proportions. Estimating measurement error is not particularly mysterious, and is a basic aspect of scholarly reporting.

A simple way to visualize the problem of measurement errors on continuous scales is to consider the smallest interval you used to distinguish your observations. If you have measured a projectile point with a 12-inch ruler that has no intervals smaller than a quarter-inch, for example, are you justified in reporting that the point is 6-1/16 inches long? Probably only 6 inches ± 1/4 inches is reasonable in this case. Now assume that you had a metric ruler and measured the point to the nearest millimeter. Here you might arrive at 152 mm ± 1 mm. Now if you measured five more projectile points with electronic calipers accurate within 0.01 mm, and wanted to pool your data with the earlier 152 mm one and take an average, would it be reasonable to report a resulting mean of 71.24 mm ± 0.01? Since, in principle, your 152 mm measurement could represent a "true" length anywhere from slightly over 151 mm to slightly less than 153 mm, it would not. It would be best to remeasure the first artifact with the more precise calipers before calculating the mean if you consider precision to 0.01 mm to be important. Alternatively, round the mean off to 71 mm. We will return to the issue of rounding off measurements shortly.

In many of the scales that archaeologists use it is not as simple to conceptualize error. As we will see in chapter 3, assessing measurement error in discrete measurements is a little less obvious, dealing as it does with the problem of **misclassification**. But when the measurement is of something less tangible than artifact length or mass, perhaps of social inequality, of motivation, or of the distribution of gender roles, it is perhaps easier to think of *uncertainty*. In these cases, rather than talk about error in terms of some hypothetical difference between our measurement and a "true" value, we may simply talk about how confident we are in our measurement and interpretations based on it. Although uncertainty in this sense seems rather subjective, it can still be quite useful (see chapter 4).

Accuracy, Precision, and Reliability

It is important to recognize the difference between Accuracy and Precision.

Accuracy concerns the degree of **bias** in measurement — i.e., systematically recording observations that are higher or lower on an ordinal or interval scale than they should be, or systematically classifying objects in the wrong category of a nominal one. If, for example, you measured some stone tools with calipers that were improperly made, or had been filed down, or measured the size of a feature with a tape that had been stretched, you would not get accurate measurements. Consequently, you might consistently underestimate lengths, and the extent of this underestimate would be the bias. Similarly, tending to make the error of classifying Type A pots as Type B, but rarely or never the reverse, would also result in bias.

Precision concerns the range of results you get if you repeat the measurement several times — the "spread" in a set of repeated measurements. If a measurement is precise, you would expect to get a very closely similar measurement if you or someone else re-measured it. A precise measurement, however, will not necessarily be accurate.

Reliability, meanwhile, is the extent to which a measurement gives the same result in different situations, such as when made by different researchers. It is the proportion of the total variability in the measurement that is due to the actual variability in what we are measuring. The remainder is variability due to such things as inter-observer differences.

For example, when the Black Mesa project (Plog, 1986:42-48; Plog et al., 1978:414) had five crews independently measure site size and ceramic density during an archaeological survey in northeastern Arizona, the crews disagreed substantially in their measurements (table 2.1). Presumably these measurements hovered

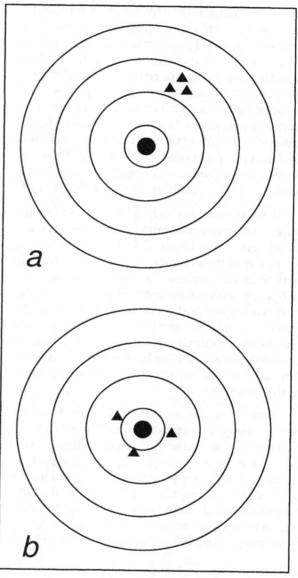

Figure 2.1. The three triangles in **a** indicate three arrows shot precisely, but not very accurately, while the three in **b** are fairly accurate, but less precise.

Table 2.1. Variability between crews in estimates of site size and artifact density on Black Mesa, Arizona (after Plog et al., 1978:414)

Crew Number	Mean Site Size (m²)	Mean Ceramics per m²	Percentage Site Areas < 100 m²
1	803	1.2	29.1
2	507	1.7	44.2
3	838	1.6	48.1
4	464	0.9	42.9
Mean	653 ± 195	1.4 ± 0.4	41.1 ± 8.3

around the actual site sizes and densities, and so the average of the measurements would probably be reasonably accurate estimates, but the substantial variation in measurement (here measured by the **standard deviation** after the ±) indicates that they were not very precise or reliable. Below we will consider why this may have happened, but in general it is important to remember that observations on continuous scales are always approximations. Ideally, these are reasonably accurate and precise, as well as appropriate to the questions we are asking (valid).

A useful analogy to help you remember the difference between accuracy and precision is a an archery target (figure 2.1). If you shoot three arrows, and they cluster very tightly, your aim is precise but, unless the arrows hit near the bull's eye, not very accurate. If your shots result in three arrows scattered in the vicinity of the bull's eye, but not very close together, they are reasonably accurate, but not very precise. Of course the ideal is to be both precise and accurate, with all three arrows hitting in or very close to the bull's eye.

When there are several sources of error, they can be **compensating** or **cumulative** errors. If you want to measure the area of a site by overlaying a map with graph paper and counting squares, for example, you can count squares that appear more than half within the site boundaries and exclude ones that appear half out. In this case your errors tend to cancel out, or compensate, and the results are fairly accurate,

but not necessarily precise. You can also count only those squares that are completely within the site boundaries. In this case you may get a very precise measurement, but you would underestimate the site size, because the errors would be cumulative, or non-compensating. A common source of this kind of bias occurrs when people doing archaeological survey crudely measure site size by multiplying length times width, which is fine so long as the site is rectangular, but substantially overestimates the size of elliptical and irregularly shaped sites. Again, the errors are non-compensating, leading to substantial bias in the estimate of site size.

If we have been careful and used appropriate measurements, the errors are reasonably small and the observations are accurate enough for our purposes. Sometimes we are forced to use other people's data with unrecorded but possibly large errors, and a useful skill is to be able to assess the reliability of these data.

Significant Digits

This brings us to the issue of significant digits. Many students of archaeology abdicate responsibility for the number of digits to their electronic calculators. Just because your calculator displays a result to 6 decimal places, however, does not mean that it is appropriate to display your results that way.

The problem with such statements as, "the mean blade length is 71.327496 mm" is that it

Table 2.2. Examples of measurements and their significant digits

Measurement	Scientific Notation	Significant Digits
26.01 cm	2.601×10^1	4
26010 g	2.601×10^4	4
0.0026 kg	2.6×10^{-3}	2
14 artifacts/m^2	1.4×10^1	2
14.00 cm	1.400×10^1	4
140.0 mm	1.400×10^2	4
101 $^{\circ}$C	1.01×10^2	3
100 dn	1×10^2	1

implies a level of precision that is dishonest. In essence, reporting 71.327496 mm constitutes the claim that the "true" mean length has a large probability of being between 71.327495 and 71.327497. In fact the actual standard error on this mean (see below, p. 21) is probably many times larger than ± 0.000001. It also implies that you actually measured artifacts to this level of precision, which seems highly unlikely. If your actual measurements were all made only to the nearest 0.5 mm, then do not report your measurements, or statistical summaries based on them, in such a way as to imply greater precision than that. Simply put, never end up with more significant digits than you started with.

But significant digits are not equivalent to the number of decimal places either. Decimal places are too dependent on the units used to make your measurement. For example, 2.1 km is a measure with two significant digits, meaning essentially that the distance we are trying to represent is somewhere between 2.0 and 2.2 km, but probably close to 2.1. The measure, 5.6 mm also has two significant digits. Both 2.1 km and 5.6 mm are distances measured to one decimal place and two significant digits, but they have substantially different units. If we convert 2.1 km into mm, the resulting measure, 2,100,000 mm, now has no decimal places but it still has two significant digits. The zeroes following the digit, 1, are only there to tell you where the decimal place would go, or the "order of magnitude" of the measurement. Similarly, we could represent 5.6 mm in km. But 0.0000056 km, although it has seven decimal places, still has only two significant digits. Essentially the measure tells you that the actual distance is somewhere between 0.0000055 km and 0.0000057 km. If you find this confusing, or are unsure how to decide how many significant digits a measurement has, convert it into scientific notation. This is the notation that uses powers of 10 to indicate the order of magnitude of the measure. In scientific notation, 2.1 km is 2.1×10^3 m, while 5.6 mm is 5.6×10^{-3} m. Meanwhile, 5.60×10^{-3} m has three significant digits, because the trailing zero is not marking the position of the decimal place, but telling us that the "true" measure is somewhere between 5.59×10^{-3} m and 5.61×10^{-3} m. Scientific notation makes it easy to see how many signifi-

cant digits there are because everything in front of the multiplication sign is significant. Table 2.1 provides examples that may help to clarify this.

One way to define significant digits is that they consist of *all the certain digits plus the first uncertain one.*

Other Sources of Error

We should not assume that the measuring device, such as a ruler, tape, or caliper, is the only source of error in their measurement and that, consequently, it is appropriate to cite measurements to the smallest increment on that device. This leads to a false sense of accuracy and precision. Suppose, for example, that you are involved in an archaeological survey, like the one that Plog and his colleagues carried out on Black Mesa, and two of your measures are the length and width of each site you encounter. Suppose that you have really well crafted steel tapes and that you can control for the effects of temperature on the steel, so that you can measure even long distances within 1 cm. Would it be appropriate or useful to claim that a site was 93.16 m in length? Here the degree of precision lies, not in the tape, but in our ability to determine consistently where the edge of the site lies. Most archaeological sites have very indistinct edges, such as a gradual diminishment in the density of scattered artifacts, and no two archaeologists are likely to agree on the exact location of a site's boundary or on the orientation of its long axis. Another archaeologist making the same measurement with the same tape might arrive at 106.05 m, or 88.70 m, depending on his or her interpretation of where that boundary lies and what constitutes the long axis, just as the Black Mesa survey teams arrived at different results. Even though the measuring device, the tape, is very precise, there are other factors that would not lead us to expect very precise results.

In cases like this, it is important to ask yourself how much measurement precision is warranted. Will it really alter our intepretation of the site if our measurement of its size is out by 3%, by 5%, or by 10%? Will our ultimate use of the data involve lumping sites into ordinal categories? In most cases, we will find that rounding off such field measurements to only a couple of significant digits is more honest than implying high degrees of precision and accuracy that are in fact quite meaningless.

You should also be aware that combining measurements that have errors, as when you multiply a length by a width, actually adds a little more error. We will return to this adjustment in the section on descriptive statistics.

Outliers

Sometimes in a set of data we encounter one or a few measurements that are very surprising, so different from the rest of the data that we find it hard to believe that they could be correct. Sometimes it is fairly obvious that they result from human error, such as an error in copying data from a recording sheet into a computer record, or failure to read calipers correctly. When we can plausibly interpret the **outliers** in this way, we may simply omit them from the data set, or remeasure something to check on the surprising readings.

In other cases, however, it is not so obvious that the outlier has simply resulted from human error. As we will see below and in chapters 4 and 6, even in well-behaved data we can expect extreme values to occur from time to time, in which case the surprising values are not really outliers at all. In other cases, the outliers may be the result of **contamination**: they are measurements or observations pertaining to something that does not really belong in the group (or population) we are analysing (Barnett and Lewis, 1994). In archaeology this is quite common. For example, we might be trying to date a particular layer in a Middle Woodland site in Ohio, perhaps by radiocarbon dates on pieces of charcoal (see chapter 15). Perhaps most of the dates that result are fairly close to 1600 B.P., but one date, surprisingly, is 2700 ± 70 B.P. Statistically it is highly improbable that a piece of charcoal from wood that was cut around 1600 B.P. would produce such a date, and the more likely scenario is that the outlier belongs to charcoal that was **residual** in the sediment (see chapter 12). That is, the charcoal had already been on the site for a long time, perhaps the remnant of some ancient forest fire, when Middle Woodland people began to occupy the site and cut some trees for fuel or building material. Of course contamination is usually only noticeable when it shows surprising values, as in this example. If a residual piece of charcoal yielded a radiocarbon date fairly close to the other dates, it would usually be accepted quite happily, because we would have no way of knowing that it did not belong in the data set. Fortunately, in that case, it at least does not seriously affect our interpretations.

Direct and Indirect Measurement

Not only do we need to consider the scale, precision and accuracy of archaeological measures, we need to consider what they really mean. Are we measuring what we are interested in measuring?

Direct measurement involves straightforward measurements such as length, where we can directly compare an object of interest with a standard scale. For example, we can measure the length of a projectile point by reference to a ruler or calipers. A quantity can be measured directly only if it can be measured without measuring some other quantity (Kyburg 1984: 90-112).

Indirect measurement involves measuring one phenomenon as a way of deriving a measure of some other concept. It is an extremely common type of measurement in some fields, such as social anthropology, but crops up frequently in archaeology as well. Even measurements of speed and temperature are indirect, being based on measurements of distance and time in the former and the length of a column of mercury in the latter case (Kyburg, 1984:100, 113-42).

The simplest and most straightforward indirect measures are ratios. For example, we generally do not measure sherd or lithic density on a site directly, instead you usually count the sherds (**enumeration**), and also measure the area where we collected the sherds (usually by measuring directly the lengths and widths of a rectangle or the radius of a circle). We then divide the number sherds by area and create a new measure, "sherds per square meter."

Often ratios make no reference to any units, because they cancel out during division. So the ratio of the frequencies of lithic blades to flakes (e.g., 1:1.4) or the proportion of Deverel-Rimbury pottery in a ceramic assemblage (e.g., 0.29 or 29%) is a unitless indirect measure ("percent" is not a unit, but simply shows that you have multiplied a proportion by 100).

Systematic inaccuracies (biases) in direct measures are compounded by arithmetic operations such as division and multiplication, so that the accuracy and precision in your original measurements are doubly important when you convert them into ratios.

In addition to ratios, there are conceptually indirect measures, which are sometimes called proxy or surrogate measures. The following measurements, all to be found in archaeological literature, are impossible for prehistorians to measure directly, and so they instead measure a proxy that they think might be associated with the phenomenon of interest:

- Number of people who inhabited an Anasazi pueblo

- Wealth of a Bronze Age household

- Social status of the occupant of a grave or tomb

- Degree of interaction between neighbouring settlements

- Volume of traffic in an obsidian exchange system

- Amount of deer meat in a prehistoric diet

- Variation in the magnitude of prehistoric rainfalls

- Conservatism in pottery decoration

To measure prehistoric population sizes, for example, archaeologists have proposed many different indirect measures based on such direct and indirect measures as site area, roofed floor area, number of hearths, number of burials per unit of time, length of longhouse, and even average volume of cooking pots multiplied by number of hearths (Hassan, 1984). Each of these measures is supposed to have some predictable relationship with the site's population size. For example, you would have to account for average life expectancy, whether all or only some people were buried, and the duration of a site's occupation to base population on the number of burials in a cemetery. Alternatively, you might multiply house area by a mean floor area per person in an ethnographic sample. We would expect all these measures to have relatively large, but quite different, sources of error.

Even if we could measure site size very precisely and accurately, for example, estimates of population based on site size would have errors introduced by the following:

- There may be a large degree of variation in the ethnographic examples used as a basis of the estimate

- There may be errors in the selection of ethnographic examples. You may have inappropriate analogues for prehistoric settlement or a biased sample of them

- Possibly not all of the site was occupied simultaneously, leading you to overestimate the ancient population size

- Possibly not all of site was used for domestic settlement. There may have been special industrial areas, gardens, etc., so that you overestimate population size

- Possibly the site we have measured is simply not very typical. It is an **outlier** that does not obey whatever equation we have for calculating population size

- The correlation between site size and the number of people occupying sites is not very strong, or other factors, such as the length of time people anticipate they will occupy the site ("anticipated mobility") may be more strongly correlated (Kent, 1991:39).

In some archaeological jargon, measuring things we cannot observe directly is met with "operational definitions" that simply use easily measurable or observable criteria. For example, some archaeologists who have adopted "decision theory" or "optimal foraging theory" to help them understand the behavior of prehistoric hunter-gatherers, being unable to measure the total "cost" or "benefit" of acquired game, instead estimate the amount of energy used to capture it or contained in its meat. Finding it equally difficult to measure "taste," they instead measure the amount of fat in the meat. The operational definitions are proxies, different from, but related to, the thing that interests us. Energy is not all there is to the cost and benefits of game, and fat content is only one aspect of taste, but we expect these to be reasonable substitutes.

The extent to which an indirect or proxy measurement is a good approximation of the measurement of interest is its **validity**. We have "face validity" if we simply have widespread agreement among researchers that a measure is valid, not a very strong indication of validity. "Content validity" occurs if the measure appears to contain all the important concepts and behaviors we would expect to find in the phenomenon of interest. This is rather difficult to assess, so content validity is also a somewhat weak measure of validity. "Criterion validity," by contrast, involves comparison of the measure with a standard or testing its ability to predict. For example, we can test a measure of population based on roofed floor area by applying it to ethnographic cases where we already know the number of inhabitants.

Even in cases where the indirect measure may be appropriate or "valid," you should not forget to consider errors intrinsic to it. For example, many people like to use Narroll's (1962) constant of 10 m^2 of roofed floor area per person to estimate the number of people that occupied a house or a settlement. But the relationship between roofed floor area and number of people, even in Narroll's original data, is not very "tight" — the points are scattered widely around the **regression** line — so that the 10 m^2 constant allows us to estimate population size only with a large margin of error (see figure 2.12). Archaeologists who have adopted Narroll's formula or similar ones do not always cite errors for the population estimates that result, although this should be routine.

Uncertainty in estimating the wealth or status of a prehistoric family, or the proportion of its subsistence produced by women's labor, would be even greater. As indirect measures of wealth or status, for example, we might look at the number or quality of grave goods, the size

and cost of houses, or osteological evidence for nutrition, none of which, by itself, is a completely valid measure of wealth or status. It is not difficult to find in modern cultures many cases of wealthy people having simple burials, the occupants of mansions falling on hard times, or people whose nutrition and general health in no way reflect their wealth or status. Furthermore, some archaeologists argue that material culture, and particularly burial practice, can often be used as a social strategy to contradict or deny social reality. For example, a very egalitarian ethic in burial practices could be meant to obscure or deny in death extreme wealth differences that existed in life. In spite of such difficulties, however, we make the most we can of indirect measures, combining different ones where possible, because they often help us to understand some of the most interesting aspects of past cultures.

Lest I seem to put indirect measurement in a bad light, it is worth mentioning that there are many examples where indirect measurement is even to be preferred to direct measurement. Quite often we can measure more easily or more precisely with indirect measurement. For example, even though we can measure area directly, perhaps by tiling the area with unit rectangles or triangles and counting them, for many geometric shapes, and especially rectangles, we find it more convenient instead to measure length and width. Even length is measured indirectly when we want to be very precise: we measure temperature to calibrate a steel tape or we measure the time it takes for a laser beam to reflect off a target. Theoretically, we could measure temperature directly, but we can do so much more precisely indirectly, by measuring the length of a mercury column (Kyburg, 1984:141).

Possibly you are wondering why I stress these basic measurement concepts. First, you should never begin research without clearly thinking about how you will measure the variables that are important to your research goals. Later, if you do statistical tests (see chapter 6) and cannot reject the hypothesis that patterns in the data are due only to measurement error, you have a serious problem. Second, too many people do not think about what different researchers' measures really mean when they pool data for regional synthesis or comparative analysis. They may be "comparing apples with oranges." For example, perhaps project A measured site population size by multiplying the number of pueblo rooms they found by a constant, project B measured site population by multiplying the number of hearths by a constant, and project C measured it by multiplying site area and a constant. If a researcher uses data from all three projects to infer population change over time or differences in population density between regions, it is possible — in fact quite likely — that any differences this researcher sees are simply due to variations in the measurement methods, and not in actual population sizes. Third, too few archaeological publications describe measurement methods in detail or provide estimates of measurement errors. This makes it virtually impossible for us to evaluate the reliability or validity of the results or to tell whether differences in the measurements are statistically or intellectually significant.

A final aspect of data collection that archaeologists need to consider is, how many and what kinds of measurements (data) are relevant to their research problems. This is a matter of research design, and we will return to it in chapter 4.

Descriptive Statistics

Inevitably, archaeologists want to summarize their data, if only because the number of individual artifacts or observations is far too large to show them all in a publication, or even too large for us to recognize any patterns in the data. There are several major ways we can produce such summaries, some of which will be the subject of subsequent chapters. Broadly speaking, we can summarize data verbally, numerically, or graphically.

Verbal summaries are common in archaeological reports and once constituted the bulk of archaeological reporting. In a verbal summary, an archaeologist simply describes "typical" data, such as the most common kinds of pottery in a site, as well as noteworthy anomalies that give the reader some impression of variation in the data. Sometimes verbal summaries can be richer, and usually they are more interesting, than nu-

merical summaries, and they have the advantage that they can convey some of the researcher's thought processes and goals (Hodder, 1989), but they are not amenable to accurate comparison of data sets and it is virtually impossible to apply statistical tests to them. They have an important place in archaeology, but should not be the exclusive means of archaeological reporting.

Numeric summaries of interval or ratio-scale data are what archaeologists usually mean by **descriptive statistics**. These are measures intended to sum up, in only one or two numbers, the "typical" or "central" characteristics of the data, or the amount of "spread" in the data. They include such common numerical summaries as the **mean** or "average," as well as other measures of central tendency, and measures of spread in the data, such as the **range**. We often summarize nominal-scale data with measures of relative abundance such as percentages, but we are more limited in how we can show central tendency or "spread" in nominal data. Although descriptive statistics may seem somewhat tedious, it is necessary to review them here.

Measures of central tendency, indicate the position along a scale about which the data tend to be centred. Measures of dispersion, meanwhile, refer to the amount of variation, or spread, around this location.

The most common measure of central tendency in interval and ratio scales is the average, or **arithmetic mean**. We use this statistic in all kinds of everyday applications, such as when we refer to mean annual rainfall in mm, average income in dollars, or average fuel consumption in miles per gallon. The mean is easy to calculate, as we only have to sum the values of all our observations and then divide by the total number of observations. For a **population** (the totality from which we may have taken a sample), the statistical expression for this simple process is,

$$\mu = \frac{\Sigma X_i}{N}$$

where μ is the population mean (average), ΣX_i is the sum (Σ) of all the data (X_i) values in the population and N is the number of observations or measurements in the population. For samples that we can expect to have characteristics similar to the population (see chapter 4), a good estimate of μ is the sample mean, x̄:

$$\bar{x} = \frac{\Sigma x_i}{n}$$

where Σx_i is the sum of all the data values in the sample, and n is the number of observations in the sample.

The mean turns out to be something like a "centre of gravity" for the distribution. Consequently, the values to either side of it "cancel out" or sum to zero when expressed as differences from the mean. For example, if our data consist of the nine numbers 25, 32, 45, 22, 28, 38, 5, 12 and 18, their mean is 25. The deviations from the mean turn out to be:

$$25 - 25 = 0$$
$$32 - 25 = 7$$
$$45 - 25 = 20$$
$$22 - 25 = -3$$
$$28 - 25 = 3$$
$$38 - 25 = 13$$
$$5 - 25 = -20$$
$$12 - 25 = -13$$
$$18 - 25 = -7, \qquad \Sigma = 0$$

When our data are not measured at the interval or ratio scales, or when the data are distributed very unevenly, we need to use a different measure of central tendency. The simplest alternative is the **mode**, which is simply the value of the highest peak in a frequency distribution. For data measured at the nominal or ordinal scale, the mode is the most common category, or the category with the greatest number of observations. The **median**, on the other hand, is the value that divides the total number of observations so that half of the observations are greater, and half are less than the median. On a frequency distribution, then, the median is the point on the x-axis that has equal numbers of observations to its left and right. The median is only applicable to ordinal, interval and ratio scales because you cannot have higher or lower values on a nominal scale. When you have an even number of observations, the median is the average of the central two values; when you have an odd number of observations, it is equal to the middle value.

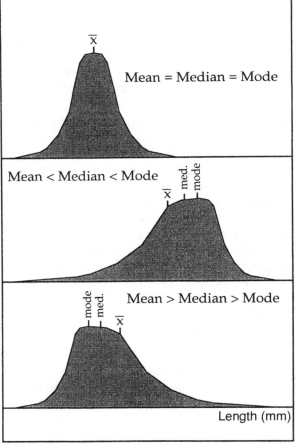

Figure 2.2. The effect of symmetry and skew on measures of central tendency.

Even when you have interval or ratio measurements, the mean is not always the best measure of central tendency, because it is much affected by extreme values and by the symmetry of the distribution of observations. In a perfectly symmetrical distribution peaked in the middle (figure 2.2), the mean, median and mode are all equal. This happens in the **normal distribution** or "bell curve," to which we will return in chapter 6. If, instead, the distribution has some extreme values toward the right, that is, it is skewed to the right or positively skewed, the mean will be greater, sometimes much greater, than the median, which will itself be greater than the mode. If it is negatively skewed, with extreme values to the left, the mean will be less than the median, which in turn is less than the mode. In these cases, since the values in the skewed "tail" of the distribution pull the mean away from the main part of the distribution, the mean no longer

Central Tendency for Grouped Data

Sometimes when we want to measure central tendency, we have to use someone else's data that have been published only in graphic or tabular summaries. We can still calculate a mean (or mean centre, in the case of choropleth maps) quite easily. We take advantage of the fact that we know the frequency of observations that fall within each interval, that the sum of all these observations is equal to n, and that within each interval the average of all the observations should be close to the midpoint of that interval. For the simple histogram in figure 2.3, for example, where x_i = the value of the midpoint of a bar, and f_i = the frequency (height) of each bar:

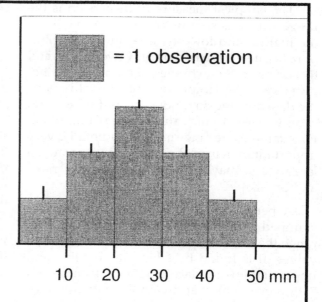

$$\bar{x} = \frac{\Sigma x_i f_i}{\Sigma f_i} = \frac{5+(2*15)+(3*25)+(2*35)+45}{1+2+3+2+1} = \frac{225}{9} = 25$$

Figure 2.3. A histogram showing lengths to be used (ticks on top of bars) in calculating a mean from grouped data.

gives us a very good idea of where most of the data tend to be clumped. Social scientists will typically use median income, rather than mean income, as a measure of central tendency in income distributions because only a few cases of enormous incomes can pull the mean far to the right. In extremely irregular distributions, the mode may be more useful than either mean or median, while some distributions may be bimodal or even multi-modal, requiring us to record more than one mode.

So far we have looked at measures of central tendency in one dimension, but it is also possible to measure central tendency in two or more dimensions simultaneously. In the case of two dimensions, the mean, for example, will be at the coordinates $(\bar{x}, \bar{y})$, where $\bar{x}$ is the mean along the x-axis and $\bar{y}$ the mean along the y-axis. When we find these coordinates on a map, the measure of spatial central tendency that results is called the mean centre. It is even more analagous to a centre of gravity, as it is the location on a map where all the distances away from it sum to zero when divided into positive and negative halves,

or the point where a map would balance when all the data points on it have equal weight. The areal median is difficult to define, and can only be approximated with a tedious process of trial and error. The areal mode, meanwhile, is quite easy to determine. Once a map has been divided up into units similar to the bar widths on a histogram (but in two dimensions instead of one), as happens whenever we put a grid on a map, we can make a "stepped statistical surface," the height or colour of each quadrat corresponding, perhaps, to the number of sites or artifacts found in that quadrat (see figure 2.15). The areal mode is the grid quadrat with the highest frequency.

Measuring Dispersion

If we are going to represent a large body of data with a single statistical summary, such as the mean, then we are going to have a rather poor idea of how the data are distributed unless we also include some measure of how they are spread out. This is where measures of dispersion come in.

The simplest measure of dispersion is the **range**, which is simply the difference between the highest and lowest values in the distribution. Because it is based on only two values, and these values are extremes, the range does not give a very good impression of how "clumped" the data are, and so is not very useful except in cases where extreme values are very important. For example, the range in annual rainfall is very important in marginal environments because a large range may make agriculture very risky and unreliable.

A better measure of where the data are clumped is the **interquartile range**. This is the range that includes the middle 50% of the data values. It is found by taking the median and upper and lower quartiles (25th percentile and 75th percentile), that divide the data into four equal numbers of observations (lower 25%, next 25%, next 25% and upper 25%).

One measure of spread in data that may seem obvious would be an average deviation from the mean. But because all the deviations from the mean sum to zero, this doesn't work. We could take the absolute values of all the deviations from the mean (simply removing the minus-signs) to solve this problem, but the result is a measure that turns out to have poor statistical usefulness.

A better way to get rid of the minus-signs is to square the deviations from the mean and sum them. This results in a useful measure of dispersion called **variance**. Algebraically, we usually represent variance as σ^2 (for populations) or s^2 (for samples), and indicate that it is the sum of the squared differences from the mean divided by number of observations or sample size:

$$\sigma^2 = \frac{\Sigma(\mu - X_i)^2}{N} \text{ and } s^2 = \frac{\Sigma(\bar{x} - x_i)^2}{n-1}$$

Note that for samples we divide by n-1 instead of n.

However, the units of variance are not the same as those of the mean. For example, if the mean is measured in meters, the variance would be in square meters. Fortunately, it is easy to compensate for this simply by using the square root of variance. We call the measure of dispersion that results the **standard deviation**, represented as either σ or s (for samples):

$$\sigma = \sqrt{\sigma^2} = \sqrt{\frac{\Sigma(\mu - X_i)^2}{N}} \text{ and}$$

$$s = \sqrt{s^2} = \sqrt{\frac{\Sigma(\bar{x} - x_i)^2}{n-1}}$$

You may find it useful to think of it as something like an average deviation, with the minus signs removed by squaring, but the standard deviation retains the useful statistical properties of the variance (see chapter 6).

For interval data that we would summarize with a mean, the standard deviation is an extremely useful measure of dispersion. In many applications, however, we will use instead a similar measure that is essentially a standard deviation that takes sample size into account. This measure is known as the **standard error**, and, as we will see later, is extremely important when we want to make predictions on the basis of samples.

The standard error of the mean is simply the ratio of the standard deviation to the square root of the sample size (n). Consequently we can represent it algebraically as

$$SE = \frac{\sigma}{\sqrt{n}}$$

but in samples, since we can only estimate σ, we must estimate SE as,

$$SE = \frac{s}{\sqrt{n}}$$

Finally, it is important to mention that when, as often happens in archaeology, we are interested in densities, such as the number of lithics per square meter, or the number of radiocarbon decays per five minutes, the standard deviation is rather different. We will return to this point in discussion of the Poisson distribution in chapter 6 and radiocarbon dates in chapter 15. For now I will simply mention that in these cases the standard deviation is simply the square root of the mean. To remind you of this difference, I will refer to the mean of counts per unit area or unit time as λ, instead of μ, and to its standard deviation as $\sqrt{\lambda}$.

Accumulating Errors

Now that we have seen some basic measures of dispersion, we can return briefly to the problem of carrying out arithmetic operations on measurements that have errors. We should expect the error on the result of adding, subtracting or multiplying two measurements to be a little larger than the errors on the original measurements, because there is a chance that the two errors will be cumulative. An estimate of the total error on the sum of two measurements is the square root of the sum the squares of the individual errors. For example, for the operation, 10.0 + 5.0 mm, if both measurements had estimated errors of ± 0.5 mm, we would estimate the error of the sum as $\sqrt{(0.5^2 + 0.5^2)} = \sqrt{(0.25 + 0.25)} = 0.7$. Consequently, we should report the sum as 15.0 ± 0.7 mm. For multiplication and ratios, we sum the squares of the relative or proportional errors before taking the square root. For an artifact density, for example, we might count 100 ± 10 artifacts in an area of 20 ± 1 m^2. That makes relative errors of 10% and 5%, respectively. The density, then, would be 100/20 or 5.0 artifacts/m^2, with a relative error of $\sqrt{(0.1)^2 + (0.05)^2} = \sqrt{0.01 + 0.0025} \cong 0.112$. Consequently we could report the density as 5.0 ± 0.6 artifacts/m^2. Estimating cumulative errors for more than two measurements simultaneously is somewhat more complicated.

GRAPHIC SUMMARIES OF DATA

Graphics *reveal* data. Indeed graphics can be more precise and revealing than conventional statistical computations (Tufte, 1983:13, italics in original).

Graphics allow us to display data visually. If used effectively, graphs can help us to communicate complex information easily, in ways that the viewer can interpret accurately. If used inappropriately, however, graphs can also be confusing or downright misleading. There are many kinds of graphs that have archaeological applications and it is important to select the right graph for the kind of data you have and the point you are trying to make. Many of the computer graphing packages typically designed for business applications make it very easy to generate inappropriate and sometimes very misleading graphs. Remember that sales and marketing people have very different goals than archaeologists, and communicating accurately is not necessarily one of them!

Among the criteria that you should use to help you select the correct kind of graph are the following:

- What scale or scales of measurement have you used in your data?

- Are the data continuous or discrete?

- How many dimensions (scales) must you show on a single graph? Most graphs are only appropriate for showing one or two dimensions.

- Who will use the graph? Is it for publication of your final results, or to help you plan your own research strategy for analysis of the data?

- How will viewers want to use the graph? Will they want to be able to extract detailed information from it, perhaps to use in a statistical test, or just compare it with another graph? Will they need to know what proportion of the data lies within a particular range of values, or just get an impression of how the data are distributed?

Tables

Sometimes all you really need to display some data is a simple table. When you are only showing a few values for a small number of attributes, a table can be a very effective way to make a point. The rows and columns in the table should be labelled in such a way that viewers can interpret it easily, and you can always put the values to which you would like to draw particular attention in bold type, or perhaps in color.

One thing you should *not* do, unless you want to lose your viewers, is to present a huge table with a sea of numbers that no one can interpret without considerable time and effort. Large data tables have their place, principally in storing large quantities of information (see chapter 3), but they are not very useful for disseminating complex information clearly and quickly. In these cases it is advisable to substitute a graph of one of the types described below. Alternatively you could make several small tables with excerpts or summaries of the data that emphasize the points you want to make.

Box-and-Dot Plots and Stem-and-Leaf Plots

For comparing batches of data quickly and without losing detail in the data, a box-and-dot plot or stem-and-leaf plot can be very useful. Both are often used as tools in "exploratory analysis"(Tukey, 1977) because they can help you visualize your data in ways that might help you plan a research design.

Both kinds of plot are used for data along a single dimension, measured on an interval scale.

The stem-and-leaf plot is appropriate if you have a small body of interval data and you want a quick way to tally it manually, with pencil and paper, that does not lose any of the original measurements. The plot begins with a scale ranging from just below the lowest measurement to just above the highest one, consisting of a list of values at ten- or five-unit increments, and omitting the last significant digit (figure 2.4). You then build up the plot by recording the last significant digit of each measurement next to its appropriate interval. For example, in figure 2.4, there are two artifacts with recorded lengths of 127 mm, and those are each indicated by a "7" next to the upper "12" on the plot. There are also two artifacts measuring 128 mm, and those are represented by the two "8"s next to the upper "12." An artifact measuring 124 mm and another two measuring 122 mm are represented by the "4" and two "2"s next to the lower "12." Meanwhile, a large artifact with a recorded length of 207 mm is represented by a "7" next to the "20" at the top of the graph. The result is something like a tally or a histogram, but it preserves all of the original measurements.

A box-and-dot plot summarizes the data more completely, so that you lose the individual measured values but retain a fairly good impression of how the data are distributed (figure 2.5). Now we see only the position of the highest 25% of values, the lowest 25% of values, the upper quartile, median and lower quartile. The box encloses the middle 50% of values (i.e., it is bounded by the upper and lower quartiles), and the line segment subdividing the box marks the median. This kind of plot is useful both in exploratory analysis and for some kinds of archaeological presentations, such as when you want to compare the size distributions of houses from several sites (figure 2.5) and the number of houses from each is small or may not be normally distributed.

Bar Graphs

Archaeologists sometimes confuse bar graphs, intended for discrete (usually nominal) data, with histograms, which are intended for continuous data. Bar graphs can be effective graphic replacements for small tables of data because they visually present the numbers or proportions of observations, or both, in a number of categories. Most computer spreadsheets and statistics packages, as well as dedicated graphing software, will generate a bewildering array of bar graphs, often incorrectly labelled as histograms. You should avoid selecting bar graphs that are too complicated or with too many embellishments that will distract your viewers.

A bar graph shows you how observations are distributed across a number of categories or discrete intervals, so it is a kind of frequency distribution. The bars are separated from each other to signal that the observations are discrete, not continuous. The height of each bar is proportional to both the number and proportion of observations for the category or value that the bar is intended to represent. At least one scale, usually on the left side, allows users to measure the heights of bars to infer the number of observations represented. It is possible to use two scales, however. Where the viewer will find it useful, you may want to have a scale for number of observations on the left and proportion or percentage of observations on the right. Since this may make your graph somewhat "busy," use an extra scale only if it has a purpose.

The y-axis is usually a linear scale, but could be logarithmic, square-root, or something else. Make sure that the label on the scale and title make this clear if it is not a linear scale. Below we will discuss cases where "transforming" the data with a non-linear scale may be useful.

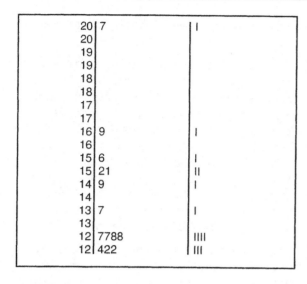

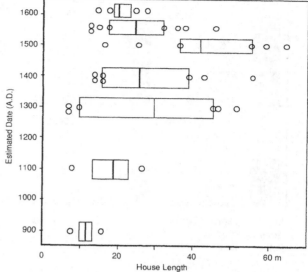

Figure 2.4. Comparison of a stem-and-leaf plot (left) with a simple tally (right). The former includes all the raw data that were measured, while the latter, like a histogram, only tells you how many observations fell within each interval.

Figure 2.5. Box-and-dot plots of house lengths at seven Iroquoian sites of varying ages (after Warrick, 1996: 18). Note how the chronological relationships of the box-and-dot plots are portrayed.

Sometimes it is tempting to put too many kinds of observations on a single bar graph. This usually only confuses the viewer and makes it difficult to compare data in meaningful ways. Each bar graph should really only show a single dimension. If you need to show several dimensions, it is usually better to draw several bar graphs to the same scale than to put bars with different colours or hatching on a single bar graph. Think carefully about what kinds of comparisons viewers will probably want to make and set up your graph or graphs to facilitate those comparisons (figure 2.6). Most viewers will want to compare bar heights, so put bars that are likely to be compared on the same horizontal axis, rather than offsetting them with a "3-D" look that is popular in business graphics packages. If you have several groups of data to compare in the same graphic, divide them into meaningful sub-graphs and arrange them in ways that facilitate comparison, rather than shuffling all the data into a single bar graph.

One of the more common archaeological variations on the bar graph is the "battleship plot" used in seriation (figure 2.7). This is really a series of bar graphs rotated 90° and reflected about the x-axis so that each bar is actually

shown twice. Arguably this reflection is visually appealing, but it is also redundant, and makes the graph take up nearly twice as much space on a page as is necessary. It could easily be omitted (figure 2.8). The rotation is a useful device, however, as it allows us to communicate visually that some categories are older (lower or deeper) than others.

Histograms

Histograms are an appropriate means for displaying the frequency distributions of continuous data in a single dimension on an interval or ratio scale. Although they look much like bar graphs, one of the important characteristics of histograms is that their bars are adjacent to one another to signal to the viewer that the data are continuous, rather than having separate bars (figure 2.9-2.10). Another extremely important characteristic is that the frequencies of observations are indicated by *area* on the graph, and not height of the bars. This is easy to overlook, which can lead to substantial misinterpretation of data.

In a histogram, the horizontal x-axis is a continuous interval or ratio scale, and if you were to construct one manually, rather than with a com-

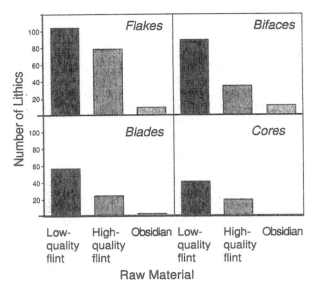

Figure 2.6. Four separate bar graphs are used here to compare the distributions of items measured on nominal scales.

puter, you would have to group your data much as you would to create a bar graph. Because the data are continuous, however, you have to make an arbitrary decision of what interval to use to group your data. The procedure is as follows.

■ Select an interval. Generally you will want an interval that is narrow enough to give you an idea of variation in the data, but large enough to create peaks and valleys. You may have to try several different intervals before you get one that presents your data effectively, but you might start with an interval that will give you 10 or 12 bars from the lowest to highest value among your observations.

■ Uniquely define the groups. For example, it does not help to say that your intervals will have values of 0-5, 5-10, 10-15, and so on, because some of your recorded observations may lie exactly on the boundaries (at the level of precision you used), creating ambiguity. Instead define your intervals in a way that will separate your data even at the greatest number of significant digits you recorded. For example, you might have intervals of 0-4.9, 5.0-9.9, 10.0-14.9, and so on.

■ Tally up the number of observations in each interval by simply counting them.

■ Draw the histogram so that the area of each bar is proportional to the number of observations in each interval. Of course the easiest way to do this is to measure the heights and keep the widths of the intervals constant but, as we will see below, it is not always appropriate for the widths to be constant. Make sure that the bars are contiguous, to signal that the data are continuous. Technically the height of the bar is measured in units of observations per interval.

■ Draw a rectangle somewhere in a blank area of the graph that has an area proportional to one unit, or ten units, or the like, to indicate the scale of the areas on the graph. Most archaeologists would instead show the scale as increments along the vertical y-axis, but this assumes that the heights of the bars are proportional to the number of observations that they represent, which is not always the case. If you must indicate magnitude on the y-axis, show it in "observations per interval" units to account for the effect of bar width. For example, you might have "number of artifacts per 5 mm interval." You can indicate the scale in numbers of observations, proportions, or both. Tell the viewer how many observations were used to make the graph with an indication like the "n=22" on the graph in figure 2.9.

■ As with all graphs, make sure that the scales are labelled, including their units, where appropriate, and give the graph a title. Do not clutter the x-axis with too many labelled increments. Three or four labels at regular intervals are usually sufficient for the reader to appreciate the scale of measurement.

Because histograms express frequency by area, you will probably get into trouble if you try to use a non-linear scale for any of your measurements. If you want to use transformations (see below), you should express them on a histogram with transformed units, so that the proportionality of area will be preserved.

As I have already hinted, there are cases when it does not make sense for the intervals

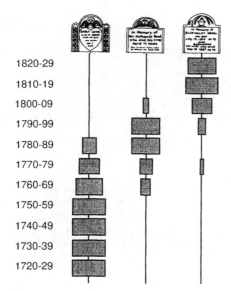

Figure 2.7. Vertical bar graphs with symmetrical bars used in a seriation of headstones from New England (after Deetz, 1967).

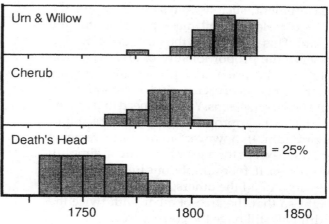

Figure 2.8. The same data rotated 90° and shown, without the symmetry, as a histogram to reflect the fact that the dates along the x-axis, in this case, are actually on a continuous scale.

along the x-axis to be equal. This has also led to some grievous errors in histograms published in archaeological reports. Two kinds of situations in which this often occurs involve chronological scales and grain-size distributions.

Commonly, archaeologists want to show change is some variable, such as settlement intensity, over time but we are often forced to assign observations to intervals of time that are not equal in length. Let us say, for example, that we want to show how the number of sites (our indirect measure of human population perhaps) varies over a period of many centuries, but we can date the sites much more precisely in recent times than we can in more ancient ones, and this is reflected in our grouping of sites into "periods" or "phases" of varying numbers of years (an interval scale). If we display the data in a histogram with bars of equal width, as in figure 2.9a, we will give the incorrect impression that human population was actually greater in the earlier (longer) periods than in the more recent (shorter) ones. If we correct for the interval widths, but indicate number of sites by bar height instead of area, we will still give misleading impression of changes in the intensity of settlement (figure 2.9b). In figure 2.9c, the inter-

vals are shown correctly and the area of each bar, not its height, is used to indicate the number of sites in each period.

Similarly, if we want to make a histogram showing the distribution of soil particles, or the like, sorted by size, typically we would pass the soil through a series of screens of gradually decreasing aperture. Even if we have an impressive collection of screens, the increment in screen aperture will not be constant. In fact, it is likely that we would consider a difference between 1.0 mm and 1.4 mm to be much more significant than the difference between 10.0 mm and 10.4 mm, and so would not want to make all the increments equal even were this possible. For this reason soil scientists regularly use special non-linear particle-size scales instead of scales in mm (see chapter 11). But if we showed the abundance of soil caught on each screen with bars of equal width in mm on a histogram, it would give the impression that large particles (which typically are captured by screens with larger increments in aperture) are much more common than small ones, when in fact the reverse may be the case.

Most of the commercial computer packages do not give you the option of having unequal intervals. If we need to draw a histogram with unequal intervals manually, the procedure is the same as before but with a small complication. We need to transform the data into a ratio measurement, such as "sites per year" for the first example or "soil mass per mm" for the second. This will give us the heights we need to preserve the proportionality of area when the bars' widths are made proportional to the number of years of each period or the size increment between screens. You then need to "stretch" each bar to the appropriate width, using a graphics program. If, however, all of our increments are equal except for one or two, we can simplify the process. If, for example, one interval is twice the width of all the others, we simply halve its height so that the area of a bar with twice the width will still have the correct area.

Before leaving histograms, it is necessary to mention how the arbitrary selection of interval width and boundary of intervals affects overall histogram shape. Even a small change in one or both of these can sometimes make a bimodal (two-peak) distribution seem unimodal, or change the location of the modes dramatically (cf. Whallon, 1987:144-47). Given this, you should be wary of making too much of histogram shape, especially if sample size is small or the intervals are very small or large relative to dispersion in the data. For example, it might be ill advised to use three modes in a histogram of data in a small pilot sample to define the ordinal categories you will use for a much larger project unless those modes are fairly reproducible in several changes of interval width. At the same time, this dependence of histogram shape on interval placement and width does not prevent the histogram from being a very useful graphic device. It is an excellent way to display general trends in continuous data, as long as you view the graphs with a critical eye, and also has close similarity to the probability distributions we will see in chapter 6. In cases where it is critical to avoid this flaw in histograms, one should instead consider using an ogive or cumulative frequency distribution (below).

Line Graphs

Line graphs are correctly used in cases where we want to show changes over a continuous scale. In some ways they are similar to histograms, but they are not frequency distributions. That is, rather than showing how many or how much of some item occurs in each interval along

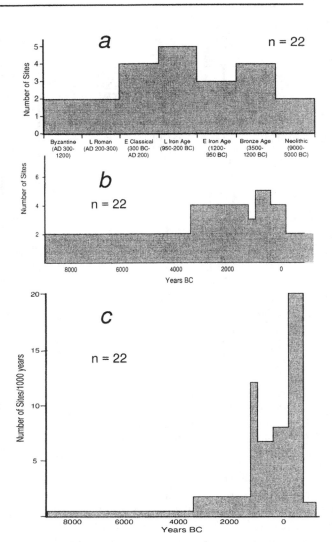

Figure 2.9. The histogram in **a** is misleading because the time intervals are of equal width, the time scale is in reverse order, and site number is given by height, rather than area. In **b** the interval width is corrected but the graph still misrepresents changes in settlement intensity by using heights. The graph in **c** gives a more realistic indication of relative settlement intensity through proportionality of area.

the scale, it shows how a particular statistic (such as population size, proportion of decorated pottery, or mean temperature or house size) varies up and down as we vary the value of the x-axis, and, in archaeology, usually the x-axis represents time. In that case, the line graph can be called a **"time-series."** Another difference between line graphs and histograms, which stems from the fact that they are not frequency distributions, is that it is the height of any point along the line, as measured by the y-axis, that determines its value, and not the area under the line. Usually you can get away with showing two or even three different measurements on the same line graph without making it too confusing, as long as each line is clearly labelled or coded with a key.

Often, it is impossible for us to make continuous measurements along this x-axis, and instead we have a sample of measurements made at different times and have to interpolate between them. A typical, non-archaeological example might be measurements of outdoor temperature at noon over a period of several months, but made not quite daily. We would simply mark points at the coordinates appropriate for each combination of x- and y-values (date and temperature), then join the points with line segments to show how noon temperature varies over the period in question.

Appropriate uses of line graphs are not as common in archaeology as those of other graph types. We could use a line graph to indicate, for example, changes in population over time (figure 2.10). The fact that we are usually unable to measure population (or one of its proxies) at a single point in time, however, makes it difficult or impossible for us to know where each point on the graph should lie, and we should show **error bars** on the points. These are line segments that extend out from the point to show the size of the estimated error. The graph in figure 2.10 has bars to show the estimated error in population size, but not in date.

Cumulative Frequency Graphs (Ogives)

The cumulative frequency graph, or **ogive**, is very useful if you want to know what percentage or proportion of your data lie above or below a certain value, or what proportion lies between two values. It is also very useful when it is important to know whether a particular distribution is relatively even or uneven, and for comparing distributions.

The graph has at least an ordinal, and usually a continuous interval scale along the x-axis and a measure of relative abundance (proportion or percentage) along the y-axis. It works

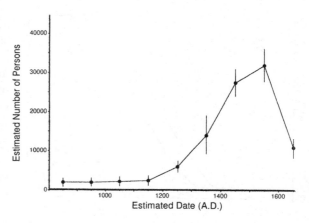

Figure 2.10. A Line graph showing changes in estimated human population over time (after Warrick, 1996:17).

much like a histogram except that the values accumulate, rather than going up and down. This characteristic is described as "monotonic" (one-way) "increasing." The graph is relatively easy to draw. You go through most of the procedure you would follow for a histogram, except you make a y-axis ranging from 0 to 1.0 or from 0% to 100% and you add each new value, going from left to right across the x-axis, to the previous ones so that the line gradually rises from near 0 at the bottom left corner of the graph, to 100% at upper right (figure 2.11).

One of the important applications of this kind of graph is in a non-parametric statistical test, the Kolmogorov-Smirnov test (Shennan, 1988:53-61) that is useful for many archaeological problems that involve comparing two distributions of observations on the ordinal, interval or ratio scale. In fact, the reason that the cumulative frequency graph became popular with lithic analysts was that you could put two or more cumulative step-lines (one for each assemblage) on a single graph and use the maximum vertical difference between the two lines as a measure of how different the assemblages were.

A more common use of such a graph is to allow viewers easily to see what proportion of houses were greater than 30 m², for example, or what percentage of graves had less than three grave goods. In the former case, we might find the place along the x-axis corresponding to 30

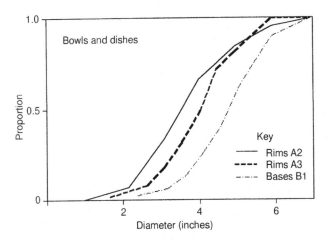

Figure 2.11. An ogive, or cumulative frequency graph, for the diameters of the rims and bases of pot sherds (after Orton, 1980:171).

m², draw a line vertically until it meets the step-line, and then horizontally from that point to the y-axis, where we might read off 80%. This would tell us that 100-80 or 20% of houses were bigger than 30 m². In the latter case, a line drawn upwards from 3 on the x-axis and then across to the y-axis might give 65%, telling us that 65% of the graves had less than three grave goods.

Clive Orton (1980) shows a good example of how a cumulative frequency graph, with rim and base diameter on the x-axis, can help us to compare differences in the proportions of size classes in pottery assemblages (figure 2.11). Orton makes the somewhat bold attempt to figure out what bases go with what rims by arguing that, if x% of rims are smaller than 6 inches and x% of bases are smaller than 3 inches, then probably the 6-inch rims belong to the same vessels as the 3-inch bases. The shapes of the cumulative frequency plots would be very different if this theory for associating bases with rims was far off, while close similarity between the two step-lines would lend it some support.

In non-archaeological applications, social scientists often use this type of graph to show income distributions. A fairly straight line would show that income varies fairly evenly, with relatively equal numbers of poor, middle-income and rich people or families, a concave distribution would indicate that there were very many poor families, and a convex distribution would

indicate that there was an abundance of middle-income or rich families. Social scientists often then use something called the Gini coefficient to measure the degree of convexity or concavity in the distribution. Some archaeologists have used the Gini coefficient in a similar way to measure the degree of inequality in grave goods in a cemetery (e.g., Morris, 1987: 141-43).

Cumulative frequency graphs have often been used to publish distributions in lithic assemblages since François Bordes popularized his approach in the 1960s. This is actually an inappropriate use of them (Thomas, 1976: 52) because the x-axis on the graph is only an arbitrarily ordered list of artifact types. If you changed the ordering of the type-categories, the shape of the cumulative frequency graph could change dramatically.

Scatterplots

Scatterplots are the most appropriate means for showing data along two, or occasionally three, dimensions on an interval or ratio scale. They are particularly useful in exploratory analysis, when we are attempting to group data or find relationships between dimensions.

Usually a scatter plot has two axes, both with continuous interval or ratio scales. The plot then consists of a number of points, or dots, at the intersections of all the (x, y) combinations. For example, following an analysis of the trace elements in a number of obsidian artifacts, we might plot the abundance of zirconium in parts per million (ppm) in each along the x-axis and the abundance of barium, also in ppm, along the y-axis. Each point on the graph represents the particular combination of zirconium and barium for each artifact, and we can search the graph for signs that points tend to cluster into groups (figure 3.7). We can show errors of the measurements by small bars (error bars) extending out from the dots. We can also add a third dimension, usually on a nominal scale, by using different symbols for the points to indicate the category to which each belongs, such as the site it came from or the source of the obsidian, if known. If we are very lucky, points with the same symbol might fall into the same cluster on the graph, while points with different symbols fall in different groups. This is a useful exploratory way to see what pairs of characteristics (in this case pairs of elemental abundances) might help us to define meaningful groups (see "grouping" in chapter 3).

Scatterplots are especially useful when we want to look for meaningful relationships between two dimensions. For example, if we plot flake width along the x-axis and flake length along the y-axis and the result is a group of points stretched roughly along a diagonal line, stretching upward from left to right, we would conclude that all of the flakes are fairly constant in shape (or at least width/length ratio), and simply vary in size. This kind of relationship is linear association, or **correlation**, and the extent to which two variables are correlated can be described with a descriptive statistic called the correlation coefficient, represented by the letter r.

One famous example of the use of a scatterplot in archaeology involves the attempt to find a relationship between the roofed area of dwellings and the number of people who inhabited them (figure 2.12, Narroll, 1962). The plot shows a fairly linear relationship between these two measures, and allowed Narroll to extract an equation for the line that fits the data observations with the minimum squared error. This equation predicts that there will be one inhabitant roughly for each 10 m² of roofed area. This fitting of a "best fit" line to the data in a scatter of points to extract an equation for predicting y when x is known is called **regression**. Note, incidentally, that the points are scattered rather widely around the $y = 10x$ line, indicating that the correlation is not especially good, and we would expect a fairly large degree of error in this particular indirect measure of human population size (LeBlanc, 1971; cf. Read, 1987:162).

Pie Charts (Circle Graphs)

Pie charts are a popular way to show proportions of things measured on a nominal scale. They are now easy, perhaps too easy, to generate with computers. They are constructed by radiating a number of line segments from the center of a circle, with the angles between radii

proportional to the proportion of each category. They are particularly common to display faunal data in the archaeological literature (figure 2.13).

The trouble with pie charts is that, although the relative areas of the pie slices are proportional to the proportion of each category represented, just as the area of bars on a bar graph, the human eye finds it much easier to estimate and compare the areas of rectangles than circles or wedges (Tufte, 1983:55). Consequently, pie charts are usually not as easy to interpret accurately as bar graphs and are easily replaced by them in most cases. Often, users of pie charts try to compensate for this deficiency by putting labels on each wedge, showing the proportions numerically. This, however, makes the graph redundant, and begs the question of why the author did not simply use a table. In addition, the frequency of this type of graph in the popular media probably has more to do with the editors' low opinion of readers' sophistication than with the graphs' effectiveness (note especially the insulting "slice of your tax dollar" type of graph). In most cases, I would suggest that you use bar graphs instead of pie charts.

One exception is when you want to show how the abundance and distribution of items varies at a number of sites on a map. Assume, for example, that you have four pottery types that occur at ten sites in a region. You can draw a circle at the location of each site on the map such that the area of the circle is proportional to the total number of sherds in your sample from that site. Then you can divide each circle into four wedges, coloured or hatched to indicate which type each wedge represents and proportional to that type's abundance in the site assemblage. When used sparingly, this can sometimes be an effective way to present complex data and allow the viewer quickly to compare the distributions of artifact types across space.

Windflowers and Rose Plots

Windflowers are named for their use to indicate prevailing wind directions. They are essentially radial bar graphs, each bar radiating out from the center and with its height proportional to the amount of time the wind blew from a particular direction. Of course the direction in which the

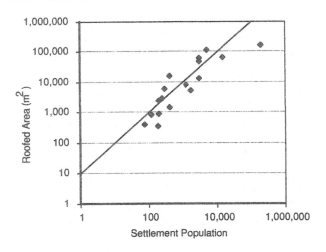

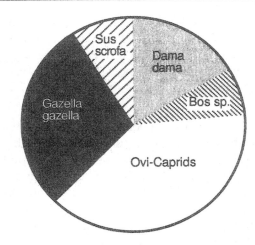

Figure 2.12. Scatterplot to display a relationship between roofed area and numer of people in an ethnographic sample, with the regression line for y=10x (after Narroll, 1962). Note that both axes have logarithmic scales in this example.

Figure 2.13. Example of a pie chart used to illustrate proportions of faunal bones.

bar radiates is analogous to the wind direction itself, so the windflower is appealing in that it conveys the idea of wind direction better than a standard bar graph would, even though it contains exactly the same information as a bar graph.

Some archaeologists have used windflowers and similar graphs called rose plots to show, for example, the distribution of orientations of the long axis in houses, the entryways in temples or houses, and the head position in graves. When excavators have recorded the individual orientations of lithics on surfaces, they can also be used to show the orientations or dip angles of the distal ends of flakes and blades (figure 2.14). Their attraction over a bar graph is that they convey the actual directionality of the patterns quite well.

Spatial Histograms and Isopleth Maps

Many kinds of archaeological data have an explicitly spatial component, and so it is often useful to combine the concept of a probability distribution with that of a map. Instead of showing variation in artifact size, for example, by using the usual histogram, we may want to show their distribution across a house floor we have excavated according to some kind of grid.

These maps, which we might call **spatial histograms** or stepped statistical surfaces, show variations in the density of artifacts or other materials across the grid. We can think of the density of artifacts across the surface as continuous, even though the actual artifacts themselves are discontinuous, and, as with a histogram, on each axis of the grid we decide on an interval (often we must select the interval in the field), and count the number of artifacts in each square. We could then represent this number by a bar that extends upward from the square, as in a three-dimensional bar graph, or simply shade or color each square according to a key to indicate the abundance of artifacts in each (figure 2.15). Note that, as with regular histograms, if the spatial units are not of equal size, we need to ensure that the data are shown as densities -- numbers of artifacts per unit of area or volume — to avoid giving an inflated impression of abundance for the larger spatial units.

An alternative that is better at capturing the feeling of continuity in the data, where that is appropriate, is to use an **isopleth map**. This looks much like a contour map used to illustrate topographic variation except that the contour lines represent, not equal heights above sea

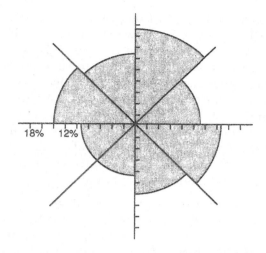

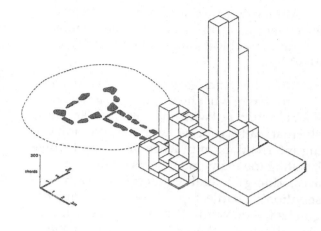

Figure 2.14. A type of rose plot used to indicate the angles of inclination (dip) of lithics in an Upper Paleolithic site (after Petraglia, 1993:102). The radial increments are 2%.

Figure 2.15. Spatial histogram or "stepped statistical surface" of potsherd densities at the entrance to grave 9 at Fjälkinge (Shanks and Tilley 1987:166).

level, but equal densities of artifacts, or isopleths. This type of map is appropriate in cases where an archaeological site-formation process has resulted in reasonably continuous changes in artifact density over space, so that we can reasonably interpolate artifact densities even in places where we did not actually do any measurements. What this means is that our measurements of artifact density across the surface must, of necessity, be discontinuous — normally we would count the number of artifacts in some unit of area at several places across the surface either systematically or opportunistically — but we then interpolate between our discontinuous measurements to estimate the densities in the space between them. This will only work in cases where we would expect fairly even fall-off in artifact density away, for example, from an activity area. In many archaeological cases the distributions are in reality very discontinuous. As with histograms, a small shift in the placement or interval of observations can have substantial effect on the form of the resulting "surface." In these cases, creating an isopleth map requires artificial, mathematical "smoothing" methods if we are to avoid misleading results.

General Principles in Creating Graphs

This summary does not exhaust the graphing methods you could use to display archaeological data, but does present principles for the use of the graph types most commonly encountered in the archaeological literature.

In addition to using the right kind of graph for your particular application, you should think about some general principles. It is easy to make even the correct kind of graph confusing, misleading, or downright dishonest.

An excellent guide for improving the effectiveness of graphs is Edward Tufte (1983; 1990). He emphasizes that graphs are to communicate information, and that they should do so clearly, precisely and efficiently. They should make large bodies of data accessible and coherent in a small space, balance fine detail with overall pattern, and encourage people to draw comparisons or identify patterns. They should have a clear purpose and should be integrated with the statistical and textual presentations with which they are associated. They certainly should not distort the data or mislead the viewer, and should encourage viewers to think about the data's substance rather than about the graph itself (Tufte, 1983: 13).

Among the aspects of graphs that affect their effectiveness, in his view, are the "data-ink" ratio and graphical integrity (Tufte, 1983:53-77, 91-106).

When he criticizes graphs for having a low data-ink ratio, what he means is that the graph is far too cluttered with lines, labels, or anything else that really is not necessary for communicating information. In practice, this may involve labelling too many increments on the x- and y-axes, adding bilateral symmetry to a graph (as in seriation's "battleship curves"), making bar graphs too decorative by making them appear three-dimensional, adding many and sometimes jarring combinations of color or hatching, or adding grid lines that are not really necessary. When graphs are decorative in the extreme, Tufte (1983:107-121) refers to them as "chartjunk." Unfortunately, commercial graphing software, whose primary market is the business communit,y makes it is all too easy for chartjunk to dominate. All this does is distract viewers from the information that the graph is intended to convey. Keep it simple.

On the other hand, it is also a mistake to remove so much labelling that the viewer has to search through a lengthy caption to interpret the graph. Include enough increment labels on your axes that what the axis is measuring, its scale, and its units are clear. Give your graph a title, and show other pertinent information, including, where relevant, a key, a scaling icon, or one or two descriptive statistics (such as n [sample size] or median).

One of the greatest threats to graphical integrity results from scaling the data in misleading ways. There are several ways in which presenters of data can mislead us. One is to hide the baseline of a bar graph or histogram so that, not only is zero not at the bottom of the graph's y-axis, but it is not very clear where zero is. This technique can be used both to inflate the impression of differences between bars (i.e., only showing the top part of the bars and truncating the bottom), and in an attempt to hide important differences and giving the graph a greater impression of stability (Tufte, 1983:54). In an honest bar graph, the height of the bars is proportional to the magnitude of the measure-

ments they indicate. In a line graph with interval rather than ratio data, however, it may not be necessary to show the zero value, as it is not a "real" zero anyway. For example, in a line graph displaying changes in temperature over time, 0°F and 0°C are only conventional temperatures and need not be shown if they are outside the range of observations. Similarly, a time scale across an x-axis need not include A.D. 1 (there is no such year as A.D. 0) or 0 B.P. unless it is included in the time range of interest.

Another threat to graphical integrity is to distort the graph by removing the proportionality of area. As we have seen already, in our discussion of histograms, it is the area of a portion of the histogram (not the height) that should be proportional to the number of observations in a particular interval. As it happens, most people find it easier to compare lengths and rectangular areas than to compare curves, circles, and angles, and systematically tend to underestimate growth in a circle's area (Tufte, 1983:55). Some of the computer graphic packages offer the option of making graphs look three-dimensional. Unless you are actually displaying three-dimensional data, however, this distorts the proportionality of area on the graph, and sometimes also offsets bars so that you cannot even compare heights properly. It is inadvisable to use such an option unless, as in spatial data, the third dimension actually contributes to the viewer's understanding.

Tufte suggests two basic principles to preserve graphical integrity. First, the representation of numerical quantities should be directly proportional to those quantities. Second, the axes and units on the graphs should be clearly labelled, with labels on the graph itself, rather than only in a caption or key, and important "events" in the data, such as modes and sudden changes of slope, should also be labelled, to call the viewer's attention to what is important (Tufte, 1983:55-56).

Many of the options that modern computer graphics software offers, including perspective views with foreshortening, distort the area of bars considerably, or automatically shift the zero (origin) of the graph out of view. You should ensure that you overrule such distortions.

Transformations and Problems of Scale

Sometimes it is difficult to make a single graph display a set of data effectively because some of the observations are many orders of magnitude larger than others. If we follow Tufte's advice not to distort the scale of the y-axis on a bar- or line-graph, in these cases, either the large observations are lost off the top of the graph, or the small observations become nearly invisible.

A common way to resolve this problem is to put a break in the y-axis, indicated by a jagged or wavy line. Although this would violate Tufte's principal of proportionality, the jagged line signals to viewers that part of the scale has been removed.

Another way to handle the problem is to transform the data. A data **transformation** typically involves using the square root or the logarithm of your measurements, either of which has the effect of "pulling in" the high values and "stretching up" the low values. Other kinds of transformations may also be desirable. Essentially, transformation is like expressing your data in different units. The logarithmic scale, however, has no zero (it increments in powers of ten), and consequently cannot be used in cases where you need to display zero values (see figure 2.12). In order to make it clear to the viewer that you have transformed the data, and that the heights displayed on the graph are consequently not proportional to the linear values of the measurements, you should label the axis and the graph accordingly. Sometimes patterns that are not clear in the raw data become much clearer or easier to interpret after data transformation, as in cases where an exponential relationship appears linear after transformation.

In addition, there may be more substantive reasons for transforming data than making the data fit the graph. Some relationships between two or more variables can form extremely clear patterns only when they are transformed. In an attempt to discover pattern in many linear measurements made on a number of artifacts, for example, we may find that the untransformed data suggest groupings by size categories, while a simple transformation results in data that suggest groupings by shape. Data transformation is a standard procedure in some kinds of analysis, such as principal components analysis (chapter 3).

References Cited

Barnett, V., and Lewis, T., 1994, *Outliers in Statistical Data.* John Wiley & Sons, New York.

Coombs, C. H., 1964, *A Theory of Data.* John Wiley, New York.

Deetz, J., 1967, *Invitation to Archaeology.* Doubleday & Co, New York.

Hodder, I., 1989, Writing archaeology: site reports in context. *Antiquity* 63:268-74.

— 1990, *The Domestication of Europe. Structure and Contingency in Neolithic Societies.* Blackwell, Oxford.

Kent, S., 1991, The relationship between mobility strategies and site structure. In *The Interpretation of Archaeological Spatial Patterning*, edited by E. M. Kroll and T. D. Price, pp. 33-59. Plenum Press, New York.

Kyburg, H. E., 1984, *Theory and Measurement.* Cambridge University Press, Cambridge.

LeBlanc, S., 1971, An addition to Narroll's suggested floor area and settlement population relationship. *American Antiquity* 36:210-11.

Morris, I., 1987, *Burial and Ancient Society. The Rise of the Greek City-state.* Cambridge University Press, Cambridge.

Nance, J. D., 1987, Reliability, validity, and quantitative methods in archaeology. In *Quantitative Research in Archaeology, Progress and Prospects*, edited by M. S. Aldenderfer, pp. 244-93. Sage Publications, Newbury Park, CA.

Narroll, R., 1962, Floor area and settlement population. *American Antiquity* 27:587-89.

Orton, C., 1980, *Mathematics in Archaeology.* Cambridge University Press, Cambridge.

Petraglia, M. D., 1993. The genesis and alteration of archaeological patterns at the Abri Duflaure: An Upper Paleolithic rockshelter and slope site in southwestern France. In *Formation Processes in Archaeological Context*, edited by P. Goldberg, D. T. Nash, and M. D. Petraglia, pp. 97-112. Prehistory Press, Madison, WI.

Pirsig, R. M., 1974, *Zen and the Art of Motorcycle Maintenance: An Enquiry into Values.* Morrow, New York.

Plog, S., ed., 1986, *Spatial Organization and Exchange: Archaeological Survey on Northern Black Mesa.* Southern Illinois University Press, Carbondale.

Plog, S., Plog, F., and Wait, W., 1978, Decision making in modern surveys. *Advances in Archaeological Method and Theory* 1:143-82.

Read, D., 1987, Archaeological theory and statistical methods: Discordance, resolution and new directions. In *Quantitative Research in Archaeology, Progress and Prospects,* edited by M. S. Aldenderfer, pp. 151-184. Newbury Park, CA: Sage Publications.

Shanks, M., 1992, *Experiencing the Past. On the Character of Archaeology.* Routledge, London.

Shanks, M., and Tilley, C. 1987, *Re-Constructing Archaeology. Theory and Practice.* Cambridge University Press, Cambridge.

Stapert, D., 1994, Intrasite spatial analysis and the Maglemosian site of Barmose I. *Paleohistoria* 33/34:31-51.

Sullivan, A. P., 1978, Inference and evidence in archaeology. *Adances in Archaeological Method and Theory* 1:183-222.

Thomas, D. H., 1976, *Figuring Anthropology.* Holt, New York.

Tufte, E. R., 1983, *The Visual Display of Quantitative Information.* Graphics Press, Cheshire, CT.

— 1990, *Envisioning Information.* Graphics Press, Cheshire, CT.

Tukey, J. W., 1977, *Exploratory Data Analysis.* Addison-Wesley.

Warrick, G., 1996, Evolution of the Iroquoian longhouse. In *People Who Lived in Big Houses: Archaeological Perspectives on Large Domestic Structures,* edited by G. Coupland and E. Banning, pp. 11-26. Prehistory Press, Madison, WI.

Whallon, R., 1987, Simple statistics. In *Quantitative Research in Archaeology, Progress and Prospects,* edited by M. S. Aldenderfer, pp. 135-50 . Sage Publications, Newbury Park, CA.

3 Systematics, Compilations, and Database Design

As we have seen, compilations are the result of collecting, compiling, cataloguing, or organizing data into arrangements. Compilations can be simple lists, indexed lists, or computer databases. Alternatively, they can be tables, graphs, collections of pictures, or statistical summaries. Compilations can be used simply to record and summarize information, or to organize that information in either arbitrary or meaningful ways.

To summarize data we can use any one or a combination of the following tools. Lists are the simplest kind of compilation; they have no particular order, and so are difficult to use either to manage data or to seek patterns in data unless we use high-speed computers to sift through them. Whether computerized or not, lists are much easier to use when they are indexed. Keywords or some other symbolic devices, such as color codes, can be used to "look up" information that is arranged in alphabetical or numerical order, for example. Often data are presented in the form of tables. These impose order and dimensions on the data and sometimes emphasize particular kinds of data over others. Graphs, meanwhile, simplify and make visual large quantities of data that we would otherwise have to present as virtually unmanageable lists or tables of numerical information. Further simplification results in statistical summaries, such as averages, medians, and proportions or percentages, and other ratios, which replace the lists of many numbers with only a few that characterize trends, "central tendencies," or typical distributions in the data.

But any kind of useful compilation more complex than a simple list must have units with

which to order data and find similarities and differences. The ways to formulate and structure such units constitute the methods of **systematics**. Archaeologists typically describe most or all of these methods as "classification" or "typology," almost interchangeably, but they can also result in non-classificatory arrangements — groups or clusters. As Dunnell (1971) emphasizes, classification as an intellectual process is quite distinct from grouping, and the distinction is worth preserving. In addition, it is useful to distinguish classifications generally from particular kinds of classifications that I will call typologies.

This chapter introduces a classification of the tools archaeologists use to order their data, through systematics. It also introduces the issues they must address when they use computer databases to record and manipulate their data. The latter section deals with databases in the abstract rather than attempting to describe any particular database management system.

SYSTEMATICS

Systematics operates on the nominal scale of measurement. Our need for systematics stems from the fact that everything on which we would like to make observations is unique: it has its own particular combination of values on an infinite number of characteristics or **attributes**. When we try to carry out an analysis, however, it is not very useful to treat each object as unique or to clump everything into a single group that comprises the whole population or sample. Categories or **classes**, and **groups** with members that share some attributes or are similar in some way, help us to make sense out of data, not to mention saving publication costs. Being able to group observations or assign them to categories is a necessary step in making comparisons. If we literally treated every artifact, burial, or site as a unique observation, we would have no way to find commonalities between artifact assemblages. There simply would be none. At the same time, to say that two artifacts belong to the same class, group, or type does not mean that they are identical in all respects, only that they share certain characteristics that we deem important.

One of the characteristics of systematics is that it is, philosophically speaking, completely arbitrary. That is not to deny that we have good reasons for organizing data the way we do, but to recognize that the number of possible ways to define categories or group information is infinite. Our research goals may guide us to design systematics in particular ways — for example, the goal of elucidating evolutionary relationships leads us to use a taxonomic classification of living things that at least mimics their evolutionary histories — but in principal, no one arrangement is any better or more valid than any other. Only our theoretical orientations, research goals, and methods lead us to select one arrangement over another. Quite often archaeologists change their arrangement of data as their research progresses or interests change.

As I noted in the introduction, archaeologists tend to describe the products of systematics as classifications or typologies, using both terms somewhat indiscriminately. Even mathematicians are far from consistent in their use of terms for systematics. I prefer to follow Dunnell (1971) in distinguishing classification from grouping and I attempt to expand on Gardin's (1980) distinctions by treating typologies as special cases of classifications and groupings. While other ways of describing and distinguishing archaeological units of analysis are certainly possible (e.g., Adams and Adams, 1991), I think it is useful to encourage a clear and consistent use of terms, and Dunnell's (1971) *Systematics in Prehistory* provides one possible basis for this consistency.

Classification is the intellectual process whereby we assign items, either real or imag-
ined, to categories in a pre-arranged system, or classification, much as though we were putting the items into boxes or trays. Adams and Adams (1991) would call this process "sorting" when it involves classifying actual *things*, such as artifacts. Hand (1997) would call it "supervised classification." For each category, there is a rule or set of rules to determine whether any item belongs or does not belong to that category and, if the rules are defined carefully, there is no ambiguity about the category to which a particular item should be assigned. The rules state the conditions that are *necessary* for a particular item or concept to qualify for membership in the class: failure to meet even one condition would disqualify it. Furthermore, satisfying those conditions is *sufficient* for membership in the class: as long as the item meets the necessary conditions, no other conditions have any bearing on its membership. To begin with a simple example, we could have a set of boxes, each labelled "flint," "pottery," "bone," or "other," and assign artifacts from an excavation to these boxes according to the material from which they are made. A classification is an abstract arrangement with which we conceptualize the categories, or **classes**, to which we are assigning items, that is, with which we create the units of a nominal scale.

Grouping, on the other hand, is a different kind of intellectual process. Here there is no pre-arranged system for ordering the phenomena of interest independent of the phenomena themselves, even though individual researchers will have preconceived ideas about how to proceed. It may involve something as simple as depositing a collection of artifacts onto a table and moving them around into piles in such a way that items in the same pile seem more similar to each other than they are to items in other piles. The important thing, philosophically, is that the starting-point is not an abstract model of how to conceptualize the items, but rather an actual collection of items. You can have classifications that have no members (although that would be a rather unproductive excercise!) because classifications are abstract, but you could never have **groups** without members. Hand (1997) would describe grouping as "unsupervised classification" or "pattern recognition."

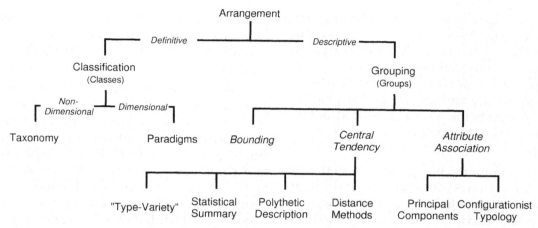

Figure 3.1. A taxonomic classification of arrangements.

Both classification and grouping belong to what Dunnell (1971:43) would call more generally, **arrangement**: a procedure that orders data into units, an organizing device. It is important to remember that arrangements are completely arbitrary; just as the number of attributes with which we might describe a particular object is infinite, the number of possible ways we may construct arrangements is also infinite. Although we routinely have some theoretical justification for preferring one arrangement over another, from the formal standpoint one arrangement is just as real and as valid as any other.

Even if it is not immediately apparent, the difference between classification and grouping is important because it affects our research designs from the beginning. If our research design calls for us to anticipate the kinds of data we will collect and how we will collect them, as it often does, we would typically employ classification, the only means at our disposal for precisely anticipating categories of information. If we are conducting exploratory analysis of a pre-existing collection of artifacts, then we might use grouping methods to get some insights into the collection that might lead to the formation of new hypotheses. Typically, archaeologists use both at various stages of their research. For example, they may begin a new project by grouping artifacts that seem intuitively similar, or whose characteristics seem to vary by context, then examine the groups to identify the attributes that seem to contribute the greatest similarities within and differences between groups. Then

they can use these attributes to construct a new classification, apply it to the original artifacts as well as to others they may collect, and test the classification's usefulness for a particular purpose, such as chronology.

Let us examine the differences between grouping and classification in more detail.

Classifications, as we have seen, are abstract. A classification consists of a number of categories, or **classes**, each defined by one or more criteria. In terms of the measurement theory we examined in chapter 2, a classification allows measurement on a nominal scale. To measure a particular object on this scale, we simply compare it with the criteria for each class until we find the class to which it belongs, that is, where there is a match between the class's defining criteria and the object's attributes. Consequently, we can say that classification is a matter of redundancy, in that two objects can be said to belong to the same class if they both meet all the criteria.

More formally, the class definition states the conditions that are both *necessary and sufficient* for membership in the class. No item can be a member unless it meets *all* the criteria, and no item can be omitted as long as it meets those criteria. For classifications to work properly, definitions need to be formulated in a way that makes the classes mutually exclusive: no one artifact should meet the definitions for two different classes simultaneously, nor should there be any ambiguity about the class to which it belongs. Because classes have definitions (i.e., rules for membership), we can also say that classification is definitive. One important characteristic of classifications is that they are independent of the things they classify. Whether or not there are any artifacts that belong to a particular class, whether you add artifacts or take some away, the rules defining that class remain the same.

Grouping methods, by contrast, start with things. These things could be real or imaginary. Instead of being definitive, as in classification, grouping is descriptive, as it simply describes particular groups, or clusters, of things. We can describe these groups by enumerating their members, by stating their boundaries in space or time, or by summarizing the characteristics of each group statistically. As an example of description by enumeration, a group of people can be described simply by listing their names and addresses. A common way in which archaeological groups are described by stating their boundaries is when artifacts are grouped by the stratigraphic levels or excavation areas in which they were found. A simple example of a statistical description might be a group composed of lithics that tend to be from 3 cm to 5 cm in length, that have length/width ratios close to 1.7, and edge angles around 18°. The thing to note here is that, unlike the definitions for classes, the measures here are "tendencies." Just because the average length for the group might be 3.3 cm doesn't mean that there are no members with lengths of 2.9 or 5.2 cm, only that the majority of group members cluster around that average. One of the major ways in which grouping differs from classification is that groups cannot exist independently of their members and, if you change the membership of a group, the group's definition also changes. For example, if one of the defining characteristics of a group is an average length of 33 mm, and you add a new member that is 37 mm long, the average length, and thus the group definition, will be different. Consequently, group descriptions are restricted to the set of phenomena with which the groups were originally constituted, and any addition or subtraction of information always changes these descriptions (Dunnell, 1971:89). That is not nec-

essarily a problem, but requires caution when we want to compare assemblages of artifacts, for example, that were not grouped by the same descriptions.

The distinction between classification and grouping does not always appear clear-cut. For example, in everyday practice we classify things along a scale of color, with values such as "red," and "brown." Yet our description of a particular object, perhaps a pottery sherd, as either red or brown may be far from unambiguous. It may seem "reddish-brown" or different researchers may assign it to different classes. This may stem in part from human differences in perception, in part to our failure to define the boundaries between classes carefully enough, but it is also a very real aspect of archaeology that our categories are often somewhat "fuzzy." We may only be able to assign a sherd to a particular class with a particular probability, and the definition of the class may begin to look like the statistical definition of a group. This is a problem that we can approach either through the concept of measurement error (chapter 2), in which case we refer to **misclassification**, or through something called 'fuzzy sets' (Kempton, 1978; Zadeh, 1965). Fuzzy sets deserve more attention in archaeology, as they may describe some aspects of real archaeological classifications (Adams and Adams, 1991:72). The theory behind fuzzy sets, however, is beyond the scope of this book. The basic distinction between classification and grouping, however, remains a useful one.

As there are many possible ways to go about designing classifications or grouping phenomena, it should come as no surprise that we can make a classification of these methods. Dunnell (1971:44) describes two major classes of classifications and two major classes of grouping methods. Of course other ways to classify classifications and grouping methods are possible (e.g., Adams and Adams, 1991:216-28), but Dunnell's classification provides a useful starting-point. The classification that follows is inevitably arbitrary, especially in the way I have subdivided some of the statistical grouping techniques, but I hope that the classification reveals some of the common elements of these techniques without need to describe them in detail.

Paradigmatic Classification

Paradigms operate by the intersection of nominal or ordinal scales that we can describe as dimensions because the classes on each scale are mutually exclusive: no item could belong to more than one category on each scale. The intersections of a number of these dimensions define classes in the same way as X, Y, and Z measurements (Cartesian coordinates) can define any portion of space. Readers who have studied languages will be familiar with paradigms because they are used, for example, to classify verbs. One dimension could be "tense," with classes for "past," "present," and "future." Another dimension could be "gender," with classes for "feminine," "masculine," and "neuter." A third could be "number," with classes for "singular," "plural," and, perhaps, "dual." Yet another could be "person," with "first person" ("I" or "we"), "second person" ("you"), and "third person" ("he," "she," "it," or "they"). By intersecting these dimensions we get classes to which we can assign such items as "he said" (third-person singular, masculine, past) or "we will go" (second-person plural, neuter, future). In an archaeological case, we might create a paradigm for measuring pottery relative to the dimensions, "exterior surface color," "temper," "decoration," "hardness," and others. It is worth noting that the nominal scales of measurement that we use to measure attributes, even ones used in non-classificatory arrangements, are usually paradigms, and often one-dimensional ones.

Paradigms have some important characteristics. Paradigmatic classifications, because they are dimensional, are non-hierarchical and unweighted. All dimensions contribute equally to the classification. In addition, it is possible, in fact quite likely, that a paradigmatic classification will contain many "empty" classes; that is, some combinations of criteria on the various dimensions will define objects that we are unlikely to encounter or even that could not possibly exist. In this sense, paradigms are not as efficient as some other kinds of arrangements, and consequently they are rarely used for complex typologies intended for large collections of material.

Dimension 1 (Temper)

Dimension 2 (Painting)	Shell-tempered	Not Shell-tempered
Black-on-Red		
Not Black-on-Red		

Figure 3.2. Example of a simple, two-dimensional paradigmatic classification of pottery with four possible classes (after Watson et al., 1971:128-130).

Taxonomy

Taxonomic classification is the kind of classification that Linnaeus used to categorize plants and animals and that botanists and zoologists still use to classify life. Rather than employing intersecting dimensions, taxonomies work by a series of distinctions or dichotomies, resulting in major categories, smaller categories, sub-categories and sub-sub-categories. They are hierarchical and assignment to a particular class is like running through a program from the top of the hierarchy on down.

An example will illustrate this point. One possible taxonomy for lithics could begin at the top with a distinction between tools and waste products. For a tool, at the next level down we may need to distinguish between core tools and flake tools. For flake tools we may further distinguish flakes with retouch on the dorsal side, ventral side, or both. For flake tools with bifacial retouch, we may distinguish ones with one retouched edge, two retouched edges, and more than two retouched edges. And so on, until we have assigned the flake to its proper category. At each level in the hierarchy, the classifier must make some distinction, on a nominal (and sometimes dichotomous) scale, such as "lithic" or "not lithic," or "small," "medium," or "large," and the final class to which an item is assigned is arrived at by winding through a sequence of such distinctions.

Among the characteristics of taxonomies are the following. Taxonomies are inherently hierarchical, with weighted criteria for assignment to classes. That is, defining criteria near the top

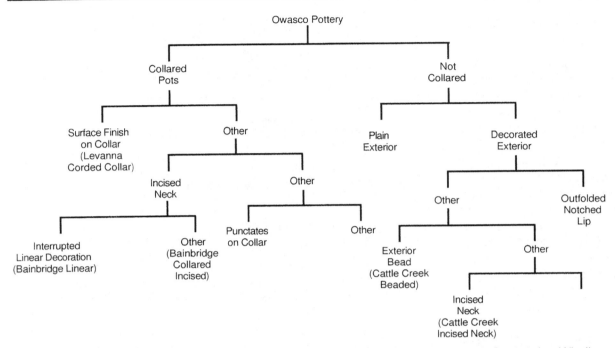

Figure 3.3. Example of a taxonomic classification for Owasco pottery from New York State (after Whallon, 1972: 17). Note that the distinctions made in the left side of the "tree" are quite different from those on the right. The taxonomy could easily be simplified by removing redundant "others." For example, there is no reason why "punctate on collar" could not move up to the same level as "incised neck."

of the hierarchy have much more influence over the class to which an item will be assigned than ones near the bottom. Taxonomies are rarely symmetrical; all the "branches" are independent of one another and need not employ the same or even similar criteria for making finer distinctions. In a lithics taxonomy, we would not expect the criteria for sub-dividing **debitage** to be the same as those for subdividing tools, while in a pottery taxonomy, we would not expect the sub-categories of rim sherds to be the same as those for handles or bases. Taxonomies need have no "empty" classes; we simply would not use any distinctions that would create classes for items we would never expect to encounter, however rarely.

Grouping

Dunnell (1971) also recognizes two basic classes of grouping methods, or "non-classificatory arrangements," which he calls "numerical taxonomy" and "statistical clustering." Superficially, the former looks like a taxonomy, but, in fact, quite different procedures are involved in its construction. The latter actually

begins with a paradigmatic classification. To limit ourselves to these two classes, however, omits some of the richness of grouping methods, among them even those based on archaeological context or on intuition that archaeologists use everyday. Consequently I propose the modified terminology that follows (see also figure 3.1), distinguishing grouping methods based on boundaries from those based on central tendency and attribute association.

Bounded Grouping

The simplest grouping method, which archaeologists use unconsciously all the time, is simply to group things by some boundary, typically a contextual (or **extrinsic**) boundary in space or time. By extrinsic we simply mean attributes that lie outside the objects being grouped or classified, such as their date of manufacture, while **intrinsic** attributes are ones inherent in those objects, such as their length or color. This is such a routine and critical kind of grouping, the backbone of any archaeological recording system, that we tend to take it for granted. It is also important in that, consciously or not, most archaeologists begin a new artifact typology by grouping artifacts by context and searching for within-group similarities and between-group differences. Once recognized, these similarities and differences can serve as the basis for a more formal classification, such as a taxonomy, or for another kind of grouping.

I label this type of grouping as bounded grouping because membership of the group is described by the boundaries of some unit, typically the two-dimensional or three-dimensional spatial boundaries of some part of a layer, feature, excavation unit, site, or survey unit. We will return to this aspect later in the chapter in connection with computer databases. The boundaries can be non-spatial, however, as when we group together artifacts of the 17th century (chronological boundaries). It is also possible for the boundaries to lie in some intrinsic dimensions. An example of this is grouping archaeological sites by partitioning a site-size distribution. In this case, as with interval widths in histograms, the arbitrary selection of boundary placement can have a significant effect (above, p. 26 and Whallon, 1987:144-47). Containment by the boundaries is a necessary condition for membership in the group, but not a sufficient one: many items included within the boundaries may be excluded from the group for reasons ranging from being suspected **intrusive** artifacts to being unhelpful for the purposes of the typology (cf. Adams and Adams, 1991: 100-102). As with any type of grouping, the description of groups can change if new information is added. For example, we may continue to excavate in the same context and find more artifacts, decide that two groups from adjacent excavation squares should be considered as a single group, or add new sites to a site-size group by further survey. We often try to place boundaries where we perceive "natural" discontinuities, such as a change in color or texture of sediment, but the exact placement of boundaries can be somewhat uncertain. In some cases, the boundaries can be described with reasonably small error. In others, however, the boundaries can be rather fuzzy (Adams and Adams, 1991:71-72), tending to lead us into the next class of grouping method.

Central-Tendency Methods

This class of grouping methods places less emphasis on boundaries of groups and more on central tendency, and is typically based on *intrinsic* attributes of group members rather than contextual (or extrinsic) ones. It includes a large range of variation, from intuitive groupings based on an archaeologist's mental image of a "type" through more explicit statistical descriptions of typical group members to complex computer-generated groupings based on distance measures. In some cases it may involve keeping a collection of "ideal" type members — a type collection — with which artifacts can be compared. Type collections are particularly common for assigning pottery sherds to fabric types, in part because the detailed analysis of pottery fabrics is time-consuming and requires special training (see chapter 8), while pottery collections are often much too large to allow such detail. The more formal central-tendency methods have features that make them seem very similar to classifications: there can (but need not) be pre-arranged (one is almost tempted to say "abstract") types to which new artifacts are matched much as we would match them with the definitions of categories in a nominal scale of measurement. There are, however, important differences that make it appropriate to classify these methods, at least formally, among grouping rather than classification.

The characteristics of central-tendency methods that determine their membership in a class of grouping methods include, most importantly, the way types are "defined." Unlike the definitions in true classification, the criteria for assignment to one of these types are not both necessary and sufficient for membership in the class. They are only tendencies. A certain type of pottery may *usually*, but not always, have a red slip; it may *tend* to have an inverted neck, but with exceptions; it may *typically* have a rim diameter of about 15 cm, but some examples could be less than 12 or more than 20 cm in diameter; and so on. In part these rather fuzzy "definitions" are forced on us by the nature of the material, which is usually so fragmentary that we cannot expect all the attributes that might help define a class even to be observable. Yet, in part, it has to do with our uncertainty about where boundaries lie and our willingness to modify our typologies as new specimens turn up. The "definitions" are really descriptions, sometimes explicitly statistical descriptions, that summarize the characteristics of the most "typical" exemplars of the type while recognizing that members vary in each of their attributes. It is tempting to treat the type description as a Platonic ideal, or a prehistoric culture's "mental template," to which each real artifact is an approximation. Really it is just a statistical summary, like a multidimensional mean and standard deviation or mode and range.

The central-tendency methods have other characteristics that plant them squarely in the realm of grouping methods. Even when they are structured to appear as pre-arranged systems, they begin with actual things, such as bone tools, ceramic pots, or archaeological sites, that provide the initial exemplars to which we will compare later finds. Consequently, the types are not abstract classes, and you would never have a type for which you would expect no members. Further, while class definitions are immutable within a given classification, type descriptions are constantly refined as new exemplars are found and examined. For example, the type whose description includes "usually red-slipped" may come to be described as "usually red- or black-slipped" as more and more black-slipped exemplars are found or, alternatively, be split into two groups with different slips.

Statistical types and type-variety typologies: Many of the typologies that archaeologists have used for a long time are based on descriptions, sometimes statistical ones, of the modal characteristics of the type, with the expectation that actual examples will vary somewhat around this mode. In some cases, as with pottery fabrics, we may keep a collection exhibiting the range of variation we would expect within each type, and use it to match up un-typed specimens. In other cases, we may just publish descriptions of each ware type (e.g., Goren, 1992; Kenyon and Holland, 1982). We might also use a set of pictures exhibiting the modal shape for each type and the range of expected variation in shape to assign artifacts to morphological types. In much Old World archaeology, for example, large num-

bers of inked drawings of pottery profiles often serve to show exemplars of these modal types, and archaeologists routinely refer to the drawings published by their colleagues in their attempt to group their own artifacts with others' types, and also to group sites with similar assemblages (contra Adams and Adams, 1991:237). Unfortunately the "rules" for using these illustrated types and information on variability around the mode are usually missing, and admittedly much ink has been used to illustrate every single "diagnostic" sherd in some cases. Alternatively, we would match the statistical summaries for the type with the measurements recorded for individual specimens. Most of the attributes emphasized in these typologies are ones we can measure on an ordinal, interval, or ratio scale, simply because these are the scales in which we can most easily express central tendency and dispersion (see chapter 2). Quite often these typologies are hierarchical, with some types considered more similar to one another than they are to other types at a higher level in the hierarchy.

Some cases of grouping entities by the modes in a multimodal distribution arguably belong to this group. For example, when there is a clearly multimodal distribution of site sizes, we might, failing better evidence, have grounds for labelling sites falling close to each mode as "camps," "farms," "hamlets," "villages," and so on.

Polythetic descriptions: David Clarke (1968:189-90) introduced to archaeological systematics the concept of "polythetic definition," to describe a kind of grouping that archaeologists had been doing for many decades. The key feature of polythetic descriptions is that they are based on a set of conditions or attributes, none of which is *necessary or sufficient* for attribution of any item to the group. Instead, we only expect each member of the group to share *a large number* of these attributes and each attribute to be shared by a large number of the group's members.

A classic early use of what we would now call polythetic descriptions is V. Gordon Childe's definition of an archaeological "culture". He formally defined it as a complex or assemblage of regularly associated types that illustrate more than one aspect of human behavior (Childe,

1929:v-vi; 1956:16, 33). Yet he recognized that it was unrealistic to expect every archaeological site of a given culture to exhibit all the important characteristics of that culture (Childe, 1956:33). For example, you might expect to find certain kinds of artifacts at a farming village, such as grinding stones, that you would not expect to find at other kinds of sites, such as hunting camps, used by the same people. Childe viewed an archaeological culture as a whole that exhibited a constellation of attributes, only some of which would appear at each individual site, but each of which would occur at at least two sites belonging to that culture and be represented by more than one example.

Polythetic groupings are conceptually similar to the statistical types just mentioned in that the description of each type, with respect to a number of attributes, is rather flexible. The main difference is that polythetic typologies use attributes measured on a nominal scale, so that we can record each attribute as either present or absent. Members of the same group are similar to one another in the sense, not that they vary only slightly from the mode or mean in each attribute, but that they are identical (on some nominal scale) with respect to some large but unspecified number of attributes, while differing in others. Even when attributes were measured on an ordinal or ratio scale, they are reduced to a nominal (often dichotomous) scale for the purposes of polythetic definition. Polythetic grouping involves a clustering of nominal attributes; statistical grouping involves a clustering of the attribute's values, as measured on at least an ordinal scale, around some mode.

One of the problems with polythetic description is simply an exaggerated version of a problem common to most grouping methods. Because the criteria for membership in a group, unlike the definitions in a classification, are quite flexible, there is no way to predict in what way any two members of a group may be similar or different. For example, items A, B, and C could constitute a group with attributes *abcdef*, *cdefgh*, and *efghij*, each sharing two-thirds of its attributes with at least one other member of the group, and the attributes *c*, *d*, *e*, *f*, *g*, and *h* occurring in two-thirds of the group's members.

Yet the ways in which A is similar to B are quite different from the ways in which B is similar to C, and A and C have only two attributes in common.

In spite of this problem, many archaeologists would argue that polythetic descriptions come very close to the kinds of type "definitions" that archaeologists routinely use, both consciously and unconsciously (Adams and Adams, 1991:226; Williams et al., 1973).

Distance methods: The class of grouping methods commonly called "clustering" or "cluster analysis" in the literature, and which Sokal and Sneath (1963) call "numerical taxonomy," has as its distinguishing feature the grouping of items by "distance." In this case, distance refers to dissimilarities between items in a multi-dimensional space, rather than distances in the everyday geometrical sense. Central tendency for each group is achieved by finding the solution that minimizes the "distances" between pairs of group members. In essence, these methods are mathematical attempts to capture the kind of within-group similarity found in the intuitive and statistical variants of the statistical/type-variety methods and in polythetic descriptions. Common sub-classes of distance-based clustering include hierarchical clustering, optimal partitioning (including the k-means technique), density seeking, and multidimensional scaling (Aldenderfer and Blashfield, 1984; Everitt, 1974; Sokal and Sneath, 1963). These involve mathematical operations well beyond the scope of this book, and that we would never carry out manually, but hierarchical clustering in its simplest form serves as an illustration of their basic principles.

The essence of hierarchical clustering is that a set of objects or other phenomena are compared with respect to a large number of attributes, and those that are most similar to one another are grouped together, while very dissimilar ones are put into different groups. Such comparisons are only practical with the use of computers, and the design of the computer database is critical to the result (see below). The product of hierarchical clustering is presented as a tree-like and hierarchical diagram, thus lending superficial similarity to taxonomic classifications. Here, however, we start with real or imagined objects, rather than class definitions or a programme of hierarchical distinctions, and the grouping of items within "branches" of the tree is based on the relative distances (or dissimilarities) between them.

The following description of procedures is simply intended to give an idea of how a very simple form of hierarchical clustering works, not to encourage you to attempt it manually. It is worthwhile to read through it, but not to focus too much on methodological details. More detailed discussion can be found in Shennan (1988:190-240).

Typically, hierarchical clustering begins with a long list of attributes measured on a dichotomous scale, such as "present"/"absent" (table 3.1). Items are compared by means of a coefficient of similarity or dissimilarity, such as the ratio of the number of "agreements" between each pair of items to the total number of attributes on which they were compared. For example, we might compare ceramic rim sherds with the list of attributes in table 3.1 and, for each sherd, score a "1" if the attribute is present on the sherd and "0" if it is not. If two sherds are both scored "1" on 15 attributes, both scored "0" on another 15, but show different scores on another 70 attributes, we would calculate a *similarity coefficient* of ([15 + 15]/[15+15+70]) = 0.3. Having done this for a number of sherds, we can then construct a matrix with the artifact numbers arranged along two axes (table 3.2). Each cell in the matrix can be used to record the similarity coefficient for the pair of sherds represented by its combination of row and column but, because the matrix is diagonally symmetrical, we actually only have to compute this coefficient for the cells in one half and, of course, the cells in the diagonal (where the cells show the comparison of each item with itself), the similarity is always a perfect 1.0 or 100%.

Another way to look at the result is to use *dissimilarity* coefficients — these are simply the difference between 1 and the similarity coefficient — because the degree of dissimilarity is a kind of distance between items. In fact, with a small number of items we might be able to plot the items as points separated by these distances but, in a typical case, it would not be possible to represent all the points on a piece of paper because the "space" in which the points lie is multi-dimensional.

Where we go after calculating a similarity (or dissimilarity) coefficient depends on exactly what criterion for grouping we use. All the methods are based generally on the principle that pairs of items with high similarity coefficients should be grouped together, but things can be more complicated when we try to group more than two items. What if we already have a group consisting of two very similar clay pipes, for example, and want to add a third that has a high similarity coefficient with one member of the pair, but not the other?

The simplest, although not very practical, method is called **single-link clustering**, an agglomerative, hierarchical type of numerical clustering that serves to demonstrate how the similarity coefficients can result in groups. We begin by searching the matrix for the highest similarity coefficients that are not on the diagonal. In table 3.2, this would be 0.95 for the pair (5, 6). We then group artifacts 5 and 6 together at the similarity level of 0.95, as in figure 3.4a. We then search for the next-highest values and find a pair with a coefficient of 0.90, (1, 2), so we add these to the graph as in figure 3.4b. The next-highest coefficient is 0.85 for the pair (2, 3), but should we add sherd 3 to the group already containing sherds 1 and 2? In single-link cluster analysis, we only have to find a high degree of similarity with at least one member of an existing group for an item to qualify for membership in that group. So we do, even though the pair (1, 3) has a similarity coefficient of only 0.80, and sherd 3 is added to the graph in figure 3.4c at a similarity level of 0.85. We continue the process until all items are linked up at some level of similarity, and the result is a tree-like graph, or dendrogram, that represents a hierarchy of similarity. We then arbitrarily decide what level of similarity we will use as the "cut-off" for distinguishing groups, represented by the horizontal, dashed line on the graph in figure 3.4f, or decide on the basis of disjunctions or jumps in similarity how many groups we should have and where the breaks should be. Then the branch segments of the dendrogram above the cut-off (representing the highest levels of similarity) or the disjunctions are placed in the same group. In figure 3.4f, we have selected a similarity level of 0.75 as our cut-off and, as the dashed line intersects three branches, three groups result, with artifacts 1, 2 and 3 in one group, 5, 6 and 7 in another, and 4 standing on its own.

As with polythetic descriptions, single-link clustering produces groups whose members shared characteristics, and dissimilarities, are individually quite unpredictable. Just because a particular item is sufficiently similar to, in this case, a single member of an existing group to qualify for membership in that group, does not mean that it is very similar at all to other members of the group. To return to the hypothetical artifacts, A, B, and C, that illustrated this problem in polythetic descriptions, in single-link clustering it can be quite exaggerated because it is based on sharing attributes with only one other member of the group. For example, we could add a fourth member, D, with the attributes *ghijkl*; this would also share two-thirds of its attributes with one other member, C, but would share absolutely no attributes with A and be only one-third similar to B. This problem is sometimes known as **chaining**, because you can have a series of items linked by similarity, but items at either end of the chain that are not similar at all.

This is why analysts turned to other agglomerative methods, such as , double-link, total-link, or average-link cluster analysis, or "Ward's method." These versions of the method are more restrictive, requiring that each new member of a group have at least some minimum level of similarity with at least two, or with all previous members of the group, or that membership is based on the average of all the similarity coefficients of all possible pairs in the group. Ward's method agglomerates clusters in such a way as to minimize the increase in intra-group variability (or "sum of squares") when items are added to the group. The extra restrictions make it less likely that an added item will have nothing in common with some other members of that group, but do not guarantee that any two members will be greatly similar to each other, either. The

Table 3.1. Example of a matrix to record the presence (Y) and absence (N) of various attributes on six pottery sherds

	Artifact Number					
Attributes	1	2	3	4	5	6
Collar	Y	N	N	Y	N	Y
Punctate collar	Y	N	Y	N	Y	Y
Incised neck	N	Y	Y	Y	N	N
Interrupted lines	N	Y	N	N	Y	Y
Exterior punctates	N	Y	Y	N	Y	N
Exterior cord markings	Y	N	Y	Y	Y	Y
Notched lip	N	Y	N	N	N	N
Punctate lip\	Y	N	Y	Y	N	Y
Exterior herringbone	Y	Y	Y	Y	Y	Y
Exterior horizonal lines	N	N	N	N	N	N
Oblique lines exterior	N	Y	N	Y	Y	N
Vertical lines exterior	N	N	Y	N	N	N
Castellation	Y	Y	N	Y	N	Y
Sharp shoulder	N	N	N	N	N	Y
Lines on interior lip	Y	N	N	Y	N	N
Rouletted lip	N	Y	Y	N	Y	Y
Wavy rim	Y	Y	Y	N	Y	Y
Effigy on collar	Y	N	N	N	N	N
Ridge below collar	N	Y	N	N	Y	Y
Punctate row below collar	Y	Y	Y	N	Y	N

Table 3.2. Example of a similarity matrix for seven artifacts (after Orton, 1980:48-49). The rectangle marks the highest similarity score

	Artifact Number						
	1	2	3	4	5	6	7
1	1.0	.90	.80	.65	.40	.40	.30
2		1.0	.85	.60	.40	.30	.30
3			1.0	.50	.25	.25	.20
4				1.0	.70	.60	.55
5					1.0	.95	.80
6						1.0	.80
7							1.0

calculations for these methods are more tedious than for single-link clustering, but modern computer software makes it easy to carry out this type of grouping.

One of the characteristics of numerical clustering, as with polythetic sets, is that, although each member of a group has a certain level of similarity with other members of the group, the *way* it which it is similar to one member can be completely different from the way it is similar to another. To return once again to the primitive example above, item B is similar to A in that both have attributes cdef, but B is similar to C by sharing, not cdef, but efgh, and to D only in that both have gh. In other words, although all members of the group share a certain number of

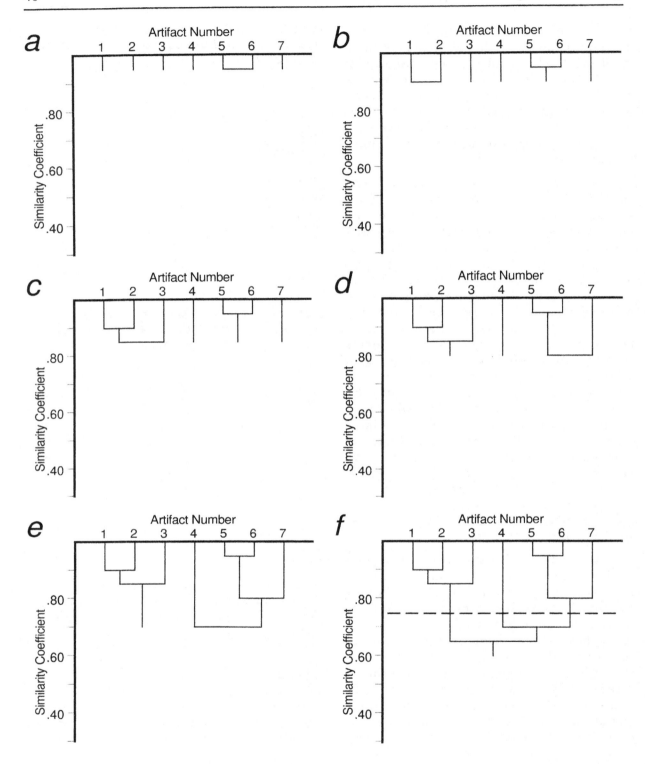

Figure 3.4. Steps in single-link cluster grouping using the data in table 3.2 (after Orton, 1980:48-49).

characteristics with other members of the group, they are not necessarily the same characteristics in each case. There is no way to predict in what ways any two members will be similar, although in groups formed by Ward's method or average-link clustering this will be less of a problem. Consequently, the groups formed by numerical clustering also have polythetic descriptions and constitute polythetic sets, even though different methods were used to form them.

The most serious objections to average-link clustering and similar hierarchical agglomerative methods is that a small change to one of the coefficients could result in a substantial change to the whole dendrogram, and not just to one or two branches (Jardine et al., 1967). If there is some uncertainty in the calculation of the coefficients (resulting from missing data and the selection of attributes), this is an undesirable characteristic, making many archaeologists reluctant to use numerical clustering for anything but exploratory analysis. Others, however, note that many objections to clustering are really objections to poor applications of it, and often specifically to poor choices of clustering method (Aldenderfer, 1987:24).

A common problem you should try to avoid if you do numerical clustering goes right back to your definition of attributes. You should define these very carefully and try to avoid redundancy and interdependence of attributes (Read, 1982). For example, if one of your attributes is "collar present" and another is "collar absent," you are really measuring the same thing twice and the two attributes are not independent of one another. A "Y" on one of these attributes must be matched by a "N" on the other. Similarly, if one of your attributes is "collar" and another is "punctates on collar," a "N" for the former must always be accompanied by a "N" on the latter, so they are not independent. This is a problem you can find in table 3.1. You should also try to avoid very rare attributes that would result in a score of "N" in almost every case. This can sometimes lead to artifacts being grouped together just because they all get "N" scores for lacking the same very unusual features. Those who have applied cluster analysis to characterize pottery by their chemical compositions have recognized the problem of highly correlated

data for a long time, but it does not always get sufficient attention in other applications.

As a result of problems with this kind of cluster analysis, archaeologists interested in grouping artifacts turned to other methods that were not based only on pairs of items, and Hodson (1970) introduced the **k-means technique** to archaeology. This method, also known as "locational clustering" (Kintigh 1990) partitions the items into a specified number (k) of clusters in such a way as to minimize the squared distance (dissimilarity) between each item and the centre of its group in "space." As it happens, two items that are members of the same group when there are, say, three groups (k=3) might be in different groups when there are four (k=4). You must decide what value of k seems reasonable, or repeat the method with different values of k. Then you can create a graph that shows how the relative error of fit (the average squared distance of the objects from the group centres as a percentage of their average squared distances from the centre of all the objects) is affected by increasing the number of groups, k (figure 3.5). The "best" number of groups is usually where we find a sharp bend, or "elbow," in the graph, indicating that there has been a marked improvement in fit over lower values of k, but that increasing k further results in relatively little improvement in fit.

Multidimensional scaling is another alternative among the distance-based methods. It more literally takes advantage of the fact that we can treat the dissimilarities between artifacts as distances in a multidimensional space. Unfortunately, we cannot accurately illustrate these distances by showing points on a map-like graph, because maps are only two-dimensional. But if we are willing to accept some distortion, much as we routinely distort Earth's geography to fit a spherical surface onto two-dimensional maps, we can try to illustrate these distances at least crudely. For example, we might allow a distortion so long as it correctly represented the rank-order of the distances (Orton, 1980: 55). Sometimes we must distort the map still further to make points representing the artifacts fit on it (figure 3.6). The technique requires use of a computer, even to group modest numbers of artifacts.

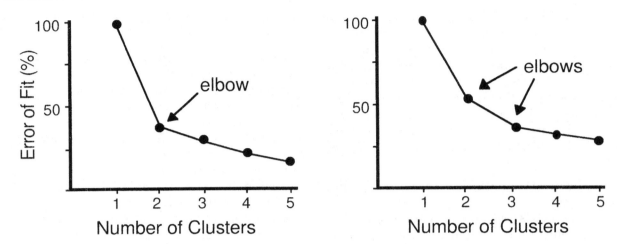

Figure 3.5. Plotting the error of fit in the k-means technique to find the best number of clusters. At left the elbow occurs at 2 clusters (k=2), while at right there are two elbows and, arguably, the best number of elbows is 3 (after Orton, 1980:53).

Generally speaking, the mathematical distance methods for grouping items have disappointed archaeologists who had hoped that they would provide an "objective" systematics. The results are far too sensitive to our initial decisions about what attributes to measure, how many to measure and how to measure them, to small errors in measurement, and to small changes in the population of items to which we apply the methods, for us to yield the consistent and "objective" results that some archaeologists expected. However, that does not mean that they are of no use at all, and they continue to be used, for example, in chemical characterization of artifacts, where there is greater agreement over the selection of attributes and identification of those that may be correlated.

A number of archaeological and non-archaeological works (e.g., Aldenderfer and Blashfield, 1984; Baxter, 1994) provide good introductions to other numerical clustering methods that are not as familiar to most archaeologists but in some cases deserve serious archaeological attention. Some are based, for example, on partitioning or density searching rather than hierarchical agglomeration or division, yet they share the characteristic that individual objects are treated as points in a multidimensional space, and the idea is to form groups in that space such that distances are minimized among group members, and are longer between members of different groups.

Attribute Association

The other major class of grouping methods Dunnell (1971:95-98) calls statistical clustering, but we will include it among *attribute association* to avoid, I hope, confusion with numerical clustering.

In attribute association, the key to the recognition of groups is associations between attributes. This is an extension of archaeologists' intuitive feeling that an artifact "type" can be defined or described by some recurring combination of attributes (as is the case with paradigmatic classifications and polythetic sets). For example, in classical archaeology one basic morphological type is the *amphora*, which has a narrow neck, two handles, one on either side of the neck, a body considerably wider than the neck, tapering to a pointed base or a knob at the bottom. We could define an amphora paradigmatically by a combination of attributes based on neck/body ratios, number of handles and so on. Attribute clustering is instead based on the idea that if we took a collection of Greek pottery we would find a large number of pots that showed a particular set of statistical relationships between neck width and body width, neck height and total height, and other sets of attributes, and that all the pots in this group would be *amphorae*. We expect there to be enough redundancy in the attributes of a type that we could use our knowledge of some of the attributes to predict the values of other attributes.

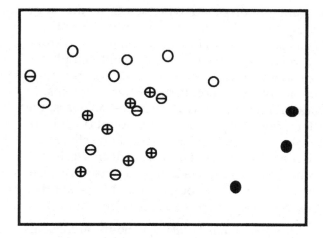

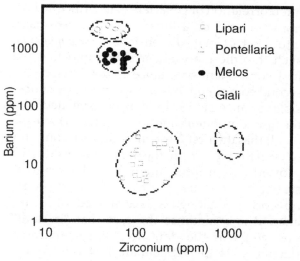

Figure 3.6. Two-dimensional "map" to illustrate the dissimilarities (distances) between 21 artifacts (after Hodson et al., 1966).

Figure 3.7. Relative concentrations of barium and zirconium in obsidians known to come from Lipari, Pontellaria, Melos, and Giali help to define clusters that can then be used to infer the sources of archaeological obsidians in the Mediterranean region (after Dixon et al., 1968).

Among the common informal applications of this approach is the attempt to group artifacts by associations between concentrations of elements or isotopes in their raw materials by the visual inspection of graphs. Here we look for distinct clusters in the ratios between various elements or isotopes that appear to be "fingerprints" for a particular source of raw materials. The classic example of this approach, as in figure 3.7, was the fingerprinting of obsidian sources, the first step both in studies of prehistoric exchange of obsidian and in obsidian hydration dating (Dixon et al., 1968). What makes the clusters important for our purposes is that samples taken from known sources consistently fall within distinct clusters or show similar ratios. If we have done a good job of sampling all possible sources, and if these sources are fairly homogeneous in their trace-element compositions, we can then be fairly confident that archaeological samples that fall into the same cluster as one of the "known" samples also had the same source. In other words, we can predict the value of an **extrinsic** attribute (source of material) as long as we know the values of the other interrelated, **intrinsic** attributes. As a result of this kind of clustering, archaeologists have had considerable success at identifying the most likely sources

for artifacts made of obsidian, silver, lead, bronze, pottery, and other materials.

Examples such as these demonstrate what the results of attribute association have in common with the central-tendency methods. It is often true that the distances between points grouped together in the "space" of the graph, as in figure 3.7, are small relative to the distances between points in different groups. The difference lies in the way we arrive at the groupings. In the central-tendency methods we concentrated on those distances (or on their opposites, similarities), while in attribute association we instead concentrate on the interplay between dimension. Attribute association, like paradigmatic classification, is dimensional. Having used this interplay in an exploratory way, however, many **archaeometrists** attempting to group artifacts by their trace-element chemistry would go on to employ either one of the hierarchical cluster methods already mentioned or one of the following methods.

Principal Components Analysis (PCA): This is a more formal multivariate technique based on attribute associations, which works well with data, such as the chemical compositions of pottery fabrics, that tend to show a lot of intercorrelation or covariance. Its principle is to transform the data linearly and orthogonally into a set of new dimensions, or *components*, such that these are uncorrelated and that the first component's variance is maximized, the second component has the second-highest possible variance, subject to being uncorrelated with the first component, and so on. This can have the result that the first few components account for most of the variance in the data, and these can be plotted on graphs much like the original scatterplot. Because the axes of the graph are now oriented along the axes of maximum variance, it is sometimes the case that "natural" groupings in the data are better separated (Baxter, 1994:48-99; Shennan, 1988:245-70). Because it is more often used in seriation than in grouping, we will return to this method in chapter 14.

Correspondence Analysis (CA): Although sometimes described as a technique competing with PCA, correspondence analysis is in fact a kind of PCA that is appropriate for non-negative, discrete data, such as artifact counts (see Baxter 1994:100-107; Shennan 1988:283-86). The method is quite popular among archaeologists in continental Europe, but only beginning to make inroads in Anglo-American archaeology.

Factor Analysis: This is another multivariate technique that works well on data tables containing considerable intercorrelation or covariance (Lawley and Maxwell, 1971). Like PCA, factor analysis expresses the data by new dimensions but, unlike PCA or CA, it does so by reducing the large number of dimensions of variation between the artifacts to a few composite dimensions, or "factors," that are something like summaries of several covarying or correlated attributes at once (for detailed discussion, see Shennan, 1988:271-80). When two dimensions are highly correlated (either negatively or positively), this implies the possibility that they are merely *aspects* of some other dimension. For example, if length and width of a group of artifacts are positively correlated, this implies that the artifacts differ from one another in size, but not much in shape. Length and width, in that case, are aspects of the component, size. In other cases, the exact nature of the component may be less obvious with some dimensions, perhaps,

negatively correlated with others in the same component. The chemical compositions of artifacts such as pottery can be expected to show correlations between some elements simply because those elements combine in a constant ratio in one of the minerals the pottery contains. In addition, when, as with chemical analyses, the data consist of proportions (amounts in percent or parts per million), increase of one element is necessarily associated with a decrease in another. None of the data, in this sense, are independent of one another, and this is another reason to expect correlations in the data.

Configurationist typology: Some archaeologists have advocated using a particular version of attribute association, with data at the nominal, or even dichotomous, scale, in the hope of discovering "natural" types. The founding proponent of this approach is Albert Spaulding , who argues that "a pronounced association of two attributes is the minimum requirement" to demonstrate that a type exists (1953:306). Here a type is "a group of artifacts exhibiting a consistent assemblage of attributes whose combined properties give a characteristic pattern" (Spaulding, 1953:305).

This method begins with a paradigmatic classification, often with only dichotomous scales in each dimension, and in a sense it is a test of the paradigm. Following classification of a collection of artifacts from a single **assemblage** with this paradigm, one proceeds to analyze the resulting groups (members of each class) for statistically significant associations between attributes. While attributes may be arbitrary in the sense that they are selected from an infinity of possibilities, adherents of the Spaulding method argue that statistical tests will show whether "valid types" exist in the classification (Watson et al., 1971:126-132). According to this view, a type only exists if there is a non-random relationship between those attributes. This means that, if we know the value of an artifact's measurement in one dimension, we can *predict* its value in another dimension.

For example, in figure 3.8, the paradigm at top, with the number of sherds that fall into each class shown, has no non-random relationship between the two dimensions. If we know that a particular sherd is shell-tempered, we cannot predict whether or not it has black-on-red decoration with much better than a 50% success rate; in other words, we can only guess, and would conclude that the paradigm provides no "valid types." In the lower paradigm, the class memberships are quite different. Here we could predict, with a high degree of success, that any shell-tempered sherd will have black-on-red decoration, and that any sherd that lacks black-on-red decoration will probably not be shell-tempered. "Black-on-red, shell-tempered," in this case, is a valid type, and the typology is verified. The statistical test that can be used to test the validity of the paradigm is the chi-square test, but we will not pursue that here (see Drennan, 1996:187-92; Shennan, 1988:65-76).

Those who follow Spaulding's approach do not accept that archaeological typologies are only arbitrary classifications or abitrary sets of groups, designed for archaeologists' own purposes. Instead, they assert that systematics is a "process of discovery of combinations of attributes ... not an arbitrary procedure of the classifier" (Spaulding, 1953: 305), and that the statistical approach just described tests the validity of these types. Some archaeologists have interpreted this as meaning that the method discovers "emic" categories of the prehistoric makers and users of the artifacts. **Emic** categories are ones that native (in this case prehistoric) informants would accept as valid or true, as opposed to **etic** categories, constructed by the (outside) observer, that can be validated analytically or scientifically. The terms (Pike, 1954) come from the linguistic distinction between phonemics (a native speaker's perception of distinct sounds) and phonetics (a linguist's system of distinct sounds). As attribute association is itself a scientific method constructed by outside analysts without information from native informants, however, its products are actually etic, even in the somewhat unlikely event that they approximate categories that a prehistoric person would recognize.

We can highlight some problems with this approach by turning to interval scales instead of the nominal ones that its users favor. Spaulding was looking for association between dimen-

sions. If he encountered data with a good correlation, as in figure 3.9a, presumably he would conclude that there were two valid types, long, wide projectiles and short, narrow ones. The data in figure 3.9b would lead him to the same conclusion, but here, unlike the previous case, we at least see two distinct clusters, much as we did with the data on trace elements in obsidian (figure 3.7), and it is relatively easy to decide how to partition the data. In figure 3.9c, however, we have two distinct clusters again, but with data reduced to nominal scale, as usually happens, we would not recognize any types, because there are approximately equal numbers of observations in each quarter of the graph. Even at the interval scale, the correlation coefficient for this case would not be very high because there are two distinct relationships between the two dimensions that would be "blended" by a simple correlation. Furthermore, it is questionable if even the data in figures 3.9a and b make good types. What we may have is a good example of **autocorrelation**. Length and width are correlated not necessarily because makers of the projectile points thought of the particular length and width combination as a distinct kind of projectile point, but because these are really "sub-dimensions" of a third dimension, size, as in Factor Analysis. So there are big projectiles and small ones, and they all have about the same width/length ratio, but there is nothing in this correlation to lead us to define two types — long-wide and short-narrow — rather than one, as there is a contiuum from small to large. Not all pairs of attributes that show good correlations result in useful, or even common-sensical, types.

In addition, some typologies that are intuitively appealing and have explanatory utility fail to show the kinds of associations that the Spaulding approach requires. Hodson (1982) draws our attention to a cross-culturally useful classification of human social roles that the Spaulding approach would not verify. Here, a fairly typical sample of people, and a paradigm with the dimensions of sex and age, would lead to their distribution among the categories, "men", "women," "girls," and "boys" in a way that is not statistically distinguishable from a random distribution. Consequently, we would have to conclude that our everyday classification of people by these four categories is not a valid typology and does not reflect the emic categories of Western cultures. Only if our sample of people came from a context in which such issues as sexual division of labour and child-rearing perhaps gave us a rather unusual distribution of people would we find any statistically verifiable associations between sex and age. We will return to this issue of "natural" and arbitrary types in the next section.

Grouping methods, with their more flexible yet less precise criteria for membership, often serve either as useful exploratory methods to help us construct the rules for a classification, or to provide a more practical alternative to formal classification (cf. Adams and Adams, 1991). Most archaeologist's work on systematics is iterative, or dialectical. That is, there is a back-and-forth interplay between conceptual categories or modal types and archaeological data, as units are abandoned or refined. We might start out with a number of groups of artifacts, perhaps initially based on stratigraphic context, and then try to ascertain what attributes most members of each group share, and that seem to distinguish them from other groups. We could subsequently use patterns in these attributes to construct the rules for a classification that we can apply to other artifacts that were not members of the original groups. It is possible and even likely that, during this process, we will find some members of some groups that lack characteristics that most of the other group members share. Consequently these items do not qualify for membership in the same class as other group members. This is an important aspect of the differences between grouping and classification. Alternatively, we might eschew formal classification in favor of more carefully described groups. It is even necessary to admit that some typologies defy the classification just presented by combining classification principles at higher levels in a hierarchy with grouping principles (such as central tendency) at lower levels. In some cases, however, we require a nominal scale that is as unambiguous as possible and that is not altered by new observations, as in defining fields in databases, when only classification principles will suffice.

	Shell-tempered	Not Shell-tempered
Black-on-Red	26	25
Not Black-on-Red	22	27

	Shell-tempered	Not Shell-tempered
Black-on-Red	(64)	8
Not Black-on-Red	7	(44)

Figure 3.8. Paradigmatic classification with the same dimensions as in figure 3.2 but two different sets of members. At top (after Watson et al., 1971:128), there is no predictable relationship between shell tempering and painted decoration. At bottom, shell-tempered pots are more likely to have black-on-red decoration, leading to the definition of two "types" (circled).

Types or Classes?

In the last section, I began to use the terms "typology" and "type" without distinguishing them from "classification" or "grouping" and "class" or "group." Indeed, that is what most archaeologists do. Here, however, I would like to offer a narrower definition of typology that, perhaps, gets us out of the dilemma of what makes a "valid type." It differs from other definitions in the archaeological literature (e.g., Adams and Adams, 1991:91).

If classification and grouping are arbitrary, how do we decide on the definition of useful types for an archaeological systematics?

For many years some archaeologists have assumed or maintained that archaeological types have inherent meaning that we need only discover. This is the position of configurationist typologists, some of those employing statistical clustering methods, and others. V. Gordon Childe (1956:9), for example, claimed that "types are just creations of individuals that have been approved, adopted, and objectified by some society," expressing a normative definition of type that was common at the time, and associ-

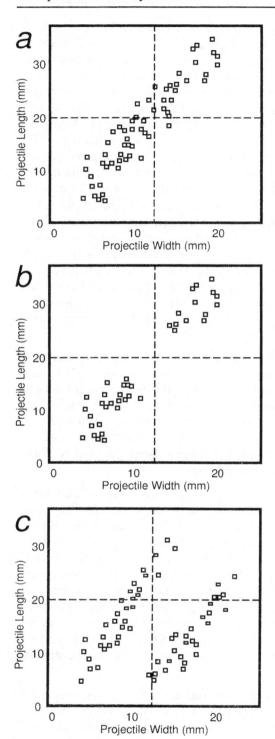

Figure 3.9. Three different relationships between the length and width of fictitious projectile points, with dashed lines dividing the field up into four quarters analogous to the cells in a paradigm with dichotomous dimensions.

ated types with a cultural group, such as ethnic group. Even then, however, there were authors who maintained that types were abstractions that we, as archaeologists, constructed for our own purposes, such as chronology or determining function (e.g., Steward, 1954). Some archaeologists assume that there is inherent or natural meaning in the types, but still focus on particular kinds of meaning. For example, Read (1974:217) argues that the data should be partitioned in such a way as to group artifacts that were used in particular activities. At present there is little agreement about what consititues a type or typology.

I propose that a **typology** should be defined as *a classification or grouping that has explanatory (or meaningful) relationships with attributes that are not intrinsic to the classification or grouping itself.* A typology is an explanation in Gardin's (1980) sense of the word, and not merely the structure for a compilation. To create one archaeologists use relevant extrinsic attributes of spatial, chronological, social, economic, functional, and symbolic context (cf. Adams and Adams, 1991: 175-76). Non-random associations with one or more of these dimensions tend to verify the typology. My usage of "typology" is reminiscent of Adams and Adams' (1991:157-68) recognition that archaeological typologies are used for particular purposes, such as chronology, and that the classes have relevance and meaning with respect to those purposes (1991:35-38). However, they use the term, "typology," to refer to the sorting of artifacts into classes (1991:47), or the partitioning of artifacts into categories that are mutually exclusive and non-hierarchical (1991:78-80; 91-92, 214). That is not the usage here. In fact, their usage resembles measurement of artifacts with a nominal scale.

What makes a typology explanatory is that there are non-random associations, not between the *intrinsic* attributes, but between its classes and one or more *extrinsic* attributes that have to do with context.

When we say that a type "works," or serves a purpose, we nearly always mean that it co-occurs or co-varies with something that is external to itself. A pottery type is found only during a certain time period, or a presumed ritual object is found only in certain locations, or a tool type only occurs in association with certain other tool types. The more consistently this is true, the more clearly it indicates that there is "something going on"; i.e. that there is an inherent order in the data that has not simply been imposed by us (Adams and Adams, 1991: 68).

For example, what makes the groupings in figure 3.7 useful is not any statistical association between levels of barium and zirconium, but that obsidians from the same source all show very similar ratios of barium to zirconium, while differing from obsidians from other sources in this ratio. Thus there is a non-random association between the barium/zirconium ratio and the spatial context of the raw material source. If the four clusters in figure 3.7 each contained a mixture of obsidians from various sources, the groupings would be useless because it would not allow us to predict the sources of unprovenienced obsidians. They would have no *meaning*, or at least none that we have discovered.

The same is true of the examples that Spaulding (1953) and Watson et al. (1971; 1984) cite. A statistical association between the intrinsic attributes of a collection of artifacts does not verify a typology, but a statistical association between the categories of a typology and the spatial, chronological, social, functional, or ideological context of the categories' members would indicate that the typology was useful in our attempt to construct explanations or discover meaning. Even Spaulding hinted at, or at least allowed, this when he recognized that provenience could be considered an attribute that might be relevant to type definition:

> Thus a site might yield two kinds of vessels [that] differed only in the presence or absence of a single physical attribute, say a lip flange on one. If nothing but physical [intrinsic] properties were considered, both kinds would be included in one pottery type…. But if the flanged lip appeared only on vessels found in graves and the plain lip was confined to village debris, it would be obvious that the potters had in mind two types with different functional connotations (Spaulding, 1953:311).

To go back to the example in figure 3.8, if we were to add a third dimension, but this time an extrinsic one, we might conceivably obtain the distribution in figure 3.10. Here we assume that

the collection is from two assemblages instead of one, from stratigraphic layers called Stratum I and Stratum II. The exact same distribution of pottery as in the top of figure 3.8 now takes on some interesting properties. Now almost all of the black-on-red, shell-tempered sherds and most of the sherds that are neither black-on-red nor shell-tempered come from Stratum I, while Stratum II shows the opposite pattern. Here I have constructed an extreme distribution to make the point, but the important thing is that what makes this particular classification a typology is that it helps us identify change over time. If we know the combination of tempering and decoration on a sherd, we can predict with a high degree of confidence to which stratum it belongs. We can explain the distribution of sherds across the categories by reference to stratigraphic context and, indirectly, time (cf. Adams and Adams, 1991:179-80).

Other typologies are explanatory because they show non-random associations between groups or classes and the functions for which tools were designed, the uses to which they were put, the age, class, gender, or ethnicity of their makers or users, the technology used to make them, the mechanisms that led to their deposition, and so on.

Archaeologists have recognized this for a long time in their use of "types of types," such as morphological types, historical-index types, functional types, and chronological types (e.g., Childe, 1956:14-15; Ford, 1954; Steward, 1954). It is important to remember that the goal-oriented construction of these typologies involves intentional bias. Typologies that are designed to have chronological usefulness, for example, stress discontinuities over time and tend to omit or gloss over attributes that might show continuity.

Post-processual archaeologists, who are critical of positivist, science-based approaches to archaeology, have not spared typology. One criticism pertains specifically to chronological typologies, which, according to Shanks and Tilley (1987:10-11), involve a "commodified time" that obscures meaningful differences between things and suggest that the mere assigning of artifacts to some distant period is a satisfying explanation in itself. Certainly all systematics reduce the complexity of the real world to a simple representation, as treating every observation as unique would make it impossible for us to compare assemblages or even count things. The other criticism is rather out-of-date. Although I would classify chronological typologies as explanatory only on the grounds that they have meaning in terms of extrinsic dimensions, most modern archaeologists would consider this only a first step toward more interesting explanations, such as explaining *why* social or economic circumstances changed over time. A more serious criticism by the post-processualists focusses on those assertions that it is possible to "discover" types or discern their meaning. Rather than define types that are assumed to reproduce the single, emic, past meaning of objects, post-processualists describe multi-dimensional variability, the "type" varying with context. A single artifact can have quite different meanings depending on this context, a concept they call **multivocality**. For example, a particular artifact may have been a "stylish serving bowl" to its first user 7000 years ago, a "gift" to its second user, "rubbish" to the same user some years later, "Yarmoukian, herring-bone incised" to a modern archaeologist, a curiosity or even ash-tray to a modern pot-hunter, an "art object" to a museum curator, and an investment to an art dealer. Some archaeologists have exploited possible changes in meaning to explain artifact distributions and the introduction of new types (Bradley, 1984:70-73). Few archaeologists today would maintain that any single artifact typology is universally valid, let alone that it captures the emic categories of prehistoric makers or users of the artifacts. At the same time, this does not mean that we cannot construct typologies that are meaningful in that they help us to recognize and understand patterns in data, observed in the present, that are relevant to the past.

Practical Considerations in Typology

Before moving on, it is also important to recognize the practical dimension of archaeological typology. Whether we use them to order data about sites, artifacts, cultures, concepts, or features, our typologies must be usable as well as useful.

a

Dimension 1 (Temper)

Dimension 2 (Painting)	Shell-tempered	Not Shell-tempered
Black-on-Red	26	25
Not Black-on-Red	22	27

Stratum I

b

Dimension 1 (Temper)

Dimension 2 (Painting)	Shell-tempered	Not Shell-tempered
Black-on-Red	25	3
Not Black-on-Red	11	20

Stratum II

c

Dimension 1 (Temper)

Dimension 2 (Painting)	Shell-tempered	Not Shell-tempered
Black-on-Red	1	22
Not Black-on-Red	11	7

Figure 3.10. The same distribution of pottery as in figure 3.8 has a different significance when we add the stratigraphic dimension.

Among the things we need to consider is how easily we can recognize or measure the attributes that are important in defining or describing types. Some attributes that would be very useful are only rarely preserved on individual (and often fragmentary) specimens. Often it is helpful to have attributes that are regularly observable on almost every specimen, to avoid overuse of the "unknown" category. In addition, an attribute that would otherwise serve our typology's purpose quite well might be quite useless if only a handful of highly-trained specialists was capable of distinguishing it, or if its measurement was very time-consuming or expensive (cf. Adams and Adams, 1991:237). For example, we are rarely able to do chemical analyses on all our artifacts, making chemical composition impractical as an attribute for any but the smallest collections.

Another consideration is redundancy. Even if chemical analyses are possible, there would be no point in conducting expensive or time-consuming analyses if the resulting data contributed nothing to the typology but confirm groupings already well established by other attributes (Adams and Adams, 1991:236). We need to consider carefully how many attributes are really necessary to define or describe a useful set of types.

Further, it is impractical to elaborate a typology until there are thousands of types. Each type should have a purpose (Adams and Adams, 1991:242). For classifications we may prefer sets of categories to which we can expect to assign reasonably large numbers of items, rather than having many "empty" classes. However, our initial exploration of the data often requires making observations of many attributes, and defining or describing many categories or types, that later on turn out to contribute little to our typology's purpose. Because it is impossible to determine this until after we have tested the typology with real data, real archaeological databases, as we will see later in the chapter, often include categories that are partly conventional. We use certain categories to record information because other archaeologists have found them useful for a particular purpose and we may, or may not, find them so.

A further factor is distinctiveness, with respect to the typology's purpose. We prefer types and attributes that allow us to be confident and precise about their meaning. For example, for a chronological typology we would prefer types that only occurred over very short periods of time to ones that changed little or not at all over very long periods. Archaeologists sometimes call the former types, "highly diagnostic" (or even "type fossils").

We might also prefer attributes whose boundaries are reasonably sharp and reproducible, from observer to observer, to ones whose boundaries are fuzzy or ambiguous as long as those attributes are just as useful with respect to our typology's purpose. Hand (1997:99, 109-115) would describe the desirable characteristic of having easily distinguishable categories as *separability*. Separability is high when categories are perfectly separated, as happens when certain attributes are uniquely associated with one class in a classification, as I define it in this chapter. Grouping methods, because they are **polythetic**, or have overlapping sets of attributes, can result in low separability. Clearly it is desirable to select attributes that result in reasonably high separability.

We will want to consider whether to use our typology to sort all our evidence, or only some of it. Projects that only have a few hundred artifacts to deal with may not need to worry about this, but some archaeological excavations result in tens of thousands of artifacts that could not practically be sorted in great detail.

Still other considerations are consistency and accuracy. Although we would like all the people working in the laboratory to type material in the same way, we must expect some error and inconsistency. We need to decide just how much error is tolerable, and find ways to keep errors from exceeding this limit (e.g., Prentiss, 1998; Whittaker et al., 1998). For example, having the same artifacts typed by several analysts will serve as a check on consistency. At the same time, we do not need to waste resources on reducing the degree of error below that limit. For example, William Adams found that 90% agreement between sorters was sufficient for him to use his chronological typology of Nubian pottery effectively (Adams and Adams, 1991:238). However, you should still report your estimates of measurement and typological error, as emphasized in chapter 2. For errors of **misclassification**, we may refer to the **error rate**, which is simply the proportion of misassignments. The approach treats the error of misclassifying a Combed Beaker as a Corded Beaker, for example, as equivalent to the error of misclassifying a Corded Beaker as a Combed Beaker. All misclassifications are assumed to be equally serious (see also Nance, 1987:258-67). More sophisticated measures of misclassification may account for the fact that some kinds of error are more serious than others. For example, to misclassify a Corded Beaker as "unknown" may be less serious than misclassifying it as a Combed Beaker. In such cases, misclassification error may refer to the expected costs or risks of different kinds of misclassifications, and may employ a "confusion matrix" for the classification rules (Hand, 1997).

Another practical aspect concerns the second half of this chapter. If we require categories either for whole archaeological entities or for their attributes that have unambiguous and unchanging definitions, as happens when we construct computer databases, we need systematics based on classification, or at least groups with standardized descriptions and very high separability. Even if grouping might seem to express the nuances of a type more effectively, in a given context, it simply would not do to have database fields with definitions that changed from one season of excavation to the next. The usefulness of the whole database for making comparisons and detecting patterns depends on reasonable consistency of definition for its fields. These definitions should be recorded in a data dictionary (see below).

Finally, we even need to consider whether typology is the most effective tool with which to achieve our goal. For example, although we might be able to sort sites or layers within a site chronologically with a typology, in principle it is possible that a series of radiocarbon dates and careful stratigraphic analysis might accomplish the job more cheaply or more effectively (Adams and Adams, 1991: 234).

COMPILATIONS: DATABASE DESIGN

Now that we have considered the systematics that are used to order compilations, we can turn to the ways modern compilations are structured and manipulated. Although compilations can be very simple, such as a collection of file cards each showing the picture of an artifact along with a few identifying labels and measurements, most archaeological compilations require some sophistication. Modern archaeological compilations are frequently computer databases, but the same principles are involved in other kinds of indexed compilations.

The purpose of this section is not to give instruction in the use of any particular type of computer hardware or database software — these change far too quickly — but to introduce

some important principles that guide the effective use of these tools in archaeological applications.

Information Language

Compilations often require us to construct an information language for the consistent and efficient recording of relevant observations, while measurement in the broad sense consists of comparing the item to be measured with a standard scale and representing the comparison symbolically. Natural language is generally too ambiguous, too inconsistent or too wordy for many analytical purposes, although it has its strengths as well.

For archaeologists, an information language is simply a system of representation. Although archaeologists have used various information languages almost since the inception of the discipline, it was the application of computers to archaeological work that caused some archaeologists to think about information languages more explicitly. Especially in the early years of archaeological computing, when computers were primitive by today's standards and archaeologists had to describe sites or artifacts with codes of no more than 80 characters, it was necessary to devote considerable attention to systems for reducing a theoretically infinite number of observations to a small set of numbers or letters that could be manipulated electronically. Today, although modern computers allow us to make these observations with something much nearer to natural language, efficient and meaningful analyses still require a consistent information language, even if it sometimes bears considerable resemblance to English or some other natural language.

Graphical Information Languages

Archaeologists have used graphical methods for simplifying the description of archaeological objects and making these descriptions consistent for more than a century. Maps and technical drawings are always simplifications of reality, because they omit details that are not relevant to their makers' or users' purposes, while they also typically depict information that would not be

Figure 3.11. Example of a technical drawing of lithics (drawings by J. Pfaff).

apparent in a photograph. Archaeologists' maps and section drawings all employ information language in this way, but their drawings of artifacts are perhaps the most obvious examples of graphical information language.

Take lithic drawings, for example. Archaeologists have had the option of publishing photographs of lithics for more than a century, but have almost always decided instead to publish drawings in which certain important attributes are encoded (figure 3.11). First, lithic analysts use strict conventions or rules about the orientation of lithics, and so drawings of flakes typically show one ventral and one dorsal view, side by side, both oriented with the proximal end (the end nearest the striking platform) at the bottom. Where it is relevant, they may also show one or more edges, oriented so as to match up with the dorsal or ventral view. On each drawing, they typically show the edges of flake scars as solid lines and use series of curved, tapering lines to simulate the rippling that occurs on knapped flint as the result of shock waves trav-

elling through the material during manufacture, and to indicate the direction of flake removal. They may use stippling to indicate cortex, and will have other conventions to represent some materials, such as basalt or quartz, as well as damage or polish on the artifact's surface. Finally, there may be special symbols to indicate something of how the tools were made. The most common example is a small arrow to indicate the position and direction of spall removal on burins and other tools for which production involved the burin technique. Some of the best lithic drawings may seem like beautiful works of art or bear remarkable resemblance to real tools, but in fact even these both simplify reality and emphasize aspects thought to be particularly relevant to lithic researchers (see chapters 7 and 17).

Pottery drawings also provide excellent examples of graphical information language. Particularly in modern archaeological publications, ceramic illustrations usually bear very little re-

PLATE 36

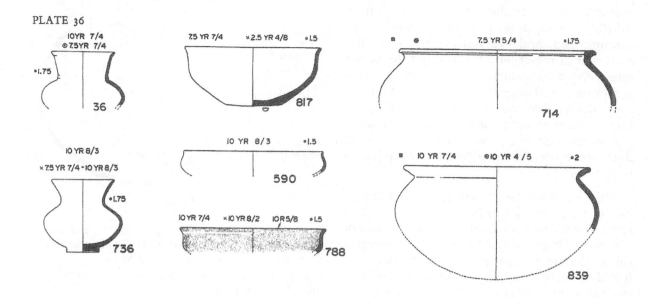

Figure 3.12. Example of drawing conventions for pottery from Pella, Jordan (from Smith, 1973). Note how the drawings show the exterior, interior and a vertical section through the pot, and encode information about surface finish and color.

semblance to the fragments of vessels on which they are based. First, ceramic illustrators typically use information from the curvature of a sherd (fragment) to estimate the diameter of the vessel from which the sherd was originally a part, and then to reconstruct a view of the whole pot over as much of the profile (in the vertical axis) as is preserved (figure 3.12). Furthermore, this reconstructed view is conventional and highly stylized, with a cutaway allowing us to see the exterior, interior, and section of the pot simultaneously. European publications typically put this cutaway on the left, while American ones typically put it on the right. The illustrator also has conventions for showing surface treatments (e.g., paint, burnish, patterned slip), carinations, decoration, damage, and uncertain reconstructions. Typically handles are shown with sections in a different axis than the cutaway, to indicate whether they are strap-like, tubular, or some other shape, and some special features may warrant close-ups or additional views, as for mat-impressed bases or decorated rims. Some information languages also show symbols on the drawing itself that encode information on fabric, colour, firing, and so on (e.g., Smith, 1973; figure 3.12).

It may seem at first glance that these are simply drawings, but they are in fact coded representations of lithics and pottery. If they did not display more of the information that is important to us than would a simple photograph of a flake or sherd, we would not be using them. That the technical drawings show information that a photograph cannot has even led some archaeologists to show the drawing and photograph side-by-side in publication (e.g., Rast, 1978).

Digital Information Languages

While the graphical information languages are excellent at depicting and storing information about the shapes of artifacts, they do not offer a very efficient way for us to sort and retrieve particular kinds of artifacts. If I wanted to find examples of a particular rim profile in a graphical database of pottery, I would have to sift through each and every drawing to identify ones that fit my criteria for that profile, or use relatively cumbersome and complex pattern-recognition software that would probably be even slower than me. In data processing, we ideally want to make retrieval of information just as easy as storage, and that is why electronic databases have come into their own in archaeology.

In data processing, an information language can be used either for reducing complex objects to a conventional representation in a database or for amplifying a simple query into alternative forms that may represent it in the database (Gardin, 1980). The former makes it easier to store large quantities of information; the latter, the ability to ask questions of the database, is essential for retrieval of information.

The tactics of information language may involve not only some kind of vocabulary or **lexical units** (geometrical shapes, edges, brush swirls, etc.), but also **orientation rules** to lay down a standard position for the objects being studied, **segmentation rules**, which account for the conventional division of an object into separate parts (e.g., pottery segments, figure 3.13), and **differentiation rules** that determine the kinds of the distinctions we will record for each segment (Gardin, 1980). It is worth noting what these concepts mean in terms of systematics. Lexical units are the symbolic representations of attributes and categories or types, differentiation rules are related to the definition of categories, and rules for orientation and segmentation ensure reasonable consistency in the way we measure attributes. You will note that the usual assumption here is that we are using classification, not grouping: the rules are *definitions* intended to make classes that are *mutually exclusive* and *unambiguous*, where at all possible. Although it is possible to have database queries that are more forgiving — for example, ones that would show you artifacts that are similar to the specific type you asked for — most databases will not do this, and even a simple spelling error in a type name will lead to the omission of data. We have already seen some of these rules being used in

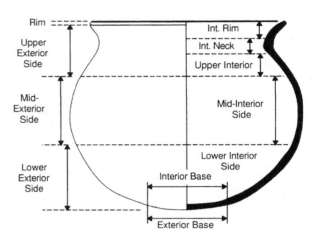

Figure 3.13. One possible way to divide a pot into segments (after Skibo, 1992:114). The definitions for these segments would constitute the segmentation rules for an information language used to describe pots.

graphical information languages. Now let us turn to examples of their use in electronic databases.

Pottery can be described by an infinity of attributes, many of which are discussed in chapter 8. For now, let us consider some very basic lexical units, orientation rules, segmentation rules, and differentiation rules we might consider in creating an information language for describing pottery. Typically, analysts consider vessels to consist of a number of segments, such as "rim," "neck," "shoulder," "body," "base," and "handle," although many more or somewhat fewer segments may be necessary for a particular ceramic assemblage, and the definitions vary. Differentiation rules define how each sherd should be assigned to a segment, just as other differentiation rules assign it to a chronological or functional type. For example, you would need a rule to allow you to assign, say, a sherd with portions of both rim and handle to a particular segment category in a consistent, unambiguous way. Orientation rules for pottery are usually fairly simple, requiring that the sherd be "stanced" in the position it would have when it was part of a whole pot, standing vertically, but also with conventional definitions of interior and exterior and orientation of decoration. The lexicon would usually include some symbolic representation of the different categories

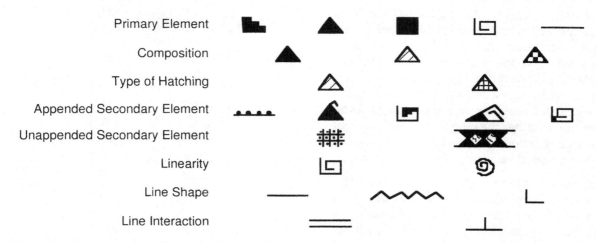

Primary Element				
Composition				
Type of Hatching				
Appended Secondary Element				
Unappended Secondary Element				
Linearity				
Line Shape				
Line Interaction				

Figure 3.14. One possible set of differentiation rules for pottery decoration that includes primary and secondary decorative elements (after Plog, 1980:51).

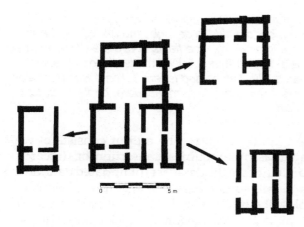

Figure 3.15. Possible segmentation rules for the description of house plans at the Samarran site of Tell as-Sawwan, Iraq (Banning, 1997).

for such things as rim shape, form of decoration, or non-plastic inclusions in the fabric, as well as the labels for the various segments and axes of orientation. Differentiation rules — essentially classification rules — help analysts assign a particular sherd to a particular category unambiguously by defining that category in a careful way. Often this involves a step-by-step, hierarchical procedure that results in a taxonomic classification, but paradigmatic classification is also common, particularly as computers can categorize materials by many attributes simultaneously.

For lithic materials information language works in much the same way. Lithic analysts typically employ such segments as "dorsal" and "ventral" sides, and will have explicit orientation rules that define the axes of length and width and the position of retouch. The lexicon will include the terms for segments and orientation as well as labels for categories of retouch, angles, raw material, platform shape, and so on (see chapter 7).

Decoration on pottery, basketry and other materials poses special problems, and archaeologists have found many ways to deal with it. Often the orientation and segmentation rules for decoration have to be very complicated in order to make the kinds of distinctions that the analyst thinks will be important (figure 3.14); in other cases, analysts construct a simple, yet rather lengthy lexicon that corresponds with a nominal classification for whole decorative patterns, rather than taking tiny segments of decoration separately. Although the same principles are relevant to decoration on other materials, and even tatoos, we will deal with decoration in more detail in the chapter on pottery (chapter 8).

Ancient Mesopotamian cylinder seals provide one of the most ambitious examples of archaeologists' attempts to apply an information language. Digard et al.(1975) created a large lexicon for the symbols, figures, and other objects depicted on the seals, along with detailed segmentation rules for distinguishing elements depicted on different parts of each seal, and a complex grammar that actually allows us to distinguish how the different lexical elements are related to each other. For example, on cylinder seals showing a king, a god, a throne, and a star, we can tell whether the king or the god is on the throne, whether the king is to the left or right of the god, is kneeling or standing, and how the star is positioned relative to the other elements.

Information language can be just as important in describing architecture. In building up a database of structures or building plans, we would want orientation rules to distingish between the long axis, short axis, front, sides, and back of each building or each room, as well as each building's compass orientation. We would need lexical units with which to label various rooms, features, post arrangements, doorways, and so on (figure 3.15). We might want ways to describe the relationships between rooms much as Digard et al. (1975) described the relationship between images on cylinder seals, or to describe the "depth" of each room relative to the outside of the building or to other rooms (Hillier and Hanson, 1984). Other lexical items might include room size, building area, building shape, wall material, construction method, and so on.

Database Design

A **database** is a reservoir of information that supplies users with the data from which they make decisions, inferences, interpretations, explore patterns, or test hypotheses. A database can be something like a telephone book or index card file — that is, it can be synonymous with what we have been calling, following Gardin (1980), a compilation. But nowadays the term database most often refers to an integrated body of data accessible through automated processing. An integrated database is a collection of interrelated data stored together with controlled redundancy to serve one or more applications independent of programs that use the data.

Most databases share some basic kinds of input and output. Users will want to make inquiries, add or modify data (transactions), or add or modify the database itself, all of which

SITES	
Site Number	
Site Name	A
Site Size	N
Map Coord.	A
Elevation	N
Survey Date	D
Sampled?	B
.	.
.	.
.	.
.	.
Comments	T

Figure 3.16. Depiction of a "Sites" file, with a number of fields to describe the attributes of each site in a survey. The fields above the dashed line are "key attributes," used to identify each record uniquely. The bolded letters indicate whether fields are alphanumeric, numeric, date, boolean, or text fields.

are kinds of input. The output consists of responses to the inquiries, transaction logs (records of changes to the database) or updated data, and an updated database. For example, an archaeologist's input to a database might consist of typing the description of a pit feature in the "fields" of a "record," resulting in an updated database. Later another archaeologist may make a query of the database (input) by asking which pit features in the database were found to have contained charred plant remains, and the output would be a list of those pit features that the computer generates.

Too often archaeologists planning to set up an archaeological database begin by sitting in front of a computer and defining fields. The result is often a database that requires many revisions before it is even minimally acceptable and leads to much frustration for the database's users.

Just as with research design and systematics, the design of a good database requires that we first consider our objectives and expectations. To what use will we put the database? Who will the users be? Will it be used only a short time, for a single project, or do we expect it to serve a number of uses over a long period? If the latter, who will maintain it? What kinds of research questions will we want to ask of it? Are the data types typically available in a commercial database product sufficient for our purposes? Or will we have to define our own data types? Are we presented with an existing database that is still useful or are we beginning a new database from the ground up? If the former, what is the current system like and what are its limitations?

Whether you are the principal or only user of a new database that you are designing, or are working with others, you should begin to create a logical design for your database before you even begin to think about its physical characteristics. In other words, you should carefully lay out how you expect the database to work and how it should be structured to facilitate your future use of it before you even think about what kind of hard drive or processor you may need.

Database Structure

Databases can be very simple, **flat-file databases**, similar to a collection of file cards, or can be very complex, **relational databases** in which different files automatically communicate with one another.

All databases consist of one or more files, each of which has a number of fields and contains a number of records. A **field** is used to contain information on a particular attribute, or characteristic, of a particular item. A **record** is analogous to a single file card in a card catalogue: it describes a single site, artifact, or some other phenomenon by displaying the contents of several fields. For example, a file for describing "Sites" may contain 100 records for 100 different sites discovered during an archaeological survey, while each record may describe a single site by reference to fields for "Site Number," "Site Size," "Map Coordinates," "Elevation," and so on (figure 3.16). A file for "Lithics," meanwhile, might have fields for "Artifact Number," "Invasiveness of Retouch," "Number of Used or Retouched Edges," "Loca-

tion of Polish," "Platform Shape," and so on (figure 3.17).

For large archaeological projects, a simple flat-file database is unlikely to be very satisfactory. Instead we use relational databases (Date, 1986; Weinberg, 1992) in which controlled redundancy allows us to make use of the relationships between different classes of data, including spatial and stratigraphic context, in an efficient, hierarchical manner.

To illustrate how this works, refer to the structure diagram in figure 3.17. If we are interested in including information about stratigraphic context and lithics in our database, we could just mix all of this information into a single big file, but this would be extremely inefficient. The main reason for this is that many of the lithics will have virtually identical contextual information; in other words, there will be extreme redundancy. For example, part of the context might involve using a field labelled "soil colour." All of the lithics found in the same sediment layer will have the same information entered in this field, and so attaching this information so literally to each lithic record would be extremely wasteful. In addition, it does not make a lot of sense to record sediment attributes in a file on lithics. Instead we make two separate files, one for lithics, the other for the characteristics of their contexts, and make a **relation** between them.

The relation simply tells the computer where to go and look up the sediment characteristics for whatever lithic record we are currently examining. The computer knows which record in the file we've called "Contexts" is appropriate because an **attribute pointer** (a special field for recording these relations) in the Lithics file, "Layer Number," matches a **key attribute** (a field used to index the records in a file) in the Contexts file. Every record in a file should have a unique entry in its key attribute field, while it is quite common for many records in a file to have duplicate entries in the attribute pointer fields. That is simply because it is common for there to be many different lithics from the same sediment layer, or many layers in a single Excavation Unit, or many Excavation Units in a single site. In order to help us keep straight which file is pointing where in a particular relation, we connect the two files on a diagram with an arrow drawn from the attribute pointer in the "Many" file to the key attribute of the "One" file (figure 3.17). Remember this by reminding yourself that there are many contexts in one site, or many sites in one survey area.

When we draw a diagram to represent the database structure, as in figure 3.17, we are making what is known as a **structure chart**. Conventionally, the files are each represented by rectangles with the file name at the top, separated from the rest of the rectangle by a line segment. Below we list the names of fields, beginning with the key attribute, with attribute pointers next and then, below another dashed or dotted line segment, the rest of the fields. Often we show an abbreviation to indicate what kind of data (the data type) each field represents.

In any database, each record describes something with information contained in a number of fields. Today's commercial database management systems (DBMS) make quite a number of different **data types** available for these fields, but these do not always correspond exactly with the scales of measurement discussed in chapter 2, and are not always archaeologically appropriate, either. Let us look at some of the data types that are typically available in the better databases and then consider some data types that we would expect to find in archaeological databases of the future.

Probably the most common types of field that you will find in databases have the **alphanumeric**, **numeric**, and **boolean** data types.

An **alphanumeric** (or "character") field allows the input of any characters typically available on a computer's keyboard, including numbers, but input is usually limited to a specified number of characters. If you have defined a particular alphanumeric field as having eight characters, the computer will store eight characters for each record even if no one has input any data. Consequently you should give careful thought to how many characters you will need unless you can afford to be cavalier with disk space. The more sophisticated databases allow you to place "filters" on alphanumeric fields, that prevent certain kinds of data entry errors,

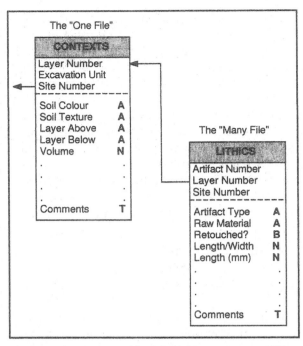

Figure 3.17. A Structure Chart depicting a relation between a "Lithics" file and a "Contexts" file for an archaeological excavation. Only some of the fields are shown. A: alphanumeric fields; B: boolean fields; N: numeric fields; and T: text fields.

such as inconsistent spelling, or allow standard entries to be selected from a list or menu, rather than spelled out.

A **numeric** field only allows users to input numerals. Many databases will specify this data type more closely, with **integer** or **real** ("float") data types. Integer numeric fields are useful for discrete data, and in most commercial databases we must select the "real" data type if we want a continuous scale. Both allow negative, as well as positive numbers, but the databases do not have separate categories for interval and ratio data. In other words, the computer has no way of distinguishing "real" zeroes from arbitrary ones unless you write a special program (or "procedure") to make the distinction yourself.

In the old days, people used to "code" nominal scale data with numbers instead of using their alphanumeric labels, because the codes took less storage space. Today's computers typically have so much more disk space that this is not necessary, but some people still prefer it. Unfortunately, the commercial database management systems will treat these codes just the same as any integers if you enter them into numeric fields, which could lead to some really embarrassing statistical errors if you are not careful. Consequently you should make absolutely sure that even numeric codes, including site numbers, layer numbers, and square numbers, are entered with the alphanumeric data type.

One aspect of numeric fields that can be important to archaeologists is that we can use software to record ratio-scale measurements directly from electronic calipers, electronic balances, and similar measuring devices. This has the advantage of eliminating one step in the recording process — typing the data from a keyboard — and makes recording errors less frequent. Typically a "serial" interface like the one you would use with a modem connects the computer to the calipers or balance.

Boolean fields are for what we would call dichotomous scales. As far as the computer is concerned, a boolean field is like a switch: it can only register true or false (i.e., 1 or 0). In our applications, however, we can use it for such dichotomous scales as yes/no, female/male, above/below, present/absent, left/right. The boolean data type is very useful for such purposes, but it is extremely important that you be sure that a dichotomous scale is really what you want if you plan to use it. If there is any chance that you should be anticipating "grey areas," such as "probably female," or might need to add a third option, you do not want to choose this data type because, unfortunately, it is not an easy matter to change your data type after the fact. Changing a dichotomous scale into a nominal one with three or four categories may sound simple enough, but in your database this would require that you write a small program (a "script" or "procedure") that transforms all your existing dichotomous data into the new three-category scale and saves it in a new field. And, in practice, you could end up with some errors.

Another data type that is commonly available is *text* or comment. This is a field that is alphanumeric but does not have alphanumeric's limitation on number of characters. It is ideal for situations where you might expect some

records to have little or no information to record on a particular attribute, but others to require several pages of information. Typically it is used for a "comments" area or a log area on each record, where users are free to write as much text as they like, or none at all, or where they can make notes on such things as when or why they modified a record. One of the advantages of text fields is that they only take up as much storage space on disk as the actual text they contain — empty text fields don't "cost" us anything — in contrast to alphanumeric fields, which store all the characters that have been assigned to them, even if they are empty. Text fields, then, allow us the freedom to write richer, more nuanced prose about our observations when that is desirable (cf. Hodder, 1989).

The kinds of operations that you can apply to data depend on data type. For numeric fields you can apply all the usual arithmetical and appropriate (and sometimes inappropriate) statistical functions, including such operators as "greater than," "sum," "product," "square root," "average," and so on. For alphanumeric and text fields you can use such operators as "contains" and "does not contain." For example, you could ask the computer to show you all the records in which the field, "Site Name," contains the *string* (sequence of characters), "Koster Site," but whose field, "Flotation Results," contains "" (i.e., is empty). This is called a *search*. The computer would return all the records from the Koster Site for which the flotation results had not yet been entered, making it easier for you to begin entering where you left off, perhaps, or simply to identify how many flotation results were missing. Another common operation is to *sort* records by one or more attributes in a particular order.

But many of the kinds of data that archaeologists use and the operations that they can be expected to make on them are not simple arithmetic or text-string ones (Ryan, 1992). For example, a lot of archaeological data specifically involve the concept of time as measured in radiocarbon years, calendar years, stratigraphic order, or cultural periods. If information such as "Neolithic" is simply entered as nominal information in an alphanumeric field or "layer 6" is just entered as a 6 in an integer field, our options will be extremely limited. If, for example, we ask the computer to sort stratigraphically or chronologically, it has no way of knowing whether the Neolithic should come before or after the Paleolithic, while the stratigraphic order of several layers is often quite different from the integer order of the numbers used to label those layers. Consequently, in these examples we could not ask the computer to show us all the records that are older than the Neolithic or more recent than layer 6. Chronological data are extremely important in archaeology, but the sort would simply put the time periods into alphabetical order and layers in numerical order. How do we get around this problem? The solution is what we can call an **abstract data type** (ADT).

Commercial DBMS now routinely have **date fields**, one of the most common ADTs. These allow you to enter data in day/month/year or month/day/year or year/month/day formats and the computer can respond to such operators as "earlier than" or "contemporary with" to tell you, for example, which records were last modified after 10 September 1996 or which records describe layers that were excavated in 1992. The former would be an example of a **transaction time** (the time when someone entered or modified a record, usually measured by the computer's internal clock); the latter is an example of a **valid time**. While many current DBMS support date fields capable of measuring time in this way, archaeologists also need user-defined time to handle such things as radiocarbon dates and such "fuzzy" dates as "Archaic," or "Late Chalcolithic." We also need special temporal operators that go beyond "earlier than" to include "overlap," and "extend" (for temporal databases and ADTs that they involve, see Cheetham and Haigh, 1992). Ideally, archaeologists should be able to search their databases to find, for example, all the records with radiocarbon dates within one standard deviation of 5000 bp, requiring what Cheetham and Haigh (1992:12) would call a "statistical date type." Since this is not available commercially, archaeologists must instead write procedures or scripts (small programs) to accomplish this.

Today's DBMS do typically offer ADTs for date fields that are useful for transaction times and some kinds of valid times, as well as for archaeologically less useful time fields (which allow you to enter hours/minutes/seconds), money fields, and telephone numbers. Some also have picture fields that allow you to insert an illustration into a record, but not to use characteristics of the picture as search operators. For example, commercially available DBMS will not allow you to search a database to find all the records with pictures showing pots with handles. If you might want to search for the records of pots with handles, you will need another field, probably alphanumeric, that records this information. Ryan (1992) points out that archaeologists require other ADTs that would be useful, for example, to record the kinds of spatial data archaeologists use, including site coordinates and the shapes of objects. He calls for archaeological databases that incorporate many of the functions currently found in Geographic Information Systems (GIS), and that would automate many of the tasks that concern spatial provenience.

> Such a query might ask for all drawings covering an area of the site within five meters of the centre of a context. If the bounding volume of a photograph is recorded it would be possible to request all photographs including a chosen point, and taken within so many days of the context excavation date (Ryan, 1992:5).

Unfortunately, commercially available database management systems were designed for use by the commercial sector, where money is available to pay for software development, and not to meet the somewhat unusual demands of archaeologists or other researchers with data that are not as well-behaved as payroll records (Cheetham and Haigh, 1992: 7). Because the market for dedicated archaeological software is much smaller than the business sector, in the immediate future the only way for us to acquire database structures that are more suitable for archaeological applications is to design them ourselves, or in collaboration with sympathetic programmers. For the moment, most of us will go on adapting the commercial software to our needs, and fortunately the more sophisticated packages do allow considerable customization.

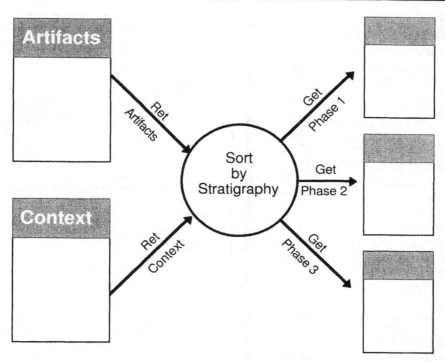

Figure 3.18. An example of part of a Data Flow Diagram (DFD) to sketch out what happens when you sort data on artifacts by their stratigraphic context. The ARTIFACTS file would contain information describing each artifact along with some attribute pointer that matches a key attribute in the CONTEXT file. The CONTEXT file would also have information on how the individual contexts should be ordered stratigraphically. By a matching process, the process SORT BY STRATIGRAPHY would cause the data on the artifacts to flow into different groups on the basis of this stratigraphic information.

Data Flow Diagrams

Data Flow Diagrams (DFDs) are the basic tools of Structured Analysis and Structured Design in computer science (Weinberg, 1992). The DFD provides a logical model of an information system, irrespective of its physical form, and depicts its logical processes and the flows of data between processes. It is quite possible to use a DFD to model the activities and even flows of artifacts (and not just abstract data) in an excavation project, for example, but it is especially useful to use it to model how you or others will make use of data in your database *in the planning stage*, to ensure that you set up your database in a way that will facilitate, rather than frustrate, you and other users. It is very tempting to sit down in front of a computer and begin to design a database without planning it ahead of time on paper, but you should avoid this temptation. A DFD is a very useful tool to help you think about how you will need to make use of data, so that you will design it with these purposes in mind.

The DFD is made up of processes (the activities that you will carry out with or on the data), flows (the movement of data between processes or from files to processes and back to files or other entities), and such data-storage entities as files and reports. Quite simply, you can use a labelled arrow to represent the flow of data, a labelled circle to represent a process, and usually a labelled rectangle (as in the structure chart) to represent a file or data storage device (e.g., figure 3.18).

At this stage, do not worry too much about how to make a complex DFD, but simply treat it as a way to sketch out the kinds of things you would like to do with your data, perhaps beginning with some fairly simple parts, and building it up afterward. For example, will you need to be able to retrieve information on the characteristics of the sediments in which each artifact was embedded? Will you need a quick way to locate field photos that might help you relate the artifacts to their contexts? Will you need some proc-

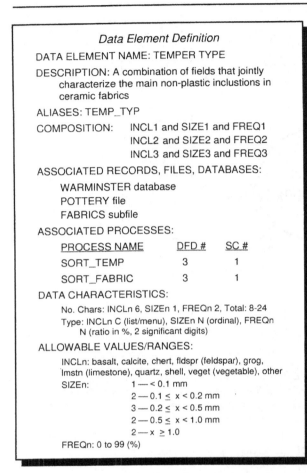

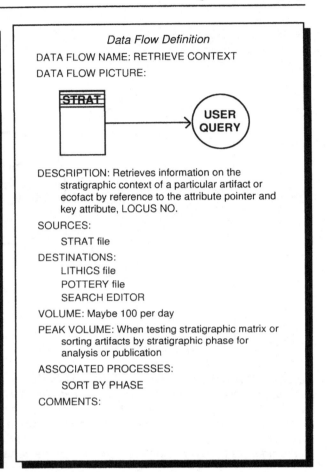

Figure 3.19. Two examples of pages from a hypothetical data dictionary, with a data element definition for the composite attribute, "temper type" and a data flow definition for the "look-up" of stratigraphic context. Note that not all data dictionaries will look like this. Especially note that most data elements are simpler than this compound attribute (made up by stringing together several smaller fields for the three most common kinds of inclusions, each with its particular average size and frequency).

esses or procedures that allow you to mimic an abstract data type, such as overlapping dates or stratigraphic order? A process as seemingly simple as "Sort in Stratigraphic Order" could require some tricky programming in cases where stratigraphic order is in fact quite different from the numerical order of labels assigned to layers! Fortunately this is one area where someone has written software that is helpful (see chapter 13). The DFD can make it easier for you to recognize where problems might occur before you waste too much time designing the database structure or, even worse, entering large amounts of data. It is always a lot more difficult and costly to fix a database that is not working the way you would like than it is to design it properly in the first place.

Data Dictionaries

No matter how well you have designed your database, if you have not documented it properly it may be impossible for others to use, especially without your assistance. In fact, if your database is at all sophisticated, you yourself may forget how it is structured or how various attributes were defined. A data dictionary is simply documentation of your database's information language; it records the lexical units (e.g., files, attributes, values, data flows) and database structure (relations, indices, attribute pointers) and all other aspects of the database that are relevant to its design, use, and maintenance.

Although no particular system for documenting your database is universally valid, at a minimum you should document your database "entities" — the files and fields — and would be wise to document the data flows and logical processes in the database. The data dictionary should tell the reader where these can be found, where they are typically used, what they are used for, how often they are likely to be used, and how they are structured. For entities that are fields, that includes the attribute's scale of measurement, the number of characters it takes up, whether these are alphanumeric or something else, and what limitations, if any, there may be on the kinds of values it can take (e.g., figure 3.19).

Hypermedia and Hypertext

Hypermedia is a kind of computerized compilation that has mushroomed in its application during the last decade, in part because of its use in CD-ROMs and on the internet.

"Hypertext" is a non-sequential system for reading and writing information that links different nodes in the text. In its more recent manifestations, hypermedia also allow non-sequential links of graphics, sounds, animation, and external applications. Hypermedia began to be widely available following Apple's introduction of HyperCard™ in 1987, and HyperCard began to incorporate hypertext capability — the ability to link keywords in the text to other nodes — in 1990. Later, similar products became available on other platforms and are used, especially, on CD-ROM disks. Then the demand for hypermedia on the World Wide Web led to the widespread use of HTML software, another kind of hypermedia.

At their simplest, hypermedia and hypertext employ concepts and techniques that closely parallel the kinds of things that authors and librarians have done for decades. In a hypertext, the author links a word or paragraph in one page of a file to some other related information on a different page or in a different file, much as some printed media use indexing techniques and references. Adapting this concept to computerized media essentially increases the speed and ease of making the connections. Rather than

being linear and sequential, a good hypertext system encourages readers to browse and search for information. Modern hypermedia works go a step further than hypertext, allowing authors to link text, data, graphics, video, animation, simulations, and sound. Most hypermedia works allow users to navigate through information with the aid of a "hypermedia map" (a visual metaphor that organizes the information) and graphic icons or "buttons." Users of the system use a mouse to select graphics or text or to click buttons that will reformat data in ways users specify or will bring up, almost instantly, new, related information that users request. Anyone who has "surfed the Web" will be familiar with these concepts. The archaeological use of hypermedia to publish results is growing rapidly (Banning, 1991; 1993; Barceló, 1992; Rahtz et al., 1992), and some field projects now make their results and even field diaries available rapidly on the World Wide Web (for example, the Çatal Hüyük web site at http://catal.arch.cam.ac.uk/). There are also other applications (e.g., Boast and Chapman, 1991).

The software, such as HyperCard, used to make hypermedia is what software engineers call an authoring tool, which helps users write applications themselves, without the specialized knowledge that would be required to programme them in one of the usual programming languages.

Hypermedia and Relational Databases

When they were first introduced, because hypermedia works are so difficult to describe, they were compared to flat-file and relational databases. The card-file metaphor, in addition to the use of fields on hypermedia "cards" or "pages" encourages this comparison. In other ways, however, hypermedia are different, making them less useful than database applications in some contexts, and more useful in others.

One difference lies in the way hypermedia and databases store individual pieces of information. In databases, data in fields are stored, essentially, as lists. While the software may provide an entry template that looks somewhat like a hypermedia card, the data are, in fact, quite separate from this template, while in hypermedia most data are integral to each "card" or web page and almost all attributes are linked either to them or their backgrounds. This means that databases can be more efficient, less hungry for storage space, or more flexible. For example, most databases allow you to design a customized report that displays a selection of fields in the data base, and omits others, while in hypermedia users are largely confined to the display formats that their authors have designed for them.

Another lies in the way the two share data between files. Relational databases partition data in distinct files (e.g., one file for lithic data, another for ceramics), and provide sophisticated 'lookup' or indexing functions that allow users to access data in one file while working in another. In hypermedia, by contrast, a card or web page that needs to incorporate data from another file in fact stores a duplicate of that information rather than doing a "lookup" in the other file, or else simply sends you to the other web page rather than showing you an excerpt from it. On the one hand this has the advantage that corruption of data or accidental deletion in one place has no effect on the duplicate data elsewhere. On the other, however, relational databases have the advantage that editing or updating information in one file causes that information to be updated throughout the database, and not only locally.

For publications that their authors do not expect users to edit or update, however, hypermedia provide a distinct advantage over relational databases, as well as over traditional forms of archaeological publication (Banning, 1991; 1993). Databases impose a rather rigid structure of formally defined fields, sometimes with fixed lengths and data types. Relations in these databases are generally possible only between like fields, and sometimes only in one direction. In hypermedia, by contrast, it is possible for authors to establish any links they please, even if the links are arbitrary. This means that they can easily provide links that anticipate where users might want to look at a map of the site they have highlighted in a text field, look at the lithics associated with the stratigraphic level they are currently viewing, or look at the distribution of animal bones from the same context as

a particular stone tool. That is one of the reasons that HTML has become so popular on the World Wide Web. In a relational database, these kinds of links are only possible if its designer has expended a great deal of effort to build them into the database structure.

It is still possible for hypermedia to read data from a traditional database or graphics file, making some combination of hypermedia and external files an attractive strategy where the volumes of data are particularly large. The details of such a combination, however, are beyond the scope of this introduction.

Hypermedia and Multimedia

What has made the web very popular is that hypermedia can incorporate, not just the text, data fields, and computer graphics discussed above, but color photographs, video, sound, and animation. "Multimedia" are simply works that incorporate this mix of media, but hypermedia software allows us to add the non-sequential aspect that is missing from normal video. Software external to the hypermedia itself but linked by a button can run animated sequences or display video. The thing that distinguishes hypermedia from ordinary multimedia, films, or videotapes is that they are interactive instead of linear; viewers choose what they want to see and in any order they desire. This has made hypermedia a very popular vehicle for business and classroom presentations and for educational workstations, but also has implications for the publication of research in disciplines, such as archaeology, that rely heavily on images. Software such as QuickTime™, for example, allows you to view the color photograph of an artifact in a window, and rotate it 360°.

Conclusion

Compilations of data are the cornerstone of archaeological analysis, but are often large and complex. Ensuring that our data are in a form that is suitable for our use and are organized in a way that facilitates analysis requires careful consideration of the lexical units we will use to categorize data (systematics) and the kinds of relationships we will want to explore in the data.

Database design principles help us ensure that our compilation is useful and easy to maintain.

Systematics involves a wide array of classification and grouping methods that either define abstract nominal scales or attempt to detect patterns in the similarities and differences between actual things. Classifications or groupings that have meaning and relevance with respect to phenomena of interest that lie outside the class definitions or group descriptions (i.e., context), can be described as typologies.

Databases can be graphical or digital, and simple or relational. Relational databases, with their controlled redundancy, have many advantages but can become very complex and difficult to maintain. It is critical to plan out the abstract structure of a database before setting up its physical structure, to give adequate attention to the definition of useful fields and relations, and the processes with which you are likely to manipulate the data. It is also extremely important to document all aspects of the database with a Data Dictionary, as otherwise it may become confusing or even useless to you and others. The wide array of database management software currently available gives you many options to create a database with the level of complexity you need, but typically these are designed for business applications and are not ideal for archaeological ones. Spending the time to learn how to adapt a more sophisticated software package, by writing small programs or "scripts," is usually worthwhile.

References Cited

Adams, W. Y., and Adams, E. W., 1991, *Archaeological Typology and Practical Reality, A Dialectical Approach to Artifact Classification and Sorting.* Cambridge University Press, Cambridge.

Aldenderfer, M. S., 1987, Assessing the impact of quantitative thinking on archaeological research: historical and evolutionary insights. In *Quantitative Research in Archaeology, Progress and Prospects*, edited by M. S. Aldenderfer, pp. 9-29. Sage Publications, Newbury Park, CA.

Aldenderfer, M. S., and Blashfield, R. K., 1984, *Cluster Analysis.* Sage Publications, Beverly Hills, CA.

Banning, E. B., 1991, The Wadi Ziqlab HyperCard Project. *Society for American Archaeology Bulletin* 9 (5):8-9

— 1993, Hypermedia and Archaeological Publication: The Wadi Ziqlab Project. In *Computing the Past: CAA 92, Computer Applications and Quantitative Methods in Archaeology*, edited by J. Andresen, T. Madsen and I. Scollar, pp. 441-47. Aarhus University Press, Aarhus, Denmark.

— 1997, Spatial perspectives on early urban development in Mesopotamia. In *Aspects of Urbanism in Antiquity, From Mesopotamia to Crete*, edited by W. E. Aufrecht, N. A. Mirau, and S. W. Gauley, pp. 17-34. Sheffield Academic Press, Sheffield.

Barceló, J. A., 1992, Programming an intelligent database in hypertext. In *Computer Applications and Quantitive Methods in Archaeology, 1991*, edited by G. Lock and J. Moffett, pp. 21-27. BAR International Series S577. Tempus Reparatum, Oxford.

Baxter, M. J., 1994, *Exploratory Multivariate Analysis in Archaeology.* Edinburgh University Press, Edinburgh.

Binford, L. R., and Binford, S. R., 1966, A preliminary analysis of functional variability in the Mousterian of Levallois facies. *American Anthropologist* 68:238-95.

Boast, R., and Chapman, D., 1991, SQL and hypertext generation of stratigraphic adjacency matrices. In *Computer Applications and Quantitive Methods in Archaeology, 1990*, edited by K. Lockyear and S. Rahtz, pp. 43-51. BAR International Series 565. Tempus Reparatum, Oxford.

Booch, G., 1991, *Object Oriented Design with Applications.* Benjamin, Redwood, CA.

Bradley, R., 1984, *The Social Foundations of Prehistoric Britain. Themes and Variations in the Archaeology of Power.* Longman, London.

Cheetham, P. N., and Haigh, J. G. B., 1992, The archaeological database — new relations?. In *Computer Applications and Quantitive Methods in Archaeology, 1991*, edited by G. Lock and J. Moffett, pp. 7-14. BAR International Series S577. Tempus Reparatum, Oxford.

Childe, V. G., 1929, *The Danube in Prehistory.* Clarendon Press, Oxford.

— 1956, *Piecing Together the Past: The Interpretation of Archaeological Data.* Routledge and Kegan Paul, London.

Clarke, D. L., 1968, *Analytical Archaeology.* Methuen, London.

Date, C. J., 1986, *Relational Database: Selected Writings.* Addison-Wesley, London.

Digard, F., Abellard, C., Bourelly, L., Deshayes, J., Gardin, J.-C., le Maître, J., and Salomé, M.-R., 1975, *Répertoire Analytique des Cylindres Orientaux.* CNRS, Paris.

Dixon, J. E., Cann, J. R., and Renfrew, C., 1968, Obsidian and the origins of trade. *Scientific American* 218(3):38-46.

Dunnell, R. C., 1971, *Systematics in Prehistory.* The Free Press, New York.

— 1986, Methodological issues in Americanist artifact classification. *Advances in Archaeological Method and Theory* 9:149-207.

Everitt, B., 1974, *Cluster Analysis.* Heinemann, London.

Ford, J., 1954, The type concept revisited. *American Anthropologist* 56:42-54.

Gardin, J.-C., 1980, *Archaeological Constructs.* Cambridge University Press, Cambridge.

Goren, Y., 1992, Petrographic study of the pottery assemblage from Munhata. In *The Pottery Assemblages of the Sha'ar Hagolan and Rabah Stages of Munhata (Israel)*, by Y. Garfinkel, pp. 329-48. Association Paléorient, Paris.

Hand, D. J., 1997, *Construction and Assessment of Classification Rules*. John Wiley & Sons, New York.

Hillier, B., and Hansen, J., 1984, *The Social Logic of Space*. Cambridge University Press, Cambridge.

Hodder, I., 1989, Writing archaeology: Site reports in context. *Antiquity* 63:268-74.

Hodson, F. R., 1970, Cluster analysis and archaeology: some new developments and applications. *World Archaeology* 1:299-320.

— 1982, Some aspects of archaeological classification. In *Essays on Archaeological Typology*, edited by R. Whallon and J. A. Brown, pp. 21-29. Center for American Archaeology Press, Evanston, IL.

Hodson, F., Sneath, P., and Doran, J., 1966, Some experiments in the numerical analysis of archaeological data. *Biometrika* 53:311-24.

Jardine, C. J., Jardine, N., and Sibson, R., 1967, The structure and construction of taxonomic hierarchies. *Mathematical Biosciences* 1:173-179.

Kempton, W., 1978, Category grading and taxonomic relations: a mug is a sort of a cup. *American Ethnologist* 5(1):44-65.

Kenyon, K. M., and Holland, T., 1982, *Excavations at Jericho IV: The Pottery Type Series and Other Finds*. London.

Kim, K., 1990, *An Introduction to Object-Oriented Database Systems*. MIT Press, Cambridge, MA.

Kintigh, K. W., 1990, Intra-site spatial analysis in archaeology. In *Mathematics and Information Science in Archaeology: A Flexible Framework*, edited by A. Voorrips, pp. 165-200. Holos-Verlag, Bonn.

Lawley, D. N., and Maxwell, A. E., 1971, *Factor Analysis as a Statistical Method*, 2nd ed. Butterworths, London.

Nance, J. D., 1987, Reliability, validity, and quantitative methods in archaeology. In *Quantitative Research in Archaeology, Progress and Prospects*, edited by M. S. Aldenderfer, pp. 244-93. Sage Publications, Newbury Park, CA.

Orton, C., 1980, *Mathematics in Archaeology*. Cambridge University Press, Cambridge.

Pike, K., 1954, *Language in Relation to a Unified Theory of the Structure of Human Behavior*, Part 1. Summer Institute of Linguistics, Glendale, CA.

Plog, S., 1980, *Stylistic Variation in Prehistoric Ceramics. Design Analysis in the American Southwest*. Cambridge University Press, Cambridge.

Prentiss, W. C., 1998, The reliability and validity of a lithic debitage typology: Implications for archaeological interpretation. *American Antiquity* 63:635-50.

Rahtz, S., Hall, W., and Allen, T., 1992, The development of dynamic archaeological publications. In *Archaeology and the Information Age, a Global Perspective*, edited by P. Reilly and S. Rahtz, pp. 360-83. Routledge, London.

Rast, W. E., 1978, *Taanach I, Studies in the Iron Age Pottery*. American Schools of Oriental Research, Cambridge, MA.

Read, D., 1974, Some comments on typologies in archaeology and an outline of a methodology. *American Antiquity* 39:216-42.

— 1982, Towards a theory of archaeological classification. In *Essays in Archaeological Typology*, edited by R. Whallon and J. A. Brown, pp. 56-92. Center for American Archaeology Press, Evanston, IL.

Ryan, N., 1992, Beyond the relational database: managing the variety and complexity of archaeological data. In *Computer Applications and Quantitive Methods in Archaeology, 1991*, edited by G. Lock and J. Moffett, pp. 1-6. BAR International Series S577. Tempus Reparatum, Oxford.

Shanks, M., and Tilley, C. 1987, *Re-Constructing Archaeology. Theory and Practice*. Cambridge University Press, Cambridge.

Shennan, S., 1988, *Quantifying Archaeology*. Edinburgh University Press, Edinburgh.

Skibo, J., 1992, *Pottery Function. A Use-Alteration Perspective*. Plenum Press, New York.

Smith, R., 1973, *Pella of the Decapolis, the 1967 Season of the College of Wooster Expedition to Pella*. College of Wooster, Wooster, OH.

Sokal, R. R., and Sneath, P. H. A., 1963, *Principles of Numerical Taxonomy*. Freeman, San Francisco.

Spaulding, A., 1953, Statistical techniques for the discovery of artifact types. *American Antiquity* 18:305-13.

Steward, J., 1954, Types of types. *American Anthropologist* 56:54-57.

Watson, P. J., LeBlanc, S., and Redman, C., 1971, *Explanation in Archeology. An Explicitly Scientific Approach*. Columbia University Press, New York.

Weinberg, V., 1992, *Structured Analysis*. Yourdon, New York.

Whallon, R., 1972, A new approach to pottery typology. *American Antiquity* 37:13-33.

— 1987, Simple statistics. In *Quantitative Research in Archaeology, Progress and Prospects*, edited by M. S. Aldenderfer, pp. 135-150. Sage Publications, Newbury Park, CA.

Whallon, R., and Brown, J. A., eds., 1982, *Essays in Archaeological Typology*. Center for American Archaeology Press, Evanston, IL.

Whittaker, J. C., Caulkins, D., and Kamp, K. A., 1998, Evaluating consistency in typology and classification. *Journal of Archaeological Method and Theory* 5:129-64.

Williams, L., Thomas, D. H., and Bettinger, R., 1973, Notions to numbers: Great Basin settlements as polythetic sets. In *Research and Theory in Current Archaeology*, edited by C. L. Redman, pp. 215-37. John Wiley & Sons, New York.

Zadeh, L. A., 1965, Fuzzy sets. *Information and Control* 8:338-53.

See also the journal, *Archives and Museum Informatics*.

4 Research Design and Sampling

As we have seen, data do not simply leap out at us. In general we only see and record those data that we are preconditioned to see and that we consider worthy of documentation. Our selection of data depends on **theory**, and the way we plan research from a particular theoretical perspective constitutes research design.

Earlier this century, guides to archaeological method (e.g., Woolley, 1930) made no mention of theoretically informed research design. Facts were supposed to speak for themselves, and interpretation of archaeological remains was supposed to be self-evident. That this approach was not very effective is clear from the numerous debates in the archaeological literature over questions that might have been solved quite simply had the excavators of sites been looking for the right kinds of information.

One of the contributions of the "New Archaeology" or **processual archaeology** in the 1960s and 1970s was the recognition that archaeological research was not an unstructured or "objective" collection of facts, but was driven by the archaeological problems we wish to solve. Lewis Binford (1962; 1964) and others spearheaded the movement to construct explicit research designs with the object of testing specific hypotheses or deciding between two or more competing hypotheses.

Soon influential publications by Binford (1962; 1968), Clarke (1968), and Watson et al. (1971) had pursuaded a large proportion of North American archaeologists, although only some of their European colleagues, that the appropriate intellectual method for archaeological research was the Hypothetico-Deductive method

(H-D). This, they asserted, was the method that physical scientists used to construct and test hypotheses, and should be adopted by archaeologists who wished to be recognized as scientists. They described H-D as a kind of cycle: an archaeologist would not simply gather facts haphazardly, but would begin with an hypothesis derived from previous experience or imagination, "deduce" what kinds of evidence should occur in the archaeological record if the hypothesis is true, and then test the hypothesis by collecting new data (by excavation or survey, for example) to see if they matched the deduced patterns (figure 4.1). If there was a match, the hypothesis was provisionally accepted, meaning not that it is true, but that it could be true; if there was not a match, the hypothesis was rejected, and the new data could be used to formulate a new hypothesis that then became the target for new tests. The general structure of this process is similar to Gardin's (1980) cycle of processes, and was implicit in most earlier archaeological work that was not simply aimed at collecting art and antiquities.

The adoption of this research model had a number of positive effects. It encouraged researchers to consider alternative hypotheses and to make active attempts to reject their favorite hypothesis. This reduces the risk that they will select only data that tend to support their hypothesis and make research a selffulfilling prophesy. Ideally, this also forces us to consider our own biases and perspectives and how these may affect our formulation of hypotheses and our perceptions of data. In principle, it required researchers to make explicit decisions, before fieldwork or laboratory work, on the design of that fieldwork, including what kinds of data to collect and how to collect them. This reduces the risk that data crucial to the evaluation of a hypothesis will be accidentally omitted.

Although there were also problems with archaeologists' use of H-D (Courbin, 1988; Salmon, 1982:39-42; Shanks and Tilley, 1987), its emphasis on explicit research design was a lasting contribution.

Research Design

A research design is an explicit plan by which an investigator ensures that the research will accomplish its objectives (Binford, 1964; Boismier, 1991; Goodyear et al., 1978; Redman, 1973). It begins with identifying one or more research problems or hypotheses that will focus the research. It includes review of relevant method and theory, the context in which the research will take place, and previous work on the same or similar problems. These help researchers refine their research problems to generate more specific questions and to identify the kinds of methods and data necessary to answer them in the context of a particular project. These are the "problem domains" of the research. We also need to decide what kinds of data analysis could help us answer the questions and select those that are appropriate given the limitations of the research context and the kinds of data we expect to be available.

Considering the context of the research is an important step. Copying a research design from a project on Hohokam sites in Arizona will not help you with research on Iron Age sites in France, even if the research problem is similar, because the research context is so different. Some kinds of data that will be available in the one area will be rare or absent in the other, or different natural and cultural site-formation processes will make comparison meaningless. Furthermore, previous work in your own research area will be much more relevant to your specification of problem domains.

In the scientific cycle, problem domains specify the research problems in ways that allow us to evaluate them with the kinds of data we can expect in the context of a project. This often includes specifying indirect measures for

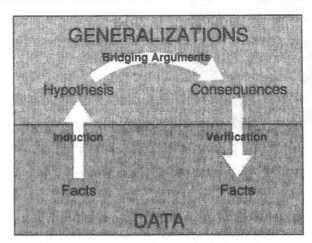

Figure 4.1. Schematic of the "scientific cycle."

phenomena we cannot observe directly and a variety of models that might account for aspects of the data (chapter 6 and Buck et al., 1996). A general research problem about the economy of a settlement, for example, might generate a long list of detailed questions about how archaeological materials are distributed and cultural and noncultural factors that may have concentrated, dispersed, displaced, or destroyed particular categories of plant and animal remains. Each model will predict how a particular process can be expected to affect the data: the "expectations" or "consequences" of the model.

Problem domains will help you select, not only what data to collect, but the methods and strategies to collect them. For example, for your work on that site's economy, you may need to estimate how many storage pits you will need to analyse to assess the **ubiquity** of maize, what volume of sediment from each you will need to process to get an adequate sample of plant remains, and what mesh size you will need to detect fish remains. You may need to decide whether you need a probability sample, or whether flotation or dry-screening will do least damage to any fragile remains you anticipate. For a use-wear analysis or a chemical residue analysis, you might decide that you need to bag each artifact separately during excavation so as to avoid edge damage or chemical contamination.

The research design should also specify analytical procedures. These will include how to classify or group data for analysis, and what kinds of quantitative or qualitative analysis to carry out. It is important to select procedures that are appropriate to the data you can expect. Applying powerful statistical techniques to meager data sets is like "using a Howitzer on a field mouse." Other chapters cover many of the analytical decisions, such as selecting means of quantification or ways to compare assemblages, you may need to make. Many research designs include an exploratory stage in which simple univariate (i.e., single-variable) analyses are used to help specify the design of more complex analyses (Tukey, 1977).

Failure to consider these factors in advance can lead to costly returns to the field or wasteful remeasurement in the laboratory.

A common misconception is that explicit research designs force us to ignore information that we did not anticipate. Sometimes we can even *expect* new information to arise during the course of research that makes it desirable to revise our research design. Many researchers use "multi-stage" designs that use a preliminary or pilot stage to refine the research questions or methods and expectations about the data (e.g., Redman, 1973; Redman and Anzalone, 1980). Furthermore, research designs do not prevent us from recording anything we happen to notice during the course of making other observations.

SAMPLING

Contrary to what Binford's (1964) early work suggests, H-D is not the only, or even the dominant method of the physical sciences (Salmon, 1982:34-42). The research designs of most processual archaeology, in fact, involved testing statistical, or probabilistic, hypotheses (see chapter 6), and to do this they emphasized probabilistic sampling as an aspect of research design (e.g., Binford, 1964; Watson et al., 1971).

We are sampling whenever we attempt to make inferences about a **population** on the basis of some subset of that population. In statistical jargon, we want to learn about one or more **parameters** of the population, such as the mean blade length among all the stone tools made by a particular culture or the proportion of deer

bones among all the bones that survive in an archaeological site. From a subset, or **sample**, of the lithics or bones we can derive sample **statistics**, such as the sample mean of blade length in a lithic sample or the sample proportion of deer bones in a faunal sample. If the sample was designed to be "representative" of the population, these statistics allow us to estimate the parameters with a known degree of error and at a particular level of confidence. In modern political polls, for example, we hear that the result is accurate within one or two percentage points 19 times out of 20. This is a statement of the error and confidence level of the reported results, which are typically based on a sample of only one or two thousand voters. The confidence level and error estimate are crucial for making comparisons between samples later on. If we do not know the degree of error, we can never know whether apparent differences between samples are due to real differences between the populations from which they were drawn, or only to variation within a single population.

Most archaeologists are familiar with the basic aspects of sampling theory. They distinguish the sample, the set of elements on which we actually make observations, from the population, the whole of which our sample is only a part, that we would like to describe or characterize. They distinguish **probability samples**, in which the selection of observations is based on probability theory, from **purposive samples**, in which the selection of observations is guided by other factors. They also distinguish **simple random samples**, probability samples in which every member of the population has an equal probability of selection, from **systematic** ones, in which only the first element is random and all the others are strictly determined by a spacing rule. The slightly more sophisticated ones may use more complicated sampling designs and may even account for **cluster sampling** (see below).

In addition to these, however, it is important to give adequate attention to defining the population and to the choice of **sample elements**, **sample frame**, and sample size, which is quite different from **sampling fraction**. We should also remember that the purpose of sampling is not merely to reduce the costs of data acquisition, although this is one advantage of sampling, but to make inferences about the larger population (to estimate **parameters**) on the basis of sample **statistics**, and that there are some archaeological research goals that probability sampling cannot help us address.

Defining Populations of Interest

The population that we sample can be finite in space and time or be conceptually infinite, such as the population of all the lithic debitage that a modern flint-knapper could conceivably produce over the next ten years. It can consist of a set of artifacts, such as the population of all chert blades in a particular archaeological site, although, as we shall see below, there can be problems with sampling such a population. It can be the set of all pit features or house structures on a site. It can also consist of a space on a map or the volume of deposits in a site. In fact, archaeologists most often sample spatial populations. We can even have temporal populations, which are distributed in time instead of space. Especially when we use spatial or temporal populations, we need to think carefully about the population's boundaries. Do they correspond with some cultural unit of interest, or are they relevant in some other way, or are they only arbitrary? If we are attempting to do *rank-size analysis*, for example (e.g., Johnson, 1980), selecting boundaries that omit part of the settlement system of interest, or that combine parts of two distinct settlement systems, will distort the shape of the rank-size distribution, possibly leading to incorrect inferences about urbanization.

Sampling Frame and Sample Elements

When our population consists, say, of a collection of pots on a museum's shelves, sampling is easy. We can simply make a list of all the pots and then use this list as the **sampling frame**, the ordered set of sample **elements** that is used as the basis for drawing a sample. For example, we might number all the pots on the list sequentially and then randomly select numbers. When the population is a spatial or temporal one, however, deciding on the sampling frame and sample elements can be more difficult.

In temporal populations, our sample elements are units of time. If we are measuring the radioactivity of a charcoal sample for the purposes of radiocarbon dating, for example, we may want to measure the number of radioactive decays of ^{14}C (carbon-14). Our sample element may be an interval of one minute, or five minutes, and our sample size consists of the number of such time intervals. Temporal sampling is uncommon in archaeology, but could be useful, for example, in evaluating the practical efficiencies of field methods or in some kinds of **experimental archaeology**.

Spatial populations, by contrast, are predominant in archaeology, and so archaeologists need to think about the kinds of spatial elements they will use and how they should be arranged into a sampling frame. Typically, archaeologists use rectangular grids as the sampling frame for space with, for example, 1 km x 1 km quadrats arranged over a regional population or a 5 m x 5 m or 1 m x 1 m grid arranged over an individual site. There is, however, nothing sacred about squares, and some archaeologists, such as McManamon (1981), instead use long rectangles, perhaps 100 m x 200 m or 1 m x 3 m, as sample elements in two dimensions. In some contexts, units that are triangular or hexagonal might have practical or theoretical advantages (Wobst, 1983). As Steve Plog et al. (1978) have pointed out, very long rectangles (i.e., transects), have higher edge:area ratios, and consequently are more likely to intersect sites or other spatially scattered materials, making them useful for prospection. When you use transects for parameter estimates, however, you should take care to account for this characteristic (e.g., you might only count sites whose centers lie within the rectangle, or might measure the site area that actually occurs within the rectangle rather than total site area) so as to avoid bias. For volumetric sample elements, you also need to decide on the third dimension, so that your elements could be, for example, 1 m x 1 m x 0.05 m. But you should also remember that there is no statistical law that your sample elements must be of equal size or shape. Just as the pots on the museum shelves can be of different sizes and shapes, but still serve nicely as sample elements, spatial and volumetric sample elements can be stream ter-

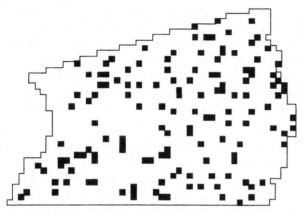

Figure 4.2. Sampling frame used for the Reese River Survey, Nevada (after Thomas, 1973). 10% of the 500 m x 500 m squares were selected without replacement in three environmental strata (not shown here).

races (Banning, 1996), hill tops, beach ridges, house floors, middens, pits, layers, or any natural or cultural deposits that may be relevant to your research. Furthermore, making spatial sample elements equal in area or volume does not mean that they will contain equal numbers of lithics, sherds, bones, seeds, or anything else of archaeological interest. It is always better to use sample elements (and populations) that make sense in terms of your research goals than to use arbitrarily defined, geometrical units. Finally, the elements of a spatial sample can even consist of points, such as the x- and y-coordinates of a map.

For spatial populations, you also need to consider the physical size of the sampling element. For example, if you are interested in characteristics of house structures, such as their size, a sample frame that consists of a 1 m x 1 m grid is unlikely to allow you to measure the size of even a single house. At a minimum you would need to supplement the statistical sample with a broadening of excavation areas to reveal the unsampled portions of houses so that you could measure at least their length and width, or the diameter of round houses. In many instances, however, you might want sampling elements that were large enough that it was highly likely that each would contain a large portion of at least one house.

In the algebraic expressions that statisticians use, the number of elements in the sampling frame of a population, the population size, is usually expressed as N. The number of elements included in the sample is n.

Sampling Strategies

Having decided what your population and sample elements are, you need to decide what strategy to use to draw a sample. If you are not interested in drawing statistical inferences about the population, you may opt for a **purposive** sample, which you consciously select in order to meet your objectives, perhaps intentionally creating bias by, for example, increasing the probability that you will find certain items of interest. This is a good idea when you are prospecting. There are also many situations in which probability sampling is impractical or impossible, an issue to which we will return later in this chapter. But even if you decide, instead, on a probability sample, you have some choices. The concepts of probability itself will be discussed in more detail in chapter 6).

The simplest strategy is to draw a simple, **random element sample**. In random sampling, each element in the population has equal probability of being selected at each draw, and the selection of any one element has no effect on the probability that any other element will be selected. Technically, this is called *epsem* sampling. Here you would enumerate all the elements in the population and select a number of them randomly, usually by assigning a number to each element and then referring to a random number table or using a computer to make a random selection for you. For spatial samples (figure 4.2), you might randomly select the x- and y-coordinates of each sample element or, if you have a set sampling frame consisting of quadrats or transects, you might just assign them a series of numerical or alphabetical labels and select a subset at random. The simple random sample is a sample with replacement, meaning that after you draw each element and record it, you return it to the sampling frame so that it is possible for it to be selected again. It is the only kind of sample that is truly random because, at each and every drawing, *every element in the* *population has an equal probability of being selected.* If, instead, we sample without replacement, as is common in archaeology, elements drawn later have higher probabilities of selection, and so, technically, this basic principle of equal probability of selection is lost. For example, if we draw a sample of ten from a population of 100, without replacement, on the first drawing all elements have a probability of 1 in 100 (0.01) of being selected. But, at the second drawing, not only is the probablity increased to 1 in 99, but the 99 elements left after the first drawing have a second chance to be selected, while the first element had only one chance. By the time we get to the tenth element in the sample, its probability of selection is $1/100 + 1/99 + 1/98 + 1/97 + 1/96 + 1/95 + 1/94 + 1/93 + 1/92 + 1/91$, or about 0.105, a probability considerably higher than the 0.01 that the first element had. Fortunately, any ordering of the ten observations is equally probable, so that sampling without replacement also works quite well.

Of course, sampling with replacement does not mean that we necessarily have to resurvey a spatial unit or remeasure an artifact (although there are some cases, such as evaluating our methods, where that would be useful), but only that we should allow for the possibility that the same element is selected two or three times, and simply enter the measurements twice for any element that is selected twice. In practice, this repetition of measurements we have already made in fact speeds up analysis.

Random sampling without replacement is, however, more common in archaeology. In some cases it is difficult to avoid, as, for example, in systematic sampling (see below). Because any ordering of the sampled elements is equally probable, sampling without replacement still provides unbiased estimates of population parameters, such as the mean. In fact, although sampling with replacement is simpler, sampling without replacement is more efficient. By this we mean that the variance in our estimates of population parameters is smaller for a given sample size (n) when the population is small (or sampling fraction large). In these cases, sampling without replacement takes advantage of

large sampling fractions. When the population is nearly infinite in size, or the sampling fraction is low, however, the gain in efficiency is negligible. Consequently, sampling without replacement may be preferable, for example, when we are sampling a map with a relatively small number of spatial elements, so that the population consists of, say, 40 squares.

If we sample without replacement, however, we need to use somewhat different equations to calculate variance and confidence intervals than the ones we use for simple random sampling. For example, the equations in Drennan's (1996) *Statistics for Archaeologists* all assume sampling with replacement, while those in Barnett's (1991) *Sample Survey Principles and Methods* all assume sampling *without* replacement. You should use the correct equations if you sample without replacement.

Another sampling strategy that is popular with archaeologists is **systematic sampling**. Here only the first element is selected randomly, and all other members of the sample are strictly determined by a regular interval along the sampling frame. For example, if our sampling frame is a list of artifacts, and we want a sample of approximately one-tenth of the artifacts, we can randomly pick a number from 1 to 10. If the number turns out to be 3, for example, we would select the third element on the list, and then every tenth element from then on — the 13th, 23rd, 33rd, and so on — until the list is exhausted. In systematic samples, all elements in the population have equal probability of being selected at the first drawing, but from then on, elements that correspond to the sampling interval have probabilities of 1.0 and all others have probabilities of zero. To sample systematically in space, we simply use a set interval along the x- and y-axes of a map, while to sample systematically in time, we take measurements at set intervals of seconds, minutes, or days. Systematic samples are more convenient than random samples in many situations. However, they are not random samples because not all possible samples of size *n* have an equal chance of occurring. Consequently, they also pose problems for estimating variance unless we assume that the

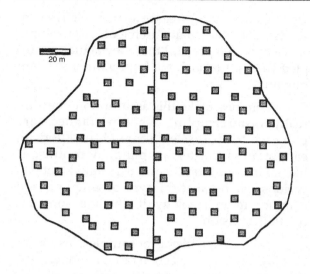

Figure 4.3. "Systematic stratified unaligned" spatial sample of the site of Girikihaçiyan, Turkey (after Redman and Watson, 1970).

sample is sufficiently unordered that we can treat it as no different from random (or "quasi-random").

Another strategy that archaeologists frequently employ is **stratified sampling**. Here we divide the population into two or more subpopulations that are relevant to our research goals. For example, if we are sampling a region for evidence of patterns in the location of sites with respect to soil types, it would be unfortunate if our sample did not contain some of the soil types. To ensure that our sample was spread fairly evenly across all the soil types, we could take a map that showed their distribution in space, treat each soil type as a separate **stratum** (or sub-population) of the population, and take a random or systematic sample from each. Or, if you are sampling a large collection of Roman pottery for a time-consuming analysis, you might want to sample with typological strata, thus ensuring that your sample included meaningful numbers of *terra sigillata*, amphoras, cooking pots, and so on. Typically, archaeologists use proportionally stratified samples, so that if, for example, grey slope soils constitute 10% of the surface area of the population, or amphoras made up 10% of the pottery, you would draw 10% of your sample elements from there. In some instances it may be better to use disproportionate stratified samples, especially if some

of the strata are very small, to optimize the balance between the cost and efficiency of the sample, or to ensure that you have an adequate sample size from each (for sample size questions, see below). Stratified sampling is discussed at length in Som (1973).

One of the most popular "cookbook" archaeological sampling strategies is described as "systematic, stratified, unaligned" sampling, which many designers of surveys have copied from an article by Redman and Watson (1970). In reality, this is a variation of the stratified random spatial sample, with the strata defined arbitrarily as square units. For example, Redman and Watson divided the tell of Girikihaciyan into a grid of blocks, each containing 5 m x 5 m squares, and then picked two random numbers for each grid square (figure 4.3). These were then used as the x- and y-coordinates for the sample element from each block. This strategy ensures that the elements selected are spread fairly evenly across the map. Some people imitating the method take the short-cut of only selecting a random number for each row and column in the grid, but this has the disadvantage of not producing a truly random sample because the sample elements are not independent of one another: the selection of one element does indeed affect the selection of other elements. It would be better to select a different random pair of x- and y-coordinates for each quadrat, as Redman and Watson did, so that the elements would all be independent of one another. Better still, we could stratify the site in a more meaningful way, rather than arbitrarily using a grid of squares, perhaps by dividing the site up by topographic features (Portugali, 1982) or by traces of architecture visible at the surface, or by attempting to account for site-formation processes (Reid et al., 1975).

A term that has not seen much use in archaeology is *PPS sampling*. PPS is an abbreviation for "probabilities proportional to their sizes" and refers to cases where a spatial sample is biased in favor of larger objects. In archaeology this can occur when we use a series of randomly selected points (x- and y-coordinates) or transects (line segments) to sample a map or a thin section through a pottery sherd, for example. In sampling a map for a regional survey, the points or transects in the sample will be more likely to intersect large sites than small ones, while in sampling the thin-section slide, the sample is more likely to include large-grained inclusions than small ones. In thin sections, in fact, even the plane of the thin section itself exposes a sample surface that is biased in favor of thicker inclusions. This sounds like a serious problem but, in some cases, as when we are trying to estimate a ratio and two parameters are highly correlated, it can in fact be an advantage. Naroll's estimate of the ratio of roofed habitation area to number of inhabitants (above, chapter 2) would be an example where this would be the case. Readers interested in this approach should consult more specialized literature (e.g., Barnett, 1991:36, 102-103; Som, 1973:59-74; Thompson, 1992:46-51)

The Paradox of Archaeological Sampling

As everyone knows, the easiest way to take a random sample of artifacts or sites is simply to enumerate them, and either use a random-number generator to select a subset of the numbers or simply put the numbers in a hat, mix them around, and arbitrarily pull out a few. The trouble is that, in archaeology, we can almost never number artifacts, features, or sites in advance, because we have not yet found them, and do not know exactly where they are. Furthermore, if we could number them it would imply that we already had knowledge of the whole population and probably would have no need for sampling. Virtually the only time this simple kind of sampling will work in archaeology is when we want to sample an existing collection. When the population consists of a large number of pots sitting on a museum's shelves, for example, we can simply list the pots and then randomly or systematically select a subset for detailed analysis; when the population consists of an unknown number of pots buried in the ground, we cannot.

What do we do? In general, archaeologists do not sample pots, or lithics, or even sites. Instead, we sample areas or volumes of space. In a regional survey, for example, our population may consist of all possible spatial units 200m x 200m in size. In an excavation, it might consist of all possible 1m x 1m areas or all possible 1m x 1m x 0.1m volumes. Many archaeologists sample space and then pretend that they actually sampled sites, artifacts, bone fragments, and plant remains.

When they make this assumption, they are really **cluster sampling**. While in stratified sampling we tried to select some observations in each stratum, cluster sampling, by contrast, is like taking one stratum and using all the observations in it. Because this type of sampling is so common in archaeology, it warrants some in-depth discussion.

In well designed cluster samples, instead of making a random selection of all members of a population, we concentrate on a spatially (or temporally) restricted subset of that population that we can reasonably expect to approximate a "microcosm" of the whole population. In other words, we would expect the one or two or 100 exposures of a large archaeological site that we excavate to include almost all the variation we would likely get if we excavated the whole site, and statistics that are close to the site's parameters. To put it in more statistical terms, cluster sampling can work well in cases where the variance in the clusters is large relative to the variance in the population. In fact, under those conditions and with roughly equal numbers of observations in each cluster, cluster sampling is actually more efficient (i.e., has less sampling error) than simple random sampling.

In a sense there are now two distinct kinds of populations. If N is the population of sampling elements (e.g., 1 m x 1 m squares), we also have M, the population of, say, rim sherds in the site. Consequently, the number of observations in our sample is still n squares, but these squares contain a total of m rim sherds.

Archaeologists often unconsciously use cluster samples because the population and elements that they are trying to analyse is not the same as the population and elements that they actually sampled. They sample n spatial elements and then act as though they sampled m lithic, ceramic, or faunal elements. That is, they take the entire set of lithics from the sample of spaces and, irrespective of what space they came from, measure them and calculate statistics. It may not seem intuitively obvious, but a collection of lithics from a random sample of spatial quadrats on a site is not exactly the same as a random sample of lithics from that site.

Typically in archaeological cases, the number of observations in each cluster varies. In one excavation square we might find 50 rim sherds, for example, and in others only 5. In such cases, our estimates of population means and proportions, e.g., mean diameter of pots or proportion of *terra sigillata*, are biased when based on cluster samples. In some instances, fortunately, the bias is small if we use the appropriate estimator.

Statisticians have devoted considerable attention to cluster sampling, so it is well known which estimators are least biased and which most efficient (e.g., Thompson, 1992:115-18). Drennan (1996:243-54) also provides an excellent introduction to the archaeological use of cluster samples. As it turns out, the best estimates of population means and proportions for cluster samples are the same as for simple random samples. The mean is just the sum of all the measured x_i values in all the clusters divided by the number of items in all the clusters (m):

$$\overline{x} = \frac{\sum x_i}{m}$$

This is called the cluster mean. The proportion belonging to a particular type i would simply be the total number of that type summed over all the clusters, divided by the total number of all items:

$$p = \frac{\sum m_i}{m}$$

This is called the cluster proportion.

The remainder of this section is for somewhat more advanced readers, but you should try to follow it. The equations are really not as difficult as they may appear.

There are other ways we could try to estimate population means and proportions. The solution that comes most easily to mind would be to take the individual estimates of means and proportions for each of the n clusters, and aver-

age them. After all, each cluster is itself a sample of the population on which we could base our estimates. However, the mean of the cluster means and mean of the cluster proportions are biased measures. You can see in table 4.1 that the means of 10 estimates of a proportion, taken from 10 clusters in a cluster sample, do not agree with the proportions calculated when we pool all the data. For site A, for example, the proportion of *Sus scrofa* (pig) bones can be estimated as $16/56 = 0.286$. But the mean of the 10 individual estimates is only 0.226. One reason why the mean of the cluster parameters does not provide good estimates is that the individual clusters have much smaller sample sizes than all the clusters taken together. In this case, the fact that many clusters have either 0 or 1 pig bones has depressed the estimate, creating bias. Pooling the data over all the clusters has the intuitively appealing result that clusters with larger sample sizes, which we would normally expect to give better estimates of parameters, contribute more to the result. Consequently, the cluster mean and cluster proportion are to be preferred, because their bias is smaller.

However, archaeologists are well aware that the conditions for "good" cluster sampling are almost never met. In fact, we generally assume the opposite: that there are activity areas and other kinds of spatial and temporal patterning on the site. Most archaeological sites provide good examples of **spatial autocorrelation**; essentially this means that artifacts found close together are more likely to be alike (in their functional, chronological, stylistic or, especially, contextual characteristics) than ones found far apart. In some cases this is because they were involved in the same activity, such as cooking or flint-knapping, and in others they may even be different fragments of the same pot, bones from the same animal, or flakes from the same core. The result is that there is less variation (and less variance) in the clusters than in the population. Under these circumstances, cluster sampling is less efficient (i.e., has more sampling error) than simple random sampling.

Obtaining only minimally biased estimates of means and proportions depends on the assumption that the population of potential observations is well "mixed." Spatial autocorrelation, however, often ensures that it is not well mixed. Let us say, for example, that of ten random quadrats on a site, nine produced only three or four blades each, while one — perhaps it intersected a blade-knapping activity area — produced almost 100 blades. If we lump all 130 or so blades together, the blades from the blade-knapping area, perhaps all made by a single individual over a very short time, will have a substantial effect on the value of such statistics as mean blade length and width and, if this flint-knapper's work is not typical of all flint-knappers on the site, these statistics could be quite far off the site population parameters, creating bias. The way in which we calculate variance (and thus standard error) for cluster samples takes this sort of situation into account, in that large variation between clusters in the sample will lead to larger estimates of variance, and larger standard errors.

Variance for cluster samples is calculated from sum of the squared deviations from the cluster mean or cluster proportion of all the clusters, divided by the number of clusters (see Drennan, 1996:247-53). To return to table 4.1, then, even though we calculated the proportion of *Sus scrofa* by pooling all the data, so that site A had $16/56 = 0.286$, we calculate the variance, and thus the standard error, by looking at how each individual cluster's estimate of the proportion differs from this value. For cluster 1, then, the proportion is $1/7 = 0.143$. That results in a deviation of $0.286 - 0.143 = -0.143$. For cluster 2, the proportion is $0/4 = 0$. That results in a deviation of -0.286. We continue on down the list in this way, square each deviation, and then sum them, finally dividing by $(10 - 1)$ to result in the cluster variance. To get the standard error we need to take the square root of the variance divided by the square root of n (i.e., multiply by $1/n$ before taking the square root):

$$SE_{cl} = \sqrt{\frac{1}{n}\left(\frac{\sum \left(\frac{x_i}{m_i} - p_x\right)^2 \left(\frac{m_i n}{m}\right)^2}{n - 1}\right)}$$

In cases where the value of N — the number of grid squares we sampled, for example — is low, we would also use the finite population corrector, multiplying the variance by $(1 - n/N)$ before taking the square root:

$$SE_{cl} = \sqrt{\frac{1}{n}\left(\frac{\sum \left(\frac{x_i}{m_i} - p_x\right)^2 \left(\frac{m_i n}{m}\right)^2}{n - 1}\right)\left(1 - \frac{n}{N}\right)}$$

where n is the number of clusters in the sample, N is the number of clusters in the population, x_i is the number of items of a particular type in the sample from one cluster, m_i is the total number of items in one cluster, p is the estimated proportion of type x in the population M, and m is the total number of items in all the clusters.

There are cases where it may be necessary or useful to use **multi-stage cluster samples**. In such cases, rather than examine all the objects in the clusters, we only examine a sample of them. In other words, we are sampling at at least two levels. First we sample, for example, space, selecting n excavation or survey units. Then, within each excavation or survey unit, we sample again, selecting m_i bags of sediment, perhaps, within each of the n clusters, a process called sub-sampling. Within each of the m bags, we may make observations on some number (l_i) of artifacts, seeds, bones, or the like. Such multi-stage sampling designs can be expected to be useful in cases where the number of potential observations is great, but analysis costs are also substantial, as in paleoethnobotany, and it is useful to reduce the analytical effort devoted to each cluster while still ensuring that all clusters in the cluster sample are given adequate attention.

But in many cases there is an easy way to avoid the problems of poor cluster samples. Often it is not difficult to ensure that the elements you are analysing are the same as the elements you actually sampled. In many instances, for example, we are interested in the densities of artifacts, charred seeds, and so on. Since the spatial units, not artifacts, are the sample elements in a typical excavation or survey, we simply treat our observations on the densities of artifacts, bones, or seeds as *measurements of attributes of the spatial units*. To return to the data in table 4.1, for example, if we treat the number of *Sus scrofa* bones in each excavation unit as an *attribute* of that unit, the average number of *Sus scrofa* bones per unit in our sample will be an unbiased estimate of the density of these bones in the entire population of all possible spatial quadrats, as long as all the excavation units are of equal size. From the data in table 4.1 we would estimate the density of Sus scrofa as 16/10 = 1.6 per unit area at site A and 26/10 = 2.6 per unit area at site B. For bones of all types we would estimate a density of 56/10 or 5.6 at site A and 81/10 or 8.1 at site B. We will also have a standard error on that estimate, measured in the usual way for means, that allows us to evaluate whether differences in density from one site to another are significant, and we calculate it with the same equation we would use for any random sample (see above, p. 20). For *Sus scrofa* densities, for example, we have 1.6 ± 0.60 at Site A and 2.6 ± 0.79 at Site B. Furthermore, if we know how many excavation units there would be in the entire sampling frame (N), all we need to do is multiply the density, and its standard error, by N to estimate the number of *Sus scrofa* bones in the entire site. If, for example, the sampling frame at site A consisted of 1000 excavation units, all of equal size, our estimate of the total number of *Sus scrofa* bones there would be 1000(1.6) = 1600 ± 600. The number of all bones

would be 1000(5.6) = 5600 ± 980. This can be very useful in many kinds of archaeology. It is an approach that should be particularly attractive to paleoethnobotanists, who often quantify plant remains by their density per unit volume of sediment (e.g., Hastorf and Popper, 1988).

Incidentally, we can also use this information to go back to our question about the proportion of *Sus scrofa* in the population. If we can estimate the number of *S. scrofa* bones as 1600 and the total number of bones as 5600, then the proportion of *S. scrofa* must be 1600/5600 = 0.286. This is exactly the same result we got with the cluster proportion, above.

As an aside, another advantage of using samples that consist of large numbers of spatial units, which serve as both sampling and analytical elements, is that they are useful for measuring **diversity** and **ubiquity** (see chapter 5), two measures that are particularly popular among archaeobotanists, but are useful in other types of research too.

Table 4.1. Determining the the proportions and densities of Sus scrofa bones, along with their standard errors, in two sites with cluster samples of ten equally-sized units each. Although these are densities (bones per sample element), the standard deviation (s) shown is somewhat higher than √λ (the standard deviation of Poisson distributions)

	Site A				Site B		
Sample Element	No. of S. scrofa	Total NISP	Prop. of S. scrofa	Sample Element	No. of S. scrofa	Total NISP	Prop. of S. scrofa
1	1	7	0.143	11	2	4	0.500
2	0	4	0.000	12	1	5	0.200
3	4	12	0.333	13	4	6	0.667
4	2	8	0.250	14	1	6	0.167
5	1	3	0.333	15	6	13	0.462
6	0	3	0.000	16	7	9	0.778
7	1	4	0.250	17	0	4	0.000
8	1	5	0.200	18	0	3	0.000
9	0	2	0.000	19	4	16	0.250
10	6	8	0.750	20	1	15	0.067
Total	16	56	**0.286**	Total	26	81	**0.321**
Mean	1.6	5.6	0.226[a]	Mean	2.6	8.1	0.309[a]
s	1.9	3.1		s	2.5	4.9	
SE	0.60	0.98	0.376	SE	0.79	1.5	0.195

[a]Note that the mean of the proportions is shown here only to show how it differs from the cluster proportion immediately above it.

An Example of the Effect of Autocorrelation on Cluster Samples

Let me illustrate some of the potential pitfalls of cluster sampling with an example from my own past mistakes. In my original analysis of a low-intensity survey of Wadi Ziqlab, northern Jordan in 1981, I treated 1 km x 1 km quadrats as sampling elements (randomly selecting 23 of them with replacement), but subsequently treated sites as analytical elements. Consequently, I was cluster sampling, but without well conceived clusters. Sites found together often represented closely related settlements, at least during the most intensively inhabited periods, and were likely to occupy similar soil and topographical circumstances. As a result, there was considerable spatial autocorrelation. Because I was interested in looking for correlations between sites and environmental variables, I should have recognized that as a serious problem. Unfortunately, I at first overlooked this and, like some other researchers (e.g., Zarky, 1976), began to cross-tabulate actual and "expected" site locations by soil type, slope, and other variables (Banning, 1985). If one of my 1km x 1km quadrats happened to turn up, say, five sites of the Roman period, it was highly probable that all five, or at least three or four of them, occurred on the same soil type, topographical zone, bedrock, and rainfall zone. Consequently, they were not independent of one another, contributing to bias in my sample of sites and rather poor results. To make matters worse, for some periods, the total number of sites was very small, meaning that my sample sizes were pathetic.

The better approach, as I learned, would have been to treat the quadrats (or better, the actual transects that we walked within those quadrats) as both sampling elements and analytical elements. For each quadrat I could measure such attributes as the density of Iron Age sites, the total area of all Iron Age sites, the area covered by the Terra Rossa soil type, the number of Iron Age sites that occur on Terra Rossa soil, the total Iron Age site area that occurs on Terra Rossa, or the area of all Terra Rossa soil in the quadrat that occurs within 200m of any Iron Age site. I could then use these measures from the 23

quadrats in my sample to arrive at means and standard errors for the population of all 1km x 1km quadrats in Wadi Ziqlab. In addition, I could explore the relationship between site area and amount of Terra Rossa soil. In all instances, no matter how many sites I had found, my sample size, n, would be 23, still small but no longer suffering from the effects of spatial autocorrelation.

Sampling Fraction and Sample Size

Having decided our population, our sample element, and what kind of sample to make, how do we decide how *much* to sample?

Clearly a sample of only one or two observations from a large population is likely to provide very poor estimates of the population's parameters, while a sample that consists of the entire population would provide perfect estimates. A typical sample should be somewhere between these extremes, and most archaeologists have assumed that the *sampling fraction*, the proportion of the whole population that is included in the sample (n/N), is an important contributor to the accuracy and precision of estimates. There has been an unfortunate tendency to use "cookbook" sampling fractions — 5% and 20% seem to be very popular — while some authors have been so bold as to declare that certain sampling fractions, as high as 50%, were necessary in quite common archaeological situations if wild inaccuracy was to be avoided. But the surprising thing is how *little* effect sampling fraction really has on the precision and accuracy of estimates, except when the whole population is itself quite small. Certainly a sampling fraction close to 100% is much better than one close to 10%, but a sampling fraction of 30% typically isn't much better than one of 20% and often not worth the additional cost of analysis. In short, the whole sampling fraction issue has been a red herring.

The most important contributor to the precision of estimates for most populations is, not sampling fraction, but sample *size*. This is not a proportion of the population, but the absolute number of observations, and has a very predictable, and quite substantial effect on the standard error of estimates. If we drew histograms of the distribution of values from a random sample, the histogram would look more and more like the normal ("bell curve") distribution as sample size increases, and the standard error would get smaller and smaller (figure 4.4). The **mean square error** of this distribution is negatively associated with the number of observations (usually represented algebraically as *n*), while the standard error decreases roughly by the square root of that number ($\sqrt{n}$). This should be obvious from the formula for the standard error, which has $\sqrt{n}$ in its denominator. What it means is that, if you want to double your precision (i.e., cut your standard error in half), you have to increase your sample size roughly by a factor of four. If you want to reduce the error to one-tenth, you need to increase sample size by a factor of 100.

But that still does not tell us exactly what our sample size should be. Again, many archaeologists tend to use "cookbook" sample sizes of 30, or 100, supposing that these are large enough, in most situations, to provide suitably small standard errors. Unfortunately, the standard error is not based only on sample size, which occurs in the denominator, but on the population's standard deviation, which occurs in the numerator. Consequently, in a population that has a relatively small standard deviation (i.e., relatively little variation) for a particular parameter, you can get away with a much smaller sample size than in a very diverse population.

The problem of deciding what sample sizes are appropriate is well understood by statisticians, and texts such as Thompson (1992:31-34, 38-40) explain the procedure clearly. Among the few archaeologists who have explicitly dealt with this issue in print are McManamon (1981), van der Veen and Fieller (1982), Shennan (1988:306-309) and Drennan (1996:132-34), who point out that we should decide on our sample size through consideration of the likely standard deviation in the population, the confidence level we plan to use when applying our estimates, and the amount of error or relative error we can tolerate. Relative error is the standard error divided by the mean. Since we are unlikely to know the amount of variation in the population, or its mean, in advance (the population standard deviation, σ), we either have to guess it or substitute the sample standard deviation (s)

of a small pilot sample as a rough estimate of σ. The formula is almost like doing a t-test (chapter 6) backwards, and solving for n instead of for t.

The remainder of this section is for readers prepared to follow the equations. Where we would like to control our relative error, perhaps limiting it to 5% of the population mean, and where the population is large relative to the sample, we would calculate sample size as follows.

$$n = \frac{(\sigma t)^2}{(r\mu)^2}$$

where r is the relative error and t is the number of standard deviations associated with the confidence we would like to have in our results. For 95% confidence, for example, t = 1.96 (for large samples). However, because we do not know the values of the population mean, μ, or the population standard deviation, σ, we must substitute estimates for them. This is something of a problem, as we must either guess, perhaps basing the guess on other samples we have made on populations that might be similar, or we must first make a small pilot sample, to give us rough estimates of μ and σ. Generally the latter is preferable, and we then estimate sample size as,

$$n = \frac{(st)^2}{(r\bar{x})^2}$$

or, if we want to control for the absolute size of the error range,

$$n = \frac{(st)^2}{d^2}$$

where s of a pilot sample is used as a rough estimate of the population σ, t is the "z-score" for the selected confidence level (e.g., t = 1.96 for 95% confidence for large samples, but t = 2.26 for samples of ten), r is the desired relative error (perhaps 5%), and $\bar{x}$ is the mean of a pilot sample being used to estimate the population mean μ. Where you want to fix the absolute size of the standard error, rather than use the relative error, d is the maximum size of the difference between the estimate and the "true" value you are willing to accept (perhaps, ± 2 sites or ± 0.05 in the proportion of deer bones).

Determining sample sizes for estimating parameters other than means, and when the population is small, is much the same. For example, sample size for a proportion, controlling for absolute error, d, is

$$m = \frac{t^2 p(1-p)}{d^2}$$

for large populations, with p representing the proportion in a pilot sample (our best estimate of the population proportion). Here I have described the sample size as m, instead of n, to avoid confusion in case we have a cluster sample with n clusters. When the population is small so that the finite population correction is necessary, it would instead be

$$n = \frac{Np(1-p)}{(N-1)\frac{d^2}{t^2} + p(1-p)}$$

The worst-case scenario is when the expected proportion is close to 0.5; that is the case that requires the largest sample size.

Things are a little more complicated if you want to estimate several proportions simultaneously, as when we wish to know the proportions of several taxa of plant remains, animal bones, or pottery (see Thompson, 1987; 1992:39-40). This usually results in a very large estimated sample size, sometimes much too large to be very practical, and it is simpler (and more cost-effective) to calculate the sample size for the taxon that comes closest to a proportion of 0.5, this being the proportion that requires the largest sample size (van der Veen and Fieller, 1982:294).

The methods outlined here still force you to make some seemingly arbitrary decisions. How much error is acceptable? How confident do you want to be of your results? That one is hard to answer, and we will deal with it in more detail when we come to testing hypotheses (chapter 6), but generally the golden rule, at least in classical statistics, is to be conservative. That means picking a confidence level that makes it easier for you to falsify your pet hypothesis or harder to reject a hypothesis you are trying to discredit. Deciding on the relative or absolute size of your

standard errors is much easier, so long as you have done a few pilot samples. Simply think in terms of the differences you would expect to find between the entities you will later want to compare. For example, if you plan do an isopleth map (chapter 2) with contour lines representing equal densities of artifacts, think in terms of the contour interval you plan to use on this map. Will there be a line for every increment of 1 artifact per m², or only for every 5 artifacts per m²? If, instead, you plan to compare faunal assemblages from two sites, would you expect differences between faunal assemblages in the order of 20%, or only 5%? Determining whether or not such differences are statistically significant would require quite different sample sizes.

Those who would like to work through an example can refer, once again, to table 4.1. Here we have two sites, each of which has contributed a pilot sample of ten sample elements (probably contexts) containing faunal bone, and from each sample element we can estimate the proportion of pig bones (*Sus scrofa*). The sample size, n, for each site is therefore 10 (although the number of bones, m, is 56 at site A and 81 at site B), and it is too small for us to be sure that any apparent difference between the two sites is meaningful. In fact the standard errors on the estimated proportions are extremely large, with 0.29 ± 0.38 and 0.32 ± 0.20, and overlap so much that the difference between 29% and 32% is not at all convincing (see chapter 6). Let us assume that we would like to have errors of only 0.03. If we want to be 95% confident of a difference as small as ± 0.03 (or 3%), we would need a new sample from each site, presumably much larger than n = 10.

One way to tackle the problem, and the most common approach, is to think of how many identifiable bones should be in our sample (m). For Site A, we would determine m as:

$$m = \frac{t^2 p(1-p)}{d^2} = \frac{(2.26)^2(0.286)(0.714)}{(0.03)^2} = 1159$$

Consequently we would want our sample to include 1159 identifiable bones, instead of the mere 56 of the pilot sample (cf. van der Veen and Fieller, 1982).

However, this does not tell us how many excavation units (n) we need to obtain an adequate estimate of the proportion of *Sus scrofa*. One solution is to divide the figure of 1159 by our estimate of bone density (i.e., 1159/5.6) as determined above. This results in an estimate of n = 207 bags, contexts or excavation units. Because our estimate of density is itself rather imprecise (note the large standard deviation), this can only be a rough guide.

Another solution is to use the densities, instead of proportions, as your measures of interest, keeping in mind that you can multiply the density by N to estimate the total number of *Sus scrofa* bones in the population. In that case, your pilot sample tells you that the mean density of identifiable *Sus scrofa* elements is 1.6 per unit, with a standard deviation of 1.3. Under those circumstances, retaining the confidence level of 95%, and assuming a maximum acceptable error on the estimate of ± 0.3, we would have

$$n = \frac{(st)^2}{d^2} = \frac{(1.3)^2(2.26)^2}{(0.3)^2} = 96$$

So we would probably need a sample of about 96 units from Site A to allow us to make comparisions *of density* with Site B at the desired levels of precision and confidence. We might take a sample of 100 to play it safe, since we used what are probably poor estimates of the population's mean and standard deviation.

There are other ways to optimize your sample size, including a **sequential sampling** approach with which you keep increasing your sample size until some predetermined criteria, such as reaching a particular relative error, are met. The sequential approach is intuitively very appealing because, ideally, it allows us to optimize the balance between the cost of taking bigger and bigger samples and the risk of ending up with bad estimates of population parameters. At its simplest it involves a basic "stopping rule" such that we keep making observations until we encounter some boundary, and our estimate is based on the total of the observations we have made at that point. In practice it often involves some rather complicated mathematics

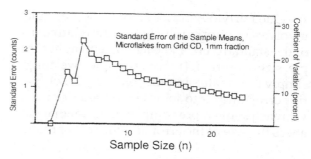

Figure 4.4. The standard error on the mean density (counts per 3 cc) of microflakes from a Neolithic floor in Jordan as it falls with increasing sample size.

if we are truly to optimize and is not necessarily less costly than a well planned, fixed-sample design (Wetherill and Glazebrook, 1987:5, 97-127).

For some time some palaeoethnobotanists have used simple sequential designs with a "stopping rule" typically based on sample richness or a plateau in the frequencies or proportions. For example, the analyst may keep counting charred seeds or charcoal fragments in a sample until the total number of taxa encountered reaches some predetermined limit or, more typically, may keep counting as long as he or she is encountering new taxa, but stop after some predetermined number of observations that contain no new taxa (Fasham and Monk, 1978; Green, 1979). Van der Veen and Fieller (1982:288-89) describe what they call "cumulative sampling" as gradually increasing sample size until the values of sample statistics, such as proportions or frequencies, "settle down." In terms of sequential sampling, these are not optimal designs because the analyst may have to count well beyond the point of recording at least one example of every taxon or reaching a steady proportion or frequency, while a run of several observations without new taxa or much change to a frequency does not guarantee that additional observations would not change this frequency or add new taxa. Furthermore, the use of a stopping rule based on richness can produce biased estimates of the proportions of various taxa because it involves investing extra effort to record the rare ones.

One fairly obvious kind of "stopping rule" involves monitoring changes in the relative size of the standard error at each increment in sample size (figure 4.4). For example, we might simply terminate sampling once the SE or relative error shrinks to some target value, or when we reach some more complicated goal that balances the size of the error and the cost of reducing it.

Nonrandom Samples and Exchangeability

Earlier in the chapter, purposive samples were introduced as a kind of nonrandom sample designed to meet some particular requirements that have nothing to do with probability theory. Most of the archaeological samples that do not conform to classical probability samples, however, are not consciously designed as purposive samples. In some cases they are "grab bag" or haphazard samples, meaning simply that the members of the sample were selected with no explicit thought to sample design at all. This type of sample is very common in archaeology, especially with the content of so many archaeological collections and databases dictated by chance discoveries, "rescue" archaeology, and practical limitations in the field, or having been accumulated many decades ago, when archaeologists did not think in sampling terms. One might get the impression, from the previous discussion, that these samples were not useful for anything at all.

In fact, we can still make use of samples that do not meet the ideal standards of classical probability sampling. We would do this through careful consideration of the kinds of bias we would expect in a haphazard or purposive sample (see Drennan, 1996:89-93). For example, a haphazard sample of pottery sherds in a surface survey in the American Southwest might be expected to include a higher proportion of large sherds and a higher proportion of decorated sherds than in the population of the site. That is because large, decorated pottery tends to attract the surveyor's eye. Obviously, we would not want to use such a sample to estimate the proportion of decorated pottery at the site, as it is clearly biased in this respect, and the degree of bias is unknown. However, this does not mean that the sample will be biased with respect to the inclusions in the sherds, or the trace elements in their chemistry. It is even possible that the decorated pottery in the sample is fairly representative of the various types of decoration, although we would need to be cautious about that. In addition, even when we have cause to believe that the sample is biased, it may be possible, with suitable caution, to compare the sample with other samples that we have reason to believe contain the same biases. Sometimes archaeologists describe samples that were not selected through probability theory, but that we believe are probably not very different from a random sample in some respect, as *quasi-random samples*.

Bayesian statisticians deal with these sampling problems through the concept of **exchangeability** (Buck et al., 1996:72-77). Rather than worry about the formal properties of the methods used to sample a population (in some cases no consistent method at all), they concern themselves with whether there is any *a priori* evidence to suggest that one member of the population is any different from other members with respect to the property we wish to measure. If there is not, then it really does not matter which members of the population we select, and we can even decide to select the ones that are most conveniently available. In situations, by contrast, where we have reason to believe that different members could be quite different with respect to some characteristic of interest, for example, when they might come from different activity areas on a site or from different sites, we would not consider them to be exchangeable, and would want to ensure that our sample included members from each activity area, for example. One way to do this, which is similar to stratified sampling, is simply to consider the population to consist of subpopulations, the members of each subpopulation being exchangeable. Because Bayesian statistics considers all probabilities to be conditional (see chapter 6), errors that might be due to careful application of the concept of exchangeability are too small to be worrisome.

Checklist for Sampling

"Cookbook" schemes for sample size and sampling fraction are not the way to design your research, while deciding between random, systematic, stratified, and other sampling strategies is only a small part of the sampling picture. I have tried to stress in this chapter that there is no simple answer in the design of research or samples, and so what follows is not a list of step-by-step instructions. Rather, it is a set of questions you should consider when making decisions about the design of a sample. Of course there will be many other questions related to the archaeological content of your research problem that will also have a bearing on your sample design, not to mention consideration of cost.

1. Is a statistical sample what you really want? Will you be estimating population parameters or comparing samples with respect to their sample statistics in an attempt to see if they come from the same or different populations? If, instead, you are prospecting for sites, describing a small collection of artifacts, or trying to reveal spatial structure, probability sampling in the usual sense may be ill advised.

2. What is the population of interest? How do you define this population and its elements? If you are to avoid making poorly conceived cluster samples, you might try to define these in ways that ensure that your sampling elements are identical to your analytical elements. If you prefer a cluster sample, how will you attempt to ensure that it represents a microcosm of the whole population?

3. What is your sampling frame? Is it a spatial grid, a list of artifacts, or a set of topographical features or sediment volumes? How should you orient it or order it? For elements that are spaces or volumes, how large should they be and how should they be shaped? Will each element be physically large enough that you can reasonably expect to make the measurements of interest?

4. Do you have relevant information that could help you stratify the sample? How many strata (subpopulations) should there be and how will you define them? Will you sample the strata proportionally, or sample some strata more intensively than others?

5. Will you make a simple random selection within the population (or in each stratum or cluster), or a systematic one? If you select a systematic strategy, what interval will you use and how will you select the first sample element (the only random one)?

6. What sample size will you use to achieve a sufficiently small standard error for the problem you plan to investigate? Will you sample with or without replacement? Remember that sampling with and without replacement requires slightly different equations for some statistics, such as variance and standard error.

7. What measurements will you make on each sample element that are relevant to your research problem? Are your sample elements defined in such a way that you can reasonably expect to be able to make this measurement in almost every case? Or will you probably have many zeroes or "missing data" observations? Perhaps rethinking your sampling frame will help you avoid missing data.

Most sampling designs represent a compromise between research cost, convenience, avoiding bias, controlling the magnitude of sampling error, making sense in terms of a research problem, or even balancing the requirements of several research problems simultaneously. Although you should seek the advice of a statistician for some of the statistical aspects — statisticians have devoted much attention to balancing cost with efficiency, for example — only you can really decide how to balance these competing requirements so that the sample meets your needs.

Nonsampling Research

Not all archaeological research is amenable to sampling in the classical sense (cf. Shennan, 1988:327-28). When we are not interested in population parameters, random sampling can in fact serve us rather poorly. For example, the investigation of "town planning" in archaeological sites is a research problem that centres on spatial structure, not on such parameters as average house size or the proportion of structures that have stone foundations. In order to see and recognize any patterning in the spatial arrangement of structures and other features or facilities on the site, we need to have broad exposures, not a random sample of 1m x 1m squares or the like. In a very large settlement, we may still need to sample because of the extreme cost that would be involved in exposing the whole site, but then we might opt for a cluster sample, exposing large expanses in only one or two areas of the site that we have reason to believe might be representative of the whole or where we have reason to believe there is structurally interesting evidence (c.f., Redman and Anzalone, 1980). Sometimes a small pilot sample could be used to guide the planning of the larger cluster sample or a carefully planned purposive sample.

The same applies to investigations of spatial structure at the regional scale. In Nearest Neighbour Analysis, for example, we want to know the mean distance between each site and its nearest contemporary neighbour, a population parameter that happens to tell us something about spatial structure (how clustered or dispersed the settlement pattern is). Even though this is a parameter of the population of all sites, it is not possible for us in archaeological situations to make a random sample of sites along with their nearest neighbours — generally we do not have advance knowledge of where they are — while a random sample of spatial units, even if fairly large, would undoubtedly omit many, or even most, of the nearest neighbours, leading us to make gross overestimates of the parameter. Here we would instead have to opt for concentrating on a smaller, spatially restricted population that we can study in its entirety, and be very careful not to miss any of the near

neighbours, or use a different statistic, such as Morisita's index of dispersion (Rogge and Fuller, 1977), that is based on densities in sample units.

Besides spatial structure, other archaeological goals that may be ill served by probabilistic sampling include prospecting for sites or other archaeological materials, and unravelling the stratification of individual sites. If you simply want to find a particular kind of site that is suitable for excavation, and that will help you solve a particular problem, you should take advantage of all the information you have about the typical locations of such sites to help you find one, or at least narrow your search with a purposive sample or by using a very narrow definition of your population. Here a random sample of space would be a very poor use of your time, since most surveyed areas would not contain the site of interest. In stratigraphy, furthermore, the last thing you would want is a random sample of deposits across a site. In order to infer stratigraphic order you ideally want an uninterrupted sequence of superimposed deposits and associated interfaces, but certainly not a series of noncontiguous deposits. Consequently, archaeologists typically use strategically placed trenches designed to reveal all, or nearly all, of the site's stratigraphic sequence. When one location will not reveal the entire stratigraphic sequence, perhaps because of erosion, it is necessary to make a careful selection of sequences that overlap one another in time, enabling us to reconstruct a sequence. Sampling theory would not help us make such selections.

It may seem surprising, but most archaeological research, and especially field research, continues to be guided by principles other than sampling. It is still possible to think of this research as a kind of sampling, for example, by considering the population to consist of all the stratigraphic sections that an archaeologist could conceivably observe in southwestern France or all the village settlements that ever occurred during the Middle Woodland period, including those of which no traces remain (cf. Drennan, 1996:261-67). Or we could adopt a Bayesian approach to the problem, as mentioned above. Some kinds of archaeological research, furthermore, is particularistic, without explicit reference to any population larger than the site or problem at hand.

Conclusion

The key to good research design is not to copy someone else's idea of research, but to anticipate the kinds of data that are likely to help you resolve a particular research question, or evaluate a particular hypothesis, and then use or develop methods to acquire those kinds of data. Often this involves what some archaeologists call a "multi-stage" research design (Redman, 1973) in which researchers periodically reassess their progress, refine hypotheses or define new kinds of data with which to test them, and introduce new hypotheses that unexpected results may suggest. Other archaeologists characterize their research as cyclical, dialectical, or **hermeneutic**. While these approaches differ in detail and theoretical underpinnings, they share a cyclical or back-and-forth revision of hypotheses in light of new data and search for new data from the perspective of revised hypotheses (e.g., Gardin, 1980; Hodder, 1992; Johnsen and Olsen, 1992). The idea is that research is an iterative process that, to some researchers' minds, gradually "homes in" on a meaningful understanding or a satisfying hypothesis, although perhaps never quite reaching it. For **interpretive archaeologists**, it homes in on one possible understanding, while other archaeologists with other interests or theoretical perspectives will approach quite different meanings or understandings, as long as they are not incompatible with the data (Hodder, 1992). Whether the data are from statistical samples or carefully selected observations, or are quantitative or not, depends entirely on the nature of the problem at a given stage in the research.

References Cited

Banning, E. B., 1985, *Pastoral and Agricultural Land Use in the Wadi Ziqlab, Jordan: An Archaeological and Ecological Survey*. Ph.D. thesis, University of Toronto.

— 1996, Highlands and lowlands: Problems and survey frameworks for rural archaeology in the Near East. *Bulletin of the American Schools of Oriental Research* 301:25-45.

Banning, E. B., and Racher, P., n.d., Sampling theory and microrefuse analysis: Neolithic house floors in Wadi Ziqlab, Jordan. Paper presented at the 1997 Society for American Archaeology meetings, Nashville, TN.

Barnett, V., 1991, *Sample Survey Principles and Methods*. Wiley, New York.

Binford, L. R., 1962, Archaeology as anthropology. *American Antiquity* 28:217-25.

— 1964, A consideration of archaeological research design. *American Antiquity* 29:425-44.

— 1968, Archaeological perspectives. In *New Perspectives in Archaeology*, edited by S. R. Binford and L. R. Binford, pp. 5-32. Aldine, Chicago.

Boismier, W. A., 1991, The role of research design in surface collection: An example from Broom Hill, Braishfield, Hampshire. In *Interpreting Artefact Scatters: Contributions to Ploughzone Archaelogy*, edited by A. J. Schofield, pp. 11-25. Oxbow, Oxford.

Buck, C. E., Cavanagh, W. G., and Litton, C. D., 1996, *Bayesian Approach to Interpreting Archaeological Data*. John Wiley & Sons, New York.

Clarke, D. L., 1968, *Analytical Archaeology*. Methuen and Co, London.

Courbin, P., 1988, *What is Archaeology? An Essay on the Nature of Archaeological Research*. University of Chicago Press, Chicago.

Drennan, R. D., 1996, *Statistics for Archaeologists: A Commonsense Approach*. Plenum Press, New York.

Fasham, P. J., and Monk, M. A., 1978, Sampling for plant remains from Iron Age pits: Some results and implications. In *Sampling in Contemporary British Archaeology*, edited by J. Cherry, C. Gamble and S. Shennan, pp. 363-71. BAR 50. British Archaeological Reports, Oxford.

Gardin, J.-C, 1980, *Archaeological Constructs. An Aspect of Theoretical Archaeology*. Cambridge University Press, Cambridge.

Goodyear, A. C., Raab, M. L., and Klinger, T. C., 1978, The status of archaeological research design in cultural resource management. *American Antiquity* 43:150-173.

Green, F. J., 1979, Collection and interpretation of botanical information from Medieval urban excavations in southern England. *Archaeo-Physika* 8:39-55.

Hastorf, C. A., and Popper, V. S., eds., 1988, *Current Paleoethnobotany: Analytical Methods and Cultural Interpretations of Archaeological Plant Remains*. University of Chicago Press, Chicago.

Hodder, I., 1992, Interpretive archaeology and its role. In *Theory and Practice in Archaeology*, by I. Hodder, pp. 183-200. Routledge, London.

Johnsen, H., and Olsen, B., 1992, Hermeneutics and archaeology: On the philosophy of contextual archaeology. *American Antiquity* 57:419-36.

Johnson, G., 1980, Rank-size convexity and system integration: A view from archaeology. *Economic Geography* 56:234-47.

McManamon, F. P., 1981, Probability sampling and archaeological survey in the Northeast: An estimation approach. In *Foundations of Northeast Archaeology*, edited by D. Snow, pp. 195-227. Academic Press, New York.

Metcalfe, D., and Heath, K. M., 1990, Microrefuse and site structure: The hearths and floors of the Heartbreak Hotel. *American Antiquity* 55:781-97.

Nance, J., 1983, Regional sampling in archaeological survey: The statistical perspective. *Advances in Archaeological Method and Theory* 6:289-356.

Nance, J., and Ball, B. F., 1986, No surprises? The reliability and validity of test pit sampling. *American Antiquity* 51:457-83.

Plog, S., Plog, F., and Wait, W., 1978, Decision-making in modern surveys. *Advances in Archaeological Method and Theory* 1:384-421.

Portugali, Y., 1982, A field methodology for regional archaeology (the Jezreel Valley Survey, 1981). *Tel Aviv* 9:170-88.

Redman, C. L., 1973, Multistage fieldwork and analytical techniques. *American Antiquity* 38:61-79.

Redman, C.L., and Anzalone, R. D., 1980, Discovering architectural patterning at a complex site. *American Antiquity* 45:284-90.

Redman, C. L., and Watson, P. J., 1970, Systematic, intensive surface collection. *American Antiquity* 35:279-91.

Reid, J. J., Schiffer, M. B., and Neff, J., 1975, Archaeological considerations of intrasite sampling. In *Sampling in Archaeology*, edited by . W. Mueller, pp. 209-224. University of Arizona Press, Tucson.

Rogge, A. E., and Fuller, S. L., 1977, Probability survey sampling: Making parameter estimates. In *Conservation Archaeology*, edited by M. B. Schiffer and G. J. Gumerman, pp. 227-38 . Academic Press, New York.

Salmon, M., 1982, *Philosophy and Archaeology*. Academic Press, New York.

Shanks, M., and Tilley, C., 1987, *Re-Constructing Archaeology, Theory and Practice*. Cambridge University Press, Cambridge.

Shennan, S., 1988, *Quantifying Archaeology*. Edinburgh University Press, Edinburgh.

Simms, S. R., and Heath, K. M., 1990, Site structure of the Orbit Inn: An application of ethnoarchaeology. *American Antiquity* 55:797-813.

Som, R. K., 1973, *A Manual of Sampling Techniques*. Heinemann, London.

Thomas, D. H., 1973, An empirical test of Steward's model of Great Basin settlement patterns. *American Antiquity* 38:155-176.

—1978, The awful truth about statistics in archaeology. *American Antiquity* 43: 231-44.

Thompson, S. K., 1987, Sample size for estimating multinomial proportions. *The American Statistician* 41:42-46.

— 1992, *Sampling*. John Wiley & Son, New York.

Tukey, J. W., 1977, *Exploratory Data Analysis*. Addison-Wesley.

Van der Veen, M, and Fieller, N. R. J., 1982, Sampling seeds. *Journal of Archaeological Science* 9:287-98.

Watson, P. J., LeBlanc, S., and Redman, C., 1971, *Explanation in Archaeology. An Explicitly Scientific Approach*. Columbia University Press, New York.

Wetherill, G. B., and Glazebrook, K. D., 1987, *Sequential Methods in Statistics*. Chapman and Hall, London.

Wobst, H. M., 1983, We can't see the forest for the trees: Sampling and the shapes of archaeological distributions. In *Archaeological Hammers and Theories*, edited by J. A. Moore and A. S. Keene, pp. 37-85. Academic Press, New York.

Woolley, L., 1930, *Digging Up the Past*. Ernest Benn, London.

Zarky, A., 1976, Statistical analysis of site catchments at Ocos, Guatemala. In *The Early Mesoamerican Village*, edited by K. V. Flannery, pp. 117-30. Academic Press, New York.

5 Quantification: Abundance and Other Measures in Archaeology

Once we have agreed on a classification for a particular kind of archaeological material, we usually want to assess each class's absolute or relative abundance. Sometimes it is sufficient to say simply that two sites share a particular type of pottery or that four out of five deposits contained at least one cow bone, an approach some archaeologists call "presence analysis." More often we would prefer to compare the abundances or proportions of pottery or bones or seeds at two sites or in several contexts from the same site. We need to be able to quantify archaeological materials before we can carry out seriation of pottery, study the "fall off" of obsidian away from its source, estimate the contribution of deer meat to a prehistoric community's diet, or even distinguish activity areas on sites.

Unfortunately, most archaeological remains are not easy to quantify in a meaningful way. Even if we can count pots, bones, and seeds accurately, however, we cannot always justify such statements as "12% of the pottery at the Red Butte site is Kayenta White Ware." Orton et al. (1993:209) note that a high percentage of coarse cooking sherds over fine table ware, for example, does not prove that cooking pots were more common in the "life population" of pots in use at any one time. Fine table ware could have been treated with more care ("curated"), while cooking pots were considered cheap and expendable or even disposable. A kitchen might have had ten times as many fine dishes as it had cooking pots, even if the middens now contain three times as many sherds from cooking pots.

This problem has to do with the degree of fragmentation. Rather than whole pots or animals, archaeologists deal mainly with sherds and bone fragments. Does a sherd have meaning in terms of whole pots? Does a bone fragment have meaning in terms of whole bones or whole animals? Two bone fragments could be from the same bone, from two different bones in the same animal, or from two different animals. Other problems are variations in archaeological recovery, and in the number of countable elements in each entity of interest. For example, some bones are more likely to be overlooked by the archaeologists excavating them, while some whole animals have more bones in their bodies than others. How do you compare branches or chunks of wood charcoal with seeds, pollen, or phytoliths? This is surely the classic "apples and oranges" problem.

Furthermore, are pots, plants, or animals really the elements of interest? Sometimes what we really want to know is the amount of food stored or cooked in the pots, or the amount of meat people ate. Nunamiut hunters, for example, think in terms of *parts* of dismembered animals, such as hind quarters, and not whole animals (Binford, 1978:70).

In spite of these difficulties, it is worthwhile to attempt quantification, rather than be satisfied with "presence analysis," which reduces the richness of evidence to the mere presence or absence of taxa. The quantification problems can sometimes be minimized if you do not need to know the absolute quantities of vessels, meat, or flour at one site, but only how the relative abundances (proportions) compare in two assemblages. In some cases, the appropriate choice of measure will indeed allow you to estimate accurately, with confidence intervals, the number of animals in the population of animals whose carcasses contributed to a deposit, or the proportion of a particular pottery type in an assemblage. At least in some instances, the opportunities for quantification are much brighter than we might expect.

With few exceptions, researchers who have dealt with archaeological quantification have discussed the measures only in the context of faunal remains or, more rarely, pottery or plant remains (e.g., Egloff, 1973; Fieller and Turner 1982; Gautier, 1984; Gilbert and Singer, 1982; Orton, 1993; Poplin, 1976; Popper, 1988; Ringrose, 1993a). Palynologists have also devoted much attention to the relationship between pollen statistics and vegetation (Faegri and Iversen, 1989). More general treatment of quantification in archaeology is still unusual. Some confusion over the relative advantages of different measures has resulted from failure to distinguish the measures' purposes. Some measures are only simple ways of counting (enumerating) or measuring objects in a particular sample; others are more sophisticated indirect measures or estimates of population parameters based on a sample (Fieller and Turner, 1982). Some of the former that are perfectly adequate for simply describing the number of some entity are often inadequate for the purposes to which they are usually put, namely estimating without bias the *relative* abundance of taxa, such as the *percentage* of deer or wheat or decorated pottery in a population.

At present, the archaeological literature shows a wide variety of quantification measures, although some are only applicable under special circumstances. The common measures for simply describing samples are fragment counts or "Number of Identified Specimens" (**NISP**), weight or **mass**, Minimum Number of Individuals (**MNI**), Minimum Number of Elements (**MNE**), and Minimum Animal Units (**MAU**). Parameter estimates include "Pottery Information Equivalent" (**PIE**), "Bone Information Equivalents," the Krantz estimator, the **Peterson index**, and other less common measures. In addition, **ubiquity** and **diversity**, do not actually measure abundance at all, but some researchers treat ubiquity as an indirect measure of abundance or simply fail to recognize the

distinction. It is important to recognize the strengths and weaknesses of each, as well as what they *really* measure.

This chapter will review these measures with examples of how the most important ones work, beginning with simple descriptive measures for samples of **fossil assemblages**, followed by indirect measures for deposited assemblages, and parameter estimates for populations (**death assemblages** or **deposited assemblages**, see chapter 9 for discussion of taphonomic assemblages). Ubiquity and diversity will come at the end. Some parts may seem daunting, but concentrate on the discussion rather than the equations if the latter prove an obstacle.

ASSESSING ABUNDANCE IN SAMPLES

Number of Identified Specimens (NISP)

The oldest and most obvious method for quantifying archaeological materials is simply to count them. The absolute number of identifiable potsherds, seeds, bones, and bone fragments is often described as NISP (Chaplin, 1971: 64-67; Payne, 1975; Grayson, 1978).

NISP, however, does not count or estimate the number of whole entities, such as animals or pots, that are represented in a sample or that were in the population. The value of NISP does depend on the number of such entities (N), but also on recovery probability (r), the number of countable elements (usually bones or seeds) expected in each whole entity (s), and the degree of fragmentation (f). Consequently, we might expect NISP = Nrsf (Chase and Hagaman 1987). In other words, the original number, N, has been reduced by r (r<1), increased by s (s≥1), and either increased or decreased by f. Fragmentation that resulted in each of the s elements being broken into an average of five fragments, for example, would mean that f=5. Although all these factors prevent NISP from providing an estimate of the population N, one could hope that by controlling rsf we might be able to estimate the *proportions* of taxa in the preserved or even deposited population:

$$\frac{n_i}{\text{NISP}_{total}}$$

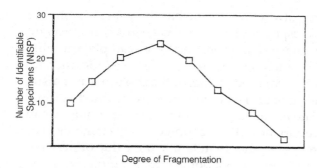

Figure 5.1. Relationship between degree of fragmentation and NISP. At first, fragmentation increases the number of identifiable fragments, but eventually some pieces become too fragmented to be easily identifiable, causing NISP to decline.

Most researchers have worried most about the degree of fragmentation, as an assemblage of N entities that is badly broken up will certainly have a much higher NISP than one that is well preserved, except when fragmentation is so extreme that most elements are unidentifiable (figure 5.1). Fewer have investigated ways to control this factor, which is usually negatively associated with physical density (but see PIE below, and Lyman, 1984). Compensating for variation in s is relatively simple, and is the basis for some of the measures below.

The most difficult variable to control is r. This is actually a combination of probabilities: probability that a particular specimen will be deposited on the site, that it will survive in the site's deposits until excavated, and that the archaeologists will find, save, and record it. We have no prior knowledge of the pre-excavation probabilites, although future research should attempt to estimate them (Kadane, 1988; Hubbard and al-Azm, 1990). The probability that a particular surviving specimen will be included in an archaeological sample, however, is a function of sampling fraction, the proportion of the archaeological deposit that we excavate and analyse. Where we have excavated, perhaps, 12% of a deposit, this component of r would simply be 0.12. This is the only component that is constant for all items, however, which means that NISP depends, not on r but on mean r ($\bar{r}$) for different categories of items.

NISP has several advantages. First, it is easy to calculate, because you only need to keep a tally of specimens as you catalogue them. Second, NISP values are additive. This means that when you increase your sample size at a site or combine two samples, you only need to add new NISP values to the old ones or add two NISP values together. Some alternative methods of quantification do not allow you to do this. Third, NISP is better than some of the other measures for comparing proportions of fragmentary remains in two assemblages. Although it is not unbiased in this situation, it often gives more realistic views of relative magnitudes between assemblages, so long as the samples were reasonably large, included the same taxa, and factors that affect recovery rates, such as curation, breakage, or butchering patterns were approximately the same.

But there are many problems with NISP, too. As mentioned above, researchers have focussed on the effects of fragmentation (f). Up to a point, pots or bones that break into a larger number of fragments, for example, will be overrepresented by NISP relative to ones that break into fewer pieces (Chaplin, 1971:65-66; Orton et al., 1993:209). The preservation of bones, for example, varies with the bones' density and shape (Lyman, 1984). This means that f is not the same for all types of entity or even different parts of the same entity, and that NISP in fact depends not on f but on mean f ($\bar{f}$) for all of these parts. Because changes in the proportions of different taxa will affect the value of $\bar{f}$, this makes it difficult to use NISP to compare sites that differ substantially in the distribution of taxa. As we will see, many researchers' preference for other measures is due to their belief, not always justified, that these measures avoid or at least substantially reduce the adverse effects of differential fragmentation.

Ringrose (1993a) would take account of these interelement variations to express NISP as

$$\text{NISP} = \sum_{i=1}^{s} \text{Nr}_i\text{f}_i$$

with r_i and f_i as the recovery and fragmentation rates for the i-th element of s elements. This means that NISP is the sum, for all s elements, of each element's rf values multiplied by the original number of animals.

Zooarchaeologists have emphasized a number of other problems with NISP. NISP of bones overestimates taxa that have more bones in their bodies (higher s), but this can be corrected (see below). More importantly, NISP overrepresents species that tend to be brought to archaeological sites intact over those, usually large ones, that tend to be butchered at the kill site, because only selected, usually meat-rich, parts of the latter may be returned to the site. This means that, for animals of which only partial carcasses were brought to the site, some elements might have fairly high r_i values, but for other elements, $r_i = 0$. A statistical objection to NISP is that some bone fragments come from the same animal, or sherds from the same pot, and so on, violating the assumption of independence of observations in the sample.

For plant remains, the problems with NISP can appear daunting. Different taxa of plants produce vastly different numbers of seeds, pollen, and phytoliths (varying s), all of which reach archaeological sites and other deposits through widely varying combinations of transport (gravity, wind, harvesting, defecation, etc.), only to experience variation in preservation. All these affect r. Some species found at a site may be represented by seeds, others by charcoal or phytoliths, and others not at all. There is consequently need for research on estimating r, s, and f, and to be careful about interpreting relative abundance, through understanding the ecological interrelationships of whole plant communities.

The Shotwell Measure and WAE

Shotwell (1955) introduced to faunal quantification the simple expedient of compensating for the different numbers of identifiable elements in whole skeletons. He simply divided the NISP by the number of identifiable elements, s, in a whole animal:

$$NI_s = \frac{NISP}{s}$$

Because there are two tibiae in each mammal, for example, we simply divide the number of, say, distal tibiae by two. This would seem to control at least one of the factors in Nrf, but it is

not always obvious what the value of s should be, especially if whole carcasses were not brought to the site (Grayson, 1984). For example, a number of vertebrae that are usually fused together are often counted as one, or the proximal and distal ends of broken long bones are counted as separate elements, so it is necessary for analysts to report how they counted such elements. For remains other than fauna, the value of s is even more elusive. For pottery, for example, we could not expect pots always to have the same number of separate parts, although in some cases we might know, for example, that each pot had exactly two handles or one spout. Otherwise, we would have to be satisfied with the average s for each type of vessel ($\bar{s}$), which is really a function of fragmentation ($\bar{f}$). For pottery, the **PIE** (below) is much preferable.

Holtzman's (1979) "frequency of elements" (FE), and Binford's (1978:70) "MNI" are really element-wise equivalents of Shotwell's measure. Chase and Hagaman (1987) take this up, under the name of "weighted abundance of elements" (**WAE**), as a step on the way to their TMAU measure (below). In effect, they count all nonredundant examples of s types of elements and divide by s. They claim that WAE = Nrs/s = Nr, yet, because r will vary by element, they replace it with the better expression, based on the sum of the individual elements' Nrs,

$$WAE = \frac{\sum_{i=1}^{s} Nr_i s}{s}$$

with r_i as the recovery rate for the i-th element of s elements. The value of f does not appear in the equation because WAE only considers fairly intact individual elements and fragments that have some landmark to ensure that the same element will not be counted twice. In essence, WAE is the average Nrs for s well-preserved elements. Chase and Hagaman (1987:80) notice that this would lead to biased estimates of N. If used to estimate relative abundances among taxa, any interpopulation differences in r would lead to bias. Furthermore, because the number of bones cannot take negative values, at low values of N (i.e., rare taxa), WAE overestimates.

Nonetheless, WAE is important in that it represents an attempt to control for most of the factors that distort the relationship between NISP and N.

Somewhat analogous to WAE and the Shotwell measure are attempts by **palynologists** (see chapter 10) to account for the effects of differential pollen production and transport on the pollen abundances in sediments (Faegri and Iversen, 1989:3, 118-20, 141-46; Moore et al., 1991:183-84). Because some species produce far more pollen than others, and some pollen drops within a few meters while others travel hundreds of kilometers, the percentage of pollen grains of any species is not proportional to that species' abundance in nature. One approach has been to find "correction factors," R (or representativity factor), much like Shotwell's s or the r in the Nrsf mentioned above. It is based on the ratio of pollen density in surface samples to the abundance of the species in the nearby vegetation (Davis, 1963; 1965). The deposition of the species' pollen "rain" in the modern sample will depend on what other plants are in the vicinity and a host of other factors, so that different R values are necessary for different plant communities and different regions. R values for pine, for example, vary in the literature from 6.6 to 200. Because palynologists often have to use relative abundances (percentages), this adds the additional complication that the percentage of one taxon will go up or down merely because of changes in other taxa. The representativity factor for these cases is

$$R_{rel} = \frac{P_{surf}}{V}$$

where P_{surf} is the percentage of pollen of a taxon found within a particular catchment on the modern surface, and V is the percentage of the taxon in the vegetation surrounding the catchment. This approach has had some success (Moore et al., 1991:184), but the R values cannot easily be generalized or extended beyond the kind of context in which they were measured. Commonly, palynologists instead group taxa into those, like pine, that tend to be overrepresented (type A), a middle group (type B), and underrepresented taxa (type C). They can then adjust the counts of each type by a correction factor before calculating percentages so as to prevent group A from swamping the other taxa on the graphs (Faegri and Iversen, 1989:126-27).

It is also possible to employ an approach similar to the Shotwell one to standardize plant macrofossils that have differing numbers of seed per plant or fruit, or seeds that represent differing amounts of food (e.g., MacNeish 1967; Monckton, 1992:84-85).

Mass

The oldest alternative to quantifying archaeological materials by the number of fragments or specimens is to "weigh" them. Although many people call this the "weight method," in practice archaeologists use the objects' mass, as measured in grams, which is inherent in the objects, rather than the weight, which depends on the gravitational field in which the object is measured. An artifact has the same mass, but quite different weight, depending on whether you measure it on Earth or on the Moon.

The rationale for measuring the mass of pottery, bone fragments, charcoal, and other archaeological materials is that it is much less sensitive to differences in fragmentation (Solheim, 1960). Except when the materials are so badly fragmented that identification is uncertain or impossible, it does not matter whether a particular pot or a particular block of charred wood is in one piece or a hundred; its mass should be the same except for a small proportion of material lost during the fragmentation process.

Mass is the most common measure of the abundance of charcoal from archaeological deposits. Because differential preservation during burial, and even treatment during excavation and curation, can have such substantial impact on the degree of fragmentation of charcoal, archaeobotanists tend to report the mass of charcoal instead of or in addition to the number of pieces from each context. Others have given up on reporting abundance altogether in favor of reporting ubiquity (see below). In cases where we have reason to believe that our charcoal sample represents the residue of fuel, mass is probably a more appropriate measure than most of the alternatives. The wood's original mass (now transformed by r and f) would have been related to the heat it produced during combustion. However, some taxa may combust more completely than others, while firing conditions also affect the degree of combustion, so that there is not a one-to-one correlation between mass of fuel consumed and mass of charcoal that results.

Some faunal analysts have favored mass measures in the hope that the mass of bone fragments belonging to a particular species or a particular element can be related to the mass of meat the bones once carried (Barrett, 1993; Chaplin, 1971:67-69). Although Chaplin mentions several problems with this approach, the most serious one is in the allometric ratio between bone mass and carcass mass for animals of different sexes and ages, a problem to which we will return later in the chapter. Problems with using bone mass as an indirect measure of some other attribute, such as carcass mass, in no way forces us to dismiss it, however, as a straightforward measure of abundance. When used in this way, we do need to keep in mind, however, that a single large animal, such as a cow, could contribute a much larger mass of bone to an assemblage than a large number of birds or hares, for example. This makes mass a poor measure of the relative number of individual animals unless we attempt to compensate for this with a factor that accounts for bone mass differences between species, sexes, and ages.

Ceramic analysts have sometimes been reluctant to use mass as their basis of quantification because they fear that it will overrepresent thick-walled, heavy vessels over thin-walled ones. Certainly this will be the case if we are interested in the numbers of vessels, but arguably this is a desirable characteristic in cases where we are really interested in the volume of food or other materials that may have been stored in those vessels. Pottery mass, therefore, may be a good indirect measure of the volume of food stored in large jars. For example, if we are interested in estimating the proportion of wine relative to olive oil in the cargo of a wrecked

ship, and can reasonably assume that the large amphoras of a particular type contained wine and another type of jar contained oil, the proportions of the two pottery types by mass might be a much better approximation than the proportion by NISP in some cases. In others, we may have prior information on the typical mass of whole pots of a given type and, much as with the Shotwell index, can just divide total mass by this average to estimate the number of "vessel equivalents" (see below). If there is reason to believe that pots of the same size varied in wall thickness, dividing total mass by mean thickness (Hulthén, 1974) will create a new indirect measure, with units of grams per centimeter, that is proportional to surface area (see area measurement, below).

The principal problem of mass as a measure of abundance is that post-depositional processes, such as leaching, mineralization, and corrosion, can remove mass from or add it to buried materials. After several centuries or millennia of burial, a bone could have substantially more or substantially less mass than it had originally, depending on its burial environment. Metal artifacts, such as coins, often gain mass through oxidation, a problem that has made numismatists and metrologists cautious about inferring ancient weight standards. Artifacts of almost any material can gain mass through mineralization or the deposition of minerals, such as calcium carbonate, during burial. This adds an error term that we would have to estimate.

To put the mass measures into terms like those we have used in previous sections, we could define the relationship between total mass and these factors as

$$\text{mass} = \sum_{i=1}^{N} Nr_i \overline{w} \varepsilon$$

where $\overline{w}$ is the average mass of the N whole pots, for example, and ε is the error introduced by leaching, mineralization, and other post-depositional factors.

Mass may be preferable in many cases when we are trying to measure, not the number or proportion of individuals, but amounts of the food, fuel, or other materials they represent. In quantification of osteological assemblages, for example, when preservation is good the most abundant identifiable bones may be the vertebrae of small fish, so that NISP overrepresents both the abundance of whole fish from which they came and the quantity of food they represented. Quantifying these fish by their mass may come closer to reflecting the proportion of meat these fish contributed to prehistoric diet, as long as we take the problems just mentioned into account, even though there is no simple linear relationship with meat mass.

Area Measurement

A less common means for quantifying fragmented remains is to measure surface area. Hulthén (1974) recommends this approach to quantify pottery when we want to account for the sizes of the pots that contributed sherds. She notes that neither NISP nor an estimated vessels approach will accurately represent the fact that large vessels contribute more to the sample than small ones. Mass comes much closer to accomplishing this, but mass depends on variations in sherd thickness, as well as the fabric's physical density and the surface area of the pot. Surface area itself, she suggests, provides a "meaningful" measure for comparing ceramic assemblages. She does not discuss what advantages there may be to knowing this quantity — in fact most other ceramic researchers would prefer a measure that removes or lessens the impact of vessel size in favor of vessel number — but, as just discussed for mass, there are cases where the contributions of larger vessels are of greatest interest.

Because it is somewhat tedious to measure the outer or inner surface area of a sherd directly, she recommends an indirect measure based on mass, mean thickness, and density, which we could express as

$$\widehat{A_j} = \sum_{i=1}^{n_j} \frac{g_i}{t_i r_i}$$

where $\widehat{A_j}$ is the estimated total surface area in cm^2 of all sherds of type j, n_j is the number of sherds of type j, g_i is the mass of each sherd in grams, t_i is the thickness of each sherd in cm, and

r_i is the density of each sherd in g/cm^3. For some pottery assemblages, variation in fabric density is negligible, allowing us to disregard it in the calculation, so that we have

$$\widehat{A_j} = \sum_{i=1}^{n_j} \frac{g_i}{t_i}$$

Byrd and Owens (1997) instead use an "effective area" (EA) based on the number of sherds captured in each increment of a series of screens:

$$EA = \sum nz^2$$

where n is the number of sherds on each screen and z is the aperture size of each screen, summing over all screens.

The most obvious application of these approaches would appear to be in comparing the "importance" of storage or transport vessels, as large ones, presumably, would contain more. In most cases, however, area would be only a very indirect measure of volume, and a transformation to vessel volume would be preferable to vessel area if enough information were available on vessel shape. It is not clear that the area approach is any better at representing the relative volumes of containers than mass in such cases. Another possible use of area would be in calculation of "vessel equivalents" (see PIE, below).

Density and Ratios

Another problem with using NISP or mass of items found in a volume of sediment for quantification is that analysts typically want to look for variations in the proportions of taxa. A classic example is the paleobotanist's pollen diagram (figure 5.2), which shows fluctuations in the relative abundance of the pollen of various taxa over depth in a soil column (an indirect measure of time). The trouble with relative abundance is that, when the percentage of one taxon goes up, others must go down, as the whole must add up to 100%. In other words, the various relative abundances are not independent of one another and, even if one of the taxa had a constant abundance over a time interval, it would appear to fluctuate because of changes in other taxa. In

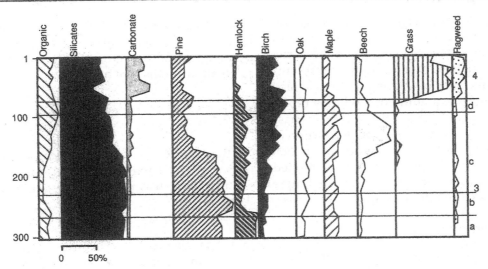

Figure 5.2. Pollen diagram from the Wye Marsh, Ontario (after Monckton 1992).

addition, if any taxon has a percentage close to 100%, its fluctuations will be almost undetectable (Faegri and Iversen, 1989:123-26; Moore et al., 1991:170-74).

One way to deal with this problem is to show variations in the densities of the pollen, seeds, bones, or potsherds, instead of their proportions. To do this, all we have to do is count or estimate (by sampling) the items of interest in a particular volume of soil, by NISP or mass, measure the volume of sediment, and take the ratio to end up with a measure of seeds per liter, bones fragments per cubic meter, or kilograms of pottery per cubic meter, for example. There are complications with this approach, too, because variations in density are due, not only to variations in the production, transport, deposition, and preservation of the items of interest, but also to sediment deposition and erosion rates, soil stoniness, and so on. Some paleoethnobotanists, however, favor the density approach in their research (Miller, 1988:73-74).

Palynologists have made the greatest strides in this area. In cases where they can use closely spaced radiocarbon dates or **varves** to date the deposition rates quite closely, they calculate the **Absolute Pollen Frequency (APF)**. This is really a density measure. The raw pollen counts are first converted into volumetric densities

(counts per unit volume of sediment). The estimated deposition rate (depth per year), based on carbon dates, then allows conversion to estimated influx (counts per cm^2 per year), the same unit used for pollen "rain" in modern samples (Davis, 1965; Faegri and Iversen, 1989:120-23). On the influx diagrams, even though they look much like the percentage diagrams, each taxon varies independently of the others, making interpretation much easier. The approach can only be used where we can measure deposition rates.

Another way to escape the interdependence of taxa is to use a standardized ratio, consistently dividing the abundance of each taxon by the abundance of one standard taxon, rather than by total abundance. For archaeobotanical assemblages, for example, it is sometimes useful to put the abundance of charcoal in the denominator of the ratio, at least in cases where much of the charcoal is from hearth fuel, and sampled deposits represent hearth sweepings in middens (Miller 1988:75-76). Binford (1978:71-72) scored MNE values (below) as a percentage of the MNE of the most abundant bone element.

Both density and ratio approaches still require us to decide what measure (NISP, mass, etc.) to use in the ratio. Consequently they do not entirely escape the quantitative considerations discussed in other sections.

Minimum Number of Individuals (MNI)

MNI is way of counting the number of individual pots, animals, or fruit *that are represented in* (*not* that originally contributed to) an assemblage. MNI is used principally in faunal analysis, where the idea is to calculate the smallest number of animals that could account for the bones and bone fragments in a sample. There have been attempts to apply variations of it to samples of plant remains as well (e.g., MacNeish 1967; Monckton, 1992).

In faunal applications, the simplest form of MNI is based on the assumption that, unless two bones or fragments are demonstrably from animals of different age or size or duplicate a unique part, they belong to the same animal (Casteel, 1977). For example, a sample consisting of four left distal humeri would have an MNI of 4, identical to its NISP, because each individual can have only one left distal humerus. In a typical sample with different skeletal parts, including some with both left and right sides, you need to count each part and side separately, and the greatest value (that is the number of the most common part and side) is MNI. In short, MNI is the abundance of the most common element. The underlying assumption is that a left and a right of an element, such as a humerus, belong to the same animal. We could represent this for the paired elements as max(L,R) where L is the number of left and R the number of right specimens of a particular element.

A more rigourous version of MNI goes further. Instead of simply assuming that the left and right of a particular element belong to the same individual, pairs are compared to see if some of the lefts and rights of paired elements might belong to the same individual by reason of size, sex, or age. This is usually called "matching" and always results in a somewhat higher value of MNI than does the simpler method. If P is the number of elements that can be paired or "matched" by this method, while L is the number of left and R the number of right elements, then MNI is calculated as the highest value for L + R - P among all the element categories (Chaplin 1971:71). In practice, one tends to assume that paired elements are matched unless there is

evidence that they are not (Chaplin, 1971:73). "Matching" can be a time-consuming process of visually comparing all possible pairs, or involve a computer algorithm based on some attribute, such as length (Ringrose, 1993a).

MNI is unaffected by the practice of bringing only partial carcasses of some animals, but whole carcasses of others, back to the site, because each animal contributes only one bone, the most abundant element for the taxon, to the count. In the past, most faunal analysts also considered MNI to be relatively insensitive to preservation problems. This seems intuitively to be so, because tiny fragments are ignored in favour of the most abundant element for each taxon. As Grayson (1978; 1981; 1984) has shown, however, MNI does not escape the preservation problem. It is correlated with NISP, and values tend to fall off to zero when fragmentation becomes extreme and identification of elements difficult.

As with all attempts at quantifying fragmentary remains, there are also problems with MNI. First, we need to remember that it is not an "estimated number of individuals," but a minimum value, representing the low extreme of a range. There are good statistical reasons to expect that MNI grossly underestimates the actual numbers of animals that contributed to a sample (Lie, 1980). The very fact that not all elements are found in the sample, and that not all lefts are matched to rights, proves that preservation (r) is low, and that many animals that were in the deposited assemblage are represented by no bones at all. Only where faunal preservation was exceptionally good, so that every animal that contributed to the deposit has at least one bone in the sample, would MNI = N. MNI is not a measure of central tendency, and has no probability distribution, confidence limits, or standard error. This is not a problem in MNI's original application, to estimate the minimum number of animals that could account for a catastrophic kill of extinct animals, most represented by substantially intact skeletons. It is, however, a serious problem if we use MNI to calculate taxonomic proportions in typical archaeological assemblages. In these situations, MNI overestimates the abundance of rare animals, because it only takes a single identifiable bone fragment to produce an MNI of 1, while hundreds of bones of more common taxa are ignored because they are not the most abundant element for their taxon. It is also a problem whenever we want to compare assemblages, because we have no way to assess whether apparent differences in MNI are due to real differences between populations, or simply to statistical variation within a single population.

Another important problem is that MNI is sensitive to degree of aggregation (Grayson 1978; 1984). What this means is that MNI values will differ if you calculate MNI for each soil deposit or excavation unit separately, for small groups of such units, or for a whole component or whole site. That is because a taxon's most abundant element at one level of aggregation may be outnumbered by other elements at a different level of aggregation. This problem is acute if the provenience units are arbitrary, such as adjacent excavation squares that may have parts of the same animal. Today archaeologists take care to ensure that their level of aggregation makes sense.

Similarly, MNI is affected by sampling fraction. Much as an estimated number of individuals can lead to large differences in proportions of taxa due only to differences in sampling fraction, whenever those taxa have different rates of fragmentation (Orton et al., 1993:169-71), proportions based on MNI may also reflect nothing more than the percentage of a site excavated. For example, a hypothetical 1% sample might contain a single identifiable duck bone and ten deer bones, each of different elements. We would calculate the MNI of both duck and deer as 1, even though it can be shown statistically that most of the ten deer bones probably came from different animals. A proportion based on these MNI would put duck at 50%. Meanwhile an 80% sample from exactly the same site might have 80 duck bones with MNI of 5 and 800 deer bones with MNI of 20. Even though both MNI values may still underrepresent the number of animals deposited at the site, their ratio now gives only 20% duck even though the ratios by NISP (and by the unknown number of actual animals) are exactly the same.

A more mundane problem with MNI is that different researchers calculate it somewhat differently, so that MNI values are not always comparable. It is important to find out how exactly each analyst calculated MNI. For example, some ignore fragmentary bones, others count them if they are identifiable, while still others count the fragments as proportions of whole bones, in an attempt to account for fragmentation (f). Furthermore, Binford (1978:69-70) uses the term "MNI" to mean something quite different.

MNI is best used in cases similar to its original paleontological application, when we are interested in the number of animals that likely contributed to a single catastrophic kill or that were processed in a single butchering episode. For historical and other reasons, including problems with alternative methods of quantification, zooarchaeologists tend to report MNI along with NISP and other measures. One thing for which it should not be used, however, is to calculate the *proportions* of taxa. This leads to biased proportions that overrepresent rare taxa and reflect sampling fraction as much as abundance.

Minimum Number of Elements (MNE)

Sometimes we are interested less in the number of animals represented in a sample than in how body parts are distributed. While MNI ignores all elements except the most abundant one for each taxon, the "minimum number of elements" (**MNE**) is based on a range of elements or parts of elements (e.g., left distal humerus epiphysis).

MNE is something like an MNI by element. For each element, you count only the most commonly occurring (or surviving) portion, such as the distal end of a humerus. The goal is to ensure that, if some of the fragments may have come from the same bone, no bone is counted twice (Bunn and Kroll, 1986). The goal is to account for fragmentation. MNE, in turn, is the unit used to calculate other indices useful in zooarchaeology, such as **MAU** and utility indices. The latter will be discussed in chapter 9.

Table 5.1. Example of selected MAU values (MNE adjusted for s) from two spring kill-butchering sites and a village site in Alaska, rounded to two significant digits (after Binford, 1978:78, 196)

Anatomical Part	Anavik MAU	Anaktiqtauk MAU	Village MAU
Antler	53	58	0
Skull	44	46	1.0
Mandible	39	27	7.5
Cervical vertebrae	42	15	1.5
Pelvis	23	10	1.0
Ribs	14	9.0	0.92
Sternum	15	7.0	4.8
Scapula	18	7.5	0.50
Distal humerus	17	8.0	0.50
Distal radio-cubitus	25	9.0	2.0
Distal metacarpal	32	37	0.50
Distal femur	9.0	3.5	3.5
Distal tibia	14	8.5	2.5
Proximal metatarsal	37	18	3.0
Phalanx	36	33	0.5

Lewis Binford introduced the term "minimum animal units" (MAU) to zooarchaeology (Binford, 1981; 1984). This measure is similar to the Shotwell index, in that it involves dividing the MNE for each element by the frequency of that element in the animal's body (s). Using MNE, rather than NISP, helps account for fragmentation (Table 5.1). As with Shotwell's measure, it is not always obvious what the value of s should be (Grayson, 1984), so analysts must report what value of s they use and why. In addition, whether or not shaft fragments from broken long bones are included in the MNE calculations has a significant effect (Marean and Frey, 1997).

These measures are used to interpret differential deposition of animal parts. By comparing the relative abundances of elements, you can attempt to learn, for example, whether prehistoric hunters were preferentially carrying hind quarters of deer to base camps, ignoring less desirable body parts, but whole birds and rabbits. Other patterns could emerge, for example, in butchering or in the distribution of meat (see chapter 9).

ESTIMATES OF POPULATION PARAMETERS

Unlike the measures discussed in the last section, which only quantify abundances of items found within a sample, the following measures represent attempts to infer abundances in the populations from which the sample was drawn.

The Krantz Estimator

Krantz (1968) made the first attempt to provide an estimator for the actual number of individuals, N, in the population ("death" assemblage for animals) from which an archaeological sample has been drawn. Krantz's method is only applicable to paired elements in skeletal remains (or, theoretically, anything that occurs naturally in pairs). Thus, while all the quantitative measures mentioned above count only what is in the sample in hand, which has been decreased by the factor, r, Krantz's estimator provides an estimate of the actual number of animals originally contributing to the deposit at the site, including animals that do not occur in the sample at all.

At first it may seem difficult to imagine how this could be done, but the Krantz estimator (like the Peterson estimator, below) cleverly takes advantage of information contained in the distribution of left and right elements and matched pairs. Krantz noted that in a sample that consisted only of paired bones, for any skeletal element the number belonging to the left side, the number belonging to the right side, and the number of pairs would all be equal: L = R = P, to use the abbreviations already encountered for MNI. Under this unlikely scenario, there would be no reason to assume that any of the bones had been lost, and it would be reasonable to conclude that the sample included all the bones of that element of all the animals that originally contributed to the sample. In other words, the sample was a 100% sampling fraction for that element (r = 1), and we could also conclude that L = R = P = N. A sample of 16 matched pairs of left and right mandibles, then, must have come from a population of 16 animals.

In most archaeological samples, however, many elements have been lost through various site-formation processes. The fact that some of the potentially paired elements are missing their partners, that is, when some left elements have no right elements to match them, is proof that elements are missing (Lie, 1980). It is possible that they have not been preserved, that they have been carried off the site, or simply that they are still buried in part of the deposit that has not been excavated. Use of MNI involves the implausible assumption, in spite of this evidence that many bones are missing, that bones must have come from the same animal unless there is evidence to the contrary. Krantz instead takes the evidence for missing bones quite seriously.

If we assume that the processes that removed bones of a particular element and taxon acted randomly, all elements of that type have an equal probability of *not* occurring in the sample. In that case, we expect some animals to be represented by only the left element, some by the right, some by both, and some by neither. Many individuals are almost certainly not represented in the sample at all.

The Krantz estimator makes intriguing use of this information. If, for example, the attrition processes at work in the site removed 80% of the left bones (i.e., L/N = 0.2), we should also expect that 80% of these left bones should have no matching rights, so than L/N = P/L, where P is the number of pairs. By rearranging the terms of this equation, we get an estimator for N as

$$N_L = \frac{L^2}{P}$$

Because we also expect the probabilities of left and right bones being removed from the sample to be equal, we would also have R/N = P/R and

$$N_R = \frac{R^2}{P}$$

Krantz takes these two separate estimates and averages them to provide the estimator,

$$N_K = \frac{L^2 + R^2}{2P}$$

The Krantz estimator provides consistently higher estimates than the Peterson estimator except when L = R, in which case they provide the same result (Fieller and Turner, 1982). Because it is very similar to the Peterson estimator in concept, we will leave discussion of its advantages and disadvantages to the end of the next section.

The Peterson Estimator

The Peterson Estimator (also known as Lincoln Index) represents another attempt to estimate the number of individuals in a population from which a sample was drawn, rather than describe a minumum number in a sample (Fieller and Turner, 1982; Poplin, 1976; Wild and Nichol, 1983). It resembles the Krantz estimator, but is modelled after the "sample-resample" estimates that ecologists and wildlife managers use in wildlife censuses.

If we want to estimate how many bears there are in a national park, for example, we do not round up all the bears and count them. Instead, game wardens go into the park and attempt to sample the bear population randomly, tagging each bear they encounter before its release. Let us say that in the first sample they find, tag, and release 100 bears. Then, after just enough time to allow the tagged bears to be "well mixed" into the general bear population, they go back into the park and sample the bears again. This time, let us say that they again encounter 100 bears. Now in this sample, some of the bears will be wearing the tags that show that they were members of the first sample. Let us say that 20 of the bears in this second sample were wearing tags. If the second sample is a random sample of the bear population, we would then conclude that tagged bears represent 20% of the population. As it happens, we already know that there are 100 tagged bears and, if 100 bears are 20% of the population, then the whole population of bears must be 500. We may express this more generally as

$$N_P = \frac{n_1 n_2}{p}$$

where n_1 is the number of bears in the first sample, n_2 the number in the second, and p the number of tagged bears in the second sample.

In applying this sample-resample methodology to archaeological assemblages, we have to make some modifications. We cannot tag potsherds or bones and then mix them up in a site prior to a resampling. As an analogue for the resampling, faunal analysts use paired elements. They assume that a matching pair of left and right elements is analogous to a bear being caught by both samples in the wildlife census, and then use the same reasoning to estimate the total population of animals from which the elements were derived. The equation for estimating N, then, is

$$N_P = \frac{LR}{P}$$

As mentioned above, the Peterson estimator will give a slightly lower estimate of N than the Krantz estimator, except when L = R.

The main advantage of the Krantz and Peterson estimators is that they provide genuine estimates of a population parameter, with a probability distribution and confidence limits. If the number of animals or the relative abundance of animals is what you want to know, then the Peterson estimator is worth considering.

We can calculate the confidence interval for the Peterson estimator with the hypergeometric distribution. While this is extremely cumbersome to do manually, we are fortunate that computer software will calculate the intervals for us. Fieller and Turner (1982) offered use of their program, POPSIZE, that contained an algorithm for calculating the cumulative hypergeometric probabilities.

The approach has limits, however. First, it is only applicable to paired elements; while pairs may often be identifiable in faunal assemblages, it is more difficult to see how we could use the Peterson estimator on other types of assemblages. Even with pots that consistently have two handles, for example, it is unlikely that we could routinely distinguish "left" from "right" handles, let alone handles that were paired, except in nearly whole vessels. Second, as with Chaplin's MNI, we can rarely be certain that matching left and right elements actually came from the same animal, except when they are still attached, as in pelvises or mandibles. When they are attached, meanwhile, the observations lack independence and could lead to underestimates of the population parameter, although the estimate will still be higher than MNI. In fact, the estimate depends on the assumption that the left and right elements are randomly mixed in the deposit, and finding partially articulated skeletons violates this assumption. Binford (1978:70) even reports cases of butchering bias in the distribution of lefts and rights. Finally, in cases where different paired elements, say *humeri* and *tibiae*, give different estimates of N_p, we need more discussion of how to decide between them. Fieller and Turner (1982:55) make the useful observation that this might tell us something about the reliability of our measure or "reveal patterns of differential deposition." In such cases, however, we seem to have a contradiction with the measure's claim to estimate "the original killed population size" (Fieller and Turner, 1982:54) rather than the fossil or deposited assemblage size (Ringrose, 1993a).

Where feasible and when the number of killed individuals is an appropriate quantity, the Peterson estimator seems superior to other measures in that it estimates, with confidence intervals, a quantity in which archaeologists are interested. In some circumstances, it can also be transformed to produce estimates of meat or relative abundances of different species. When evidence for pairing is unavailable (as in most nonfaunal assemblages) or some of the assumptions are not met, estimating the original number of individuals may elude us. In those cases we may need to estimate some other quantity of interest, such as the relative abundance of taxa, or the relative abundance of some anatomical part. As we will see below, the PIE is one such measure for pottery.

In addition, the technique of sample-resample on which the Peterson estimator is based can itself be useful in palaeoethnobotany and microrefuse studies, where the trick is to estimate the abundance of pollen, small seeds, or microscopic fragments of flint or shell in soil volumes. Rather than attempt to count everything in these sediment volumes, we can add a known number of some "exotic" particle — palynologists often add *lycopodium* spores to their pollen samples, while microrefuse analysts could add tiny plastic beads or the like — that is analogous to the first sample of tagged bears. Then when we count pollen or microdebitage in small subsamples, we also count the *lycopodium* spores or plastic beads. If we know in advance that there are 1000 plastic beads mixed into the sample, and 200 of the plastic beads occur in a subsample, by simple arithmetic we can estimate that our subsample contains one-fifth of the particles, with a known degree of error, that occur in the sample of deposit. We could express this as

$$N_i = \frac{E n_i}{n_e}$$

where N_i is the total number of particles of a particular kind, E is the number of exotics added to the subsample, n_i is the number of the particle of interest in the subsample, and n_e is the number of exotics in the subsample. The confidence limits on the estimate are also calculated the same way as for the paired faunal elements.

Completeness Indices and Estimated Equivalents (EVE)

As we have seen, most authors' concern about the shortcomings of NISP or MNI stem from their failure to estimate the number or proportion of actual bones or pots. Clive Orton has suggested a refreshing alternative to this deadlock. Since we are often interested in the proportions of pottery types, not their absolute abundances, he argues that we should use a measure that estimates proportions accurately and forget about the absolute abundances of whole pots. We can also use an analogous pro-

cedure to account for degree of fragmentation in faunal remains (Moreno-Garcia et al., 1996). In effect the method accounts for the effect of differential fragmentation (f), but not the other effects on quantity.

We do not count sherds, but instead use a completeness index to estimate the proportion of a whole pot that each sherd represents, perhaps by surface area, and then simply add the proportions together (Orton, 1993; Orton and Tyers 1992; 1993). This is not an MNI approach — in fact you should not "round up" to whole pots as you do with MNI — as the units, "Estimated Vessel Equivalents" (EVE) are not intended to represent actual pots, but only units of abundance.

In practice, it may be difficult or impossible to know what proportion of a whole pot a particular sherd represents, especially for body sherds. In most cases, a more practical way to estimate EVE uses "rim-equivalents," "base-equivalents," or the average of the two, as units.

For rim or base equivalents, you simply use a diameter chart to estimate what proportion of the circumference of a vessel each rim or base represents, assuming pots are circular, giving a completeness index (rim-equivalent or base-equivalent) that ranges from 0 to 1.0 (or 0 to 100%). Adding these together for a particular category of pottery will yield some fractional value — 0.6 or 2.4, for example — that is transformed into a "Pottery Information Equivalent," so that 1 PIE contains as much statistical information as a single complete vessel. If we use these EVE values to calculate proportions of pottery types, they provide unbiased estimates of the relative abundance of each type in the deposit. For a deposit with only two types, and EVEs of 0.6 and 2.4, the proportion of the first would be 0.6/3.0 = 0.2 and that of the second would be 2.4/3.0 = 0.8. No matter how many sherds of each type there were, we can be confident that these are good estimates of the proportions of actual pots deposited in the context, within a range of error. More generally, the estimated proportion of each type, p_i, would be

$$p_i = \frac{x_i}{\sum_{i=1}^{t} x_i}$$

This is the ratio of the EVE value for the ith type to the sum of the EVE values for all t types. Computer software that employs this method of quantification is called the Pie-slice Package (Orton and Tyers, 1993).

If we want realistic errors on these estimates, calculating the confidence interval can be a bit complicated. Diameter charts only allow you to estimate the diameter and circumferential proportion of sherds within a few centimeters and a few percent. In fact, the two measures are associated, so a small error in estimating the diameter will lead to an error in the circumference. Consequently, you should record your estimated measurement error for the circumferential proportion of each sherd and accumulate this error. For eight rim sherds with an EVE of 0.95, for example, we might have the measures in table 5.2.

Table 5.2. Example data set for calculating EVE (rim equivalents) for eight rim sherds. Note that the total measurement error here is estimated as the square root of the sum of the squared individual errors.

Sherd No.	Rim Proportion	Measurement Error
1	0.05	0.02
2	0.10	0.02
3	0.20	0.03
4	0.15	0.02
5	0.15	0.03
6	0.12	0.01
7	0.08	0.02
8	0.10	0.01
EVE	0.95	0.06

In addition, the confidence interval would be affected by the usual sampling error. For a cluster sample (usually excavations and surveys provide samples of sediment volumes that contain clusters of sherds), we would calculate EVE and ratios based on EVE over the total of all contexts that belonged to the same assemblage. The standard error on the proportion of each type, would be based on the squared deviation of individual estimates of the proportion from the grand proportion. So, if we represent Σx_i simply as y, and the proportion of x_i as x/y, the standard error for a cluster sample would be (Drennan, 1996:247),

$$SE_i = \sqrt{\frac{1}{n}\left(\frac{\sum \left(\frac{x_i}{y}-p_i\right)^2 \left(\frac{yn}{Y}\right)^2}{n-1}\right)\left(1-\frac{n}{N}\right)}$$

The Pie-slice approach has an important advantage over NISP when we want to estimate the relative abundance of types. It accounts for differential fragmentation because rims that break into ten pieces instead of five will on average each measure only 36° of the pot's circle instead of 72°, and the differential breakage will have no effect on relative abundance.

Most importantly, proportions based on EVE are estimates of the population proportions in the fossil assemblage of vessels. Meanwhile, like NISP, EVE is additive, and so relatively easy to measure and to augment with new information, and is not affected by degree of aggregation.

The method for quantifying faunal bone fragments is similar. Much as some analysts deal with fragments for MNI calculations, we control for fragmentation by measuring a competeness index for each bone, and summing these over each element class in each context. Completeness is assessed by counting the number of "diagnostic zones" found on each bone fragment and dividing by the total number of such zones found on a whole bone (Rackham, 1986). Unlike MNI modified for completeness, you do not round up to whole bones, as this would bias the proportions. One could later divide by s (the number of elements in whole animals) to make the taxa comparable at the level of animals.

EVE appears to achieve its aim of estimating *relative* abundances of pottery (Orton, 1993). Like TMAU, for bones it will be biased by variations among species in preservation, deposition, or recovery (r).

Total Minimum Animal Units (TMAU)

In spite of its name, this is not a version of MNI or even MAU, as its purpose is, like PIE, to estimate accurately the relative abundances of species in a population (n_i/N). Chase and Hagaman (1987) begin with the WAE, note that WAE is a good estimate of $N\bar{r}_i$, except that elements such as vertebrae often have to be grouped because they are indistinguishable, so that where differences in $\bar{r}$ are very small and N is not too small we can use it to provide good estimates of the relative abundances in the population (apparently the "death assemblage"). They use the expression,

$$TMAU = \sum_{i=1}^{g} \frac{Nr_i s_i}{s_i}$$

where N is the number of animals in the death assemblage, r_i and s_i are the recovery rate and number of elements for the i-th group of elements, and g is the number of element groups. What this means, essentially, is that you divide the frequencies of elements in each group by the number of those elements in whole animals (s), and sum these modified frequencies over all groups of elements. Because different species may have different numbers of groups, however, this in itself would be biased unless you limit the measure to those groups that all the taxa have in common. A way to correct for this, which they call "relative frequency" is simply to average the values by dividing by the number of groups for each species. This gives us,

$$RF = \frac{\sum_{i=1}^{g} \frac{Nr_i s_i}{s_i}}{g},$$

which is biased by the fact that some species have more r_i values than others. Thus it is preferable, where feasible, to restrict analysis to the element groups shared by all the species. Even so, we can rarely assume that $\bar{r}$ will be nearly the same for elements belonging to different species. As Ringrose (1993a) points out, at least the TMAU approach considers the right factors.

INDIRECT MEASURES

Yield Estimates

Many archaeologists have recognized that some archaeological research is not aimed at discovering the actual number of animals or pots or some other whole entities that were killed or deposited at a site. Instead, archaeologists are often interested in an indirect measure of di-

etary preferences, for example. We may want to know whether venison or hare contributed more meat to prehistoric diet, and this is a question that the number of bone fragments or even number of animals will not answer accurately without some kind of transformation of data. Faunal analysts have invested the most research in this area, although some paleoethnobotanists have also employed conversions into food values (e.g., Monckton, 1992; Yarnell, 1974).

In these cases, researchers have typically transformed the data as quantified with one of the measures discussed above. The transformation is based on information about the amount of usable meat (or sometimes other resources) that we might expect to have occurred on each identifiable bone element or on whole carcasses (e.g., Casteel, 1974; 1978; Chaplin, 1971; Lyman, 1979; Smith, 1975; Stahl, 1982). Because they are based on other measures, the meat-yield estimates retain those measures' problems.

The main problem with these approaches, however, lies in selecting a ratio for the transformation. It seems tempting, for example, simply to multiply the mass of identifiable red deer bones by the ratio of meat/bone by mass in a living deer or its dressed carcass. The problem is that the meat/bone ratio depends on a number of factors, including the animal's nutritional state and, most importantly, its age and sex. If our faunal sample pools bones of various ages and sexes, we are likely to get a quite inaccurate estimate of meat mass (Casteel, 1978; Jackson, 1989). In addition, some studies are only based on small samples of live animals or modern carcasses, which renders yield estimates suspect (Ringrose, 1993a:148).

The study of the ratios of the metrics of body parts to one another is called **allometry**, and is the basis of this approach (Gould, 1966; Prange et al., 1979; Reynolds, 1977). For any individual living animal, we can study, for example, the relationship between its total mass and the length or cross-sectional area of its *femur*, or between its total stature and the length of its *tibia*, and note how these ratios change over the animal's lifetime (Jackson, 1989; Noddle, 1973). A plot of these changes will show a distinctive curve.

Some researchers have used multiple regressions taken from such studies and applied them to the total bone mass of a species in an assemblage. The problem with this is that it is equivalent to assuming that all the bones came from a single, enormous, and very old animal, when in fact it probably came from a large number of small, much younger animals with quite different allometric ratios than those the faunal analyst used.

Careful use of allometric methods to estimate meat yields would require that we first sort the bones into sex and age categories, so that an appropriate ratio, with error estimate, could be applied to the fragments from each group (Barrett, 1993). In cases where evidence for sex and age is elusive, this could be difficult or force analysts to omit a large portion of the evidence, but there are cases where the approach is feasible and warrants the attempt. After all, this is the only approach that tells us something meaningful about an important quantity of interest, the actual amount of meat used. The mass allometric methods seem particularly attractive for the analysis of fish remains, which are easy to age, yet difficult to quantify in a meaningful way otherwise.

NONABUNDANCE MEASURES

Ubiquity

Some archaeologists, and especially paleoethnobotanists, refer to "presence analysis" in their work. By this they usually mean that they measured ubiquity (e.g., Popper, 1988). **Ubiquity** is not a measure of taxonomic *abundance*, although it can be a useful measure nonetheless. Quite simply, ubiquity measures how commonly a particular taxon is *represented* in sample elements, but not how *abundant* it is in those sample elements.

The measure works like this. Let us assume that we have a sample that consists of 100 bags of sediment, each with a volume of 2 liters. Let us further assume that upon close examination we found maize kernels in 42 of those bags, while it was absent in the other 58 bags. We would calculate maize's ubiquity as 42/100, or 0.42. We might also find, say, wild raspberry

seeds in 80 of the samples, giving wild raspberry an ubiquity of 80/100 or 0.8. We could not conclude from this that raspberry was almost twice as abundant as maize. In fact, it could well be that the raspberry seeds occurred in very small numbers in most or all of the 80 sample elements in which it occurred at all, while the maize kernels often occurred in quite large numbers.

What ubiquity tells us, then, is not how abundant a particular taxon is, but how concentrated or spread out it is among our sample elements. Taxa that tend to be concentrated in storage pits or refuse areas will have low ubiquity, even if they are extremely abundant, while ones that are spread evenly, if thinly, over a site will have very high ubiquity. Ubiquity could be a good measure for us to use when we are investigating site-formation processes, but it is not clear how it relates to the "importance" of taxa at a site, although some authors use it that way (e.g., Boyd, 1988).

Ubiquity is very sensitive to sample size (Popper, 1988: 63). It is important for those who use ubiquity to keep in mind that the sample size is the number of units (bags, sediment volumes, excavation squares, etc.) over which the presences and absences were counted (see chapter 4). In many instances, the number of such units is far too small for us to estimate ubiquity with very much confidence or with very much precision.

As we will see in chapter 6, we can model ubiquity with the binomial distribution. Ubiquity is x/n, or the number of "presences" in n trials. The confidence limits for sampling fractions are defined the same way as for any other proportion, and so we should estimate our expected sample size with the formula for proportions in chapter 4. In many cases, such as when excavation areas form the sampling frame, N will be small enough to require the finite population correction.

Kadane (1988) shows concern that some archaeologists are losing considerable information by abandoning measures of abundance in favor of ubiquity. He notes that the belief that ubiquity is somehow less sensitive to preservation problems (differing values of r and f) is not well supported and suggests that archaeologists instead concentrate on accounting for these factors.

Diversity

Another measure that archaeologists sometimes use is **diversity**. This is never intended as a measure of abundance but does, in some sense, provide a quantifiable measure of assemblages' characteristics. A very diverse population is one that is distributed fairly evenly among a large number of nominal-scale classes, or **taxa**. In a sense, it is a measure of dispersion in the data rather than a measure of central tendency (Ringrose, 1993b). It was originally developed by ecologists who wanted to summarize the structure of biological communities (Hurlbert, 1971; Peet, 1974).

Why should we want to know about diversity? It has a number of useful applications in archaeology. Diversity can be a good way to approach the study of specialization. Sites or activity areas with low diversity are more likely to have been specialized in particular tasks. Habitation sites in which a wide array of activities were carried out, by contrast, should exhibit relatively high diversity. Low diversity in faunal or plant assemblages could indicate very focussed hunting, gathering, or farming strategies (e.g., Bonzani, 1997). By contrast, the "broad niche" that some archaeologists see as preceding the earliest domestication represents a high diversity of resources. Low diversity in lithics could indicate either a specialized activity or a very generalized tool kit, with each tool having multiple potential functions.

The simplest way to measure diversity is simply to count the number of taxa represented in an assemblage, the **richness (s)**. In other words, how many classes in a nominal scale that we are employing are represented by observations, rather than being "empty?" The trouble with this is that it is extremely sensitive to sample size and sampling fraction. Obviously a very small sample is far less likely to represent all classes in the population than would a large sample (Meltzer et al., 1992), and there is no unbiased

estimator that would allow us to estimate population richness from a sample.

Consequently, researchers interested in diversity have attempted to account for sample size or sampling fraction in various ways. One way is with computer simulations, comparing the observed richness in a sample of size n to the richness you would expect to find in a simulated sample of size n drawn from a hypothetical population with a given population diversity. By successive approximation, you can then account for the sample-size effects (Kintigh, 1989).

A richness index (dl) rather than simple richness takes some account of sample size, so that small samples result in higher indices than large ones. The index is calculated from

$$dl = \frac{s - 1}{LN(n)}$$

where s is the number of taxa in the sample and LN(n) is the natural logarithm of number of individuals in the sample. Kruz-Uribe (1988) substitutes MNI for n (note that she gives the equation incorrectly with the logarithm instead of the natural logarithm). This formula compensates somewhat for underrepresentation of richness in small samples, but overestimates richness if MNI is used for n, and is not an estimator of richness in the population. In addition, the index treats extremely small samples as though they were just as reliable as large ones. Intuitively, we would expect large samples to give much more accurate estimates of richness.

Other measures of diversity not only account for the number of classes, but also for the way individuals are distributed among the classes, or evenness. Here we assume that a population in which all classes have equal proportions of individuals is more diverse than one with the same number of classes but in which most of the individuals belong to only one or two of the classes.

We could compare the diversities of two populations with respect to both richness and evenness by drawing a graph (Ringrose, 1993b). For each population we rank the taxa in increasing order of abundance. We then plot the cumulative number of taxa (S) on the x-axis against

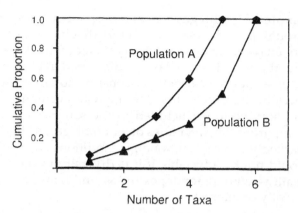

Figure 5.3. Population A is intrinsically more diverse than Population B in spite of having fewer taxa because the cumulative proportions of taxa are higher (cf. Ringrose 1993b).

the cumulative proportion of individuals on the y-axis. For example, population A has five species with relative abundances of 0.09, 0.11, 0.15, 0.25, 0.40, and population B has six species with relative abundances of 0.05, 0.07, 0.08, 0.10, 0.20, 0.50 (figure 5.3). In this example, population A is intrinsically more diverse, in spite of having fewer taxa (less richness), because greater evenness among taxa cause the cumulative proportions to be higher than for population B. However, this approach is also biased if we attempt to apply it to samples, rather than populations.

A common diversity index is called the Shannon-Wiener information function or, more simply, Shannon index (D_{sh}):

$$D_{sh} = \sum_{i=1}^{s} p_i \log p_i$$

the sum over all the s taxa of their proportions multiplied by the logarithm of their proportions. We can estimate the proportions from n_i / n in a sample, using PIE or WAE for example, but the Shannon index is a biased estimator, and there is no unbiased one. It is most heavily influenced by the most abundant taxa, a generally undesirable characteristic. Hill (1973) proposed a way to decrease dependence on the most abundant taxa. As it does not have any unbiased estimators, however, it is unlikely to be useful (Kempton, 1979; Ringrose, 1993b).

Better indices are based on Simpson's index of dominance. When expressed as a measure of diversity instead, Simpson's index (D_{si}) can be expressed as

$$D_{si} = 1 - \sum_{i=1}^{s} p_i^2$$

the difference between one and the sum of the squared proportions. A population with many taxa with very similar abundances will have a much lower sum of squared proportions than a sample dominated by one or two taxa, so this index also tends to be very sensitive to the most abundant one or two taxa. It does, however, have an unbiased estimator for samples:

$$\widehat{D}_{si} = 1 - \sum_{i=1}^{s} \frac{n_i(n_i-1)}{n(n-1)}$$

Patil and Taillie (1979) proposed another new notation that unifies the richness, Shannon and Simpson indices, but also has an unbiased estimator for samples. This family of indices can be expressed as

$$\Delta_\beta = \frac{1}{\beta} \cdot \left(1 - \sum_{i=1}^{s} p_i^{\beta+1}\right)$$

When $\beta = -1$, the index describes a version of richness, S-1 (the number of taxa less one). When $\beta = 0$, we get the value of the Shannon index, and when $\beta = 1$, the value of the Simpson index. It has an unbiased estimator for samples for any positive integer value of β:

$$\widehat{\Delta}_\beta = \frac{1}{\beta}\left(1 - \frac{\sum_{i=1}^{s} n_i(n_i-1)...(n_i-\beta)}{n(n-1)...(n-\beta)}\right)$$

Like the Shannon and Simpson indices, however, it is heavily influenced by the proportions of the most common taxa (Ringrose, 1993b).

Because the main problem with the most popular of these measures is their lack of unbiased estimators for samples, Kintigh (1989) proposes sampling simulated populations to obtain a mean and variance of diversity for a given sample size. But it is preferable to use an index that provides unbiased estimators in the first place, but without too much influence by the most abundant taxa (Rhode, 1988; Ringrose, 1993b).

Smith et al. (1979) propose an "expected species" index that does exactly this. This is the expected number of taxa in a random sample of n individuals in a population:

$$s(m) = \sum_{i=1}^{s} \left[1 - (1 - p_i)^m \right]$$

for various orders, m. When m = 2, the expected species is closely related to the Simpson index $[s(2) = 1 + D_{si}]$. In that case, then, the most abundant one or two taxa contribute the most to the value of the index. For orders of m > 2, however, taxa of medium and minor abundance contribute more and more to the value, because the value of $(1 - p_i)$, rather than p_i, is raised to a power greater than 2. For samples, an unbiased estimator for s(m) for integer values of m from 1 to n is

$$\widehat{s(m)} = \sum_{i=1}^{s} \frac{1 - C(n-n_i,m)}{C(n,m)}$$

where C(a,b) = a!/(a-b)!b! (i.e., the number of combinations of a items taken b at a time), and a! = a(a-1)(a-2)...1. This is tedious to calculate for large sample sizes, but is feasible with spreadsheet software for small samples. Typical archaeological applications would call for use of a dedicated computer program, and Ringrose offers a PASCAL program to interested researchers.

Ringrose (1993b) suggests using this estimator of s(m) to compare the diversities of archaeological samples by calculating it for all integer values of m between 2 and the smallest sample size, and then to plot the results in a graph with m on the x-axis and $\widehat{s(m)}$ on the y-axis (figure 5.4). Much as in the graph for populations in figure 5.4, any assemblage with a set of values higher than those for another assemblage must be more diverse (see also Birks and Line 1992).

Although s(m) does then seem to be the most useful diversity index, it is important to keep in mind that the diversity in archaeological

sample assemblages can vary between sites through post-depositional factors that have removed some taxa more readily than others. As with the abundance measures discussed in previous sections, we need to be sensitive to differences in the probability that any class of item will survive to be included in the sample (r). Comparing the diversities of assemblages with markedly different taphonomic conditions, then, would not be advisable if it is diversity in the **death assemblage** or **deposited assemblage** that is really of interest.

Conclusion

Quantifying the abundances of items that archaeologists find interesting is not trivial. Counts of potsherds, animal bones, seeds, or phytoliths, for example, have no simple relationship to the number of pots, animals, or plants or the amount of food that the archaeological remains represent. Research on identifying and controlling factors that affect the relationship between the quantities of real interest and the quantities we are able to measure allows us to "correct" for some of these factors. Palynologists, for example, correct for differential pollen production and transport, while the Shotwell index corrects for the number of bones in whole animals. In addition, we can sometimes take advantage of paired elements in faunal assemblages to estimate the number of animals in the population that contributed to the assemblage (the Peterson estimator). For pottery it is common to cite both numbers of sherds and sherd mass, but the Pottery Information Equivalent provides an effective way for us to achieve unbiased estimates of the proportions of pottery types. For bones, a similar approach is possible. Although the quantitative problems are serious, archaeologists have increasingly sophisticated ways to deal with them.

In addition, measures of ubiquity and diversity have become common in archaeology. Neither of these measures abundance. Ubiquity can be very useful for identifying classes of things that occur very consistently, as opposed to ones that may be fairly abundant, but occur only infrequently, in clusters or hoards. Diversity is something like a measure of dispersion for nomi-

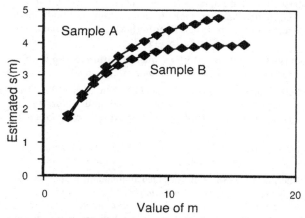

Figure 5.4. Sample A shows more diversity than sample B when quantified by s(m) over a range of values of m (cf. Ringrose 1993b).

nal scales. Since archaeologists have often considered diversity in food spectra and diversity in manufactured items to be important clues to the beginnings of agriculture and craft specialization, quantifying diversity can be quite important. The effect of sample size on diversity has been a problem, but the "expected species" index accounts for this.

References Cited

Barrett, J. H., 1993, Bone weight, meat yield estimates and cod (*Cadus morhua*): A preliminary study of the weight method. *International Journal of Osteoarchaeology* 3:1-18.

Binford, L. R., 1978, *Nunamiut Ethnoarchaeology*. Academic Press, New York.

— 1981, *Bones: Ancient Men and Modern Myths*. Academic Press, New York.

— 1984, *Faunal Remains from the Klasies River Mouth*. Academic Press, New York.

Birks, H. J. B. and Line, J. M., 1992, The use of rarefaction analysis for estimating palynological richness from Quaternary pollen-analytical data. *HOLOCENE* 2 (1):1-10.

Bonzani, R. M., 1997, Plant diversity in the archaeological record: A means toward defining hunter-gatherer mobility strategies. *Journal of Archaeological Science* 24:1129-39.

Boyd, W. E., 1988, Methodological problems in the analysis of fossil non-artifactual wood assemblages from archaeological sites. *Journal of Archaeological Science* 15:603-19.

Bunn, H. T., and Kroll, E. M., 1986, Systematic butchery by Plio-Pleistocene hominids at Olduvai Gorge, Tanzania. *Current Anthropology* 27:431-52.

Byrd, J. E., and Owens, D. D., 1997, A method for measuring relative abundance of fragmented archaeological ceramics. *Journal of Field Archaeology* 24:315-20.

Casteel, R. W., 1974, A method for estimation of live weight of fish from the size of skeletal elements. *American Antiquity* 39:94-98.

— 1977, Characterization of faunal assemblages and the minimum number of individuals determined from paired elements: Continuing problems in archaeology. *Journal of Archaeological Science* 4:125-34.

— 1978, Faunal assemblage and the 'weigemethode' or weight method. *Journal of Field Archaeology* 5:71-77.

Chaplin, R. E., 1971, *The Study of Animal Bones from Archaeological Sites*. Seminar Press, London.

Chase, P. G., 1985, Whole vessels and sherds: an experimental investigation of their quantitative relationship. *Journal of Field Archaeology* 12:213-18.

Chase, P. G. and Hagaman, R. M., 1987, Minimum number of individuals and its alternatives: a probability theory perspective. *Ossa* 13:75-86.

Cruz-Uribe, K., 1988, The use and meaning of species diversity and richness in archaeological faunas. *Journal of Archaeological Science* 15:179-96.

Davis, M. B., 1963, On the theory of pollen analysis. *American Journal of Science* 261:897-912.

— 1965, A method for determination of absolute pollen frequency. In *Handbook of Palaeontological Techniques*, edited by B. G. Kummel and D. M. Raup, pp. 647-86. Freeman, San Francisco.

Drennan, R. D., 1996, *Statistics for Archaeologists, A Commonsense Approach*. Plenum Press, New York.

Egloff, B. J., 1973, A method for counting ceramic rim sherds. *American Antiquity* 38:351-53.

Fægri, K., and Iverson, J., 1989, *Textbook of Pollen Analysis*, 4th ed. Blackwell Scientific Publications, Oxford.

Fieller, N. R. J. and Turner, A., 1982, Number estimation in vertebrate samples. *Journal of Archaeological Science* 9:49-62.

Gautier, A., 1984, How do we count these bones, let me count the ways? Problems of archaeozoological quantification. In *Animals and Archaeology*, edited by C. Grigson and J. Clutton-Brock, pp. 237-51. BAR International Series 227. British Archaeological Reports, Oxford.

Gilbert, A., and Singer, B. H., 1982, Reassessing zooarchaeological quantification. *World Archaeology* 14:21-40.

Gould, S. J., 1966, Allometry and size in ontogeny and phylogeny. *Biological Review of the Cambridge Philosophical Society* 41:587-640.

Grayson, D. K., 1978, Minimum numbers and sample size in vertebrate faunal analysis. *American Antiquity* 43:53-65.

— 1981, The effects of sample size on some derived measures in vertebrate faunal analysis. *Journal of Archaeological Science* 8:77-88.

— 1984, *Quantitative Zooarchaeology*. Academic Press, Orlando, FL.

Hill, M. O., 1973, Diversity and evenness: A unifying notation and its consequences. *Ecology* 54:427-32.

Holtzman, R. C., 1979, Maximum likelihood estimation of fossil assemblage composition. *Paleobiology* 5:77-89.

Hubbard, R. N. L. B. and al-Azm, A., 1990, Quantifying preservation and distortion in carbonized seeds; and investigating the history of friké production. *Journal of Archaeological Science* 17:103-106.

Hulthén, B., 1974, On choice of element for determination of quantity of pottery. *Norwegian Archaeological Review* 7:1-5.

Hurlbert, S. H., 1971, The nonconcept of species diversity: A critique and alternative parameters. *Ecology* 52:577-86.

Jackson, H. E., 1989, The trouble with transformations: Effects of sample size and sample composition on meat weight estimates based on skeletal mass allometry. *Journal of Archaeological Science* 16:601-10.

Kadane, J. B., 1988, Possible statistical contributions to paleoethnobotany. In *Current Paleoethnobotany, Analytical Methods and Cultural Interpretations of Archaeological Plant Remains*, edited by C. A. Hastorf and V. S. Popper, pp. 206-214. University of Chicago Press, Chicago.

Kempton, R. A., 1979, The structure of species abundance and measurement of diversity. *Biometrics* 35:307-21.

Kintigh, K., 1989, Sample size, significance and measures of diversity. In *Quantifying Diversity in Archaeology*, edited by R. Leonard and G. Jones, pp. 25-36. Cambridge University Press, Cambridge.

Klein, R. G., and Cruz-Uribe, K., 1984, *The Analysis of Animal Bones from Archeological Sites*. University of Chicago Press, Chicago.

Krantz, G. S., 1968, A new method of counting mammal bones. *American Journal of Archaeology* 72:286-88.

Kruz-Uribe, K., 1988, The use and meaning of species diversity and richness in archaeological faunas. *Journal of Archaeological Science* 15:179-96.

Lie, R. W., 1980, Minimum numbers of individuals from osteological samples. *Norwegian Archaeological Review* 13:24-30.

Lyman, R. L., 1979, Available meat from faunal remains: A consideration of techniques. *American Antiquity* 44:536-46.

— 1984, Bone density and differential survivorship of fossil classes. *Journal of Anthropological Archaeology* 3:259-99.

— 1985, Bone frequencies: differential transportation, in-situ destruction and the MGUI. *Journal of Archaeological Science* 12:221-36.

— 1992, Anatomical considerations of utility curves in archaeology. *Journal of Archaeological Science* 19:7-22.

Lyman, R. L., Savelle, J. M., and Whitridge, P., 1992, Derivation and application of a meat utility index for Phocid seals. *Journal of Archaeological Science* 19:531-55.

MacNeish, R. S., 1967, A summary of the subsistence. In *The Prehistory of The Tehuacan Valley*, volume 1, *Environment and Subsistence*, edited by D. S. Byers, pp. 290-309. University of Texas Press, Austin.

Marean, C. W., and Frey, 1997, Animal bones from caves to cities: Reverse utility curves as methodological artifacts. *American Antiquity* 62:698-711.

Marshall, F. and Pilgram, T., 1991, Meat versus within-bone nutrients: Another look at the meaning of body part representation in archaeological sites. *Journal of Archaeological Science* 18:149-63.

— 1993, NISP vs. MNI in quantification of body-part representation. *American Antiquity* 58:261-69.

Meltzer, D. J., Leonard, R. D., and Stratton, S. K., 1992, The relationship between sample size and diversity in archaeological assemblages. *Journal of Archaeological Science* 19:375-87.

Metcalfe, D., and Jones, K. T., 1988, A reconsideration of animal-part utility indices. *American Antiquity* 53:486-504.

Miller, N. F., 1988, Ratio in paleoethnobotanical analysis. In *Current Paleoethnobotany, Analytical Methods and Cultural Interpretations of Archaeological Plant Remains*, edited by C. Hastorf and V. Popper, pp. 72-85. University of Chicago Press, Chicago.

Monckton, S. G., 1992, *Huron Paleoethnobotany*. Ontario Archaeological Reports 1. Ontario Heritage Foundation, Toronto.

Moore, P. D., J. Webb and M. C. Collinson (1991). *Pollen Analysis, A Laboratory Manual*. Oxford: Blackwell.

Moreno-Garcia, M., Orton, C., and Rackham, J., 1996, A new statistical tool for the comparison of animal bone assemblages. *Journal of Archaeological Science* 23:437-453.

Morlan, R. E., 1983, Counts and estimates of taxonomic abundance of faunal remains: Microtine rodents from Bluefish Cave 1. *Canadian Journal of Archaeology* 7:61-76.

Noddle, B. A., 1973, Determination of the body weight of cattle from bone measurements. In *Domestikationsforschung und Geschichte der Haustiere*, edited by J. Matolsci, pp. 377-89. Akadémiai Kiadó, Budapest.

Orton, C., 1980, *Mathematics in Archaeology*. Collins, London.

— 1993, 'How many pots make five? - an historical review of pottery quantification' *Archaeometry* 35:169-184.

Orton, C., and Tyers, 1992, Counting broken objects: The statistics of ceramic assemblages. *Proceedings of the British Academy* 77:163-84.

— 1993, *A User's Guide to Pie-slice*. University College London, Institute of Archaeology, London.

Orton, C., Tyers, P. A., and Vince, A. G., 1993, *Pottery in Archaeology*. Cambridge University Press, Cambridge.

Patil, G. P., and Taillie, C., 1979, An overview of diversity. In *Ecological Diversity in Theory and Practice*, edited by J. F. Grassle, G. P. Patil, W. K. Smith, and C. Taillie, pp. 3-27. International Co-operative Publishing House, Fairfield, MD.

Payne, S., 1975, Partial recovery and sample bias. In *Archaeolozoological Studies*, edited by A. T. Clason, pp. 7-17. American Elsevier, New York.

Peet, R. K., 1974, The measurement of species diversity. *Annual Review of Ecology and Systematics* 5:285-307.

Poplin, F., 1976, Rémarques théoretique et pratiques sur les unites utilisées dans les études d'ostéologie quantitative, particulièrement en archéologie préhistorique. In *Union Internationale des Sciences Préhistoriques 9e Congrès, Themes Specialisées*, pp. 124-41. Nice.

Popper, V. S., 1988, Selecting quantitative meaurements in paleoethnobotany. In *Current Paleoethnobotany, Analytical Methods and Cultural Interpretations of Archaeological Plant Remains*, C. Hastorf and V. Popper, pp. 53-71. University of Chicago Press, Chicago.

Prange, H. D., Anderson, J. F., and Rahn, H., 1979, Scaling of skeletal mass to body mass in birds and mammals. *American Naturalist* 113:103-22.

Rackham, D. J., 1986, Assessing the relative frequencies of species by the application of a stochastic model to a zooarchaeological database. In *Database Management and Zooarchaeology*, edited by V. Wijngaarden-Bakker. Journal of the European Study Group of Physical, Chemical, Biological, and Mathematical Techniques Applied to Archaeology, Research Volume 40.

Reynolds, W. W., 1977, Skeletal weight allometry in aquatic and terrestrial vertebrates. *Hydrobiologist* 56:35-37.

Rhode, D., 1988, Measurements of archaeological diversity and the sample-size effect. *American Antiquity* 53:708-716.

Ringrose, T. J., 1993a, Bone counts and statistics: A critique. *Journal of Archaeological Science* 20:121-57.

— 1993b, Diversity indices and archaeology. In *Computing the Past. Computer Applications and Quantitative Methods in Archaeology, CAA92*, edited by J. Andresen, T. Madsen, and I. Scollar, pp. 279-85. Aarhus University Press, Aarhus.

Shotwell, A. J., 1955, An approach to the paleoecology of mammals. *Ecology* 36:327-37.

Smith, B. D., 1975, Toward a more accurate estimation of the meat yield of animal species at archeological sites. In *Archaeozoological Studies*, edited by A. T. Clason, pp. 99-106. North-Holland Publishing Company, Amsterdam.

Solheim, W. G., 1960, The use of sherd weights and counts in the handling of archaeological data. *Current Anthropology* 1:325-29.

Stahl, P. W., 1982, On small mammal remains in archaeological contexts. *American Antiquity* 47:822-29.

Wild, C. J. and Nichol, R. K., 1983, Estimation of the original number of individuals from paired bone counts using estimators of the Krantz type. *Journal of Field Archaeology* 10:337-44.

Yarnell, R., 1974, Plant food and cultivation of the Salt Cavers. In *Culture Change and Continuity*, edited by C. E. Cleland, pp. 113-22. Academic Press, New York.

6 Probability and Testing Statistical Hypotheses

We have seen that we can make measurements on samples, organize our data, and estimate the parameters of populations. These help us describe our samples and characterize, with a degree of error, the populations from which they come, but this is rarely enough. Most archaeological research requires us to compare samples either with each other or with some characteristics we would expect to find if a particular theory, or hypothesis, were true. For example, we might compare samples of plant remains or faunal remains from a site that we think is pre-agricultural with ones from a site that we think has early agriculture on the assumption that they should not only be significantly different, but in ways consistent with theories about the development of agricultural economies. We make these comparisons to test the hypothesis — that is, attempt to show it is either true or false — or to evaluate the strength of the hypothesis relative to competing hypotheses. We may refer to this process as "verification," or "hypothesis testing," even if we can never be absolutely sure that any hypothesis is true.

Generally, we can only say that one hypothesis is more probable than another, and archaeologists therefore turn to probability and inferential statistics. This chapter will review probability and some basic ways to test statistical statements. You can skip it if you already understand statistical concepts quite well. If you have not studied statistics at all, you should consult a basic text. Drennan's (1996) *Statistics for Archaeologists* is an excellent introduction and reference, while Fletcher and Lock's (1991) *Digging Numbers* is perfect for those who are put off by jargon and equations. This chapter will

only provide a few examples of ways that we can assess a hypothesis's probability, while the books just mentioned and other texts introduce kinds of statistical tests for which we do not have room here.

"Verifying" Hypotheses

One verification approach that has become almost synonymous with the "New Archaeology" or processual archaeology, a movement that became dominant in Anglo-American archaeology in the 1960s and early 1970s, is the hypothetico-deductive (HD) method. In this method, we have a hypothesis, and then logically deduce from this hypothesis what outcome should happen, upon experiment, if the hypothesis is correct. This entails anticipating, before carrying out the test, all possible outcomes of the experiment or observation, and deducing which of these outcomes must occur if the hypothesis is true. It requires us to agree that any other outcome would result in rejection of the hypothesis, so we must agree in advance on a method of observation that should not itself affect the "success" or "failure" of the outcome. That is, should the test result in rejection, the rejection will not be due to incorrect observation method. This is a common problem in archaeology. We then conduct the experiment or observation and, if we do not observe the outcome we would expect if the hypothesis were correct, we reject the hypothesis.

For example, our hypothesis might be that the Natufian complex of the Middle East represents the material culture of a pre-agricultural group that had no domesticated plants or animals. We could deduce from this that assemblages of this complex should not contain *any* evidence of domesticated plants or animals. We would then take a representative sample from Natufian components of some sites that were excavated carefully, so that we can be sure, for example, that there was no contamination of Natufian deposits by later, agricultural deposits, and we would carefully examine the sample for any evidence of domestication. We would have to agree in advance on what such evidence might be, such as particular morphological and metric attributes in animal bones and plant remains. When the examination is complete, even a single piece of evidence for a domesticated plant or animal would force us to reject the hypothesis that Natufian was pre-agricultural. Failure to find such evidence, however, would not prove that the hypothesis was correct — in fact, additional samples might turn up some evidence that we simply did not include — but only that the hypothesis *could be* correct.

Unfortunately, the hypothetico-deductive (HD) method of verification has few non-trivial applications in archaeology, and rarely describes what archaeologists really do when they try to interpret a site. That is because we can almost never deduce exact outcomes of archaeological hypotheses; our hypotheses only predict *probable* outcomes. Using our example from the Natufian, most archaeologists when presented with a single domesticated grain or bone of a domestic goat found among a huge sample of Natufian remains would be reluctant to reject the hypothesis that the Natufian was pre-agricultural. Instead they would make special pleading — the bone is intrusive or genetically anomalous or its identification uncertain, or wild cereal stands contain small numbers of plants with the "domestic" mutation — that is strictly not allowed under the HD method. Even if we have been very careful to agree in advance on a sample and a method that does not allow for such possibilities as intrusion or misidentification, we would have to admit that we cannot entirely control for them. Consequently, we feel more confident about such statements as, "If Natufian sites are pre-agricultural, we would *probably* not find any bones of domestic animals in their assemblages." This is the form of statistical statements, which are much more common in archaeological research than true use of the hypothetico-deductive method, and leads us into the subject of probability and inductive statistics.

In statistical hypotheses, we always have to balance the risk that we will incorrectly reject a true hypothesis with the risk that we will incorrectly accept a false one. The former, rejecting a true hypothesis, is called a **type I** (or α) error, while failing to reject a false hypothesis is called a **type II** (or β) error.

Probability

Most of us have at least an intuitive feel for probabilities. In essence they are proportions, representing the number of times, over the long run, we would expect a particular outcome to occur divided by the total number of tests or observations. Consequently, we have already been dealing implicitly with probabilities when we considered sample proportions as estimates of population proportions in chapter 4. For example, if the population proportion of red-painted pot sherds in a particular assemblage is 0.30 (or 30%), then the probability that any sherd we might randomly select from that assemblage is red-painted is also 0.30. Sometimes we have theoretical grounds to believe that some outcome has a particular probability. For example, in coin-flipping experiments, there are only two possible outcomes, heads and tails, and in most coins we would expect these two outcomes to have equal probability. Consequently the probability of flipping "heads" should be 1/2 or 0.5. Similarly, in a faunal assemblage, for any bones that occur in pairs (left and right), we would expect that the probability that a particular bone is from the left side should be 0.5. We can call these kinds of probabilities *a priori* probabilities. Of course in any real sample, we would not expect the actual proportion of left *humeri* to be 0.5, but only that the proportion of left elements would come close to 0.5 if our sample were large enough. In this case, we would call 0.5, the proportion that our sample approaches with increasing sample size, the **limit**. The limit is the proportion of successful trials (heads or left elements) in a very large sample.

Because we are sampling, however, we only know the sample proportions and not the population proportions. Consequently we can only estimate the *a priori* probabilities except in cases, as with coin-flipping and dice-throwing, when we can establish them on theoretical grounds. When we know the *a priori* probabilities, however, we can take advantage of some useful mathematical properties that they have.

The following statements of these properties may seem daunting to the uninitiated, but they are actually simpler than you think and you should at least try to follow them. They are really just short-hand for rather common-sense principles.

First, because they are proportions, probabilities always range from 0 to 1. Mathematically, we would represent the probability of a particular outcome A, or "probability of A," as $p(A)$, so

$$0 \le p(A) \le 1.0$$

Where $p(A) = 1$, the outcome is certain to occur. Conversely, $p(A) = 0$ indicates that the event A is impossible.

In cases where two different possible outcomes are mutually exclusive (i.e., the coin cannot be heads and tails simultaneously), we can easily add probabilities. The probability that a single roll of a die will produce either a 1 or a 2 is simply $1/6 + 1/6 = 1/3$, because a single roll cannot be 1 and 2 simultaneously. Mathematically, we would write this *addition rule* as

$$p(A \text{ or } B) = p(A) + p(B),$$

"the probability of getting an A or a B equals the sum of the probability of A and the probability of B."

The sum of all possible, mutually exclusive outcomes must be 1.0, so that where there are only three possible outcomes, $p(A) + p(B) + p(C) = 1.0$. The probability that a particular outcome will *not* occur, then, must simply be equal to the sum of the probability of all other outcomes, which means that

$$p(\text{not } A) = 1.0 - p(A).$$

For example, if somehow we knew that the probability that a projectile point taken from a particular population was notched was 0.4, we could deduce that the probability of an unnotched point was $1.0 - 0.4 = 0.6$.

Often, however, outcomes are not mutually exclusive. For example, we might be interested in the probability of a potsherd coming from a jar, as well as its probability of being red-painted. There is no *a priori* reason to assume that these are mutually exclusive options. In this case we must modify the addition rule as follows.

$$p(A \text{ or } B) = p(A) + p(B) - p(A \text{ and } B)$$

The reason for subtracting the $p(A \text{ and } B)$ is to avoiding counting the "overlap" between A and B twice. If the probability of a sherd being from a jar is 0.13 and its probability of being red-painted is 0.05, we need to make sure that we do not count sherds from red-painted jars twice. If sherds from red-painted jars make up 2% of the population, then the probability of a sherd being either a jar or red-painted (and possibly both), would be $0.13 + 0.05 - 0.02 = 0.16$.

If we wanted to add the probabilities of multiple, overlapping outcomes, we would have to modify the rule still further. For three outcomes, for example,

$$p(A \text{ or } B \text{ or } C) = p(A) + p(B) + p(C) - p(A \text{ and } B) - p(A \text{ and } C) - p(B \text{ and } C) + p(A \text{ and } B \text{ and } C).$$

We can also multiply probabilities, which is how we obtain the probability that two outcomes that are not mutually exclusive will co-occur. For any two outcomes, A and B, the probability of getting both A and B simultaneously is equal to the probability of one of these outcomes times the "conditional probability" of the other. The conditional probability is the probability that the one event will occur *given that* the other event occurs. If, for example, you are interested in the probability that any sherd will be both from a jar and red-painted, the conditional probability could be the probability that it is red-painted, *given that* it is from a jar:

$$p(A \text{ and } B) = p(A) * p(B \mid A) = p(B) * p(A \mid B),$$

where "$A \mid B$" should be read as "A given B."

So, the probability that any sherd we randomly select will be from a red-painted jar is $0.13 * 0.15 = 0.02$ or $0.05 * 0.40 = 0.02$. This may be easier to see if you think of the probabilities as population proportions. 13% of the pottery consists of jar sherds, 5% of the pottery is red-painted, 15% of the jars have red paint, and 40% of the red-painted sherds are from jars. All of the proportions are interrelated by the multiplication rule.

An important statistical concept that this interrelationship brings up is the concept of independence, which already cropped up in the discussion of random sampling in chapter 4. Two events or outcomes are independent of one another only if the occurrence of one *in no way affects the likelihood* that the other will occur. Mathematically, this means that $p(A \mid B) = p(A)$ and $p(B \mid A) = p(B)$. In our pottery example, clearly we do not have statistical independence, because the probability of getting a jar is 0.13, but the probability of getting a jar if we know it is red-painted is 0.40! These are far from equal probabilities, and suggest that there is some interesting pattern in our pottery population, the kind of pattern, in fact, that is used in configurationist typology (chapter 3). Identification of such patterns is one of the things that interest archaeologists.

In the special case in which events are indeed independent, however, we can simplify the multiplication rule to leave out the conditional probabilities:

$$p(A \text{ and } B) = p(A) * p(B)$$

For example, since the colour of a playing card is independent of its value, the probability of getting a red queen would simply be $1/2 * 1/13 = 0.038$.

We will return to the application of these probability rules in discussion of Bayesian analysis, below, but for now let us launch into more straightforward statistical tests that are based on these principles.

Parametric Tests

Many statistical tests involving interval- or ratio-scale data involve comparing measurements made on a sample with a theoretical sampling distribution, such as the binomial distribution, student's t distribution, Poisson distribution, or, commonly, the Gaussian or "normal" distribution. These distributions are mathematical **models** of the way we expect data to behave in certain situations.

We have already noted how repeated sampling and measurement on a continuous scale, followed by plotting the distribution of the means for each sample, will result in a symmetrical, unimodal distribution with mean of μ and variance of s^2/n (or standard deviation of $s/\sqrt{n}$ = standard error). This is a normal or **Gaussian distribution**, which serves as our model of repeated continuous measurement. The distribution gets narrower (standard error decreases) as sample size increases. If repeated samples of size n are taken from any population, even if the population is not normally distributed, with a mean of μ and variance of σ^2, then the sampling distribution of the sample means will approach a normal distribution with mean of μ and variance of σ^2/n. This, the **central limit theorem**, describes a very useful property, as it means that we can use the normal distribution even to test hypotheses about many distributions that are not normally distributed. If you have trouble picturing why this should be the case, remember that you would expect most of the samples to yield a mean that is reasonably close to the population mean. Consequently, the mean of the distribution of many means on samples drawn from the same population should be extremely close to the population mean μ. Furthermore, because most of the sample means are themselves quite close to the population mean, the amount of dispersion in the distribution of sample means is also much less than the dispersion in individual samples; that is why the standard error decreases as sample size increases.

Furthermore, the normal distribution that results is useful in that it is really a probability distribution. The area under any portion of the curve represents the sum of the probabilities of all corresponding outcomes on the x-axis of the graph. If, for example, in a sampling distribution for repeated samples of projectile length, we draw a line vertically from the 5 cm mark on the x-axis, the area under the curve to the left of this line will represent the total probability that any projectile point from the population will be less than 5 cm long, while the area to its right represents the probability that it is longer than 5 cm. In general, we would expect any projectile we draw from a sample to be fairly close to the mean, since this is the peak of the distribution and measurements close to it consitute the most probable outcomes. But we can quantify this nicely by measuring the area under the curve for any range of outcomes on either side of the mean so that, perhaps, we estimate a probability of 0.4 that any projectile will be somewhere between 6 cm and 10 cm long.

The Z-Test

We can take advantage of all these properties to test the hypothesis that a particular sample belongs to a particular population. Let us assume for the moment that the whole population of projectile points is well known (an unlikely assumption), so that we know that $\mu = 11.5$ cm and $\sigma = 1.5$ cm. Let us further assume that we have taken a sample of 100 artifacts from this population and found its mean to be 11.9 cm. Is it possible that there is something wrong with our sample? Or is this just a typical result of statistical variation in random sampling? It seems possible that our sampling method is creating bias in favor of larger projectile points. We could test the hypothesis as follows.

First, we would have to make some assumptions. We assume that the sample is random (here that is really the hypothesis we are trying to test). If our sample is not very large, we also must assume that the population is randomly distributed, which is not too unreasonable in measurements of projectile points. We assume a continuous scale of measurement, which is fine for lengths of artifacts measured in centimeters. Finally, we assume that $\mu = 11.5$ cm and $\sigma = 1.5$ cm.

Second, we would employ the normal distribution as our sampling distribution. We can

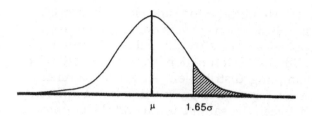

Figure 6.1. The rejection region for a one-tail Z-test at a significance level of 0.05.

either use normal tables from a statistical text or, more likely, some computer software that employs normal distributions.

Our working hypothesis is that there is something suspicious about our sampling methods. But the hypothesis that we actually test will be the "null hypothesis" (sometimes represented as H_o), that there is no significant difference between our sample and a random one from the population. Mathematically, this would mean that there is no significant difference between the population mean μ and the sample mean, $\bar{x}$.

Next, we must decide on a **significance level**, which has to do with the level of confidence we would like to place on the result of our test. In other words, it has to do with our willingness to make a type I or type II error. We should weigh the relative costs of these errors in their effect on our use of the test result: if we incorrectly conclude that there is nothing wrong with our sampling methods, will it mean that we have to do weeks of work all over again at some later date? If so, this may outweigh the cost of incorrectly concluding that our current sample is defective, which would simply require us to tighten up our methods right now. If, for example, we decided on a significance level of 0.05, this would mean that we are willing to risk a type I error 1 time out of 20, making us 95% confident that rejection of the hypothesis is justified. But if the costs in later resampling are daunting, we might instead opt for a significance level of 0.10, with a greater chance of a type I error, but less chance of type II, incorrectly accepting the hypothesis that our measurements are accurate. In addition, we need to decide whether to conduct a one-tail or two tail test, and to know what "Z-value" needs to be exceeded at this level of significance for rejection of the hypothesis to result. Here we suspect bias in one direction — oversampling large projectile points — so we would make it a one-tail test, with a rejection region in the upper tail of the sampling distribution. At a 0.05 significance level, for example, we would need a difference between the sample mean and the population mean of at least 1.65 "Z-scores" before we would reject the null hypothesis, meaning that we would expect our sample statistics to fall into the upper 5% of the area of the normal curve.

What the Z-test essentially does is to convert our measurements into "Z-scores," which are simply units of standard error, rather than units of centimeters or the like. To compute the test statistic, we first need the standard error for a sample of size 100 from this population, as follows.

$$SE = \frac{\sigma}{\sqrt{n}} = \frac{1.5}{\sqrt{100}} = 0.15$$

Next we need to measure the difference between the mean projectile length in our sample and the known population mean in Z-scores, instead of centimeters.

$$Z = \frac{\bar{x} - \mu}{s/\sqrt{n}} = \frac{11.9 - 11.5}{0.15} = 2.67$$

As it happens, 2.67 is considerably greater than 1.65, so that the null hypothesis is rejected at a significance level of 0.05. It also exceeds 2.33, the Z-score needed for rejection at the 0.01 significance level.

Consequently, we conclude that our sample does indeed overrepresent long projectiles, and we try to design a new sampling method that avoids this shortcoming.

In most cases, of course, we do not know the population parameters in advance and so we cannot carry out a **one-sample test** such as the one we just did. Much more common are **two-sample tests** in which we compare two samples in order to infer whether they could have come from the same population, or two different ones.

Commonly, this involves testing for a difference of means in two samples, and so the test is called a **difference-of-means** test. One of its common applications in archaeology is in comparing radiocarbon dates. *Uncalibrated* radiocarbon dates satisfy the conditions for this test because, although radiocarbon disintegrations are actually described by the Poisson distribution (see below), the means are so large and sample size so great that their probability distribution is an excellent approximation of the normal distribution. The date is based on the mean number of ^{14}C counts (atoms or their disintegrations) in a unit of time, and the standard deviation is calculated from the square root of these counts (as for all Poisson distributions, see below). It would be a big mistake to apply a difference-of-means test to calibrated dates, because they are generally not even close to being normally distributed (see chapter 15), but we can use other tests that do not depend on normal distributions.

More commonly, archaeologists compare, not means, but proportions among sites or assemblages. For example, we might want to compare the proportion of deer bones between two faunal assemblages. Here we can employ a **difference-of-proportions test**, which works much the same way as a difference-of-means test but with a different way of calculating the standard error.

Most often, the faunal remains from sites come from cluster samples, and are only reported in the literature as a single group for each assemblage. That is, we are told what proportion of deer bones there was among the total of all the identifiable bones recovered from the assemblage (the cluster proportion), but not how these were distributed in different sample volumes or excavation units across the site. Let us say the reports show 57% deer in a sample of 150 identifiable specimens at one site and 46% in a sample of 124 in another.

Because we do not know how the proportion of deer bones varied from one excavation context to another, we cannot calculate variances and standard errors the way we normally would for cluster samples (above, p. 82). If the number of bones is large, we can estimate the standard error of a proportion as

$$SE = \sqrt{\frac{p(1-p)}{m}}$$

with p representing the proportion, and m representing the total number of bones in the sample (distinguished from n, the number of clusters in the cluster sample). Using the reported proportions of 0.57 and 0.46 as estimates of the population proportions (since we do not know the population parameters either), our two estimated standard errors are 0.04 and 0.045.

When we compare two proportions to see if they are significantly different (i.e., could come from different populations), we would divide the difference between the two proportions by the standard error of the differences of proportions. As it turns out, the variance of the distribution of differences of proportions (or means) is equal to the sum of the two individual variances. Therefore the standard error for the distribution of differences, with $q = (1 - p)$, is

$$SE_{i-j} = \sqrt{\frac{\sigma_i^2}{n_i} + \frac{\sigma_j^2}{n_j}} = \sqrt{\frac{p_i q_i}{n_i} + \frac{p_j q_j}{n_j}} = 0.06$$

As before, we would make some assumptions, including that the proportions are of measurements on a dichotomous scale (deer or not deer), that the two samples are random and independent, and that the null hypothesis is that $p_i = p_j$ (i.e., the two proportions are estimates of the same population proportion). We will select a significance level, say, 0.10 with a rejection region for a two-tail test (since we have not predicted which of the two sites should have more deer bones if the null hypothesis is false) of 1.65.

To get a reasonable estimate of the population proportion and variance (if the two samples are from the same population, as the null hypothesis suggests), we calculate a pooled proportion:

$$p = \frac{n_i p_i + n_j p_j}{n_i + n_j} = 0.521$$

This simply means that we add the number of deer bones from site i and the number from site j and divide by the total number of bones from both sites. The proportion of bones that are not deer would then be $1 - p = 0.479$.

Consequently, to calculate the difference as "standardized" to Z-scores, we would find

$$Z = \frac{p_i - p_j}{SE_{i-j}} = \frac{0.57 - 0.46}{0.0609} = 1.8$$

Since 1.8 exceeds the 1.65 value we selected for our significance level of 0.10 (two-tail), we may reject the null hypothesis and *tentatively* conclude that the difference between the two samples reflects real differences in the population from which they were drawn.

A better application of the difference of proportions test is as follows. Suppose, for example, we have excavated 50 randomly located test pits, each 1 m x 1 m in area, on each of two Late Woodland sites in New York state, and we are interested in the density of habitation on the site. Let us further suppose that sediment characteristics and the positions of pits and post holes allow us to tell which test pits have at least 50% of their area included within Late Woodland longhouses, and which lie outside. Consequently, we can estimate the proportion of test pits assigned to the "inside" of longhouses by counting them and dividing, in this case, by 50. If Site A had 22 test pits "inside" longhouses and Site B had 34 pits "inside" houses,

$$p_A = \frac{22}{50} = 0.44 \text{ and } p_B = \frac{34}{50} = 0.68$$

and standard errors of

$$SE_A = \sqrt{\frac{0.44(0.56)}{50}} = 0.07 \text{ and}$$

$$SE_B = \sqrt{\frac{0.68(0.32)}{50}} = 0.066$$

If the sampling frame of 1 m x 1 m squares was fairly small, the SE would also incorporate the finite population corrector (multiply by [1 - n/N] before taking the square root). The two estimates are several standard errors apart, indicating that the habitation densities at the two sites are probably different. We can test this with the difference-of-proportions Z-test, but would probably actually use the very similar t-test because our sample sizes are only 50. We would use the same approach in "presence analysis" or ubiquity (chapter 5). For example, we might be

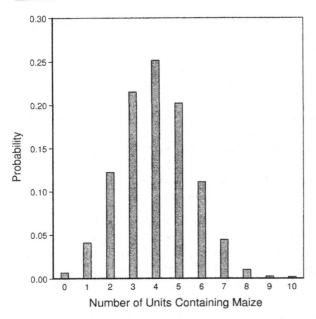

Figure 6.2. Binomial distribution with the parameters n = 10 and p = 0.4. As we would expect from these parameters, there is a high probability that three, four, or five excavation units will contain maize, and very low probability that less than two or more than seven will contain maize.

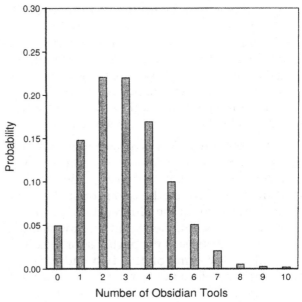

Figure 6.3. Poisson distribution with the parameter λ = 3. As we would expect from this parameter, there is a relatively high probability that we will find three obsidian tools in a particular excavation unit, but very low probability that we will find as many as ten.

interested in the proportion of test pits that contained charred maize kernels.

Tests Based on Other Distributions

Some other statistical tests work much the same way as the Z-test except that they are based on distributions other than the normal distribution. In other words, they employ different models. Most common among these is the **t-test**, based on the t distribution. This is similar to the normal distribution, but is wider and flatter when sample sizes are relatively small, while virtually identical to the normal distribution for sample sizes of more than 100. If you are not sure if your sample size is large enough to warrant a Z-test, but meets its other assumptions (including measurement on a continuous interval or ratio scale), use the t-test.

The distributions most appropriate to model many cases of *discrete* archaeological phenomena are the Binomial distribution and the Poisson distribution. The following section introduces these useful distributions and it is worthwhile to

read through even if you struggled somewhat with the Z-test.

You may already be familiar with the **Binomial distribution** as the probability model that describes coin-flipping experiments. It applies to cases where we have a fixed number of independent observations, and where each observation can have one of only two outcomes, such as heads or tails. In the case of coin-flipping, we assume *a priori* probabilities of 0.5 for heads and 0.5 for tails because we would expect, in the long run, to get equal numbers of each. For an experiment involving flipping a coin ten times and counting the number of heads, the parameters of the binomial distribution are n = 10 and p = 0.5, and we abbreviate the distribution as B(10,0.5), meaning, "Binomial distribution with ten trials and a probability of 0.5 in any one trial."

In archaeology there are many possible applications of the binomial distribution. For example, the measures of ubiquity that paleoethnobotanists use (see above, p. 109 and chapter 11) involve fixed numbers of samples or features that either do or do not contain particular plant taxa. Let us say that the probability of finding one or more maize kernels in a $1m^2$ excavation unit at a particular site is 0.4, and that we excavate 10 such excavation units. We could model this with the distribution B(10,0.4). When we excavate the ten units, we might actually find maize in only one unit (i.e., ubiquity = 0.1). Would this indicate that something unusual is happening in our excavation units — perhaps maize preservation is unusually poor or we have missed the part of the site where maize was processed — or is it just a function of the statistical nature of our sample?

We can attempt to answer this question by reference to a graph of the distribution in figure 6.2. The probability of finding maize in only one of ten excavation units turns out to be 0.0404, so that it would appear unlikely, although not impossible, that we would get these results by chance if the parameter, p = 0.4, is correct. Note that for p = 0.4 the binomial distribution is not symmetrical; it would only be symmetrical if, as for coin-flipping experiments, p = 0.5. The mean of the binomial distribution is np; here that would be 10(0.4) = 4. Consequently, we might have expected to find maize in four of the ten units if the estimate of the parameter p was correct. The standard deviation is

$$s = \sqrt{np(1-p)} = \sqrt{10 * 0.4(0.6)} = 1.55.$$

Note how similar this is to the standard deviation for a proportion. The only difference is that the proportion variance is multiplied by n.

Another useful distribution for discrete observations is the **Poisson distribution**, which models random events per unit time or space when there is theoretically no upper limit on the number of such events. In radiocarbon dating, for example (see chapter 15), the number of disintegrations of radioacitive ^{14}C in ten minutes is described by the Poisson distribution. The number of obsidian tools found in a volume of sediment (a unit of space) can also be modelled with the Poisson distribution. For example, suppose that we have excavated part of a site in units that are $1 m^2$ in area and 0.1 m in thickness, giving each a volume of $0.1 m^3$. The probability

that any given unit will contain a particular number of obsidian artifacts is

$$p(x) = \frac{e^{-\lambda}\lambda^x}{x!} \quad \text{for } x = 0, 1, 2, \ldots.$$

This means, simply, that the probability of getting x obsidian tools depends on the parameter λ (the mean or expected number of obsidian tools per unit) and e (= 2.718...). x! (pronounced "x factorial") is the product of all the integers from x to 1. If $\lambda = 3$, then the probability of finding two obsidian tools in a unit is

$$p(2) = \frac{e^{-3}3^2}{2!} = \frac{(2.718\ldots)^{-3}9}{2*1} = \frac{0.448}{2} = 0.224$$

We can calculate this for other values of x to get the distribution in figure 6.3. Note that the graph does not show bars for values higher than 10, but it really should because, even though there is very low probability of getting more than ten obsidian tools, one could theoretically find a cache of dozens of them. The graphs shows us that we would expect such caches to be very rare, however. Note that this is the major difference between the Poisson and binomial distributions. In our binomial example, we could not have values higher than ten because we only excavated ten units. In the Poisson example, however, we could theoretically have even hundreds of obsidian tools, even though that would be a very unlikely outcome.

As noted already, the mean of the Poisson distribution is λ. As it happens, the standard deviation is $\sqrt{\lambda}$. For example, if the expected number of obsidian tools in our excavation units is nine (for the population), we can express this as 9 ± 3. To estimate λ from a sample, we can use $\bar{x}$, which is an efficient estimator with n as the number of units in space or time in which we counted x_i events or objects. Alternatively, if we decided on a particular sample size m (of events or objects), we can use sequential sampling, increasing the amount of space or the length of time until the minimum number of events has been observed (Haight, 1967: 83).

As Kadane (1988) has pointed out, recognizing that many archaeological observations fit the Poisson model has important implications for optimizing sample sizes and interpreting the effects of differential preservation. Furthermore, we really should be using tests based on the Poisson distribution when we are comparing the frequencies of relatively rare items in units of space.

Where λ is very large, however, as happens when we use accelerator mass spectrometry to count millions of carbon atoms over a period of an hour, the shape of the Poisson distribution approximates the normal distribution. Although it is discrete, rather than continuous, the increments in the graph are so small as to be mistaken for continuous data.

An excellent source illustrating applications of Binomial and Poisson distributions to archaeological problems is *Bayesian Approach to Interpreting Archaeological Data* (Buck et al., 1996).

There are many other mathematical models besides the Gaussian (normal), Binomial, Poisson and t-distributions that are applicable to some kinds of archaeological problems. Among those that are implicit in many archaeological analyses are the uniform distribution (sometimes called the rectangular distribution), which models ranges (see chapter 15), Beta distribution (a continuous analogue to the Binomial distribution), and Exponential distribution (a continuous analogue to the Poisson distribution). The last would model, for example, the *rate* of ^{14}C decay in disintegrations per minute or the *rate* at which we encounter artifacts on the surface during a pedestrian survey (Buck et al., 1996:105-107). We could also use the Hypergeometric distribution to model the combinations of left and right elements in an assemblage of animal bones (Lie, 1980).

Bayesian Inference

The basic multiplication rule of probability, p(A and B) = p(A) * p(B | A), which we saw on p. 120, has an interesting property that is critical to a particular analytical approach called Bayesian analysis (Buck et al., 1996: 65; Salmon, 1982). This section is for readers who were able to weather the probability section quite well.

When we simply interchange A and B in the basic multiplication rule, we get,

$$p(B \text{ and } A) = p(B) * p(A \mid B),$$

and, because A and B are interchangeable, we can deduce that

$$p(A) * p(B \mid A) = p(B) * p(A \mid B), \text{ and that}$$

$$p(A \mid B) = \frac{p(B \mid A)}{p(B)} p(A)$$

This last is known as Bayes' theorem and serves as the basis of a whole approach to analysis. In essence, the theorem tells us what effect a new piece of information, which we have been calling B, has on another piece of information, A. The *prior probability*, p(A), is based on our original knowledge, while the probability of A *given B*, p(A | B) is known as the *posterior probability* of A.

> In a nutshell Bayes' theorem is a formal way of expressing how probability changes in the light of new information: how we update our knowledge (Buck et al., 1996:66).

Another way we might put it is that the posterior probability of A is its revised probability in the light of what we now know about B.

The satisfying thing about Bayesian analysis is that, rather than forcing us into a mold of simple yes-no hypothesis tests, typically based on only one source of information at a time, the Bayesian approach takes multiple lines of evidence into account and allows us to see whether new information either strengthens or weakens a hypothesis, while also allowing us to reject hypotheses that are very improbable.

For, example, rather than simply compare two uncalibrated radiocarbon dates from an archaeological site with a Z-test, to see if they probably pertain to the same event or same occupation, we can simultaneously consider all the *calibrated* radiocarbon dates from the site, in conjunction with information about their stratigraphic order and, if we wish, information about the chronologically sensitive artifact types associated with them. This can result in very precise understanding of site chronology (see chapter 15), but the approach is not by any means limited to dating problems. Cullberg et al. (1975), for example, use a Bayesian approach to group lithic assemblages.

The Bayesian approach also provides an alternative way of evaluating hypotheses. Rather than simply rejecting or provisionally accepting a hypothesis on the basis of new evidence, in the Bayesian approach new data either weaken or strengthen the hypothesis (Salmon, 1982). For an example of this, let us return to the problem of whether or not Natufian sites in the Middle East were agricultural, which served above to illustrate the hypothetico-deductive form of hypothesis testing. We will represent the probability that the Natufian culture had agricultural subsistence as $p(A)$, the probability that it did not as $p(H)$, the probability of finding identifiable charred remains from domesticated plants at a Natufian site as $p(D)$, and the probability of finding these domesticated plant remains at a Natufian site if the Natufian culture was agricultural as $p(D \mid A)$.

As our next step, we must estimate some probabilities, a step that might seem unusual to readers accustomed to the hypothetico-deductive method. Because most experts in the field and the weight of evidence at present suggest that it is very unlikely that the Natufian was agricultural (Bar-Yosef, 1989), setting $p(A)$ at 0.1 is, if anything, a generous estimate. The probability of the alternative hypothesis, $p(H)$, then, must be 0.9. We might estimate $p(D \mid A)$ by analogy to sites of the later Pre-Pottery Neolithic B, as it is generally accepted that PPNB sites had a partly agricultural economy. Certainly not all excavated PPNB sites yield unambiguous evidence for agriculture, and the published literature might suggest that $p(D \mid A)$ should be about 0.5. We would expect the probability of finding domesticated remains at a Natufian site if the Natufians had no agriculture to be very low. Perusal of evidence from Kebaran sites, which most archaeologists would accept as the sites of hunter-gatherers, and where the excavators used recovery methods that would have detected any domesticated remains (technically this is another "given that"), might suggest that $p(D \mid H)$ should be 0.05. This summarizes our belief that nineteen times out of twenty you would not find any domesticated plant remains at such sites, but that occasionally there might be contamination from later deposits or errors of identifica-

tion, for example. From these estimates we can calculate $p(D)$, because it is the total probability of finding domesticates, whether Natufian sites had agriculture or not, as $p(A)p(D \mid A) + p(H)p(D \mid H) = (0.1)(0.5) + (0.9)(0.05) = 0.095$.

In reality, the problem is more complicated than this. For example, we might want to separate the probability of finding domesticated remains at a Natufian site that has PPNB remains stratified above it, $p(D \mid Neo)$, from the probability of finding them at a single-period Natufian site. But this will serve as an example. Now we simply put our estimated prior probabilities into Bayes' theorem as follows.

$$p(A|D) = \frac{p(D|A)}{p(D)}p(A) = \frac{(0.1)(0.5)}{0.095} = 0.53$$

The posterior probability that the Natufian culture had agriculture, given what we know about the discovery of domesticated plant remains, is now 0.53. This is quite a bit higher than our estimate of the prior probability, $p(A)$. Here the result is somewhat dramatic, simply because the result of finding domesticates at the site was surprising, and the denominator, reflecting our belief that finding domesticated plant remains was quite unlikely, is so low. The exact value of the result, however, is not really important. What is important and intuitively satisfying is that, after more and more research, we would expect other excavations at Natufian sites to add still more information that we can use to calculate new posterior probabilities. The more often excavators find domesticated plant remains at these sites, the higher the probability that Natufian sites are agricultural will become. If, on the other hand, most of the new excavations do not find any domesticated plant remains, the new posterior probabilities will get lower and lower, strengthening our conviction that the Natufian was not, after all, agricultural.

It is important to remember, however, that here we used only one simple model of probabilities. It would be much better to construct several alternative models relevant to the finding of domestic plant remains and to test them with Bayesian techniques. For example, one such model might describe the probabilities of contamination, another the probabilities of natural mutations in a wild crop stand. After testing them we reject those that are extremely improbable and evaluate the remainder further.

Conclusion

Although many archaeologists today would say that they are not testing hypotheses or using statistical inference, it remains true that all archaeologists want to present plausible hypotheses based on patterns they identify, and that they typically search for these patterns in samples of some larger population. To make these hypotheses plausible, we at least have to show that the patterns are not due to the vagaries of chance, and tests of statistical models are the way to do this.

References Cited

Bar-Yosef, O., 1989, The Natufian in the Levant: An overview. *Paléorient* 15:57-63.

Blalock, H. M., 1979, *Social Statistics*. McGraw-Hill, New York.

Buck, C. E., Cavanagh, W. G., and Litton, C. D., 1996, *Bayesian Approach to Interpreting Archaeological Data*. Statistics in Practice. John Wiley & Sons, New York.

Cullberg, C., Odén, A., Pehrsson, N.-G., and sandberg, B., 1975, Some quantitative methods applied to flake-measuring problems. *Norwegian Archaeological Review* 8:81-97.

Drennan, R. D., 1996, *Statistics for Archaeologists. A Commonsense Approach*. Plenum Press, New York.

Fletcher, M., and Lock, G. R., 1991, *Digging Numbers: Elementary Statistics for Archaeologists*. Oxford University Committee for Archaeology, Oxford.

Haight, F. A., 1967, *Handbook of the Poisson Distribution*. John Wiley & Sons, New York.

Kadane, J. B., 1988, Possible statistical contributions to paleoethnobotany. In *Current Paleoethnobotany. Analytical Methods and Cultural Interpretations of Archaeological Plant Remains*, edited by C. Hastorf and V. Popper, pp. 206-14. University of Chicago Press, Chicago.

Lie, R. W., 1980, Minimum numbers of individuals from osteological samples. *Norwegian Archaeological Review* 13:24-30.

Salmon, M. H., 1982, *Philosophy and Archaeology*. Academic Press, New York.

7 Basic Artifact Conservation

The purpose of this chapter is not to introduce remedial or intrusive measures to deal with corroded or fragile artifacts. Most kinds of conservation require considerable background knowledge of the chemistry of the artifacts, of their environment, and of the substances used to restore or stabilize them, and there are no simple "recipes" for the conservation of the objects (Cronyn, 1990:xv). Nor is it to suggest methods for dealing with conservation in the field. Instead this chapter focusses on basic care and handling of artifacts, including storage and monitoring of collections. Discussion of remedial action will be restricted to the most unproblematic cleaning and refitting of fragmented pottery. The reader should consult sources in the bibliography for other aspects of conservation.

The basic purpose of artifact conservation is to stablize artifacts in a stable state, while interfering as little as possible with the archaeological evidence (Cronyn, 1990:9). Maintaining an environment that will not accelerate their deterioration is one of the most important aspects of stabilization. More aggressive treatments, such as removal of corrosion on metal or applying consolidants, may make the artifact useless for some kinds of archaeological, and especially archaeometric, analyses, making more passive methods preferable where possible.

In addition to the ethic of minimal intervention, the ethic of reversibility is very important. Although no treatment is completely reversible, conservators aim to select treatments that cause as little permanent alteration to the nature of the piece as possible. At the same time, one kind of treatment, namely the labelling of artifacts, should be reliable and stable (Pye, 1992:398). While a conservator should be able to remove the labels, we would not want them to fall off accidentally, with loss of information about archaeological context.

A third important ethic of artifact conservation is to maintain accurate records of any actions taken to clean or preserve the artifacts, as well as of any observations about the artifact that might be important, and especially observations of things that might not survive or need to be removed. For example, if we refit pottery fragments with an adhesive, these three ethics dictate that we should use an adhesive that causes minimal alteration to the chemical and physical nature of the sherds, and that we can easily remove, and we should document what adhesive it was. The documentation ensures that a future conservator will know what procedure to use to remove it, should that prove necessary. Fourth, artifact conservation needs to be collaborative (Cronyn, 1990:10); conservators work with archaeologists, museum curators, and others.

Artifacts in the Burial Environment

When artifacts are deposited in sediments or bodies of water, and even while they are still in use, various physical, biological, and chemical processes begin to alter their condition (Cronyn, 1990:14-29; Dowman, 1970:4-47). Handling during use (e.g., Skibo, 1992) and movement of particles in sediments abrades the artifacts' surfaces. Percolation of water through sediment, and alternation of wet and dry conditions, can dissolve some chemicals and remove them by leaching or deposit them by precipitation, leading in some cases to the mineralization, or fossilization, of wood and bone. In other cases, consistent wet or very dry conditions allow organic materials to survive for extremely long periods, albeit in altered form, by preventing bacterial action. The form of the wooden members of sunken ships, for example, can be preserved almost perfectly even though the contents of the cells in the wood have been completely replaced by sea water (Cronyn, 1990:26; McCawley, 1977; Pearson, 1981). The environment's pH is very important (Dowman, 1970:18-28). Inorganic materials, especially metal, often deteriorate in acid environments. Organic materials are often degraded in basic environments. Bone, antler, and ivory have organic components that "prefer," but inorganic components that are degraded by, acidic environments (Bradley, 1992). This is one reason why archaeologists should record sediment pH. Salinity, climate, and organisms also affect materials. Although many destructive processes are slow and continue indefinitely, quite often the artifacts stabilize in a state that changes very little, after a brief, initial period of rapid deterioration. Excavation of the artifact disturbs its equilibrium with its environment and accelerates deterioration (Cronyn, 1990:29; Dowman, 1970:4). Consequently, often the best thing we can do is to leave it where it is or keep it in conditions that mimic its burial environment until stabilization at a new equilibrium.

Collecting Artifacts in the Field

Because the most radical change to artifacts' environment typically occurs when archaeologists or others remove them from their burial environment, the way we collect artifacts in the field has a critical effect on their possibility of survival.

We can at least improve vulnerable artifacts' chances of survival by ensuring that the transition from the burial to the storage environment is as gradual as possible. An artifact can experience considerable shock when it is removed from fairly moist sediment, and then set out into bright sunlight to dry, for example. Buried or underwater artifacts have not been exposed to sunlight for a long time, and the sun's radiation can quickly alter the temperature and humidity of the artifact's environment. It is therefore better to let artifacts dry more slowly in a shaded location, and to use bags that "breathe" to prevent the build-up of condensation.

Some kinds of artifacts require especially careful removal from the sediments in which they are found. Extremely fragile ones may need to be lifted along with some of their surrounding sediment, often with the aid of a consolidating material, such as acrylic, or physically supported with gauze strips and some kind of under-support. Ones that we expect to be subject to chemical analysis, radiometric dating, or DNA analysis may require special care to avoid contamination, such as removal from their sediment with clean tweezers or trowel, and collection of associated sediment samples as a check on potential sources of contamination.

Handling Artifacts in the Laboratory

Because artifacts are often rather fragile, and some kinds of archaeological analysis require care to avoid contamination, the way we handle artifacts in the laboratory is extremely important. The temptation to handle an interesting artifact casually with bare hands should be avoided (Bradley et al., 1990).

One of the greatest risks from handling artifacts is breakage. Some artifacts, even without seeming so, are so fragile that simple handling could reduce them to crumbs in your hands. Generally these artifacts need to be held, not in the hands, but on some kind of support, such as a tray with gauze or other soft, stable material to support weak points or irregularities of shape, but that will not stick to or catch on the object. Before you decide to pick up an artifact, you should assess its probable strength and vulnerabilities. Do not grasp objects by projecting parts, such as handles, as these might break off. Instead try to support artifacts under their center of gravity, preferably with something that cushions them (Miles, 1992).

Even relatively stable and sturdy artifacts are susceptible to breakage if dropped on a hard surface. In spite of your best efforts to handle artifacts carefully, there is always the chance that you will drop an artifact some time, so always hold artifacts over a cushioned surface that will absorb much of the shock of impact. One of the best ways to avoid unecessary breakage is to cover laboratory surfaces where artifacts are handled with sheets of padding, such as nalgene, polyethylene, styrofoam, bubble pack, or carpeting. Ideally you want a material that lies flat, with minimal curling of edges, and that will not slide on the lab counter. Note that not all such padding would be appropriate for use in long-term storage (see below).

Some kinds of artifacts should never be handled with bare hands. The skin in your hands will leave oils and organic acids on surfaces that can actually etch into metal surfaces slightly, providing sites for future corrosion, and can contaminate surfaces with substances that react chemically with some kinds of materials, especially metal artifacts (Shearman, 1990). In some cases these contaminants will also confuse attempts at archaeometric analysis or radiometric dating. An artifact scheduled for any kind of chemical, isotopic, or genetic analysis should only be handled with clean tools, such as tweezers, made from an inert material or one that would not jeopardize the results of analysis if it left small amounts of residue on the artifact's surface, or with latex gloves. Disposable latex gloves are available in boxes of 100 or more pairs, and are a good investment. Metal artifacts should be protected from the oils and acids on your hands by clean cotton gloves. Even while wearing gloves, you should minimize the chance of causing wear on the surfaces of metal artifacts, especially coins, by holding them only by their edges. Also remove any jewelry before you handle artifacts.

If you have to transport the artifacts more than a few feet, carry it in a tray, or box, or on a wheeled cart. Boxed artifacts should also have a packing list, and artifacts in the box should not be wrapped in paper that might be thrown away, as this creates the risk that small objects could accidentally be discarded with the paper.

Simple Cleaning of Artifacts

Some kinds of artifacts, such as lithics and well-fired pottery fragments from moderate burial environments, may be sufficiently stable to allow straightforward cleaning without intrusive or complicated conservation procedures. You should test them to see if this is the case. As long as the artifacts will not be used for a kind of analysis for which chemical contamination must be avoided, and have fairly hard surfaces, you can remove loose dirt by brushing with a soft brush and then carefully remove tougher dirt mechanically with a fine tool, such as a scalpel, bamboo stick, or dental pick. You should use brushes that suit the situation — soft ones for loose dirt or vulnerable surfaces — and never use metal brushes, vigorous brushing, or scraping, or you will damage the surface of pottery or edges of lithics. If you still find it difficult to avoid damaging delicate slips on the surface of sherds, you should record any damage you have done and any observations you would have wanted to make on the slip, such as its thickness and color (chapter 9).

Where the dirt is very hard, and the artifacts are able to withstand water (test them first), you may use water to soften and loosen it before and during brushing and other mechanical removal. Where there has been deposition of very hard carbonates or other minerals on the surface, and you are unable to remove them with water and simple mechanical lifting, it may be necessary to use a relatively gentle acid, such as acetic acid (vinegar) or dilute hydrochloric acid. In such cases, you should consider safety issues and seek the advice of a conservator to ensure that use of such acids would not damage the artifacts, which are often chemically very similar to the carbonates you are trying to remove. In addition, it is generally better to drip the acid onto stubborn precipitates with an eye-dropper, rather than to immerse the artifact in dilute acid, which might destroy it before you are able to remove it and stop the acid's action. Finally, it is important to neutralize and remove all traces of the acid to prevent it from continuing to act on the artifact. Use distilled water to rinse away residues.

Storage of Archaeological Collections

Artifacts that survive removal from their burial environment reasonably well can still find themselves in very inhospitable storage conditions. Archaeologists and collections' curators must take reasonable care to preserve both the physical and archaeological integrity of the artifacts. This means protecting them from conditions that could accelerate their physical deterioration or result in loss of archaeological, including contextual, information (Bradley and Daniels, 1990; Leigh, 1982; Partington-Omar and White, 1981; Pye, 1992; Tate and Skinner, 1992; UKIC Archaeology section 1983; 1984).

To protect information about archaeological context after artifacts have been taken from the field to the laboratory, it is critical to label them. As soon as any artifact is removed from the labelled bag or box in which its excavator first placed it, there is a risk that it will be separated from its contextual information, its archaeological significance lost. Somewhat ironically, it is often the most remarkable artifact whose exact context is lost, simply because it was separated from the other artifacts for photography, illustration, or to show colleagues.

Unless we keep each artifact in its own labelled bag, with the risk that it will still somehow get separated from its label, we must put the label on the surface of the artifact itself. We must ensure that it is both legible and stable enough to prevent accidental removal, but still reversible and only minimal in its physical alteration of the artifact. Packaging should also be labelled (Pye, 1992:398).

In the case of pottery and flint or stable glass, we can coat a small area of the surface, in a spot where it will be least obtrusive to later analysis, with a patch of acrylic, such as Paraloid (or Acryloid) B72, which will harden to leave a smooth surface on which we can write fairly easily. This will adhere to the surface reliably, but can be removed with acetone. Subsequently, we can carefully write the label with a fine-tipped technical pen, using black India ink on light-colored but white ink on dark-colored surfaces, and then, after the ink dries, protect the label with another coat of the acrylic. The ink must be light-fast and not soluble in acetone. Even this kind of label, under poor storage conditions, may occasionally detach from the artifact's surface, which makes regular collection monitoring essential (below). Detachment is especially likely if the artifact is not dry before application of B72, as water in its pores prevents the consolidant from penetrating properly.

Once the artifacts have been labelled, they need to be stored under conditions that minimize the rate of processes that deteriorate them. This involves maintaining an environment that is moderate and stable in its temperature and humidity and in which the artifacts are protected from sudden movement, friction, and vibration. The storage area should by dry, clean, secure, away from traffic and heating systems, but accessible with trolleys for carrying large trays and boxes (Pye, 1992:400-401; Tate and Skinner, 1992). It should be away from direct sunlight, and fluorescent lights should have UV filters or be left off in "dead storage."

High temperatures accelerate chemical reactions, but extremes of heat and cold are fairly easy to avoid by curating artifacts in a climate-controlled building, with temperature held close to 20°C.

Humidity can also be a problem. A simple way to prevent humidity from climbing too high, especially where metal artifacts are concerned (Knight, 1982; Shearman, 1990), is to put the artifacts in a sealed polyethylene box, creating a "microclimate," along with silica-gel, which absorbs water from the air in the container into its micropores until it comes into equilibrium with the surrounding air (figure 7.1). The silica-gel will become saturated after some months, so that it no longer works. You must revitalize it by heating it in an oven at 105°C for 10 hours to drive off the accumulated water molecules, letting it cool for another 10 hours before returning

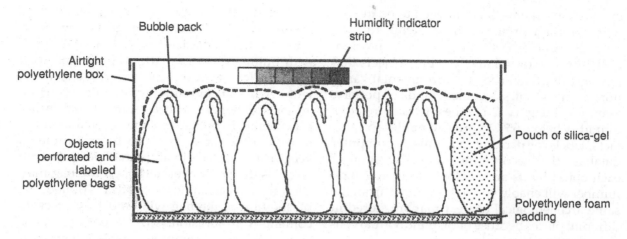

Figure 7.1. Packaging for metal artifacts or other artifacts that need careful maintenance of low relative humidity (after Cronyn 1990:75). The bag labels should be near the top, just below the fold, to facilitate retrieval of particular bags with minimal disturbance to the others.

it to the artifact container. To signal you when this needs to be done, you can either put a humidity strip, a small paper strip that indicates by color changes relative humidities as low as 20%, into the box (Ramer, 1981) or use an "indicator" silica-gel, which changes color when it needs to be changed. For very vulnerable artifacts, such as iron, you need enough silica-gel in the container, and to rotate it often enough, to keep relative humidity between 10 and 20% (Cronyn, 1990:75). A recommended amount is 1 kg of silica-gel for each 0.012 m³ of volume to be dessicated (Watkinson, 1987). Leaving a hygrometer in the container allows you to monitor humidity more precisely, and ensure that they remain within acceptable ranges. The usefulness of silica gel is related to its surface area, so a broad layer of it in the bottom of the box is more effective than a small pouch, but more difficult to rotate. You also need to consult the WHMIS safety sheet for silica gel.

Apart from atmospheric conditions, the physical means for containing and organizing artifacts is the most important storage factor affecting their preservation. Ideally, the storage system should organize the artifacts in a way that facilitates their location and retrieval, allows easy and safe removal and replacement of artifacts, minimizes their exposure to movement, friction, and abrasion, facilitates monitor-

ing of the collection's condition and environment, and maintains the collection's environment within the safe zone. We need to consider the materials with which the storage system is constructed, the shape and size of units within it, how robust and chemically active the artifacts are, how and how often artifacts must be examined or removed. Within the parameters of our decision to select a storage system, we may consider various types of shelving and cabinetry, drawers, trays, boxes, and bags. Today we are fortunate that a wide variety of storage alternatives are available, and many of the containers are constructed from inert materials that will not release harmful acids or other chemically active agents into the artifacts' environment.

The storage system needs to make sense archaeologically, facilitating the collection's use by archaeologists. Separating artifacts by categories of varying fragility or vulnerability and with different environmental needs is also critical (Cronyn, 1990:79-80; UKIC Archaeology Section, 1982). Category A is for the most unstable materials, for which control and monitoring of environmental conditions is most important. These artifacts, often of metal or organic material, need to be kept in enclosed containers with their own sealed and carefully controlled environments. Category B refers to less sensitive objects, such as bone, that can be kept in more open environments, but still need to be treated with care and protected from damp, fungus, pests (Stansfield, 1985), and physical abrasion. Category C is for relatively robust objects that have greater tolerance of environmental variation, such as lithics and most kinds of pottery. Even for Category C it is best to keep relative humidity below 65% to prevent mildew on artifacts, labels, or packing materials. A computer database that records the storage location of each object by its archaeological identification number will enable you to find things from the same archaeological context that are stored in different places because of their individual conservation needs (see chapter 3).

One of the oldest archaeological storage systems consists of sturdy wooden shelving to support wooden or cardboard boxes and trays in which artifacts are piled or arranged in rows or bags. The shelving is arranged in rows in a dry room around 20°C. The boxes are arranged on the shelves in a sensible order, and each box has a label on the end facing out, summarizing its content to facilitate location and retrieval. This storage system has proved effective for the "dead storage" of rather robust artifacts (Category C) that are no longer undergoing analysis, but has disadvantages that make it inappropriate for more vulnerable artifacts or active analysis. The wooden framework, typically a softwood such as pine or fir, contains resins and exudes acidic vapours that could be deleterious to metal artifacts. Plywood and particle-board, which are often used in the shelving, contain glues that also may give off small amounts of harmful fumes. Cardboard boxes are themselves susceptible to water damage, are usually made of very acidic paper and glue, and do not protect their contents very well. Friction and jostling of artifacts against each other as boxes are moved on or off the shelves cause abrasion of surfaces and encourage fragmentation. If the boxes are heavy, the difficulty of moving them will increase opportunities for abrasion. We can compensate for some of these problems by covering surfaces with an aluminum foil barrier or substituting metal shelving and plastic boxes for the wood and cardboard but these are still best only for dead storage.

Where you will retrieve and replace artifacts frequently, you want a storage system with drawers that minimize the friction associated with pulling them in and out. Each time you open or close a drawer, however, the artifacts within will shift and suffer wear, unless you line artifact containers with a material that either prevents artifacts from moving or cushions them from hard surfaces. This can be as simple as keeping the artifacts in individual polyethylene bags inside the drawer; although the bag may slide around each time the drawer is pulled, the plastic film of the bag will tend to protect its contents from abrasion. An excellent but expensive storage system employs metal cabinets with doors that seal, to isolate each cabinet's environment and help maintain constant humidity, and with many shallow, adjustable metal drawers. The drawers can be subdivided into rows and small polyethylene bags or small trays lined with safe cushioning material, such as polyethylene foam, can be arranged within them. Labels on the drawer fronts facilitate location of specific artifacts. For artifacts that are particularly susceptible to damage from abrasion, cutting form-fitting holes in a polyethylene foam pad and placing each artifact in its appropriate hole will prevent them from shifting when the drawer is moved. Any padding used to prevent movement should be as nearly as possible chemically inert, such as polyethylene (Pye, 1992:396). Cotton wool has the disadvantage of catching on microscopic spurs on the surface of artifacts, and polyether sponge degrades (Cronyn, 1990:79). The padding should also be firm enough to prevent objects from jostling about, yet allow easy retrieval of artifacts for study; otherwise you risk damaging things as you unwrap them from their packing.

A similar storage system employs many tray-like plastic boxes that either slide along closely-spaced metal shelves or have flanged edges that slide along tracks. As with the metal cabinets, it is necessary to prevent artifacts from sliding around inside the plastic trays, but closely fitting, transparent lids allow each tray to be fairly well sealed, isolating the artifacts' environment within. If a pouch of silica-gel is left in each and monitored, this environment can be kept at a low relative humidity. The clear lid allows you to check the gel without opening the tray.

Collection Monitoring and Condition Census

Even if you think you have stored artifacts under nearly ideal conditions, there is always the possibility that they will begin to deteriorate. To address this problem, it is necessary to schedule regular checks on the collection's condition, recording changes that may have occurred to any artifacts, and to keep tabs on environmental conditions. This is called **monitoring** (Bradley and Daniels, 1990), and the records of the artifacts' conditions constitutes a condition census. Note that silica-gel is useless if left unmonitored.

Conservation Documentation

As we saw at the beginning of this chapter, it is extremely important to record information about an artifact before and during any conservation treatments, as well as to record the treatments themselves and the storage history. As with archaeological recording (chapter 3), no one recording system necessarily presents itself, but conservation recording systems (e.g., Bradley, 1983; Corfield, 1983) tend to have many features in common.

In addition to any information required by the archaeologists' database, such as context and details of form or decoration (especially if those might be affected by treatment), a typical conservation record includes a brief description of the artifact and its condition before treatment, photographs, a record of how the conservator examined the artifact, what he or she noticed, and each step of treatment that the conservator carried out, often with photographs or diagrams to illustrate these steps. The treatment record would include details of investigative cleaning, methods of stabilization (including materials used), and the condition that results. The record would also usually include recommendations for further treatment, if necessary, and requirements for environmental control (Cronyn, 1990:94-95).

Pottery Refitting

One of the few remedial conservation measures that archaeologists routinely carry out without intervention by a professional conservator is to refit the fragments, or sherds, of a broken pot into as much of a whole pot as possible. This requires careful attention to the shapes, coloration and any decoration on individual sherds to see which ones most likely fit together. It requires more thought than you would imagine, while physical joining of the sherds with an adhesive may not even be necessary.

Before beginning to refit pottery you should give serious thought to a number of questions (Cronyn, 1990:157). Is physical refitting warranted, or is it sufficient to discover which pieces fit together and to reconstruct the vessel on paper? Is the fabric of the broken vessel able to withstand reconstruction? Flaking sherds and vessels of porcelain or stoneware are not good candidates for reconstruction. Are the breaks free of dirt and encrustations of salt or carbonates? Are the sherds sufficiently dry? The water in damp artifacts would prevent some common consolidants from penetrating the pottery fabric. What previous conservation treatments have the sherds undergone? Answers to these questions will guide whether and how to go about reconstruction.

The first step in refitting is to lay out the sherds, all with the outer (or inner) surface up, and to attempt to determine their orientation and, if possible, position on the pot, and to group sherds together that appear to be from the same vessel. For example, any rim sherds should be placed near the top, with the rim horizontal, and any base sherds near the bottom. Differences in fabric or rim diameter are among the clues you would use to group sherds. If there is any surface decoration to guide you, such as painted bands, you may be able to arrange many of the body sherds into zones between the rim and base sherds. For wheel-thrown and sometimes coil-built or wheel-smoothed vessels, you can also use the parallel ridges and valleys in the sherds' microtopography, which should be horizontal, in order to orient body sherds. The sizes, edge-shapes, and sometimes surface features, such as decoration and color variations due to firing, will help you find pairs of sherds that might fit together. Then you can test them, if the edges are clean, by gently fitting them together, without adhesive, to see if they fit snugly. Sherd color can, however, be extremely deceptive, as sherds that fit perfectly often have acquired quite different colors from their burial environments.

Once you have identified sherds that appear to fit together, it is important to document which ones these are. This not only makes it unnecessary to go back over old ground if your refitting is interrupted, but can be very important in helping to understand site-formation processes. If all the sherds belonging to one vessel were found in the same archaeological context, this would suggest, among other things, that the context had not been disturbed substantially since the pot's deposit, while finding joins between sherds from many different contexts might tell you something about how the broken pottery was discarded, about which contexts were likely contemporary, and about activities, such as pit-digging or plowing, that may have spread artifacts around.

If you decide to rebuild a vessel at this point, you should plan out your reconstruction carefully (Cronyn, 1990:158-59). If the broken edges of the sherds are not clean, you must clean them mechanically to remove any dirt or encrustation that could prevent a snug fit. It may also be advisable to prime the edges with a dilute (5%) solution of Paraloid (or Acryloid) B72 in acetone (consult the WHMIS guide first). After the consolidant has dried, but before you begin to use any adhesive, plan the order in which you will join the sherds. This is important to avoid "locking out" sherds that cannot be fit in because of previous joins you have made. For whole vessels, it is often advisable to start with the base and build upwards to ensure that the curvature around the circumference is correct. Otherwise you may find, as you join sherds in sequence around the pot, that they do not meet at the far side of the circle. If you have no base, begin with rim, if possible. Join each pair of sherds with an adhesive of about 25% B72 (Koob, 1986). Apply the adhesive in a thin trail along the edge of one sherd, with a fume extraction system to protect you from the acetone fumes, and then press the two sherds snugly together. You may have to rock the sherds back and forth a little to get a tight join. After holding the sherds firmly together for a few minutes, stand them in a "sandbox," carefully positioned so that gravity is perpendicular to the join, until the adhesive dries. Sand is actually not the best material for the "sandbox," as sand may stick to the adhesive at the joins. It is better to use small sand-bags, or dried beans or peas, which are easier to separate from the adhesive. Leaving open boxes of beans in the lab, however, will attract pests, such as mice, so store them in a sealed container. Some people also reinforce the joins temporarily with adhesive tape. This is fine for many fabrics as long as it is not left on long, but removal of tape could lift off slips or consolidants, so is best avoided except where necessary. Except in cases where the intervening sherds are missing, build up each vessel from only one part (generally the base). If you attempt to work on several parts of the vessel simultaneously, you will probably find the curvature on one or more pieces slightly out, so that the various parts will not go together and you need to remove your joins and start over.

The reason that conservators recommend Paraloid (Acryloid) B72 for use as an adhesive is that we can reverse the joins by dissolution in acetone, yet it holds the sherds together extremely well otherwise. If small errors in the angle of joins between sherds accumulate so that, as reconstruction becomes almost complete, the final few joins do not meet, it is possible to correct the problem. Had a non-reversible adhesive been used, such an attempt would likely involve rebreaking the sherds, but with acetone we can soften the joins to alter the curvature until the vessel can be closed. When the acetone evaporates, the joins will harden again. Some adhesives, such as the popular "white glue," are also reversible, but will not hold the pot's shape under hot or humid conditions. White glue will also contaminate sherds with collagen, making them unsuitable for residue analysis. If you use solvent to dissolve joins too often, you may stain the fabric in the area around the join (Cronyn, 1990:159).

Removing Samples for Analysis

Although the conservator's usual concern is to stabilize artifacts and prevent any further damage, sometimes archaeological analysis, like archaeological excavation, is invasive, and some destruction is unavoidable. For example, petrographic analysis of pottery or lithics requires thin sections, which we make from pieces we have sawn from the artifacts. Furthermore, many kinds of chemical analysis and dating require us to remove small amounts of material. Clearly in these cases we want to minimize the extent of destruction, as well as to maximize the effectiveness of the analysis. Where possible, we should select cutting and drilling sites so as to minimize damage to the artifact, or to avoid decorative features and the like, as long as they still fulfill their analytical functions (e.g., by giving a correct radial section). In some cases, aesthetic or ethical concerns may exclude the possibility of sample removal altogether.

For thin sections, it is important to select locations to cut where the sections will intercept important structural features and will reveal the most information, for example, on the orientation of inclusions in pottery (chapter 9) or the thickness of the hydration rind on an obsidian flake. Usually this involves radial sections of potsherds and cuts perpendicular to the edges of flakes.

One of the ways to maximize the benefit that results from the admittedly destructive sectioning of pottery is to take advantage of the radial cut section to facilitate drawing (chapter 16) and to make macroscopic observations in the cut of such features as slip thickness and variations in paste color that are related to firing conditions.

Many kinds of analysis, such as neutron activation analysis and X-ray diffraction, are typically done with powdered samples removed from the artifact by drilling. In these cases it is important to avoid contamination by using a clean drill bit made of a material that does not interfere with measurement of the constituents of interest, and to discard the first material drilled out, in case it is contaminated by surface contact. It is important to keep in mind that a single drilling site may not always characterize the artifact's composition very well, as some materials can be heterogeneous, or even have different parts intentionally made with different characteristics. One should also remember that discarding the materal closest to the surface does not guarantee immunity to diagenetic contamination; buried bone, for example, can absorb chemicals from surrounding sediment deeply into its structure (Hancock et al., 1989).

Ethical Issues

Curation of specimens is not only a matter of their preservation; it also entails broader ethical issues. Today the most noteworthy ethical issues for archaeological curators involve the curation, use, and potential repatriation of artifacts and human remains claimed by indigenous peoples. It is also important to ensure that collections meet the conditions of the authorities that issued the excavation and survey permits used to collect them, as well as the laws of the country or state of origin and such international conventions as the UNESCO convention.

Any artifacts or specimens that may be culturally sensitive should be treated with respect, and there should be a protocol for the legitimate repatriation of items the ownership of which is in dispute or that can be shown to be associated with or culturally important to extant indigenous groups. It is simply not acceptable, for example, to display the bones of someone's ancestors in a frivolous manner, nor is it appropriate to treat sacred objects carelessly. In their cultures of origin, it was often the case that certain sacred objects were kept hidden except on particular occasions, or could only be viewed by particular people. Some museums now accomodate these restrictions by keeping particular items out of public view except in cooperation with indigenous groups that use them in public ceremonies. Many museums and universities now also have protocols for the return of artifacts and skeletal remains, many of which were originally collected in the 19th century, to descendents of the peoples from which they were taken. Some repatriation policies are available on the World Wide Web, with that of the Smithsonian Institution, for example, at http://www.nmnh.si.edu/anthro/repatriation/repat.htm.

The terms of archaeological excavation permits may place restrictions on the way artifacts are curated, including where they should be stored and how long they can stay in the archaeologist's possession before being repatriated or moved, for example, to a country's national museum. In addition, where bringing artifacts to the laboratory involves crossing international borders, you will need to declare the contents of the collection to customs officials. In countries that are signatories to the UNESCO convention, you should expect to be asked to show a permit for the export of the artifacts from their country of origin. If you plan to bring sediment samples, plant remains, and the like across international borders, customs officials will expect you to have a soil import permit, the terms of which may require you to dispose of the samples, after analysis, by incineration.

References Cited

Bradley, S., 1983, Conservation recording in the British Museum. *The Conservator* 7:9-12.

— 1992, Conservation aspects of storage and display. In *Manual of Curatorship, a Guide to Museum Practice*, 2nd ed., edited by J. M. Thompson, pp. 468-73. Butterworth-Heinemann, London.

Bradley, S., and Daniels, V., 1990, Environment. In *A Guide to the Storage, Exhibition and Handling of Antiquities, Ethnographia and Pictorial Art*, edited by S. Bradley, pp. 1-14. British Museum Occasional Paper 66. The British Museum, London.

Bradley, S., Uprichard, K., and Munday, V., 1990, General guidelines on the handling of objects. In *A Guide to the Storage, Exhibition and Handling of Antiquities, Ethnographia and Pictorial Art*, edited by S. Bradley, pp. 15-17. British Museum Occasional Paper 66. The British Museum, London.

Clarke, R. W., and S. N. Blackshaw, eds., 1982, *Conservation of Iron*. Maritime Monographs and Reports 53. National Maritime Museum, London.

Corfield, M., 1983, Conservation records in the Wiltshire Library and Museum Service. *The Conservator* 7:5-8.

Cronyn, J. M., 1990, *The Elements of Archaeological Conservation*. Routledge, London.

Dowman, E. A., 1970, *Conservation in Field Archaeology*. Methuen & Co., London.

Hancock, R., Grynpas, M., and Pritzker, K., 1989, The abuse of bone analyses for archaeological dietary studies. *Archaeometry* 31:169-79.

Hodges, H. W. M., 1987. Conservation treatment of ceramics in the field. In *In Situ Archaeological Conservation*, edited by H. W. M. Hodges, pp. 144-49. J. Paul Getty Trust, Century City, CA.

Jespersen, K., 1985, Extended storage of waterlogged wood in nature. In *Waterlogged Wood: Study and Conservation*, pp. 39-54. Proceedings of the 2nd ICOM Waterlogged Wood Working Group. Centre d'Etude et de Traitement des Bois Gorgés d'Eau, Grenoble.

Knight, B., 1982, A note on the storage of freshly excavated iron objects. *Conservation News* 17:19.

Koob, S., 1981, Conservation with acrylic colloidal dispersions. In *Preprints of the AIC 9th Annual Meeting*, pp. 86-94. American Institute for Conservation, Washington, DC.

— 1986, The use of Paraloid B72 as an adhesive: Its application for archaeological ceramics and other materials. *Studies in Conservation* 31:7-14.

Leigh, D., 1982, The selection, conservation and storage of archaeological finds. *Museums Journal* 82:115-16.

McCawley, J. C., 1977, Waterlogged artifacts: The challenge to conservation. *Journal of the Canadian Conservation Institute* 2:17-26.

Miles, G., 1992, Object handling. In *Manual of Curatorship, a Guide to Museum Practice*, 2nd ed., edited by J. M. Thompson, pp. 455-58. Butterworth-Heinemann, London.

Partington-Omar, A., and White, A. J., eds., 1981, *Archaeological Storage*. Society of Museum Archaeologists, Lincoln.

Pearson, C., 1981, The use of polyethylene glycol for the treatment of waterlogged wood: Its past, present and future. In *Conservation of Waterlogged Wood*, edited by L. H. de Vries-Zuiderbaan, pp. 51-56. Proceedings of the International Symposium on the Conservation of Large Objects of Waterlogged Wood. Ministry of Education and Science, The Hague.

Phillips, P., ed., 1985, *The Archaeologist and the Laboratory*. CBA Research Report 58. Council for British Archaeology, London.

Pye, E. M., 1992, Conservation and storage: archaeological material. In *Manual of Curatorship, a Guide to Museum Practice*, 2nd ed., edited by J. M. Thompson, pp. 392-426. Butterworth-Heinemann, London.

Ramer, B. , 1981, The use of colour change relative humidity cards. *Conservation News* 16:10.

Sease, C., 1992, *A Conservation Manual for the Field Archaeologist*, second ed. Archaeological Research Tools 4. University of California, Los Angeles, Los Angeles.

Shearman, F., 1990, Metals. In *A Guide to the Storage, Exhibition and Handling of Antiquities, Ethnographia and Pictorial Art*, edited by S. Bradley, pp. 18-26. British Museum Occasional Paper 66. The British Museum, London.

Skibo, J. M., 1992, *Pottery Function. A Use-Alteration Perspective*. Plenum Press, New York.

Stansfield, G., 1985, Pest control: A collections management problem. *Museums Journal* 85:97-100.

Tate, J., and Skinner, T., 1992, Storage systems. In *Manual of Curatorship, a Guide to Museum Practice*, 2nd ed., edited by J. M. Thompson, pp. 459-67. Butterworth-Heinemann, London.

UKIC, 1983, *Guidance for Conservation Practice*. United Kingdom Institute for Conservation, London.

UKIC Archaeology Section, 1982, *Excavated Artefacts for Publication: U.K. Sites*. Guidelines 1. United Kingdom Institute for Conservation, London.

—— 1983, *Packaging and Storage of Freshly-Excavated Artefacts from Archaeological Sites*. Guidelines 2. United Kingdom Institute for Conservation, London.

—— 1984, *Environmental Standards for the Permanent Storage of Excavated Material from Archaeological Sites*. Guidelines 3. United Kingdom Institute for Conservation, London.

Watkinson, D., ed., 1987, *First Aid for Finds*, 2nd ed. Rescue/ UKIC Archaeology Section, London.

8 Analysing Lithics

The best preserved and most abundant evidence for 95% of the human career consists of stone tools and the debris left from making them. Needless to say, archaeologists have spent considerable time and effort learning how to interpret this evidence.

In this chapter we will consider briefly the technology of stone tool production, the description of lithic artifacts, sourcing lithic raw materials, the replication of simple tools, the determination of tool use, problems posed by post-depositional alteration of lithics, and the questions of economy and style in stone tools. We will concentrate on tools that were shaped by flaking, but will briefly deal with tools made with other reduction techniques, such as grinding. Readers interested in lithics should refer to some of the works listed among the references, especially Andrefsky (1998), Debénath and Dibble (1994), Inizan et al. (1992), and Whittaker (1994).

La Chaîne Opératoire

There are many ways to approach the study of stone tools, including a long-standing typological approach that focusses on the form and retouch of finished tools. Many researchers today use primarily a technological approach, sometimes emphasizing the sequence of activities that were involved in the production of artifacts (e.g., Schiffer 1976). Recently, one such approach for studying lithics and, indeed, any kind of artifact, called the **chaîne opératoire**, has gained prominence. This "operational chain" refers to all the processes involved in people's use of materials, from the discovery, selection, and processing of raw materials, through manufacture, use, and reuse of artifacts, to recycling and eventual discard of the artifacts, their remnants, and the debris from their manufacture. Unlike some similar approaches, it also refers to the strategies that people use in these processes, the decisions they make at each stage, and the "gestures" they have learned through immersion in their culture. For archaeologists, it is a methodological framework for helping to understand variability in lithic and other assemblages or to "read" the signs left by the decisions of the tools' makers and users (Chazan, 1997; Inizan et al., 1992:12-13; Sellet, 1993).

When applied to lithics, the chaîne opératoire approach treats flint-knapping as a subsystem of a larger technological system. It considers the particular characteristics of tools, manufacturing debris, and other debris as the result of physical actions and people's motor abilities, and of skills (*savoir faire* or know-how), knowledge (*connaissance*) and experience, as expressed in ability and performance.

Lithic Raw Material

One of the principal limitations on the manufacture of stone tools is raw material. The makers of stone tools appreciated the differences that raw materials made to ease of flaking, sharpness of edge, tools' ability to hold an edge, and even aesthetic appearance. One indication of this is that tools that appear to have had different functions are often made of different materials, with basalt and quartzite, for example, used for heavy chopping tools, and obsidian for making very sharp knives. Selection and acquisition of raw material were early stages in the *chaîne opératoire*, and prehistoric flintknappers sometimes favored raw materials that could not be found locally, importing highly regarded material over many hundreds of kilometers.

Although many stone and glass materials are useful for making chipped stone tools, the most commonly used material for cutting and scraping tools is flint or chert. This is a microcrystalline (usually 2 to 50 μ) silicate (SiO_2) rock, formed as nodules or layers in limestone, that behaves in many ways like a super-cooled fluid (Hodges, 1964:99), similar to glass. It is formed over millions of years from concentrations of silica in ocean sediments. Broadly defined, any sedimentary rocks composed mainly of microcrystalline quartz can be considered chert, including flint, chalcedony, agate, jasper, and hornstone (Luedtke, 1992).

For many applications that require an extremely sharp edge or great control over fracture mechanics, obsidian is the preferred material. Obsidian is a volcanic glass, and glass is in fact a super-cooled fluid. While obsidian flakes have very sharp edges, they are also brittle.

Quartzite is a hard material that is not as easy to flake as fine-grained flint or obsidian, but can be useful for a variety of heavy tools, such as choppers and hoes.

Quartz is a material that was commonly used in parts of North America and Africa where fine-grained cherts and obsidian were not available. A crystalline silicate, many flaws in the crystal structure of quartz make it much more difficult to flake predictably. Quartz tools are usually small and rather irregular, but still quite functional because quartz does hold a sharp edge.

Basalt is a coarse volcanic rock that can also be flaked, but not with the fine control of flint or obsidian. In spite of its difficulties, Palaeolithic knappers sometimes used basalt for flaked tools. In addition, basalt has often been the prefered material for ground-stone tools.

Even hard, dolomitic limestone and other sedimentary and metamorphic rocks can be flaked, although these rocks are not very suit-

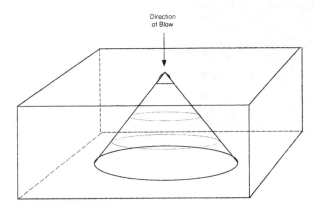

Figure 8.1. Schematic of conchoidal fracture in a block of flint or glass.

able for most kinds of cutting tools. More commonly, masons would use flaking techniques to shape them into building stones, or tool makers would use flaking simply to rough out the shape of a tool that they would finish with pecking and grinding.

Lithic analysts have made some headway both into recognizing prehistoric preferences for particular raw materials and into the identification of their sources. The latter allows us to recognize prehistoric, long-distance exchange or transport (e.g., Dixon et al., 1968).

For many decades, archaeologists tried to identify the sources of raw materials simply by outward appearance, especially color, banding, and graininess. Presumably this was much the way that prehistoric flintknappers also did it, but in the last 30 years archaeologists have increasingly relied on chemical and microscopic attributes for lithic identification and sourcing.

Variation in trace elements in the material can sometimes give it a "signature" that is recognizable. X-ray fluorescence, instrumental neutron activation analysis, and other spectroscopic techniques are commonly used to detect the abundances of these traces in tools or debitage, which can then be compared with samples of raw material from known sources. This sounds very straightforward, but sometimes the sources themselves show considerable internal variability. In addition, until there is sufficient survey of sources to convince skeptics that no sources go unanalysed, there is always the possibility that two or more sources have very similar signa-

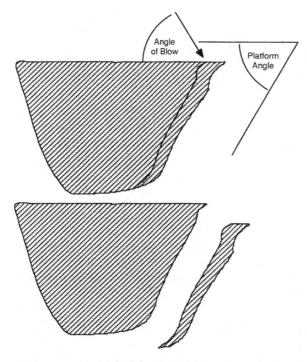

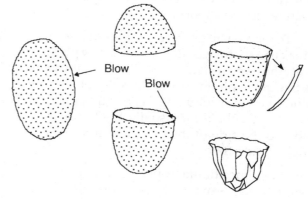

Figure 8.3. Starting a pyramidal core from a cobble.

Figure 8.2. Removal of a flake from a core.

tures. Just finding what seems to be a match, then, is not entirely convincing.

In spite of these problems, archaeologists have been quite successful in some regions in identifying the sources of high-quality knapping materials, such as obsidian in Greece, the Near East, western North America, Mesoamerica, and the southern Pacific, and moderately successful at identifying some high-quality chert, such as Rama chert in eastern Canada.

Fracture Mechanics and Stone Tool Manufacture

Lithic manufacture is fundamentally a *reductive* technology. The flintknapper shapes artifacts by *removing* material from a core or flake. In particular, he or she does this by striking the core or flake at a particular angle and location, the idea being to cause **conchoidal fracture**. This kind of fracture involves a shock wave that radiates through the material from the point of impact in a conical fashion (figure 8.1). In flint, the angle between the direction of the impact and the sides of the cone is usually in the range of 120° to 160° (Hodges, 1964: 99), and flintknappers took advantage of this predict-

ability to make thin flakes of flint by directing the blow near an edge with an angle less than 90°. This truncated the cone so that the resulting flake had a surface nearly parallel to one surface of the core (figure 8.2).

To allow this, flintknappers often prepared cores so that they had shapes suitable for producing predictable flakes or blades. To make a simple **pyramidal core** suitable for making big flakes, all that was necessary was to find a good-size, roughly egg-shaped river cobble and break it in half by a sideways blow (figure 8.3). This left a flat area, called a **platform**, on each half that would serve as the surface upon which the flintknapper would direct subsequent blows. Note that the angle of the edge between the platform and the sides of the cobble is around 70° or 80°. Now, striking the platform near this edge at an angle of 70° or 80° in the opposite direction causes the cone of the shock wave to pass though the material at an angle 70° to 80° to the platform (~ 150° - 75°), nearly parallel to the side of the core. When the flint fractures along this wavefront, then, a thin flake will detach. Removing more flakes in a similar fashion around the perimeter of the core will gradually give it the shape of an upside-down pyramid or faceted cone, and eventually the angle between the platform and the sides of the core will become too great, or the core will get too small, for the core to continue to be useful. If the latter, the core will be "exhausted" and discarded; if the former, it could be discarded or, in some cases,

rejuvenated by creation of a new platform or even reused as a tool.

To rejuvenate a core, the flintknapper had to break it in such a way as to create a new platform with the appropriate platform angle, the angle between the platform and the sides of the core. Much as with producing the original platform on the river cobble, this usually involves a strong blow to the side of the core, but at a different angle (figure 8.4).

Sometimes flintknappers maintained more than one platform on the same core, alternately removing flakes first from one, and then another.

The basic techniques of core reduction that flintknappers used were hard-hammer percussion, soft-hammer percussion, indirect percussion, and pressure flaking.

Bipolar reduction is a simple way to produce many flakes, chips, and chunks with little control over their size or shape. It involves placing the core on an anvil and striking it from above with a large hammer to shatter it.

Hard-hammer percussion involves striking the core near the edge of the platform with a stone hammer, such as a rounded pebble.

Soft-hammer percussion involves striking the core with a hammer made of antler, bone, wood, or a material with similar characteristics. This kind of hammer is called a **billet, baton,** or **percussor.**

In **indirect percussion**, the flintknapper strikes, not the edge of the platform, but the upper end of a **punch** that has its lower end placed carefully near the platform's edge. This allows the flintknapper to control the location and angle of force very accurately, thus improving the predictability of the resulting flake or blade. The punch can be made of antler, but these wear out quickly, and modern flintknappers tend to use copper-tipped punches. Indirect percussion is commonly used to produce long blades from blade cores.

Pressure flaking works by pressing a flaker perpendicular to the edge of a flake rather than striking it, as you would with hard- or soft-hammer percussion. Although you cannot ap-

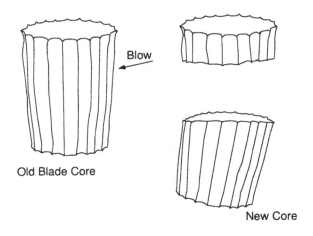

Figure 8.4. Rejuvenating a blade core by an angled blow to the side. Note that the resulting core (lower right) has a more acute platform angle on the right side.

ply as much force with pressure flaking, accuracy of flake removal is much improved. Pressure flaking is especially useful for **retouching** tools' edges — fine-tuning their shape, sharpening them where you want them to cut, or blunting them where you want to insert them into a haft or bind them with cord.

It is important to note that cores were not only used to remove flakes for use as tool blanks, but were often shaped into tools themselves. Such tools are called **core tools,** and include a variety of **bifaces** (core tools flaked on two sides) as well as other types.

The Anatomy of Flakes

Although there remain some differences in terminology, lithic analysts have developed some widely accepted, standard terms for the products of flintknapping and for features on them.

The main products of most kinds of flintknapping are **cores** or core tools and **flakes** that have been removed from cores. Flakes that are at least twice as long as they are wide are conventionally called **blades.** In France, where the term originated, and in the chaîne opératoire approach, **debitage** is the term for all the material removed from a core, including ones that result from shaping the core, flakes that could be used as tools or tool blanks, and unusable flakes

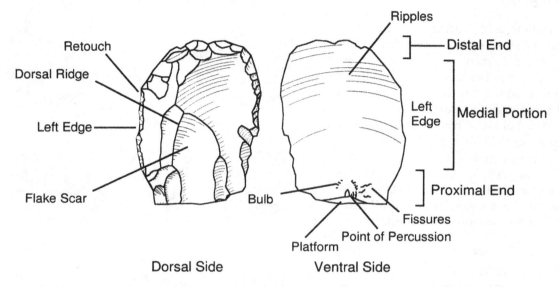

Figure 8.5. Common terms (segmentation rules) for describing the parts of a flake or blade.

and chunks called **debris** (Inizan et al., 1992:84). In North America, many lithic analysts use the term debitage differently, to refer to the waste products of core reduction, including discarded cores. Here we will attempt to avoid confusion by refering to debris and discarded cores as **waste**. Parts of broken flakes and cores are called **fragments**, and sections of snapped blades are called **segments**.

Flakes and cores exhibit some common features. Among these are **cortex**, consisting of the weathered surface that originally covered the raw material, the **platform** (on flakes, of course, you only find a tiny portion of the platform, and only on complete flakes or proximal fragments), and **scars** that resulted from previous flake removals (figure 8.5).

Complete flakes and blades (elongated flakes) that are the products of flintknapping typically show several distinctive features that help us to distinguish them from naturally broken stone or glass. At the **proximal end** we find a small portion of the striking platform. Next to this on the **ventral surface** (the face toward the center of the core) we usually find a small lip, and the **bulb of percussion**, a raised bump that results from compaction under the force of striking, especially by the hard-hammer technique. Sometimes there are several lines on the bulb, radiating away from the point of percussion on

the platform, called **radial fissures**. Then we find ripples that extend away from the point of percussion and the bulb like the waves in a still pond. These continue all along the ventral surface to the **distal end** (the end farthest from the point of percussion) and are very distinct in obsidian or fine-grained flints, less distinct in coarser flints and cherts, and nearly invisible in coarse materials. The side of the flake or blade that was on the outer part of the core prior to detachment is called the **dorsal surface**, and shows cortex, if the flake is from the outermost part of the core, or the traces of previous flake removals, called **flake scars**, or both. The sharp ridge that marks the border between flake scares is called an **arris** or **dorsal ridge**. Flakes that show any cortex at all on their dorsal surface are called **cortical flakes** or **primary flakes**. They are quite important because they provide information on some of the first steps in core reduction. Although some naturally broken flakes may show bulbs of percussion, ripples, or radial fissures, this happens relatively rarely. Any assemblage of flakes that shows these features quite consistently is almost certainly the product of artificial flaking. Naturally shattered flint, often produced by weathering, tends instead to have lots of right-angles and flat surfaces that follow the planes of the material's crystalline structure.

Lithic Attributes

Although there is an infinity of attributes that we could measure on any lithic artifact, lithic analysts routinely measure some attributes that they believe are relevant to understanding how tools were made, what they were designed to do, and to what complex or culture an assemblage might belong. They also measure ones that help them to identify the sources and characteristics of raw materials, to discover the way tools were actually used, and to solve other problems that will be discussed in later sections. Some are attributes that occur on all kinds of flakes or blades, others only on certain kinds of tools (e.g., Dibble, 1987), and others are specific to waste (Burton, 1980; Henry et al., 1976). The following is a sample of very basic attributes used to characterize the technology and design of stone tools and the waste products of their manufacture, with emphasis on ones that are fairly straightforward to measure.

Attributes of Cores

Generally speaking, archaeologists find cores that were discarded once they were approaching, or reached, the point where they were no longer useful. The latter are *exhausted cores*. Occasionally we find the flakes that had been removed from these cores and can refit them to find out what the core looked like in earlier stages of reduction, or we find cores that were discarded before exhaustion. Yet even exhausted cores can show us some clues as to the strategy or strategies used to reduce them.

Among the kinds of technological attributes we can observe on cores are the raw material, the type of core preparation, if any, the number of platforms, the means of flake removal, the directions from which flakes were removed, overall core shape, and the intensity with which raw material seems to have been used.

As we have seen, we could use a simple cobble as a core, but some technologies involved intentionally shaping the core so that flake removals would be more predictable. For example, **Levallois** technology involved preparing cores by removing flakes bifacially around the perimeter, so that the "production face" is less

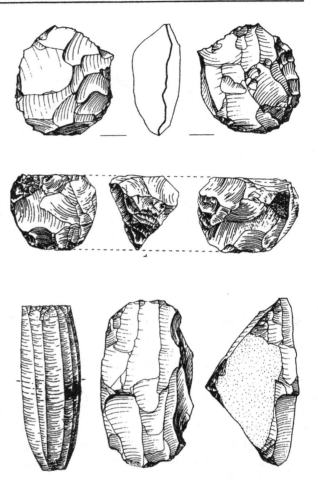

Figure 8.6. Some classes of cores: discoidal (top), amorphous (middle), bullet or pyramidal blade core (lower left), and "naviform" bidirectional blade core.

convex than the "platform face," and then removing blanks from the production face (Boëda, 1995; Van Peer, 1992). In other cases, only the platform was carefully shaped, to make it easier to control the location of percussion, for example.

In addition to single-platform cores, there are bidirectional cores (with a platform at each end), multi-directional cores, and "amorphous" cores (figure 8.6). In the Near Eastern Pre-Pottery Neolithic B, for example, blade blanks were made on narrow, boat-shaped, bidirectional cores that allowed the flintknapper to remove very consistent blades alternately from the two platforms.

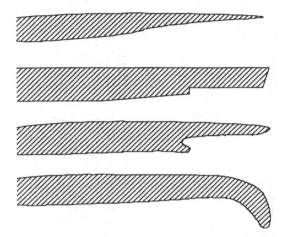

Figure 8.7. Fracture terminations: feather, step, hinge, and plunging.

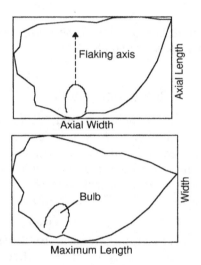

Figure 8.8. Alternative ways to measure a flake's "length" and "width."

By studying the platform angles and negatives of the bulbs of percussion, we attempt to determine whether core reduction was by hard- or soft-hammer or indirect percussion, or by punch.

Attributes of Flakes and Blanks

When a satisfactory flake detaches from a core, the tool maker can discard it, save it for potential use in future, use it as is, or use it as a **blank** for making a retouched tool.

Conventionally, archaeologists use a nominal scale to characterize the forms of flakes. Common categories include blade and triangle. They also use measures on the ratio scale, but researchers vary in how they characterize size and shape (Cullberg et al., 1975; Dibble, 1985; 1987). For example, they use different orientations for the axes of linear measurements. Length can be measured along the longest axis, or along the axis of flaking ("debitage axis") (figure 8.8). Width can be measured perpendicular to the axis of length, or along a different axis, and at the artifact's widest part, or midway along its length. Measurement of thickness can vary substantially in its location. A common practice is to record maximum thickness, but there are alternatives. The most common shape measure is the simple ratio of length/width. It is used, among other things, in the most common definition of blades as any flake with a length/width ratio of 2.0 or greater. Some other shape measures are intended to summarize the "pointedness" of flakes and finished tools (figure 8.12). Because the exact definitions of these measures can vary, it is extremely important to make it clear to your readers how you defined the measures you made.

Some nominal-scale measures are related to the technology of flake production. Platform shape, as viewed from above the proximal end of a flake, may tell us something about core preparation and the blow used in striking. Whether the dorsal flake scars show that previous flake removals were all from the same direction as the current flake (unidirectional), or from two directions but parallel to the flaking axis of the current flake (bidirectional or alternate), or at right angles to the axis of the current flake, or from many directions, will also tell us something about how cores were prepared or used. The nature of the flake termination at the distal end is also conventionally measured on a nominal scale. The flake may show a **feather fracture**, a **hinge fracture**, or a **step fracture**, for example (figure 8.7). In addition, a blade may show that the crack from flaking went too far and curved in towards the core, producing what is called an **overshot** or **plunging termination**. In that case the distal ends's dorsal surface shows the bottom surface of the core and the distal end is often

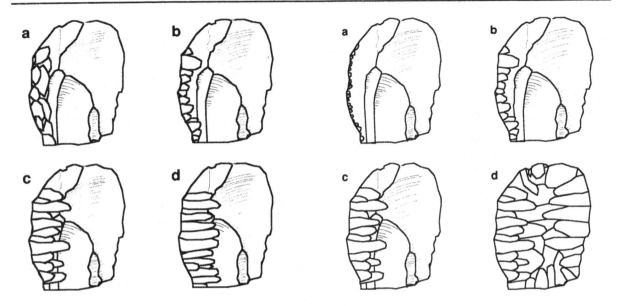

Figure 8.9. Retouch flake scar types: scaled (a), stepped (b), sub-parallel (c), and parallel (d).

Figure 8.10. Extent of retouch: short (a), long (b), invasive (c), and covering (d).

quite thick. These kinds of information not only help us infer how particular tools were made, and how knappers dealt with flaking errors, but are relevant to the kinds of activities that took place at the site.

Prominence of the bulb of percussion can be measured on an ordinal scale with at least a loose relationship to the force and technique of striking (strong blows with a hard hammer produce more prominent bulbs). However, it is also possible to measure the position and height of the bulb on a ratio scale (Gallet, 1998:35).

Some of the important measures related to flaking technology are angles measured on either ordinal or ratio scales. The exterior platform angle, often simply described as **platform angle**, is the angle between the plane of the platform and the exterior (dorsal) surface of a flake or core (figure 8.2). It will almost always be less than 90°, because it is impossible to create proper flakes with platform angles greater than a right angle. Other angles on the platform may also be important (Gallet, 1998:33).

Attributes of Retouched Tools

Once a blank has been retouched, it is recognizably a tool. Unretouched tools, by contrast, can only be recognized if they show traces of use, such as polish or micro-scratches, or were produced through very controlled core reduction, as with unretouched Levallois points.

Typological approaches to stone tools resulted in many nominal categories for the shapes and retouch characteristics of retouched tools. These include bifaces (made from cores or thick flakes), lunates, and many kinds of points. Lithic analysts often use variations of standardized classifications that were designed for a particular group of lithic complexes, such as the European Paleolithic (Bordes, 1961) or North African Mesolithic (Tixier, 1974). Historically, archaeologists have tended to assume that these morphological types were related to the intended function of the tools, but more recent lithic analysts urge caution in equating form with function. The types are also used to compare assemblages and measure their cultural similarity.

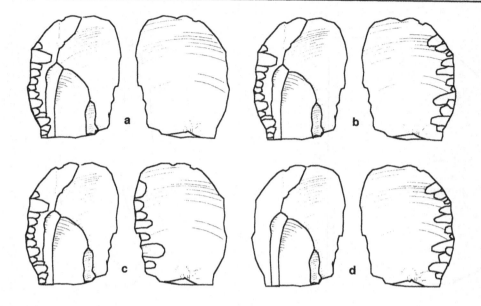

Figure 8.11. Position of Retouch: Direct (a), Bifacial (b), Alternate (c), and Inverse (d).

We can also use a nominal scales for the location and type of retouch (figures 8.9, 8.11). An endscraper, for example, has steep retouch at one end that will hold its shape even under the stress of heavy scraping work. A backed blade has steep retouch, or **backing**, along one of its long edges, presumably to prevent it from cutting into fingers or hafting material. Common categories for retouch are direct, inverse, alternate, and bifacial (figure 8.11). We measure location of retouch relative to the axis of flaking and the point of percussion. Although it is possible to measure the latter in degrees with 0° along the axis of flaking, this is not a ratio-scale measure. You are simply labelling a location with a convenient number that happens to have some common-sense order, just as with compass directions and map coordinates, and it would be nonsense to suggest that a retouch location of, say, 190° is in any sense greater than one of 40°. If, however, you measured *length* of the retouched area in degrees, rather than in millimeters (thus using a length definition based on the radial extent of an arc rather than on a line segment), that would be a ratio-scale measurement. A retouched edge that extends over 80°

would be twice as long, relative to the size of the artifact, as one that extends over 40°. Because retouch typically occurs during the final shaping, hafting, and resharpening of tools, these retouch measures tend to be highly relevant to the designed functions and final uses of the tools.

Some of the ordinal-scale measures are related to both flake production and retouch. Steepness and invasiveness of retouch, for example, are often measured on ordinal scales (figure 8.10).

Steepness of retouch is the angle between the flat plane of a flake and a retouched surface. On a unifacial flake this might simply be the angle between the ventral surface and the retouched surface. Note that this retouch angle is likely to vary along a retouched edge, so you should measure it more than once and average the results (with appropriate error estimate) if you are using a ratio scale.

Attributes of Waste and Debris

Waste and debris are becoming increasingly important to our understanding of prehistoric technologies. Because debris consists of chips

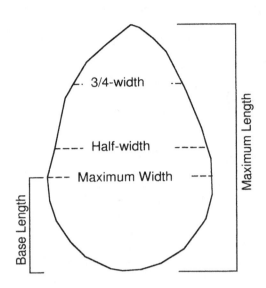

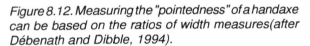

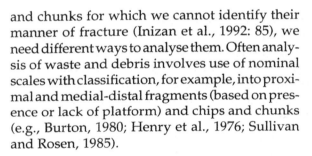

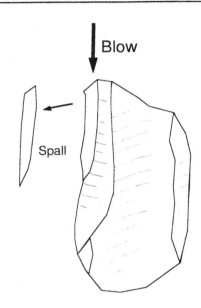

Figure 8.12. Measuring the "pointedness" of a handaxe can be based on the ratios of width measures (after Débenath and Dibble, 1994).

Figure 8.13. Removal of a burin spall.

and chunks for which we cannot identify their manner of fracture (Inizan et al., 1992: 85), we need different ways to analyse them. Often analysis of waste and debris involves use of nominal scales with classification, for example, into proximal and medial-distal fragments (based on presence or lack of platform) and chips and chunks (e.g., Burton, 1980; Henry et al., 1976; Sullivan and Rosen, 1985).

For example, a site with lots of evidence for hard-hammer primary core reduction of a particular kind, but no evidence for finishing tools, might be a place where flintknappers roughed out cores that they would use to make finished tools somewhere else. Another assemblage in which technological evidence indicated a lot of retouch and modification of finished tools, but no primary core reduction, might be a place where hunters repaired their hunting kit while waiting in ambush for their prey. A third might have a technology that suggests extremely economizing behavior in the use of the raw material, indicating, perhaps, that the material was difficult to obtain.

Illustrating Lithic Attributes

Technical drawings of lithics summarize many of the important nominal and ratio measurements. Some of the conventions used on lithic illustrations are worthy of mention (see chapter 16). For example, an arrow is used on drawings of burins to indicate the location and direction of a burin spall's removal (figure 8.13). A burin is a tool, often thought to have been used as an engraving tool, that has a small, chisel-like working edge produced by removal of a **spall**. Fine stippling may be used to indicate the location and extent of silica polish on sickle blades (figure 8.14), while coarser stippling usually indicates the extent of cortex on cores and cortical flakes. You should consult chapter 16 and published guides (e.g., Addington, 1986; Chase, 1985) if you are planning to draw stone tools.

The Replication of Stone Tools

Since the 1960s, one of the key skills that lithic analysts have sought to acquire has been the ability to knap flint. Flintknapping gives researchers a "feel" for the material and its potential, some understanding of the design problems that prehistoric flintknappers probably encountered, and, incidentally, an appreciation for the

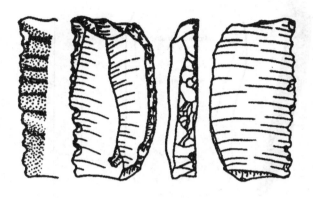

Figure 8.14. "Sickle polish" indicated by stippling next to the polished edge of a blade segment (drawing by J. Pfaff).

skill and artistry of prehistory's best flintknappers. Experimental flint-knapping can be used to test hypotheses about how certain tools *may* have been made, or about the relationships between particular kinds of tool manufacture and the debitage they produce. The products of flintknapping, replicated tools, are also useful for experimental work to test their usefulness for particular tasks, such as tree-cutting (Steensberg, 1980), or to study the relationship between such tasks and the use-wear that results (see below).

There is no substitute for actual practice with lithic raw material, hammerstones, and batons, under the supervision of a skilled flintknapper, but there is some very good literature on the replication of stone tools. Crabtree (1972) was one of the pioneers of modern flintknapping, while Whittaker (1994) is an accessible and excellent introduction to the subject. Safety is an important issue in this kind of research.

GROUND-STONE TOOLS

Archaeologists conventionally distinguish flaked stone tools, which have been the focus of this chapter up to this point, from what they call ground-stone tools, even though many of these tools were neither manufactured through grinding nor used for grinding. They range from minimally modified cobbles used to break nuts or to hammer flakes from a core, through intricately shaped sculptures and ornaments. Most of the ground-stone artifacts with which archaeologists concern themselves, however, are much simpler ornaments and milling tools that were used to process foodstuffs, including nuts, maize, wheat, and legumes, as well as pigments, pharmaceuticals, pottery temper, and other materials.

While these milling tools can have many functions, they attract particular interest for their probable role in the beginnings of food production. Grinding seeds into flour makes them easier to digest, facilitates their use in new kinds of food, such as bread, reduces cooking time, and increases their nutritional value (K. Wright, 1992; 1993a; 1994).

The Manufacture of Ground-Stone Tools

In spite of their common name, ground-stone tools are made of a variety of materials and by a variety of manufacturing techniques. Nor are they all "grinding stones." Basalt, sandstone, dolomitic limestone, slate, and other stones are common raw materials (Moore, 1983). The function for which the tool was intended may sometimes have dictated use of a harder or softer stone, or one that was vesicular (basalt) or coarse-grained (sandstone) to make the tool more abrasive, or fine-grained to allow a smoother surface. As with flaked core tools, shaping the tool often began with flaking, unless a cobble that already had approximately the right shape could be found. After roughing out the shape, however, the tool-makers could employ a combination of pecking, grinding, drilling, cutting, and polishing to achieve the desired shape and surface characteristics (Hayden, 1987; Horsfall, 1987; Huckell, 1986; Schneider et al., 1996; E. Wright, 1988; K. Wright, 1992).

Reconstructing the reduction sequence for ground-stone tools, however, can be more difficult than for flaked ones because there may be little debitage to aid us while later stages of reduction and use typically eradicate traces of earlier manufacturing techniques. Information on manufacture often comes from analysis of quarry waste (Huckell, 1986; Nelson, 1987; Schneider et al., 1996).

Because some ground-stone tools are only slightly modified natural cobbles, it is sometimes difficult, especially in the field, to be certain that a particular stone is an artifact at all. The smoothed surface of a stone that had been used with a grinding or polishing motion, for example, may show a flattened surface that truncates the natural irregularities in the stone's surface, instead of rounding them as erosion would do.

The Anatomy of Common Ground-Stone Tools

The immense variety of "ground-stone" tools makes it difficult to create a consistent scheme for describing them, so terms tend to be specific to particular kinds of tools. Here we will concentrate on some of the most common kinds: grinding slabs or querns (also called *metates* or lower milling stones), handstones or *manos*, mortars, and pestles. Ground-stone ornaments, hammers, axes, maces, shaft-straighteners, spindle-whorls, weights, pipes, and other tools require quite different terminology (cf. K. Wright, 1993b).

In general, these kinds of tools, variously used for pressing, pounding, crushing, pulverizing, or grinding seeds and many other materials, occur in sets of two distinct tools. One is a relatively fixed, lower tool, its use surface generally upward; the other is an upper tool, its use surface mainly downward, which its user moves up-and-down, back-and-forth in a repetitive motion or in a circular motion against the use surface of the lower tool. Hand stones are the upper members associated with grinding slabs, while pestles are the upper members for mortars. In some cases, there may be a rotating upper or lower member, as with the millstones of Roman or mediaeval Europe (Carelli and Kresten, 1997), or the upper member may roll in a tight circle, as in some European olive presses.

Grinding slabs, querns, or *metates* are relatively large, generally elongated and fairly flat pieces of stone with a table-like or concave use surface upon which the material to be ground

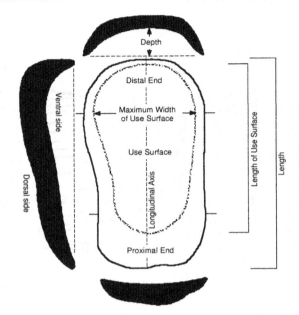

Figure 8.15. Orientation and terminology for describing a grinding slab or quern. The ticks indicate the positions of the two transverse sections. The longitudinal section is along the longitudinal axis (modified from Wright, 1992:497-98).

can lie. In use, the quern would be oriented with its long axis pointing away from its user, and use surface either upward or sloping down away from the user, sometimes with one end resting on knees. The user would lean forward to push a handstone across the quern's surface so that seeds or other materials were crushed between them, and the ground material was pushed off the far end to fall into a container. Where this is the case, the end resting on the knees may be thinner (until the stone has experienced considerable use-wear), or the end away from the user may show accentuated concavity or wear close to the edge, allowing us to distinguish the distal and proximal ends of the quern. The use surface occurs on the ventral side, which normally is oriented upwards, while the unused and often rather rough surface is the dorsal side (figure 8.15). To either side of the use surface are the lateral sides or edges.

Mortars have most of the same features as querns except that they are round or nearly round in plan view, so that there are no ends or lateral sides. The ventral (upward) surface shows

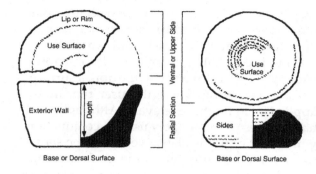

Figure 8.16. Some terminology for describing a mortar. As with drawings of pottery or bottles (chapter 17), we show a radial section or "cutaway" on one half of the lateral or side view, but also show a ventral view of the use surface (modified from Wright, 1992:497-98).

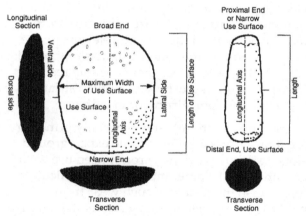

Figure 8.17. Some terminology for describing unifacial handstones (left) and bidirectional pestles (right) (modified from Wright, 1992:497-98).

a bowl-like concavity or opening, often more pronounced than in querns and sometimes very deep, while the dorsal surface can be a flat base or be more convex (figure 8.16). The use surface may be the entire surface of the concavity, or only its lower portion, distinguished by battering or wear that may not occur in the upper part of the opening. Some tall mortars have relatively thin and nearly vertical side-walls, having been shaped much like deep pottery bowls. Others are more squat with sides that are rounded in radial section. In some cases, prolonged use of a mortar has worn through its bottom, resulting in a perforation. In some cases, mortars were permanent facilities in bedrock, rather than portable artifacts, in which case they

have no dorsal surface. Some very small artifacts shaped like mortars may actually be the cap stones for bow drills, used as the socket in which the drill shaft rotated.

Handstones are ovoid, domed, or bun-shaped stones, usually with a fairly flat or slightly convex ventral use surface and a convex dorsal arch that is high enough to provide a useful grip (unifacial handstone, figure 8.17). Bifacial handstones have use surfaces on two opposite sides, so that we cannot distinguish ventral from dorsal. Typically handstones are somewhat elongated, but it is usually impossible to distinguish proximal from distal ends, especially as users may have turned them from time to time to discourage uneven wear, except arbitrarily or by width (narrow and broad ends). In other cases they are rather circular in plan, so that we cannot distinguish ends at all.

Pestles are elongated, cylindrical, or conical tools with one or two convex use surfaces that occur on the ends. In some cases there may be additional features, such as decorative ends. Only where there was a single use surface can we distinguish the distal end (at the use surface) from the proximal end, which provides a handle (figure 8.17). In conical pestles, the use surface and distal end often occur at the wider end, but this is not universal.

Some Attributes of Ground-Stone Tools

As stressed in previous chapters, the attributes you would measure on ground-stone tools would depend on your research questions, but this section will briefly present a few ideas on how you might proceed.

Among the research questions that might be of interest we might include the following: What properties of the stone itself made it suitable or desirable for this particular processing task? Where did the stone come from? How was the grinding stone made? What was the material processed with the grinding stone? What motion was used to process it? Was the processing intended to crush the material slightly, or to pulverize it? Was the material wet or dry? How much of the material could be processed in one hour? How long had the tool been used?

Many of these questions we can approach with exactly the same methods as for chipped-stone tools, such as the sourcing of raw materials, or chemical analysis of use-residues (Yohe et al., 1991). Others involve only modifications of those approaches, such as examination for use traces that might distinguish crushing from grinding or back-and-forth from circular grinding (Adams, 1988; 1989). A few may require methods specifically tailored to ground-stone tools.

Among the last we might include design features related to the substance being ground or pounded and the motions used to accomplish the task. We would expect characteristics of the use surface to be particularly important in this respect, but should keep in mind alterations that may have occurred during use as well. The dimensions, curvature, and texture or roughness of the use surface are among these (Cotterell and Kamminga, 1990: 151-55).

For querns, we might expect the length of the use surface to be related to the length of stroke for a single pass of the handstone, while its overall area may be loosely associated with the amount of material being ground. The thickness of querns at their two ends, and striations on the use-surface itself, may provide clues to the way they were used. Vessicular or coarse querns may have ground some materials more quickly, but more finely textured querns may have been more suitable to mill flour for human consumption.

For mortars, we might consider the total volume of the concavity to have some relationship to the volume of material being pounded or pulverized, and the thickness of the mortar's walls relative to the use surface may provide some indication of the amount of force it was expected to withstand from the pestle. Whether the use surface shows chipping, circular striations, or both will tell us something about the motion of the pestle against the use surface. The diameter of the opening can be estimated for fragmentary mortars by using a diameter chart, just as with pottery (see below, p. 285).

For hand stones we might consider their overall mass, the area of the use surface, and the curvature of the use surface to be relevant to the way these stones were used. As with the other tools, striations on the use surface may help us decipher the motion of use, and whether this was unidirectional, circular, or multidirectional (Adams, 1988). Even wear on the dorsal surface, perhaps occurring where the user repeatedly applied force, might be relevant. Although most hand stones were probably used in conjunction with lower grinding slabs, we should be sensitive to the possibility that some, such as small, coarse ones, were used alone to remove hair from hides or for personal grooming, while other, smooth ones may have been used to burnish pottery.

For pestles we would again expect the overall mass to have some bearing on the force they were expected to apply to the material being pounded or ground. The area and curvature of the use surface might also be relevant to use, while careful examination might show small chips on the use surface that probably resulted from pounding or crushing, or circular striations that resulted from stirring or grinding.

Because pounding and especially grinding are abrasive processes, we would expect ground-stone tools to experience pronounced use wear (Adams, 1988). Sometimes it will be difficult to distinguish the results of such wear from original design features of, for example, the curvature of a mortar's use surface. Among the measurements that might be relevant to the design or use-life of grinding stones are the depth and curvature of querns and mortars. Presumably, they get deeper with use, and in querns the wear may occur disproportionately at the distal end. An easy way to quantify the depth of the concavity in either a quern or a mortar is to place a straight-edge across the ventral surface, and then measure the perpendicular distance from the straight-edge to the deepest part of the concavity, taking care to avoid minor irregularities in the surface. If the concavity is hemispherical, and you also measure its width or length where the straight-edge is resting (this length is called the *cord*), you will have all the information you need to measure indirectly the overall curvature of the use surface along one axis. If r is the radius of curvature, 2a is the length of the cord, and d is the depth perpendicular to the cord,

$$r = \frac{a^2 + d^2}{2d}$$

Detailed analysis of ground-stone tools has had a much shorter history than that of chipped stone, and we should expect many new developments in this area in the next decade.

RESEARCH ON CHIPPED AND GROUND LITHICS

The Function and Use of Stone Tools

Although archaeologists have traditionally used functional names for some kinds of stone tools — scraper, projectile point, axe, chopper, and drill, for example — in fact the intended and actual uses of these tools is often far from obvious. Today, although we continue to use these labels, we do not assume that they necessarily describe the tools' actual functions. In some cases, such as common grinding stones that have abundant relevant analogies among ethnographically documented people, the argument for their function by analogous morphology may be so strong that few archaeologists would bother to challenge it. Even then, although we might agree that the tool was used for grinding, it might not be obvious whether it was used for grinding nuts, maize, pharmaceuticals, minerals, or some other material.

Here we should make a distinction between the intended use or designed function of a tool — the function that the flintknapper had in mind when he or she made it — and the actual use (or even last use) of the tool. This is particularly important because tools can have more than one designed function and, furthermore, can be used for many purposes that their designer never envisaged. An oft-cited example from our own culture is that screwdrivers, although designed for driving screws, are also the usual tool for opening paint cans. Even though they were never designed for this purpose, they are very effective at it. Ethnographic and ethnoarchaeological studies have shown that many relatively modern users of stone tools viewed them as multi-purpose tools (e.g., White, 1967).

Having replicated a type of stone artifact and, in some cases, having hafted it in a plausible manner, an archaeologist can get some idea of how it *might* have been used by experiment. For example, you could try to chop down trees with an axe-like tool (Steensberg, 1980) or try to harvest wheat with a sickle made from blades (Unger-Hamilton, 1985). In some cases you might find that the tool does not work very well at all. This means either that you have hypothesized the wrong function for the tool, or that you have hafted it incorrectly, or that you are not using it properly (wrong force or motion). If, on the other hand, it works quite well, you have only demonstrated by analogy that it *could* have been used that way, and there may be hundreds of other functions for which it would be equally suitable.

In an attempt to strengthen the hypothesis that a tool was used for a particular function, lithic analysts have increasingly turned to a combination of experiment and examination of microscopic evidence of scratches, wear, polish, and residues to infer the use of stone tools.

This involves argument by analogy. Having used replicated stone tools on a number of different materials, and with different motions and number of repetitions, analysts examine the microscope traces of damage on the replicated tools edges and surfaces and compare them with those on prehistoric tools (Bamforth et al., 1990; Grace, 1988; 1996; Kamminga, 1982; Keeley, 1980; Odell and Odell-Vereecken, 1981; Shea, 1988; Tomenchuk, 1988; Young and Bamforth, 1990). If they can find one or more good matches, this allows a stronger inference of use than would be possible by either morphological analogy or experiment alone. The more care the analyst has taken to exhaust the possible motions of use and materials on which the tool is used, the stronger the inference. Failure to be exhaustive, just as in trying to source raw materials, leaves open the probability that there are alternative possible uses or motions of use that remain to be explored. Even if failure to find a match rules out a particular use, finding a match does not assure that the correct use has been identified, although it sometimes results in very strong probability.

Researchers who study use-traces on stone tools usually fall into one of three groups. One group uses high magnification and even Scanning Electron Microscopes (SEM) to study polish and extremely small scratches and striations (Jensen, 1988; Keeley, 1980). A second group is sceptical of the "high-power" approach and concentrates on scratches and striations that are visible under low magnification (e.g., 8x to 30x). A third attempts to identify organic residues that might come from the blood of butchered animals or the resins used as adhesives in hafted tools (Anderson, 1980; Hardy et al., 1997; Kooyman et al., 1992; Loy and Wood, 1989). Some researchers combine these approaches.

All these approaches have only recently gone through the early phases of development, scepticism, and revision, and should be applied with care. For example, post-depositional alteration (including wear in archaeologists' collection bags) could confuse analysis of use traces or obliterate the traces altogether. Careful sampling of lithics in the field specifically for these purposes, and protecting the sampled items by isolation in individual bags, is therefore necessary. Samples for chemical and DNA residues require protection from contamination both in the field and in the laboratory (see also Smith and Wilson, 1992).

Economizing Behavior and Design in Stone Tools

Some of the attributes that interest lithic analysts are ones that they believe are relevant to the costs and benefits of tools that differ in their design (Bamforth, 1986; Horsfall, 1987). These attributes are of particular interest to archaeologists who have adopted an economic-materialist theoretical perspective, and assume that hunters, farmers, flintknappers, and others in prehistory made decisions based on their rational evaluation of known alternatives that had different costs and benefits as measured in time, energy, effort, risk, or some other "currency." For example, for some hunting strategies, it may be desirable to have weapons that are highly reliable, while for other strategies it may be more important for the weapons to be easily and quickly maintainable (Bleed, 1986; Hughes, 1998; Hutchings, 1991; Knecht, 1997).

For a long time lithic analysts have observed variations in lithic assemblages that could be interpreted as evidence for increases in the economic "efficiency" of tool makers. For example, Mesolithic flintknappers were able to get many meters of usable edge out of the same nodule of flint that a Lower Paleolithic knapper would use to obtain only a few centimeters of edge.

More generally, lithic analysts tend to conclude that knappers practiced economizing behavior when average implement size is small, indicating either an intention to produce more flakes or blades from the same core, or there was repeated resharpening or reworking. The tendency to have several distinct usable edges, and different edge angles, per tool, also suggests that the same tool was used for several different tasks (Vierra, 1995).

Style in Stone Tools

Even though intended function, available technology, and raw materials place limitations on how a flintknapper makes a tool, there are still many ways to accomplish the same task that vary either substantially or in detail. Archaeologists often call **style** any variation in a tool that they cannot explain by variation in material, technology, or function (Close, 1978). They often assume that gross aspects of style are passed from generation to generation, although in gradually distorted form, by flintknappers teaching others their craft, but archaeologists differ in how they conceive of style.

Sackett (1977; 1982; 1990) offers a model for what he calls **isochrestic style**. He suggests that a number of alternative ways to make a tool would all satisfy its function, and that the form archaeologists find represents the tool-maker's choices among these alternatives in a particular context. We presume that this context included the traditions, knowledge, habits, and values of the person or group that made the tool, and so the selection among functionally equivalent alternatives was restricted. Thus, we would not expect two social groups widely separated in space and time to exhibit the same choices, while the degree of similarity between related groups would depend on the degree of social interaction. As in evolutionary theory, we essentially have selection operating on a set of variations. Sackett would call more deliberate use of style to signal group membership and other information symbolically, **iconic style**. Sackett (1990) notes that many researchers seem to restrict iconic style to "adjunct" aspects of form — the decorative or non-instrumental aspects — but iconic information can also be found latent in the isochrestic choices. Archaeologists who make use of design theory or evolutionary approaches often favor some version of the isochrestic model (e.g., Sheppard 1987).

Yet some ethnographic research indicates that style is not so passive. A high degree of social interaction, rather than leading to stylistic similarity, sometimes leads to stylistic divergence, as people, intentionally or not, emphasize social boundaries (Davis, 1990; Hodder, 1982; Wobst, 1977). Wiessner (1983; 1985; 1990) suggests that style constitutes a premeditated behavior meant to communicate social messages. She considers style to be variation that results from the human cognitive process of comparing styles and social identities. Like Sackett, she would say that style is found in both decorative and functional attributes, and calls styles with very distinct symbolic referents, **emblematic style**, while those with only vague associations with social identity, **assertive style**.

In addition, some research focusses on the most idiosyncratic levels of style, which appear to be due to individuals' differing motor habits and abilities (Hill and Gunn, 1977). These use methods much like those of handwriting analysis or the detection of art forgeries with the aim of identifying the output of individuals or workshops rather than ethnic or other large social groups.

It is important to note that the chaîne opératoire's emphasis on gesture and sequences of gestures, as embedded in learned cultural behavior, is very similar to some of these approaches to style (White, 1993).

Non-Use Alteration of Lithics

Although flint, chert, and other lithic raw materials are quite hard, making lithics one of the most abundantly preserved traces of prehistoric activities, they are not immutable. They can be damaged by a number of processes, including burning, trampling, weathering, and other cultural and geological processes. Some kinds of damage are visible with the naked eye; others are detectable with microscopic techniques.

Burning, which can result from the discard of flakes in a hearth or from the heat-treatment of chert to improve its flaking characteristics (Domanski and Webb, 1992; Flenniken and White 1983), often results in distinctive scars called **potlid fractures**. These are crater-like pits that result when when marked temperature differentials force round, dome-like flakes from the surface of the chert. In frost-prone regions, freezing and thawing may also cause potlids. Burning can also cause crazing, which looks like a network of small cracks on the surface. There are also archaeometric methods for detecting heat-treatment (Borradaile et al., 1993; Pavlish, 1978; Robins et al., 1978).

Trampling, especially where herd animals frequent the surface of an archaeological site, not only chips off the edges of flakes to destroy or obscure the prehistoric form, retouch, and use traces (Shea and Klenck, 1993), but can simulate intentional retouch with sometimes alarming success . Repeated stepping on a flake that has an edge resting on a small pebble can even result in notching. In areas where trampling by humans or animals is likely, you need to be very careful that any retouch you are measuring is the product of the prehistoric flintknapper and not of goats' hooves, for example.

Weathering can have a variety of effects. The principal one is hydration of the outer skin of the flint by humidity in the air and soil. This can result in a **patina** on the surface that has quite a different color than that of the underlying chert or flint (Nadel, 1993), so you should beware of sourcing raw materials on the basis of surface colour unless your lithics are unweathered. I have seen grey and brown flints from Syria take on a deep black patina around natural springs, while dark brown flints from some parts of Jordan have a white patina. Patina can take a long time to form, making it a very crude indicator of age, but the rate of weathering depends on environmental variables, especially temperature. Obsidian hydration dating is a dating method that depends on this rate. However, some assemblages presumably deposited at the same time have lithics both with and without patina. Flints that lie on the surface of deserts where they are exposed to bright sunlight and blowing sand can end up with potlid fractures from rapid heating on their upward surfaces, and sometimes show both abrasion on formerly sharp edges and a distinctive **desert varnish**, a thin, lustrous coating on the stone that results from the action of lichens or micro-organisms (Watson and Nash, 1997:90-91).

Conclusions

Lithics represent the most easily preserved artifacts that archaeologists ever encounter, and occur at sites ranging from well over a million years to only a few decades in age. Consequently they are one of the most important sources of evidence for human activities and cultural development over the human career. Lithic analysis, especially in combination with lithic replication and experimental archaeology, tends to focus on technological aspects of the evidence, as reflected by the bulk of the attributes that lithic analysts commonly measure. Other approaches, such as stylistic and use-oriented ones, are also common, however. And while most of the attention has been on chipped stone, many of the same analytical approaches, and new ones, are beginning to become common for "ground stone" tools. We can expect the latter to be important to our understanding of the food-producing revolution, so further research into grinding and pounding technologies is likely to be very rewarding.

References Cited

Adams, J. L., 1988, Use-wear analysis on manos and hide-processing stones. *Journal of Field Archaeology* 15:307-15.

— 1989, Methods for improving ground stone artifact analysis: Experiments in mano wear patterns. In *Experiments in Lithic Technology*, edited by D. S. Amick and R. P. Mauldin, pp. 259-76. BAR International Series 528. British Archaeological Reports, Oxford.

Addington, L. R., 1986, *Lithic Illustration. Drawing Flaked Stone Arfifacts for Publication*. University of Chicago Press, Chicago.

Anderson, P., 1980, A testimony of prehistoric tasks: Diagnostic residues on stone-tool working edges. *World Archaeology* 12:181-94.

Andrefsky, W., 1998, *Lithics: Macroscopic Approaches to Analysis*. Cambridge University Press, Cambridge.

Bamforth, D., 1986, Technological efficiency and tool curation. *American Antiquity* 51:38-50.

Bamforth, D., Burns, G. R., and Woodman, C., 1990, Ambiguous use traces and blind test results: New data. *Journal of Archaeological Science* 17:413-30.

Bleed, P., 1986, The optimal design of hunting weapons: Maintainability or reliability. *American Antiquity* 51:737-47.

Boëda, E., 1995, Levallois: A volumetric construction, methods, a technique. In *The Definition and Interpretation of Levallois Technology*, edited by H. Dibble and O. Bar-Yosef, pp. 41-68. Prehistory Press, Madison, WI.

Bordes, F., 1961, *Typologie du Paléolithique Ancien et Moyen*. Publication de l'Institut de Préhistoire de l'Université de Bordeaux. Memoire 1. Imprimeries Delmas, Bordeaux.

Borradaile, G. J., Kissin, S. A., Stewart, J. D., Ross, W. A., and Werner, T., 1993, Magnetic and optical methods for detecting the heat treatment of chert. *Journal of Archaeological Science* 20:57-66.

Burton, J., 1980, Making sense of waste flakes, *Journal of Archaeological Science* 7:131-48.

Carelli, P., and Kresten, P., 1997, Give us this day our daily bread: A study of Late Viking Age and Medieval quernstones in south Scandinavia. *Acta Archaeologica* 68:109-37.

Chase, P. G., 1985, Illustrating lithic artifacts: Information for scientific illustration. *Lithic Technology* 14(2):57-70.

Chazan, M., 1997, Redefining Levallois. *Journal of Human Evolution* 33:719-735.

Close, A. E., 1978, The identification of style in lithic artifacts. *World Archaeology* 10:223-36.

Cotterell, B., and Kamminga, J., 1990, *Mechanics of Pre-Industrial Technology*. Cambridge University Press, Cambridge.

Crabtree, D. E., 1972, *An Introduction to Flintworking*. Occasional Papers No. 28. Idaho State University Museum, Pocatello.

Cullberg, C., Oldén, A., Pehrsson, N.-G., and Sandberg, B., 1975, Some quantitative methods applied to flake-measuring problems. *Norwegian Archaeological Review* 8:81-97.

Davis, W., 1990, Style and history in art history. In *The Uses of Style in Archaeology*, edited by M. Conkey and C. A. Hastorf, pp. 18-31. Cambridge University Press, Cambridge.

Debénath, A., and Dibble, H. L., 1994, *Handbook of Paleolithic Typology: Lower and Middle Paleolithic of Europe*. University Museum, University of Pennsylvania, Philadelphia.

Dibble, H. L., 1985, Technological aspects of flake variation. *American Archaeology* 5:236-40.

— 1987, The interpretation of Middle Paleolithic scraper morphology. *American Antiquity* 52:109-17.

Dixon, J. E., Cann, J. R., and Renfrew, C., 1968, Obsidian and the origins of trade. *Scientific American* 218(3):38-46.

Domanski, M., and Webb, J. A., 1992, Effect of heat treatment on siliceous rocks used in prehistoric lithic technology. *Journal of Archaeological Science* 19:601-14.

Edmonds, M., 1995, *Stone Tools and Society. Working Stone in Neolithic and Bronze Age Britain*. B. T. Batsford, London.

Flenniken, J. J., and White, J. P., 1983, Heat treatment of siliceous rocks and its implications for Australian prehistory. *Australian Aboriginal Studies* 1:43-47.

Gallet, M., 1998, *Pour une Technologie des Débitages Laminares Préhistoriques*. Dossier de Documentation Archéologique 19. CNRS Editions, Paris.

Gero, J. M., 1991, Genderlithics: Women's roles in stone tool production. In *Engendering Archaeology*, edited by J. Gero and M. W. Conkey, pp. 163-93. Basil Blackwell, Oxford.

Grace, R., 1988, *A Multi-dimensional Approach to the Study of the Function of Stone Tools*. Unpublished Ph.D thesis, Institute of Archaeology, University of London.

— 1996, Use-wear analysis: The state of the art. *Archaeometry* 38:209-29.

Hardy, B. L., Raff, R. A., and Raman, V., 1997, Recovery of mammalian DNA from Middle Paleolithic stone tools. *Journal of Archaeological Science* 24:606-11.

Hayden, B., 1977, *Lithic Analysis*. Academic Press, New York.

— 1987, Traditional metate manufacturing in Guatemala using chipped stone tools. In *Lithic Studies among the Contemporary Highland Maya*, edited by B. Hayden, pp. 8-119. University of Arizona Press, Tucson.

Henry, D., Haynes, V., and Bradley, B., 1976, Quantitative variations in flaked stone debitage, *Plains Archaeologist* 21:57-61.

Hill, J. and Gunn, J., eds, 1977, *The Individual in Prehistory* Academic Press, New York.

Hodder, I., 1982, *Symbols in Action: Ethnoarchaeological Studies of Material Culture*. Cambridge University Press, Cambridge.

Hodges, H., 1964, *Artifacts. An Introduction to Early Materials and Technology*. John Baker, London.

Horsfall, G. A., 1987, Design theory and grinding stones. In *Lithic Studies among the Contemporary Highland Maya*, edited by B. Hayden, pp. 332-77. University of Arizona Press, Tucson.

Huckell, B., 1986, *A Ground Stone Implement Quarry on the Lower Colorado River, Northwestern Arizona*. USBLM Cultural Resource Series 3. U. S. Bureau of Land Management, Phoenix.

Hughes, S. S., 1998, Getting to the point: Evolutionary change in prehistoric weaponry. *Journal of Archaeological Method and Theory* 5:345-408.

Hutchings, W. K., 1991, *The Nachcharini Composite Projectile Point: Design Theory and the Study of Hunting Systems Technology at Mugharel-Nachcharini in the Post-Natufian Levant*. M.A. thesis, University of Toronto.

Inizan, M.-L., Roche, H., and Tixier, J., 1992, *Technology of Knapped Stone*. Préhistoire de la Pierre Taillée 3. Cercle de Recherche et d'Etudes Préhistoriques and CNRS, Meudon.

Jensen, J. H., 1988, The functional analysis of prehistoric tools by high-power microscopy: A review of the West European approach. *Journal of World Prehistory* 2:52-87.

Johnson, J. K., and Morrow, C. A., eds., 1987, *The Organization of Core Technology*. Westview Press, London.

Kamminga, B., 1982, *Over the Edge: Functional Analysis of Australian Stone Tools*. Occasional Papers in Archaeology 12. University of Queensland, Brisbane.

Keeley, L., 1980, *Experimental Determination of Stone Tool Uses: A Microwear Analysis*. University of Chicago Press, Chicago.

Knecht, H., ed., 1997, *Projectile Technology*. Plenum Publishing, New York.

Kooyman, B., Newman, M. E., and Ceri, H., 1992, Verifying the reliability of blood residue analysis on archaeological tools. *Journal of Archaeological Science* 19:265-69.

Loy, T. H., and Wood, A. R., 1989, Blood-residue analysis at Çayönü Tepesi, Turkey. *Journal of Field Archaeology* 16:451-60.

Luedtke, B. E., 1992, *An Archaeologist's Guide to Chert and Flint*. Archaeological Research Tools 7, Institute of Archaeology, University of California, Los Angeles.

Maggi, R., Campana, N., Negrino, F., and Ottomano, C., 1994, The quarrying and workshop site of Valle Lagorara (Liguria — Italy). *The Accordia Research Papers* 5:73-96.

Mellars, P., 1996, *The Neanderthal Legacy. An Archaeological Perspective from Western Europe*. Princeton University Press, Princeton.

Moore, D. T., 1983, Petrological aspects of some sharpening stones, touchstones, and milling stones. In *The Petrology of Archaeological Artefacts*, edited by R. C. Kempe and A. P. Harvey, pp. 277-300. Clarendon Press, Oxford.

Morrow, T. M., 1996, Lithic refitting and archaeological site formation processes. A case study from the Twin Ditch site, Greene County, Illinois. In *Stone Tools. Theoretical Insights into Human Prehistory*, edited by G. H. Odell, pp. 345-73. Plenum Press, New York.

Nadel, D., 1993, Patination of flint artefacts: Evidence from Bikta, a submerged prehistoric occurrence in the Sea of Galilee, Israel. *Journal of the Israel Prehistoric Society* 25:145-62.

Nelson, M. C., 1987, Site content and structure: Quarries and workshops in the Maya Highlands. In *Lithic Studies among the Contemporary Highland Maya*, edited by B. Hayden, pp. 120-47. University of Arizona Press, Tucson.

Odell, G. H., ed., 1996, *Stone Tools. Theoretical Insights into Human Prehistory*. Plenum Press, New York.

Odell, G. H., and Odell-Vereecken, F., 1981, Verifying the the reliability of lithic use-wear assessment by "blind tests": The low-power approach. *Journal of Field Archaeology* 7:87-120.

Pavlish, L. A., 1978, Thermoluminescent (TL) determination of prehistoric heat treatment of chert artefacts. *Science* 197:1359-62.

Pelcin, A. W., 1997, The formation of flakes: The role of platform thickness and exterior platform angle in the production of flake initiations and terminations. *Journal of Archaeological Science* 24:1107-13.

Robins, G. V., Seeley, N. J., McNeil, D. A. C., and Symons, M. R. C., 1978, Identification of ancient heat treatment in flint artefacts by ESR spectroscopy. *Nature* 276:703-704.

Sackett, J. R., 1977, The meaning of style in archaeology. *American Antiquity* 42:369-80.

— 1982, Approaches to style in lithic archaeology. *Journal of Anthropological Archaeology* 1:59-112.

— 1990, Style and ethnicity in archaeology: The case for isochrestism. In *The Uses of Style in Archaeology*, edited by M. Conkey and C. A. Hastorf, pp. 32-43. Cambridge University Press, Cambridge.

Schiffer, M. B., 1976, *Behavioral Archaeology*. Academic Press, New York.

Schneider, J. S., Lerch, M. K., and Smith, G. A., 1996, Quarrying and production of milling implements at Antelope Hill, Arizona. *Journal of Field Archaeology* 23:299-310.

Sellet, F., 1993, Chaîne Opératoire: The concept and its applications. *Lithic Technology* 18:106-112.

Shea, J., 1988, Methodological considerations affecting the choice of analytical techniques in use-wear analysis: Tests, results and applications. In *Industries Lithiques: Traceologie et Technologie*, edited by S. Beyries, pp. 83-97. BAR International Series 411. British Archaeological Reports, Oxford.

Shea, J. J., and Klenck, J. D., 1993, An experimental investigation of the effects of trampling on results of lithic microwear analysis. *Journal of Archaeological Science* 20:175-94.

Sheppard, P. J., 1987, *The Capsian of North Africa. Stylistic Variation in Stone Tool Assemblages*. BAR International Series 353. British Archaeological Reports, Oxford.

Smith, P. R., and Wilson, M. T., 1992, Blood residues on ancient tool surfaces: A cautionary note. *Journal of Archaelogical Science* 19:237-41.

Sullivan, A. P., and Rozen, K. C., 1985, Debitage analysis and archaeological interpretation. *American Antiquity* 50:755-79.

Steensberg, A., 1980, *New Guinea Gardens: A Study of Husbandry with Parallels in Prehistoric Europe*. Academic Press, London.

Tixier, J., 1974, Glossary for the description of stone tools with special reference to the Epipaleolithic of the Magreb. *Newsletter of Lithic Technology* 1.

Tomenchuk, J., 1988, The effect of loading rates on the reliability of engineering use-wear models. In *Industries Lithiques: Traceologie et Technologie*, edited by S. Beyries, pp. 99-114. BAR International Series 411. British Archaeological Reports, Oxford.

Unger-Hamilton, R., 1985, Microscopic striations on flint sickle blades as an indication of plant cultivation. *World Archaeology* 17:121-26.

Van Peer, P., 1992, *The Levallois Reduction Strategy*. Prehistory Press, Madison, WI.

Vierra, B. J., 1995, *Subsistence and Stone Tool Technology: An Old World Perspective*. Anthropological Research Papers. Arizona State University, Tempe.

Watson, A., and Nash, D. J., 1997, Desert crusts and varnishes. In *Arid Zone Geomorphology. Process, Form and Change in Drylands*, edited by D. S. G. Thomas, pp. 69-107. John Wiley & Sons, New York.

Whittaker, J. C., 1994, *Flintknapping. Making and Understanding Stone Tools*. Unversity of Texas Press, Austin.

White, J. P., 1967, Ethnoarchaeology in New Guinea: Two examples. *Mankind* 6:409-14.

White, R., 1993, Introduction to *Gesture and Speech* by A. Leroi-Gourhan, translated by A. B. Berger. MIT Press, Cambridge.

Wiessner, P., 1983, Style and social information in Kalahari San projectile points. *American Antiquity* 49:253-76.

— 1985, Style or isochrestic variation? A reply to Sackett. *American Antiquity* 50:160-66.

— 1990, Is there a unity to style? In *The Uses of Style in Archaeology*, edited by M. Conkey and C. A. Hastorf, pp. 105-12. Cambridge University Press, Cambridge.

Wobst, M., 1977, Stylistic behavior and information exchange. *Anthropological Papers of the University of Michigan* 61:317-342.

Wright, E. M., 1988, Bee hive quern manufacture in the southeast Pennines. *Scottish Archaeological Review* 5:65-77.

Wright, K. I., 1992, *Ground Stone Tool Assemblage Variation and Subsistence Strategies in the Levant, 22,000 to 5,500 B.P.* Ph.D thesis, Yale University.

— 1993a, Early Holocene ground stone tool assemblages in the Levant. *Levant* 25:93-111.

— 1993b, A classification system for ground stone tools from the prehistoric Levant. *Paléorient* 18:53-81.

— 1994, Groundstone tools and hunter-gatherer subsistence in Southwest Asia: Implications for the transition to farming. *American Antiquity* 59:238-63.

Yohe, R. M., Newman, M., and Schneider, J. S., 1991, Immunological identification of small mammal proteins on aboriginal milling equipment. *American Antiquity* 56:569-666.

Young, D., and Bamforth, D. B., 1990, On the macroscopic identification of used flakes. *American Antiquity* 55:403-409.

Young, D., and Bonnichsen, R., 1984, *Understanding Stone Tools: A Cognitive Approach*. Peopling of the Americas Process Series 1. Center for the Study of Early Man, University of Maine at Orono, Orono, ME.

9 Analysing Pottery

One of the most common materials that archaeologists process and analyse is ceramic.[1] Ceramic vessels or, more commonly, their fragments (sherds) are ubiquitous on Holocene archaeological sites in much of the world. This ubiquity is due to the combined factors of relatively cheap manufacture, short use-life, and resistance to many mechanisms, such as bacterial decay and oxidation, that cause other materials to deteriorate in archaeological environments. Archaeologists also encounter ceramics with functions unrelated to containment, such as bricks, drain or roof tiles, writing tablets, and sculpture, but here we will concentrate on ceramic containers, or **pottery**. Many of the problems surrounding the analysis of ceramic artifacts, including sampling, fragmentation, and quantification, are common to most kinds of artifacts and ecofacts that archaeologists analyse, but ceramics present unique problems as well.

Archaeological investigations tend to focus on three primary dimensions of variation — technological, functional, and stylistic — that may themselves be interrelated and have associations with chronological, spatial, social, economic, and ideological variability. Any of these studies depends on fundamental principles for defining and recording attributes (recall measurement theory and systematics, chaps. 2 and 3).

Technological analyses of pottery and other ceramics, as with lithics, focus on the selection and preparation of raw materials, the manufacturing methods and sequences, modification or recycling of finished pieces, and their ultimate failure and post-depositional modifications. Technological variations can be related to differences in the costs or availability of raw materials, in the skills, knowledge, preferences, and motor habits of individual potters, in the anticipated functions of the finished products, and in their anticipated use-life.

Functional variability results from the varying design considerations that affect the usefulness of pots for various tasks, such as containment, temperature control, transport, distribution, social display, and disposal, as well as their actual use in these tasks. Although some pots represent considerable investments of design, they remain quite versatile and can be used for many tasks for which the designer did not intend them. A Greek amphora designed for the containment, transport, and pouring of wine, for example, could be recycled as a container of fish paste or even as building material in a wall or roof. Design criteria often include technological details and the morphology and size of the vessel or its parts. Determining the use or uses of pots involves both analysis of probable design features and identification of residues and use-related damage, just as with stone tools.

Stylistic variability is not restricted to decorative attributes, but concerns variations that do

---

[1] Here I use the term, "ceramic," in the non-technical sense to include earthenwares, terracottas, stonewares, porcelains, and other materials of fired-clay. In materials science it has a different usage to include any solid made of compounds of metallic elements and non-metallic, inorganic ones (cf. Kingery, Bowen and Uhlmann 1976: 3; Rice 1987: 3-4).

not have substantive effects on the vessels' utilitarian functionality (although often on social or ideological function). Stylistic differences range from the unconscious variations due to individual potters' unique motor habits to deliberate symbolic content.

The Anatomy of a Pot

Any archaeological information language requires segmentation and orientation rules, while attributes and classes or categories require unambiguous definition. While the exact definitions vary from researcher to researcher, depending on their research questions and idiosyncracies of the assemblages they are studying, they share some aspects of ceramic terminology.

At first glance, orientation rules for pottery seem simple. We simply orient the pots in the way they would be used, with the **orifice** or opening at the top and horizontal, and the **base**, which would normally be in contact with any surface on which the vessel rested, at the bottom. We call this orientation "at stance." In reality, however, things are not always so simple. Some pots have unusual or asymetrical shapes, with orifices that are not horizontal, with side orifices, with multiple orifices, or without a clear base. Some vessels that actually functioned as lids may be formally indistinguishable from bowls, so that archaeologists risk misorienting them by 180°. Other ceramics, such as drains and smoking pipes, were designed to have orifices at both ends, and were oriented almost horizontally during use. More commonly, the problem is fragmentation; it would be difficult to demonstrate convincingly that a loop handle on a sherd showing no trace of either rim or base was oriented vertically and not horizontally, or even diagonally, when it was still attached to the whole vessel. In addition, pots can be oriented differently during different uses or different stages of the same use. For example, a cooking pot may be stored or dried with its orifice downward, used to boil stew with its orifice upward, and used to roast beans with its orifice tilted 45° (e.g., Skibo, 1992:64-73).

Archaeologists therefore adopt conventions for orienting ceramics and their fragments, even when though these conventions will not always describe the way vessels were oriented during use. Except when there is evidence to the contrary, they make such assumptions as the following.

- Rim sherds are oriented so that the vessel orifice is upwards and horizontal. In this case, the rim is "at stance." In addition, we normally assume that the orifice is circular in plan view.

- Base sherds (except round or pointed bases) are oriented downward in such a way as to maximize contact between the base and the surface on which it rests. This puts them "at stance."

- Pointed bases are oriented so that their long axis is vertical (unless the point is one part of a tripod).

- Round bases are oriented so that the thickest part of the base touches the surface on which the base lies.

- Body sherds, where possible, are oriented so that any signs of coil construction, smoothing, or rouletting are predominantly horizontal. This still leaves undetermined which way is up. One possibility is to assume that the thickest half of the sherd (when divided along the horizontal axis) is closer to the base, or the lower half.

- Handles, spouts, or knobs that are not attached to a rim or base that could provide evidence for orientation are oriented in the direction that predominates in more complete vessels in the assemblage. An unintended consequence of this assumption is that orientations that appear atypical will be recorded even more rarely, reinforcing the original assumption about predominant orientation even if it is not correct.

For most measurements of rims and bases, the most important element of orientation is the **stance**. As we have seen, this is the position that, ideally, orients the pot the way it would typically be positioned while resting on a surface. To stance a rim, hold it against a flat surface and rock it back and forth until you find the position that puts all or most of the lip in contact with that surface. The flat surface is then assumed to represent the horizontal plane of the pot.

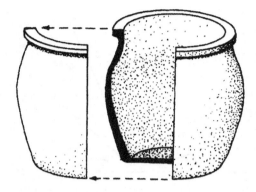

Figure 9.1. Conventional pottery illustrations are based on the concept of cutting away a quarter-section of a whole pot. The cross-section (black) is a radial section and the exterior view is a lateral view. The top and base of the pot are in the transverse plane (Newlands and Breede, 1976:127).

For purposes of describing slices through vessels or their sherds, it is also useful to refer to the **radial plane**, any slice radiating out from the vertical axis of the pot's (radial or bilateral) symmetry, the **transverse plane**, any slice along a plane parallel to the stance, and the **lateral** or **tangential view**, any view or slice that is tangent to the surface of the pot (figure 9.1). In addition there is the **plan view**, showing the pot or one of its parts as it would appear from above (i.e., in the transverse plane), and the base view, showing it from below (see also drawing conventions, chapter 16).

The segments of the vessel (e.g., figure 3.13) conventionally include the **rim** (adjacent to the main orifice), the base (on which the vessel normally rests), the **body**, and sometimes the neck, shoulder, **carination**, handle, spout, or **castellation**. The exact definition of the segments depends on the characteristics of the particular assemblage under study, but the definitions that follow provide examples applicable to many kinds of pottery.

- Lip: The point most distant from the base as measured along the center of the vessel walls.

- Rim: The portion of the vessel closest to the orifice (including lip).

- Neck: A vertical (often cylindrical) restriction of the vessel orifice above the maximum diameter of the body or shoulder (cf. Rice, 1987: 212).

- Shoulder: The region above the body's maximum diameter but below the neck or rim.

- Handle: An appendage attached to the exterior wall of the body, neck, or rim. There may be more than one handle on each vessel.

- Base: The portion from the lower boundary of the body to the surface that would normally be in contact with a surface when the vessel is at rest (including, in some cases, the foot or tripod).

- Foot: An appendage attached along the circumference the base that raises the body.

- Tripod: Set of three leg-like or knob-like supports attached individually along the circumference of the base that raises the body.

- Spout: Neck-like appendage restricting a secondary orifice that occurs to one side of the vessel's vertical axis (typically on the upper body or shoulder).

If some or all of a pottery assemblage exhibits decoration, it is also necessary to define orientation and segmentation rules for the decorated area or areas (figure 9.2).

Measuring Vessel Form

Having devised orientation and segmentation rules, the next step in describing pottery typically involves devising a set of attributes whose values you will measure (see chapter 3).

Some attributes can pertain to whole-vessel shape, in those fortunate cases in which whole or restorable vessels are fairly common. A common way to do this involves the ratio between orifice diameter and vessel height. Vessels with large orifices relative to their height are called **open**, while ones with relatively small orifices are called **closed** or **restricted vessels** (figure 9.3). Although an alternative simple shape measure would be the ratio of maximum diameter to height, the relative openness of the orifice has the advantage of being relevant to the accessibility and restriction of vessel contents. These things pertain directly to the function of vessels, as with all facilities.

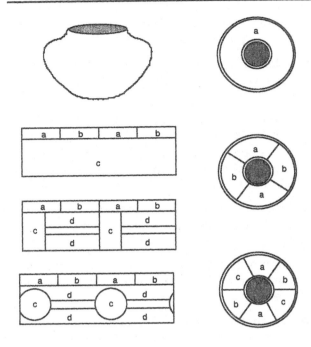

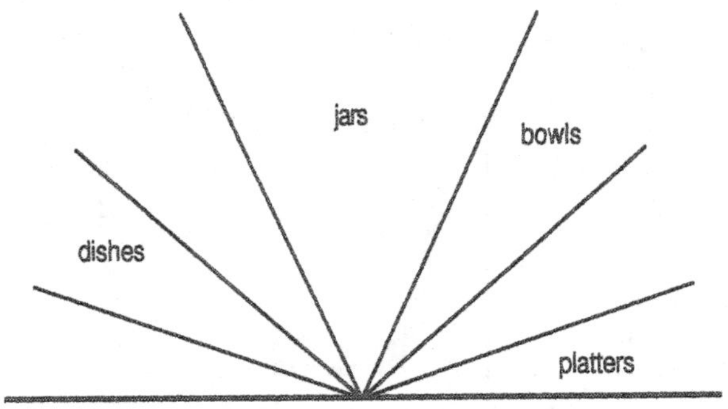

Figure 9.3. A simple template for classifying vessels by the degree to which they are open or closed (after Orton, 1980:34). The radii originate at the bottom center of the vessel interior and extend to the top of the rim of the orifice.

Figure 9.2. An example of segmentation rules for painted decoration on Pueblo pots (after Bunzel, 1972). Whole vessels like the one at upper left are divided into zones of decoration vertically and radially. The rectangles show the segmentation of panels as viewed from the side (laterally). The circles show radial segments as viewed from above.

CERAMIC TECHNOLOGICAL ANALYSIS

Matson (1965) pioneered the concept he called "ceramic ecology" as a framework for studying pottery from the perspective of its manufacturing steps and use. Although this is not the only way to approach the study of pottery, many modern ceramic analysts have followed his lead. These structure their research around the selection, acquisition, and pre-processing of materials, the forming, finishing, and decoration of the pot, as well as its drying, firing, and cooling. You will recognize the parallel with the **chaîne opératoire** mentioned in the last chapter and, as with lithics, not all pots undergo the same manufacture sequence, so it may be necessary to reconstruct that sequence for each pot.

Owen Rye (1981) provides a good summary of attributes that help us identify manufacturing methods and sequences, only some of which will be outlined here.

The main materials for pottery are water and clay, which together provide plasticity, and one or more fillers, known as **"temper,"** which alter the physical characteristics of the fabric in various ways. Clay itself is a very complex and diverse material. The potter may blend temper into the wet clay to prevent the pot from collapsing under its own weight before or during firing, to control shrinkage during drying, or to increase the porosity or resistance to crack propagation in the finished product. Particular choices of temper can alter the result substantially. Since all natutally occuring clays contain non-clay inclusions, it is not always possible to determine which, if any, inclusions the potter intentionally added as temper. It is important to understand how potters prepare and mix threse materials (e.g., Rye, 1981:16-20).

Many archaeological analyses are aimed at the identification of pottery materials, their sources (figure 9.4), and whatever desirable properties they may have given either the unfinished or finished pot. The analyses can involve the identification of chemical signatures, with Neutron Activation Analysis and X-Ray Diffraction as their main tools, or optical mineralogy, with thin-sectioning equipment and polarizing microscopes as the main tools. Experimental studies, meanwhile, attempt to discover the effects

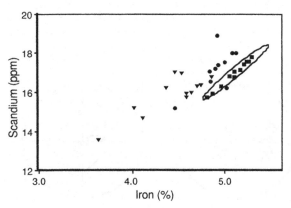

Figure 9.4. Scatterplot intended to help explore possible groupings of pottery by their clay sources. It shows the relationship between the concentration of iron and traces of scandium in parts per million in ceramic wasters from different sites in northeastern Syria, marked by different symbols. The ellipse shows the 95% confidence interval for wasters from Leilan (after Blackman et al., 1993).

of different materials on pottery performance (e.g., Bronitsky, 1986; Bronitsky and Hamer, 1986; Feathers, 1989; Hoard et al., 1995; Kilikoglou et al., 1998; O'Brien et al., 1994; Skibo et al., 1989; Vekenis and Kelikoglou, 1998).

Here we will not deal with chemical characterization in detail, and refer the reader to more specialized sources on archaeometry, notably the journal, *Archaeometry*. The bulk of a ceramic's raw material consists of clay minerals, which result from the weathering of silicate rocks containing significant amounts of alumina (Al_2O_3), notably feldspar (Rice, 1987:34-35). Among the clays are kaolinite ($Al_2(Si_2O_5)(OH)_4$), halloysite ($Al_2(Si_2O_5)(OH)_4 \cdot 2H_2O$), montmorillonite ($\left(Al_{1.67}\dfrac{Na_{0.33}}{Mg_{0.33}}\right)(Si_2O_5)_2(OH)_2$), and illite ($(Al_{2-x}Mg_xK_{1-x-y})(Si_{1.5-y}Al_{0.5+y}O_5)_2(OH)_2$) , but the inclusions have their own chemical constituents and both the clay and inclusions include impurities (Rice 1987: 40-51). Thus a bulk chemical analysis of a ceramic will show large quantities of the elements that form the crystals of the clay minerals and main inclusions, such as silicon (Si), aluminum (Al), magnesium (Mg), potassium (K), iron (Fe), and calcium (Ca), as well as minute amounts of other elements, or "trace elements." Analysts look for grouping in the ratios of **trace elements** (figure 9.5), once

they have accounted for the mixing of clays and tempers by examining the ratios of the main elements, in the hope of identifying different clay sources or different tempering practices that may be archaeologically significant (Rice, 1996; Rye, 1981:47-49).

Characterization of the fabric (especially inclusions) by optical techniques is still the most broadly useful way to study a ceramic's raw material, especially in regions with considerable geological diversity and wide range of potential inclusions. Where the researcher's goal is to distinguish pottery fabrics with different clay sources, it may also be useful to analyse the trace elements (e.g., Stewart et al., 1990; Vitali, 1989) or even **diatom** content (Jansma, 1977).

Optical petrographic techniques are based on the ways in which light interacts with the crystals through which it passes in thin sections (Nesse, 1986: 3-108). Light is considered to act like a wave with peaks and valleys at right angles to the direction in which the light ray is moving. The wavelength is simply the distance from one peak to the next one and in visible light ranges from about 400-700 nm (nanometers). The frequency of the light is simply the number of waves, or cycles, per second, and this is constant no matter what material the light passes through. The speed of the light and its wavelength, however, do change. Mineralogists refer to materials as **isotropic** when they show the same velocity of light in all directions, and **anisotropic** when the velocity of light through the material is different in different directions. Isotropic materials include glass, such as obsidian, while quartz, for example, is an anisotropic mineral. One of the ways we identify minerals is based on the properties of **polarized light**. While normal light waves "vibrate" in all directions perpendicular to the direction of travel, plane polarized light "vibrates" in only one direction. On a mineralogical microscope, we polarize the light that reaches the thin section by passing normal light through a polarizing film (the lower polar), that only lets light through that vibrates in a particular plane. If we then look at the polarized light through another polarizing film (the upper polar), we will not see any light at all unless the two polarizers are lined up in the

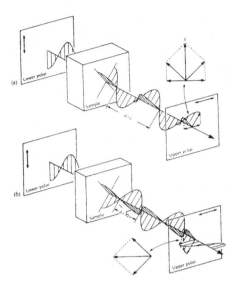

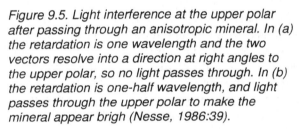

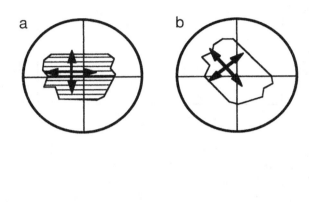

Figure 9.5. Light interference at the upper polar after passing through an anisotropic mineral. In (a) the retardation is one wavelength and the two vectors resolve into a direction at right angles to the upper polar, so no light passes through. In (b) the retardation is one-half wavelength, and light passes through the upper polar to make the mineral appear brigh (Nesse, 1986:39).

Figure 9.6. When the vibration directions of the mineral are parallel to the lower and upper polars, the mineral is dark between crossed polars (a), while rotating the grain (b) allows light to pass through (after Nesse, 1986:44).

same plane. You can demonstrate this for yourself by taking two pairs of polarized sunglasses and looking through both at once while one is turned at right angles to the other. But when polarized light passes through an anisotropic crystal, it is split into two rays "vibrating" at right angles to one another, and "twisted" relative to the original direction of vibration (figure 9.5). The ray with the lower index of refraction is called the **fast ray**, and the other is the **slow ray**. **Birefringence** is the difference between their two indices of refraction. By the time the slow ray exits the crystal, the fast ray will be ahead of it by a distance called the **retardation**. The two rays can also interfere with one another, resulting in different colours being viewed at the upper polar. But when the vectors of the two rays' vibrations resolve into a direction at right angles to the upper polar, no light passes through the upper polar and the mineral appears dark. By rotating the thin section on the microscope's rotating stage, we can find the extinction angle: the angle through which you must rotate the crystal from its cleavage axis or length to make it go "extinct" or dark (figure 9.6).

Preparing a sample of pottery for this type of analysis involves making a *thin section* from one or more pieces cut from a sherd with care to represent the planes that will reveal useful information about manufacturing practices. Radial and lateral (or tangential) sections both tend to be useful. The cut piece is mounted on a glass slide and consolidated to prevent it from crumbling. Then the appropriate radial or lateral surface is polished with a polishing wheel and a graded series of abrasives until the sherd has been reduced to a thickness of about 30μ, which allows light to be transmitted through it. University Geology departments usually have facilities for making thin-sections.

Body Preparation

Only rarely will a naturally occurring, wet clay, such as you might find in a stream-side, be suitable for making pottery because it will not contain the right combination of particle sizes in the right proportions. Most people would be surprised to learn that potters usually begin with dry clay, which looks like rock, and prepare it carefully before using it for pottery construction.

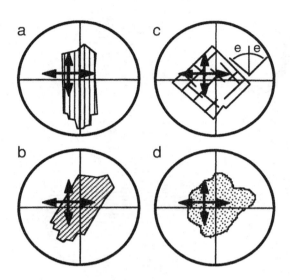

Figure 9.7. Categories of extinction angle: (a) parallel, (b) inclined, (c) symmetrical and (d) no extinction angle (after Nesse, 1986:45).

Dried clay is broken up into small pieces and coarse contaminants, such as plant material and rocks, are removed. The potter can use a stone or pestle to pulverize the clay lumps, and may use a sieve to remove some of the rootlets and other plant fragments. A crude sieve can be made from basketry, cloth, or perforated rawhide (Rice, 1987: 118).

The next step is *slaking*. Here the potter adds water to the pulverized dry clay in a shallow pit and disintegrates the remaining lumps, sometimes over several days. Adding more water to the slaked clay and stirring with a stick or paddle puts the clay particles into suspension and facilitates removal of coarse particles.

Since prehistoric potters may not have had fine sieves through which to pour the suspended clay, they probably separated the fine clay particles from coarser particles by *settling* or levigation. The former involves simply letting the suspension sit in a vat. The coarser, heavier particles sink more rapidly and can be left behind when the remaining suspension, now containing only the lighter particles, is poured off or ladled out. *Levigation*, or elutriation, is a method

in which the potter allows the suspension to flow along a shallow trough that has a series of low walls that trap the heavier, coarser particles as they move downward, while the finer, lighter particles flow all the way through. Levigation can produce extremely fine clay, with particle sizes less than 50μ (Rye, 1981:36-37; Rice, 1987:118). Not all potters worried about attaining such fine clay, however.

Once the settled or levigated clay has been left standing long enough for much of the water to evaporate, leaving a plastic clay, the potter adds temper to improve workability, prevent the vessel from collapsing during construction, reduce shrinkage, ensure that it could withstand firing, and alter the physical characteristics during firing and in the finished pot. Temper can be sand of suitable size distribution, or materials that the potter has pulverized down to a suitable size, such as rock, shells, old sherds, or chopped fibrous material, such as chaff or hair. The latter typically burns out during firing, leaving voids in the fabric of distinctive shape. When the temper consists of sharp, angular particles, this suggests that the potter crushed rock or other material to use as temper, while rounded particles could be natural sand from a stream bed. Sometimes the temper will be sieved to remove the coarsest particle sizes (Gibson and Woods, 1997:27-37; Rye, 1981:37).

The potter blends suitable proportions of temper and clay by one of two methods. Usually a volume of temper is added to a volume of clay that has been wet just enough to make it plastic, and then kneads the two together on a flat surface or shallow bowl, often with a little fine temper sprinkled on it to prevent sticking (a parting agent). An alternative method sometimes used to prepare large amounts is to add the temper to the clay while it is suspended in water, and then letting the excess water evaporate (Rye, 1981:38-39).

In either case, the tempered clay or "body" must then be kneaded thoroughly, or "wedged," to eliminate air bubbles and make sure that the distribution of moisture and inclusions is uniform. Thoroughly kneaded material will have very few voids in the finished pottery except those left by organic temper, while badly

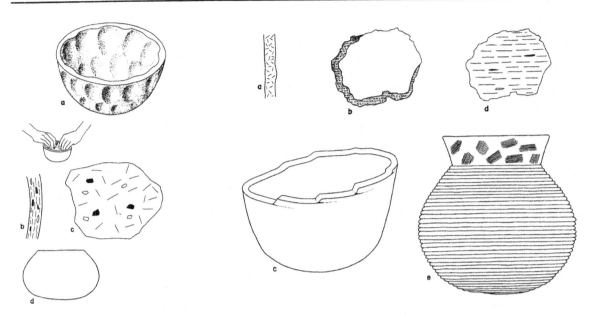

Figure 9.8. Physical characteristics of pinching (Rye, 1981).

Figure 9.9. Physical characteristics of coiling (Rye, 1981).

kneaded material may result in more and larger voids (Rye, 1981:39-40; Rice, 1987:119).

Construction of the Vessel

Forming methods can be crudely divided among hand-forming, molding, and wheel throwing, with many finer distinctions. In addition, it is useful to distinguish primary from secondary forming.

Primary Forming

Hand-made pots may be constructed by one of several techniques or with several in combination. Each technique leaves a physical fingerprint that we can recognize if we examine the right combinations of attributes.

Pinching is the simplest technique for forming small hemispherical bowls and the bases of round-bottomed pots. The potter takes a ball of the tempered clay and squeezes it manually into a bowl shape, rotating the piece and continuing to squeeze at intervals along the circumference to thin the vessel walls. Traces of pinching can include regularly spaced, shallow indentations left by finger or thumb, especially on the interior. These tend to be oriented vertically and are

roughly the size of a human fingertip. In horizontal cross-section, this results in almost sinusoidal waviness in surface profile unless the surface was later modified. Inclusions in the clay will tend to be drawn upward by the squeezing, with the result that they can have a slightly preferred vertical orientation when viewed in a section cut along the pot's radial plane, and a tendency for the long axis of particles to be parallel to the surface, but in the lateral view, in an X-radiograph of a sherd, for example, orientation appears random (figure 9.8; Rye, 1981:52).

Drawing is a technique very similar to pinching. It begins with the potter driving a fist into a lump of tempered clay, then squeezing it and pulling or stretching it upwards. As with pinching, it results in a series of finger-width indentations around the pot's circumference, but longer and with a more strongly vertical orientation. Later finishing may disguise or obliterate evidence for these grooves, but there may still be wavy variations in the thickness of the vessel wall when viewed along a horizontal section. In the lateral view, a tendency for inclusions to be oriented vertically, as a result of their being dragged upwards, is discernible.

Coiling is is mainly a primary forming technique. The potter can begin by patting a ball into a disk to serve as a flat base, and setting it on a small mat, or by pinching out a round base and then supporting it in a shallow hole in the ground or some kind of ring or bowl (often a broken pot base). The next step is to roll another small ball of tempered clay into a snake-like cylinder, pinch one end of it onto the base, and then coil it around the base's circumference. After pinching it securely to the edges of the base all around, another coil is built onto the previous one and pinched into place, and so on. By continuing to add coils, the potter gradually increases the vessel's height and can control its general shape by splaying newly added coils inward or outward. Alternatively, the potter can make a round- or pointed-bottom pot by starting it upside-down with a coil arranged in a broad circle, gradually decreasing vessel diameter while building upwards with additional coils. Unless secondary forming and finishing have removed the "bumps" at the center of coils, coil-built pots have noticeable variations in wall thickness along a radial section (figure 9.9a). When the vessel breaks, the sherds may have irregular or meandering edges or, may break along coil junctions to make "false rims" (Gibson and Woods, 1997:39-42; Rice, 1987:128), sometimes resulting in a stepped fracture (figure 9.9c). Because the rolling out of coils tends to squeeze inclusions so that their long axes are parallel to the coil, the particles and voids have a strong tendency to horizontal orientation in the lateral view, as in an X-radiograph of a sherd, while a radial section tends to show the particles end-on, and with random orientation (figure 9.9a, d; Gibson and Woods, 1997:37-42; Rye, 1981:67-69).

Slab-building also involves building up the vessel with separate pieces of tempered clay and is mainly a primary forming technique. Here the pieces are not cylinders, but flat slabs made either by patting the tempered clay out by hand or by rolling it out on a flat surface with a rolling pin. Construction begins by shaping one slab into a base. Additional slabs are joined onto the edges of the base, at an appropriate angle, by pinching them together to make a seam and smearing the seam to make it smoother. Once the first row of slabs has dried just enough that it can support some weight, another row of slabs is built onto the first, and so on, up to the rim of the vessel, much as mud bricks are used to build a house. Although slab-building can be used for the primary forming of all or part of many vessel shapes, it is particularly well suited to construction of rectangular vessels, or boxes, and very large, immovable containers, such as ovens and grain silos. Individual slabs can exhibit a very smooth surface as a result of being rolled out on some kind of table, but there are usually many surface markings, from scraping or combing the seams in an attempt to obliterate them and even out differences in the thickness of slabs. If the slabs were rolled out with a rolling pin under enough pressure, inclusions will be flattened so that they are parallel to the surface in radial and horizontal sections, but randomly oriented in lateral X-radiographs. Fracture may sometimes occur along seams, but rolling out under pressure can also result in a laminar structure that later results in fracture parallel to the lateral surface, with layer-like pieces of the surface flaking off (figure 9.10; Rye, 1981:71-72).

Molding involves either pressing plastic raw material into a mold or sloshing a liquid slurry (clay suspended in water) around in the mold so that the clay adheres in a gradually thickening layer on the mold's surface, as the porous mold draws water away from the slurry. The former method was more common prehistorically; the later is used in much modern pottery.

Molding can be very simple. For example, one of the easiest ways to make a crude bowl is to dig a shallow pit in the ground that will serve as the mold, and then simply press some plastic, tempered clay into it. After smoothing off the rim and waiting for the bowl to dry, you then remove it to dry further prior to firing. Pressing clay into a bowl or large sherd can be used to form the base of a vessel to be completed by coiling or slab-building.

Commonly, the mold is specially carved or constructed to leave designs in raised relief on the ceramic's surface. The mold must be carefully designed to taper so that, once the plastic clay is pressed into it, it can still be removed. In addition, a parting agent, such as fine ash, dry clay or sand, is dusted on the mold's interior

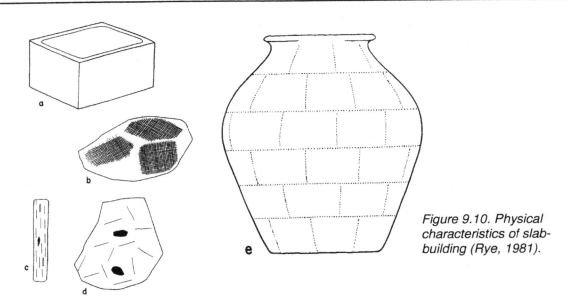

Figure 9.10. Physical characteristics of slab-building (Rye, 1981).

surface to prevent the molded clay from getting stuck. Molding is well suited both for relief and for complex shapes, the latter often requiring several mold-made pieces that are later fitted together much as with slab-building (figure 9.11).

Molding of the sophisticated kind is easy to recognize. The molded surface reproduces in relief the design that is intaglio in the mold (figure 9.12), while the opposite surface may show finger impressions where the potter forced clay into the mold or, in more complex molding, the impression of the other side of a two-part mold. There will either be thickened seams between different molded parts, or signs that these were cut or scraped away (figure 9.11). There may also be traces of the parting agent embedded in the molded surfaces. Inclusions sometimes respond to the pressure applied in forcing clay into the mold by aligning themselves parallel to the surface (in radial or horizontal section), but are otherwise random in orientation (Rye, 1981:81-83). Potters sometimes prefer the particle size of inclusions to be small, to avoid imperfections in the carefully designed relief surface.

Wheel-throwing is qualitatively different from all the hand-forming techniques and from molding. Although the potter manipulates the tempered clay much as with pinching and drawing, the difference is that the hands serve mainly as barriers to the outward thrust of the material under centrifugal force caused by rotation between 50 and 150 rpm. Throwing is particularly well suited to mass production of standardized pots that are approximately circular in plan view.

To begin to throw a number of vessels, the potter will place a large lump of tempered clay onto the wheel-head and center it by pressing inwards with wet hands while the wheel rotates, resulting in a volcano-like cone of material. The potter then "opens" this cone by pushing thumbs or a fist into its center, making a hole that widens the top of the cone into a bowl shape. Squeezing and drawing the material upwards, either between thumb on the inside and fingers on the outside, or between two hands, is called **lifting**. This simultaneously thins the walls and increases their height. The material is frequently wetted with water to lubricate it. Moving the hands inward or outward, meanwhile, shapes the vessel by decreasing or increasing its diameter. With both hands outside, applying inward pressure while the wheel rotates at high speed, a process called **collaring**, narrows the vessel to form a neck or to close it in completely, as when making a base on an upside-down vessel(figures 9.13, 9.14). The potter may apply additional pressure after the basic lifting to finish shaping the vessel; **shaping** involves changing the vessel diameter anywhere

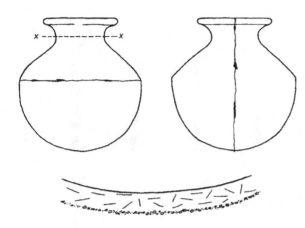

Figure 9.11. The mold-made vessel at upper left not only shows a seam at the shoulder, where upper and lower parts were joined, but the rim above the x-x line also had to be formed separately, to avoid undercutting in the mold. The one in upper right has a vertical seam showing that it was entirely mold-made in two halves that were later joined. The section of a sherd at bottom shows small particles at the lower surface left by the parting agent that prevented sticking to the mold (Rye, 1981:81).

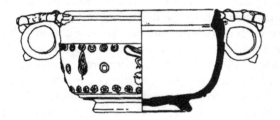

Figure 9.12. Roman-period mold-made skyphos probably made in Syria or Cilicia around AD 50-80 (after Hayes, 1976:80).

along its profile without significantly altering the height. **Folding** is a special kind of shaping in which the potter flares a rim outward or bends it inward, and then rolls it down to double its thickness and sometimes create a complicated profile. Sometimes folded rims are hollow or clearly show the fold in cross-section. When the potter has finished shaping the vessel or vessel section, she or he cuts it off of the hump of tempered clay by drawing a string or wire through while the wheel is still spinning (Rye, 1981:74-75).

Physical traces of some of these operations make it fairly easy to identify thrown vessels. Opening tends to leave spiralling thumb indentations on the inside of the base and, if the potter does not expect these to be visible, they will remain (figure 9.15). Lifting not only leaves spiral finger grooves, or **rilling**, up the walls of the vessel, but also gives the inclusions a preferred diagonal orientation in the lateral view (figure 9.15). Removal of a vessel can result in a "string-cut" base, typically showing spiral or shell-like drag marks from the string or wire (figure 9.16) as well as fingerprints on the lower exterior walls where the potter picked the vessel up, unless later finishing removed these (Rye, 1981:75; Rice, 1987:129).

There are other characteristics that help to identify wheel-made vessels. Often the lower walls will be thicker than the upper ones but there will not be noticeable differences in thickness along the circumference. Wetting the clay during lifting and shaping can leave a slurry of clay on the surface that is sometimes described as a "self-slip." It will be less regular in its thickness and distribution than most intentional slips. The particle size of inclusions is proportional to mean wall thickness, with inclusions typically less than 1 mm in diameter in sherds 5 mm thick, while thorough kneading followed by throwing leaves only a few small voids. S-shaped cracks on the base and spiral fracture of vessel walls are common. Wheel-thrown vessels are rarely perfectly circular in plan but, even if the potter has pushed the rim in or out to make small spouts or a sub-rectangular plan, it is usually obvious that the vessel started out nearly circular. If the potter did some finishing or decorating while the vessel was still on the wheel, typically the tool marks will be neatly horizontal and regular or continuous and sinusoidal or spiralling (Rye, 1981:75-80).

It is not at all unusual for a single pot to be made with a combination of these primary forming techniques.

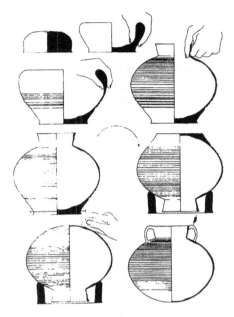

Figure 9.13. The reconstructed construction sequence of a thrown cooking pot (Franken and Kalsbeek, 1975).

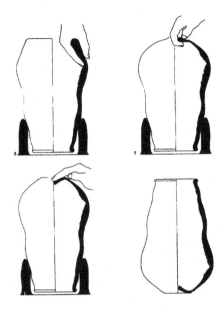

Figure 9.14. Closing the base of a tall jar on the wheel (Franken and Kalsbeek, 1975).

Secondary Forming

Often primary forming is insufficient to produce the desired shape, wall thickness, or surface texture, or leaves undesirable traces, so secondary forming follows the initial roughing out of the vessel's shape by one or more of the above methods.

Large or complicated vessels often have to be made in several pieces, that are then **joined**. The join will result in a thickened seam, as in slab-built or some molded vessels, although the potter will try to smooth or scrape away this seam where it is visible. On the interior of necked jars, however, the seam where the neck was added is sometimes quite prominent. Many large, globular, wheel-thrown vessels are made in two bowl-like pieces joined along their "rims," and the seam sometimes occurs at a "carination," a sharp turn in vertical profile.

Beating, paddling, or hammer-and-anvil, is an effective way to thin and even out the walls of coil- or slab-built vessels after they have partially dried to "leather" hardness, as well as to apply surface texture and improve bonding between coils. The "anvil" can simply be the potter's hand or fist, or a stone or other tool; it is inside the vessel to support it while, with the other hand, the potter repeatedly beats the outer surface with a stick or paddle. Beating can also be used without an anvil to help close a wheel-made vessel or to push tempered clay into a mold. Sometimes the paddle is carved or covered with cloth or cord to add decoration or texture to exterior walls. Beating leaves rounded indentations of the anvil on the interior and facets on the exterior that reflect the shape and texture of the paddle (figure 9.18) and result in regular variations in wall thickness. If the paddle was wet, it might make an irregular "self-slip" on the surface. Because beating puts local stresses on the leather-hard fabric, there may be star-shaped compaction cracks around large inclusions, while cross sections will show the preferred orientation of inclusions to be parallel to the surface and there will be a laminar structure that can lead to the spalling off of lens-shaped flakes. Beating is a popular method for the secondary forming of medium-size, globular forms because it is easy to rotate them around one fist while beating the outside (Rye, 1981:84-85; Rice, 1987:137).

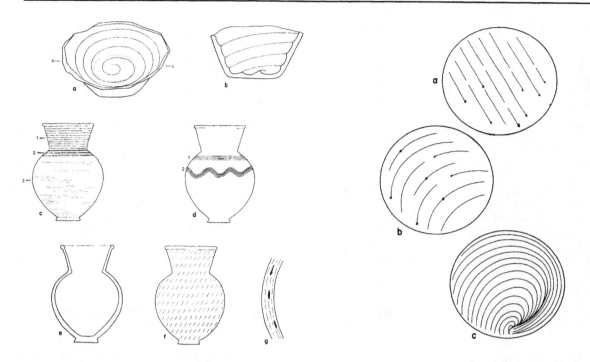

Figure 9.15. *Physical characteristics of thrown vessels (Rye, 1981).*

Figure 9.16. *Drag marks on string-cut bases of thrown vessels (Rye, 1981).*

Scraping involves thinning vessel walls by removing material with a tool held almost perpendicular to the surface, usually when the clay is still somewhat plastic, but nearly leatherhard. Sometimes the tool has a serrated edge, as a sea-shell. Even scraping with a smooth-edged tool produces prominent drag marks as it pulls large inclusions along the surface (figure 9.18). The tool also leaves facets on the surface, which can end abruptly (Rye, 1981:86).

Trimming or fettling, like scraping, involves cutting material away from the surface with a tool, but in this case the tool, often a knife, is used at an acute angle to the surface while the vessel is leather-hard (figure 9.19). A common use of trimming is to remove the ridge at the seam between parts of a mold-made or piece-made vessel (Rice, 1987:137). Trimming can leave drag marks, especially in a gritty fabric, but the most prominent evidence, if it is not removed by later finishing, consists of fairly smooth facets with sharp or torn edges where a curl of material was pulled away. Facets may be elongated and irregular in size and distribution (Rye, 1981:87).

Turning is a form of trimming analogous to wood-turning on a lathe. The vessel is rotated at about 150 rpm on a wheel while the trimming tool is held fairly still at an acute angle, and long curls of material are removed. The tool facets consequently form a fairly continuous spiral pattern that typically shows rotation in the opposite direction as the lifting (usually turning is used to thin parts of wheel-thrown vessels) because the vessel is often turned upside-down to thin the base and lower walls. Drag marks oriented along the rotation spiral are common when the fabric is gritty. Sometimes the potter tries to hide signs of turning with burnishing; if this is also done on a wheel, the burnish marks will also be spiralling. Because the vessel will not be centered exactly as it was when originally thrown, there is often an eccentricity in the thickness of walls where the vessel was turned. Turning is an ideal technique for cutting horizontal grooves and sharp carinations on the body, for hollowing out the base, and for bevelling and shaping thickened rims (Rye, 1981:87-88).

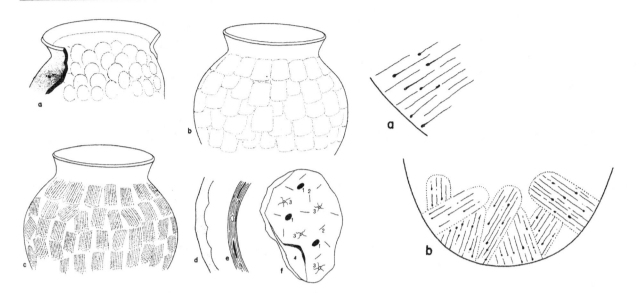

Figure 9.17. Physical characteristics of beating (Rye, 1981).

Figure 9.18. Physical traces of scraping (Rye, 1981).

Finishing Techniques

Once formed, vessels may undergo one or many techniques to alter their surface characteristics. These can involve displacing or impressing material at the surface, applying thin coats of slip, paint, or other materials, or removing small amounts of material from the vessel by cutting or carving. Some of the secondary forming techniques, such as beating and trimming, resemble these finishing methods.

Smoothing and **burnishing** are two techniques that only slightly displace material near the vessel surface. Both involve rubbing the surface with a tool while the vessel is leather-hard or dry, but not yet fired. Smoothing is less aggressive and leaves the surface matte, while burnishing, often performed on a slip (see below) with a smooth bone or pebble, results in a hard, reflective and less porous surface because it compacts and reorients the clay particles near the surface (Rice, 1987:138). Burnishing typically shows the streaks of tool motion, which themselves are often used as a decorative element. For example, sometimes the potter will make a net pattern by intersecting widely spaced burnish marks. Burnishing all over a vessel's surface is sometimes used to simulate the appearance of metal containers (often in combination with a copper-colored slip).

Greater displacement is caused by **impressing** the plastic or leather-hard surface with a tool. Impression with fingernails, fingertips, edges of shells and seals is often called **stamping**, while **punctate** decoration results by impressing with ends of sticks, bones, canes, porcupine quills, and other narrow objects (figure 9.20).

Rouletting is like impressing except that the tool is rolled over the vessel surface. The tool can be a carved stick, cylinder seal, gear-like wheel (Rye, 1981:92-93), or cord-wrapped stick (figure 9.22; Hurley, 1979). Rouletted decoration repeats itself over patches of the vessel surface or even around its whole circumference. If the roulette is used over a substantial portion of the vessel's surface, resulting in a "corrugated" vessel, the result is a roughened surface that provides a good grip and a greater surface area that may improve heat transfer in cooking (Rice, 1987:138).

Combing and incising are techniques that displace material from the vessel surface aggressively. In **incision**, a narrow tool cuts into the surface, displacing material slightly to either side, and is then dragged along, generally displacing more material toward the final end of a linear or curvilinear mark. Incisions are made while the vessel is leather-hard or only slightly

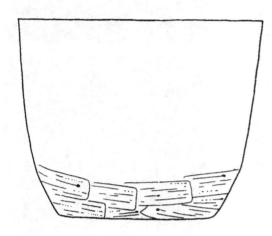

Figure 9.19. Physical traces of trimming (Rye, 1981).

plastic. **Combing** is the same as incision except that the tool has multiple cutting prongs, so that several parallel marks can be made simultaneously (figure 9.22). As with incision, it is often fairly easy to see where the mark began and where it ended, as a small raised mound of displaced material occurs near the final end of the cutting stroke. Careful study of the incisions can reveal the shape of the tool used and sometimes it can be identified quite precisely. British prehistoric sites have yielded denticulated bones that were probably for combing pottery (Gibson and Woods, 1997:47).

Although there can sometimes be unintentional coatings on the vessel surface, including "self-slip" and various residues from firing and use, often potters intentionally coat part or all of the surface with slip, paint, pigment, glaze, resist, or some other treatment.

A **slip** is simply a suspension of clay particles in water. When most ceramic analysts use the term, "slip," however, they refer to a thin layer of fine clay adhering to the surface of a vessel and fired with it. It may have the same color as the underlying fabric or a different color. Applying a different color of slip to only a portion of the surface may be a decorative effect. Slips show up as a distinct layer in cross-sections through sherds, while "self-slips" that result

from wetting the surface of the vessel during construction may not be so distinct. Slips may also show a fine network of rather hexagonally oriented fractures that do not continue down into the fabric (Rye, 1981:54). Slips can be applied by dipping, dripping, wiping, or brushing. Only dipping is effective at giving the entire vessel surface a very uniform coating of slip, the others showing variations in distribution and thickness. Slips make the vessel surface smoother and less permeable, hide large inclusions, and prepare the surface for burnishing.

Paint is a material that the potter applies to the surface either before or after firing to decorate it, and Rye (1981:40) would say that it can be a slip, pigment or other material, paint's definition being based on the potter's intent rather than the material involved. Others prefer to limit the term, "paint," to **pigments**, media containing coloring agents, such as metallic oxides, and sometimes organics, such as oils, that make it easier to brush the color on and make it adhere to the surface (Shepard, 1961:177). It is usually better to brush the pigment onto a dry surface, because the vessel walls quickly absorb any water used to suspend the colorant and the decorative elements will have crisp edges (Rye, 1981:41). Some pigments will contain significant proportions of clay to make them flow better and adhere better. High-clay pigments, often showing hexagonal networks of cracks from shrinkage during drying, are often designated as "slips," showing that the distinction is somewhat arbitrary.

A **glaze** is a thin coating of glass fused to the vessel surface. Most ceramic glazes consist of silica (SiO_2) and fluxes, such as potassium, sodium, calcium, magnesium, and lead, that bring the melting temperature down from more than 1700 °C to 900-1300 °C (Rye, 1981:44-46). Often clear glazes are applied over pigment or slip, but glazes may contain coloring agents as well.

A **resist** is any material that the potter applies to the surface to prevent the adhesion of slip, paint, or glaze, so that uncoated regions are left as a decorative device. A wax resist burns off during firing, while resists made from leaves and other materials can be stuck onto the vessel and then removed again after the slip or paint

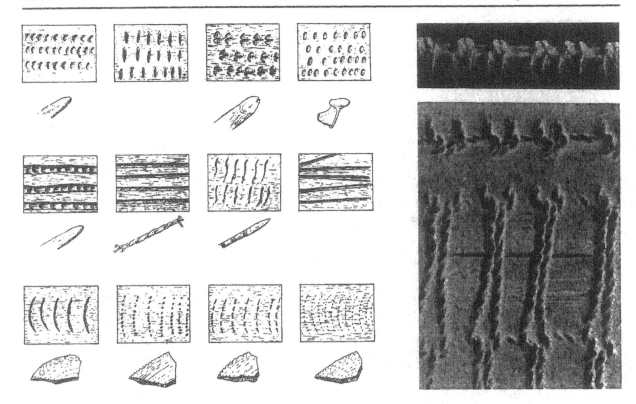

Figure 9.20. A variety of punctate and impressed motives created with sticks, small mammal's condyle, cord, quills, and notched shell fragments and different motions (Sampson, 1988:55).

Figure 9.21. Example of rouletting using a cord-wrapped stick (Hurley, 1979:97).

has been applied, but before firing (Shepard, 1961:206-13; Rye, 1981:43-44).

Some vessels show other coatings applied after firing, such as lime or pitch used to make the vessel more waterproof, as well as residues acquired during use.

A number of finishing techniques involve removing material from the vessel walls. These include **piercing** or perforating them when they are leather-hard, drilling through them after they are fired, and **carving** away areas in a decorative pattern (Rye, 1981:91-92).

Appliqué is a finishing technique that involves joining shaped pieces of plastic clay to a nearly leather-hard surface by pressure. The applied pieces can be functional, as with handles, or decorative, as with "rope" decoration and modelled figures (figure 9.23; Rye, 1981:93-95). Often, because the bond is somewhat weak, the vessel fractures along the boundary between the vessel and the appliqué.

Drying and Firing the Vessels

Carefully drying the formed vessels before firing is essential. Drying must be gradual and takes days or weeks, depending on weather conditions and the type and texture of inclusions. Warming unfired pots artificially to about 100°C helps dry them in inclement weather. It is also possible to raise the firing temperature very slowly to make sure that all moisture is out of the vessel walls before they are subjected to high temperatures (Gibson and Woods, 1997:46-47; Rice, 1987:152).

Firing the vessels to high temperatures (above 500-800°C) breaks down the clay minerals and transforms them into a ceramic material. The duration and atmosphere of firing, and not only the temperature, are responsible for the physical characteristics of the resulting ceramics (Rice, 1987:80-81). These range from relatively poorly fired earthenwares, with mainly crystalline and rather porous fabric, to porce-

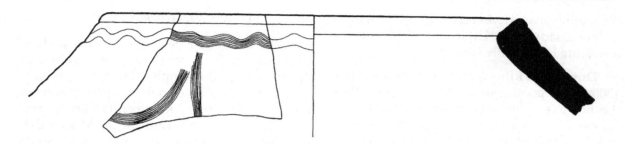

Figure 9.22. Example of a sherd with curvilinear, horizontal wavy, and vertical combing on the exterior of a rim sherd from an early Islamic site in northern Jordan (drawing by J. Pfaff).

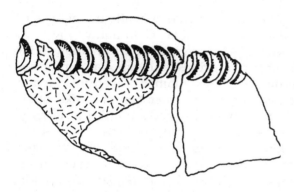

Figure 9.23. A band of appliqué decoration on a Chalcolithic sherd from Jordan (drawing by J. Pfaff).

lains, with predominantly vitreous, translucent, and non-porous fabric (table 9.1). Simple earthenwares can be made by open firing, in which vessels and fuel intermingle, while kiln firing, with vessels and fuel separated, is generally used for stonewares and porcelains.

With open firing, dried vessels are arranged on top of fuel, usually in a shallow pit, and more fuel is piled around them. Potters may leave spaces between pieces of fuel to permit better airflow around the vessels, which is necessary to get the temperature much above 800°C, but the temperature and atmosphere are likely to vary substantially in various parts of the fire, maximum temperature rarely exceeding 1000°C even in the hottest places. The temperature also varies considerably over time, going up and down as fuel is added or rearranged or the draft changes. Commonly vessels with broad apertures are fired upside-down, so that ash will insulate their rims and cause them to cool more slowly, thus preventing the rims from cracking through differential cooling rate (Rye, 1981:98).

This may result in reduction of the interior and rim surfaces, making them grey or black, while the remainder of the surface appears oxidized (cf. Lucas, 1962:373). It is extremely difficult to create a reducing atmosphere except in these small areas, however, and Rice (1987:81) characterizes the atmosphere in a typical open firing as "incompletely oxidizing." Maximum temperature is usually reached within 20 minutes, and then falls off slowly for more than 2 hours, and the potters typically use the color of the hot pots as a guide to the progress of the firing (Rice, 1987:157-58). Open firing is successful because the most pronounced physical changes in production of a ceramic, including loss of water, organics, carbonates, sulphates, and sulfides, occur at temperatures well below 900°C, and even sintering and vitrification, with the collapse of the clays' crystal structure, require temperatures only in the range of 900 to 1000°C (Rice, 1987:86-92, 153-58).

In a kiln, the fuel combusts in a firebox and the resulting hot gases pass through flues into a chamber that contains the vessels to be fired. Kilns allow potters to achieve temperatures of 1000 to 1300°C, control the rate of heating, and control the atmosphere by disrupting or increasing the flow of oxygen. The former creates a reducing atmosphere, containing CO and CO_2, while the latter produces an oxidizing one, with CO_2 and O_2 (Rye, 1981:98; Rice, 1987:81).

The **updraft kiln** (figure 9.24) has the chamber above the firebox, the whole resembling a chimney, airflow controlled at the stokehole. Mayes (1962) notes that it is difficult to create a reducing atmosphere in updraft kilns, although the potter can blacken the pottery by closing the stokehole and letting the fuel smoulder during the cooling phase (Rye and Evans, 1976). A more serious disadvantage is that updraft kilns do not distribute heat evenly (Rye, 1981:100).

Downdraft kilns allow temperatures up to 1300°C and good control of atmosphere. Here the hot gasses flow from the firebox over a "bagwall," downwards through the chamber, and through bottom flues into a chimney (figure 9.25). The chimney is necessary to draw the flame over this long distance. Downdraft kilns are used to produce porcelain and reduced stoneware (Rye, 1981:100).

Potters determine whether or not ceramics have reached the desired temperature by observing their color or by using "draw trials," small pieces that can be removed to test how well they have been fired and whether they are reduced or oxidized.

During the firing, the vessels undergo a series of physical changes culminating in cooling of the ceramic fabric (Rye, 1981:105-110; Rice, 1987:86-98).

The result of this firing is a hard material that falls into one of several commonly used categories of ceramics (table 9.1), depending mainly on the temperature of the kiln.

Several different methods can help us to estimate the maximum firing temperature of an ancient ceramic, but it is important to remember that the distinctive changes that we correlate with temperature are also affected by differences in firing atmosphere and in composition of the body (Rice, 1987:81-82). Rice (1987:82-85) notes that it is the duration of exposure to the maximum firing temperature that matters most.

Tite (1969) and Matson (1971) discuss ways we can estimate the firing temperatures of ancient pottery, but we can gain some idea of the atmosphere and duration of the firing and cooling by looking for a core in cross-sections of sherds that were fired below 1000°C. A ceramic fired for a long time in an oxidizing atmosphere will be well fired, and generally light-colored (pink, red, or yellow) throughout. A black or grey core will be visible if oxidation is incomplete and there were organics in the clay body, or if the atmosphere was reducing (figure 9.26; Rye, 1981:112-116).

FUNCTIONAL ANALYSIS

As with lithics, one aspect of pottery that archaeologists typically want to know is the function of the vessels. At the simplest level, the primary **utilitarian function** of pottery is containment. Like such other containers as pits, silos, boxes, and baskets, pots prevent the accidental dispersal of their contents, while still allowing some access for the intentional removal or addition of materials. Even pipes are containers in that their bowls contain tobacco while the opening on the bowl allows introduction of tobacco and removal of ash and smoke, while the pipe-stem allows egress of smoke. Commonly, however, we would like more specific information about containers' functions, and especially information on what they contained or were intended to contain. We must remember that, like other tools, they could have had multiple functions or have been used for purposes their makers did not intend. For example, a vessel used to make or store beer might also be used to serve or drink beer, to show hospitality, to display information through its decoration (e.g., ethnic or status markers, or even modern advertising), or to contain my car keys. Some archaeologists like to distinguish between utilitarian functions, such as mundane use of the pot to contain water or cook food, and symbolic or social functions, but any artifact can have several functions at once.

Archaeological investigations of function tend to take one of two general courses. One is to consider the properties of the artifact in terms of its design, on the assumption that the designer or maker of the artifact, in this case a pot, consciously selected design attributes to make the artifact as useful as possible for an intended

Table 9.1. Classification of ceramic bodies (after Rice 1987: 5)

Body	Porosity	Firing Range	Characteristics
Terra-cotta	High	<<1000°C	Coarse, porous
Earthenware	10-25%	900-1200°C	Nonvitrified
Stoneware	0.5-2%	1200-1350°C	Vitrified
China	<1%	1100-1200°C	Vitrified
Porcelain	<<1%	1300-1450°C	Hard, fine, white, translucent

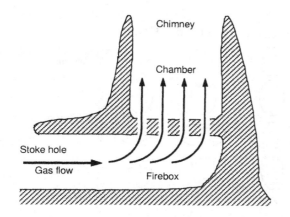

Figure 9.24. Cross-section through an updraft kiln.

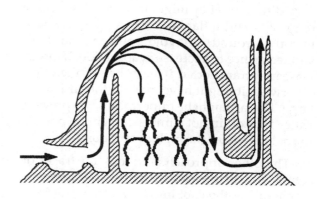

Figure 9.25. Cross-section through a downdraft kiln (after Rye, 1981).

task, under the constraints imposed by cost and competing design attributes (Braun, 1983; Henrickson and McDonald, 1983; Scholfield, 1948; Smith, 1985). The other is to investigate the use or uses of the artifact (or its last use prior to deposition) through examination of use traces, much as with "use-wear analysis" of stone tools.

The design approach involves anticipating certain features that might make a pot more useful for a particular task and then testing a hypothesized function by examining pots for the expected constellation of attributes and contextual associations. In many cases the hypothesized function is itself suggested by patterning in other attributes and context.

For example, a well-designed cooking pot needs to be able to withstand the thermal shocks associated with sudden heating and cooling. It also needs to be large enough to accomodate a typical meal of the type for which it was intended, with an opening large enough for stirring, adding ingredients, and removing the cooked food. It may need to have handles or some other device to make it easier to lift and manipulate while hot. Accomodation for a lid, such as rims that are bevelled or ledged on the interior, may be a good design feature to reduce the escape of heat from the orifice. A round bottom may provide more efficient heat transfer from an open flame if the pot is designed to be suspended or perched over stones or a tripod.

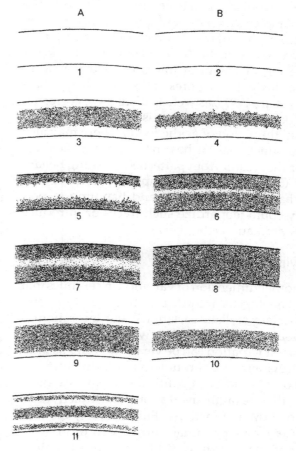

Figure 9.26. Cross-sections through sherds with fine-textured (A) and coarse clays (B) ranging from oxidized without organics (1-2), through oxidized with organics (3-4), reduced (5-6), reduced with possible organics (7-8), reduced, cooled in air (9-10), and reduced, cooled rapidly in air, and reduced again (11) (Rye, 1981:116).

The design features of a water jar would be very different. They might include a low center of gravity and a flat base (or digging the base into the ground) to avoid spillage, and a restricted orifice to decrease evaporation. If the jar was rarely transported, it might have no handles; otherwise, it might have many if the jar is very large. The jar might be impermeable, to prevent water loss, or, in hot climates, might be porous to cool the water through evapration.

The other approach is to look for traces of actual use on the vessels or their fragments. Again, using the cooking pot as an example, it may show signs of thermal spalling on parts of the vessel exterior that result from drying wet vessels near an open fire and from rapid heating during cooking. It may be soot-blackened on the lower exterior walls, and quite oxidized on the bottom where it was in direct contact with flame. It may show visible traces of burned food on the interior, or chemical traces of food that were absorbed into the pores of the fabric (e.g., Charters et al., 1997), as well as distinctive corrosion on parts of the interior vessel walls that results from the action of acidic foods. There may also be distinctive scratches on the interior and exterior that result from patterned washing behavior (Skibo, 1992). It is important to note that archaeologists' washing and handling of pottery could jeopardize such traces or introduce contamination (chapter 7).

Stylistic Analysis

Another dimension of variation in ceramics that archaeologists frequently study is **style**, and especially stylistic variation in the decoration on vessels. Many researchers would agree that this form of variation can be very important as indirect evidence for chronology, social institutions, ideology, and even political strategy, but there is rather less agreement about what exactly style is or how it functions. Furthermore, the rich variety and potential complexity of stylistic variation make the careful definition of analytical elements and selection of segmentation, differentiation, and orientation rules all that much more important. Although style can be manifested in anything from lithics (Close, 1978) to Jesuit finger rings (Cleland, 1972), ceramic analysts have shown particular interest in style.

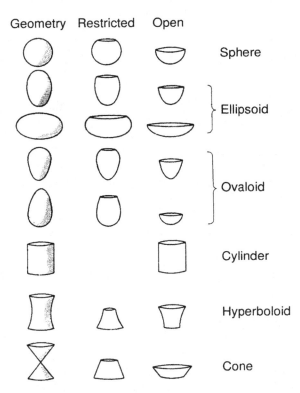

Figure 9.27. The geometry of overall form can have both functional and stylistic importance (Shepard, 1961).

Style can occur in many different attributes of pottery, and is certainly not limited to decoration, yet decorative style particularly lends itself to stylistic analysis.

After decades in which decorative style was used mainly to define chronological and geographical groups, several archaeologists (e.g., Deetz, 1965; Hill, 1970; Longacre, 1970) began to exploit it in the 1960s as evidence for social relationships, such as post-marital residence patterns. While many of the assumptions of these landmark studies have not withstood scrutiny, they still marked a watershed in the archaeological use of style (Graves, 1998; Skibo et al., 1989a).

Archaeologists differ on whether style is the result of the unique motor habits of individuals, of habits passed on through apprenticeship, or of conscious or sub-conscious social strategies, or is simply all the variation left over that cannot be explained functionally (see chapter 8).

The first sort of variation occurs because no two people will hold or use a tool, such as a paint brush or incising stylus, in exactly the same way, or execute the brush strokes, incisions, or impressions in exactly the same order (figure 9.28; Hardin, 1977; Hill, 1977; 1978). Prehistorians' use of this approach is similar to that of hand-writing analysts and art historians, who had already used small variations in various ratio-scale measurements of letters and brush strokes to identify the work of individual artists. For example, Hackett (1984) used minute details of brush-strokes to analyse the epigraphy of the Deir 'Alla inscription, an Aramaic document from Jordan that probably dates to the late eighth century B.C. Similar kinds of measurements can be made on the smallest discrete elements of a painted or incised design, or even on some aspects of rim shape, in an attempt to identify individuals' habits. Archaeologists who take this approach assume that the small variations are unconscious or subconscious rather than intentional, so that a novice pot-decorator would not necessarily duplicate the style of his or her teacher or mentor.

Most archaeologists, however, have treated style as learned behavior, passed from teacher to student, master to apprentice, or mother to daughter. Assuming that style is transmitted this way is attractive because it allows us to attempt to infer social structure, to measure social interaction, and to explain changes in style over time. Classic studies by Deetz (1965), Hill (1970), and Longacre (1970), for example, adopted the assumption that potters were women who learned potting skills and decorative designs from their mothers so that they could associate spatial clustering of design motives with matrilocal residence pattern. Assuming that style is a body of ideas that can be learned also allows us to associate the degree of stylistic similarity between pottery assemblages with the degree of social interaction between potters. Distinct discontinuities in the spatial distribution of styles, then, may represent "barriers to social intercourse" (Binford, 1965: 204). It also allows a very simple explanation of stylistic change as resulting from error in the transmission of the ideas, analogous in many ways to genetic drift (Binford, 1963; Cleland, 1972).

In addition to basic skills and design shapes, learning can transmit concepts or basic structures about the way new designs can be imagined, created, manipulated, or changed. Some authors (e.g., Kintigh, 1985; Muller, 1973; 1977; Shanks and Tilley, 1987:157-71; Washburn, 1977) have adopted a structuralist approach through which they attempt to discern the rules, almost a "grammar," that could have generated particular designs. For example, in figure 9.29, we can represent the vertical structure of decoration in the upper vessel as "ABCD" and that of the lower one as "ABACAD," meaning that the decoration of each band is different in the former, but that the zig-zag line alternates with other design elements in the latter. They then sometimes attempt to associate the designs' "lexical" elements and rules ("syntax") with aspects of the artists' social or physical context.

Archaeologists of the 1980s began to see style as a more active element in individuals' or groups' repertoire of social strategies (Shanks and Tilley, 1987). Already Wobst (1977) had suggested that style encoded information about group membership, which is particularly important in the context of ethnic or class conflict. "Stylistic messaging," Wobst (1977:327) says, "defines mutually expectable behavior patterns and makes subsequent interaction more predictable and less stressful," particularly for individuals who are not usually in verbal contact with one another. Hodder (1977; 1982) similarly discussed cases where individuals did not adopt the styles of their parents' social group, but used decorative styles actively to send messages about how they wanted themselves perceived. He also found that stylistic display was more intensive in boundary regions where people of different ethnicity were more likely to encounter one another. Bradley (1984:70-73) reinterpreted pottery that previous researchers had identified with supposed ethnic groups. Bradley sees them as conscious markers of status, with emerging or established elites adopting distinctive styles to distinguish themselves from those of lower status. Those who wished to enhance their own status through emulation later also adopted the same status markers. This forced elites continually to adopt new fashions in order to maintain their stylistic distinctiveness. In later Neolithic

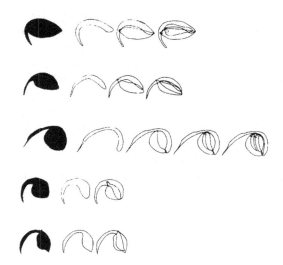

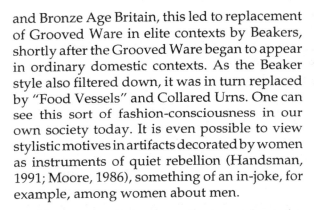

Figure 9.28. Variation among five artists in the sequence and number of brush-strokes used to paint a curved leaf on Mexican pottery from San José (Hardin, 1977:121).

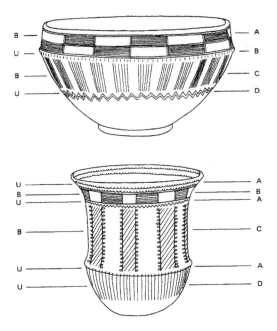

Figure 9.29. The sequence of distinctive bands of decoration from top to bottom of a Swedish Neolithic vessel can be treated as a sort of code (here each design type represented by a letter) to infer the structure of a design, irrespective of the actual design elements used in the bands of decoration (Shanks and Tilley, 1987:160).

and Bronze Age Britain, this led to replacement of Grooved Ware in elite contexts by Beakers, shortly after the Grooved Ware began to appear in ordinary domestic contexts. As the Beaker style also filtered down, it was in turn replaced by "Food Vessels" and Collared Urns. One can see this sort of fashion-consciousness in our own society today. It is even possible to view stylistic motives in artifacts decorated by women as instruments of quiet rebellion (Handsman, 1991; Moore, 1986), something of an in-joke, for example, among women about men.

No matter what perspective one adopts for the study of style, it is necessary to be very careful about the definition of analytical elements, orientation rules, and segmentation rules. Among the problems inherent in some of the classic stylistic studies are that there was no unambiguous way to decide what constituted a "design element," as well as a failure to ensure that different dimensions of stylistic variability were treated separately (Plog, 1980:41-43). For example, Hill's (1970) classification of design elements includes a number of different geometric shapes, as well as lines of different thicknesses, as though a thick line and a thin one were different values of the attribute "shape." In reality, these are identical on the dimension of shape, and vary only in the dimension of size.

Some kinds of stylistic analysis are only applicable to whole vessels (e.g., Bunzel, 1972; Friedrich, 1970; Washburn, 1977), and we have to be either particularly careful or less ambitious if we are forced to deal with sherds. For example, decoration may be restricted to a particular part of a vessel, such as the shoulder or the region below the rim, or decoration may occur in bands or panels, with different designs in each (figures 9.2, 9.30). Consequently, the absence of a particular motif or treatment in the decoration exhibited on a sherd does not mean that it was absent on the whole vessel prior to fragmentation. Quite often the distribution of stylistic elements over different zones, bands, or panels of distribution can be very interesting and potentially informative, but this kind of analysis is not suitable for the vast majority of ceramic collections, which consist mainly of sherds.

Defining the elements of decoration and the ways in which they can vary is quite challenging but absolutely necessary for consistency in analysis (Plog, 1980:42).

Plog (1980:47-53) advocates a hierarchical definition of the elements used to classify and analyse ceramic decoration on sherds (figure 3.14), but it could also be viewed as a multi-dimensional (paradigmatic) approach. Under the influence of previous work by Carlson (1970) and Friedrich (1970), he identifies *primary design units*, which are the most obvious motives in the design and are typically geometric shapes, such as rectangles, triangles, and line segments. *Secondary units* are optional shapes that do not occur except in combination with primary units, and their location depends on the location of the primary units, as would happen if the primary units were created first, and the secondary ones added in, on, or around them (Friedrich, 1970:335). Secondary units can be *appended*, as in the case of ticks added around the margins of a geometric shape, or *unappended*, as in the case of dots placed in or between geometric shapes. Plog also records the *composition* or fill of the primary and secondary units; the composition could be, for example, solid, open, hatched, cross-hatched, checkerboard, or stippled. Another dimension is *linearity*; essentially the same primary or secondary unit can sometimes be found in both rectilinear and curvilinear varieties. Yet another dimension, reminiscent of some of the structuralist approaches, is the way in which secondary or primary units are combined, or their *interaction*: they can be isolated, doubled, interlocked, reflected, repeated, and so on.

Plog is quite right to emphasize the careful definition of design elements or "differentiation rules" (above, p. 60), but this is only part of the picture. First, it may still be quite difficult to define them unambiguously, while different researchers who think they are following Plog's rules may still classify the same motif differently. It is necessary for individual researchers to make the rules for such distinctions as clear as possible if their work is to be reproducible. Second, for some types of design the orientation of design elements may be as important as their content. In assemblages that preserve some evidence for orientation, we may need orientation rules. In figure 9.24, for example, where preservation of the rim just above the applied decoration allows us to determine which way is up, it may be important that some jars have scalloped or lunate appliqué oriented with the curve on the left, and others on the right. This variation could be due to individual motor habits or to learned behavior in the placement of the half-disks of clay.

OTHER APPROACHES TO POTTERY

While it is impossible to be exhaustive here, some studies do not fit the characterizations as "ceramic ecology," functional analysis, or stylistic analysis. One of the issues with which archaeological ceramicists are sometimes concerned is the issue of craft specialization. Although stylistic and technological analyses both contribute to such studies, an approach that lies in their intersection is to look for evidence of standardization. A very small standard deviation in some of the attributes of vessels that may have been mass produced, for example, may be the result of specialization among potters (e.g., Blackman et al., 1993). Another one is gender. Many archaeologists in the past made the assumption, based only loosely on modern ethnographic literature, that hand-made pots were made by women and that mass-produced, wheel-made pots were made by men. Only recently have some researchers given serious attention to the factors that may have led to women specializing in pottery production in some cultures, men in others, or to no specialization, or specialization among both sexes in still others (R. Wright, 1991). Some archaeologists now suggest that stylistic elements in pottery, in cultures in which women were the potters, could encode messages that contrast markedly with those found in male-dominated public spheres. Still other researchers have investigated the seasonality of pottery production, particularly where the annual schedule revolved around agricultural duties. Seed impressions on pottery lead Howard (1981) to argue that Neolithic pottery from Windmill Hill in Britain was made in autumn, for example.

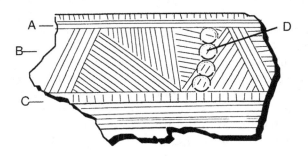

Figure 9.30. Examples of design elements on an incised Iroquoian sherd of a type called "Durfee Underlined": straight line border (a), alternately hatched band (b), appended ticks (c), and appended punctate circles (d).

Conclusions

Fragments of pottery are probably the most abundant macro-artifacts to be found on sites of the last 2000 years or more and, on average, they tend to be preserved almost as well as lithics. Because pottery is a plastic medium, it lends itself to a tremendous variety in vessel shape and decoration. Historically, archaeologists have depended on this variety in pottery to order archaeological cultures in time, determine their distribution in space, and identify interactions between regions. More recently, archaeologists investigating pottery have focussed on what it can tell us about technological change, the use of pottery, craft specialization, social roles, strategies, and relationships.

References Cited

Arnold, D. E., 1974, Some principles for paste analysis and interpretation: A preliminary formulation. *Journal of the Steward Anthropological Society* 6:33-47.

Binford, L. R., 1963, "Red ochre" caches from the Michigan area: A possible case of cultural drift. *Southwestern Journal of Anthropology* 19:89-108.

— 1965, Archaeological systematics and the study of culture process. *American Antiquity* 31:203-210.

Blackman, M. J., Stein, G. J., and Vandiver, P. B., 1993, The standardization hypothesis and ceramic mass production: Technological, compositional, and metric indexes of craft specialization at Tell Leilan, Syria. *American Antiquity* 58:60-80.

Bradley, R., 1984, *The Social Foundations of Prehistoric Britain. Themes and Variations in the Archaeology of Power.* Longman, London.

Braun, D. P., 1983, Pots as tools. In *Archaeological Hammers and Theories*, edited by J. Moore and A. Keene, pp. 107-134. Academic Press, New York.

Bronitsky, G., 1986, The use of materials science techniques in the study of pottery construction and use. *Advances in Archaeological Method and Theory* 9:209-76.

Bronitsky, G., and Hamer, R., 1986, Experiments in ceramic technology: The effects of various tempering materials on impact and thermal-shock resistance. *American Antiquity* 51:89-101.

Bunzel, R. L., 1972, *The Pueblo Potter, a Study of Creative Imagination in Primitive Art.* Dover Publications, New York.

Carlson, R. L., 1970, *White Mountain Redware, a Pottery Tradition of East-Central Arizona and Western New Mexico.* Anthropological Papers of the University of Arizona 19. University of Arizona Press, Tucson.

Charters, S., Evershed, R. P., Quye, A., Blinkhorn, P. W., and Reeves, V., 1997, Simulation experiments for determining the use of ancient pottery vessels: The behaviour of epicuticular leaf wax during boiling of a leafy vegetable. *Journal of Archaeological Science* 24:1-7.

Cleland, C. E., 1972, From sacred to profane: Style drift in the decoration of Jesuit finger rings. *American Antiquity* 37:202-210.

Close, A. E., 1978, The identification of style in lithic artifacts. *World Archaeology* 10:223-37.

Deetz, J., 1965, *The Dynamics of Stylistic Change in Arikara Ceramics.* Illinois Studies in Anthropology 4. University of Illinois Press, Urbana.

Engelbrecht, W., 1971, *A Stylistic Analysis of Iroquois Pottery.* Unpublished Ph.D dissertation, University of Michigan.

Feathers, J. K., 1989, Effects of temper on strength of ceramics: Response to Bronitsky and Hamer. *American Antiquity* 54:579-88.

Franken, H. J., 1974, *In Search of the Jericho Potters.* North-Holland Ceramic Studies in Archaeology 1, Leiden.

Franken, H. J., and Kalsbeek, J., 1969, Excavation at Tell Deir 'Alla, Volume I: A Stratigraphic and Analytical Study of the Iron Age Pottery. H. J. Brill, Leiden.

— 1975, *Potters of a Medieval Village in the Jordan Valley.* American Elsevier Press, New York.

Friedrich, M., 1970, Design structure and social interaction: Archaeological implications of an ethnographic analysis. *American Antiquity* 35:332-43.

Gibson, A., and Woods, A., 1997, *Prehistoric Pottery for the Archaeologist.* Leicester University Press, London.

Glock, A. E., 1975, Homo Faber: The pot and the potter at Taanach. *Bulletin of the American Schools of Oriental Research* 219:9-28.

Graves, M. W., 1998, The history of method and theory in the study of prehistoric Puebloan pottery style in the American Southwest. *Journal of Archaeological Method and Theory* 5:309-43.

Hackett, J. A., 1984, *The Balaam Text from Deir 'Alla.* Scholars Press, Chico, CA.

Hamer, F., 1975, *The Potter's Dictionary of Materials and Techniques.* Pitman Publishing, London.

Handsman, R G., 1991, Whose art was found at Lepenski Vir? Gender relations and power in archaeology. In *Engendering Archaeology: Women and Prehistory*, edited by J. Gero and M. Conkey, pp. 329-365. Basil Blackwell, Oxford.

Hardin, M. A., 1977, Individual style in San José pottery painting: The role of deliberate choice. In *The Individual in Prehistory*, edited by J. Hill and J. Gunn, pp. 109-36. Academic Press, New York.

Hayes, J., 1976, *Roman Pottery in the Royal Ontario Museum*. Royal Ontario Museum, Toronto.

Henrickson, E., and McDonald, M., 1983, Ceramic form and function: An ethnographic search and archaeological application. *American Anthropologist* 85:630-43.

Hill, J. N., 1970, *Broken K Pueblo: Prehistoric Social Organization in the American Southwest*. Anthropological Papers of the University of Arizona 18. University of Arizona Press, Tucson.

— 1977, Individual variability in ceramics and the study of prehistoric social organization. In *The Individual in Prehistory: Studies of Variability in Style in Prehistoric Technologies*, edited by J. N. Hill and J. Gunn, pp. 55-108. Academic Press, New York.

— 1978, Individuals and their artifacts: An experimental study in archaeology. *American Antiquity* 43:245-57.

Hoard, R. J., O'Brien, M. J., Khorasgany, M. G., and Gopalaratnam, V. S., 1995, A materials science approach to understanding limestone-tempered pottery from the Midwestern United States. *Journal of Archaeological Science* 22:823-32.

Hodder, I., 1977, The distribution of material culture items in the Baringo district, western Kenya. *Man* 12:239-69.

— 1982, *Symbols in Action. Ethnoarchaeological Studies of Material Culture*. Cambridge University Press, Cambridge.

Howard, H., 1981, In the wake of distribution: Towards an integrated approach to ceramic studies in prehistoric Britain. In *Production and Distribution: A Ceramic Viewpoint*, edited by H. Howard and E. Morr, pp. 1-30. BAR British Series 120. Oxford: British Archaeological Reports.

Hurley, W. M., 1979, *Prehistoric Cordage*. Manuals on Archeology 3. Taraxacum, Washington, DC.

Jansma, M. J., 1977, Diatom analysis of pottery. In *Ex Horreo*, edited by B. L. van Beek, R. W. Brandt and W. G. Waateringe, pp. 77-85. Universiteit van Amsterdam, Amsterdam.

Jizba, Z. V., 1971, Mathematical analysis of grain orientation. In *Procedures in Sedimentary Technology*, edited by R. E. Carver, pp. 313-33. John Wiley and Sons, New York.

Kempe, R. C., and Harvey, A. P., eds., 1983, *The Petrology of Archaeological Artefacts*. Clarendon Press, Oxford.

Kilikoglou, V., Vekenis, G., Maniatis, Y., and Day, P. M., 1998, Mechanical performance of quartz-tempered ceramics: Part I, strength and toughness. *Archaeometry* 40:261-79.

Kingery, W. D., Bowen, H. K., and Uhlmann, D. R., 1976, *Introduction to Ceramics*, 2nd. ed. John Wiley, New York.

Kintigh, K. W., 1985, Social structure, the structure of style, and stylistic patterns in Cibola potter. In *Decoding Prehistoric Ceramics*, edited by B. A. Nelson, pp. 35-74. Southern Illinois Press, Carbondale.

Longacre, W. A., 1970, *Archaeology as Anthropology: A Case Study*. Anthropological Papers of the University of Arizona 17. University of Arizona Press, Tucson.

Lucas, A., 1962, *Ancient Egyptian Materials and Industries* (fourth edition). Edward Arnold, London.

Matson, F. R., 1965, Ceramic ecology: An approach to the study of the early cultures of the Near East. In *Ceramics and Man*, edited by F. R. Matson, pp. 202-17. Thames and Hudson, London.

— 1971, The study of temperatures used in firing ancient Mesopotamian pottery. In *Science and Archaeology*, edited by R. Brill, pp. 65-79. MIT Press, Cambridge, MA.

Matson, F. R., ed., 1965, *Ceramics and Man*. Viking Fund Publications in Anthropology 41. Aldine, Chicago.

Mayes, P., 1962, The firing of a second pottery kiln of Romano-British type at Boston, Lincolnshire. *Archaeometry* 5:80-85.

Menzel, D., 1976, *Pottery Style and Society in Ancient Peru*. University of California Press, Berkeley.

Moore, H. L., 1986, *Space, Text and Gender. An Anthropological Study of the Marakwet of Kenya*. Cambridge University Press, Cambrdige.

Muller, J., 1973, *Structural Studies of Art Styles*. Ninth International Congress of Anthropological and Ethnological Sciences, Chicago.

— 1977, Individual variation in art styles. In *The Individual in Prehistory*, edited by J. Hill and J. Gunn, pp. 23-39. Academic Press, New York.

Nesse, W. D., 1986, *Introduction to Optical Mineralogy*. Oxford University Press, Oxford.

Newlands, D. L., and Breede, C., 1976, *An Introduction to Canadian Archaeology*. McGraw-Hill, Toronto.

O'Brien, J., Holland, T. D., Hoard, R. J., and Fox, G. L., 1994, Evolutionary implications of design and performance characteristics of prehistoric pottery. *Journal of Archaeological Method and Theory* 1:259-304.

Orton, C., 1980, Mathematics in Archaeology. Cambridge University Press, Cambridge.

Peacock, D. P. S., 1970, The scientific study of ancient ceramics: A review. *World Archaeology* 1:375-89.

Plog, S., 1978, Social interaction and stylistic similarity: A reanalysis. *Advances in Archaeological Method and Theory* 1:143-82.

— 1980, *Stylistic Variation in Prehistoric Ceramics. Design Analysis in the American Southwest*. Cambridge University Press, Cambridge.

Rands, R. L., 1961, Elaboration and invention in ceramic traditions. *American Antiquity* 26:331-40.

Redman, C. L., 1977, The "analytical individual" and prehistoric style variability. In *The Individual in Prehistory: Studies of Variability in Style and Prehistoric Technologies*, edited by J. N. Hill and J. Gunn, pp. 41-53. Academic Press, New York.

Rice, P. M., 1987, *Pottery Analysis: A Sourcebook*. University of Chicago Press, Chicago.

— 1996, Recent ceramic analysis : 2. Composition, production, and theory. *Journal of Archaeological Research* 4:165-202.

Rye, O. S., 1981, *Pottery Technology. Principles and Reconstruction*. Taraxacum, Washington, DC.

Rye, O. S., and Allen, J., 1976, New approaches to Papuan pottery analysis. *Prétirage: IX Congress, Union Internationale des Sciences Préhistoriques et Protohistoriques*. Colloque XXII: La Préhistoire Océanienne, pp. 198-222.

Rye, O. S., and Evans, C., 1976, *Traditional Pottery Techniques of Pakistan: Field and Laboratory Studies*. Smithsonian Contributions to Anthropology 21. Smithsonian Institution, Washington, DC.

Sackett, J. R., 1982, Approaches to style in lithic archaeology. *Journal of Anthropological Archaeology* 1:59-112.

Sampson, C. G., 1988, *Stylistic Boundaries among Mobile Hunter-Foragers*. Smithsonian Institution, Washington, DC.

Scholfield, J. F., 1948, *Primitive Pottery*. Handbook Series 3, The South African Archaeological Society, Capetown.

Shanks, M., and Tilley, C. 1987, *Re-Constructing Archaeology, Theory and Practice*. Cambridge University Press, Cambridge.

Shepard, A. O., 1961, *Ceramics for the Archaeologist*. Carnegie Institution Publication 609. Carnegie Institution, Washington, DC.

Sinopoli, C. M., 1991, *Approaches to Archaeological Ceramics*. Plenum Press, New York.

Skibo, J. M., 1992, *Pottery Function. A Use-Alteration Perspective*. Plenum Press, New York.

Skibo, J., Schiffer, M. B., and Kowalski, N., 1989a, Ceramic style analysis in archaeology and ethnoarchaeology: Bridging the analytical gap. *Journal of Anthropological Archaeology* 8:388-409.

Skibo, J., Schiffer, M. B., and Reid, K. C., 1989b, Organic-tempered pottery: An experimental study. *American Antiquity* 54:122-46.

Smith, M., 1985, Toward an economic interpretation of ceramics: Relating vessel size and shape to use. In *Decoding Prehistoric Ceramics*, edited by B. A. Nelson, pp. 254-309. Southern Illinois University Press, Carbondale.

Smith, R. H., 1972, The sectioning of potsherds as an archaeological method. *Berytus* 21:39-53.

Stewart, J. D., Fralick, P., Hancock, R., Kelley, J. H., and Garrett, E., 1990, Petrographic analysis and INAA geochemistry of prehistoric ceramics from Robinson Pueblo, New Mexico. *Journal of Archaeological Science* 17:601-25.

Textoris, D. A., 1971, Grain-size measurement in thin-section. In *Procedures in Sedimentary Petrology*, edited by R. E. Carver, pp. 95-107. John Wiley and Sons, New York.

Tite, M. S., 1969, Determination of the firing temperature of ancient ceramics by measurement of thermal expansion: a reassessment. *Archaeometry* 11:131-44.

Vekenis, G., and Kelikoglou, V., 1998, Mechanical performance of quartz-tempered ceramics: Part II, Hertzian strength, wear resistance and applications to ancient ceramics. *Archaeometry* 40:281-92.

Vitali, V., 1989, Archaeometric provenance studies: an expert systems approach. *Journal of Archaeological Science* 16:383-91.

Washburn, D. K., 1977, *A Symmetry Analysis of Upper Gila Area Ceramic Design*. Papers of the Peabody Museum of Archaeology and Ethnology 68. Peabody Museum, Cambridge, MA.

Whallon, R., 1969, *Reflections on Social Interaction in Owasco Ceramic Decoration*. Bulletins 27 and 28:15. Eastern States Archaeological Federation, Andover, MA.

Williams, D. F., 1983, Petrology of ceramics. In *The Petrology of Archaeological Artefacts*, edited by R. C. Kempe and A. P. Harvey, pp. 301-29. Clarendon Press, Oxford.

Wobst, H. M., 1977, Stylistic behavior and information exchange. In *Papers for the Director: Research Essays in Honor of James B. Griffin*, edited by C. E. Cleland, pp. 317-42. Anthropological Papers of the Museum of Anthropology 61. University of Michigan, Ann Arbor.

Wright, R. P., 1991, Women's labor and pottery production in prehistory. In *Engendering Archaeology*, edited by J. Gero and M. W. Conkey, pp. 194-223. Basil Blackwell, Oxford.

10 Analysing Osteological and Other Faunal Remains

In some archaeological sites, the bones, shells, and other relatively robust remains of animals constitute one of the most completely preserved classes of macroscopic archaeological materials. Because they are often preserved better than plant remains, they have attracted considerable attention from archaeologists hoping to reconstruct the natural environments, hunting and herding behaviors, and dietary preferences of prehistoric people, and the season in which their settlements were located.

As with other chapters in this book, the limitations of an introduction require omission of many topics that would appear in a thorough reference. Although the osteological study of ancient humans has much in common with that of non-human mammals, in this chapter we will focus on comparing the latter with birds, and introduce only the most common types of fish and mollusc remains. The processes by which human remains accumulate in archaeological sites (often intentional interment) differ, in most but not all cases, from those responsible for the distribution of faunal remains. Research on human burials, furthermore, usually has quite different research goals than research on archaeological fauna. Human remains also entail ethical issues that are better dealt with in courses on physical anthropology. For detailed treatment of human remains see Brothwell (1981), Roberts and Manchester (1995), and Ubelaker (1989).

There are many labels attached to archaeologists who study the surviving evidence of animals. Some texts refer to them as zooarchaeologists, others as archaeozoologists, still others as faunal osteologists, faunal osteo-archaeologists, or simply faunal analysts.

Types of Faunal Remains

It is tempting to jump to the conclusion that an analysis of faunal remains is an analysis of bones. In fact, bones are only one of the categories of fossils that zooarchaeologists analyse. Although bones are often the best preserved and most obvious fossil evidence of animals with bony endoskeletons, it is sometimes also possible to detect and recover fragments of cartilage, skin and hair, muscle tissue, certain stomach contents, and coprolites (fossil feces), especially in sites that are waterlogged or very dry. Teeth may be preserved much more reliably than bone in typical site environments. In some sites the fragmented shells of birds' eggs may occur (Keepax, 1981). Meanwhile insects sometimes leave parts of their exoskeletons, parasites have left eggs, while snails and various sea animals leave shell, and some animals leave antler, hoof, or horn. Insects and worms may even leave distinctive traces of tunnelling or nests. Some archaeologists have attempted to identify pastoral sites on the basis of microscopic **phytoliths** and **spherulites** from plants that are deposited on sites in the animals' manure. A very productive line of research is to identify the mineral concretions called **otoliths** (ear-stones) from fish. This chapter, however, will emphasize the analysis of bone, teeth, otoliths, and mollusc shell.

Taphonomy and Faunal Assemblages

As with other classes of archaeological remains, it is important to remember that the sets of fossils that archaeologists study are not equivalent to the sets of either bones or animals that existed in the past. Archaeologists do not directly study past populations of animals; instead they study modern samples of bones and bone fragments. Not only does this force us to pay attention to the quality and size of the sample (see chapter 4), but we must think about the ways in which our modern sample became a distorted remnant of the original past population. It is useful to view this as a sequence of selections that gradually reduced the large original population of living creatures to a sample of their remains.

Taphonomy is the study of the processes by which living animals in the biosphere are transformed and eventually become (through fossilization) part of the earth's rock or lithosphere (Efremov, 1940; Gifford, 1981; Lyman, 1994). Taphonomists try to strip away the "biases" in a fossil assemblage in the hope of reconstructing the structure of the population of animals at the time they died. By studying factors that concentrate or destroy bones in modern environments and in laboratories, they attempt to understand these biases. Taphonomy has much in common with the study of what Schiffer (1976; 1987) would call site-formation processes. Taphonomic research includes various kinds of geoarchaeological, analogical, and experimental work, including moving bones by water flow through a laboratory flume (e.g., Hanson, 1980), ethnoarchaeological observations of recent scavengers, hunters, and butchers (Binford, 1978; 1981; Brain, 1975; 1976; 1981), and experiments with bone trampling and dog consumption (Gifford, 1981; Payne and Munson, 1985). Taphonomic processes are the actions whose forces modify the physical characteristics and distribution of animal carcasses and tissues, while a taphonomic effect is the trace of such a process (Lyman, 1994: 35).

Modern zooarchaeologists now distinguish among a number of quite sets of fauna, only one of which is normally directly observable. Klein and Cruz-Uribe (1984: 3), following Clark and Kietzke (1967), Meadow (1980) and others, propose the following distinctions.

1. The **life assemblage**: This is the living community of animals, a population from which the fossils are ultimately derived.

2. The **death assemblage**: This is the population of carcasses that results when members of the life assemblage die. Except when there is a catastrophic kill of the whole community, we would not expect the proportions of animals of various ages, sexes, and health status in this assemblage to be the same as in the life assemblage for the simple reason that death is not equally probable for animals of different age or health. This is the population whose size (N) the Peterson estimator (chapter 5) estimates.

3. The **deposited assemblage**: This is the set of carcasses or body parts that are deposited on an archaeological site through the action of humans, non-human predators, and scavengers such as hyaenas, rats or owls, and other agents of bone-accumulation (e.g., water flow, gravity, erosion).

4. The **fossil assemblage**: This is a subset of the deposited assemblage, consisting of those animal parts that survive in the site's deposits until found by a modern researcher. Environmental conditions, such as pH of the sourrounding sediments (see chapter 12), have a substantial effect on the character of this assemblage. In terms of sampling, this (or some spatial volume that encloses it) is the population that archaeologists sample (see chapter 4).

5. The **sample assemblage**: This is the portion of the fossil assemblage that was excavated or collected and then analyzed (in fact, the sample assemblage is sometimes only a portion of what was excavated). Archaeologists' field and laboratory methods have a great impact on the character and size of this sample.

At each stage from the life assemblage to the sample assemblage, the absolute number of bones and other animal remains decreases and, even more importantly, the distribution of remains by sex, age, body part, and health status changes. Both diseases and hunting behavior select victims unequally; bone accumulators, including humans, preferentially bring certain animal parts to a location, and the work of scavengers and various natural agents (e.g., chemical leaching, erosion, trampling) destroys some kinds of bone more easily than others. Finally, the behavior of the modern researchers, including how carefully they excavated, inspected, or screened the sediments (Clason and Prummel, 1977; Payne, 1972a), affects the likelihood that certain kinds of bones in the fossil assemblage (and particularly very small ones) will get into the sample assemblage. As with archaeobotanical work, zooarchaeologists spend a great deal of time worrying about how to compensate for the effects of poor preservation, principally fragmentation, during the transition from the deposited assemblage to the fossil assemblage.

Animal Taxonomy

Carl von Linné, an 18th-century anatomist, developed the basic structure of the taxonomic classification of organisms that biologists still use. All organisms are classified in a hierarchy with **kingdom** at the first level, down through the levels **phylum** (or division), **class**, **order**, **family**, and **genus** to **species** and sub-species. In the kingdom, Animalia (the other kingdoms are Protista and Plantae), Mammalia is a class of the phylum, Chordata (animals possessing a spinal chord). Because there is an evolutionary, that is, historical, basis for the hierarchy in this taxonomy (although von Linné was himself ignorant of the evolutionary history), the taxonomic relationships mimic relationships of descent. Animals descended from the same ancestor tend to share quite a few characteristics. This is very helpful to zooarchaeologists trying to identify animals on the basis of fragmentary evidence. Even when they do not have enough evidence to identify a fossil to species, often they can at least narrow down the possibilities to a given genus (plural, genera) or family because of these familial similarities. The taxonomic category to which we assign a particular animal or bone is called its **taxon** (plural, taxa), whether that is a species, genus or more general category.

Mammalian Anatomy

Through common evolutionary descent, all mammals (members of the class, Mammalia) have largely the same skeletal anatomical parts, even though their skeletons vary in the total number of bones. For describing parts of skeletons, zooarchaeologists employ the same segmentation rules and analytical elements that zoologists use (see figure 10.1). In addition to the names for whole bones and teeth, there are also terms for their parts and various surfaces: **epiphysis** (bone end) and diaphysis (bone shaft or centrum), **proximal** and **distal** ends (toward or away from the body), **medial** and **lateral** position (near or away from the midline), **anterior** and **posterior** (roughly "front" and "rear"), **dorsal** (toward back) and **ventral** (toward stomach), and **buccal** (cheek-side) and **lingual** (tongue-side) for the mouth and teeth. But there are also names for groups of bones within the structure of the skeleton. Conventionally, biologists divide the skeleton into the **axial** (skull, vertebral column, ribs, and sternum) and **appendicular** parts. Appendicular includes the fore-limbs, hind-limbs, **pectoral girdle** (shoulder region), and **pelvic girdle** (hip region).

Although this is the basic system of segmentation rules that zooarchaeologists use, where we have some information about butchering practices, as in historical archaeology, it is sometimes useful to supplement it with the butchers' system of segmentation. For example, in recent times in England a butcher would subdivide a pig's carcass into such portions as loin, belly, shank, forehock, and gammon (Davis, 1987). Data organized by segments such as these is sometimes more informative about past butchering activity than those organized in the standard zoological manner.

Bone and cartilage are the supporting tissues in vertebrate organisms. Bone is a living tissue that consists of cells and their products, blood vessels, and nerves. The inorganic materials that the cells deposit include calcium phosphate ($Ca_3(PO_4)_2$), calcium carbonate ($CaCO_3$), magnesium, fluorine, chlorine, and iron. These are the materials that sometimes survive in fossil assemblages long after the organism is dead and most of the organic constituents have decayed away. In addition, the fossilization process itself deposits minerals while gradually converting the bone into a stone. Bone cells also deposit fibrous protein material, similar to that found in cartilage, of which collagen is very important. All red and many white blood cells are produced in the long bones. Cartilage is durable and generally more flexible than bone. It consists of cells in a matrix of protein, carbohydrates, and fibres.

Bone is formed by **ossification** over the lifetime of a vertebrate animal. Early in the animal's life, the "bones" are in fact composed entirely of cartilage. Ossification begins midway between the proximal and distal ends of the bone and later occurs at the two epiphyses. The bone-forming cells remain alive within the matrix materials that they secrete, and the first bone that they form is spongy (*cancellous*), but is later replaced by more compact bone tissue as concentric layers of bone are deposited on the inside surface of channels along the *periosteum* (outside of the bone). The channels thus become narrowed over time, forming canals through which lymph and blood vessels run. Once bone has stopped growing, the bone-forming cells occupy cavities in the bone, where they maintain the bone. The central cavity of long bones contains marrow (Lyman, 1994: 72-78).

Antler is an outgrowth of bone and is structurally similar to long bone. The outer cortex is compact and bone-like, but the inner part is similar to cancellous bone, rather than marrow-filled. Following seasonal growth, antler ossifies and is shed annually.

Horns, on the other hand, are instead an outgrowth of epitheleal tissue, like skin. Horn is made up of a fibrous material, called keratin, also found in hooves and claws. The horn grows as keratin is laid down in layers over the horn-cores, which are protuberances of cancellous bone that project from the skull. Consequently, horns tend to have distinct layers of fibrous material that can flake off during burial. Rhinoceros horns do not have horn cores.

In common speech we tend to think of the teeth as part of the skeletal system, but they are actually part of the digestive tract and not bones at all, having been formed from tooth "buds" formed in the epithelial tissue that lines the mouth. They are composed of dentine, enamel, and cementum, with a central nerve cavity. Elephant ivory is almost entirely dentine (the enamel only occurs on the tips of the tusks of young elephants).

Axial Parts

The axial skeleton consists of the skull, vertebral column, ribs, and sternum.

The skull is constructed of the cranium, which protects the brain, and facial bones that shape and protect the eyes, nose, and mouth. Normally, in adults, only the mandible is movable, the *sutures* in the cranium being immovable joints. At the base or back of the skull, the *foramen magnum* is an opening that permits the spinal chord to enter. Near it, two bony projections called *occipital condyles* serve much as hinges on the *atlas* and *axis* at the top of the spinal column. With two condyles we can nod our heads up and down. The dome (*calvaria*) of the skull contains a frontal bone, left and right parietal bones, left and right temporal bones, an occipital bone, sphenoid bone, and ethmoid bone. The face includes two maxillae (upper mouth), a mandible (jaw), two zygomatic (cheek) bones, and two nasal bones, among others that are not visible.

The vertebral column consists of a stack of vertebrae (sg., vertebra), separated by intervertebral discs made of cartilage, that protect the spinal nerve and provide support for the animal's weight. Conventionally, we segment the vertebral column into cervical (neck), thoracic (upper back), lumbar (lower back), sacral (hip area), and caudal (tail) regions. Although they vary in detail, each vertebra has a body, on which the discs rest, and a vertebral arch, which encloses the spinal canal or foramen and is surrounded by processes that radiate out from it, including the transverse processes and the spine. The transverse processes are attachments for muscles and, in the thoracic vertebrae, ribs. Openings allow nerves to branch out from the spinal chord to various parts of the body.

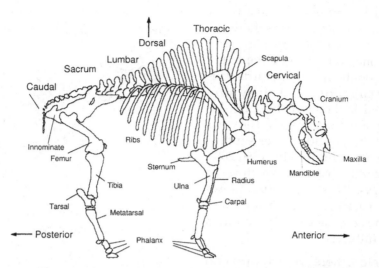

Figure 10.1. *Right lateral view of the skeleton of a North American bison (Bison bison), to illustrate the major skeletal parts of ungalates (after Lyman, 1994:88). The fibula is hidden behind the tibia.*

Given that the sternum and ribs function mainly as protection for the heart and lungs and to aid breathing, it is not surprising that they are important in mammals.

Appendicular Parts

The pectoral girdle consists of the scapula (shoulder blade), which serves as a broad attachment for muscles, and sometimes the clavicle (collar bone) and coracoid (as in birds).

The forelimb consists of the humerus, radius, and ulna, carpals, metacarpals, phalanges, and sometimes sesamoids.

The pelvic girdle (innominate) consists of the two ilia, two ischia, and two pubis bones, all fused together and joined to the sacrum (fused sacral vertebrae) in the vertebral column. The males in some species also have a baculum (penis bone).

Each hindlimb consists of the femur (pl., femora), patella, tibia and fibula, tarsals, metatarsals, and phalanges.

Teeth

Mammals typically replace their deciduous (primary) teeth only once, having to make do with their permanent teeth through their adult lives. Mammal teeth include incisors, canines, premolars, and molars.

A mammal's tooth consists of the crown, exposed above the gum, and the root. The surface on the crown that makes contact with its opposite during chewing is called the occlusal surface, which itself has one or more projections called cusps. Enamel covers most of the crown in most species, but is absent, for example, on the lingual side of rodents' and rabbits' incisors. It is generally the cusps that are most helpful in identifying the animal to which a tooth belonged.

Anatomy of Birds

Birds belong to the class, Aves. Although the overall skeletal structure of birds is similar to that of mammals, and they have many bones in common, avian skeletons also have unique features and features they share with reptiles, especially the subclass Archosauria, which includes dinosaurs and crocodiles. Among these are features that allow them to run on their hind legs, leaving the forelimbs available for evolution into wings (figure 10.2). As a further aid to flight, the skeleton is lightened by pneumatization. This means that many bones are hollow and contain air sacs (Bellairs and Jenkin, 1960:243, 289-93). Most of the zoological literature on avian skeletons is old and widely scattered (e.g., Fürbringer, 1888; Shufeldt, 1909), but there are some recent guides for archaeologists working in western Europe and North America (Cohen and Serjeantson, 1986; Gilbert et al., 1981; Olsen, 1972).

The avian skull has several reptilian and other unusual features. In some birds there is a craniofacial joint that allows the upper jaw, and not only the lower one, to move relative to the braincase. To accomodate their eyes, birds usually have extremely large orbits that rarely form full circles (King and McLelland, 1984:46). Instead, there is a ring of 10 to 18 tiny, overlapping bones, *scleral ossicles*, to provide stiffer support for the eyeball (Bellairs and Jenkin, 1960:288). Birds' tongues actually have a skeleton, or *hyobranchial apparatus*. This apparatus allows birds to probe into narrow spaces for food. Birds, with only one *occipital condyle,* can turn their heads almost full-circle.

In the axial skeleton, there is much variation in the number of vertebrae but the actual number in each portion of the column is often uncertain because of widespread fusion of vertebrae and the difficulty of distinguishing cervical from thoracic vertebrae (King and McLelland, 1984:51). Thoracic, lumbar, sacral, and anterior caudal vertebrae are frequently fused, making the trunk very rigid to support birds in flight. The cervical vertebrae compensate by being generally more numerous and more mobile than in mammals. Unlike most vertebrates, the articular surfaces of the vertebrae are saddle-shaped, with the anterior surface concave in the transverse but convex in the dorso-ventral plane, and are arranged in a way that allows the anterior part of the neck to move mainly in a forward direction, and the middle part backward, so that the neck tends to be S-shaped (Bellairs and Jenkin, 1960:249; King and McLelland, 1984:52). All the cervical vertebrae except the atlas have ribs or vestiges of ribs, mainly fused with the vertebrae, but sometimes the last one or two vertebrae have long and movable ribs articulated with them. The thoracic ribs, as in some reptiles, have *uncinate processes*, small bones at an angle to the ribs that provide extra muscle attachment. In flying birds and penguins, the sternum usually has a pronounced keel (*carina*) that strengthens it with a cross-section like a steel girder and provides muscle attachments for large pectoral muscles. Finally, there are often five to eight free caudal vertebrae and up to ten fused elements that form an upturned rump-post, or *pygostyle*, for moving the bird's tail feathers.

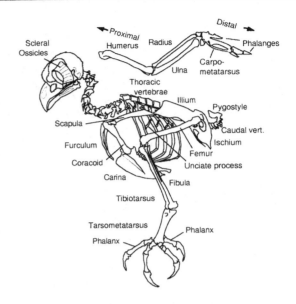

Figure 10.2. Avian skeletal elements illustrated with an owl, Bubo bubo, with wings and one leg removed, and, upper right, left wing of swift (Micropus apus)(redrawn after Bellairs and Jenkin, 1960).

The pectoral girdle and forelimbs are usually adapted for flying. The girdle is strong to deal with compression stresses during flight, and the coracoids and clavicles (often fused into a furculum or "wishbone") act as struts that hold the wings away from the sternum. The scapula is usually long. A bird's wings are supported mainly by the "arm" bones — the humerus, radius, and ulna — rather than the "hand" bones that are important in the wings of bats and pterosaurs (Bellairs and Jenkin, 1960:255). The proximal end of the humerus is flattened and has two prominent crests for muscle attachment. The ulna generally shows small knobs where quills of feathers are attached. Fusion of distal carpals with three of the metacarpals creates the compound structure known as the *carpometacarpus*.

The pelvic girdle and hindlimbs are similar to those of some dinosaurs. The sutures between pelvic bones tend to disappear, while the illium is fused to the synsacrum, the whole thus becoming a rigid structure that carries the bird's weight when it is walking. In most birds the ilium and ischium do not meet ventrally in a symphysis. This makes the pelvic outlet more open, allowing the passage of hard-shelled eggs

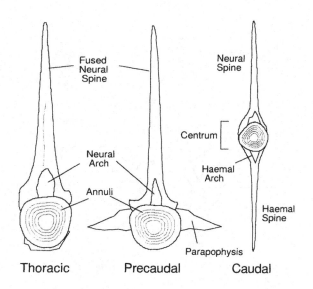

Figure 10.3. Generalized anterior view of thoracic, precaudal, and caudal vertebrae of bony fish.

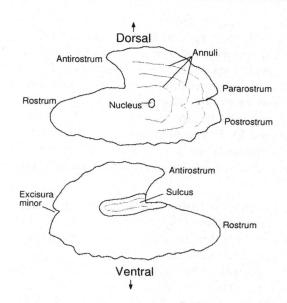

Figure 10.4. Anatomy of a sagittal otolith, in lateral (top) and medial (bottom) views (after Casteel, 1976:22).

in females. The *acetabulum*, into which the head of the femur fits, is completely perforated instead of a cup-like socket, and a facet on the ilium, above the acetabulum, prevents the femur from pushing through when there is weight upon it. The more distal parts of the hindlimb include the *tibiotarsus* (fusion of tibia with the proximal tarsal bones), with an anterior extension called the *cnemial process*, and fibula (usually much reduced in size), sometimes a patella, and a *tarsometatarsus* (fusion of distal tarsal bones with elongated metatarsals). Because the distal end of the last is made up of three fused metatarsals, it branches into three pulley-shaped processes called *trochleas* (Bellairs and Jenkin 1960: 263). Sometimes (as in fighting cocks) there is also a spur on the inner side of the tarsometatarsus. Birds vary considerably in the arrangement of their feet, most birds having four toes with three, four, and five phalanges but others having three or even two.

Anatomy of Bony Fish

Unlike the skeletons of mammals, those of bony fish do not experience re-modelling or resorption; the bones simply keep growing throughout the fish's life. Like reptiles, fish continually

replace their teeth because they also have a lifelong supply of tooth buds. The rate of fish's bone growth varies seasonally, resulting in distinct growth rings. As we will see below, this is extremely helpful in determining the fish's age at death and even the season in which it died. There are also many differences in skeletal anatomy, although many of the major classes of body part found in mammals and the terms for orientation can also be used for fish. The body parts of greatest importance to archaeologists are the otoliths (ear stones) and vertebrae, because these are more often preserved. In some contexts and with careful recovery, however, even scales can be very useful sources of data.

Fish vertebrae (figure 10.3) consist of a spool-shaped *centrum* to which a number of *spines* are attached. The concave face or faces of centra show annuli, or annual growth rings. Casteel (1976:77-78) recommends classifying fish vertebrae according to nine classes, extending posteriorly from the basioccipital, where the skull articulates with the spinal column. These are the proatlas, the atlas, the second vertebra, the Weberian vertebrae, the thoracic vertebrae, the precaudal vertebrae, the caudal vertebrae, the penultimate vertebra, and the ultimate vertebra. The spines are not always preserved in archaeological specimens, but can include the neural spine on the dorsal side of the centrum, parapophyses or transverse processes that extend laterally from the centrum, and two haemel spines (or ribs) flanking the centrum's ventral surface, which can sometimes be fused. The passage for the spinal cord is the neural arch. The ultimate vertebra has a urostyle at the posterior end, where it begins the fanning out of the tail.

Often more important than fish vertebrae as sources of archaeological evidence are **otoliths**, small concretions of calcium salts, principally calcium carbonate, that occur in the inner ear. They appear to be part of the animal's control over balance, or to help with depth perception or hearing (Casteel, 1976:17-18). The smallest otoliths are not very helpful for identification, but the larger ones, called statoliths, occur in three pairs. These are the *sagittae, asterisci,* and *lapilli.*

The outer face of most otoliths is flat or concave, sometimes with concentric rings or *annuli,* but with little relief, while the inner face is highly sculptured in ways that facilitate identification, sometimes to species level (figure 10.4). Both the sagitta and the asteriscus tend to show a groove, called a sulcus, extending roughly horizontally across the inner surface and often bordered by a ridge. Two protrusions, the anterior rostrum and the antirostrum, which juts out on the anterior dorsal edge, flank the anterior end of the sulcus.

Anatomy of Molluscs

Mollusc shells constitute the only invertebrate remains that archaeologists routinely collect, although analysis of archaeological insect remains is becoming more common. The major classes of molluscs (phyllum mollusca) are the Monoplacophora, the Amphineura (including subclass Polyplacophora), the Gastropoda (including snails, slugs, limpets, and abalone), the Scaphopoda (including Dentalium or "tusk" shells), the Bivalvia or Pelecypoda ("bivalves" such as clams and oysters), and the Cephalopoda (including squid, octupi, nautilus, and extinct ammonites)(Wilbur and Yonge, 1964). Molluscs'

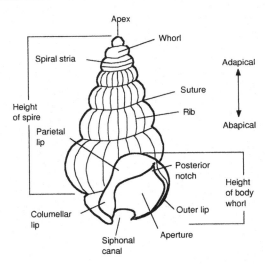

Figure 10.5. Anatomy of a helicocone (after Fretter and Graham, 1962:56-66).

hard tissue occurs, if at all, in the form of one or more exoskeletons, or shells, formed from deposited calcium carbonate, that serve as external protection for the animal's soft, unsegmented body (Waselkov, 1987).

The shells occur in a number of major varieties (Fretter and Graham, 1962:49-82). Gastropods, for example, can have an overall helicoid (a long cone wound around a shorter cone) shape, but be described as ventricose, if each whorl bulges outward between sutures, flatsided, if the whorls are flattened, or turreted, if the upper part of each whorl projects outward below the suture line. Other gastropods have shells shaped like simple cones. In bivalves the two shells are hinged, each valve a mirror-image of the other, and occur in a wide variety of symmetrical and asymmetrical shapes. Good introductions to shells include Wye (1991) and Claassen (1998).

As you would expect, the terminology for the parts of molluscs shells is quite different from that for skeletal elements.

As illustrated in figure 10.5, helicoid gastropod shells are oriented relative to the apex, vertically along the axis of the spiral, with apex at top. The coiling is normally upwards and clockwise (dextral) when viewed from the apex, but there are exceptions with sinistral coiling or

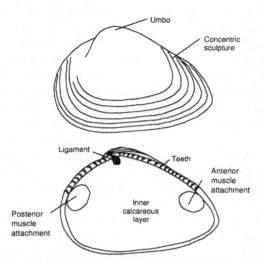

Figure 10.6. Anatomy of a bivalve shell (after Yonge and Thompson, 1976:147, 150), here the outer right valve (top) and inner left valve of Nucula nucleus.

with the spire extending downwards. In helicocones that lay new whorls so that they touch the central axis, a solid or hollow central pillar, called the *columella*, is visible in a broken shell. In hollow *columellae*, the lower opening is called the inferior *umbilicus*. The protoconch is the original shell, secreted while the animal is embryonic or larval, at the innermost part of the shell's helicocone. The mouth, or aperture, is near the bottom of the shell and its growing edge, or *peristome*, includes an outer lip, or *labrum*, away from the axis of the shell and inner columellar lip or *labium*, close to the shell's axis. Where part of the peristome lies over the previous whorl, it is called the *parietal lip*. An important attribute for identification is the angle of the outer lip relative to the shell's axis. Other features of the aperture can include the siphonal or anterior canal, which allows the gastropod to suck water into its mantle cavity, and which can be an elongated tube in some species. At the adapical (towards apex) end of the aperture there may be a posterior notch or canal, which facilitates the discharge of feces. The youngest (largest) whorl, forming one complete turn of the helicocone, is the *body whorl*; all other whorls combine to make the *spire*. The maximum diameter of the body whorl is known as its periphery. Tiny spiralling folds on the surface of the whorls are known as *striae*, while periodic thickenings of shell along the length of the helicocone are

ribs, which appear to intersect the striae. Where the ribs appear parallel to the axis of the shell, they are orthocline ribs. If their adapical ends are turned toward the direction of growth, they are prosocline, and if turned in the opposite direction, they are opisthocline. At the microscopic level, there are also tiny growth lines created by secretion along the peristome, which can be seasonal, allowing the age of the animal to be counted in the lines. In some species, there are long spines protruding from the ribs, or series of out-turned flanges, called *varices* (sg. *varix*), both of which originate in an out-turning of the outer lip. In some species, mature animals stop growth of the helicocone and instead secrete bosses (denticles or teeth) on the inside of the aperture. A *septum* (pl. *septa*) is an interior growth of shell, extending from the *columella*, to block off the uppermost whorls of the spire when the animal no longer occupies them (Fretter and Graham, 1962:50-66; Wye, 1991: 16)

Bivalve shells are oriented relative to the umbo (beak) and nearby ligament (hinge), inner and outer surfaces, anterior and posterior ends, and left and right valves (figure 10.6). The shell of a bivalve grows from the margin of the mantle, as in gastropods, but the mantle is divided into two symmetrically arranged lobes, from which shell growth must be identical to ensure that the margins of the two valves meet when the shell is closed. The mantles' margins have three parallel folds, of which the outer secretes the peristracum and outer calcareous layer of the shell, the middle has sensory functions, and the inner controls water flow into the mantle cavity. The shell itself has three major layers: the outer, horny periostracum, made of protein, the outer calcareous layer, consisting of calcium carbonate in a matrix of protein conchiolin, and the inner calcareous layer, which sometimes has the iridescent quality of mother-of-pearl. Along the bivalve's mid-line, an uncalcified, elastic ligament serves as a hinge. While the ligament is rarely preserved in fossil assemblages, hinge "teeth," ridges and grooves on either side of the ligament are often important attributes in bivalve identification. Each tooth fits into its corresponding groove or socket on the opposing valve. The teeth ensure that the two valves line up properly when the shell is closed, and that they will not slip against one another (Yonge and Thompson, 1976:142-49).

As with fish, seasonal variations in temperature and food availability affect shell growth in many species of molluscs. For some, there may be no shell growth at all in winter (Davis, 1987:83-90). Molluscs accumulate shell when specialized parts of the mantle secrete an organic base, conchiolin, and inorganic salts of calcium around its growing edge. Later deposition of calcareous material thickens the shell over its whole inner surface. But shell deposition is not always constant. Some bivalves, for example, only secrete shell when the animal is submerged and the shell is open. In interdital bivalves, such as the cockle, there is a new increment of shell at each high tide. Hundreds of these small increments, separated by thin dark lines, accumulate during each growing season (generally summer) and are separated by grooves, or "growth cessation rings," when only extremely thin increments, or none at all, are added to the shell. Some gastropods also show seasonal increments, representing either winter cessation of growth due to cold, or summer cessation to avoid dessication. As we will see later, these growth increments have important implications for the analysis of seasonality at archaeological sites.

Identifying Taxa

One of the basic activities of the zooarchaeologist, although it is only a first step, is to try to identify the taxon to which a particular fossil belongs.

As we have seen, animals with similar evolutionary histories tend to have similarities in the presence and morphology of body parts. We can take advantage of this fact in our attempt to identify fossils. The first step is to determine to what skeletal part a particular fossil belongs. Once we have done this, we may be able to note morphological idiosyncracies that allow us to narrow down the taxonomic possibilities to a particular family, genus or species.

Although osteological reference books can be helpful for identifying the more common animals (e.g., Cornwall, 1964; Glass, 1973; Hall and Kelson, 1959; Olsen, 1972; Pales and Garcia, 1981; Pales and Lambert, 1971; Schmid, 1972;

Walker, 1985), a critical tool in faunal identification is a *reference collection*. This is a collection of modern skeletal elements, teeth, shell, and horn or antler from reliably identified specimens of known species, age, and sex (determined before or shortly after the animal's death). It is also useful for the reference material to show such information as the place and date of each animal's killing or capture, and its mass and other useful size measures (e.g., length or stature) at that time. Because most of the species of archaeological interest will have evolved only very slowly, the modern specimens should be a very good guide to most archaeological specimens, although evolutionary changes will be more important in very old assemblages. Since most of the collections in museums of natural history are neither complete enough nor formed with archaeologists in mind, it is usually necessary for zooarchaeologists to build up specialized reference collections. This may require hunting, trapping, fishing, finding cooperative zoos and butchers or slaughterhouses, making exchange arrangements with other reference collections, and scouring roadsides for road-kill or beaches for dead birds. Where you are unable to obtain whole animals, however, you need to make special arrangements to ensure you have accurate information about the sources of body parts.

It is then necessary to deflesh the animals (sometimes dissecting them to study their anatomy first), and there are several ways to accomplish this messy and smelly task (Anderson, 1965; Casteel, 1976:8-16; Hangay and Dingley, 1985:326-65; Hildebrand, 1968). A common method is a combination of defleshing manually, simmering the partly defleshed specimen just below boiling, often with some detergent or enzyme in the water (Ossian, 1970), and maceration (allowing the partly defleshed specimen to rot in the water). This is fairly slow and is best accomplished under a fume hood to evacuate the steam and very unpleasant odors that result. Safe disposal of water containing rotted tissue and enzymes can also be a problem, and simple disposal down the drain may violate health-and-safety regulations or municipal law. Dermestid beetles will clean articulated specimens quite well, but this method is even slower and the beetle colonies require careful maintenance. Another, available only at coastal laboratories, is to place eviscerated specimens in perforated containers in the intertidal zone of the sea, where marine isopods will deflesh them fairly quickly (Casteel, 1976). Nested screens should be used to capture the disarticulated remains from all these methods, to avoid losing the smallest elements, and when these are clean and dry they need to be labelled accurately by species, sex, age, and specimen number and stored safely where you can easily retrieve them. This may require thousands of plastic or other insect-proof and rodent-proof boxes of various sizes, considerable shelving, and good climate control (see chapter 7). Ideally, you will want enough specimens of each taxon to represent not only various ages and both sexes, but other within-species variations in size and shape.

Shape differences among taxa can be subtle and only differ from within-taxon variation by degree (Davis, 1987:37-38). Often they may allow us to differentiate by genus but not species. We can attempt to separate these taxa by making careful measurements of skeletal parts and calculating ratios between them. In cases of rather similar taxa, we often find that animals in a population consisting of one species will show the same or closely similar ratio between two measurements, while groups of animals of different species will tend to differ in these ratios. This is a matter of **allometry**, the scaling of body parts in animals. If we are to depend on such measurements to distinguish taxa, however, we must be careful to be very consistent in the way we make them. Angela von den Driesch (1976) provides one guide to the measurement of mammals and birds from parts of the Old World. The use of such ratios, often presented graphically in a scatterplot, can help us make subtle distinctions between elements of such closely related taxa as sheep and goats (Davis, 1987:33; Payne, 1968) or horses, donkeys, and onagers. In the most difficult cases, we may now use DNA analyses to distinguish these species as long as DNA is reasonably well preserved (Loreille et al., 1997).

Not all variation in size and shape is due to interspecific difference. Bones are modified over the life of an animal, but especially in its youth.

As you would expect, we can use some of the changes that occur in the development of the skeleton to determine the age at which a particular animal died. In addition, some parts of the skeleton may show *sexual dimorphism* (patterned differences between males and females). When this happens, and the sexually diagnostic parts are preserved, we can identify both the age and the sex of the animal from which the bones came.

Determining Sex

Some parts of the skeleton, such as the pelvic girdle, and teeth or antlers that are used in sexual display, vary by sex in their size and shape. For example, in equids (horses), the males usually have large canine teeth, while females usually either lack canines or have only vestigial ones, while in both cervids and bovids, females usually either lack horns or antlers or have ones that are different in shape from those on males. The pelvis frequently shows differences related to birthing. In most mammals, males' bones tend, on average, to be larger and more robust than the same bones in females of the same age, and males often have greater overall body size. There are exceptions, however, as in hares (the doe is larger than the buck). Castration of males, furthermore, slows epiphyseal fusion and allows more longitudinal growth. Sometimes bones that are good indicators of sex are those that support the extra weight of the male animal's large horns or antlers, as these may well exaggerate the sexual dimorphism. One must be careful, however, not to confuse size differences due to sex with those due to age. Comparing fused ephiphyses, for example, controls for age (Klein and Cruz-Uribe, 1984:40). Using size as an indirect measure of sex works well in species with strong sexual dimorphism, such as goats, cattle, and seals, but in some species there is too much overlap between the size distributions of males and females for us to determine the sex of any but the most extreme cases in the sample assemblage. Even when we cannot be certain about each individual bone element, however, it may still be possible to recognize assemblages that show, for example, predominant culling of males.

Age at Death

There are several sources of evidence for determining the age-at-death of animals from which we have bones or teeth (Iscan, 1989).

One is fusion of the epiphyses. As we have seen, bone formation begins in the mid-shaft and two epiphyses, and the epiphyses remain separated from the shaft by a layer of cartilage for quite some time. Eventually, however, ossification proceeds to the point that they become fused to the shaft, and the time when this tends to occur in modern animals is known. Bones with unfused epiphyses therefore belong to young animals, while fused ones belong to adults. We can often be more precise than this in that, for some bones, the two epiphyses fuse at different times. For example, often the distal epiphysis of the humerus fuses before the proximal one. As long as we know the ages at which fusion occurs in modern animals of the same species, we can use the ordinal scales (unfused, one epiphysis fused, both fused) to estimate age in months. This leaves us with a coarse, indirect measure of age, not always as precise as we would like (Davis, 1987:39; Klein and Cruz-Uribe, 1984:43), and we must keep in mind that unfused epiphyses are less likely than fused ones to survive centuries of burial.

Teeth provide a more precise indirect scale of age. As horse-traders have known for centuries, patterns of dental eruption and tooth wear are excellent clues to an animal's age (Hillson, 19867:176-223). Deciduous teeth are replaced on a schedule that is known in modern animals, so it is often possible to determine the age of young animals very precisely as long as their mandibles or maxillae are preserved to show the stage of tooth eruption (Deniz and Payne, 1982). Clearly, young animals should also show very little wear on the occlusal surfaces of their teeth (apart from any post-depositional wear), while old animals may show quite a lot of wear. Although tooth wear depends on a number of factors besides age, including the amount of grit and acid in the diet, it is possible to make a rough aging scale based on tooth wear (figure 10.7; e.g., Klein and Cruz-Uribe, 1984; Spinage, 1973). Where we can assume that the usual cause of death of the animal was seasonal (as in a seasonal kill site), we may be fortunate that the degree of wear in a particular tooth (say, a molar) clusters into groups that probably represent annual age-grades. In other words, teeth with almost no wear come from animals in their first year, the cluster with slightly more wear from animals one to two years old, and so on (Klein and Cruz-Uribe, 1984:45). Aging on the basis of tooth eruption and wear works much better when whole rows of teeth are available; single teeth are more difficult.

In some herbivorous animals, with high-crowned teeth whose growth stops early in life, tooth wear results in ever-diminishing crown height, as measured from the top of the root. For example, Spinage (1972) has found an exponential decrease in the crown height of zebra teeth.

An alternative is to count the growth increments (*annuli*) in mammal tooth cementum (Morris, 1972; 1978), much the way dendrochronologists count tree rings. Fortunately for zooarchaeologists and wildlife biologists, the rate of deposition of secondary dentine in the pulp cavity and of cementum on the roots varies by season in many mammals. Cementum is the concentric tissue that mineralizes collagen fiber onto the tooth's root to hold the tooth in place. Consequently, it grows throughout a mammal's life and, in thin section and polarized light, shows discrete, alternating translucent and opaque bands that we can count to determine the animal's age at death. In many species and environments, there is a strong correlation between the number of these bands and the known age of animals. Because the pulp cavity fills with dentine fairly early in an animal's life, however, zooarchaeologists focus on the cementum *annuli*, as viewed in stained thin-sections. The method does have some problems, as the deposit of cementum is not uniform in thickness, some cementum may be resorbed during life or lost through abrasion, and "secondary bands" may be mistaken for true annuli (Klein and Cruz-Uribe, 1984:44-45). In many cases, the method is more useful for estimating the season in which the animal died, rather than its actual age at death (see below).

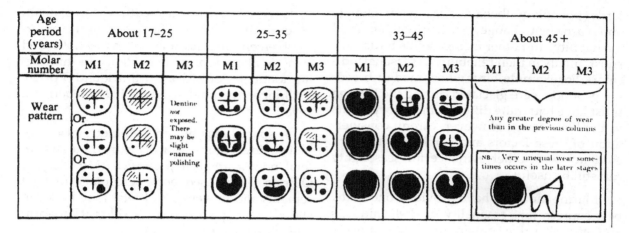

Figure 10.7. Chart for estimating the age of humans on the basis of molar wear (Brothwell, 1981:72).

Most determinations of age depend, however, on metrics (ratio-scale measurements). Not only are there gross differences in size among animals of the same sex and species but different ages, but there may also be differences in the ratios of one measurement to another (i.e., differences in shape). As already mentioned, the study of the relationships between these measurements and animals' age, sex, and weight, is called **allometry**. It is also possible to use these measures on teeth to quantify tooth wear (Klein and Cruz-Uribe, 1984:46-55).

In fish, thanks to the characteristic of constant bone growth, often rather simple allometric relationships will result in accurate estimates of the fish's size (Casteel, 1976:93-123), which is in turn a function of its age. In addition, incremental, seasonally varying bone growth results in annular rings, or *annuli*. These are quite detectable on the anterior and posterior surfaces of the centra of fish vertebrae (figure 10.3) and we can simply count them, like tree rings, to determine age in years, as has been recognized for more than two centuries (Casteel, 1976:78-83). *Annuli* also occur on fish otoliths and scales (Casteel, 1976:31-35, 65-71).

In molluscs, similarly, we can sometimes depend on constant but seasonally varying accretion of shell as a source of information on age. This is discussed more fully below, in connection with seasonality.

In many species for which it is possible to estimate age fairly precisely and sample size is fairly large, we can construct *mortality profiles* that show how the probability of death varies with age and compare such profiles. We will return to the interpretation of age profiles below (pp. 204-205).

Seasonality

Faunal remains are among the archaeologist's best evidence for the season or seasons during which an archaeological site was formed and used.

On sites that contain large samples of cervid (deer) remains, zooarchaeologists can take advantage of the fact that deer shed their antlers annually to try and estimate the season in which the cervid remains were deposited. One of the classic studies of site seasonality used the presence of shed antlers of red deer, most easily collected in April, to conclude that the Mesolithic site, Star Carr (Clark, 1954:119-22) was a camp-site occupied in winter and early spring. Subsequent authors have noted that shed antler can be curated, while other evidence points to use of the site in summer and probably other seasons as well (Andresen et al., 1981).

Some authors have tried to use evidence of migratory birds to show that a site was occupied during the season when the birds are expected to have been present. As Muñiz (1998) shows, birds' phenology (behavior relative to climate and season) can change along with climate, food availability, and other factors, while birds vary substantially in their reliability as seasonal indicators. For example, birds whose modern breeding grounds were glaciated during the Ice Age must have had quite different migratory habits in the Pleistocene. However, careful consideration of these factors and combining the bird evidence with other evidence for seasonality can still be useful.

Marine molluscs have provided one of the best sources for seasonality of shell middens and other sites that contain significant numbers of these fossils (Deith, 1985). One way in which some molluscs can inform us about season is through size. Molluscs increase fairly steadily in size as they age, and in some areas the largest age-class is likely to be molluscs less than a year old, the "young of the year" (Russo, 1998). Where we know the approximate time of year that clams, oysters, and scallops of a given taxon began their lives, and the rate of shell growth, we can use size measurements to estimate the age of a mollusc in months and add this to its probable "birthdate" to arrive at an approximate season of death. Better still, we can often rely on the fact that in some species of bivalve, increments of shell growth are separated by bands of little or no shell growth during winter or summer. For example, in quahogs (a kind of clam), Quitmyer et al. (1985) found that they could identify six different seasonal phases of shell growth depending on the thickness of the outer increment and whether it was translucent or opaque.

Mammal teeth are also a source of evidence for seasonality. For mammals born in a brief and predictable season, such as spring, we can use dental patterns to age the teeth closely enough to determine season of death. As Moore (1998) points out, this works best when we have sets of teeth representing all the ages we would expect in the population at one time (i.e., animals born one year apart). It is also difficult to use eruption and wear patterns unless a large sample, with many fairly complete sets of teeth, is available. The increments in tooth cementum are more generally useful. They are not only associated

with age in years, but also with season of death (Bourque et al., 1978). The nature of the outermost cementum band, unless it has been abraded away, will often provide evidence in thin-section for the season of death (Miracle and O'Brien, 1998; Lieberman and Meadow, 1992; Lieberman, 1998).

A special case of bone allometry also provides evidence for season of death in sites where fetal bones are well preserved. Miracle and O'Brien (1998) used both percentage of fetal remains and the lengths of fetal long bones to show that pregnant deer were killed at Badanj in late winter and early spring.

Paleoecology

Faunal remains are among the sources that archaeologists and paleontologists have used in the attempt to reconstruct extinct ecologies. In the more extreme cases, such as the change from the Pleistocene to Holocene in Europe, there may be substantial replacement of cold-climate fauna by temperate-climate fauna (Butzer, 1971:258-62).

One attempt to reconstruct changes in a site's environment on the basis of faunal remains depended on the alternation of fallow deer and gazelle hunted by humans in Kebara cave at Mount Carmel, Israel (Davis, 1977). Although the deer preferred woodland and the gazelle more open habitats, cultural preferences will have made the distribution of their remains at best a distorted reflection of their abundance in the environment. Rodents, however, may sometimes provide a more representative picture of the environment around cave sites (Tchernov, 1968). Owls may have sampled the rodent population in their hunting range and, after eating their prey, disgorged rodent bones in the cave. Changes in the relative frequencies of rodents that, in modern ecologies, prefer wetter or drier climates can then contribute to reconstruction of climatic changes within the cave's catchment area.

Land snails are often very sensitive indicators of ecological conditions, and archaeologists have taken advantage of their sometimes "fussy" requirements to reconstruct the environments in which their shells were deposited (Butzer, 1971:265-66; Evans, 1972; Thomas, 1985). Some of the factors that influence the distribution and abundance of land snails are water availability, temperature, soil pH, and calcium levels (Evans, 1972). The abundance of food (snails can be herbivores, carnivores, omnivores, or detritivores) may rarely limit snails' distribution simply because there is almost never a shortage of the foods they consider acceptable, but the quality of food may sometimes influence that distribution (Thomas, 1985:136-37). Generally, analysts combine various taxa of snails into groups based on their supposed ecological niches. For example, British zooarchaeologists group taxa into habitat-groups: "shade-loving," "open-country," "marshland," and "catholic" (able to live in a variety of habitats). Like plant taxa (see chap. 11), snails tend to occur in associations of several taxa, and it is always better to look at whole assemblages of taxa rather than placing too much emphasis on individual taxa that are supposed to be indicators of a particular kind of habitat (Thomas, 1985:140-44). For information on the extraction, identification, and analysis of snails see Evans (1972) and Preece (1981).

Insect remains can also be instructive about the habitats around a site, and even the microhabitats within it. Like snails, insects can be very particular about their environments. Where conditions permit their preservation, parts of insects' exoskeletons can then be used in an attempt to reconstruct those environments (Kenward, 1975; 1976). Kenward (1985) shows how insect assemblages can be used to distinguish indoor from outdoor archaeological contexts, which would be very valuable in cases where architecture is not very substantial or it is uncertain whether certain walled spaces were roofed rooms or open courtyards. He cautions, however, that we must take into account the mechanisms that could transport "outdoor" insects into buildings, such as wind and predation by birds. Some archaeologists have attempted to use the fossils of insect pests that infest grain to identify probable grain-storage facilities even where no plant remains are preserved.

Biostratigraphy

Biostratigraphy is a paleontological technique for the relative chronology of deposits that depends on the sets of fossils found in them and the assumption that these fossils reflect the paleoecology of a particular time and place (Butzer, 1971:261-66). In archaeology, this technique is rarely used except on Paleolithic sites for two reasons. First, other dating techniques are usually available, including relative dating by artifact typology and absolute dating by radiocarbon assay, that can date the deposits more precisely. Second, cultural effects make it unlikely that the fossil assemblage bears very close resemblance to the life assemblage.

Yet for assemblages too old for radocarbon dating to be applicable and without the volcanic ash layers that allow dating by the potassium-argon method, biostratigraphy is a useful method of relative dating. It operates on the assumption that the fossil assemblages reflect the appearance, spread, and eventual extinction of various species. A given geological deposit will contain a set of fossils that is a sample of the species that existed at that location at the time it was deposited. Deposits below and above it may show quite different combinations of taxa, as some species are added to or subtracted from the set through speciation and extinction. When two columns of deposits from different rock outcrops show similar sequences of fossil sets, then, we can correlate them to determine which deposits are approximately contemporary.

In one archaeological application of the method, Eitan Tchernov (1990) attempts to redate the Paleolithic deposits at 'Ubeidiya, Israel, to about 1.4 million years ago on the basis of similarities in the spectrum of fauna to deposits in Europe, Russia, and Olduvai Gorge, and the lack of faunal taxa from known earlier and later deposits.

Domestication of Animals

A research area that has attracted zooarchaeologists is the investigation of early animal domestication. Although archaeologists are mainly interested in the human behaviors involved in the shift from an economy based on hunting and gathering to one based mainly on herding and agriculture, quite often they rely on physical, evolutionary changes in the plants and animals that are associated with domestication as indirect evidence of these behaviors.

In the Old World, zooarchaeological research on domestication has tended to focus on the first domesticates: dogs, goats, cattle, and pigs, while in the New World it has focussed on dogs, guinea pigs, and llamas. But some animals, such as the camel (Köhler-Rollefson, 1981), were added quite late to the repertoire of domestic animals.

Domestication can be difficult to identify or even to define (Bökönyi, 1969; 1989). Generations of animals can show physical changes as they are domesticated, including changes in size, crowding of teeth and, in some animals, loss of horns or change in their shape. Some authors suggest that such changes may not appear until many generations after the domesticatory relationship between humans and animals began (Bökönyi, 1989: 25). We cannot expect domestic animals to be consistently distinguishable from wild ones (Ducos, 1989). Although many animals decreased in size over the course of domestication (Meadow, 1989:86-87), size changes can also occur in other situations, such as isolation on islands or changes in mean annual temperature (Bökönyi, 1989:25; Davis, 1981; Meadow, 1989:87). Tooth crowding in dogs and pigs, and hornlessness in sheep, seem to be rather reliable indications of domestication, but it is not clear how long it takes for these changes to evolve.

Although some zooarchaeologists are interested in tracing the origins and spread of domesticated animals (e.g., Bökönyi, 1974), others are more interested in explaining the beginnings of a mutualistic relationship between humans and animals, which must begin with describing a shift from the hunting of wild animals, to nearly complete dependence on domesticated ones, with a transitional phase that could include management of wild herds. This cannot depend on genetic changes, but sometimes pathologies, including evidence for tethering animals, can supplement anomalous mortality profiles (below) as evidence for herd management.

Taxonomic Abundance — Menu Preference

Commonly zooarchaeologists try to reconstruct the dietary choices of hunters and herders. This means trying to quantify the relative "importance" of different species on the menu, as well as preferences for animals of particular sex or age in some cases. We will leave the latter for another section and concentrate here on the choice of species.

One of the things that archaeologists have noticed for some time is that prehistoric hunters and farmers sometimes changed their subsistence strategies substantially, particularly from narrow niches (hunting mainly one or two species) to broad ones (hunting, collecting, and raising a wide range of food resources), as well as shifting their emphasis from, say, gazelle to deer or wild animals to domesticated ones. In general, although changes in environment are often factors in such shifts, this kind of research focusses on diet and, as such, should focus on the amount of the resource (typically amount of meat, but potentially also hides, etc.), and not necessarily the number of animals killed, although these two measures are related. We would not want to assume a focus on rabbits, because of their greater number among the bone counts or estimated individuals, when in fact the diet of the people who created a site was dominated by, say, bison. A single bison would produce more meat than 100 rabbits.

As we saw in chapter 5, the appropriate way to quantify faunal remains when we are interested in the relative importance of taxa is to use an estimator that provides unbiased estimates of proportions. When we are interested in the proportions of different types of animals in the deposited assemblage, then, it would be useful to use a quantification approach that accounts for bone fragmentation (f) and the number of bones in whole animals (s). When we are interested in the proportions in the death assemblage, and the size and quality of our sample warrants it, we might base the proportions on the Peterson estimator. In some instances, we might have to quantify the remains by mass, sorting elements into age classes so that reasonable transformations to meat mass are possible.

In addition, an examination of niche breadth can employ measurements of diversity, such as the Expected Species index, s(m).

We cannot assume that the remains of animals we find on archaeological sites are a simple reflection of diet. Not only can some of the skeletal remains belong to pests or pertain to non-human bone accumulators, or fail to be preserved, but humans themselves can bring animals and animal parts to sites for many purposes other than for food. Some of these purposes may be utilitarian — bringing hides for clothing or antler for tool-making, for example — while others could be ideological. Among the latter we might include skulls, whose food value is limited to the brain, but which can nonetheless have symbolic value. In Western culture, for example, mounting heads and antler racks of game is for social display and symbolizes status and mastery over nature. In other cultures, furthermore, there can be taboos requiring the remains of food animals to be buried off-site (e.g., Tooker, 1964:64, 67).

Elemental Abundance — Choice of Cut

Interpreting dietary choices is often confounded by the fact that neither hunters nor herders typically deposit entire skeletons on site, where they can become part of the deposited assemblage. Instead, they often only deposit those bones associated with selected cuts of meat, or attached to pelts that they use for clothing or bedding.

When humans and other bone accumulators kill, butcher, and consume an animal, they can alter the distribution of bones in the deposited assemblage both by selective transport of body parts and by selective destruction of bone. Hunters who make a kill at some distance from their camp or village will often butcher the animal, if it is large, on the spot, taking the most valued cuts (e.g., upper limbs, pelvic girdle) back to their settlement and abandonning the parts that have low meat/bone ratios (e.g., axial skeleton, lower limbs) unless these have value for reasons other than nutrition (Perkins and Daly, 1968). For example, parts of the lower limbs may still be attached to highly valued pelts (which can also be used as "bags" for carrying the meat back

to camp), while skulls can be saved as trophies or religious items, and antler saved for tool production. In such cases, we would find some body parts missing from the settlement site, and others missing from the kill site.

Binford (1978:72-74; 1981) and others have attempted to understand the distribution of body parts by quantifying their value with "utility indices." Binford introduced the "general utility index" (**GUI**) as a measure of each bone part's usefulness for meat, marrow, and grease, and "modified general utility index" (**MGUI**), which makes allowance for less useful elements that were probably attached to parts of higher value. Binford used patterns in the MGUI values for different skeletal parts in an attempt to infer transport of more useful body parts and to distinguish between kill sites and transported sites of hominids and other carnivores in an attempt to infer whether hominids were responsible for bone accumulations.

Other researchers have since adopted utility indices (e.g., Lyman, 1992; Lyman et al., 1992), with Metcalfe and Jones (1988) providing a simpler way of calculating what they describe as a meat utility index (MUI):

$$MUI = g - d$$

where g is the gross mass of the body part, and d is the dry bone mass of the part. In effect it measures the amount of tissue expected on the bone. This measure has the effect of giving high scores to bones that would have a large mass of tissue on them, such as *femora*, even if they might have lower ratio of g/d and be more difficult to transport (Ringrose, 1993a: 146). Ringrose instead proposes indices based on g/d, (g-d)/d, or (g-d)/g, with preference for the last. Although he has a point, there could be some cases where a large joint of meat was preferable to many small pieces of meat with higher g/d ratios.

The most serious potential problem with utility indices, once again, is differential preservation. Binford's MGUI values are inversely correlated with volume density, and the patterns that he describes as a "bulk utility strategy" are equally explicable by differences in the probability of bone survival (Lyman, 1985; 1992; Grayson, 1989).

In cases where we are more interested in explaining the differential distribution of elements, rather than taxonomic abundance, utility indices, although not without problems, are a helpful approach if the preservation issue is also addressed.

We must be wary of assuming automatically that the selective transport of body parts for food, often called the "schlepp effect," is universal, however. In some societies, in fact, the killed animal's spirit is thanked and its unused remains are given ritual disposal not unlike that accorded deceased humans. We should also not assume that any discrepancies between body parts in their abundance must have resulted from selection between the death assemblage and the deposited assemblage. Since some body parts are more durable than others, post-depositional selection also contributes to such discrepancies (Lyman, 1985; 1992).

Butchering Practices

In some cases, butchering of food animals is among the taphonomic effects that we can recognize.

Along with the elemental evidence we have just considered, cutmarks on bone have been studied as evidence for butchery since the 1970s (Aird, 1985; Noe-Nygaard, 1977). When analysed systematically, cutmarks may help us identify butchery traditions and reconstruct whether the butchers were preparing meat for immediate consumption or to preserve it for storage through smoking, drying, or salting (Maltby, 1985).

Mortality Profiles — Hunting Strategies and Herd Management

In sample assemblages that are sufficiently large, fairly well preserved and with sufficient evidence for sexing and aging a large proportion of specimens, we can sometimes get some insights into the sex-age structure of the death assemblage.

One of the most common applications of this approach is to infer hunting strategies from mortality profiles. Some authors have inferred that proportions of young animals much higher than their expected proportion in living herds indicates a kind of hunting that borders on herd management, and may even indicate early attempts at domestication. For example, Perkins' (1973) claim that sheep bones from very early Neolithic deposits at Zawi Chemi Shanidar were from domesticated sheep depends solely on an elevated proportion of immature animals.

Payne (1973), meanwhile, attempts to determine whether, in a sample assemblage of sheep and goat bones at Asvan Kale, different kill-off patterns reflected different herd-management practices (meat production, milk production, wool production). The approach is based on the idea that herders will kill off (cull) unproductive animals, such as males when milk is the desired resource, or animals that produce too little relative to the cost of maintaining them. Most dairy herders will cull males in their first few months, while a meat-producing strategy might keep them until they are about a year old to reach optimum weight and a wool-producing one might keep some of them even longer for their wool. Payne recognizes that there are numerous reasons why herders might select a "non-optimal" strategy, and both depositional and post-depositional selection could mimic herders' selection.

Even where taphonomic problems and sampling bias are minimal, and you can assume that the sample assemblage is representative of the death assemblage, this kind of analysis requires care. It is easy to confuse evidence for animal behaviour (ethology) with evidence for human exploitation. Baker and Brothwell (1980:19) have noted that claims for herd-management strategies are often unconvincing. An apparent shift toward younger animals is insufficient to demonstrate a transition from hunting to herding, while a shift toward more adults does not necessarily demonstrate milk or wool production. For example, Smith and Horwitz (1984) claim that high percentages of adult goats in the Early Bronze Age of the southern Levant indicates a shift from meat to milk products, but Payne (1973) shows that the survivorship curves for females can be identical in meat-, milk-, and wool-oriented herds. It is the treatment of males that varies. In addition, milk, meat, and wool can be complementary in a mixed pastoral strategy. Some analysts also make the assumption that males and unproductive females will be culled at the point where the ratio of feed consumed to animal weight gained begins to rise. Prehistoric farmers and pastoralists, however, may not have relied on feed, and, where climate was unpredictable, may have kept males longer than optimal as a hedge against drought.

Mortality profiles can provide useful information, but you should keep Payne's caveats in mind if you plan to interpret culling patterns.

Paleopathology

Evidence for disease, trauma, and genetics in the faunal remains from archaeological sites has great potential.

Although the literature on human paleopathology is much larger, key publications on the paleopathology of animals include Baker and Brothwell (1980) and Siegel (1976).

Evidence for trauma in animal bones can be informative about hunting methods and the handling of livestock (Baker and Brothwell, 1980:82). In addition to healed and unhealed fractures, there may even be flint fragments, embedded projectile points, or holes of distinct shape that suggest what weapon was used to dispatch an animal. Statistical anomalies in the distribution of trauma, both among taxa and among body parts, can help to reveal the causes of injury, including poor treatment of domestic stock and overcrowding of livestock (Baker and Brothwell, 1980:93-94).

Some kinds of disease and trauma in faunal remains can provide clues that herds were being managed. Paleopathological study can also show exostoses or neoplasia (abnormal growth) that might result from tethering or hobbling, and osteoarthritis of joints that can result from the stress of traction in draught animals, such as oxen and horses (Baker and Brothwell, 1980:97, 114-115). In general, herds belonging to sedentary people tend to be more prone to disease than are wild animals and the herds of nomads,

and a marked increase in pathology is probably a good indication that animals were being confined (Meadow, 1989:85), as we would expect during the first stages of domestication.

Smith and Horwitz claim that radiographic evidence of osteoporosis in the metacarpals of older sheep and goats are evidence of calcium depletion through prolonged milking. If they are right, then this provides evidence for early dairying. It is also possible that diverting milk for human consumption could have been a factor in the rapid size diminishment of early domestic animals (Meadow, 1989:86).

The treatment that people gave to the carcasses of animals that died of disease, furthermore, can suggest aspects of their ideology.

Faunal paleopathology is particularly important given the clues it can provide to the nature of human interactions with animals in the past, including domestication, and given the fact that some human diseases probably have their origins in these early interactions. One of the likely outcomes of the sedentism that accompanied the development of Neolithic food production was the proliferation of diverse pathogens and vectors that found new niches and ease of transmission among the clustered populations of humans, their livestock, and various animal pests that the villages attracted (Brothwell, 1969). Not only were some of the animal pests likely disease vectors, but the close association between humans and their herds, both probably occupying the same dwellings in some cases, provided additional pathways for disease transmission. Tuberculosis, for example, is probably a bacillus that humans first contracted from their cattle (Francis, 1947). Consequently, the study of diseases in the animals from ancient settlements has direct relevance to the history of disease in humans.

Recently, the potential of DNA analysis to solve difficult identification problems has created some excitement. As it turns out, fragments of DNA are quite often preserved in osteological remains even after millennia of burial. Sometimes even the DNA of infectious diseases can be preserved in ancient tissues.

Trace Elements, Isotopes, and Diet

Sometimes the osteological remains are not the best evidence for the relative importance of meat, fish, and plant foods in a prehistoric community's diet. The chemistry of associated human bones can sometimes be important in this context. The most common approaches have been to study variations in the ratios of carbon isotopes and variations in trace elements that are thought not too susceptible to post-depositional (diagenetic) alteration.

Osteological remains can provide evidence for the diets of deceased humans or animals in the isotopic ratios of their carbon atoms. The ratio of ^{13}C to ^{12}C in living plants and animals varies because the synthetic pathways in some plants act slightly differently on these two carbon isotopes when they absorb carbon dioxide from the atmosphere. This slight favoring of one isotope over the other is called *fractionation*, and the two groups of plants distinguished by their synthetic pathways are called C3 and C4 plants. The former include trees, shrubs, and temperate grasses, while the latter includes tropical grasses, such as maize. Generally the C3 plants are more depleted in ^{13}C than are C4 plants.

Consequently, we would expect humans or animals that eat exclusively C4 plants to be less depleted in ^{13}C than ones that eat exclusively C3 plants. In fact, things are more complicated because fractionation is not identical for all kinds of animal tissues and fractionation varies with trophic level. "Secondary fractionation" in animals and humans results in herbivore bone collagen that is less depleted in ^{13}C than the plants the animals ate. For example, in laboratory mice, bone collagen shows 0.3 to 0.4% less ^{13}C depletion than the plant foods they were fed. Furthermore, secondary fractionation leads to different isotopic ratios in different kinds of tissue in the same individual. The herbivores' protein and lipids are less depleted in ^{13}C than the collagen, and the bone apatite is even less depleted (figure 10.8). Carnivores, whose muscle tissue and collagen derives carbon from the herbivores' meat, but whose bone apatite derives it from the herbivores' meat and lipids, show still less depletion of ^{13}C. In herbivores the difference in ^{13}C depletion between collagen and bone apatite is

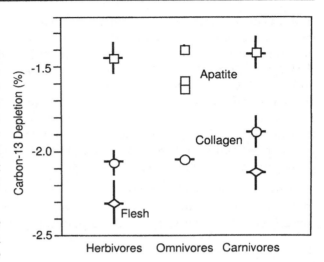

Figure 10.8. Examples of carbon-13 depletion ($d^{13}C$ values) for bone apatite (squares), collagen (circles), and flesh (diamonds) from southern African fauna (after Lee-Thorp et al., 1989:592).

much greater, on average, than in carnivores. This difference could, in principle, help us distinguish primarily vegetarian humans from substantially carnivorous ones but, oddly, omnivorous humans can show a smaller difference between collagen and apatite than carnivores (Lee-Thorp et al., 1989).

In addition, populations whose diet consists mainly of marine animals, such as salmon and molluscs, will have carbon isotopic ratios that differ from populations with terrestrial diets (Chisholm et al., 1982; Hobson and Collier, 1984; Tauber, 1981). Even though marine animals consume C3 plants, their tissues are enriched in ^{13}C relative to terrestrial herbivores.

Researchers have taken advantage of carbon isotopic differences to identify the introduction of maize into the diets of people inhabiting more northerly biomes, where C3 plants are found. This allows identification of early maize agriculture even in sites with poor plant preservation, as long as human bone is well preserved (van der Merwe and Vogel, 1978; Vogel and van der Merwe, 1977). They have also used it to identify heavy dependence on fish or marine mammals in coastal communities.

Carbon-isotope analyses such as these require fairly well preserved bone less than about

100,000 years old, and careful chemical removal of diagenetic carbonates (e.g., carbonates deposited from ground water while the bone was buried).

In some instances, trace element chemistry may also provide clues to prehistoric diet, although we must be very careful about diagenetic effects during burial that can alter bones' chemical compositions (Hancock et al., 1989; Price et al., 1992; Sandford, 1992). Some authors, for example, have used barium/strontium ratios to assess the degree of dependence on marine resources (Burton and Price, 1992). Strontium is also thought to be depleted in the bones of carnivores, and Sillen (1981), for example, attempted to use strontium levels and strontium/calcium ratios to detect changes in the dietary dependence on meat at Hayonim Cave, Israel. However, Tuross et al. (1989) have shown that strontium levels increase with time in buried bone, and that repeated washing of the samples does not completely remove this diagenetic strontium, some of which is locked into the bone apatite during recrystallization. Future use of strontium levels to infer dietary changes must take these effects into account.

Conclusion

The physical traces of animals present a rich source of evidence for archaeologists. Taphonomic processes that affect the distribution of this evidence require careful attention, and the identification and analysis of bones and other remains requires specialized training and access to a large comparative collection. The faunal remains can tell us a great deal about environment, diet, hunting, food production, seasonality, tool use, and the use of animals for traction, transportation, or non-food resources. Human remains, meanwhile, can also provide indirect evidence for their diet.

References Cited

Aird, P. M., 1985, On distinguishing butchery from other post-mortem destruction: A methodological experiment applied to a faunal sample from Roman Lincoln. In *Palaeobiological Investigations. Research Design, Methods and Data Analysis*, edited by N. R. J. Fieller, D. D. Gilbertson and N. G. A. Ralph, pp. 5-18. Symposium 5B of the Association for Environmental Archaeology. BAR International Series 266. British Archaeological Reports, Oxford.

Anderson, R. M., 1965, Methods of collecting and preserving vertebrate animals. *Natural Museum of Canada Bulletin 69*. National Museum of Canada, Ottawa.

Andresen, J. M., Byrd, B. F., Elson, M. D., McGuire, R. H., Mendoza, R. G., Staski, E., and White, J. P., 1981, The deer hunters: Star Carr reconsidered. *World Archaeology* 13:31-46.

Armitage, P. L., and Clutton-Brock, J., 1976, A system for classification and description of the horn cores of cattle from archaeological sites. *Journal of Archaeological Science* 3:329-48.

Baker, J., and Brothwell, D., 1980, *Animal Diseases in Archaeology*. Academic Press, London.

Barrett, J. H., 1993, Bone weight, meat yield estimates and cod (*Gadus morhua*): A preliminary study of the weight method. *International Journal of Osteoarchaeology* 3: 1-18.

Bass, W. M., 1987, *Human Osteology, A Field Guide and Manual*. Missouri Archaeological Society.

Behrensmeyer, A. K., 1975, Taphonomic and ecologic information from bone weathering. *Paleobiology* 4:150-62.

Bellairs, A. d'A., and Jenkin, C. R., 1960, The skeleton of birds. In *Biology and Comparative Physiology of Birds*, edited by A. J. Marshall, pp. 241-300. Academic Press, New York.

Benn, D. W., 1974, Annuli in the dental cementum of white-tailed deer from archeological contexts. *Wisconsin Archeologist* 55:90-98.

Binford, L. R., 1978, *Nunamiut Ethnoarchaeology*. Academic Press, New York.

— 1981, *Bones: Ancient Men and Modern Myths*. Academic Press, New York.

Boessneck, J., 1969, Osteological differences between sheep (Ovis aries Linne) and goats (Capra hircus Linne). In *Science in Archaeology*, edited by E. Brothwell and E. Higgs, pp. 331-58. Thames and Hudson, London.

Bökönyi, S., 1969, Archaeological problems and methods of recognizing animal domestication. In *The Domestication and Exploitation of Plants and Animals*, edited by P. J. Ucko and G. W. Dimbleby, pp. 219-29. Aldine, Chicago.

— 1974, *History of Domestic Mammals in Eastern Europe*. Akadémiai Kiadó, Budapest.

— 1989, Definitions of animal domestication. In *The Walking Larder. Patterns of Domestication, Pastoralism and Predation*, edited by J. Clutton-Brock, pp. 22-27. Unwin Hyman, London.

Bonnichsen, R., and Sanger, D., 1977, Integrating faunal analysis. *Canadian Journal of Archaeology* 1:109-33.

Bourque, B. J., Morris, K., and Spiess, A., 1978, Determining season of death of mammal teeth from archeological sites: A new sectioning technique. *Science* 149:530-31.

Brain, C. K., 1975, An introduction to the South African australopithecine bone accumulations. In *Archaeozoological Studies*, edited by A. T. Clason, pp. 109-19. American Elsevier, New York.

— 1976, Some principles in the interpretation of bone accumulations associated with man. In *Human Origins*, edited by G. Isaac and E. McCown, pp. 121-38. W. A. Benjamin, Menlo Park, CA.

— 1981, *The Hunters or the Hunted? An Introduction to African Cave Taphonomy*. University of Chicago Press, Chicago.

Brothwell, D. R., 1981, *Digging Up Bones*, 3rd ed. Oxford University Press, Oxford.

— 1969, The palaeopathology of Pleistocene and more recent mammals. In *Science in Archaeology, A Survey of Progress and Research*, 2nd ed., edited by D. Brothwell and E. Higgs, pp. 310-314. Thames and Hudson, London.

— 1989, The relationship of tooth wear to aging. In *Age Markers in the Human Skeleton*, edited by M. Y. Iscan, pp. 306-16. Charles Thomas, Springfield, IL.

Brown, T., and Brown, K., 1992, Ancient DNA and the archaeologist. *Antiquity* 66:10-23.

Burton, J. H., and Price, T. D., 1992, Ratios of barium to strontium as a paleodietary indicator of consumption of marine resources. *Journal of Archaeological Science* 17:547-58.

Butzer, K. W., 1971, *Environment and Archaeology. An Ecological Approach to Prehistory*, 2nd ed. Aldine, Chicago.

Casteel, R. W., 1976, *Fish Remains in Archaeology and Paleoenvironmental Studies*. Academic Press, London.

Chaplin, R. E., 1971, *The Study of Animal Bones from Archaeological Sites*. Seminar Press, New York.

Chisholm, B. S., Nelson, D. E., and Schwartz, H. P., 1982, Stable carbon isotopes as a measure of marine versus terrestrial protein in ancient diets. *Science* 216:1131-32.

Claassen, C., 1998, *Shells*. Cambridge University Press, Cambridge.

Clark, J. G. D., 1954, *Excavations at Star Carr*. Cambridge University Press, Cambridge.

Clark, J., and Kietzke, K. K., 1967, Paleoecology of the Lower Nodular Zone, Brule formation, in the Big Badlands of south Dakota. *Fieldiana: Geology Memoirs* 5:111-137.

Clason, A. T., 1972, Some remarks on the use and presentation of archaeozoological data. *Helinium* 12:139-53.

Clason, A. T., and Prummel, W., 1977, Collecting, sieving and archaeozoological research. *Journal of Archaeological Science* 4:171-75.

Cohen, A., and Serjeantson, D., 1986, *A Manual for the Identification of Bird Bones from Archaeological Sites*. Jubilee Printers, London.

Cornwall, I. W., 1974, *Bones for the Archaeologist*. Phoenix House, London.

Crabtree, P. J., Campana, D., and Ryan, K., eds., 1989, *Early Animal Domestication and its Cultural Context*. MASCA Research Papers in Science and Archaeology Special Supplement to Volume 6. The University Museum of Archaeology and Anthropology, Philadelphia.

Davis, S. J. M., 1977, The ungulate remains from Kebara Cave. *Eretz Israel* 13:150-63.

— 1981, The effects of temperature change and domestication on the body size of late Pleistocene to Holocene mammals of Israel. *Paleobiology* 7:101-14.

— 1987, *The Archaeology of Animals*. B. T. Batsford, London.

Davis, S. J. M., and Valla, F. R., 1978, Evidence for domestication of the dog 12,000 years ago in the Natufian of Israel. *Nature* 276:608-610.

Deith, M. R., 1985, Seasonality from shells: An evaluation of two techniques for seasonal dating of marine molluscs. In *Palaeobiological Investigations. Research Design, Methods and Data Analysis*, edited by N. R. J. Fieller, D. D. Gilbertson and N. G. A. Ralph, pp. 119-130. BAR International Series 266. British Archaeological Reports, Oxford.

Deniz, E. and Payne, S., 1982, Eruption and wear in the mandibular dentition as a guide to ageing Turkish Angora goats. In *Ageing and Sexing Animal Bones from Archaeological Sites*, edited by B. Wilson, C. Grigson and S. Payne, pp. 155-205. BAR British Series 109. British Archaeological Reports, Oxford.

Drew, I. M., Perkins, D., and Daly, P., 1971, Prehistoric domestication of animals: Effects on bone structure. *Science* 171:280-82.

von den Driesch, A., 1976, *A Guide to the Measurement of Animal Bones from Archaeological Sites*. Peabody Museum Bulletin 1. Peabody Museum of Archaeology and Ethnology, Harvard University, Cambridge, MA.

Ducos, P., 1975, Analyse statistique des collections d'ossements d'animaux. In *Archaeozoological Studies*, edited by A. T. Classon, pp. 35-44. American Elsevier, New York.

— 1989, Defining domestication: A clarification. In *The Walking Larder. Patterns of Domestication, Pastoralism and Predation*, edited by J. Clutton-Brock, pp. 28-30. Unwin Hyman, London.

Edwards, J. K., Marchinton, R. L., and Smith, 1982, Pelvic girdle criteria for sex determination of white-tailed deer. *Journal of Wildlife Management* 46:544-47.

Efremov, I. A., 1940, Taphonomy: A new branch of paleontology. *Pan-American Geologist* 74:81-93.

Evans, J. G., 1972, *Land Snails in Archaeology*. Seminar Press, London.

Francis, J., 1947, *Bovine Tuberculosis Including a contrast with Human Tuberculosis*. Staples Press, London.

Fretter, V., and Graham, A., 1962, *British Prosobranch Molluscs, Their Functional Anatomy and Ecology*. The Ray Society, London.

Fürbringer, M., 1888, *Untersuchungen zur Morphologie und Systematik der Vögel*. Amsterdam.

Gifford, D. P., 1981, Taphonomy and paleoecology: A critical review of archaeology's sister disciplines. *Advances in Archaeological Method and Theory* 4:365-438.

Gilbert, B. M., 1980, *Mammalian Osteo-archaeology*. B. Miles Gilbert, Laramie, Wyoming.

— 1989, Microscopic bone structure in wild and domestic animals: A reappraisal. In *Early Animal Domestication and its Cultural Context*, edited by P. Crabtree, D. Campana, and K. Ryan, pp. 46-86. MASCA Research Papers in Science and Archaeology. The University Museum of Archaeology and Anthropology, Philadelphia.

Gilbert, B. M., Martin, L. D., and Savage, H. G., 1981, *Avian Osteology*. Modern Printing Co, Laramie, WY.

Gilbert, R. I., and Mielke, eds., J. H., 1985, *Analysis of Prehistoric Diets*. Academic Press, New York.

Glass, B. P., 1973, *A Key to the Skulls of North American Mammals*, 2nd ed. Oklahoma State University, Stillwater.

Goldstein, K., and Kintigh, K., 1990, Ethics and the reburial controversy. *American Antiquity* 55:585-91.

Grayson, D. K., 1973, On the methodology of faunal analysis. *American Antiquity* 38:432-39.

— 1981, A critical view of the use of archaeological vertebrates in paleoenvironmental reconstruction. *Journal of Ethnobiology* 1:28-38.

Grue, H., and Jensen, B., 1979, Review of the formation of incremental lines in tooth cementum of terrestrial mammals. *Danish Review of Game Biology* 11(3):1-48.

Hall, E. R., and Kelson, K. R., 1959, *The Mammals of North America*. Ronald Press, New York.

Hancock, R. G. V., Grynpas, M. D., and Pritzker, K. P. H., 1989, The abuse of bone analyses for archaeological dietary studies. *Archaeometry* 31:169-79.

Hangay, G., and Dingley, M., 1985, *Biological Museum Methods*. Academic Press, Orlando, FL.

Hanson, C. B., 1980, Fluvial taphonomic processes: Models and experiments. In *Fossils in the Making*, edited by A. K. Behrensmeyer and A. P. Hill, pp. 156-81. University of Chicago Press, Chicago.

Hesse, B., and Wapnish, P., 1985, *Animal Bone Archeology: From Objectives to Analysis*. Manuals on Archeology 5. Taraxacum, Washington, DC.

Hildebrand, M., 1968, *Anatomical Preparations*. University of California Press, Berkeley.

Hillson, S., 1986, *Teeth*. Cambridge Manuals in Archaeology. Cambridge University Press, Cambridge.

Hirsch, A., 1883, *Handbook of Geographical and Historical Pathology*. London.

Hobson, K. A., and Collier, S., 1984, Marine and terrestrial protein in Australian aboriginal diets. *Current Anthropology* 25:238-40.

Huelsbeck, D. R., 1989, Zooarchaeological measures revisited. *Historical Archaeology* 23:113-17.

Iscan, M. Y., ed., 1989, *Age Markers in the Human Skeleton*. Charles C. Thomas, Springfield, Ill.

Kay, M., 1974, Dental annuli age determination on white-tailed deer from archaeological sites. *Plains Anthropologist* 19:224-27.

Keepax, C. A., 1981, Avian egg-shell from archaeological sites. *Journal of Archaeological Science* 8:315-35.

Kennedy, K. A. R., 1989, Skeletal markers of occupational stress. In *Reconstruction of Life from the Skeleton*, edited by M. Y. Iscan and K. A. R. Kennedy, pp. 129-60. Alan Liss, New York.

Kenward, H. K., 1975, Pitfalls in the environmental interpretation of insect death assemblages. *Journal of Archaeological Science* 2:85-94.

— 1976, Reconstructing ancient ecological conditions from insect remains: Some problems and an experimental approach. *Ecological Entomology* 1:7-17.

— 1985, Outdoors-indoors? The outdoor component of archaeological insect assemblages. In *Palaeobiological Investigations. Research Design, Methods and Data Analysis*, edited by N. R. J. Fieller, D. D. Gilbertson and N. G. A. Ralph, pp. 97-104. BAR International Series 266. British Archaeological Reports, Oxford.

King, A. S., and McLelland, J., 1984, *Birds: Their Structure and Function*, 2nd ed. Baillière Tindall, London.

Klein, R. G., and Cruz-Uribe, K., 1983, The computation of ungulate age (mortality) profiles from dental crown heights. *Paleobiology* 9:70-78.

— 1984, *The Analysis of Animal Bones from Archeological Sites*. Prehistoric Archeology and Ecology Series. University of Chicago Press, Chicago.

Klein, R. G., Allwarden, K., and Wolf, C., 1983, The calculation and interpretation of ungulate age profiles from dental crown heights. In *Hunter-Gatherer Economy in Prehistory: A European Perspective*, edited by G. Bailey, pp. 47-57. Cambridge University Press, Cambridge.

Köhler-Rollefson, I., 1981, *Zur Domestikation des Kamels*. D.M.V. diss., Tierärztlichen Hochschule Hannover.

Lee-Thorp, J. A., Sealy, J. C., and van der Merwe, N. J., 1989, Stable carbon isotope ratio differences between bone collagen and bone apatite, and their relationship to diet. *Journal of Archaeological Science* 16:585-99.

Lieberman, D. E., 1998, Natufian "sedentism" and the importance of biological data for estimating reduced mobility. In *Seasonality and Sedentism. Archaeological Perspectives from Old and New World Sites*, edited by T. R. Rocek and O. Bar-Yosef, pp. 75-92. Peabody Museum Bulletin 6. Harvard University, Cambridge, MA.

Lieberman, D. E., and Meadow, R. H., 1992, The biology of cementum increments (with an archaeological application). *Mammal Review* 22(2):57-77.

Loreille, O., Vigne, J.-D., Hardy, C., Callou, C., Treinen-Claustre, F., Dennebouy, N., and Monnerot, M., 1997, First distinction of sheep and goat archaeological bones by means of their fossil DNA. *Journal of Archaeological Science* 24:33-37.

Lyman, R. L., 1979, Faunal analysis: An outline of method and theory with some suggestions. *Northwest Anthropological Research Notes* 13:22-35.

— 1982, Archaeofaunas and subsistence studies. *Advances in Archaeological Method and Theory* 5:331-93.

— 1985, Bone frequencies: differential transportation, in-situ destruction and the MGUI. *Journal of Archaeological Science* 12:221-36.

— 1989, Bone transport, bone destruction, and reverse utility curves. *Journal of Archaeological Science* 16:643-652.

— 1992, Anatomical considerations of utility curves in zooarchaeology. *Journal of Archaeological Science* 19:7-22.

— 1994, *Vertebrate Taphonomy*. Cambridge University Press, Cambridge.

Lyman, R. L., Savelle, J. M., and Whitridge, P., 1992, Derivation and application of a meat utility index for Phocid seals. *Journal of Archaeological Science* 19:531-555.

Maltby, J. M., 1985, Assessing variations in Iron Age and Roman butchery practices: The need for quantification. In *Palaeobiological Investigations. Research Design, Methods and Data Analysis*, edited by N. R. J. Fieller, D. D. Gilbertson and N. G. A. Ralph, pp. 19-30. BAR International Series 266. British Archaeological Reports, Oxford.

Meadow, R. H., 1980, Animal bones: Problems for the archaeologist together with some possible solutions. *Paléorient* 6:65-77.

— 1989, Osteological evidence for the process of animal domestication. In *The Walking Larder. Patterns of Domestication, Pastoralism and Predation*, edited by J. Clutton-Brock, pp. 80-90. Unwin Hyman, London.

Metcalfe, D., and Jones, K. T., 1988, A reconsideration of animal-part utility indices. *American Antiquity* 53:486-504.

Miracle, P. T., and O'Brien, C. J., 1998, Seasonality of resource use and site occupation at Badanj, Bosnia-Herzegovina: Subsistence stress in an increasingly seasonal environment? In *Seasonality and Sedentism, Archaeological Perspectives from Old and New World Sites*, edited by T. R. Rocek and O. Bar-Yosef, pp. 41-74. Peabody Museum Bulletin 6. Harvard University, Cambridge, MA.

Mitchell, B., 1967, Growth layers in dental cement for determining the age of red deer (Cervus elaphus L.). *Journal of Animal Ecology* 36:279-93.

Monks, G. G., 1981, Seasonality studies. *Advances in Archaeological Method and Theory* 4:177-240.

Moore, K. M., 1998, Measures of mobility and occupational intensity in highland Peru. In *Seasonality and Sedentism, Archaeological Perspectives from Old and New World Sites*, edited by T. R. Rocek and O. Bar-Yosef, pp. 181-97. Peabody Museum Bulletin 6. Harvard University, Cambridge, MA.

Morris, P., 1972, A review of mammalian age determination methods. *Mammal Review* 2:69-104.

— 1978, The use of teeth for estimating the age of wild mammals. In *Development, Function and Evolution of Teeth*, edited by P. Butler and K. Joysey, pp. 483-94. Academic Press, New York.

Muñiz, A. M.,1998, The mobile faunas: Reliable seasonal indicators for archaeozoologists? In *Seasonality and Sedentism, Archaeological Perspectives from Old and New World Sites*, edited by T. R. Rocek and O. Bar-Yosef, pp. 25-39. Peabody Museum Bulletin 6. Harvard University, Cambridge, MA.

Noe-Nygaard, N., 1977, Butchery and marrow fracturing as a taphonomic factor in archaeological deposits. *Paleobiology* 3:218-37.

Olsen, S. J., 1971, *Zooarchaeology: Animal Bones in Archaeology and Their Interpretation*. Addison-Wesley, Reading, MA.

— 1972, *Osteology for the Archaeologist 4, North American Birds*. Papers of the Peabody Museum of Archaeology and Ethnology. Harvard University, Cambridge, MA.

— 1974, Early domestic dogs in North America and their origins. *Journal of Field Archaeology* 1:343-45.

— 1979, Archaeologically, what constitutes an early domestic animal? *Advances in Archaeological Method and Theory* 2:175-97.

Ossian, C. R., 1970, Preparation of disarticulated skeletons using enzyme-based laundry "presoakers." *Copeia* 1:199-200.

Pales, L., and Garcia, M. A., 1981, *Atlas Ostéologique des Mammifères*, vol. 2. Centre National de la Recherche Scientifique, Paris.

Pales, L., and Lambert, C., 1971, *Atlas Ostéologique des Mammifères*, vol. 1. Centre National de la Recherche Scientifique, Paris.

Payne, S., 1968, The origins of domestic sheep and goats: A reconsideration in the light of fossil evidence. *Proceedings of the Prehistoric Society* 34:368-84.

— 1972a, Partial recovery and sample bias: The results of some sieving experiments. In *Papers in Economic Prehistory*, edited by E. S. Higgs, pp. 49-64. Cambridge University Press, Cambridge.

— 1972b, On the interpretation of bone samples from archaeological sites. In *Papers in Economic Prehistory*, edited by E. S. Higgs, pp. 65-81. Cambridge University Press, Cambridge.

— 1973, Kill-off patterns in sheep and goats: The mandibles from Asvan Kale. *Anatolian Studies* 23:281-303.

— 1975, Partial recovery and sample bias. In *Archaeolozoological Studies*, edited by A. T. Clason, pp. 7-17. American Elsevier, New York.

Payne, S., and Munson, P. J., 1985, Ruby and how many squirrels? The destruction of bones by dogs. In *Palaeobiological Investigations. Research Design, Methods and Data Analysis*, edited by N. R. J. Fieller, D. D. Gilbertson and N. G. A. Ralph, pp. 31-39. BAR International Series 266. British Archaeological Reports, Oxford.

Perkins, D., 1973, The beginnings of animal domestication in the Near East. *American Journal of Archaeology* 77:279-91.

Perkins, D., and Daly, P., 1968, A hunters' village in Neolithic Turkey. *Scientific American* 219(11):97-106.

Pollard, G. C., and Drew, I. M., 1975, Llama herding and settlement in prehispanic northern Chile: Application of analysis for determining domestication. *American Antiquity* 40:296-305.

Potts, R., and Shipman, P., 1981, Cutmarks made by stone tools on bones from Olduvai Gorge, Tanzania. *Nature* 291:577-80.

Preece, R. G., 1981, The value of shell microsculpture as a guide to the identification of land Mollusca from Quaternary deposits. *Journal of Conchology* 30:331-37.

Price, T. D., Blitz, J., Burton, J., and Ezzo, J. A., 1992, Diagenesis in prehistoric bone: Problems and solutions. *Journal of Archaeological Science* 19:513-29.

Quitmyer, I., Hale, S., and Jones, D. S., 1985, Paleoseasonality determination based on incremental shell growth in the hard clam Mercenaria mercenaria, and its implications for the analysis of three southeast Georgia coastal shell middens. *Southeastern Archaeology* 4:27-40.

Reinhard, K., 1990, Archeoparasitology in North America. *American Journal of Physical Anthropology* 82:145-63.

Ringrose, T. J., 1993a, Bone counts and statistics: A critique. *Journal of Archaeological Science* 20:121-57.

Roberts, C., and Manchester, K., 1995, *The Archaeology of Disease*. Cornell University Press, Ithaca, N.Y.

Russo, M 1998, Measuring sedentism with fauna: Archaic cultures along the southwest Florida coast. In *Seasonality and Sedentism, Archaeological Perspectives from Old and New World Sites*, edited by T. R. Rocek and O. Bar-Yosef, pp. 143-64. Peabody Museum Bulletin 6. Harvard University, Cambridge, MA.

Ryder, M. L., 1969, *Animal Bones in Archaeology*. Mammal Society Handbooks. Blackwell, Oxford.

Sandford, M. K., 1992, A reconsideration of trace element analysis in prehistoric bone. In *Skeletal Biology of Past Peoples: Research Methods*, edited by S. R. Saunders and M. A. Katzenberg, pp. 105-19. Wiley-Liss, New York.

Schiffer, M. B., 1976, *Behavioral Archaeology*. Academic Press, New York.

— 1987, *Formation Processes of the Archaeological Record*. University of New Mexico Press, Albuquerque, NM.

Schmid, E., 1972, *Atlas of Animal Bones for Prehistorians*. Elsevier, Amsterdam.

Sherratt, A., 1983, The secondary exploitation of animals in the Old World. *World Archaeology* 15:90-104.

Shipman, P., 1981, *Life History of a Fossil*. Harvard University Press, Cambridge, MA.

Shotwell, A. J., 1955, An approach to the paleoecology of mammals. *Ecology* 36:327-37.

Shufeldt, R. W., 1909, Osteology of birds. *Bulletin of the New York State Museum* 130:5-381.

Siegel, J., 1976, Animal paleopathology: Possibilities and problems. *Journal of Archaeological Science* 3:349-84.

Sillen, A., 1981, Strontium and diet at Hayonim Cave. *American Journal of Physical Anthropology* 56:131-37.

Simpson, G. G., Roe, A., and Lewontwin, R. C., 1960, *Quantitative Zoology*. Brace and World, New York.

Smith, P., and Horwitz, L. R., 1984,

Speth, J. D., 1983, *Bison Kills and Bone Counts: Decision-making by Ancient Hunters*. University of Chicago Press, Chicago.

Spiess, A. E., 1979, *Reindeer and Cariboo Hunters: An Archaeological Study*. Academic Press, New York.

Spinage, C. A., 1972, Age estimation of zebra. *East African Wildlife Journal* 10:273-277.

— 1973, A review of the age determination of mammals by means of teeth, with special reference to Africa. *East African Wildlife Journal* 10:273-77.

Starks, E. C., 1901, Synonymy of the fish skeleton. *Proceedings of the Washington Acadamy of Science* 3:507-539.

Stewart, F. L., and Stahl, F. W., 1977, Cautionary note on edible meat poundage figures. *American Antiquity* 42:267-70.

Tauber, H., 1981, ^{13}C evidence for dietary habits of prehistoric man in Denmark. *Nature* 292:332-33.

Tchernov, E., 1968, *Succession of Rodent Faunas during the Upper Pleistocene of Israel*. Mammalia Depicta, Hamburg.

— 1990, The age of 'Ubeidiya Formation (Jordan Valley, Israel) and the earliest hominids in the Levant. *Paléorient* 14 (2):63-65.

Thomas, D. H., 1971, On distinguishing natural from cultural bone in archaeological sites. *American Antiquity* 36:366-71.

Thomas, K. D., 1985, Land snail analysis in archaeology: Theory and practice. In *Palaeobiological Investigations. Research Design, Methods and Data Analysis*, edited by N. R. J. Fieller, D. D. Gilbertson and N. G. A. Ralph, pp. 131-56. BAR International Series 266. British Archaeological Reports, Oxford.

Tooker, E., 1964, *An Ethnography of the Huron Indians, 1615-1649*. Washington, DC.

Tuross, N., Behrensmeyer, A. K., and Eanes, E. D., 1989, Strontium increases and crystallinity changes in taphonomic and archaeological bone. *Journal of Archaeological Science* 16:661-72.

Ubelaker, D. H., 1989, *Human Skeletal Remains : Excavation, Analysis, Interpretation*, 2nd ed. Taraxacum. Washington, D.C.

Uerpmann, H. P., 1978, Metrical analysis of faunal remains from the Middle East. In *Approaches to Faunal Analysis in the Middle East*, edited by R. H. Meadow and M. A. Zeder, pp. 41-45. Peabody Museum of Archaeology and Ethnology Bulletin 2. Peabody Museum, Cambridge, MA.

van der Merwe, N. J., 1982, Carbon isotopes, photosynthesis, and archaeology. *American Scientist* 70:596-606.

van der Merwe, N. J., and Vogel, J. C., 1978, ^{13}C content of human collagen as a measure of prehistoric diet in woodland North America. *Nature* 276:816-16.

Vogel, J. C., and van der Merwe, N. J., 1977, Isotopic evidence for early maize cultivation in New York State. *American Antiquity* 42:238-42.

Von den Driesch, A., 1976, A guide to the measurement of animals bones from archaeological sites. *Bulletin of the Peabody Museum of Archaeology and Ethnology* 1:1-136.

Walker, R., 1985, *A Guide to Post-Cranial Bones of East African Animals*. Norwich, UK:Hylochoerus Press.

Waselkov, G. A., 1987, Shellfish gathering and shell midden archaeology. *Advances in Archaeological Method and Theory* 10:93-210.

Wilbur, K. M., and Yonge, C. M., eds., 1964, *Physiology of Mullusca*, vol. 1. Academic Press, New York.

Wye, K. R., 1991, *The Illustrated Encyclopedia of Shells*. Quantum Books, London.

Yonge, C. M., and Thompson, T. E., 1976, Living Marine Molluscs. Collins, London.

Zeuner, F. E., 1963, *A History of Domesticated Animals*. Hutchinson, London.

Ziegler, A. C., 1973, *Inference from Prehistoric Faunal Remains*. Addison-Wesley Module in Anthropology 43. Addison-Wesley, Reading, MA.

11 Analysing Plant Remains

Sites with exceptional preservation, such as waterlogged sites in Europe, have attracted the attention of botanists since the mid-1800s, and pollen analysis has been common in some branches of archaeology almost as long (Greig, 1989:4). Since about 1950, archaeologists have found plant remains increasingly important for what they can tell us about diet, food production, paleoenvironment, and tool use.

The archaeological study of plant remains has variably been called archaeobotany or paleoethnobotany. Those who prefer the latter term like its emphasis on the relationship between plants and people. Here I use the terms interchangeably, and attach no value judgement to one or the other. By either name, it is related to such fields as zooarchaeology and Quaternary paleoecology, while its archaeological purposes distinguish it from paleobotany, the botanical version of paleontology. For students interested in pursuing paleoethnobotany, modern Botany departments' frequent focus on molecular biology rather than the taxonomy of vascular plants makes it difficult to acquire the skills necessary to become a competent archaeobotanist except through years of experience under the guidance of a senior practitioner. This brief chapter serves only as an introduction to its laboratory methods and what they can contribute to archaeology.

As is also the case for zooarchaeologists, archaeobotanists or paleoethnobotanists must concern themselves with the taxonomy of organisms (see p. 189 for biological taxonomy), and with taphonomic problems (see pp. 188-189, and Beck, 1989). Identification to genus or species is one of their first concerns, which is made more difficult by taphonomic circumstances that usually prevent the preservation of more than tiny fragments of particular plant parts. This makes taxonomy a greater challenge for paleoethnobotanists than for botanists who have whole, living plants at their disposal. In addition, the plant parts that taxonomists usually emphasize (typically the anatomy of flowers) are usually not preserved, while there has not always been sufficient research on the morphology and structure of those parts that are most often preserved, such as phytoliths.

Types of Plant Remains

Paleoethnobotanists typically classify archaeological plant remains as either plant macrofossils, microfossils, or chemical traces, each with its own problems and analytical methods.

Macrofossils are visible to the naked eye and their identification usually requires no more than low-power magnification. Some analysts (e.g., Ford, 1979:301) prefer to call these "macroremains," as the plant remains from most archaeological sites are not fossilized in the sense of mineral replacement of their original components. The term, "macrofossil," remains common in the literature, however. Among this type of evidence are charcoal, nuts, tubers, fruit endocarps or seeds, or their fragments, as well as pieces or artifacts of wood or basketry, each with different probabilities of preservation in different environments. Dry caves and waterlogged sediments are most favorable for preservation. Often this probability has been enhanced by charring in a reducing atmosphere, which tends to caramelize the sugars in the plant material. More rarely they are completely carbonized, with all of their organic constituents converted into pure carbon. Two of the key characteristics of carbonized remains is that they are not susceptible to bacterial attack, and that they are often light enough to float in water. Macrofossils may also be preserved in ancient feces, or coprolites (e.g., Minnis, 1989).

Microfossils require use of sophisticated separation and concentration techniques for their isolation and high-power magnification for identification. They include pollen, spores, diatom frustules, and opaline phytoliths. The study of pollen and spores is called **palynology**.

Chemical evidence for prehistoric plants includes fatty residues and amino acids on artifacts or in the matrix of pottery, DNA fragments in plant remains, and carbon isotopes and trace elements in bones.

Macrofossils

Today most macrofossils from archaeological sediments are retrieved by water separation in the field through a technique called *flotation*, and then sorted and analysed in the laboratory, but flotation is not always the best method. Flotation separates the lighter, carbonized materials from the mainly inorganic sediment matrix and concentrates them for easier analysis. Some heavier carbonized and charred material, especially fruit stones and larger pieces of charcoal, will sink into the "heavy" fraction, which may also contain small artifacts and bones. Agitation in water may destroy many of the more delicate bones and plant remains. Users of flotation tanks must also be wary of contamination from previous samples in the tank, and of potential contamination of any remains they might want to use for radiocarbon dating. Whether flotation or dry-sieving is the best method for concentrating and separating the plant remains from a particular site can only be determined by experiment. The mass and volume of sediment should be recorded prior to concentration of plant remains to preserve information about the density of remains in the sediment.

A specially designed froth-flotation tank is capable of separating plant remains from fairly large volumes of sediment, but simple "bucket flotation" is effective for processing small volumes of sediment.

The froth-flotation tank is a simple device that uses jets of pressurized water — gravity is sufficient to provide the pressure — forced through small holes in interior pipes to agitate water in a tank. A mesh submerged in the tank captures the "heavy fraction," and a lip allows overflowing water and any floating material to exit into a series of nested sieves. In regions with water shortages, the overflow water may be recaptured in settling tanks for reuse later. For very clayey or carbonaceous sediments, in which clay particles or calcium carbonate may adhere to plant macrofossils and make them sink, or clay peds may fail to break up, it may be necessary to add a deflocculant to break up the clay and carbonates. After pouring a sediment sample of known volume and mass into the tank and stirring, the analyst simply collects floating material, most of it organic, on the sieves, and then removes the internal mesh bag containing all of the heavier particles too large to pass through the mesh. In essence, the method simply removes all the finest particles, and separates the lighter particles from the rest.

Bucket flotation requires no equipment more sophisticated than the usual collection of sieves, a small tea-strainer type of sieve, and two buckets, one of which has had its bottom cut out and replaced with a mesh. With the mesh-bottomed bucket nested into the intact one, the user simply fills them about two-thirds full with water (including, where necessary, a deflocculant), and then empties a volume of sediment, up to about one liter, into the water. Grabbing the handle of the mesh-bottomed bucket, the analyst pulls it up, plunges it down and rotates it back-and-forth to agitate the water, put the sediment into suspension, and release lighter particles from the sediment matrix to float to the surface while fine silts and clays pass through the mesh and sink to the bottom of the intact bucket and large, heavy particles are caught on the bottom of the mesh-bottomed bucket. Having collected any floating material with a small, long-handled, tea strainer, and emptied it carefully onto a cloth, the analyst can then slowly remove the mesh-bottomed bucket to empty the heavy fraction onto another cloth.

Following separation by either method, the analyst then allows both the light and heavy fractions to dry slowly in cloth bags or cloth sections folded over to keep their contents from escaping. Failure to dry the samples properly could lead to attack by fungi and mildew. Generally drying takes several days, even in warm climates.

Occasionally, very dry or sandy sediments may call for screening without flotation, especially if there are fears that soaking in water may damage some of the remains. A conservator's advice is helpful in these cases. The main advantage to flotation is that it concentrates the light fraction, which saves sorting time later.

Once the plant remains have been separated from the bulk of the sediment, a zooming binocular microscope (7x to 30x) can be used to examine each fraction in small portions on a Petrie dish. Sort it gently with tweezers or fine brush into major categories of material, such as charcoal, nuts, seeds, stones, and amorphous or uncertain plant material. There may also be non-plant material, such as insect parts, small bones or lithics, that merit recording, especially in the heavy fraction. Sorting is a time-consuming step, and can take hours per kilogram of charred material. Further sorting of each category and identification to genus or species can be even more time-consuming, sometimes requiring subsampling (see chap. 4).

Identification requires a voucher collection containing samples of wood, charred wood, seeds, nuts, and other plant items that you might expect to find in the archaeological samples (Bye, 1986; Pearsall, 1989:128-44). Most paleoethnobotanists have to build their own collections, as the specimens in herbarium collections do not always show the parts (such as seeds) that are of greatest archaeological interest, and their curators are reluctant in any case to let anyone cut bits from specimens. Some of the more obvious seed specimens, such as maize, wheat, peas, and lentils, can be easy to obtain, at least in modern varieties, from bulk food stores, but not other plant parts. Assembling most of the collection requires the patient accumulation of seeds, wood, and other plant parts from carefully identified plants in the wild or in farmers'

fields. Next, the collector must char some of the collected material of each taxonomic group and plant part to make it more comparable to the archaeological specimens, most of which have usually been charred. A laboratory oven can be used to accomplish this, preferably in an atmosphere that excludes oxygen (e.g., nitrogen atmosphere).

Seeds and Nuts

The remains of fruit, most often charred or dessicated seeds or nuts or their impressions in clay, have traditionally been the most important type of plant macrofossil. In some cases other plant parts adjacent to the seeds, such as glumes and rachis fragments of cereals, are also preserved. Quite commonly these plant parts have been preserved through charring. Hulled wheats that need to be parched with heat before threshing, for example, are likely to be charred occasionally (Harlan, 1967). In other cases, an accidental fire in a house or storehouse resulted in the charring of stored cereals and legumes, or volcanic eruptions, as at Pompeii, charred whole fruit. In such cases, only plant parts that were protected from direct conflagration are preserved. There was enough heat to carbonize them, but not enough to combust them and reduce them to ash (Dimbleby, 1967). The carbonization process makes the seeds immune to bacterial action, but also changes their metric attributes slightly through shrinkage (Renfrew, 1973:10-14).

Fruit and seeds of flowering plants are formed from the flowering parts of plants after fertilization of the egg cell (in the ovule) by pollen. The fruit of a flowering plant varies depending on whether the plant is a monocotyledon or dicotyledon. A cotyledon is a modified leaf in the seed, and monocots have one cotyledon, while dicots have two. The cotyledons store food that the parent plant transmits to them, and enclose the embryo. Monocots store the food in a tissue called endosperm, and in both monocots and dicots the ovule's outer wall thickens to become the seed coat, or *testa*.

As seeds grow, the ovary becomes much enlarged, the flower's stamens and petals shrivel and fall off, and the ovary becomes recognizable as a fruit. Fruits vary widely in form, ranging from pods and dry capsules to fleshy, edible fruits, such as apples, tomatoes, cucumbers, and cherries. Blackberries and raspberries are actually clusters of many small fruits. In strawberries, the largest edible portion is actually the flower's receptacle, while the fruits are technically the small pips that cover it.

The seed of a bean illustrates the anatomy of a dicot seed (figure 11.1). The embryo consists of a root or *radicule* and a shoot or *plumule*, and is attached to two cotyledons, which store food for the embryo. Both embryo and cotyledons are enclosed within the testa. A micropyle (small hole through which pollen entered the ovule) is still visible on the testa and allows moisture to enter the seed. The *hilum* is a scar marking the place where the seed was attached to the pod. When the bean germinates, the hypocotyl (region just above the radicle) grows, arches upwards, and pulls the cotyledons and plumule out of the testa and the soil. Later the cotyledons fall off.

In grasses, including cereals, food is not stored in cotyledons but in the endosperm (figures 11.3, 11.4). The single cotyledon (grasses are monocots) remains in the seed to digest the stored food and transfer it to the embryo. The plumule as it grows straight up from the seed is at first protected by a sheath-like coleopile, and leaves the cotyledon behind in the soil.

Sometimes the seed itself is not the only part of a grass plant that is preserved archaeologically. Grains are carried at the top of a culm (stem) in a spike (e.g., wheat and barley), in a broad pannicle (e.g., oats), or the intercalary ear (only maize). A spike is made up of a central, segmented rachis, with spikelets attached alternately at the nodes. A pannicle is the same except that branches at each node are attached to the spikelets. Each spikelet (figure 11.2) has two glumes enclosing several florets attached by rachillae. In each floret, a lemma and palea enclose the grain or caryopsis, the lemma on the dorsal side and the palea on the ventral.

Maize (figure 11.5) is a highly unusual grass, being the product of domestication by humans (Chapman, 1996; Chapman and Peat, 1992). Here the axis is a tough cob, rather than delicate

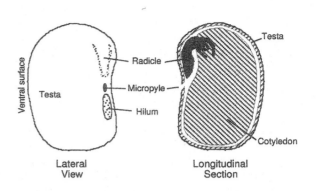

Figure 11.1. Lateral view (left) and longitudinal section of a generalized dicotyledon bean.

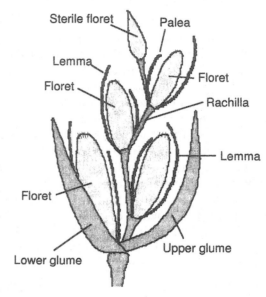

Figure 11.2. Generalized anatomy of a cereal spikelet to show how florets are arranged along the axis of the rachis (after Renfrew, 1973).

rachis, to which the grains are quite firmly attached. The glumes, lemma, and palea have become so reduced in size that the grains or kernels are naked and, instead, the entire corn ear is enclosed by leaf bases (husks). These completely preclude natural dispersal of the grains, making the plant completely dependent on humans for its reproduction. They also keep maize kernels attached to cobs that have been carbonized and preserved in archaeological deposits.

Some guides to the indentification of seeds include Lone et al. (1993), Renfrew (1973), and Shopmeyer (1974).

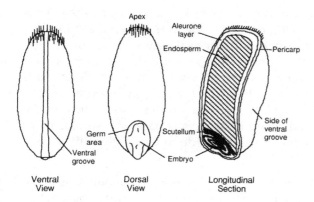

Figure 11.3. Ventral and dorsal views and longitudinal section through a wheat caryopsis.

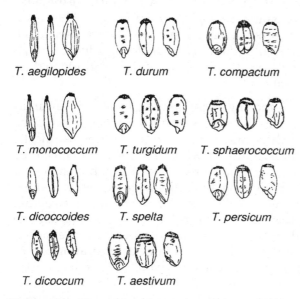

T. aegilopides   *T. durum*   *T. compactum*

T. monococcum   *T. turgidum*   *T. sphaerococcum*

T. dicoccoides   *T. spelta*   *T. persicum*

T. dicoccum   *T. aestivum*

Figure 11.4. External morphology of various species of the genus Triticum (wheat)(Lone et al., 1993:16).

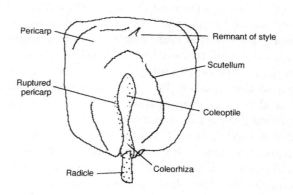

Figure 11.5. Dorsal view of a maize caryopsis during early germination.

Wood Charcoal and Parenchymous Parts

The heavy fraction from flotation often includes fragments of charcoal. Wood charcoal can be useful, not only for radiocarbon dates and dendrochronology, but to reconstruct a site's environment and human preferences for fuel and construction materials. The wood taxa represented by charcoal may not be representative of the distribution of trees around the site because wood accumulates on the site through a variety of cultural and natural processes that favor particular kinds of wood, presenting many of the same taphonomic problems we already saw with faunal remains. Some kinds of wood make better fuel, are easier to hew, make straighter timbers, or are easily found lying on the ground within easy reach of the site. Charcoal made from taxa that are particularly good for fuel may be produced in forested regions and exported to regions with fewer or poorer trees. In other areas, such as the Arctic coast, most of the charcoal found is from driftwood, which may have been transported thousands of kilometers. In some contexts, however, opportunistic collection of dead wood for fuel may have provided a nearly random sample of wood around the site. Only attention to site-formation processes and cultural practices can help us distinguish these situations.

To prepare charcoal samples for examination, it is necessary to cut or break them so that they show the **transverse, radial,** and **tangential** planes (figure 11.6). The transverse section is a

Remains of nuts are also common on archaeological sites. Nuts were exploited for their oil and meat, which can even be made into flour, and their shells could be used as fuel. Fuel uses as well as roasting to reduce tannic acid levels in some species accounts for their charring in many cases. Sometimes the tannic acid itself may have been the attractive resource in nuts, as it is useful for tanning hides. Nut fragments can be difficult to identify unless they are reasonably large, in which case Schopmeyer (1974) is a useful guide.

cross-section at right angles to the growth rings and parallel to the rays. The tangential section is along the grain at right angles to both growth rings and rays. In the transverse section, the rays appear as spokes of a wheel, while in the tangential section you see the rays end-on, and in the radial section they appear as parallel bands. Although you can make simple identifications in reflected light by examining these sections, it is useful to mount thin sections cut from them on slides. Once you have all three views exposed, you can cut a thin slice from each using a microtome or a very sharp razor blade or exacto-knife, thin enough that light will show through. A dull blade will tear at the cell structure and ruin your section. Generally you should remove several slices in each axis to be sure that you intersect diagnostic features (Friedman, 1978:2-4). You can mount the sections on a microscope slide in a 50% solution of glycerin in 95% alcohol. It is useful to keep one section of each plane on a single slide under three cover slips, with a consistent orientation and order from one to the other so that it is easy for you to switch views or slides without becoming disoriented. Of course the slide needs to be labelled clearly. Next you should heat the slide on a hot plate at 300 °F for one or two minutes to expel air bubbles.

Identification of wood charcoals depends on the recognition of distinctive patterns in the cellular structure of the wood. In charred wood, this is not a problem. Although identification to genus can be very difficult and requires detailed inspection of minute differences in cell structure, arrangement, and size in a reference collection, distinguishing hardwoods from softwoods is relatively straightforward. Hardwoods have more complex structure than do softwoods, and have vessels (pores) running longitudinally through them, which appear as tunnel-like, circular features in a transverse section (figure 11.6). The vessels can be isolated or, as in maples and birches, grouped. Softwoods lack these specialized vessels, mainly showing only the band-like variations in cell width (early and late growth) that result in tree rings, although some genera, including pine, can have longitudinal resin canals that appear as cavities surrounded by epithelial cells. They also show pits in radial section that transfer water and are very useful in

identification. Both kinds of wood also show rays that radiate out in transverse section like spokes. In softwoods the rays appear in tangential section as single or double strands of cells arranged vertically, but in hardwoods the rays can be multiseriate (have large bundles of cells arranged in vertical lenses). Identification of reeds used in baskets is based on similar principles. A useful guide to wood identification is Jane (1970).

Until recently, most archaeobotanists assumed that the remains of vegetative **parenchymous organs** (roots, tubers, rhizomes, and corms) would not typically be preserved in archaeological deposits, or simply did not have the skills necessary to recognize them. Hather (1993; 1994) notes, however, that such tissues are often much more abundant in archaeological deposits than you would think, and provides a guide to their identification.

Ignoring these tissues, especially in areas such as the tropics or Andes, where foods such as yams and potatoes were staples, would be unfortunate. As with other plant remains, they are sometimes preserved through charring or waterlogging, but often with the result that the tissues are distorted by shrinking or swelling. Consequently, the reference collections used to identify parenchymous tissues must be exposed experimentally to the same deteriorating conditions (particularly charring) for identifications to be accurate. Tissue that has dried slowly prior to charring usually shows the best preservation, while steam expulsion that results when moist tissues are heated causes fissures and large vesicles (Hather 1993:vii-ix, 3-4).

Microfossils

Plant remains that are visible to the naked eye or under low-power magnification provide only part of the picture. Pollen, spores, opaline phytoliths, and diatoms are microscopic fossils that offer quite different information and have rather different taphonomic histories. Consequently, they complement macroremains.

Pollen consists of rather heavily armored gametophytes. Male gametes (sperm cells) occur inside the pollen grain or pollen tube, and the pollen thus transmits male genetic material

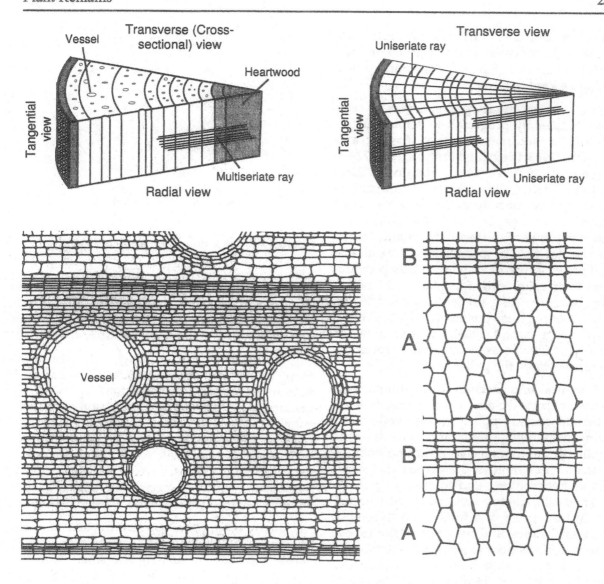

Figure 11.6. Wedges of hardwood (top left) and softwood (top right) along with magnified transverse cross-sections to depict the tubular vessels in hardwood (lower left), and the lack of vessels in softwood (lower right), which has earlywood (A) and latewood (B) zones of growth rings.

to the female gamete. The wall, or *exine*, of the pollen grain contains a substance, called sporopollenin, that is very resistant to decay. The identification of pollen grains to genus or species depends on the great diversity of shapes that the exine exhibits (Erdtman, 1943; Faegri and Iversen, 1989; Moore et al., 1991).

Both exine morphology and the relative abundance of pollen are related to the pollen's means of dispersal. *Anemophilous* (wind-borne) plants produce abundant pollen, which tends to

have features that enhance its buoyancy on the wind. Amenophilous pollens include *Pinus*, *Casuarina*, *Poaceae*, and *Typha*. *Zoophilous* (including *entomophilous*) plants produce less pollen, but have animal (usually insect) vectors that are very effective at transporting the pollen from the anthers to the stigmas of flowers. *Hydrophilous* (water-borne) and *cleistogamous* (self-pollinating) pollens rarely occur in archaeological deposits because hydrophilous pollen lacks the hard exine, while cleistogamous plants are fertilized without transport. These variations in transport mechanism complicate our interpretation of pollen distributions and need to be kept in mind.

We can concentrate pollen grains in sediment samples by progressive chemical digestion of the sediment matrix (Bryant and Holloway, 1983; Faegri and Iverson, 1989: 72-84; Moore et al., 1991: 41-46) without undue damage to the pollen they contain. Introducing a known number of polystyrene spheres, exotic *Lycopodium* spores, or *Eucalyptus* pollen into known volumes of soil facilitates quantification (see chapter 5). The proportion of exotics to fossil pollen grains of each taxon later provides a basis for calibrating the number of pollen grains and providing a reliable estimate for the total number of fossil pollen of each taxon in the sample (Benninghoff, 1966). This also allows us to monitor the success with which processing has concentrated the pollen.

Chemical and mechanical treatments that follow minimise the amount of matrix material that could obscure pollen grains, while maximizing the number, preservation, and diversity of pollen grains that survive. As any palynological treatment employs dangerous chemicals, such as hydrochloric and hydrofluoric acids (HCl and HF), safety measures are very important, including use of a fume hood to remove dangerous fumes, and wearing of gloves, eye protection, and smock to protect against splashing. Those processing the samples should also be familiar with the WHMS data sheets on all the chemicals they use. A solution of hydrochloric acid (HCl) removes calcium carbonate, potassium hydroxide (KOH) removes humic acids, hydrofluoric acid (HF) is used to digest the silicates, and an acetolysis solution (one part sulphuric acid to 9 parts acetic anhydride) can be used to remove cellulose, and tertiary butyl alcohol to remove water. The details of these processes need not concern us here, but are discussed in standard texts (e.g., Fægri and Iversen, 1989; Moore et al., 1991). The addition of safranin red stain enhances pollen visibility and a portion of the concentrated pollen can then be mounted on a warm glass slide with a pipette and covered with a cover slip. The mate-

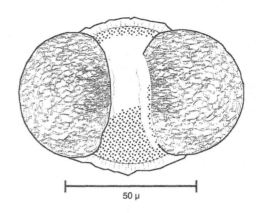

50 μ

Figure 11.7. Distal view of an exine of Pine pollen.

rial should spread out to the edges of the cover slip, and then you should seal the cover slip with varnish and label the slide, which is now ready for examination under a microscope.

A number of identification guides for pollen exist (e.g., Moore et al., 1989), but there is no substitute for a voucher collection. A palynologist needs a good reference collection of slides showing identified pollen. These can be made up from pollen collected from the field or herbarium specimens, while some can be bought from commercial firms. Even so, it is not always possible to identify to species, and some pollen can only be attributed to a "type" (Greig, 1989:65).

Quantifying what you see on one of the pollen slides involves making a series of traverses across the slide by turning the small "travel knobs" to move the microscope stage in the x- and y-axes by measurable increments. Always begin examination of the slide at the same corner. Along each traverse you count and record pollen of various taxa at various grid coordinates on the slide. For common types of pollen a mechanical or electronic counter helps prevent miscounts and speeds analysis. Grains that are not immediately identifiable require closer examination by zooming in at higher power; if you want to wait to to do this you can simply record the location of the grain by its coordinates and return to it later. While you may do counting at around 400x, close examination may require magnification around 1000x, and you may need to move the focus in and out a bit because there is little depth of field at high power (Faegri and

Iversen, 1989: 86; Greig, 1989: 65-66). Quantification of pollen on the slide is often expresssed in number of grains per unit volume or unit mass of sediment (as measured before chemical digestion), rather than simply in number of grains or percentage of grains, although the last is still commonly reported.

Sample size is an issue with pollen counting as with anything else. On a pollen slide exhibiting typical diversity, a total pollen count of about 600 grains may be sufficient (Greig, 1989: 67; Moore et al., 1991: 168). In pollen assemblages with low evenness, however, most of the 600 could conceivably come from only a few taxa. Counts of less than 150 grains in total can give misleading results unless variations in pollen spectra are extreme. Estimating the density of rarer taxa with reasonable confidence may require counting some 5000 grains in total, and involve more work than most analysts are willing to invest (Faegri and Iversen, 1989: 150-52). Use the sampling guidelines in chapter 4 to estimate the total sample size necessary to represent interesting but fairly rare taxa, but you may need to compromise on the rarer types. Alternatively, some analysts use **sequential sampling** that stops when the abundances of taxa seem to stabilize (Moore et al., 1991: 168-69).

Spores are the mainly airborne reproductive bodies released by non-flowering plants, such as fungi, ferns, and mosses. They are rarely identifiable as specifically as pollen grains, and it is more difficult to find good reference collections for these diverse plants. Fern spores are usually the most important for archaeological analysis, as many of them are distinguishable by their external morphology. Spores of ferns and club-mosses are very resistant to decay even in peat bogs in which no pollen is preserved (Dimbleby, 1985).

Complementing the evidence from pollen and spores with phytolith data is another way to deal with the problems of differential production and transport that pollen and spores present.

Phytoliths, unlike pollen and spores, are the silicified casts of cells in the leaf and stem tissues of some plants. During life, as these plants take up water, they deposit SiO_2 from monosilicic acid (Si $(OH)_4$) or soluble silica that is disolved in the water on the surfaces of some cells. Phytoliths are extremely resistant to weathering or decomposition unless they are in soils that have a pH higher than 8 or 9, so that long after the death of the plant and the decay of its organic material, these silicate outlines can be preserved, making them a unique source of evidence for the plant parts that are usually not preserved in typical archaeological conditions.

Separating phytoliths from the sediment matrix requires chemical digestion of the sediment, much as with pollen analysis. First, a combination of deflocculants, repeated decanting, and settling is used to remove clays. The silt is then screened to remove modern roots and stones, HCl (hydrochloric acid) solution is used to remove carbonates, and nitric acid to remove organic matter. Sediment is washed and centrifuged many times to concentrate the remaining sediment.

The sediment is then ready for separation (Lentfer and Boyd, 1998). One way to separate them is heavy-liquid separation, in which the particles of interest are isolated through their buoyancy in a liquid of a particular density. Phytoliths have a specific gravity (density) of 2.3 - 2.4. Many substances can be used for the separation: tetra-bromide ethylene, zinc bromide, cadmium-potassium iodide, and non-toxic sodium polytungstate, a latex-based substance that is soluble in water. Sodium polytungstate (the safest choice) is diluted until a specific gravity of 2.3 is achieved, this is added to the tubes and centrifuged at a medium setting until phytoliths float to the top. The floated sediment is then decanted into another tube and washed several times to retrieve the Sodium Polytungstate (it is expensive). Absolute ethyl alcohol is added and the suspended sediment put into small vials. Sediment is then wet-mounted onto microscope slides with a pipette, covered, and sealed.

Phytoliths can also be found fused to tooth enamel or on chert or flint tools. These require different extraction methods (Armitage, 1975).

Identification of phytoliths depends on the fact that the cellular structures of plants are highly variable. The silica casts that represent those structures thus allow us to identify the family, genus and, in certain cases, species of the plant in which they were formed. The morphology that a phytolith takes varies according to the place in the plant where the silica was deposited and, since the location of deposition is genetically controlled, phytoliths from plants of the same family or genus will tend to be similar. Phytoliths can form either in the actual cells of a plant, revealing 'casts,' or can result from the incomplete silicification of the cell lumen or interior. The latter are referred to as 'short cells' in the literature (Piperno, 1988:52). It is now possible to identify broad categories of plants by their morphology. For example, we can differentiate between dicotyledons (shrubs, herbs, and trees), monocotyledons (herbaceous plants, shrubs) and Gramineae (grasses, figure 11.8), and gymnosperms (Dahlgren and Clifford, 1982; Mulholland, 1989). Within the Gramineae family, we can also identify some species, including *Hordeum distichium* (barley) and *Triticum dicoccum* (wheat) (Blackman, 1969; Lentfer et al., 1997; Rosen, 1993). Phytolith analysts can distinguish three tribes within the Gramineae: Panicoid, tall grasses growing in cool, humid climates; Festucoid, medium grasses inhabiting humid and locally wet conditions; and Chloridoid, short grasses growing in xerophytic (or dry) conditions.

The technique of phytolith analysis is in many ways still in its pioneering stage. Identification requires a large reference collection to ensure a clear distribution of phytolith morphology across plant taxa, because different plants can produce similar phytoliths while one plant can produce a large array of different phytoliths in different plant parts. The problem is certainly not simply in the variability of the phytoliths, it is in the lack of published regional reference keys for other phytolith analysts to use. Some key references for archaeological phytolith analysis are Baker (1959), Brown (1984), Pearsall and Piperno (1993), Piperno (1988), and Rapp and Mulholland (1992).

Diatom frustules are the siliceous valves or shells of diatoms, microscopic algae that occur just about anywhere there is open water. They are very sensitive to environmental conditions, and especially salinity, and consequently are excellent for documenting changes in shorelines

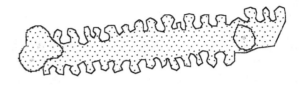

Figure 11.8. Sketch of a silica skeleton (phytolith) from grass husks. The differences between cereal species are in the relative amplitude of the sinuous edges and in the width of the long-cells, and in the ornamentation of the papillae cells found in the husk.

and estuaries. Because they occur in clays, they can also be very useful in helping to characterize and source the clays used for pottery (Battarbee, 1986; Faegri and Iversen, 1989:203-205; Gibson, 1986).

Incidentally, while looking at pollen, spores, diatoms, or phytoliths, you may also encounter parasite ova, spherulites (Brochier, 1983; Canti, 1997), and other microscopic remains that, whether botanical or not, may be valuable evidence for prehistoric diet, disease, and site-formation processes.

Chemical Traces

Sometimes the evidence for prehistoric plants is even less tangible than the skeletons of individual cells. Chemical residues of some of the organic compounds in the plants, such as fats and proteins, and even fragments of DNA and RNA, are now sources of information that can help us identify the presence of completely decayed plants in archaeological contexts. These compounds can occur, not only within macrofossils, but also on the edges of stone tools, within the pores of ceramic vessels, and on the interior surface of pipe bowls, as well as in archaeological sediments. For example, Raffauf and Morris (1960) detected alkaloids of tobacco with gas chromatography, while Jones and Morris (1960), found nicotine on the interior of a Basketmaker III pipe bowl.

On the edges of stone tools, residues provide one of the best sources of evidence for the tools' use. It is possible to identify cellulose, lignin, lipids, resins, amino acids, fibres, pollen, starch grains, and phytoliths on the surfaces of stone tools (Hall et al., 1989:138-39; Kealhofer et al., 1999) using techniques ranging from chemical staining to chromatography and Fourier Transform Infrared Spectroscopy (FTIR).

For many years archaeologists and physical anthropologists have used isotopic ratios in bones as indirect evidence of diet. One of the things that affect the ratio of ^{12}C to ^{13}C in a mammal's body is its relative dependence on C4 plants as part of its diet (see chapter 10).

Plant Taphonomy and Preservation

Like zooarchaeologists, paleoethnobotanists show great concern for taphonomic factors that affect their attempts to interpret plant remains. As in zooarchaeology, it is useful to distinguish between living populations, deposited assemblages, fossil assemblages, and sample assemblages. One difference from faunal assemblages, however, is that plants regularly deposit seeds, pollen, spores, dead leaves, and fallen branches while still living, and not only at the end of their lives.

Several kinds of taphonomic factors affect plant remains. First, different plants deposit greatly different quantitites of seeds, pollen, wood, and so on (see chapter 5). For example, black pine produces about 22,500,000 pollen grains per flower, while many oak species produce less than 1,000,000 per flower (Erdtman 1943: 176). Similarly, many plant families are poor silica accumulators or lack silica completely, while others will produce phytoliths in enormous amounts (Piperno, 1988:16). Second, the mechanisms that transport various plants and plant parts onto sites are numerous, selective, and not always well understood. Some pollen, for example, is transported by wind, others by insects, while phytoliths are deposited when a leaf falls to the ground or hay is placed in a barn, seeds may be brought onto the site by humans, or on the coats of their livestock. The result is that different taxa have radically different probabilities of ending up on the site, and some have low probability of being deposited even if they are abundant in the site's environment. Third, most plants and plant parts have very little probability of being preserved to become part of

the fossil assemblage. Seeds and vegetative parts of plants may be consumed by humans or livestock, grain and nuts ground into flour, wood burned to ash, and the remainder, including leafy parts, roots, and tubers, mainly decayed with no more than a chemical trace. Only a biased sample may be charred to improve preservation. Finally, sampling and processing of site deposits by archaeologists and paleoethnobotanists has a substantial impact on the distribution, representation, and preservation of plant remains.

Pollen analysts have contributed research on compensating for differential pollen production (Faegri and Iversen, 1989:126-29, 142-43), while some paleoethnobotanists try to account for variations in the number of seeds per fruit (e.g., Monckton, 1992:84). Production of seeds and pollen depends not only on species but on temperature, soil conditions, and water availability during the growing season, and disturbance by humans and grazing animals. It is important for analysts to be aware at least of gross differences in production from taxon to taxon.

Transport mechanisms require similar consideration in these interpretations. Fortunately, we can make some reasonable assumptions about the transport of seeds, pollen, and even wood.

Seeds of some taxa are unlikely to occur on archaeological sites unless transported there by humans, which is fortunate if the human use of these plants for food, fuel, fodder, bedding, or some other purpose is our primary interest, but makes things difficult if we are more interested in reconstructing the natural environment. Other taxa are weedy species that we can expect to occur in agricultural fields, where they would be accidentally harvested along with crop seeds, but some of these may also be plants that grow in disturbed areas, including the public spaces within settlements, where they can drop seeds directly onto the site. Still others have spiny exteriors that allow seeds to cling to the coats of livestock or the clothes of humans, and thus be brought onto the sites. Still others may be windborne. Although some of these, even once transported to a site, may have low probabilities of preservation, all of these seeds can be charred if discarded in hearths or refuse fires.

Palynologists have attempted to account for differential transport (Erdtman, 1943:177-82; Faegri and Iversen, 1989:141-46). Some pollen is very heavy, and is dropped only in the vicinity of the plant of origin (generally self-pollenating). Other relatively heavy pollen is transported by insects (entomophilous). Generally the only pollen that is transported into deposits that paleobotanists are likely to sample, especially bogs and lake sediments, is amenophilous (wind-borne). Winds will transport some light pollens, such as olive pollen, hundreds of kilometers, while carrying other, heavier pollens less than 100 m. Furthermore, some of these pollens will be carried high above the tree canopy of forests, while other pollens will be blown along closer to the ground, where they are likely to be caught by grasses and foliage before they have travelled very far. After the introduction of agriculture, the evidence from wind-borne pollen becomes more difficult to interpret as the area that contributes pollen becomes patchy (Rackham, 1976:50). It is important to keep these transport differences in mind when interpreting pollen diagrams; some of the taxa will reflect vegetation in the immediate vicinity of the pollen core, while others will only give a rough idea of what vegetation existed in a catchment, possibly hundreds of kilometers in extent.

Phytoliths, because they occur within the stems and leaves of plants, are deposited where these stems and leaves decayed (Dimbleby, 1985). As a result, phytolith analysis tends to represent local vegetation. Fire and wind can, however, move phytoliths over long distances, as the occurrence of phytoliths in atmospheric dust demonstrates. In most archaeological situations, however, phytoliths probably represent plants that either dropped leaves and branches directly onto the site, or were brought onto the site as useful resources. For example, we may expect concentrations of grass phytoliths where hay was stored or spread on a floor, while phytoliths of some plants, even if they were abundant around a site, may never have been transported onto the site in quantity because the

site's occupants either had no use for the plant, or only used parts of the plant that contained no phytoliths.

The occurrence of charcoal on archaeological sites depends on the transport of wood onto them for use in architecture, for fuel, or as raw material for wooden artifacts, such as furniture. Consequently, wood on a site may not be a random sample of the trees in a site's environment. People may select some trees for use in architecture either because the wood is strong, resistant to rot, or available in long, straight poles. They may select quite different ones for use as fuel, because of availability, ease of reduction to small pieces, relative production of heat, or the need to preserve other trees for other uses. Wood for furniture and other artifacts may be selected for its aesthetic qualitites as well as its ease of working, hardness, durability, and water-resistance (Smart and Hoffman, 1988). Of course, wood can be re-used and its last use is often as fuel. In environments in which trees are diverse and plentiful, the selection of wood will be very different than in ones in which trees are rare and wood must be conserved. Where there was opportunistic collection of dead wood, however, the charcoal assemblage may much better reflect the distribution of trees around a site.

Differential preservation is the problem that seems most to attract the attention of paleoethnobotanists. It is, however, one of the problems over which we have most control, because the context of the samples can often give us some good clues to the probability that particular classes of plant fossil will be preserved (Beck, 1989). Attention to soil pH, wet-dry cycling, temperature, and other factors, as well as variations in the preservation of different plant parts (e.g., macrofossils and pollen) and other remains (e.g., bones), can suggest what we may have lost through poor preservation. For example, we would not expect to find ancient pollen in soils with low acidity and good drainage. If we can be reasonably certain that the site's inhabitants were roasting the seeds of some taxa, grinding or pounding others, and pressing others for their oil, we would expect the first group of taxa to have much greater probabilities of preservation because accidental charring is likely. For evidence of the pressed seeds we might turn to chemical residues or the burnt remains of plant parts that would have been separated from the seeds prior to pressing. Beck (1989) employs decomposition studies to assess the relative probabilities of preservation of various plant parts of various taxa in a variety of contexts in Australia. She measures decomposition rates as the number of years it takes for 95% of the plant part's weight to be lost (much as ^{14}C's half-life is the number of years for 50% of the radiocarbon to decay). It is also important to remember that different parts of plants that humans used are more likely to be preserved at different stages of processing, and that the combination of parts is an important clue to these stages (Dennell, 1979; Hastorf, 1988; Hillman, 1981).

Sampling problems are also widespread in archaeobotany and are typically exacerbated by the fact that the analysis of most plant remains requires the tedious processing and examination of thousands of tiny or even microscopic items. In general, the sampling problems result from a combination of small sample size (i.e., too few sediment volumes analysed) and low density of plant remains within sediment volumes. Modern archaeobotanists are more sensitive than their predecessors to the need to sample a diversity of features and deposits and not just one or two obviously fossil-rich features, and palynologists have a long history of concern with sampling. Archaeobotanical sampling requires a balance between analytical effort and the need for precise estimates of fossil abundances at given confidence intervals (see chapter 4). In general, a fairly large number of small to medium-sized soil volumes is preferable to analysing a single large volume of sediment, as long as each volume contains a reasonable number of all but the rarest taxa.

In spite of the problems, plant remains inform us about a wide range of prehistoric behaviors and environmental conditions, and the following is only a brief introduction to the kinds of evidence they can provide.

Ecological Archaeology and Reconstructing Paleoenvironments

One of the earliest uses of archaeological pollen evidence was in reconstructing Europe's prehistoric environments (Barker, 1985:15-19), and other kinds of archaeobotanical evidence, including wood charcoals, have extended the usefulness of paleoenvironmental reconstruction. One of the advantages of pollen and spores over most of the other evidence in this case, however, is that they are less affected by human transport onto sites. Pollen evidence has been important for reconstructing climatic changes, documenting the invasions of new species, and identifying human impacts on the environment (Faegri and Iversen, 1989:167-70; Moore et al., 1991:185-91).

Some researchers have convincingly reconstructed North American and European woodlands by combining evidence from palynology, historical documents, and modern woodland structure (e.g., Keene, 1981; Rackham, 1975; 1976). Because plants occur in communities, it is even possible to infer unobserved species most likely associated with the species actually detected.

Reconstructing Paleodiets and Plant Use

As with zooarchaeology, reconstructing ancient diet is an important goal of paleoethnobotanists. In addition to the use of plants as food, we should pay attention to their very important uses as fuel, construction material, drugs, condiments, dyes, and poisons.

Here paleoethnobotanists tend to focus on estimating the relative abundances of taxa to reconstruct a spectrum of plant use. Their implicit aim is often to identify the staples of diet, those taxa that are numerically important. Consequently, problems of quantification and relative preservation have been a serious concern. The definition of "staple" varies widely. Some define a staple as any taxon that forms some arbitrary proportion of the plant spectrum, such as 30%, over a given period, but this is problematical because the taxon may have been used all year or for a period of only a few days. Others prefer a definition that emphasizes the use of the staple in a regular way over at least a significant portion of each year. Still others prefer to characterize resource use as having an opportunistic (potentially abundant, but infrequent and unpredictable) and "low-key" (perhaps less abundant, but more stable and reliable) components. The dependability of "low-key" resources or staples might reveal itself through repetition among a large number of archaeobotanical samples (Beck et al., 1989:8). Thus ubiquity might be better than proportion as a quantification meant to identify low-key resources. It is also important to assess the likelihood that a given taxon could have fulfilled the role of a staple; does it have properties, such as concentrating carbohydrates in an easily harvestible form, that make it suitable for use as a staple?

Many attempts to compare the dietary spectra of archaeological assemblages are unsatisfactory either because they adopt a simplistic "laundry list" approach, simply noting the presence or absence of a number of taxa, or because they take the relative abundances of taxa in very small samples too seriously. The former are attempting to avoid the pitfalls of differential preservation and quantification problems at the cost of revealing little interesting information about ancient plant use. The latter often provide no error estimates on their proportions; what seem to be large differences in the proportion of a taxon at two sites may not be statistically significant, or may be due to the contexts or characteristics of particular samples, such as caches, rather than to overall differences between sites.

Successful attempts to extract meaningful information about prehistoric plant use must depend on adequate sampling, on attention to preservation, context and statistical errors, on quantitative data, and on the natural and cultural processes that lead to particular combinations of taxa, plant parts, and other material culture. Although ubiquity and diversity are measures that are useful to address some issues (e.g., identifying "low-key" resources and weeds, and niche breadth), routinely reducing the ratio-scale data to nominal-scale data or ubiquity does not make the preservation problems go away, while it could mask meaningful differ-

ences between assemblages (Kadane, 1988). Some of these differences will not be due to differences in diet, but to functional and taphonomic differences between contexts, so attention to contextual information is essential (Pearsall, 1988).

Plant Domestication

Especially in parts of the world that were likely "hearths" of early horticulture or agriculture (Harris 1990), paleobotanists and archaeobotanists have focussed considerable attention on identifying and understanding the domestication of wheat, barley, rice, maize, millet, peas, lentils, beans, squash, and other plants that became important agricultural staples in the Neolithic or Formative and after (e:g., Blumler and Byrne, 1991; Chang, 1976; Evans and Peacock, 1981; Galinat, 1983; Harlan, 1965; 1992; Lupton, 1987; Mangelsdorf, 1986; Oka, 1988; Sakamoto, 1982; de Wet, 1992; Zohary, 1972; 1989; Zohary and Hopf, 1988). Archaeologists and others, meanwhile, have attempted to understand the human behaviors that may have led to domestication when and where it did, nearly simultaneously in widely separated parts of the world (e.g., Binford, 1968; Byrne, 1987; Flannery, 1965; 1973; Harris, 1972; McCorriston and Hole, 1991; Rindos, 1984).

Domestication is a process whereby the plant becomes dependent on humans for its dispersal just as the humans become dependent on the plant for food or some other use. Consequently, the most important morphological changes that the plant undergoes involve changes in the mechanisms for dispersing its fruit. Some of the typical changes are as follows (after Rindos, 1984: 183).

■ The plant loses its mechanism for natural dispersal. In grasses, for example, a brittle rachis that shatters when the grain is ripe to scatter it on the ground is replaced by a tough rachis that holds the grain on the stalk even when a human roughly cuts the stalk with a toothed sickle.

■ The plant part that humans use becomes enlarged. In some cases, such as apples, the fleshy fruit becomes enlarged (and may even signal ripeness with a change in color) to attract humans and other predators that will eat the fleshy part and discard the pit or core where it can grow into a new tree.

- The plant part that humans used becomes clustered. Seeds that are clustered in a pod or spike or on a maize cob are easier to harvest in quantity and this tends to attract dispersal agents, including humans.

- There is often a change in duration, from annual to perennial or *vice versa*.

- There is a tendency toward polyploidy (increase in chromosome number), often accompanying gigantism.

- There is a loss of dormancy. In the wild, only some seeds germinate the first year, others lying dormant until subsequent years as insurance against a year of bad growing conditions. In an agricultural ecology, with humans seeding and tending the plants, there is less need for this insurance mechanism.

- The plants will tend to develop simultaneous ripening. In the wild, fruit may ripen at different times over a period of several weeks, again as insurance against bad weather or predation. Simultaneous ripening is much more useful to humans, however, as they can harvest the crop all at once instead of having to return to the field several times. Thus simultaneous ripening tends to attract human harvesters, and is also a trait that they might tend to select for.

- There is loss of mechanisms, such as thorns and toxins, that protected wild plants from browsing animals. Humans may select less thorny and more palatable plants to seed, while the plants will have less need for protection once humans are tending them.

- Diversity in the form of the plant tends to increase. In the protected environment of an agricultural ecology, subtle mutations may thrive that might not have survived in the natural habitat. Humans may encourage this diversity by intentionally propagating plants with unusual features.

In general, the plants tend to change from very opportunistic (r-selected) to much more specialized (K-selected) ones because humans provide a highly dependable means for them to reproduce themselves. It is tempting to think of this as a slow process, but Hillman and Davies (1990) have shown that changes associated with domestication could have developed surprisingly rapidly under some circumstances.

Paleobotanical studies of early domestication tend to focus on the morphological changes that are observable in the plant parts most often preserved, notably the change from brittle to tough rachis, changes in the size of seeds, and clustering of fruits (notably rows of maize kernels on cobs).

In the New World, the domestication of maize is a particularly interesting area of research. Maize (*Zea mays*) has puzzled botanists for more than a century, and archaeological evidence is critical to a solution. Chapman (1996:202) describes maize as "not so much unusual as astonishing." It is unique among grasses. Its single intercalary (between-leaf) female infloresence and multiple rows of large, naked seeds on a non-shattering spike (cob) enclosed by modified leaves (husks) are only some of the differences that make maize attractive to, and dependent on, humans. Maize is genetically very flexible, with mutations common and hybridization with teosinte and *Tripsacum* easy (Chapman, 1996). The discovery of a new wild, perennial (*Zea diploperennis*) has generated new interest in maize's evolutionary history (Ilitis et al., 1979; Mangelsdorf, 1986). There are several competing theories for its evolution as a domesticate, and we cannot even be sure of its ancestor. Mangelsdorf (1958; 1961; 1986) argues that it evolved from an extinct (and undocumented) wild maize, with some genes introduced by *Tripsacum*, and that teosinte was a weed that co-evolved with it. Beadle (1980) notes that hybridization between maize and teosinte can create a series of intermediate forms that, he claims, illustrate the likely steps in maize's evolution from an ancestral teosinte. Ilitis (1983) also argues that maize evolved from teosinte, but with "catastrophic sexual transmutation" of a male tassel into a female corn ear without intermediate forms. As Chapman (1996) notes, archaeological evidence is the key to whether or not teosinte could have been maize's ancestor. Archaeological evidence of maize impressions in pottery from Ecuador and from corn molds from Peru and Mexico show that many of the modern varieties of maize already existed more than a millennium ago (Chapman 1996). MacNeish's (1985) evidence of thousands of examples of prehistoric cob fragments from central America seems consistent with the view that maize preceded teosinte, thus lending support to Mangelsdorf (1961), but the mystery is by no means solved.

Agricultural History and Land Use

Domestication is not the end of the story, but only a part of a long process of interaction between plants and humans. Among the changes that can occur to landscapes, archaeologists have shown particular interest in ones that may have been caused by humans. In particular, evidence for the rapid replacement of forest by grasses and associated weed flora, especially in combination with evidence of burning, such as fire-cracked rock, reddened paleosols, and charcoal, is often taken as evidence that humans may have been burning down forest either to clear it for agriculture or to attract animals, such as deer, to the new growth in the clearings (Dimbleby, 1985; Faegri and Iversen, 1989:170; Moore et al., 1991:189-91). Much of the effort has been devoted to recognizing the expansion of farming and the evolution of agricultural landscapes (Barker, 1985; Guilaine, 1991; McAndrews and Boyko-Diakonow, 1989). In Denmark, for example, it is possible to interpret the pollen record as showing several waves of land clearance punctuated by periods of reforestation, and increases in grasses, *Artemisia*, *Rumex*, and chenopods, among others, during these waves is probably evidence of arable cultivation (Dimbleby, 1985). Historical records, place-names and existing plant distributions, as well as the archaeobotanical evidence, can sometimes be used to reconstruct the likely distribution of ancient woodlands (Keene, 1981; Rackham, 1975; 1976). Kranz (1977) has similarly attempted to reconstruct the standing crops of ancient agroecologies.

Plant Processing and Agricultural Activity

Paleoethnobotany also has enormous potential for helping us reconstruct and understand the way ancient people harvested, processed, stored, and consumed collected and cultivated plant foods. For example, the distribution of weed seeds, and fragments of rachites and glumes in samples of cereals can provide clues as to cereals' stage of processing (e.g., winnowed or not) and sometimes to the interplanting of crops or the rotation of fields between crops (Charles et al., 1997; Dennell, 1974; 1979; 1983; Hastorf, 1988; Hillman, 1981; 1984a; 1984b; Van Zeist and de Roller, 1994). Residues on grinding slabs, mortars, sickle blades, cooking pots, and other tools can inform us about food processing. These can be combined with other kinds of archaeological evidence, including evidence of plow scars, irrigation ditches, and field lines, to reconstruct much of the prehistoric agroecology (e.g., Barker, 1985; Ford, 1981).

Seasonality

As with faunal evidence, plant remains can sometimes provide clues to the season or seasons in which a site was occupied. Both natural and cultural processes can bring plant remains onto sites that we would not expect to occur there during the season of site use, and the time of plant harvest is not necessarily the time of their use. The use of stored seeds, for example, can confuse the evidence for seasonality. In addition, as with migratory birds, plants vary in the predictability and duration of major events, such as fruit ripening (Adams and Bohrer, 1998).

In spite of these difficulties, archaeobotanical evidence can help us to reconstruct season of site use, especially as a complement to faunal evidence. Adams and Bohrer (1998) discuss the assumptions that we make when using pollen, fruit, vegetative parts, and evidence of insect predation to help distinguish short-term camps from multiseasonal sites and settlements occupied all year round in the American Southwest. For example, among seeds that must be parched or roasted shortly after harvest to prepare them for use or storage, swollen reproductive parts would suggest that processing took place im-

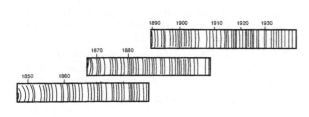

Fiogure 11.9. Crossdating tree-ring sequences.

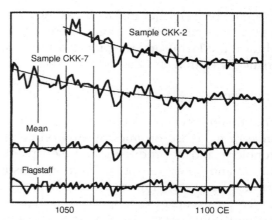

Figure 11.10. Example of a skeleton plot. Modern ones are line graphs done on compupters.

mediately after harvest. In some cases, furthermore, artifactual and other evidence from the site may indicate harvesting or fruit-processing activities that must have taken place at a predictable time of year.

Chronology

For many decades, pollen assemblages provided a method for ordering deposits chronologically through **biostratigraphic** principles (Erdtman, 1943:172-73; Faegri and Iversen, 1989:170-72). Particularly in Europe, the sequence of plant communities associated with the waxing and waning of the glaciers, the beginnings of the Holocene, and the encroachments of agriculture and animal husbandry left signatures on the pollen record that could be used to date artifacts and deposits indirectly. But this aspect of palynology has largely been displaced by better dating methods, such as radiocarbon dating.

Yet plant remains still provide one of our very best chronological tools. For most of the 20th century, one of the prime archaeological uses of wood remains, in areas where it is well preserved, has been to construct dated tree-ring sequences. A. E. Douglass (1916; 1935), an astronomer, developed the technique originally as a way to study cycles in sunspot activity, but it has become archaeologists' most precise chronological tool where written records are unavailable.

Dendrochronology depends on the fact that in some species of trees, the thickness of the successive layers of zylem growth depends on environmental conditions. In conifers growing in temperate and arctic regions, each ring consists of an inner band of light-colored cells and an outer band of thicker-walled, dark cells. The differences in cell characteristics are due to the fact that the trees are dormant in winter and highly active in spring. Species in which tree rings are fairly uniform in thickness or only show a gradual decrease in thickness with age are called *complacent*, while ones in which tree rings vary in thickness as environmental conditions change are called *sensitive*. Under ideal conditions, sensitive tree rings form a series that is closely comparable to series from other trees in the same region, and this allows cross dating of trees and, ultimately, the build-up of a long chronology from overlapping series (figure 11.9).

To carry out dendrochronological work, once again it is necessary to prepare samples so that the transverse section (or radial section) is very clear. One then measures the growth increments on each sample to build up a series on a skeleton plot or dendro-chronograph, which displays the increments' sizes as departures from the floating mean of all the increments. This is to compensate for the fact that absolute ring-width varies from tree to tree and between the inner and outer parts of the same wood (zylem growth slows down as the tree ages), so comparing absolute widths would not be useful. Today these skeleton plots are typically drawn with computer software that makes it easy to compare the "hills and valleys" of variations in ring width (figure 11.10), and the plots are analysed statistically (Litton and Zainodin, 1991).

Conclusions

Plant remains provide an extremely important source of evidence on ancient environments, chronology, and the production and use of plants for food and other purposes. Their analysis is complex, however, and even identification of taxa requires years of very specialized training and many hours of eye-straining work. Among the issues to keep in mind when interpreting archaeobotanical data are sample size, quantification, and differences in production, transportation, and preservation of plant remains of different types and in different contexts.

References Cited

Adams, K. R., and Bohrer, V. L., 1998, Archaeobotanical indicators of seasonality: Examples from arid southwestern United States. In *Seasonality and Sedentism, Archaeological Perspectives from Old and New World Sites*, edited by T. R. Rocek and O. Bar-Yosef , pp. 129-41. Peabody Museum Bulletin 6. Harvard University, Cambridge, MA.

Armitage, P. L., 1975, The extraction and identification of opal phytoliths from the teeth of ungulates. *Journal of Archaeological Science* 2:187-97.

Baker, G., 1959, Fossil opal-phytoliths and phytolith nomenclature. *Australian Journal of Science* 21:300-306.

Bannister, B., 1969, Dendrochronology. In *Science in Archaeology, a Survey of Progress and Research*, 2nd ed., edited by D. Brothwell and E. Higgs, pp. 191-205. Thames & Hudson, Leipzig.

Barker, G., 1985, *Prehistoric Farming in Europe*. Cambridge University Press, Cambridge.

Battarbee, R. W., 1986, Diatom analysis. In *Handbook of Holocene Palaeoecology and Palaeohydrology*, edited by B. E. Berglund, pp. 527-70. John Wiley, Chichester.

Beadle, G. W., 1980, The ancestry of corn. *Scientific American* 242:96-103.

Beck, W., 1989, The taphonomy of plants. In *Plants in Australian Archaeology*, edited by Beck, W., A. Clarke and L. Head, pp. 31-53. Tempus, Archaeology and Material Culture Studies in Archaeology 1. University of Queensland, St. Lucia.

Beck, W., Clarke, A., and Head, L., eds., 1989, *Plants in Australian Archaeology*. Tempus, Archaeology and Material Culture Studies in Archaeology 1. University of Queensland, St. Lucia.

Benninghoff, W. S., 1966, Calculation of pollen and spore density in sediments by addition of exotic pollen in known quantities. *Pollen et Spores* 44:332-33.

Binford, L. R., 1968, Post-Pleistocene adaptations. In *New Perspectives in Archaeology*, edited by S. R. Binford and L. R. Binford, pp. 313-42. Chicago: Aldine.

Blackman, E., 1969, Observations on the development of the silica cells of of the leaf sheath of wheat (*Triticum aestivum*). *Canadian Journal of Botany* 47:827-38.

Blumler, M. A., and Byrne, 1991, The ecological genetics of domestication and the origins of agriculture. *Current Anthropology* 32:23-54.

Bohrer, V., 1970, Ethnobotanical aspects of Snaketown, a Hohokam village in southern Arizona. *American Antiquity* 35:413-30.

Bottema, S., 1984, The composition of modern charred seed assemblages. In *Plants and Ancient Man*, edited by Van Zeist, W., and W. A. Casparie, pp. 207-12. Studies in Palaeoethnobotany. A. A. Balkema, Rotterdam.

Brochier, J.-E., 1983, Combustion et parcage des herbivores domestiques. Le point de vue sédimentologue. *Bulletin du Société Préhistorique Français* 80(5):143-45.

Brown, D., 1984, Prospects and limits for a phytolith key in the central United States. *Journal of Archaeological Science* 11:221-43.

Bryant, V. M., and Holloway, G., 1983, The role of palynology in archaeology. *Advances in Archaeological Method and Theory* 6:191-224.

Bye, R. A., 1986, Voucher specimens in ethnobotanical studies and publications. *Journal of Ethnobiology* 6:1-8.

Byrne, R., 1987, Climatic change and the origins of agriculture. In *Studies in Neolithic and Urban Revolutions*, edited by L. Manzanilla, pp. 21-34. BAR International Series 349. British Archaeological Reports, Oxford.

Canti, M. G., 1997, An investigation of microscopic calcareous spherulites from herbivore dungs. *Journal of Archaeological Science* 24:219-31.

Carbone, V., 1977, Phytoliths as paleoenvironmental indicators. *Annals of the New York Academy of Science*. 288:194-205.

Chang, T.-T., 1976, The origin, evolution, cultivation, dissemination and diversification of Asian and African rices. *Euphytica* 25:425-41.

Chapman, G. P., 1996, *The Biology of Grasses*. CAB International, Wallingford, UK.

Chapman, G. P., and Peat, W. E., 1992, *An Introduction to the Grasses (Including Bamboos and Cereals)*. CAB International, Wallingford, UK.

Charles, M., Jones, G., and Hodgson, J. G., 1997, FIBS in archaeobotany: Functional interpretation of weed floras in relation to husbandry practices. *Journal of Archaeological Science* 24:1151-61.

Dahlgren, R. M. T., and Clifford, W. T., 1982, *The Monocotyledons: A Comparative Study*. Academic Press, London.

Dennell, R., 1974, The purity of prehistoric crops. *Proceedings of the Prehistoric Society* 40:132-35.

— 1979, Prehistoric diet and nutrition: Some food for thought. *World Archaeology* 11:121-35.

— 1983, *European Economic Prehistory: A New Approach.* Academic Press, New York.

Dimbleby, G. W., 1967, *Plants and Archaeology.* London.

— 1985, *The Palynology of Archaeological Sites.* Academic Press, London.

Douglass, A. E., 1916, *Climatic Cycles and Tree Growth*, vol. 1. Carnegie Institution of Washington, Washington, DC.

—1935, *Dating Pueblo Bonito and Other Ruins of the Southwest.* National Geographical Society, Washington, D.C.

Erdtman, G., 1943, *An Introduction to Pollen Analysis.* Chronica Botanica, Waltham, MA.

Evans, L. T., and Peacock, W. J., eds., 1981, *Wheat Science. Today and Tomorrow.* Cambridge University Press, Cambridge.

Fægri, K., and Iverson, J., 1989, *Textbook of Pollen Analysis,* 4th ed. Blackwell Scientific Publications, Oxford.

Flannery, K. V., 1965, The ecology of early food production in Mesopotamia. *Science* 147:1247-56.

— 1973, The origins of agriculture. *Annual Review of Anthropology* 2:271-310.

Ford, R. I., 1979, Paleoethnobotany in American archaeology. *Advances in Archaeological Method and Theory* 2:285-336.

— 1981, Gardening and farming before A.D. 1000: Patterns of prehistoric cultivation north of Mexico. *Journal of Ethnobiology* 1:6-27.

Friedman, J., 1978, *Wood Identification by Microscopic Examination, A Guide for the Archaeologist.* British Columbia Provinical Museum Heritage Record 5. Province of British Columbia, Victoria.

Galinat, W. C., 1983, The origin of maize as shown by leaf morphological traits of its ancestor teosinte. *Maydica* 28:121-38.

Gibson, A. M., 1986, Diatom analysis of clays and Late Neolithic pottery from the Milfield Basin, Northumberland. *Proceedings of the Prehistoric Society* 52:89-103.

Greig, J., 1984, The palaeoecology of some British hay meadow types. In *Plants and Ancient Man. Studies in Palaeoethnobotany*, edited by Van Zeist, W., and W. A. Casparie, pp. 213-26. A. A. Balkema, Rotterdam.

— 1989, *Archaeobotany.* Handbooks for Archaeologists 4. European Science Foundation, Strasbourg.

Guilaine, J., ed., 1991, *Pour une Archéologie Agraire.* Colin, Paris.

Hall, J., Higgins, S., and Fullagar, R., 1989, Plant residues on stone tools. In *Plants in Australian Archaeology*, edited by W. Beck, A. Clarke, and L. Head, pp. 136-160. Tempus Monograph Series, St. Lucia.

Harlan, J. R., 1965, The possible role of weed races in the evolution of cultivated plants. *Euphytica* 14:173-76.

— 1967, A wild wheat harvest in Turkey. *Archaeology* 20:197-201.

— 1989, Self-perception and the origins of agriculture. In *Plants and Society*, edited by M. A. Swaminathan and S. L. Koxhhar, pp. 5-23. Macmillan, London.

— 1992, Origins and processes of domestication. In *Grass Evolution and Domestication*, edited by G. P. Chapman, pp. 159-75. Cambridge University Press, Cambridge.

Harris, D. R., 1972, The origins of agriculture in the tropics. *American Scientist* 60:180-93.

— 1990, Vavilov's concept of centres of origin of cultivated plants: Its genesis and its influence on the study of agricultural origins. *Biological Journal of the Linnaean Society* 39:7-16.

Hastorf, C. A., 1988, The use of paleoethnobotanical data in prehistoric studies of crop production, processing, and consumption. In *Current Paleoethnobotany*, edited by C. Hastorf and V. Popper, pp. 119-44. University of Chicago Press, Chicago.

Hather, J. G., 1993, *An Archaeobotanical Guide to Root and Tuber Identification*, Volume I, *Europe and South West Asia.* Oxbow Monograph 28. Oxbow Books, Oxford.

Hather, J. G., ed., 1994, *Tropical Archaeobotany. Applications and New Developments.* One World Archaeology 22. Routledge, London.

Hillman, G. C., 1981, Reconstructing crop husbandry practices from charred remains of crops. In *Farming Practice in British Prehistory*, edited by R. Mercer, pp. 123-62. Edinburgh University Press, Edinburgh.

—1984a, Interpretation of archaeological plant remains: The application of ethnographic models from Turkey. In *Plants and Ancient Man: Studies in Palaeoethnobotany*, edited by W. Van Zeist and W. A. Casparie, pp. 1-41. A. A. Balkema, Rotterdam.

— 1984b, Traditional husbandry and processing of ancient cereals in modern times. Pt. 1: the glume wheats. *Bulletin on Sumerian Agriculture* 1:114-52.

Hillman, G. C., and M. Davies, 1990, Measured domestication rates in wild wheats and barley under primitive cultivation, and their archaeological implications. *Journal of World Prehistory* 4:157-222.

Ilitis, H., 1983, From teosinte to maize: The catastrophic sexual transmutation. *Science* 222:886-94.

Ilitis, H., Doebley, J. F., Guzman, M. R., and Pazy, B., 1979, *Zea diploperennis*: A new teosinte from Mexico. *Science* 203:186-88.

Jane, F. W., 1970, *The Structure of Wood*, 2nd ed. Adam & Charles Black, London.

Jones, V. H, and Morris, E. A., 1960, A seventh-century record of tobacco utilization in Arizona. *El Palacio* 67:115-17.

Kadane, J. B., 1988, Possible statistical contributions to paleoethnobotany. In *Current Paleoethnobotany, Analytical Methods and Cultural Interpretations of Archaeological Plant Remains*, edited by C. Hastorf and V. Popper, pp. 206-214. University of Chicago Press, Chicago.

Kealhofer, L., Torrence, R., and Fullagar, R., 1999, Integrating phytolithis within use-wear/residue studies of stone tools. *Journal of Archaeological Science* 26:527-546.

Keene, A. S., 1981, *Prehistoric Foraging in a Temperate Forest, a Linear Programming Model.* Academic Press, New York.

Körber-Grohne, U., 1984, Über die Notwendigkeit einer Registrierung und Dokumentation wilder und primitiver Fruchtbäume, zu deren Erhaltung und zur Gewinnung von

Vergleichsmaterial f'r paläo-ethnobotanische Funde. In *Plants and Ancient Man: Studies in Palaeoethnobotany,* edited by W. Van Zeist and W. A. Casparie, pp. 237-41. A. A. Balkema, Rotterdam.

Körber-Grohne, U., and Küster, H., 1989, *Archäobotanik. Symposium der Universität Hohenheim (Stuttgart) vom 11.-16. Juli 1988.* J. Cramer, Berlin.

Kranz, P. M., 1977, A model for estimating standing crop in ancient communities. Paleobiology 3:415-421.

Lentfer, C. J., and Boyd, W. E., 1998, A comparison of three methods for the extraction of phytoliths from sediments. *Journal of Archaeological Science* 25:1159-1183.

Lentfer, C. J., Boyd, W. E., and Gojak, D., 1997, Hope Farm Windmill: Phytolith analysis of cereals in early colonial Australia. *Journal of Archaeological Science* 24:841-856.

Litton, C. D., and Zainodin, H. J., 1991, Statistical models of dendrochronology. *Journal of Archaeological Science* 18:429-440.

Lone, F. A., Khan, M., and Buth, G. M., 1993, *Palaeoethnobotany. Plants and Ancient Man in Kashmir.* Oxford & IBH Publishing, New Delhi.

Lupton, F. G. H., ed., 1987, *Wheat Breeding, Its Scientific Basis.* Chapman and Hall, London.

MacNeish, R. S., 1985, The archaeological record on the problem of the domestication of corn. *Maydica* 30:171-178.

Mangelsdorf, P. C., 1958, Ancestor of corn. *Science* 128:1313.

— 1961, Introgression in maize. *Euphytica* 10:156-168.

— 1965, The evolution of maize. In *Essays on Crop Plant Evolution,* edited by J. Hutchinson, pp. 23-49. Cambridge University Press, Cambridge.

— 1986, The origin of corn. *Scientific American* 255:80-86.

McCorriston, J., and Hole, F., 1991, The ecology of seasonal stress and the origins of agriculture in the Near East. *American Anthropologist* 93:46-69.

Miller, N., 1988, Ratios in paleoethnobotanical analysis. In *Current Paleoethnobotany: Analytical Methods and Cultural Interpretations of Archaeological Plant Remains,* edited by C. Hastorf and V. Popper, pp. 72-85. University of Chicago Press, Chicago.

Minnis, P., 1989, Prehistoric diet in the northern Southwest: Macroplant remains from Four Corners feces. *American Antiquity* 54:543-563.

Monckton, S. G., 1987, Paleoethnobotany: Some methodological considerations. In *Man and the Mid-Holocene Climatic Optimum,* edited by N. A. McKinnon and G. S. L. Stuart, pp. 59-67. Proceedings of the 17th Annual Chacmool Conference. Archaeological Association of the University of Calgary, Calgary.

— 1992, *Huron Paleoethnobotany.* Ontario Archaeological Reports 1. Ontario Heritage Foundation, Toronto.

Moore, P. D., Webb, J., and Collinson, M. C., 1991, *Pollen Analysis, A Laboratory Manual.* Blackwell, Oxford.

Mulholland, S. C., 1989, Phytolith shape frequencies in North Dakota grasses: A comparison to general patterns. *Journal of Archaeological Science* 16:489-511.

Oka, H. I., 1988, *Origin of Cultivated Rice.* Elsevier, Amsterdam.

Pearsall, D., 1988, Interpreting the meaning of macroremain abundance: The impact of source and context. In *Current Paleoethnobotany: Analytical Methods and Cultural Interpretations of Archaeological Plant Remains,* edited by C. A. Hastorf and V. S. Popper, pp. 97-118. University of Chicago Press, Chicago.

— 1989, *Paleoethnobotany.* Acedemic Press, New York.

Pearsall, D. M., and Piperno, D. R., eds., 1993, *Current Research in Phytolith Analysis: Applications in Archaeology and Paleoecology.* MASCA Research Papers in Science and Archaeology. University Museum of Archaeology and Anthropology, Philadelphia.

Piperno, D. R., 1988, *Phytolith Analysis: An Archaeological and Geological Perspective.* Academic Press, San Diego.

Powers, A. H., Padmore, J., and Gilbertson, D. D., 1989, Studies of late prehistoric and modern opal phytoliths from coastal sand dunes and machair in northwest Britain. *Journal of Archaeological Science* 16:27-45.

Rackham, O., 1975, *Hayley Wood, Its History and Ecology.* Cambridgeshire and Esle of Ely Naturalists' Trust, Cambridge.

— 1976, *Trees and Woodland in the British Landscape.* J. M. Dent and Sons, London.

Raffauf, R. F., and Morris, E. A., 1960, Persistence of alkaloids in plant tissue. *Science* 131:1047.

Rapp, G., and Mulholland, S. C., eds., 1992, *Phytolith Systematics.* Plenum Press, New York.

Renfrew, J. M., 1973, *Palaeoethnobotany. The Prehistoric Food Plants of the Near East and Europe.* Methuen & Co., London.

Rindos, D., 1984, *The Origins of Agriculture. An Evolutionary Perspective.* Academic Press, Orlando.

Rosen, A. 1987, Phytolith studies at Shiqmim. In *Shiqmim I: Studies Concerning Chalcolithic Societies in the Northern Negev Desert, Israel (1982-1984),* edited by T. E. Levy, pp. 243-49. BAR International Series. British Archaeological Reports, Oxford.

— 1989, Ancient town and city sites: A view from the microscope. *American Antiquity* 54:564-578.

— 1990, Phytoliths as indicators of ancient irrigation farming. In *Préhistoire de l'Agriculture: Nouvelles Approches Expérimentales et Ethnographiques,* edited by P. Anderson-Gerfaud, pp. 281-87. Centre des Recherches Archéologiques, Valbone.

— 1992, Preliminary identification of silica skeletons from Near Eastern archaeological sites: An anatomical approach. In *Phytolith Systematics,* G. Rapp and S. C. Mulholland, Pp. 129-47. Plenum Press, New York.

— 1993, Phytolith evidence for early cereal exploitation in the Levant. In *Archaeology and Paleoecology,* pp. 160-171. MASCA Research Papers in Science and Archaeology. University Museum of Archaeology and Anthropology, Philadelphia.

Sakamoto, S., 1982, The Middle East as a cradle for crops and weeds. In *Biology and Ecology of Weeds,* edited by W. Holzner and M. Numata, pp. 97-109. Junk, The Hague.

Schopmeyer, C. S., 1974, *Seeds of Woody Plants in the United States*. Agricultural Handbook No. 450. United States Department of Agriculture, Washington.

Smart, T. L., and Hoffman, E. S., 1988, Environmental interpretation of archaeological charcoal. In *Current Paleoethnobotany*, edited by C. Hastorf and V. Popper, pp. 167-205. University of Chicago Press, Chicago.

Smart, J., 1978, The evolution of pulse crops. *Economic Botany* 32:185-198.

van der Veen, M., 1984, Sampling for seeds. In *Plants and Ancient Man. Studies in Palaeoethnobotany*, edited by W. Van Zeist and W. A. Casparie, pp. 193-199. Rotterdam: A. A. Balkema.

Van Zeist, W., and W. A. Caspari, eds., 1984, *Plants and Ancient Man. Studies in Palaeoethnobotany*. Proceedings of the Sixth Symposium of the International Work Group for Palaeoethnobotany, A. A. Balkema, Groningen.

Van Zeist, W., and de Roller, G. J., 1994, The plant husbandry of aceramic Çayönü, SE Turkey. *Palaeohistoria* 33/34:65-96.

Western, A. C., 1969, Wood and charcoal in archaeology. In *Science in Archaeology, a Survey of Progress and Research*, 2nd ed., edited by D. Brothwell and E. Higgs, pp. 178-87. Thames & Hudson, Leipzig.

de Wet, J. M. S., 1992, The three phases of cereal domestication. In *Grass Evolution and Domestication*, edited by G. P. Chapman, pp. 176-198. Cambridge University Press, Cambridge.

Wilson, D. G., 1984, The carbonisation of weed seeds and their representation in macrofossil assemblages. In *Plants and Ancient Man. Studies in Palaeoethnobotany*, edited by Van Zeist, W., and W. A. Casparie, pp. 201-206. A. A. Balkema, Rotterdam.

Yarnell, R., 1969, Contents of human paleofecies. In *The Prehistory of Salts Cave, Kentucky*, edited by P. J. Watson et al., Pp. 41-54. Illinois State Museum Reports of Investigations 16. Illinois State Museum, Springfield, IL.

—— 1974, Plant food and cultivation of the Salt Cavers. In *Archaeology of the Mammoth Cave Area*, edited by P. J. Watson, pp. 113-122. New York: Academic Press.

—— 1982, Interpretation of plant remains. *Southeast Archaeologist* 1:1-17.

Zohary, D., 1972, The wild progenitor and the place of origin of the cultivated lentil: Lens culinaris. *Economic Botany* 26:326-332.

—— 1989, Domestication of the southwest Asian Neolithic domestic crop assemblage of of cereals, pulses and flax: The evidence from the living plants. In *Foraging and Farming. The Evolution of Plant Exploitation*, edited by D. R. Harris and G. Hillman, pp. 358-373. Unwin Hyman, London.

Zohary, D., and Hopf, M., 1988, *Domestication of Plants in the Old World*. Oxford University Press, Oxford.

12 Soils, Sediments, and Geomorphology

> … it is no more possible for us to understand the nature of the past without an understanding of soil dynamics than it is for a marine biologist to comprehend his discipline without an understanding of the nature of ocean water and its movements (Wood and Johnson, 1978:315).

By far the most abundant material that archaeologists excavate is not lithic, ceramic, or faunal; it is the soil and sediment matrix in which these things are found. This matrix is not simply a passive artifact-bearing medium to be sifted and ignored, for it preserves evidence for archaeological site-formation processes, paleoenvironment, and site chronology. This last type of evidence, principally in the form of stratification, is a topic that we will leave for chapter 13. Here we will introduce the characterization of soils and sediments, which not only helps us recognize stratigraphic episodes, but tells us about the natural and cultural processes of deposition, erosion, and disturbance. Many of the concepts discussed here would be useful during fieldwork, as well as in post-excavation analysis. For more detailed treatment of the subject, readers should consult such references as Courty et al. (1989), Goldberg et al. (1993), Griffiths (1967), Hassan (1978), Holliday (1992), Shackley (1975), and Waters (1992).

Soils and Sediments

"Soil" and "sediment" are not interchaneable terms. The basic difference between them is that soils are products of weathering the earth's crust *in situ*, while sediments are layers or collections of particles that have been removed from the place where they were originally weathered from rock and redeposited elsewhere (Shackley, 1975). Even these definitions can be somewhat ambiguous, because sediments can subsequently be weathered *in situ* to produce soils. Cultural deposits, for example, start out as sediments,

but after thousands of years of natural alteration can acquire the characteristics of soils. Geologists consider the "sedimentary cycle" to consist of weathering, transport, deposition, and post-depositional alteration of particles. Most archaeologists use the term, "sediment," in the broad sense to include soils, and reserve "soil," for cases that display clear zonation.

One of the characteristics of soils is that they show zonation with depth, called a profile, and the zones are called horizons. The *A horizon*, on top, is the richest in humus, but rainwater filtering through it has removed some soil components by a process called *leaching*. The *B horizon* is the zone in which the leached materials become redeposited. The *C horizon* consists of weathered bedrock (the parent material for the soil), but is not chemically distinct from unweathered bedrock because no leaching has either removed or redeposited chemicals there. Where there are smaller zones within these three, they are designated as A_1, A_2, B_1, B_2, B_3, etc. It is important to remember that a *profile* describes the internal structure of a uniform sediment (in the broad sense), not a sequence of stratified layers, which should instead be called a *stratigraphic series* (Shackley, 1975:4).

Lithostratigraphy and Archaeological Stratigraphy

Geologists consider the subdivisions of the earth's crust, as defined by their physical, lithologic characteristics, to be **lithostratigraphic units** (NACSN, 1983; Stein, 1987; 1992). Soil scientists also distinguish **pedological units** that consist of mineral and organic materials that climate and living organisms have altered through soil-forming (pedological) processes. In a soil profile, the various horizons are different pedological units, even though they may originally have been deposited at the same time or gradually accumulated without change in depositional process. Although not all authors would agree that pedological units are distinct from lithostratigraphic ones, soil scientists regularly subdivide soil profiles more finely than a geologist would, and pedological units do not necessarily represent separate depositional events. Stein (1992) also distinguishes **biostratigraphic units**, defined by their fossil content. Archaeologists, meanwhile, routinely divide the same record more finely still, and tend to rely on cultural content as well as lithologic characteristics in defining these units, with the result that the boundaries of their major units do not always agree with lithologic ones, sometimes combining several separate lithostratigraphic units into a single archaeological layer. Stein (1992) prefers to call these "ethnostratigraphic units," but other terms that appear in the literature include **anthropogenic** units (formed by human activity), **anthropic soils**, or **archaeological layers**, *loci*, and features (figure 12.1; Courty et al., 1989:32). Archaeological layers are sometimes defined on the basis of a combination of lithological, pedological, and material cultural criteria.

Nonetheless, in modern archaeology it is usual to define basic stratigraphic units on lithological criteria, such as color, texture and particle characteristics, rather than by the artifacts they contain.

Texture and Particle Characteristics

Describing a sediment or soil as clay, silt, or sand is a statement about its texture. Technically this is a characterization of its predominant particle size, but in colloquial usage the terms have come to signify particular sediment types. Although only a careful particle-size analysis can accurately characterize texture, it is possible to make a gross characterization of sediment texture by feel. Squeezing and working a small, wetted

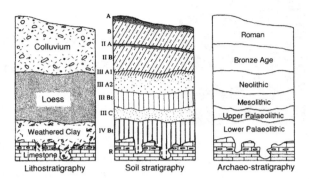

Figure 12.1. Comparison of lithostratigraphic, pedological, and archaeological units (Courty et al., 1989:33).

sample of the sediment between the fingers allows its characterization on a nominal scale (figure 12.6). Some of the major categories in this scale could be characterized as follows.

Sand — Sand has particle sizes in the range 4-0.5 ϕ, and the lack of finer material to hold it together makes it very loose, especially when it is dry, so that it is impossible to squeeze it into a ball. Instead it falls between your fingers. If you rub it into your skin, you will feel the gritiness of it, especially in coarse sand (with particle sizes of 1 to 0.5 ϕ).

Silt — Silt has a smaller particle size than sand, so that individual grains are not visible except under magnification. Although it can be somewhat gritty, it feels much smoother or silkier than sand when rubbed between your fingers.

Clay — Clay has an extremely small particle size (less than 8 ϕ). Its main characteristic is that it is sticky and plastic when wet, but dries into hard lumps that have shrinkage cracks running through them.

Sandy loam — This is a sandy sediment that contains enough clay and silt to make it hold together, rather than falling apart. Sandy loam consists of about 50% sand, 30% silt, and 20% clay (Shackley, 1975:12).

Loam — Consisting of roughly 40% sand, 40% silt, and 20% clay, loam is only a little gritty, and is more plastic than sandy loam.

Silty loam — This is a mixture of at least 50% silt and sand, and 12 to 25% clay that feels somewhat silky and forms clods when dried out. The clods break into soft, floury powder.

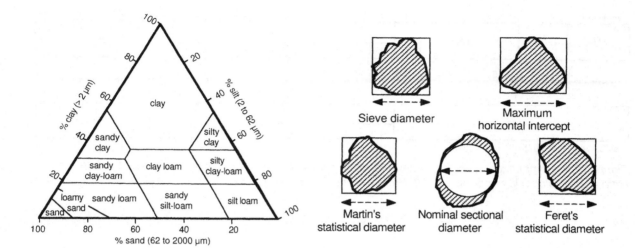

Figure 12.2. Ternary diagram to show the basic classes of sediment texture used in soil science (after Courty et al., 1989:37).

Figure 12.3. Differing definitions of particle "size" (after Shackley, 1975:89).

Clay loam — With roughly equal parts sand and clay, clay loam is a fine-grained material that is plastic and cohesive when wet, but makes hard clods when dry.

Particle size is a key piece of information to help us identify the agent, environment, and process of a sediment's deposition (Allen, 1968; Friedman, 1961; Mason and Folk, 1958), as well as to correlate stratigraphic deposits. Although "size" can be defined in many ways (Folk, 1966), and methods for analysing size that are based on volume or some indirect measure will result in quite different size distributions, here we will concentrate on a few of the simpler size measures, based on the linear dimensions of the particles.

The most common definitions of particle size are based on sieve diameter, on maximum length, on some kind of statistical average diameter, or on the diameter of the largest sphere that would fit within the particle (figure 12.3). By far the simplest of these, although by no means the best, is the sieve diameter. This can be quite deceiving because typical sediments contain particles that are far from spherical, while smaller particles sometimes adhere to larger ones to be caught in sieves through which they should, ideally, have passed. One compelling reason to use sieve diameter, at least in cases where it is not too misleading, is ease of measurement. One

need only pass a properly prepared sample through a stack of sieves of gradually decreasing mesh size, catching each increment of particle size on the way down.

Sieving sediment samples requires care and common sense. Sieve sets are available in a variety of standard aperture series, the ASTM (American Society for Testing Materials), Tyler, and British Standard series being quite common. The sieves usually consist of a shallow brass cylinder, most often 8 inches in diameter, with a mesh prepared from woven brass or steel for the coarser apertures and phosphor bronze or nickel mesh for increasingly finer apertures. For the sieves to maintain their precision, they must be treated with care. Using the same sieves for both wet and dry sieving, for example, is poor practice, and corrosion build-up on the mesh will tend to close up the apertures. Gentle brushing of the meshes after each use will help to prevent this. Careless handling, and particularly rubbing or prodding with fingers or screwdrivers can stretch and tear the mesh, allowing large particles to pass through to smaller meshes. Putting too much sediment on the sieve will stretch or tear it in the same way. You can check the accuracy of the mesh periodically either by passing standard glass beads through or by measuring portions of the mesh under a microscope with a micrometer. Sieving too long is also

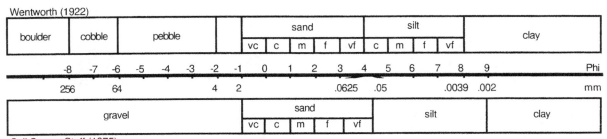

Figure 12.4. Competing scales for measuring particle sizes in sediments (after Courty et al., 1989:36). Note abbreviations very coarse (vc), through medium (m) to very fine (vf).

poor practice, as it can start to erode the larger particles as well as wear out the mesh itself. Run the screen shaker that agitates the sediment in the sieve series for only about 10 min, and no longer than 15 min (Shackley, 1975:109-111).

Sediments can be screened wet or dry, although dry sieving is usually to be preferred in archaeological situations in which wetting, followed by agitation, could destroy delicate artifacts or organic remains, such as carbonized seeds (chapter 11). You should use wet sieving for very fine-grained sediments that will clump when dry.

To dry sieve, measure the mass of each clean, empty sieve, and the collection pan, on a calibrated electronic balance and then stack the sieves in serial order from the finest, set on the collection pan, to the coarsest, on top. If you are using the entire set of sieves (as many as 21!), you will have to work with several sub-sets, beginning with the coarsest sieves. Make sure that the total volume of sediment from a sample is sufficient for a meaningful analysis. Dry the sediment sample in an oven set at about 105°C for several hours, or by leaving the sediment in a warm, dry place in clean, cloth bags for several days, unless you plan to look for organic material, such as charred seeds or charcoal. If the sediment contains a lot of clay, which would bake into hard clumps at 105°, reduce the oven temperature to about 50°C and hold it for several days. Pour the entire sample into the uppermost (coarsest) sieve, cover with a lid, and clamp the stack of sieves down to secure them. Set the timer for 10 min, and turn the screen shaker on.

After the screen shaker turns itself off, remove the sieves and remeasure the mass of each with the balance. The net mass, obtained by subtracting the masses of empty sieves from the gross mass, should be recorded.

When you have finished, carefully empty the sieves into labelled sample bags for each size fraction, and brush the sieves gently to clean them.

Although the size distributions in a sediment are a continuum, it is usual to express these on an ordinal scale, and several of these have some currency (figure 12.4). The most commonly used scales in Anglo-American archaeology are the Wentworth (1922) scale and the British Standard scale or Soil Survey Staff (1975) scale. Shackley (1975:91-92) prefers the Krumbein (1934) scale (φ units) for its logarithmic elegance.

The use of histograms to display particle-size distributions can be quite misleading if you forget that it is the area of each bar, and not its height, that conveys the abundance of particles in each size interval (see above, pp. 25-26, and Shackley, 1975:94). Since most analyses use substantially unequal size intervals, this is quite important. A common error is to show all the intervals as equal, when in fact they are far from it. Ensuring that the bars of unequal width show magnitudes by their *area* suppresses the heights of the wider bars and gives a truer representation of particle-size distribution. If you choose a graph with particle size measured in Krumbein's logarithmic φ units, you should remind viewers in the label that the units are logarithmic, not

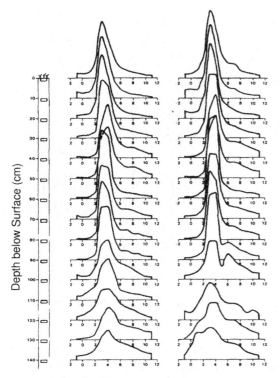

Figure 12.5. Particle-size distributions for samples taken at various depths down a soil profile (Stein, 1992:142). Samples at left have had CaCO₃ removed, while those at right are untreated.

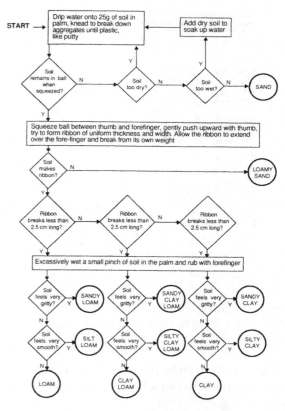

Figure 12.6. Step-by-step program to help classify sediments by texture.

linear. When properly constructed, the histogram can be helpful in revealing some general characteristics of the sediment. For example, a bimodal distribution could result from the work of two separate depositional processes (Shackley, 1975:94). In figure 12.5, Stein (1992:142) shows how the grain-size distribution (using the Krumbein ϕ scale) can vary with depth in a soil column, with larger particles being better represented at greater depth.

Other forms of presentation include triangle graphs and pictorial graphs. The triangle graph simultaneously shows the percentages of clay, silt, and sand and is a good way to characterize and compare sediment textures (figure 12.2). Pictorial graphs are popular in geology and geomorphology for presenting the broad outlines of sediment characteristics over a profile or stratigraphic series (figure 12.7). In the latter, bar graphs or line graphs are oriented vertically to produce a metaphor for the depth of the profile, and are shaded to represent visually the

gross characteristics of the sediment, with the bar height showing texture.

For most archaeological applications, it is possible to characterize the texture of sediments without tedious measurements of individual particle sizes, simply by moistening it and manipulating it in your hand. Following the program steps in figure 12.6 will allow you to characterize sediments fairly consistently.

Particle Shape

Describing the shape of particles in a sediment is, in many ways, just like describing the morphology of lithics, especially for the largest particles (pebbles, cobbles, and boulders).

One simple shape measure involves three linear measurements — the long axis (length, l), the axis perpendicular to it (width, w), and the short axis (s) — with calipers or in a right-angled measuring frame. Shape can then be characterized by ratios, especially l/w and s/w, for each

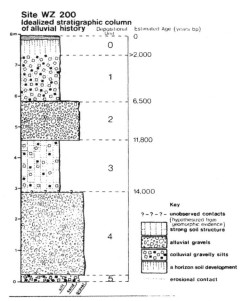

Figure 12.7. Example of a stylized profile that doubles as a kind of bar graph (Banning et al., 1992:46).

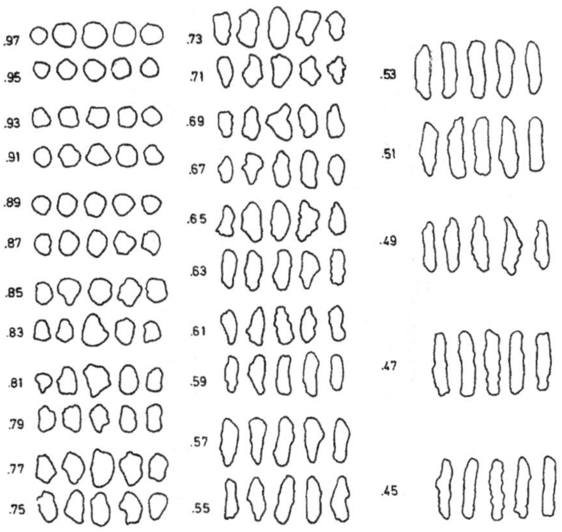

Figure 12.8. Scale for estimating sphericity visually (Shackley, 1975:50).

pebble, and the results for many particles of a given size presented in a histogram or ternary graph. Such graphs from different archaeological contexts can then be useful in attempting to tell whether the pebbles in these contexts come from the same statistical population, and therefore might belong to the same stratigraphic depositional event or be due to the same site-formation process.

In other cases, it is usual to employ a nominal scale for characterizing the shape of particles or their aggregates (**peds**) in sediments. One of the simplest such scales is as follows (see also figure 12.9).

Platy: Plate-like particles with nearly horizontal grain surfaces.

Prismatic: Prism-like blocks with well defined vertical faces (relatively high l/w ratio) and angular vertices.

Columnar: Much like prismatic, with strong vertical faces, but with rounded vertices that give the particles or peds a pillar-like shape.

Angular Blocky: Grain surfaces are fairly flat, vertices are angular, and both l/w and s/w ratios are not much greater than 1.0, so that the long axis is not all that obvious.

Subangular Blocky: Much like angular blocky, except that there are both flat and rounded surfaces and most of the vertices are rounded.

Granular: Particles are roughly spherical or polyhedral, and nonporous.

Crumbs: Aggregates of particles that are spherical or polyhedral, but porous.

One useful measure is *roundness*, which varies not only with the composition of the grain, but also its depositional history and environment (Shackley, 1975:46). It is possible to estimate roundness on an ordinal scale using a chart such as that in figure 12.10, or we can calculate roundness indices based on the radius of circles that fit into the grain corners.

Sphericity measures can also be useful, particularly in identifying sediments that have been moved through an agency that erodes the particles. As with roundness, there are indices that can be calculated from linear measures on the particles. Krumbein's Intercept Sphericity, for example, is the cube-root of the length, width, and short axis divided by the square of the length:

The simplest way to estimate sphericity, however, is again with a visual chart (figure 12.8), which is usually sufficient for archaeological purposes (Shackley, 1975:49).

Sediment Color

You are probably familiar with the way to characterize a sediment's color, as the Munsell soil chart is also used to measure the colors of pottery and other artifacts.

In the Munsell system, colors are measured along three different dimensions: *hue, value* (lightness or darkness), and *chroma* (departure from grey), making a three-dimensional paradigmatic classsification. To measure the color of a sediment sample, place a small amount on a clean trowel or spatula and hold it under the holes in the chart's pages so that you can attempt to find a matching color chip. Make sure that you do this in natural, indirect sunlight (not fluorescents or in bright, direct sunlight), unless you have special lamps designed for this purpose, and without wearing sunglasses. Generally the sample should be moist, but not wet, to bring the color out, although it can be useful to record color twice, once dry, once moist. You record the color in the order, hue, value/chroma, such as 10YR 4/6.

pH

pH is a measure of the concentration of hydrogen ions in the sediment, along a scale from 0 to 14 such that numbers less than 7 indicate acidity and ones higher than 7 indicate basic (alkali) material. Most sediments have pH ranging between 5 and 9 (Shackley, 1975:65). Since pH is one of the factors that heavily affects the likelihood that some materials of archaeological interest, such as bone and pollen, will be preserved, it is very important to record it both in the field and in the lab.

There are several ways to measure pH, ranging considerably in their precision and accuracy. The simplest, but most inaccurate and imprecise, is with litmus papers. You make a measurement by dipping the papers into a beaker containing a suspension of the sediment in distilled water, shaking off the excess liquid,

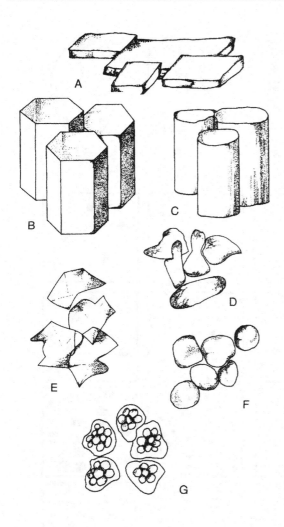

Figure 12.9. Nominal-scale classes for the description of particles and aggregates (peds): A - platy, B - prismatic, C - columnar, D - subangular blocky, E - angular blocky, F - granular, G - crumbs (Shackley, 1975:45).

$$\psi = \sqrt[3]{\frac{LWS}{L^2}}$$

Wadell's Sphericity, meanwhile, is based on the diameter of the smallest circle that will fit around the grain:

$$\psi = \sqrt{\frac{4Ad}{W^2}}$$

where A is the area of the particle, and d is the diameter of the circle.

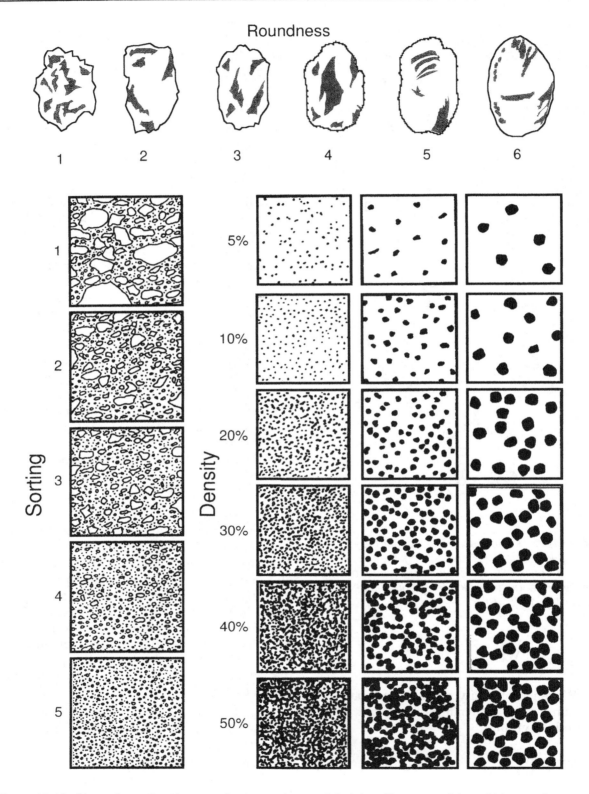

Figure 12.10. Charts for estimating roundness, sorting, and density of larger particles within a sediment (after Courty et al., 1989:69 and others).

watching the paper change color, and comparing this color with a chart. Typically this allows measurement of pH in steps of 1 pH with an error of ± 0.5 pH, especially if you check your readings against a "buffer" solution of known pH. Even if you are very careful, however, the presence of some chemicals, such as proteins, salt, or sulphur dioxide, in the sediment will result in biased measurements

A somewhat better method is to use indicator solutions. Some substances, such as phenolphthalein, change color markedly when they reach different pH levels, but are difficult to use. A "universal" indicator, such as BDH universal indicator, is easier to use. You mix a small amount of the sediment with some distilled water in a test tube and stir it into a suspension, then add a few drops of the suspension (avoiding large grains) to a piece of white, glazed tile. You then add a couple of drops of the indicator and compare the resulting color with standards (Shackley, 1975:66). Similarly, commercially available gardeners' test kits sometimes include indicator solutions that allow you to estimate pH and Nitrogen levels. You add a few milliliters of the indicator to a small amount of dry sediment and compare the color of the suspension that results to a standard color chart.

The best way to measure pH is with a pH meter. This measures the "effective" pH of the sediment, which is the electrical potential measured with a glass electrode, and is affected by all sources of hydrogen ions. The meter is calibrated by taking measures on standard "buffer" solutions, known to have pH of 4.0 and 9.0. After mixing the sediment with distilled water to make a muddy paste, you insert the glass electrode into the mud and read the digital value. Make sure that you rinse the electrode with distilled water between measurements, and never let the electrode dry out. If you are testing sediments containing carbonates, you may need to rinse the electrode with a mild acid, such as acetic acid (vinegar) periodically to remove carbonate build-up. With a pH meter, readings are easy and accurate, and modern pH meters are light and often quite precise (Shackley, 1975:66-68).

Phosphates

Phosphate content of soils and sediments can be an important piece of archaeological evidence. Elevated phosphate levels are often associated with soils and sediments that contain decayed bone or feces and, consequently, measurement of phosphates can be useful in the identification of habitation sites, middens, and graves, even when the skeletons have completely decayed. The "background" phosphate levels of some rocks and sediments, meanwhile, are often low, although some limestone-derived soils can have higher than usual phosphate from fossils. Some deposits that originally were high in phosphate could have the phosphate leached out, however, while in some areas recent use of high-phosphate fertilizers could have altered the phosphate content.

Accurate measurement of phosphate involves boiling an acid extract of the sediment with ammonium molybdate and nitric acid (Shackley, 1975:68), a procedure that requires considerable care, expertise, and equipment to complete safely, or use of a colorimeter (Shackley, 1975:69-70). However, archaeologists can estimate phosphate content more simply and safely with gardeners' soil test kits.

One simple test for phosphates is called the Gundlach test. Here you put a small amount of the sediment on a filter paper in a Petri dish and add two drops of a solution of ammonium molybdate and sulphuric acid by pipette. After a couple of minutes, you add two drops of an ascorbic acid solution. As the liquids are absorbed into the filter paper phosphates will cause a color change to yellow and then blue. The amount of color change can be used as a rough indication of the amount of total (organic and inorganic) phosphate present. Schwartz (1967) presents a scale of five color-intensity increments (Shackley, 1975:68-69).

Geomorphology and Site-Formation Processes

Although the cultural and natural processes that contribute to the formation of an archaeological site are many and complex, those that occur in the archaeological context conform to a

number of basic geological principles that gov-
ern the deposition and removal of sediment,
and analysis of the sediments in deposits provides important clues as to what those processes
were.

Some of the most basic processes involve the
erosion of rock, soils, and sediments from one
location and their redeposition as sediments in
another location (figure 12.11). The mechanisms
that remove material are often the same as those
that transport it to the new location: wind, water, gravity, and the activity of plants and animals, including humans. Quite commonly, for
example, wind, rain, and the force of gravity
remove material from the tops of hills and ridges
and move it to lower elevations, such as valley
bottoms. The soil profile upslope is truncated by
the removal of material (perhaps the A horizon
is missing), while the lower slopes and edges of
the valley may be buried with **colluvium** (formed
by the movement of material downslope by
gravity) or **loess** (formed by the deposition of
wind-borne particles). There the A horizon of
the original soil profile is buried, making it a
paleosol, while the newer deposits on top of it
will begin to be altered, eventually forming new
zonation so that there is more than one A horizon. We tend to think of most of these processes
as rather slow, but colluviation can sometimes
be quite dramatic, taking the form of landslides.
In once instance in Jordan, a recent land slump
rather suddenly moved an entire small archaeological site from one side of a valley to the other
(Field and Banning, 1998).

When water transports particles, they are
carried along watercourses until the water's
velocity is not great enough to keep them in
suspension and they settle out as **alluvium**.
Typically alluvium has large, rounded particles
where water velocity was high, and fine particles (silts and clays) downstream, where water
velocity slowed down enough to allow them to
settle (figure 12.12). But fast-moving water also
cuts into alluvium that was previously deposited and carries away particles, so that there is
typically a channel, with a levee on either side
formed from the settling of large particles when
the channel overflows, and with silts and clays
on the plain either side of the levee. As a result

of alluvial deposition, the channel is often higher
than the surrounding plain.

Particle size, rounding, sorting, and orientation of particles are all important clues as to
what sort of transport is responsible for the
deposition of sediments (Friedman, 1961; Mason and Folk, 1958; Sneed and Folk, 1958; Udden,
1898). Artifacts also act as particles, and attributes of artifact orientation and damage can
reveal such things as artifact transport and processes that selectively remove evidence from
sediments (Schiffer, 1987:267-79; Shea, 1999).

Archaeologists often describe some of the
processes that act on archaeological sites as "disturbance" because they tend to displace artifacts
from their original points of deposition. More
recently they have viewed archaeological deposits as dynamic, rather than static, so that
"disturbance" is not as useful a concept. Instead
they refer to the natural and cultural processes
that have acted or continue to act on deposits.
Schiffer (1987) refers to the natural processes as
"N-transforms" and the cultural ones as "C-
transforms." Sometimes there is an interplay
between the two. For example, human activity,
such as forest clearance, can cause a drop in
water tables or increase erosion, which in turn
have natural effects on sites, their landscapes,
and their contents.

Some natural processes act on sites on small
scales, and not just on the larger earth-moving
scale we tend to associate with geomorphology.
Among these are the action of frost and growing
plants and the activities of burrowing animals
(Wood and Johnson, 1978; Schiffer, 1987:207-
215). In areas that are prone to heavy frost,
capillary action and the expansion that water
undergoes when it freezes can lift stones out of
the soil, while in very cold weather ice crystals
will decrease in volume. Alternate freezing and
thawing over many centuries can move material
considerably, and sometimes has unexpected
effects, such as tending to sort pottery from
lithics vertically (Limbrey, 1975; Rolfsen, 1980)
or creating stone patterns that look like man-
made structures (Wood and Johnson, 1978:344-
46). **Bioturbation**, the movement of materials in
deposits by plant roots and burrowing animals,

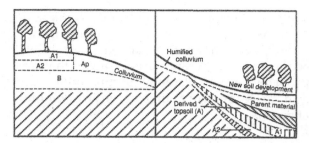

Figure 12.11. Truncation of soil profiles upslope and development of paleosols and new soil development downslope (after Butzer, 1982:133).

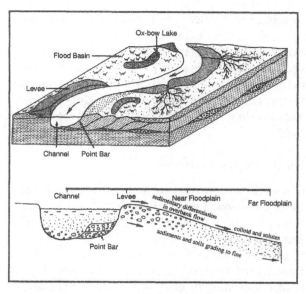

Figure 12.12. Sediments and transport in streams (Courty et al., 1989:87).

can also have substantial effect on the distribution of artifacts and other remains in those deposits. Already Darwin (1882) demonstrated how earthworms could bury ancient Roman pavements, while animals such as insects, crayfish, voles, and mole rats may not only bring older materials up to a recent surface, but also introduce recent materials into deeper levels or concentrate items in their burrows so that they could be mistaken for cultural activity areas. Tree falls can bring great masses of soil up to the surface with the roots, while root growth itself displaces sediment and artifacts, and root casts are left where roots have decayed away (Rolfsen, 1980; Wood and Johnson, 1978:318-33).

Environmental Interpretation

The processes that cause, affect, and remove deposits are not only of interest because they potentially confuse our interpretation of archaeological distributions. In their turn, these processes provide important clues to environmental conditions in the past (Hassan, 1978). Because river downcutting and transport of large particles to be deposited elsewhere as alluvium requires high water velocities, for example, it implies that there must have been, at least occasionally, fast water such as you would find in flash floods. Deposition of colluvium can occur very quickly, during landslides and mudslides caused by sudden, high rainfall, or very slowly where there is dense vegetation cover to prevent erosion by sheetwash during rains. The kind of particle transport has a relationship to rainfall intensity, valley shape, and vegetation cover.

Cultural Interpretation

Knowing something about the kinds of processes that deposited sediment in an archaeological site and affected it afterward is extremely important in archaeological interpretation. Many of these processes are cultural (Butzer, 1982:78; Hassan 1978; Schiffer, 1987:288-91). For example, careful consideration of particle-size distributions and the orientation of elongated particles might help us recognize that a rather mixed-up collection of artifacts within a large pit or within the walls of a structure occur in a fill deposit, with many more-or-less distinct basket-loads of sediment deposited over a fairly short period of time. Tipping of the basket-loads into the pit would cause size-sorting of particles at different places along the slope, for example. It might help us distinguish the surfaces that ancient people walked on from pseudo-surfaces caused by bioturbation or interfaces caused by erosion. Trampling and sweeping, for example, have a real effect on average particle size and on the spatial distribution of larger particles (Nielsen, 1991; Simms, 1988). It may help us to recognize the remnants of mud, adobe, or mud-brick architecture amid the sediments derived from decaying mud walls. It might also help us distinguish genuine activity areas from artifact concentrations made by burrowing animals. In sites ranging from single-component post-hole configurations truncated by plowing to complicated shell middens and Near Eastern tells, sediment analyses provide much-needed clues to the human and natural circumstances that led to the form and character of the deposits we excavate (e.g., Holliday, 1992; Rosen, 1986; Stein, 1992).

Stratigraphic Correlations

One of the applications of sediment analysis is to determine whether stratigraphic contexts in different excavation areas are really part of the same archaeological (or lithostratigraphic) layer. If the sediments were deposited at the same time, by the same process of transport and deposition, they may be closely similar in their sediment characteristics, such as color, texture, particle roundness, and, of course, material-culture content. On the other hand, similarity between contexts in these respects, by itself, does not absolutely guarantee that they are from the same layer, as the same combination of processes could occur more than once on the site.

Because artifacts and micro-artifacts can be among the particles in sediments, some archaeologists have used peaks in their density in a series of pits, sections, or auger-holes to identify and map buried landscape surfaces. For example, Russell Stafford (1992) reconstructed the topography of a buried Early Woodland surface around the Ambrose Flick site in the Upper Mississippi Valley by plotting the mid-elevations of density peaks in vertical artifact distributions.

Conclusions

Understanding sediments and soils is important for archaeologists because they almost always hold the key to archaeological context. We cannot be sure that artifacts and other kinds of material culture we find together are culturally associated, for example, by having been deposited during a particular activity, unless we know something about how the deposit in which they were found was formed and transformed over time. Sediment characteristics, such as particle size, shape, and sorting can help us identify such

site-formation processes as natural colluviation, frost-heaving, and tipping of refuse into a midden. In addition, they can help us associate sediments in different parts of a site that are probably portions of a single stratigraphic layer and to reconstruct ancient environmental changes.

References Cited

Allen, T., 1968, *Particle Size Analysis*. Halstead Press, London.

Banning, E. B., Dods, R. R., Field, J., Kuijt, I., McCorriston, J., Siggers, J., Ta'ani, H., and Triggs, J., 1992, Tabaqat al-Bûma: 1990 excavations at a Kebaran and Late Neolithic site in Wâdî Ziqlâb. *Annual of the Department of Antiquities of Jordan* 36:43-69.

Butzer, K. W., 1982, *Archaeology as Human Ecology*. Cambridge University Press, Cambridge.

Courty, M. A., Goldberg, P., and Macphail, R., 1989, *Soils and Micromorphology in Archaeology*. Cambridge University Press, Cambridge.

Darwin, C., 1882, *The Formation of Vegetable Mould, through the Action of Worms with Observations on their Habits*. John Murray, London.

Davidson, D. A., 1973,. Particle size and phosphate analysis — evidence for the evolution of a tell. *Archaeometry* 15:143-52.

Field, J., and Banning, E. B., 1998, Hillslope processes and archaeology in Wadi Ziqlab, Jordan. *Geoarchaeology* 13:595-616.

Folk, R. L., 1966, A review of grain size parameters. *Sedimentology* 6:73-93.

Friedman, G. M., 1961, Distinction between dune, beach and river sands from their textural characteristics. *Journal of Sedimentary Petrology* 27:3-27.

Goldberg, P., Nash, D. T., and Petraglia, M. D., eds., 1993, *Formation Processes in Archaeological Context*. Monographs in World Prehistory 17. Prehistory Press, Madison, WI.

Griffiths, J. C., 1967, *Scientific Method in Analysis of Sediments*. McGraw-Hill, New York.

Hassan, F. A., 1978, Sediments in archaeology: Methods and implications for paleoenvironmental and cultural analysis. *Journal of Field Archaeology* 5:197-213.

Holliday, V. T., ed., 1992, *Soils in Archaeology. Landscape Evolution and Human Occupation*. Smithsonian Institution Press, Washington.

Inman, D. L., 1962, Measures for describing the size distributions of sediments. *Journal of Sedimentary Petrology* 22:125-145.

Krumbein, W. C., 1934, Size frequency distribution of sediments. *Journal of Sedimentary Petrology* 4:65-77.

Limbrey, S., 1975, *Soil Science and Archaeology*. Academic Press, New York.

Mason, C. and Folk, R. L., 1958, Differentiation of beach, dune and aeolian flat environments by size analysis. *Journal of Sedimentary Petrology* 28:211-226.

NACSN, 1983, North American commission on Stratigraphic Nomenclature, North American Stratigraphic Code. *American Association of Petroleum Geologists Bulletin* 67:841-875.

Nielsen, A. E., 1991, Trampling the archaeological record: An experimental study. *American Antiquity* 56:483-503.

Rittenhouse, G., 1943, A visual method of estimating two-dimensional sphericity. *Journal of Sedimentary Petrology* 13:79-81.

Rolfsen, P., 1980, Disturbance of archaeological layers by processes in the soil. *Norwegian Archaeological Review* 13:110-18.

Rosen, A. M., 1986, *Cities of Clay: The Geoarchaeology of Tells*. University of Chicago Press, Chicago.

Schiffer, M. B., 1987, *Formation Processes of the Archaeological Record*. University of New Mexico Press, Albuquerque, NM.

Schwartz, G. T., 1967, Prospecting without a computer in southern Switzerland. *Estratto da Prospezioni Archaeologische* 2:73-80.

Shackley, M. L., 1975, *Archaeological Sediments. A Survey of Analytical Methods*. Butterworths, London.

Shea, J. J., 1999, Artifact abrasion, fluvial processes and "living floors" from the early Paleolithic site of 'Ubeidiya (Jordan Valley, Israel). *Geoarchaeology* 14:191-207.

Simms, S. R., 1988, The archaeological structure of a Bedouin camp. *Journal of Archaeological Science* 15: 197-211.

Sneed, E. D. and Folk, R. L., 1958, Pebbles in the lower Colorado River, Texas: A study in particle morphogenesis. *Journal of Geology* 66:114-150.

Soil Survey Staff, 1975, *Soil Taxonomy: A Basic System of Soil Classification for Making and Interpreting Soil Surveys*. Soil Conservation Service, U.S. Department of Agriculture, Washington, DC.

Stafford, C. R., 1992, Archeological stratigraphy and paleotopography. In *Early Woodland Occupations at the Ambrose Flick Site in the Sny Bottom of the Mississippi River Valley*, edited by C. R. Stafford, pp. 58-94. Kampsville Archeological Center Research Series 10. Center for American Archeology, Kampsville, IL.

Stein, J. K., 1987, Deposits for archaeologists. *Advances in Archaeological Method and Theory* 2:319-396.

— 1992, *Deciphering a Shell Midden*. Academic Press, San Diego.

Udden, J. A., 1898, *Mechanical Composition of Wind Deposits*. Augustana Library Publication No. 1.

Wadell, H. A., 1935, Volume, shape and roundness of quartz particles. *Journal of Geology* 43:250-280.

Waters, M., 1992, *Principles of Geoarchaeology: A North American Perspective*. University of Arizona Press, Tucson, AZ.

Wentworth, C. K., 1922, The shape of pebbles. *Bulletin of the US Geological Survey* 730-C: 91-114.

Wood, W. R., and Johnson, D. L., 1978, A survey of disturbance processes in archaeological site formation. *Advances in Archaeological Method and Theory* 1:315-381..

13 Seriation

...some professional archaeologists may be under the mistaken impression that ... seriation ... has been taken over by robots and no longer requires good judgement, careful field work, and plain common sense (Marquardt, 1978: 257).

As we saw in the last chapter, sometimes we have multilinear stratigraphic sequences so that stratigraphy, alone, is insufficient for us to ascertain which stratigraphic units are contemporary. Furthermore, we sometimes would like to put components from different sites into a relative sequence, or to find out which ones are contemporary. To solve these problems we must turn to nonstratigraphic evidence, including that from independent dating methods. A common means for ordering such contexts has been to compare their artifactual content, often with a methodology we call seriation (Laxton, 1990; Marquardt, 1978).

The first, and still classic, use of seriation was Petrie's (1899) "sequencing" of predynastic Egyptian graves. Petrie used what is now called the Concentration Principle to arrange 900 graves into a linear sequence on the basis of 804 types and varieties of pottery. The Concentration Principle states simply that arrangements that minimize the ranges of varieties over the sequence are preferred.

The purpose of seriation is to order a number of units along a single dimension (usually time is the dimension of interest) such that adjacent units are more similar to one another than to nonadjacent units. The similarities can be measured in much the same way they are measured for grouping (chapter 3). Often the attributes that archaeologists measure to compile a similarity matrix are the relative abundances of various artifact "types."

Seriation begins with a number of assumptions and a model that purports to describe the way the relative abundance of an artifact type changes over the dimension, time. The essence of the model is the assumption that each artifact type first grows in its relative abundance (incipience), following its initial introduction, reaches a mode or peak in "popularity" (fluorescence), and then declines (figure 13.1; Kendall, 1971; Robinson, 1951). We can call this unimodal distribution the Kendall model (Buck et al., 1996: 328). Ford (1962) referred to the distinct unimodal shape as a "battleship curve." Among the other assumptions are the assumptions that each archaeological unit corresponds to a relatively brief and comparable period of time, that the content of each unit is a representative sample of the artifacts that were in use during that time, that all units belong to the same cultural tradition, and that all the units come from a reasonably small region. The last two assumptions represent an attempt to ensure that the dimension along which we are ordering the units is time, rather than space or cultural affiliation, and they depend on other evidence (Dunnell, 1970; Marquardt, 1978:261, 297).

In mathematical terms, we represent the various relative abundances in a matrix of m rows and n columns, where m is the number of

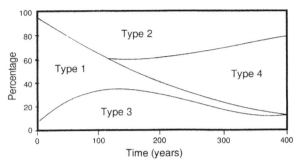

Figure 13.1. Kendall's model for the way the proportions of four types of artifact would vary over time.. Each type has a unimodal distribution so that it gradually increases, reaches a peak, and then decreases in abundance (after Buck et al., 1996:41).

archaeological units (deposits, graves, or components) and *n* is the number of artifact types. Each cell in the matrix is occupied by a figure we can represent by $a_{i,j}$, meaning the *j*th entry in the *i*th row (the number of artifacts of type *j* in the *i*th archaeological unit). We conclude that the matrix is seriated if the numbers going down each column, once they have decreased, never rise again. We refer to this property of never increasing again as decreasing **monotonically**. For example, in table 13.1 the archaeological contexts are in arbitrary order and are not seriated. In table 13.2 they have been reordered so that the relative abundance of each type (represented as percentages) never increases once it has started to decrease.

Although the seriation arranges the contexts in a linear order (4, 1, 7, 5, 3, 8, 2 and 6), the direction of ordering is arbitrary. The order, 6, 2, 8, 3, 5, 7, 1, 4 would be equally seriated.

We can also seriate with a dichotomous-scale version of the Kendall model, which comes closer to what Petrie (1899) accomplished. In this case we only record the presence (1) or absence (0) of each type and follow the rule that, once a zero follows a one, it can only be followed by more zeros, and no ones. For example, you can have 0, 0, 1, 1, 0, 0, but not 0, 1, 0, 1, 0, 0. In other words, in any one column the ones must be clustered together with no intervening zeros. In honor of Petrie's work, the result is called a "P-matrix."

In tables 13.3 and 13.4 we see a fictitious example of this kind of seriation, in which the contexts are graves and other widely separated deposits of unknown stratigraphic relation to one another, and we have recorded the presence or absence of a number of pottery types that we have reason to believe are chronologically short-lived.

There are, however, problems with the Kendall method. First, it is not always true that in correctly ordered assemblages the relative abundance of a type will never increase after it has decreased. In more realistic situations, in fact, there are usually fluctuations in relative abundance that the model does not take into account. Second, the algorithms for finding the best ordering do not account for the fact that there may be more than one possible ordering, including some that are almost as likely as the "best" one (Buck et al., 1996:329).

The former problem can be partly addressed by turning to the overall similarity or dissimilarity between the archaeological units, rather than assuming that each type will increase monotonically to a peak and then decrease monotonically. We simply make a new matrix that is *n* x *n* instead of *n* x *m*, that is, with archaeological contexts along both axes (table 13.5). For each pair of contexts we can measure the degree of similarity by Robinson's (1951) Index of Agreement (IA) as,

$$IA_{jk} = 200 - \left(\sum_{i=1}^{m} |x_{ji} - x_{ki}| \right),$$

or the sum of the absolute values of the difference between the percentages of each type for each pair of archaeological units, subtracted from 200. In other words, if two archaeological contexts have exactly the same distribution of types, the summed differences between them (a measure of dissimilarity) will be 0 and the IA will be 200. If, on the other hand, the two contexts are maximally different (i.e., when one has 100% of one type and the other has 100% of another type), the summed differences will be 200% and IA will therefore be 0. Subtracting from 200, then, simply turns a dissimilarity coefficient into a measure of agreement or similarity.

Table 13.1. An abundance matrix, showing the percentages of four different artifact types in eight different archaeological contexts

	Artifact Type			
Context	A	B	C	D
1	10	20	0	70
2	20	0	70	10
3	40	10	30	20
4	0	10	0	90
5	40	20	15	25
6	10	0	90	0
7	30	30	5	35
8	30	5	50	15

Table 13.3. An incidence matrix showing the presence (1) or absence (0) of each of four artifact types among eight different archaeological contexts

	Artifact Type			
Context	A	B	C	D
1	1	0	1	0
2	0	0	0	1
3	1	1	0	1
4	1	1	0	0
5	0	0	1	0
6	1	1	0	1
7	1	0	1	0
8	0	1	0	1

Table 13.2. The archaeological contexts from table 13.1 seriated so that the percentages never increase after reaching their peak. Archaeologists sometimes call this type of matrix a "Q-matrix" (Kendall 1971: 219)

	Artifact Type			
Context	A	B	C	D
4	0	10	0	90
1	10	20	0	70
7	30	30	5	35
5	40	20	15	25
3	40	10	30	20
8	30	5	50	15
2	20	0	70	10
6	10	0	90	0

Table 13.4. A seriation of the contexts shown in table 13.3. Note how the ones are all grouped together by column, with no intervening zeros. Archaeologists sometimes call this type of matrix a Petrie order or a "P-matrix" (Kendall 1971: 220)

	Artifact Type			
Context	A	B	C	D
2	0	0	0	1
8	0	1	0	1
6	1	1	0	1
3	1	1	0	1
4	1	1	0	0
7	1	0	1	0
1	1	0	1	0
5	0	0	1	0

Returning to the data from the matrix in table 13.1, for example, the absolute values of the differences between the four types for contexts 1 and 2 are 20 - 10, 20 - 0, 70 - 0, and 70 - 10. The sum of these differences is 10 + 20 + 70 + 60 = 160, so that IA = 200 - 160 = 40. For contexts 1 and 3 they are 30 + 10 + 30 + 50 = 120, so that IA = 80. We can continue this simple process for each pair of archaeological units to produce the matrix shown in table 13.5. We only have to fill out half of the matrix, as it is perfectly symmetrical about the diagonal, where all values of IA are 200 (perfect agreement between each context and itself).

The next step is to rearrange the row-columns so that higher IA values are clustered near the diagonal (close to the 200 values) and IA decreases toward the upper right corner. In the

case of table 13.5, some of the highest values are 160 for the pairs (2, 8) and (3, 8) and 140 for the pair (1, 4). Meanwhile, the pair (4, 6) shows no agreement at all (IA = 0), indicating that they should probably be at opposite ends of the sequence. This provides some clues to reordering the contexts with the result that appears in table 13.6.

Dempsey and Baumhoff's (1963:499) variation on Robinson's technique reduces the data to the dichotomous scale "so that the presence (or absence) of any one type contains no necessary implication concerning the presence (or absence) of any other type." They note that in Robinson's technique, by contrast, an increase in one type will force the relative abundances of other types to decrease even if their absolute abundance remained constant, and expressed the concern that this could obscure the expected pattern of incipience, fluorescence, and decline. This technique should seem familiar, as it measures similarity coefficients in the same way as in numerical taxonomies (chapter 3). Although it solves the problem of interdependence of percentages, it has the usual problem we encounter with presence/absence data: a single artifact of one type has just as much weight as hundreds of examples of another type (Marquardt 1978: 268). In addition, it has other problems, including difficulty of calculation.

There are many other variations of and alternatives to the Robinson (1951) method, most of which Marquardt (1978) reviews. Here we will only briefly mention Cowgill's (1972) variation because it involves measures of similarity, not between pairs of contexts, but between pairs of types, Wilkinson's (1974) because it treats artifacts and contexts equally, and LeBlanc's (1975) because it is based on the distributions of attributes, rather than types.

Essentially Cowgill's (1972) method involves applying multidimensional scaling to a matrix of similarity coefficients that are based on the the number of contexts in which both types of a pair occur, the number in which the first type occurs but the second does not, and the number in which the second is present but the first is absent.

Wilkinson's (1974) AXIS program orders rows and columns of a dichotomous $n \times m$ incidence matrix as follows. First it calculates the mean position of the ones in the columns and reorders the columns by reference to those means. Then it calculates the mean position of the ones in the rows and reorders the rows by reference to those means. Then it goes back to the mean position of the ones in the columns and repeats over and over until no further improvement of the matrix occurs. The "best" order occurs when the "R" score is minimized, R being the sum, for every column, of the difference between the first and last nonzero value (i.e., the range of the artifact type is minimized).

LeBlanc (1975) begins by standardizing the values for each attribute so that they each range between 1 and 100, so that rarely occurring attributes receive as much weight as common ones. In LeBlanc's example, he then creates an $n \times n$ matrix of dissimilarity indices for each attribute, where n is the number of archaeological contexts and the attributes are slip, paint, hue, and line width. He can then seriate each attribute independently or, alternatively, add the dissimilarity matrices together. LeBlanc argues that seriation on the basis of chronologically sensitive attributes provides better results than using types, but one should be careful of the effect of weighting rare attributes as highly as common ones (Marquardt 1978: 284).

Table 13.5. Matrix of the Robinson's Indices of Agreement (IA) for the data from table 13.1

Context	1	2	3	4	5	6	7	8
1	200	40	80	140	110	20	130	60
2		200	120	20	110	160	70	160
3			200	60	170	80	130	160
4				200	50	0	90	40
5					200	50	160	130
6						200	30	125
7							200	110
8								200

Table 13.6. Rearranged matrix of the Robinson's Indices of Agreement (IA) for the data from table 13.1. Note that the same order results as in table 13.2. In general, the IA values fall off from the diagonal, although there are exceptions, as in the value for the pair (4, 3)

Context	4	1	7	5	3	8	2	6
4	200	140	90	50	60	40	20	0
1		200	130	110	80	60	40	20
7			200	160	130	110	70	30
5				200	170	130	110	50
3					200	160	120	80
8						200	160	125
2							200	160
6								200

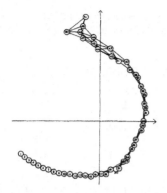

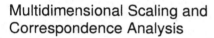

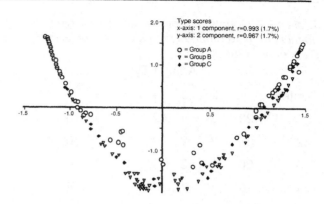

Figure 13.2. Results of multidimensional scaling on a dissimilarity matrix using Kendall's (1971) MDSCAL programme. If time is the main dimension, early units will be at one end of the "horseshoe" and late ones at the other.

Figure 13.3. Results of a correspondence analysis on a number of artifacts. If time is the principal ordering dimension, then the oldest artifacts will be at one end and the youngest at the other end of the "horseshoe."

Multidimensional Scaling and Correspondence Analysis

As we have seen, among the techniques that can help in seriation efforts is multidimensional scaling (see Boneva, 1971; Orton, 1980:84-88). Correspondence analysis is even more commonly used (Baxter, 1994:100-139). These methods help address the problem that most matrices are not ideal Robinson matrices.

Just as with similarity matrices used for grouping artifacts into "types," one way to see if there was really any order for the seriation to discover was to apply multidimensional scaling. In this technique, the idea is to draw something like a "map" representing the dissimilarities between units (here contexts, but for typology the units would be artifacts) as distances in space (see chapter 3). Because the space is multidimensional (i.e., there are many attributes or many types), it is impossible to draw these distances on a two-dimensional sheet of paper without distorting them. In multidimensional scaling, we accept a certain amount of such distortion, for example, distortions that preserve the rank-order of the distances. Typically the resulting map has a near-circular or "horseshoe" shape (figure 13.2) as a result of many units having almost the same dissimilarity (such as no types in common) with some other unit. If time is the principal dimension along which the units are spread out, then the oldest context is found at one end of the horse-

shoe and the youngest at the other, so that we have a time-ordering of the contexts.

Correspondence analysis is an alternative method that, like multidimensional scaling, results in a roughly U-shaped string of data points (figure 13.3). Again, if time is the main contributor to the ordering, then old units will be at one end, and young units at the opposite end, of the curve.

A Bayesian Approach to Seriation

Most of these techniques work well in ideal situations, such as the fictitious example provided here, but not so well with real data, which are often quite "noisy." In addition, they provide a single "best" order without considering the possibility that there are other solutions that order the data nearly as well (Buck et al., 1996:329).

Buck and Litton (1991) provide a seriation model that takes the noisy, stochastic variations in artifact abundance into account and addresses the objection that there may be several seriations that are almost as probable as the "best" one. Detailed discussion of this method is beyond the scope of this book, but suffice to say that it begins with an iterative algorithm, called the Gibbs sampler, some arbitrary starting values, and data modelled by the multinomial and Dirichlet distributions. For each context, you simulate the proportion of each artifact type,

Table 13.7. Counts (not percentages) of 7 types of artifacts from six different archaeological units (after Buck et al., 1996:332)

Context	Artifact Type						
	1	2	3	4	5	6	7
1	20	3	4	42	18	0	13
2	85	3	12	0	0	0	0
3	26	40	8	0	0	26	0
4	20	1	4	13	58	0	4
5	67	10	23	0	0	0	0
6	26	29	8	3	0	33	1

Table 13.8. Counts of artifacts from the six different archaeological units ordered by Kendall's model (after Buck et al., 1996:332)

Context	Artifact Type						
	1	2	3	4	5	6	7
2	85	3	12	0	0	0	0
5	67	10	23	0	0	0	0
3	26	40	8	0	0	26	0
6	26	29	8	3	0	33	1
1	20	3	4	42	18	0	13
4	20	1	4	13	58	0	4

Table 13.9. Counts of artifacts from the six different archaeological units ordered by correspondence analysis (after Laxton and Restorick, 1989)

Context	Artifact Type						
	1	2	3	4	5	6	7
3	26	40	8	0	0	26	0
6	26	29	8	3	0	33	1
5	67	10	23	0	0	0	0
2	85	3	12	0	0	0	0
1	20	3	4	42	18	0	13
4	20	1	4	13	58	0	4

Table 13.10. Results of the Bayesian analysis, with the five most probable orderings (Buck et al. 1996: 333)

Order of Contexts	%
2, 5, 3, 6, 1, 4	80.8
2, 5, 3, 6, 4, 1	14.0
2, 5, 6, 3, 1, 4	3.6
5, 2, 3, 6, 1, 4	1.2
2, 5, 6, 3, 4, 1	0.4

test to see whether they seriate, and repeat this process many times. The repetitions, or "iterations," allow us to discover which order is most likely, which second-most likely, and so on.

In doing so we give the archaeologist some idea of what is the most likely answer and what are the other possible orders, together with some indication of their relative importance (Buck et al., 1996:333).

When they apply their method, with 1000 iterations, to the same data set that Laxton and Restorick (1989) used to compare Kendall's method with correspondence analysis, they find that Kendall's order (2, 5, 3, 6, 1, 4) has the highest probability (0.81), but other orders also have significant probabilities (tables 13.7-13.10). Interestingly, the other possible orders do *not* include the one that Laxton and Restorick (1989) found by correspondence analysis (3, 6, 5, 2, 1, 4), indicating that it is improbable.

In this instance, there was no additional information to aid in the selection of starting probabilities, but one of the advantages of this approach is that it can incorporate any prior information that may exist about the order of contexts. For example, any stratigraphic data that put limits on the possible orders, or radiocarbon dates that might lend more support for one order than another, could be incorporated into the model.

The Use and Interpretation of Seriations

As Marquardt (1978:292-304) correctly points out, the mathematics of seriation is only part of the picture. If we are to have meaningful results, we must apply the seriation method to representative samples of artifacts from contexts that were carefully excavated and free of disturbances that introduced significant numbers of intrusive or **residual** artifacts.

Scott (1993) points out a number of other cautions. He notes that similarity coefficients are often selected without adequate consideration of their appropriateness or chronological sensitivity. He argues that giving all contexts equal weight, regardless of the size or nature of their assemblages, may distort the results of the seriation.

We must also remember that, if some of the assumptions are not justified, the dimension along which we have ordered the archaeological units may be something other than time. Possible alternative dimensions include space, function, site-formation process, and various social dimensions, such as ethnicity.

If we have successfully isolated the chronological dimension, however, seriation does allow us to make better sense of those multilinear sequences that plague stratigraphic analyses. Triggs (1997) attempts first to identify and remove nonindigenous artifacts from the stratigraphic contexts (see chapter 14) and then uses seriation to order the stratigraphic contexts from different multilinear sequences at Fort Frontenac and two other historic sites. Triggs uses Wilkinson's (1974) AXIS program and presence/absence data, as well as the Bonn Seriation and Archaeological Statistics Package™ (Scollar et al., 1992) with both incidence and abundance matrices. He tests the seriation with both broad and more finely grained types, and with both small stratigraphic units and phases (combining many smaller stratigraphic units). In his application, incidence seriation was better at resolving the ambiguous stratigraphic relationships, it was better to use phases or other units that were well separated in time, and broad typological categories worked better than attributes, "unless those attributes have demonstrated temporal significance" (Triggs, 1997:263). He also found that the seriations, when combined with stratigraphy, helped him identify site-formation processes that introduce residual or infiltrated artifacts.

Scott (1993) also notes that current methods of seriation do not help us apply existing sequences to new data. Unlike Petrie's old sequence, which is still a basis for chronological typology in Egypt, these methods do not focus on fitting new assemblages into previously established sequences. He offers a parametric method, in which he treats the age of each context as a parameter to be estimated, that has a number of advantages. Among these are that the age estimates have standard errors, so that we can judge whether pairs of assemblages are statistically different from one another, and that known dates can be incorporated into the analysis. To address the "Petrie problem," his method makes it easy to add new data as it becomes available. He models the unimodal variation in the abundance of types over time with a normal distribution, and considers the distribution of artifacts in an assemblage as Poisson. Full discussion of this method is beyond this chapter.

References Cited

Baxter, M. J., 1994, *Exploratory Multivariate Analysis in Archaeology*. Edinburgh University Press, Edinburgh.

Boneva, L. I., 1971, A new approach to a problem of chronological seriation associated with the works of Plato. In *Mathematics in the Archaeological and Historical Sciences*, edited by F. R. Hodson, D. G. Kendall and P. Tautu, pp. 173-85. Edinburgh: Edinburgh University Press.

Buck, C. E., Cavanagh, W. G., and Litton, C. D., 1996, *Bayesian Approach to Interpreting Archaeological Data*. Statistics in Practice series. John Wiley & Sons, New York.

Buck, C. E. and Litton, C. D., 1991, A computational Bayes approach to some common archaeological problems. in *Computer Applications and Quantitative Methods in Archaeology 1990*, edited by K. Lockyear and S. Rahtz, pp. 93-99 . BAR International Series 565. Tempus Reparatum, Oxford.

Cowgill, G., 1972, Models, methods, and techniques for seriation. In *Models in Archaeology*, edited by D. L. Clarke, pp. 381-424. Methuen, London.

Dempsey, P., and M. Baumhoff (1963). The statistical use of artifact distributions to establish chronological sequence. *American Antiquity* 28: 496-509.

Dunnell, R. C., 1970, Seriation method and its evaluation. *American Antiquity* 35:305-319.

Ford, J. A., 1962, *A Quantitative Method for Deriving Cultural Chronology*. Pan-American Union Technical Manual 1. Reprinted as Museum of Anthropology, Museum Brief 9. University of Missouri.

Greenacre, M. J., 1984, *Theory and Applications of Correspondence Analysis.* Academic Press, London.

Kendall, D. G., 1971, Seriation from abundance matrices. In *Mathematics in the Archaeological and Historical Sciences,* edited by F. R. Hodson, D. G Kendall and P. Tauta, pp. 215-52. Edinburgh University Press, Edinburgh.

Laxton, R. R., 1990, Methods of chronological ordering. In *New Tools from Mathematical Archaeology,* edited by A. Voorrips and B. Ottoway, pp. 37-44. Scientific Information Centre of the Polish Academy of Sciences, Warsaw.

Laxton, R. R., and Restorick, J., 1989, Seriation by similarity and consistency. in *Computer Applications and Quantitative Methods in Archaeology 1989,* edited by S. P. Q. Rahtz and J. D. Richards, pp. 229-40 . BAR International Series 446. British Archaeological Reports, Oxford.

LeBlanc, S. A., 1975, Micro-seriation: A method for fine chronologic differentiation. *American Antiquity* 40:22-38.

Marquardt, W. H., 1978, Advances in archaeological seriation. *Advances in Archaeological Method and Theory* 1:257-314.

Orton, C., 1980, *Mathematics in Archaeology.* Cambridge University Press, Cambridge.

Petrie, W. M. F., 1899, Sequences in prehistoric remains. *Journal of the Anthropological Institute* 29:295-301.

Robinson, W. S., 1951, A method for chronologically ordering archaeological deposits. *American Antiquity* 16:293-301.

Scollar, I., Herzog, I., Rehmet, J., and Greenacre, M. J., 1992, The Bonn Archaeological Statistics Package, Version 4.5. Unkelbach Valley Software Works, Remagen, Germany.

Scott, A., 1993, A parametric approach to seriation. In *Computing the Past: Computer Applications and Quantitative Methods in Archaeology, CAA92,* edited by J. Andresen, T. Madsen and I. Scollar, pp. 317-24 . Aarhus University Press, Aarhus.

Triggs, J. R., 1997, *Matrix Seriation: A Relative Dating Technique for Sites with Multilinear Stratigraphic Sequences.* Unpublished Ph.D. dissertation, University of Toronto.

Wilkinson, E. M., 1974, Techniques of data analysis — seriation theory. *Archaeo-Physika* 5:1-142.

14 Stratigraphy

An important aspect of post-excavation analysis is to order deposits and interfaces chronologically, by **stratigraphy**. Stratigraphy is the analytical process that the archaeologist or geologist carries out; **stratification** refers to the physical layering of deposits in a site.

As we already saw in chapter 12, it is useful to distinguish between lithostratigraphy, biostratigraphy, and archaeological or ethnostratigraphy. Lithostratigraphy, biostratigraphy, and archaeological stratigraphy share the assumption that we can recognize depositional events and events that remove material (erosion, pit-digging, etc.), but differ in the unit that consititutes that "event." For a geologist or biostratigrapher, the event might last thousands of years. Archaeologically interesting events may have lasted less than one day, or as much as two centuries. In this chapter we will concentrate on archaeological stratigraphy, but some discussion of lithostratigraphy and biostratigraphy is necessary. In fact, some authors (Farrand, 1984; Stein, 1992) argue that there is no need for a distinctly archaeological stratigraphy, and that lithostratigraphy is perfectly adequate for archaeological work. Although it is true that there are geological analogues for many of the processes that affect archaeological stratification, here we will follow principally the alternative view, espoused especially by Harris (1989), that the goals and shorter time scale of archaeologists, and the fact that cultural site-formation processes are sometimes quite different from geological ones, require some distinctly archaeological stratigraphic theory.

In spite of the debate between these two groups, they do agree on several points. Both adopt the three main principles of lithostratigraphy — the Principle of Superposition, the Principle of Original Horizontality, and the Principle of Original Continuity — for sedimentary deposits, although archaeological stratigraphers frequently have to deal with deposits and features created by nonsedimentary (especially cultural) processes.

The *Principle of Superposition* is that, for sedimentary deposits, deposits that were formed earliest were overlain by ones formed later, so that the ages of deposits tend to be ordered by their depth. Although deposits were laid down in that order, later events, such as earthquakes and landslides, can alter their physical ordering.

The *Principle of Original Horizontality* is that all sedimentary layers formed in bodies of water were originally deposited horizontally, as a result of gravity and other physical phenomena. Again, these layers can later become tilted and warped out of horizontal.

The *Principle of Original Continuity* is that each layer originally extended spatially as a whole, uninterupted sheet or lens, and that any discontinuities or edges that now exist are the result of erosion, faulting, and other processes that dislocate or remove portions of the layer.

One of the main differences between the two stratigraphic camps is in the importance they assign to the **interfaces** between deposits. An interface is simply a boundary between deposits, representing, for example, the surface that would have been exposed at the top of the deposit before it was covered by other deposits, or the concave surface exposed when someone excavates a pit into pre-existing deposits. Those in the lithostratigraphic camp, notably Stein (1987), argue that the deposit is the unit of importance for both archaeological stratigraphy and lithostratigraphy:

A deposit, like the "bed" of the geologists, is a three-dimensional "envelope" of sediment distinguishable from surrounding sediment on the basis of its physical properties because it was formed under a particular set of physical conditions (Stein, 1987:339). In Near Eastern archaeology, the deposit is often called a "locus" (Dever and Lance, 1978).

The other camp is just as emphatic that geological stratigraphy is inadequate for understanding deposits created by human activities (Harris et al., 1993). Rather than focus only on deposits, Harris submits that the analysis of archaeological site formation requires attention to *layers*, *features* and **interfaces**. These, he argues, are contextual units that archaeologists recognize repeatedly on all kinds of archaeological sites in all parts of the world.

Layers are essentially equivalent to deposits that geologists would recognize, if on a rather different scale. They are deposits whose horizontal dimensions are much greater than their vertical dimension, so that archaeological excavations can intersect them over some extent of an archaeological site. Layers have distinct sedimentary characteristics that allow them to be distinguished in the field, including particle shape, texture, color, pH, composition, and compaction.

Features have no close analogue in geology. They include such nonportable artifacts as hearths, pits, walls, and structures, with vertical dimensions often even greater than their hori-

zontal dimensions, and are generally smaller than layers in horizontal extent. More importantly, although some features — a purposely built mound, for example — are equivalent to deposits, others, such as pits, are in fact defined by the *removal*, rather than deposit, of sediment. Later, of course, the pit can be filled with new sediment, constituting one or more deposits, but the pit fill represents one or more events quite distinct from, and later than, the event of digging the pit. In addition, some kinds of features, notably walls built from stone, mud, or brick, constitute what Harris calls *upstanding strata*. If we were to treat these as geological deposits, they would violate the principle of original horizontality because their largest dimension is often the vertical one. Each feature is always associated with at least one interface.

Finally, there is the **interface**. This is the most important point of disagreement between Harris and the geoarchaeologists, in spite of the fact that it actually does have an analogue in geology: the unconformity. Uncomformity is the term geologists use for the upper surfaces of sediments that have been truncated by erosion or lain for some time without any deposition occurring on them. For Harris (1989), the interface represents either the upper surface of nondepostion on a layer, on which human activities took place or other deposits were laid, or the boundaries created when pre-existing sediments are removed by erosion or excavation, or when features are constructed, renovated, or repaired. Intrusive interfaces are those created by digging, burrowing, gullying, or insertion of posts.

Harris refers to intrusive interfaces such as ditches, pits, and post-holes as *Vertical Feature Interfaces*, while *Horizontal Feature Interfaces* result from the destruction or levelling of upstanding strata, such as stone or brick walls, leaving truncated walls or foundations.

Stein's (1987:355-56) principal objection to Harris's classification of stratigraphic phenomena appears to be her doubt that archaeologists are competent to recognize them consistently in the field (Harris et al., 1993:14; Triggs, 1997:29). She criticizes him for failing to provide explicit, objective criteria for assigning stratigraphic phe-

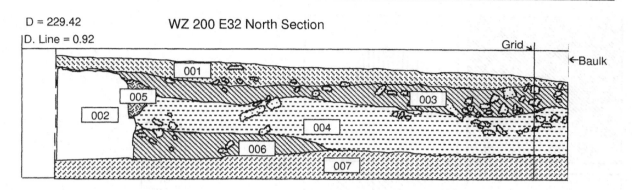

Figure 14.1. Example of a stratigraphic section drawing showing the vertical relationships between deposits that intersect the North edge of an excavated 4m x 4m square. Data from the Wadi Ziqlab Project, Jordan.

nomena to the classes he proposes.

Another point of contention is Harris's (1989) emphasis of the *single-context plan* over the stratigraphic section (figure 14.1). This is a map that depicts a complete plan of a particular stratigraphic unit (or the portion exposed by excavation) as viewed from above (figure 14.2). Harris prefers sets of these plans to stratigraphic sections because not all layers, features, and interfaces intersect the sections, and thus important stratigraphic information is omitted from the record in the sections (Harris et al., 1993:4). Consequently, archaeologists following Harris's methods, especially in the United Kingdom, tend to conduct open-area excavations rather than grid-and-baulk excavations. In the former method, the excavators remove deposits in the reverse order of their deposition, simultaneously over a wide area. The single-context plan and frequent topographic levels are their principal recording instruments, the stratigraphic units being treated much like superimposed sheets of paper (Triggs 1997: 34). In the grid-and-baulk method, excavations in different parts of a site can proceed at quite different paces because they are separated by **baulks** — strips of unexcavated sediment — and drawings of the vertical sections exposed on the sides of the baulks are their main stratigraphic recording instrument (figure 14.1).

Triggs (1997:34-35) argues for an archaeological stratigraphy that combines the interfacial views that Harris espouses with the vertical

views visible in sections. He notes that the vertical section provides clues to the site-formation processes that created and transformed the deposit that are unlikely to be visible in plan view alone.

The Harris Matrix

The archaeological stratigraphy that Harris advocates depends especially on the abstract representation of stratigraphic relationships in what is now called the Harris-Winchester matrix or the **Harris matrix**. It is built from the record of all *unequivocal* relationships between layers, interfaces, and features, and is essentially like a wiring diagram, flow chart, or lattice, rather than a matrix in the mathematical sense (Orton, 1980).

In the Harris system, each layer, feature, and interface is represented by a labelled box and the nonredundant stratigraphic relationships between them by line segments (figure 14.3). It is important to note that the purpose of the resulting diagram is to show the sequence of deposits, features, and interfaces in time, not to show physical relationships (Harris, 1989:34-36).

The stratigraphic units in the labelled boxes are any deposits, features, or interfaces that represent a distinct moment of time, whatever its duration. The boxes are connected by vertical line segments by the *Law of Stratigraphic Succession*. According to this law, any stratigraphic unit is placed on the diagram "between the undermost (or earliest) of the units [that] lie above it and the uppermost (or latest) of all the

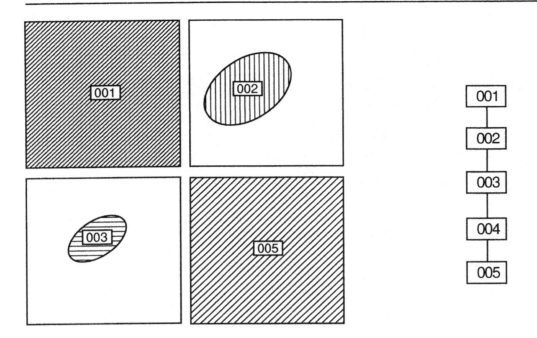

Figure 14.2. Single-context plans. Unit 005 is a layer into which a pit (interface 004) was cut, then filled by deposit 003, then 002, before the whole area was covered by layer 001. The single-context plan for interface 004 would look the same as that for pit fill 002, but with contour lines inside it.

units [that] lie below it and with which the unit has some physical contact, all other superpositional relationships being redundant" (Harris, 1989:157-58). These nonredundant superpositional relationships are indicated by the vertical line segments in such a way that the oldest unit is at the bottom of the diagram and the youngest units are at the top. It is not necessary to indicate the other physical relationships between units because they contribute nothing to our understanding of the stratigraphic sequence (figure 14.3).

This becomes clearer, perhaps, when we represent the relationships by a mathematical model. Here we might represent the stratigraphic relationships with the "> " sign, which we will take here to mean, "older than." If we make the statements,

Unit 1 > Unit 2, and

Unit 2 > Unit 3,

then we can conclude by deduction that Unit 1 > Unit 3, and that the full sequence is Unit 1 > Unit 2 > Unit 3. Consequently, we do not need to show the relationship, Unit 1 > Unit 3, as it would only tend to complicate the diagram without contributing any essential *chronological* information (figure 14.3). The Harris matrix that results from the gradual build-up of such relationships provides an extremely useful representation of all the stratigraphic units, including those that do not intersect any stratigraphic sections, along with the key chronological relationships between them.

However, it often happens that there are stratigraphic units whose relationships are uncertain because there is no physical contact between them. For example, in figure 14.4, we know that Unit 004 and Unit 005 are both older than Unit 001 and both are younger than Unit 008, but we have no stratigraphic information that would allow us to confirm or deny that Unit 004 > Unit 005. In mathematical form we would express this problem with the following statements.

Unit 008 > Unit 004 > Unit 001, and

Unit 008 > Unit 005 > Unit 001.

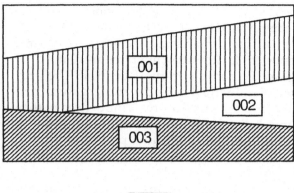

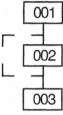

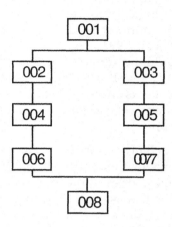

Figure 14.3. Schematic section drawing and simple Harris matrix for three superimposed deposits. The superposition of 001 over 003 is redundant (dashed lines) and so should not be included in the Harris matrix.

Figure 14.4. Multinlinearity in a stratigraphic sequence. Although we can follow the sequence confidently in each one of the two separate branches, we do not know the relationship between units on different branches except that they are all later than 008 and older than 001. Unit 008 could be a wall that separates two areas with somewhat different sedimentary histories.

From these statements we cannot deduce that Unit 004 > Unit 005, or that Unit 004 < Unit 005, or even that Unit 004 = Unit 005. We can only deduce that both date to some time between the two events represented by Units 008 and 001, and can only guess at their precise relationship unless additional information is available. When this happens we have what is called a *multilinear stratigraphic sequence*, and it is extremely common on sites that have substantial architecture because walls, ditches, and other constructed features commonly partition the site into a patchwork of regions with separate stratigraphic histories. In these cases we require nonstratigraphic information, such as reliable radiocarbon dates or evidence from the geoarchaeological characteristics, site-formation processes, or artifactual content of deposits, to help us sort out the most probable order of units in different strands of a multilinear sequence, much as geologists use fossil content, paleomagnetic reversals, and potassium-argon dates to work out the associations between noncontiguous lithological members.

Many archaeologists around the world have adopted Harris's matrix approach, but its acceptance is by no means universal and some archaeologists have modified it to suit their own purposes. In some cases the modifications result from misunderstanding Harris's purpose in omitting redundant relationships. In some cases they go so far as to try to represent many *physical* relationships rather than those relationships that have chronological importance (e.g., Paice, 1991). These may be useful attempts to represent site structure or illustrate certain site-formation processes, but they cloud the strictly chronological picture. Still others attempt to represent the relative lifespans of stratigraphic units by elongating some of the boxes or make the matrix easier to read by symbolically distinguishing layers, interfaces, and various kinds of features on the diagram (e.g., Bibby, 1993; Hammond, 1993).

Because constructing a Harris matrix for sites with numerous stratigraphic units can be a daunting task, even though the stratigraphic relationships themselves are mathematically simple, many archaeologists have turned to computer software to construct the diagrams. The Bonn Archaeological Program™ is a software package with routines designed for this purpose (Scollar et al., 1992). Here we simply enter all the individual stratigraphic relationships, such as Unit A > Unit B and Unit C = Unit D, and the computer works out all the sequences, eliminates redundant relationships, and draws a Harris diagram.

One of the chief advantages of such software is that it allows us to identify stratigraphic errors. Sometimes, for example, our first attempt to construct a Harris matrix from the set of stratigraphic relationships we have recorded in the field leads to such propositions as Unit A > Unit B > Unit C > Unit A. Clearly such a set of relationships is impossible, as no unit can be both above and below another unit. The Bonn program flags such logical inconsistencies so that we can return to the field notes and attempt to discover the recording errors that led to them. The final results of the analysis, once such errors have been corrected, can be very complex and exhibit considerable multilinearity (e.g., figure 14.5).

Grouping Stratigraphic Units

Once a Harris diagram has been completed for all the stratigraphic units on a site, typically archaeologists want to group them so that all units belonging to a fairly brief period (rather than moment) of time, and thought to be associated with a distinct human occupation of the site, are associated. This results in a larger unit that Old World archaeologists typically describe as a *phase* (not to be confused with Willey and Sabloff's [1956] usage of the term) or stratum and that New World archaeologists would usually call a *component*. Stein (1992) would call this an *ethnozone*. The phase, component, or ethnozone then becomes one of the building-blocks for comparison with other sites, creating regional sequences, and reconstructing the spatial extent of cultures or *complexes*.

Because of the common problem of multilinear sequences, phasing also tends to rely in part on nonstratigraphic information,

such as the artifact content of deposits. Yet this is complicated by the fact that we cannot assume that all the artifacts and ecofacts found in a deposit or laying on an interface are of the same age as the deposit or interface itself. The presence of individual artifacts, and groups of artifacts, in layers and features is influenced both by natural disturbance processes (see chapter 12) and cultural site-formation processes, such as discard, recycling, and pit-digging (see Schiffer, 1987:47-140). Harris (1989) distinguishes three kinds of cultural remains on the basis of their chronological relationship to the deposit in which they were found: indigenous, residual, and infiltrated remains.

Indigenous remains are those artifacts and ecofacts that were created only shortly before the deposit in which they were found.

Residual remains are those artifacts or ecofacts that had been in existence for some time before they came to rest in the deposit in which archaeologists found them. In some cases they are *curated* artifacts, such as family heirlooms or coins, that were kept or circulated for many decades before they were eventually lost or intentionally buried. More commonly, they are remains that were removed from some other sediment through pit-digging, erosion, or some other destructive process and redeposited in a new resting place, such as an artificial fill or a colluvium.

Infiltrated remains are artifacts and ecofacts that were actually created *after* the deposit in which they were found, but that somehow worked their way into it, usually from above, without leaving any obvious trace of their infiltration. Among the processes that can cause younger objects to settle into older deposits are earthworm activity, frost heaving, and root penetration.

Associating Noncontiguous Stratigraphic Units

Geologists, prior to radiometric dating, depended heavily on "type fossils" or on spectra of animal remains or pollen to establish whether spatially separated deposits were probably contemporary, or one was later than the other. The

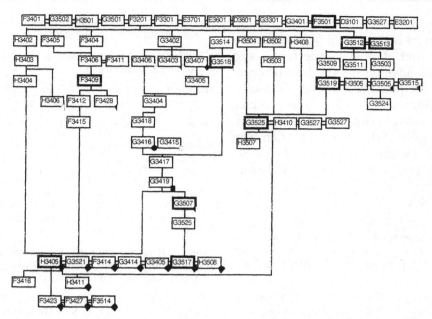

Figure 14.5. Example of part of a Harris matrix executed with the Bonn Archaeological Program™ (Blackham, 1994). Symbols on the matrix indicate walls, graves, etc.

geologists' problem was closely analogous to archaeologists' problem of multilinear sequences.

Today, archaeologists sometimes try to associate widely separated deposits on the same site or components at different sites by carrying out statistical analyses of the artifact distributions in deposits. Some of these analyses are based on seriation (see chapter 13) or clustering methods (chapter 3).

Here I will briefly mention a relatively new method based on set theory. The Unitary Association Method was developed to establish stratigraphic relationships for noncontiguous deposits on the basis of sets of fossils present in them (Guex, 1991; Savary and Guex, 1991), but Blackham (1998) has adapted it for use with archaeological assemblages. It uses the observed superpositions of artifact types in stratified series to identify the sequence of associated sets of artifacts as well as "virtual associations" that take into account the fact that any sampled deposit is unlikely to include all the artifact types that existed at the time it was deposited. A "local horizon" is the set of all associated artifact types in a layer, but those that are sub-sets of other local horizons are combined with them to create "maximal horizons." Other artifacts asso-

ciated with the members of each maximal horizon are used to define "maximal cliques," which are ethnostratigraphic units representing unique associations of artifact types. Information on the superposition of artifacts that belong to these associations is used to put the maximal cliques into stratigraphic order. A software package called *Biograph™* (Savary and Guex, 1991) resolves contradictions in this ordering and produces an ordered series of "unitary associations." Subsequently, the contents of each physical stratigraphic unit at each site must be a subset of one of the unitary associations, and so can be ordered relative to deposits with which it has no physical connection.

Conclusions

On stratified sites, our data on the ordering of events consist of observable evidence of stratigraphic superposition of deposits and features and cutting of interfaces into pre-existing deposits. Sometimes this evidence may be difficult to recognize in the field, and archaeologists spend years gaining experience in the detection of interfaces and features. Once they have entered such information into their field notes, however, we can use careful analysis of the individual observations, usually with the aid of

Harris matrices and computer software, to detect probable errors in the stratigraphic observations and to order deposits, interfaces, and features in time. Sites with complex stratigraphy, standing architecture, or many noncontiguous excavation areas are likely to produce multilinear sequences with many units of uncertain stratigraphic order. We must then turn to other methods, some of which are discussed in the following two chapters, to sort these out.

References Cited

Bibby, D. I., 1993, Building stratigraphic sequences on excavations: An example from Konstanz, Germany. In *Principles of Archaeological Stratigraphy*, edited by E. C. Harris, M. R. Brown, and G. J. Brown, pp. 104-121. Academic Press, London.

Blackham, M., 1994, *Chronological Correlations of Archaeological Stratigraphy: An Intrasite Test at Tabaqat al-Buma, Jordan*. Unpublished M.Sc. thesis, University of Toronto.

— 1998, The Unitary Association Method of relative dating and its application to archaeological data. *Journal of Archaeological Method and Theory* 5:165-207.

Courty, M.. A., Goldberg, P., and Macphail, R., 1989, *Soils and Micromorphology in Archaeology*. Cambridge University Press, Cambridge.

Darwin, C., 1882, *The Formation of Vegetable Mould, through the Action of Worms with Observations on their Habits*. John Murray, London.

Dever, W., and Lance, H. D., 1978, *A Manual of Field Excavation*. Hebrew Union College, New York.

Farrand, W., 1984, Stratigraphic classification: Living within the law. *Quarterly Review of Archaeology* 5:1.

Guex, J., 1991, *Biochronological Correlations*. Springer-Verlag, Berlin.

Hammond, N., 1993, Matrices and Maya archaeology. In *Principles of Archaeological Stratigraphy*, edited by E. C. Harris, M. R. Brown, and G. J. Brown, pp. 139-154. Academic Press, London.

Harris, E. C., 1975, The stratigraphic sequence: A question of time. *World Archaeology* 7:109-21.

— 1989, *Principles of Archaeological Stratigraphy*, 2nd edition. Academic Press, London.

Harris, E. C., M. R. Brown, and G. J. Brown, eds., 1993, *Practices of Archaeological Stratigraphy*. Academic Press, London.

Orton, C., 1980, *Mathematics in Archaeology*. Collins, London.

Paice, P., 1991, Extensions to the Harris matrix system to illustrate stratigraphic discussion of an archaeological site. *Journal of Field Archaeology* 18:17-28.

Savary, J., and Guex, J., 1991, BioGraph: Un nouveau programme de construction des corrélations biochronologiques basées sur les Associations Unitaires. *Bulletin Laboratoire Géologie, Université de Laussanne* 313:317-334.

Scollar, I., Herzon, I., Rehmet, J., and Greenacre, M. J., 1992, The Bonn Archaeological Statistics Package, Version 4.5. Unkelbach Valley Software Works, Remagen, Germany.

Schiffer, M. B., 1987, *Formation Processes of the Archaeological Record*. University of New Mexico Press, Albuquerque.

Stein, J., 1987, Deposits for archaeologists. *Advances in Archaeological Method and Theory* 11:337-93.

— 1992, Interpreting stratification of a shell midden. In *Deciphering a Shell Midden,* edited by J. Stein, pp. 71-93. Academic Press, San Diego.

Triggs, J., 1993, The seriation of multilinear stratigraphic sequences. In *Practices of Archaeological Stratigraphy*, edited by E. C. Harris, M. R. Brown and G. J. Brown, pp. 250-73 . Academic Press, London.

— 1997, *Matrix Seriation: A Relative Dating Technique for Sites with Multilinear Stratigraphic Sequences*. Unpublished Ph.D dissertation, University of Toronto, Toronto.

Wood, W. R., and Johnson, D. L., 1978, A survey of disturbance processes in archaeological site formation. *Advances in Archaeological Method and Theory* 1:315-81.

15 Interpreting Radiocarbon Dates

Although stratigraphy and seriation help us date archaeological deposits on an ordinal scale, often this is not enough. Only with an interval time scale can we determine the duration of an archaeological occupation or be confident that occupation at two different sites was contemporaneous. For sites of the last 50,000 years or so, radiocarbon dating is the method of choice for dating archaeological events on an interval scale.

This chapter will not review the physical principles behind radiocarbon dating, which are relatively well known and appear elsewhere (e.g., Aitken, 1990; Bowman, 1990; Taylor, 1987). Instead, it will concentrate on how to interpret and apply radiocarbon results.

Sometimes archaeologists have misunderstood radiocarbon dates, simply rejecting dates that do not agree with their preconceptions, or even rejecting the radiocarbon method altogether. Appropriate use of radiocarbon dates reflects the fact that they are statistical estimates, that "radiocarbon years" are not the same as calendar years, that calibration of radiocarbon dates can either decrease, or *increase*, the precision of date estimates, and that the event that the radiocarbon method dates (the death of an organism or completion of a tree ring) is usually not the same as the event of archaeological interest. Sophisticated use of suites of radiocarbon dates, when informed by stratigraphic and other evidence, can often lead to extremely precise conclusions about the absolute date of archaeo-

logical events and the duration of prehistoric processes. But intelligent use of radiocarbon dates, like any dating evidence, requires careful thought about the nature of the events that archaeologists want to date.

Kinds of Dates and Events

Conventionally, archaeologists express dates in distinctly different ways without giving the assumptions behind these dates explicit thought. Sometimes a date can be a point estimate, such as AD 55 or 500 BC, the date expressed as a single year. Note, incidentally, that in the common era, there is no such year as AD 0. The calendar goes straight from 1 BC (or BCE) to AD 1 (or 1 CE). Commonly, archaeologists instead cite a **date range**, such as "fifth century BC" or AD 1150-1300. Sometimes, as happens when we are describing the date of a deposit that is stratigraphically later than a building whose construction date is known, we express the date as a *terminus post quem*. What we are saying is that the date of interest is *no earlier* than the known date. When citing a date, we could also provide a point estimate and estimated error, such as AD 1050 ± 60. In that case we would be expressing the idea that the most probable date is close to AD 1050, and that the probablility declines as we get farther from that date. Most people think that is what happens with a carbon date. As we will see below, however, that is not exactly the case.

We can model the difference between these dates graphically by reference to a probability distribution, or "probability density function," which looks like a histogram. For dates to a single year (assuming we are confident in the date), the probability is 1.0 that the event belongs to that year and 0 that it does not, so the entire area of the distribution is lumped into a single year (figure 15.1 a). For date ranges, we only know the beginning and ending dates and indicate no preference for any particular years in between. Consequently we would model the range with a **uniform distribution** to indicate that every year within the range has an equal probability of being the year in which the event took place (figure 15.1 b). We could model a *terminus post quem* either with a uniform distribution or, to express our belief that a date close to the known date is more probable than a much more recent date, with something like an **exponential distribution** (figure 15.1 c). Note how the probability declines as we move away from the known date. Finally, we could treat a date estimate as the mean of a Gaussian or **normal distribution** (figure 15.1 d)(Buck et al., 1996:97-112; Orton, 1980:100). Other models are also possible (e.g., Bronk Ramsey, 1998a).

In addition, we can expect our date to have one or more sources of bias in addition to and quite different from the statistical error associated with the normal distribution. Most of this bias occurs because the event we actually date is not the event of interest. For example, suppose that the event of interest, or **target event**, is the construction of a room in a Pueblo. We could take a piece of wood used in the construction of the room and date it either by **dendrochronology** or radiocarbon dating. Suppose that we use dendrochronology, because it can give us very precise, point estimates of dates, and the outermost ring of the piece of wood dates to AD 1150. Does this mean that the room was constructed in AD 1150? There are many reasons why it does not. First, even if the outermost tree ring preserved on the wood was the last ring formed before the tree was cut to make timber, the **dated event** (cutting down the tree) is not the same as the target event. For all we know, the tree could have been cut two hours or 200 years before the room was constructed. Jeffrey Dean (1978:229)

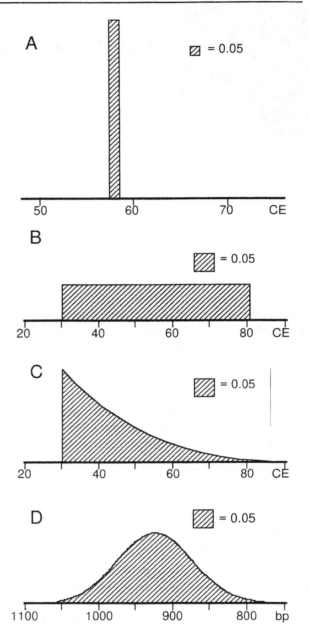

Figure 15.1. Four different models to represent dates. A — a point estimate of AD 58, B — a uniform distribution for the date range AD 30-80, C — a terminus post quem of AD 30, and D — a date of 925 ± 60 bp.

calls this kind of dating bias a **hiatus** (figure 15.2). Second, the outermost ring may not even be the last ring formed before the tree was cut. Possibly the outer part of the timber was planed down before use, or possibly the outermost rings were burned off in a fire. Dean calls this

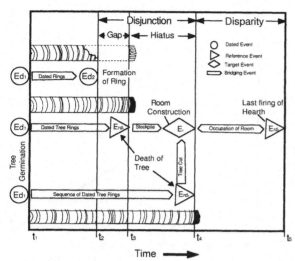

Figure 15.2. Different kinds of dating discrepancies. Disjunction leads to overestimating the age of the target event; disparity leads to underestimate (after Dean, 1978:227).

kind of bias a **gap**, representing the length of time between the formation of the dated ring and the cutting of the tree. The gap and hiatus in combination lead to what Dean calls a **disjunction**. Both gap and hiatus will lead the incautious archaeologist to overestimate the age of the room's construction. But there are also ways we can underestimate that age. Suppose we have not been careful in our choice of the piece of wood we dated, and it comes, not from a roof beam used in the original construction of the room, but from wood used much later in room repair, or even as fuel in the room's hearth. In that case the dated event (formation of the outermost tree ring) could be decades later than the target event, leading to the dating bias that Dean calls a **disparity** (figure 15.2).

Similarly, suppose our target event is the deposit of a particular sediment, and our dated event is the last firing of a pot, sherds of which occurred in the sediment. If the sherds are residual, then we could have quite a large hiatus, while, if they are infiltrated, we could have a significant disparity. For radiocarbon dates, disjunction (overestimates) can result from contamination of samples by very old carbon or from dating large pieces of charcoal whose rings could be much older than the target event, while disparity (underestimates) can result from contamination by modern carbon. We can largely

avoid disparities and disjunctions in radiocarbon dates by careful selection of material for dating (*short-lived* material, such as nuts and seeds, are preferable to charcoal from long-lived trees), by avoiding contamination during sample collection, and by careful separation of the carbon of interest from potential contaminants. Modern radiocarbon dating by accelerator mass spectrometry (AMS) makes it much easier for us to date small samples, such as seeds.

What are Radiocarbon "Dates"?

Most archaeologists recognize that radiocarbon years are not the same as calendar years. In fact, radiocarbon dates are technically not dates at all, but simply measures of ^{14}C content. Although the typical measurement is reported in a way that looks like a date in "years before present" (the "present" was standardized as AD 1950), there are several reasons why it differs from a true age. First, radiocarbon dates are calculated using an obsolete measurement of ^{14}C meanlife, 8033 years, even though it is now known more accurately as 8266 years. Second, the ^{14}C content in the atmosphere has varied over the millennia. Third, the ^{13}C and ^{14}C content of living organisms, such as trees, is not the same as that of the atmosphere, so an isotope fractionation correction is necessary. In addition, the reservoir of ^{14}C in the oceans ("marine reservoir") also differs from the atmosphere, so marine samples require a different correction. Consequently, it is only when we calibrate the radiocarbon "date" by reference to measurements on samples of known age, such as tree rings, that the ^{14}C measurement can be converted into a date.

Radiocarbon measurements are reported either in "radiocarbon years" BP or in pMC (percent Modern Carbon). These are just two different units for measuring the same thing, the relative abundance of ^{14}C in the sample. An error estimate after the ± sign accompanies the measurement. This expresses the fact, based on sampling theory, that the actual amount of ^{14}C in the sample has about a 68% chance of lying within the error range. Note that radiocarbon dates should *not* be reported in radiocarbon years BC. 1 BC is not at all equivalent to 1950 BP, so subtracting 1950 from an uncalibrated date makes no sense and leads to quite misleading impressions of age.

Archaeologists should always report the uncalibrated radiocarbon date (the BP date), as it never changes, no matter how the calibrations are updated and revised. If they want to talk about ages, however, they need to use calibrated dates, at least during the range (more than 10,000 years now) over which this is possible. The international Radiocarbon Working Group adopted "cal BC" and "cal AD" as the conventional units for calibrated radiocarbon dates. As we will see below, the calibrated dates are usually given as ranges expressing confidence limits. That is to say, a date of 1000-1150 cal AD might indicate 95% confidence that the sample dates within this range. Some archaeology journals, however, have their own conventions, such as using lower-case "bp" to indicate a measurement in radiocarbon years and BC/AD or BCE/CE for calendar years. The journals may also specify what version of the tree-ring calibration you must use, and this is not always, unfortunately, the most up-to-date one. The most important thing is to make clear to your reader what sort of "date" you are reporting.

Date Calibration

As we noted above, radiocarbon dates are measured in radiocarbon years, not calendar years, and there is no one-to-one correlation between radiocarbon measurements and calendar dates. Fortunately there are long tree-ring sequences that allow us to convert radiocarbon years into calendar years for events of the last 10,000 years, and scientists are constantly pushing back that boundary with data from corals, **varves,** and ice as well as tree rings (e.g., Geyh and Schlüchter, 1998; Jöris and Weninger, 1998; Kitagawa and van der Plicht, 1998).

Thank to this research, the data set on which calibrated dates are based is constantly changing. Since 1981, the radiocarbon community has released several updated data sets, originally in the journal, *Radiocarbon,* and since 1986 these have been available electronically. The 1998 Radiocarbon conference in Groningen led to the release of a much improved data set for terres-

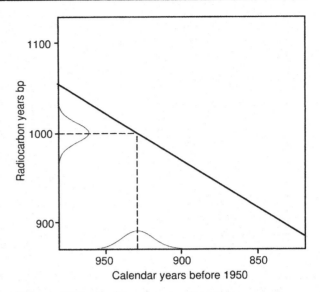

Figure 15.3. Radiocarbon calibration assuming a linear relationship between radiocarbon years and calendar years. Note that both distributions are normal, but the breadth of the calibrated probability distribution depends on the slope of the line.

trial samples (INTCAL98) down to 22,000 cal BC, a set for marine samples (MARINE98), and a special single-year interval set (UWSY98) used for "wiggle-matching" in particularly knotty parts of the calibration curve after 1510 cal AD. These are published in the special calibration issue of the journal, *Radiocarbon* 40.

We can make use of the radiocarbon calibration in a crude, manual way. If radiocarbon abundances had been constant in the past, rather than fluctuating, and the calibration line were known with certainty, a plot of radiocarbon years against calendar years would be linear, as in figure 15.3, correcting only for the errors in meanlife and fractionation. For any given radiocarbon measurement we could simply draw a line from its mean, across to the calibration line, and then down to the calendar scale to read off the calibrated date. Not only would the radiocarbon measurement's probability distribution be normal, the calibrated date's probability distribution would also be normal. Depending on the slope of the calibration line, the calibrated age would be greater than, equal to, or less than the value of the radiocarbon measure.

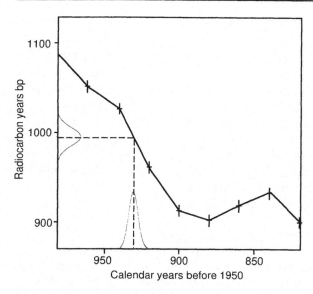

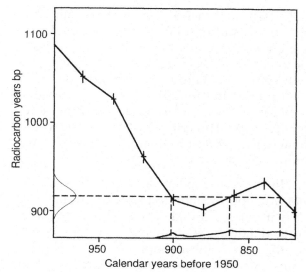

Figure 15.4. A more realistic radiocarbon calibration with short line segments joining the "knots" from radiocarbon determinations on samples of known date. Because the segment where the radiocarbon date intersects the curve is straight and steep, the calibrated date is very precise and approximately normal.

Figure 15.5. Another radiocarbon date with the same standard deviation as in 14.4 but intersecting a fairly flat area of the calibration curve with a "wiggle." The resulting calibrated date distribution is much broader and multimodal because there are three intersections.

But radiocarbon calibrations are not linear. If we plot the known, calendar ages against their radiocarbon ages as in figures 15.4 and 15.5, not only is there a range of error (confidence interval) around the resulting curve, because it is based on dates that have statistical errors, but the slope of the curve changes rapidly and frequently between the "knots" at the data points. In some places the slope is steep, in others it is fairly "flat." There are even places where the curve changes direction altogether, so that a line drawn from a radiocarbon date would intersect the calibration curve in more than one place (figure 15.5). As a result, the probability distribution of the calibrated date is not even close to a normal distribution. If we are lucky, however, and the slope of the calibration curve is steep, the calibrated date will have a narrower probability distribution, so that the region representing, say, our 68% confidence limits, will be smaller than the region delimited by the standard errors on the radiocarbon date. In this case, an error of ± 70 radiocarbon years may result in a 68% high density interval of only ± 40 or 50 years. If we are unlucky, and the radiocarbon date intersects a relatively flat region of the

calibration curve, or intersects it more than once, the original ± 70 radiocarbon years may correspond with a calibrated date with 68% confidence interval of ± 200 years or more.

This relationship between the slope of the calibration curve and the precision of calibrated dates has important implications for archaeologists. Most radiocarbon labs give you the option to request "high-precision" dates, with significantly smaller standard errors, but at significantly greater cost. Because the precision of the date is proportional to the square root of the sample size, cutting the error in half would require a counting time that is four times as long, or using four times as many targets in AMS dating. Since the cost of the radiocarbon date is roughly proportional to counting time, you would not request a high-precision radiocarbon date unless you were confident that it would lead to a higher precision in the calibrated date. Before making the decision to request a high-precision date, therefore, you should examine the calibration curve in the region you would expect the date to fall. Is the curve fairly steep and monotonic (sloping consistently) in that region? If so, your high-precision radiocarbon date has a good chance of leading to a calibrated date with equal or even higher precision. If that region of the curve is fairly flat or very wiggly, however, it is likely that your calibrated date will come out with a very broad probability distribution and multiple modes, results little better than you would have had with a measurement of normal precision. In that case you would be wiser to request normal precision and save money for other dates.

In practice, modern archaeologists would not attempt to calibrate radiocarbon dates by drawing lines on graphs of the calibration curve. Instead they use computer programs that work out the probability distributions of the calibrated dates when the calibration curve, radiocarbon measurements, and their standard errors are known (see below).

Comparing Dates

Since radiocarbon dates are really the means of statistical samples, we should never expect a single date to give us entirely satisfactory results. After all, while there is roughly a 68% chance that the "true" abundance of ^{14}C in the sample lies between the standard errors, there is also a hefty 32% chance that it lies outside them. Consequently, some archaeologists try to be more conservative by citing "two-sigma" errors that indicate the 95% confidence interval of the BP measurement. A more useful, if somewhat expensive, approach is to date the same target event with several radiocarbon dates. Not only does this help to weed out cases where residual carbon has led to disjunction, but we can have more confidence in our our date estimates when our sample size has increased by using the pooled mean of dates that are not anomalous (Ward and Wilson, 1978; 1981).

Consequently, when we do have more than one radiocarbon measure from the same deposit, we usually want to test the dates to see if they probably represent separate age estimates for the same event. That is, are the differences between them due only to the vagaries of chance? Because we can model the probability distributions of radiocarbon dates, it is very easy to answer this question statistically. For pairs of uncalibrated dates we could use the Z-test, because the sample size for radiocarbon measure-

ments is typically thousands of ^{14}C atoms or hundreds of radioactive decays, and the uncalibrated measure is normally distributed.

For example, at the Late Neolithic site of Tabaqat al-Buma, in Wadi Ziqlab, Jordan, two different pieces of wood charcoal from locus 026 (a stratigraphic deposit) were dated. The results appear in table 15.1. Can we reasonably expect both these dates to be good estimates for the date when locus 026 was deposited? Or should we conclude that one of the samples, at least, is on residual material?

Table 15.1. Radiocarbon determinations on two different samples of wood charcoal from Tabaqat al-Buma, Jordan. Note that the calibrated dates represent the 68.3% confidence intervals. Dates by IsoTrace, Toronto

Area	Locus	Sample	BP	Error	Date cal BC
E33	026	TO-4277	6490	70	5445-5330
E33	026	TO-3409	6900	70	5831-5649

The difference between the two uncalibrated measures is 6900-6490 = 410 radiocarbon years, and the standard errors are equal, 70 years. Standardizing this difference in units of standard errors (Z scores), then, gives us the following.

$$Z = \frac{6900\text{-}6490}{\sqrt{70^2 + 70^2}} = \frac{410}{\sqrt{9800}} = \frac{410}{98.99} = 4.14$$

That is, the difference is 4.14 times the size of the pooled standard error, a result that is very unlikely by chance alone. In fact, the probability of getting a difference this large by chance is much less than 0.001 (it should happen less than once in 1000 trials). We would conclude that the two samples probably do not pertain to the same event, and that the second sample is probably on residual material, leading to a disjunction. Unless we have reason to suspect infiltration by the younger charcoal, we would then prefer a date close to 5445-5330 cal BC.

Had our test instead shown that the two dates were in substantial agreement (e.g., Z value of only 0.2), we could have averaged the two radiocarbon measurements to provide a pooled estimate and then carried out a calibra-

Table 15.2. Example of output of the CALIB program

Calibration file: INTCAL93314C
Listing file: ziqlabtxt
TO2117 G402
CHARCOAL
Radiocarbon Age bp 1680 ± 60
Calibrated age cal AD 397
Cal AD/BC age ranges obtained from intercepts (Method A):
  one Sigma** cal AD 264 -282 328 - 428
  two Sigma** cal AD 238 - 539

Summary of above:
minimum of cal age ranges (cal ages) maximum of cal age ranges:
  1å   cal AD 264 (397) 428
  2å   cal AD 238 (397) 539
cal AD/BC age ranges (cal ages as above) from probability distribution (Method B):

% area enclosed	cal AD age ranges	relative area under prob distribution
68.3 (1å)	cal AD 259-291	0.17
	322-434	0.83
95.4 (2å)	cal AD 246-533	1.0

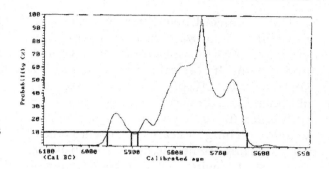

Figure 15.6. Example of output from the IsoTrace lab in Toronto, showing the total integrated probability of the calibration result for a radiocarbon date of 6900 ± 70 bp. To find the 90% confidence interval, we would extend a horizontal line from 10% on the y-axis and then down from where this line intersects the curve, as shown.

tion. There could still be a disjuction, but we hope it is small. In that case we would also need to use a pooled estimate of the standard error, which can already be found in the denominator of the Z equation, here about 99 years.

Note that, because the Z-test assumes normal distributions, we had to use *uncalibrated* radiocarbon measurements for the comparison. If we wanted to compare the calibrated dates directly, we could do so with a different kind of probablity analysis. Such analysis is available in some of the software used to calibrate dates.

Radiocarbon Software

Today there are at least six software packages that archaeologists can use to calibrate radiocarbon measurements and to manipulate the results. All of these depend on the calibration data sets released by the radiocarbon community, which needs to be up-to-date. At time of writing, they were beginning to use the 1998 INTCAL98 data set (Stuiver et al. 1998). Currently, all these programs are based on some form of probability analysis, use the same data sets, and can calibrate both terrestrial and marine samples.

Because the probability distributions of the radiocarbon measurements are known, we can determine the total probability of all the measurements by multiplying the individual probabilities together with the aim of finding the most probable age solutions. The computer programs show these solutions as peaks in a probability curve, which constitute the best estimates of date on the basis of the data, and assuming no bias (such as disparity or disjunction or contamination). The curves that the programs display also give you an indication of how probability declines away from these best estimates, but the programs differ in exactly how they display this.

A very popular calibration program is University of Washington's CALIB program, now in version 4 (Stuiver and Reimer, 1998). When you enter a radiocarbon date and its standard error, the program will use equations for the small line segments joining the "knots" in the calibration curve to work out the posterior probabilities of each possible calendar date. The computer's output displays the values representing the most probable dates as well as one or more ranges of dates that indicate the 68% and 95% high-density regions (table 15.2). In other words, it indicates that there is a 68% probability that the correct calendar date falls within one range, and a 95% probability that it falls within a broader range, of dates. It has some special features for marine dates.

The Groningen University radiocarbon laboratory offers a software package, CAL25 (van der Plicht, 1998), for MSDOS or Windows operating systems. It does calibrations in much the same way as CALIB, providing probability distributions in calibrated AD/BC years for any radiocarbon (bp) date you enter. It also will use "wiggle matching" for cases where very precise date estimates are necessary. A key stroke allows users to switch between the Groningen and Seattle (CALIB) methods.

Oxford University offers a software package that calibrates radiocarbon dates and aids in their interpretation, called OxCal 3.2 (Bronk Ramsey, 1998b), which works with Windows 95. It has a number of useful features, including the ability to simulate a radiocarbon date calibration for a particular calendar date. This allows us to see, in advance, whether or not a radiocarbon date is likely to give us a precise, unique solution to a dating problem. It also has features relevant to the next section, such as a "chronological query language" to define models and Bayesian methods to combine evidence from radiocarbon dates with that from coins or inscriptions, stratigraphic order, and tree-ring sequences, or to evaluate *termini post quem* and *termini ante quem* (Bronk Ramsey, 1998a). Combining the evidence of many radiocarbon dates is also an option. The program comes with an excellent manual (Bronk Ramsey 1998c) that provides many useful tips on the interpretation of dating evidence.

The IsoTrace laboratories in Toronto uses its own software, C14CAL, to provide its clients with a display of the integrated absolute probability (therefore ranging from 0 to 1.0) as well as the usual probability ranges (figure 15.6). Note that the curves touch the top of the box that encloses the distribution and that the y-axis indicates probability ranging from 0 to 1.0. Where the curves touch the top of the graph corresponds to the intersect, or intersects, with the calibration curve (as in figure 15.5). To use this graph to find, for example, the 90% confidence interval for the date, you would draw a horizontal line from 0.1 on the y-axis (i.e., 1.0 - 0.90) and find where it intersects the curve. Drawing ver-

tical lines from these intersects to the x-axis allows you to find the interval. It provides some special features for marine dates, and corrections for cavewater and stalagmites. C14CAL is not available for general use.

Combining Radiocarbon and Stratigraphic Evidence

In the last chapter, there was brief mention that Bayesian statistical modelling allowed us to take stratigraphic information into account while seriating assemblages. Bayesian methods for combining probabilities are what lies behind the programs just mentioned (Buck et al., 1996). Where Bayesian methods really come into their own is in combining the radiocarbon information with other dating information. In particular, where stratigraphic information or historical evidence is available, we can use the known ordering of stratigraphic units or known dates as constraints on the calibrated radiocarbon dates (Bronk Ramsey 1995; Buck et al., 1991). Intuitively, this makes sense, especially where the calibrated probability distributions are multi-modal. Sometimes the stratigraphic information makes some of the calibrated modes much less probable.

For example, consider the multilinear stratigraphic matrix in figure 15. 7, taken from Buck et al. (1996). We can represent the stratigraphic relationships by series of inequalities, assuming that the ">" sign means "older than," and θ represents the calendar date.

$$\theta_{758} > \theta_{814} > \theta_{1235} > \theta_{358} > \theta_{813} > \theta_{1210},$$

$$\theta_{493} > \theta_{358},$$

$$\theta_{925} > \theta_{923} > \theta_{358}, \text{ and}$$

$$\theta_{1168} > \theta_{358}.$$

These relationships impose constraints on the possible *combinations* of dates. For example, because the stratigraphic evidence indicates that unit 358 must be older than unit 813, we could conclude that the calibrated date on unit 358 should also be earlier than that on unit 813. One way to model the calibration in a way that takes these stratigraphic constraints into account is to use a Gibbs sampler or Monte Carlo simulation

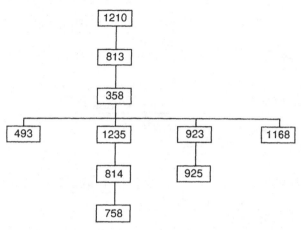

Figure 15.7. Harris matrix showing the stratigraphic relationships of contexts at the site of St. Veit-Klinglberg, Austria (after Buck et al., 1996:431).

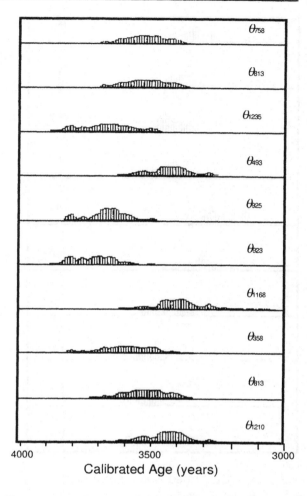

Figure 15.8. Posterior probability distributions for calibrations of the St. Veit-Klinglberg dates without considering stratigraphic information (after Buck et al., 1994:435).

methods (Buck et al. 1991; 1996; Buck, Litton and Scott 1994). The simulation program takes a calibrated date for one of the contexts, uses that as a constraint on the possible calibrated dates for the other contexts, takes one of those dates and uses it as a constraint in recalculating the calibration, and repeats many times before arriving at an estimated probability distribution. The final output may require thousands of iterations.

The results of this process can be quite startling. Note the differences between the probability distributions for the plain calibrations (figure 15.8) and stratigraphically constrained calibrations (figure 15.9) for the contexts shown in the stratigraphic matrix of figure 15.7. The very broad probability distributions in the former have been replaced with much narrower distributions that are more precise hypotheses about the contexts' dates.

Other ways in which Bayesian methods can help with the use of radiocarbon dates include estimating the time duration between stratigraphic units (Buck, Christen, et al. 1994) and of the boundaries between periods in a regional chronology (Buck et al. 1996). The latter is particularly important when there is some disagreement over whether the "periods" are really sequential, overlap slightly, or have gaps between them (figure 15.10).

Summary

Radiocarbon dating has become the premiere method for dating organic remains of the last 50,000 years, and sophisticated calibration by reference to tree-ring sequences allows us to convert radiocarbon years into calendar years for samples less than 24,000 years old. Slope changes and "wiggles" in the calibration curve can result in either very precise estimates of the calendar date or only very broad date estimates. Careful selection of datable material and the chronological constraints imposed, for example, by stratigraphic relationships can result in much better chronological control than archaeologists would have imagined only a decade ago.

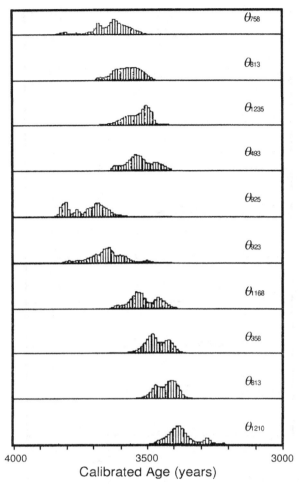

Figure 15.9. Posterior probability distributions for the calibrated St. Veit-Klinglberg dates with prior stratigraphic information considered (after Buck et al., 1994:466).

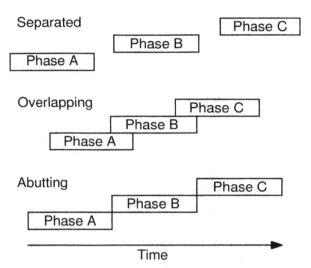

Figure 15.10. Schematic of three different models for archaeological phasing. Top—gaps between phases, middle — overlap between phases, and bottom — abutting phases (after Buck et al., 1996:218).

References Cited

Aitken, M. J., 1990, *Science-based Dating in Archaeology*. Longman, New York.

Bayliss, A., and Orton, C., 1994, Strategic considerations in dating, or 'How many dates do I need?' *Institute of Archaeology Bulletin* 31:151-67.

Bowman, S., 1990, *Radiocarbon Dating*. University of California Press, Los Angeles.

Bronk Ramsey, C. B., 1995, Radiocarbon calibration and analysis of stratigraphy: The OxCal program. *Radiocarbon* 72:425-30.

— 1998a, Probability and dating. *Radiocarbon* 40:461-74.

— 1998b, OxCal Program [www document]. URL http://info.ox.ac.uk/departments/rlaha/xcal/oxcal_h.html

— 1998c, Radicarbon calibration. Radiocarbon WEB-Info [www document]. URL http://units.ox.ac.uk/departments/rlaha/calib.html

Buck, C. E., Cavanagh, W. G., and Litton, C. D., 1996, *Bayesian Approach to Interpreting Archaeological Data*. John Wiley & Sons, New York.

Buck, C. E., Christen, J. A., Kenworthy, J. B., and Litton, C. D., 1994a, Estimating the duration of archaeological activity using ^{14}C determinations. *Oxford Journal of Archaeology* 133:229-40.

Buck, C. E., Kenworthy, J. B., Litton, C D., and Smith, A. F. M., 1991, Combining archaeological and radiocarbon information: A Bayesian approach to calibration. *Antiquity* 65:808-21.

Buck, C. E., Litton, C D., and Scott, E. M., 1994b, Making the most of radiocarbon dating: some statistical considerations. *Antiquity* 68:252-63.

Buck, C. E., Litton, C D., and Smith, A. F. M., 1992, Calibration of radiocarbon results pertaining to related archaeological events. *Journal of Archaeological Science* 19:497-512.

Dean, J. S., 1978, Independent dating in archaeological analysis. *Advances in Archaeological Method and Theory* 1:223-55.

Geyh, M., and C. Schlüchter, C., 1998, Calibration of the ^{14}C time scale beyond 22,000 BP. *Radiocarbon* 40:475-82.

Jöris, O., and Weninger, B., 1998, Extension of the ^{14}C calibration curve to ca. 40,000 cal BC by synchronizing Greenland ^{18}O/^{16}O ice core record and North Atlantic foraminifera profiles: A compariston with U/Th coral data. *Radiocarbon* 40:495-504.

Kitagawa, H., and van der Plicht, J., 1998, A 40,000-year varve chronology from Lake Suigetsu, Japan: Extension of the ^{14}C calibration curve. *Radiocarbon* 40:505-15.

Manning, S. W., and Weninger, B., 1992, A light in the dark: Archaeological wiggle matching and the absolute chronology of the close of the Aegean Late Bronze Age. *Antiquity* 66:636-63.

Orton, C., 1980, *Mathematics in Archaeology*. Cambridge University Press, Cambridge.

Stuiver, M., and Reimer, P., 1998, 1998 CALIB Version 4.0 [computer software]. URL http://depts.washington.edu/qil/

Stuiver, M., Reimer, P., and Braziunas, T., 1998, High-precision radiocarbon age calibration for terrestrial and marine samples. *Radiocarbon* 40:1127-51.

Stuiver, M., Reimer, P., Bard, E., Beck, J. W., Burr, G., Hughen, K., Kromer, B., McCormac, G., van der Plicht, J., and Spurk, M., 1998,. INTCAL98 radiocarbon age calibration, 24,000-0 cal BP. *Radiocarbon* 40:1041-83.

Taylor, R. E., 1987, *Radiocarbon Dating: An Archaeological Perspective*. Academic Press, Orlando.

van der Plicht, J., 1998, The Groningen Calibration Program Version CAL25 [computer software]. URL http://www.cio.phys.rug.nl/html-docs/carbon14/cal25.html

Ward, G. K., and Wilson, S. R., 1978, Procedures for comparing and combining radiocarbon age determinations: A critique. *Archaeometry* 20:19-39.

— 1981, Evaluation and clustering of radiocarbon age determinations: Procedures and paradigms. *Archaeometry* 23:19-39.

16 Archaeological Illustration

Archaeologists frequently use **graphical information language** to describe artifacts and other archaeological phenomena in a consistent way. Drawings of lithics, pottery, plans, and stratigraphic sections are not realistic or artistic renderings of what the artist sees, but are technical drawings that present a *selection* of information that some archaeologist considers important, while omitting many details (in fact, an infinity of them) that she or he considers less relevant to the research at hand. This is not to say that the selection of information is arbitrary; in fact, archaeologists employ a wide range of conventions for the minimal information that they expect to find in an archaeological illustration. For some kinds of archaeological observations, such as those on lithics, these conventions are fairly well developed. For others, there is less agreement on conventions. In any case, it is important for archaeological publications to include clear keys that explain what these conventions are.

Today it is increasingly common for archaeologists to use computers and graphical software to produce illustrations. We will discuss some general aspects of computer graphics later in this chapter, but it is still important to have basic facility with hand-drawn illustration. For one thing, you are likely to find yourself at some point needing illustrations when, either because of field conditions or some unforseen problem,

you are unable to use a computer. For example, you may have the unexpected opportunity to catalogue a small but really important collection of artifacts in some out-of-the-way museum while travelling without your computer. Drawing, photographing, and recording them now may save you a costly return trip. You do not have to be a great artist to produce a useful archaeological illustration, but you do need to have patience and some basic skills that are not too difficult to learn.

Early Archaeological Illustration

Early archaeological illustrations were much less conventional and more "artistic" than is usual today, with more emphasis on aesthetics than information content. Indeed, some (e.g., figure 16.1) use depictions of artifacts more as decoration than as visual support for the text, or sacrifice accuracy for romanticism.

Nonetheless, many early illustrations of ancient architecture, pottery, metal artifacts, and sculptures provide useful evidence for archaeological finds that, in many cases, have been damaged or have disappeared. Thanks to illustrators who attempted to provide realistic depictions, we can sometimes recognize attributes that the illustrators themselves might never have considered to be archaeologically important.

Styles of Representation and Basic Conventions

Archaeological illustrators of all stripes adhere to a number of conventions, while also varying considerably in illustrating style.

One of the first things you should do if you are about to illustrate a number of artifacts, plans, or sections from a project is to decide what styles you will use. Consistency in style will make the published drawings, indeed the whole publication, look much better, and also facilitates comparison of the items depicted. It is also important that the style *encodes information* that you want to convey to your audience. For example, will stippling indicate cortex on a stone tool, "sickle sheen" polish, or post-depositional damage? Will hatching indicate slip on a pot, red paint, or burnishing? Will reconstructed portions of broken objects be indicated by dashed lines, dotted lines, or grey lines? For some elements that you will use regularly, such as scales and north arrows, it is useful to make up masters that can be copied easily, whether on computer or tranfers (such as Letratone™). You also need to decide what line thicknesses to use for various purposes, taking care to remember that your drawings will probably be reduced in size.

For all types of artifact illustration, artifacts are depicted as they would look with light raking down on them from the upper left, at an angle of about 45°. This ensures that all the artifacts illustrated on a single page will be illuminated in a consistent way, facilitating comparison and making the page look more unified.

For maps and plans, it is usually best to keep North more-or-less at the top, unless you have strong reason, such as orienting buildings consistently with the door at the bottom, to do otherwise.

Basic Equipment and Supplies

Although many kinds of equipment can be helpful for archaeological illustration, some are essential. Among these is a high-intensity lamp (*not* a fluorescent lamp) to illuminate details on artifacts and create sharp shadows, and a magnifying glass to examine small details on them. A magnifyer with a large lens, some 10 cm

Figure 16.1. Illustration of vessels from British and Irish archaeological sites (Camden, 1806:plate 206).

across, is best, ideally mounted on a base or swinging arm that allows you to position it with your hands free to hold artifacts. Other tools you should have are good calipers for taking measurements on artifacts, preferably with plastic "jaws" that will not mar the artifacts' surfaces when in contact with them, metal straight-edges, preferably with bevelled edges or raised up on cork bases so that ink will not bleed along them, a drafting table and stool adjusted to comfortable working heights, a guillotine-type paper cutter, plastic triangles, good scissors, x-acto knives and carpet knives, and, of course, technical pencils and drawing pens. Technical pencils that accept 0.5 mm 5H leads work well for most applications. Drawing pens are typically Staedtler or Koh-i-Noor Rapidograph™ pens with an ink cartridge that accepts Pelican™ or similar inks and a fine, tubular point in various sizes that draws the ink onto the paper. Most graphic supply stores sell such pens in sets with pens of various sizes from 000 or 00 up to 3 or 4

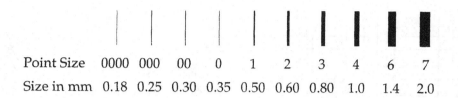

Figure 16.2. Table of point sizes for technical pens.

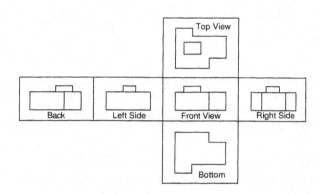

Figure 16.3. Orthographic projection of a simple shape (after Jensen and Mason, 1963:34).

(see figure 16.2). Because most archaeological illustrations are reduced for publication, you will use the larger pen sizes of 1, 3, and 4 most often. For some applications that require a variable line thickness, you should have a quill-type pen with a variety of nibs.

Equipment needs to be maintained in order to operate properly. Technical pens clog very easily and should be cleaned out after use if you do not immediately anticipate using them again. Clean them with great care, as it is easy to damage the tiny wire that transmits the ink.

In addition, you will need supplies. These include replacement leads for the pencils, ink, pen cleaner, plastic erasers, drawing paper (vellum, mylar™, or Strathmore™ single-ply), blades for the x-acto knife, drafting tape (similar to masking tape), frosted transparent tape, Pounce™ powder for keeping the drawing surface clean and dry, and lint-free, cocktail-size paper napkins. It is also extremely useful to have pencils in "nonphoto blue" or "drop-out

blue" so that you put labels on drawings that will not show up when the drawings are reproduced, Mylar™ "photo-file" pages, file folders or large manila envelopes in which to sort and store drawings, large pads of layout paper with nonphoto blue grid, and glue sticks. If you will be labelling the drawings directly, rather than on the computer, you should have Letraset™ transfer letters. You will need a variety of point sizes of the last item, and should keep in mind that the point sizes should be large enough that they do not disappear or become illegible when the illustration is reduced to publication size.

For computer graphics you should have some kind of scanner, preferably a flat-bed scanner of at least 300 dpm resolution, or a large digitizing tablet, and software that allows you to trace bit-mapped graphics from scanned images with mouse or stylus to create vector-based graphics (more on this below). You should also have a plotter or laser printer with which to print test output of your drawings and plenty of disk-storage capacity; graphics tend to take up a lot of disk space.

Lithic Illustration

An excellent guide for lithics illustration is Addington (1986). This section only introduces concepts with which she deals in considerable detail. It is important to note that producing a good lithic illustration requires basic knowledge of lithics, including the ability to distinguish the various surfaces, bulbs, platforms, burin blows, retouch, polish, and so on (chapter 8).

One of the first steps is to orient the piece. Lithics illustrations conventionally include views of the dorsal (left) and ventral (right) surfaces, sometimes with a side view between them and

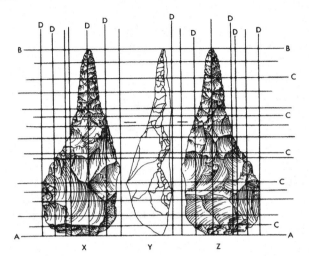

Figure 16.4. A "selective grid" used to ensure that features appearing in several adjacent views are correctly lined up (Addington, 1986).

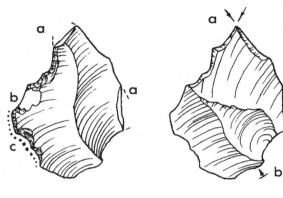

Figure 16.5. Conventions for broken (left, a), bag-retouched (left, b), and abraded (left, c) damage; and for burin blows (right, a) and atypical position of bulb (right, b) (Addington, 1986).

with end views below and above. For flakes and blades, the proximal end, where the bulb and platform would occur, is at the bottom. Bifaces (handaxes), points, drills, awls, and other pointed tools are always shown point up even when the pointed end is proximal (Addington, 1986:43, 46). Cores are oriented with a platform at the top, while choppers are shown with the cutting edge at top, burins so that the burin blows point downward, and endscrapers with the retouch at the top (Addington, 1986:44-48). The articulation of the various views in the drawing (dorsal, profile, ventral, etc.) follows standard drafting conventions by which the views can be "folded" into their correct orientation. This is called **orthographic projection**, in which each view shows the surface nearest to it in an adjacent view, but from an angle that differs by 90° (figure 16.3).

First, you will need to draw the outline of the artifact in either its dorsal or ventral view (one is simply the mirror image of the other). You should *not* do this by lying a flake on a piece of paper and tracing around it with a paper for at least two reasons. One is that even a fairly sharp pencil will add thickness to your tracing and, if the pencil edge is not exactly vertical, there will also be parallax that will distort your tracing. In either case the tracing will not be accurate and will usually tend to exaggerate the flake's size. The other reason is that your pencil will cause

edge damage to the flake that could destroy evidence for use wear or retouch in later analysis. Instead, draw a thin, near-vertical line on which you will line up two landmarks, such as pointy protrusions or small points of retouch, one near the top (distal end) and one near the bottom (proximal end), use the calipers on the artifact to establish the distance between these two landmarks, and transfer this distance to marks on your near-vertical line. With a transparent straight-edge, lined up on these two landmarks, you may be able to find a third landmark near the center of the flake, such as the junction of several flake scars on the dorsal surface, that is on the line running between the first two. Then you can measure with the calipers at right angles to the first line to establish the position of landmarks on the left and right edges relative to the central landmark. Alternatively, you may want to lay the flake on a piece of graph paper so that the first two landmarks are on a line, and then draw dots at landmarks along the edge while holding the flake close to the paper, and then filling in between the dots by eye. You can then use the outline twice (trace it in reverse) to fill in the details of the dorsal and ventral surfaces.

When drawing the dorsal surface, you need to pay close attention to the direction from which flakes were struck off, as the inked drawing

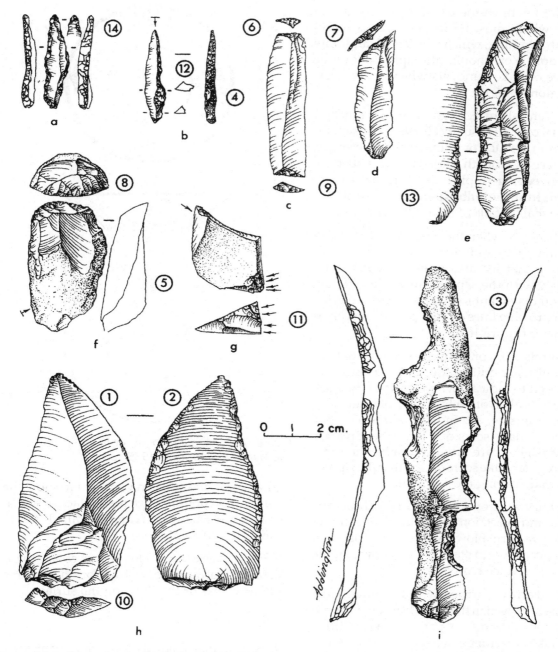

Figure 16.6. Example of a lithic plate with multiple views and correct orientation (Addington, 1986).

must have curved lines, imitating the ripples on flaked flint or glass, that extend away from the point of percussion like ripples in a pond (figures 16.5, 16.6). On fine-grained materials, these ripples are generally shown smooth; on coarse materials, such as quartz or quartzite, or on badly weathered pieces, they are often shown discontinuous, in an attempt to give an impression of the rougher surface. For the smoother cases, skilled lithic illustrators often use a quill pen to ink the ripples because it allows them to start out with a fairly thick line and gradually thin it until it disappears part-way across the flake scar. This tends to result in lithic illustrations that look very three-dimensional, as long as it is done with the left-raking light convention in mind. Sometimes there is cortex on the dorsal surface, which most lithic conventions represent with stippling, which consists of randomly placed dots. You should attempt to show the sequence of flake removals wherever possible (Addington, 1986:14).

The ventral surface can be drawn much as the dorsal one, but usually shows fewer details. Apart from retouch or damage near the edges, the surface is smooth and will need to have broad, sweeping ripples inked in that extend outwards from the bulb of percussion. Be sure to include small details of the bulb and platform.

Particularly when the edges are retouched, it is common to add side and end views. To make sure that features in each view line up accurately with the same feature in a different view, you may want to make a "selective grid" in nonrepro blue lines or light pencil that can be erased later (figure 16.4).

A number of conventions for edge details, and the like, are quite important. Dashed lines can be used to indicate where parts of the flake have been broken off, while rows of large dots, graduated in size, can indicate abrasion. "Bag retouch" — flake scars due to post-excavation edge damage — are often indicated the same way as regular flake scars except that the ripples are omitted, leaving the scar white.

On burins, arrows are used to indicate the position and direction of burin blows (figure 16.5). Where burin blows were closely spaced, it is often necessary to stagger the arrows on the drawing to reduce crowding.

Barred arrows, arrows with a "T"-like bar at their base, are used in the dorsal view to indicate the position of the bulb of percussion and direction of flake detachment whenever those are not in the "usual" position at the very bottom of the drawing and oriented vertically. This usually happens on pointed tools that are oriented point-up, shifting the bulb away from the bottom position.

Dash-like line segments between multiple views of the same piece often facilitate orientation of one view to another, although this is usually not necessary unless you deviate from the normal orthographic projection. The dashes

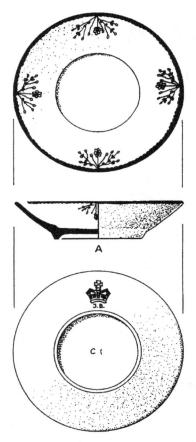

Figure 16.7. A china bowl from an historic site (Newlands and Breede, 1976:135).

are more important when you need to show the location of sections *through* the artifact, in which case they are usually short and are called "ticks" (Addington, 1986:24-25).

Sometimes conventions are necessary to indicate thermal damage, such as pot-lid fractures and fine cracks or crackling on the surface.

Pottery Illustration

Although archaeological illustrations of pottery up to the mid-19th century depicted vessels, whether whole or fragmentary, much as they would look to a person viewing them from the outside (figure 16.1), modern pottery illustrations conventionally depict the interior, exterior, and vertical section of the pot simultaneously (figures 16.7, 16.8). In addition, for sherds they reconstruct as much as possible of the whole shape of the pot rather than just the sherd itself.

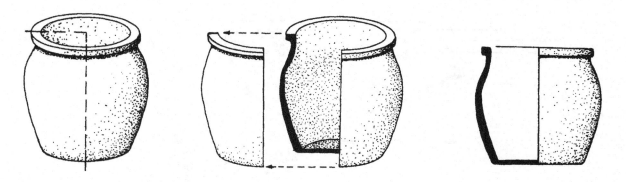

Figure 16.8. Conventional pottery illustrations are based on the concept of cutting away a quarter-section of a whole pot, although in reality the drawings are usually reconstructed from fragments (Newlands and Breede, 1976:127).

The drawing is divided in half, so that the exterior of the pot appears on one side, while the other is a cutaway view of the interior and a vertical section through the wall of the pot. Some archaeological projects (most European ones) follow the convention of putting the cutaway on the left, while others (most American ones) put it on the right. The reconstruction of the pot extends from the rim downward as far as the lowest point on the sherd, but omits the base, as there is no evidence for the form of the pot's lower portion. Sometimes a drawing of a sherd's outline is superimposed on the technical drawing to show how much was reconstructed. It may not be obvious exactly how such a reconstruction is accomplished, so let us examine the steps.

The first thing to do is to establish the inside diameter of the pot at its rim, assuming that the pot is circular in plan. Of course this will not work for pots that are oval, rectangular, or irregular in plan. For most pots, however, diameter is easily determined with a diameter chart and the sherd held "at stance" (see p. 162). Once determined, this diameter becomes the length of a horizontal line segment, the **stance line**, drawn on a piece of vellum or tracing paper, and the line is bisected by a perpendicular line segment that extends downward (figure 16.14).

Next we need to draw the profile and section of the sherd. There are several ways to do this, including complicated procedures with triangles and calipers; here we will mention two of the most common, reasonably fast ones.

One way to make an accurate tracing of the interior and exterior profiles is with a profile guage or "formaguage." This is a tool with a large number of thin, metal teeth sandwiched between metal brackets in a comb-like arrangement, and held somewhat loosely in place either magnetically or by friction. Profile guages were used by plasterers and cabinet-makers to help them reproduce the profiles of cornices and moldings, but can work just as well to record the curves of pottery surfaces. When you push the guage's teeth against an irregular surface, the teeth move to conform to its shape, and retain an image of this shape when you pull the guage away again. The guage can then be placed against the vellum to allow you to trace the profile onto paper with a sharp pencil. It is very important to be sure that you held the profile guage so that it was perpendicular to the stance plane of the rim, so that it gives you an accurate vertical profile of the sherd, and along whatever line gives you the longest profile. You will have to record the profiles of the exterior and interior separately, and then join them together in such a way as to represent the sherd's thickness accurately. To do this, measure the sherd thickness near the top, bottom, and middle of the profile with calipers and use the three measurements as a guide as to the spacing between the two profiles.

One alternative to using the profile guage to draw the profile is to trace it directly from a sherd that has been sawn along a radial section with a lapidary saw. Some archaeologists cut sherds so as to expose the interior fabric or to

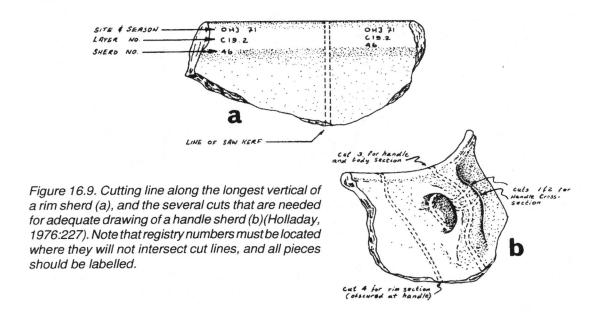

Figure 16.9. Cutting line along the longest vertical of a rim sherd (a), and the several cuts that are needed for adequate drawing of a handle sherd (b)(Holladay, 1976:227). Note that registry numbers must be located where they will not intersect cut lines, and all pieces should be labelled.

produce thin sections for mineralogical examination. As a biproduct of this analysis, the cut sherds provide ready-made radial sections and profiles that can easily be traced onto paper (Holladay 1976). If you plan to be sectioning pottery, therefore, you should consider where to make cuts so that they will also be useful for illustration (figure 16.9). Quite often, these are places where the cuts would also provide useful technological information in section. To make the tracing, first draw the stance line, and then hold a stance block (figure 16.10) so that its edge is aligned with the stance line. Place the sherd so that its rim makes continuous contact with the stance block and the section lies flat against the paper, and then trace it all around. Holladay (1976) recommends tracing with the pencil or pen refill inserted in a special block that holds the point as close as possible to the edge of the sherd (figure 16.11). Otherwise the tracing will exaggerate the thickness of the section. It is also useful to make small marks around the tracing to indicate places where there are grooves, decorative panels, or **carinations** (inflection points or sharp turns in the profile). This method results in accurate sections and profiles that can be produced much more quickly than with traditional methods that employed many measurements with calipers.

Holladay's cut-sherd method provides a correctly stanced drawing of the sherd's section. If you use a profile guage or some other method to make the section, you need to transfer it onto the drawing of the stance line in such a way that the angle between the stance line and the profile reflects the stance of the sherd itself. This can be somewhat tricky to do with a stance block and goniometer. It is generally better in these instances to stance the sherd upside-down (figure 16.13) and use a right angle triangle held along the sherd's radial plane to find the correct horizontal distance between a point on the sherd's rim and the bottom of the profile. Trace the section onto the drawing with the interior of the rim just touching the stance line (when you ink it later, the stance line should not touch) and the section arranged at the proper angle. You now have most of the cutaway half of the drawing completed.

The next step is to reflect the outer profile to the opposite side. Fold the drawing along the vertical line segment that bisects the stance line, and trace the outer surface so that it makes contact with the stance line (figure 16.14). You now have the outline of the exterior. Then draw any of the horizontal grooves that might appear on the exterior or interior on the appropriate side. Also draw lines to mark any sharp edges or

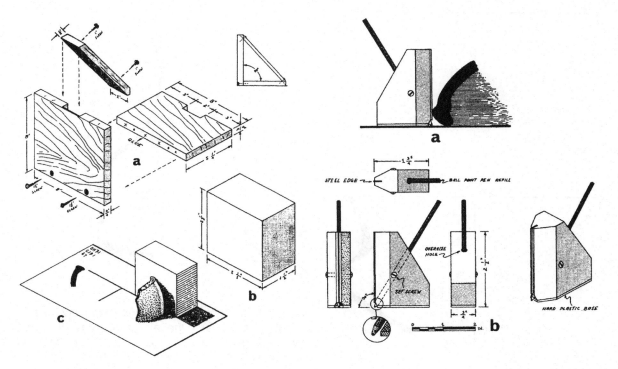

Figure 16.10. Construction of a stance block (a) for large vessels, and (b) for small sherds. Use of the stance block is shown in (c) (Holladay, 1976:226).

Figure 16.11. Holladay's (1976) design for a block, or 'circumference scriber' to hold the pencil or pen refill used to trace the outline of a sherd's section.

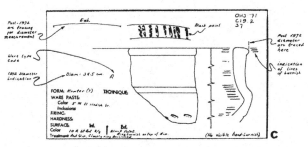

Figure 16.12. A card for recording the drawing of a sherd. Note that a tracing of the stanced rim at upper left can be used to establish the rim's diameter, and is marked "Ext" to indicate that it was traced on the exterior, not interior. The traced section is shown in correct orientation to the horizontal stance line at right, and can also be used for the exterior profile. The small "ticks" around the section can be used to mark the position of groves, carinations, and painted horizontal lines that should appear on the final drawing. Face-on views of the sherd and other details, such as the painted lip here, can also be added. Comments indicate burnish, paint colors, and so on (Holladay, 1976:227).

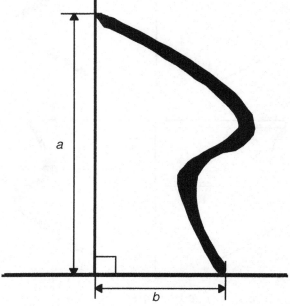

Figure 16.13. Measuring the height (a) and radial distance (b) of the sherd when stanced correctly can be used to ensure that the section is stanced correctly on the drawing.

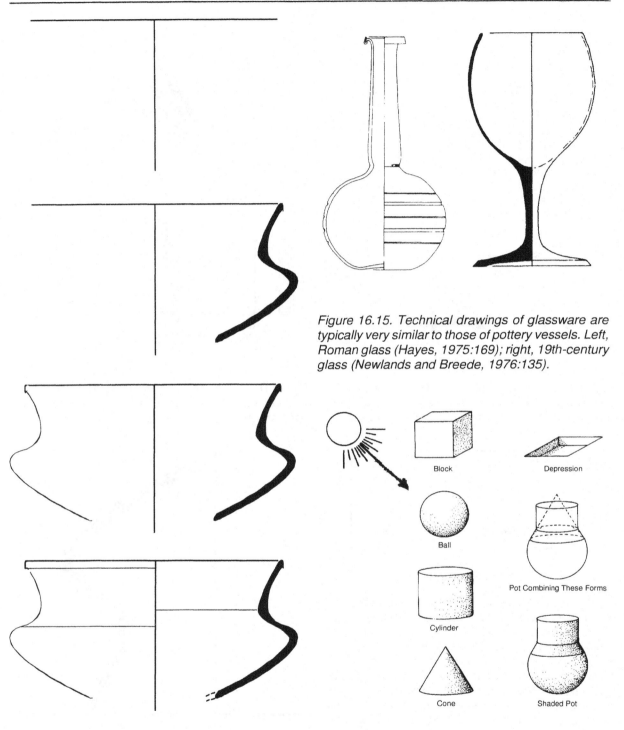

Figure 16.15. Technical drawings of glassware are typically very similar to those of pottery vessels. Left, Roman glass (Hayes, 1975:169); right, 19th-century glass (Newlands and Breede, 1976:135).

Figure 16.14. Sequence from stance line with correct diameter (top) to finished inking (bottom). Note that horizontal lines do not touch the section so as to avoid obscuring detail of lip or carination, and that the folded-over rim is not undercut on the left side.

Figure 16.16. Shading objects to simulate illumination from the upper left (Newlands and Breede, 1976:132).

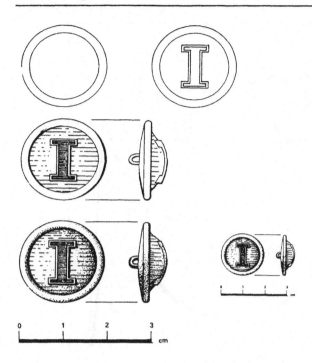

Figure 16.17. Steps in drawing a military button: drawing its outline (top), pencil drawing (middle), and finished inking (lower left), followed by reduction by 50% (Newlands and Breede, 1976:134).

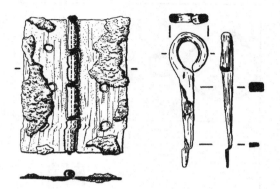

Figure 16.18. Inked illustrations of a metal hinge (left) and metal eyelet (right) with appropriate cross-sections (Newlands and Breede, 1976:135).

Illustrating "Small Finds"

Small finds are so varied that it is impossible to give a brief set of instructions that will be applicable to the illustration of all of them. Glass vessels (figure 16.15), metal and wooden tools (figure 16.18), stone beads, buttons (figure 16.17), and jewelry, and clay figurines (figure 16.18) all require their own sets of conventions for technical illustration.

Unlike pottery and lithics, which are usually drawn actual size and reduced later, small finds are often drawn at an enlarged scale in order to ensure that small details are not omitted.

One of the few conventions common to all these drawings is shading that simulates lighting from the upper left corner (figure 16.16).

Maps and Plans

Of the many sources available on cartography, a must-read is Mark Monmonier's (1991) *How to Lie with Maps*. No matter what guide you follow, it is important to remember that a map is a much simplified and often distorted model of reality. First we stretch and bend reality by trying to fit three-dimensional phenomena onto two-dimensional paper, then we omit lots of details and add new ones that are really our own interpretations.

Among the things we should keep in mind when drawing maps and plans are the degree to which they are likely to be reduced in publica-

carinations, such as protruding parts of the lip. Note that when you do this, you should continue the horizontal line all the way across, to represent the way a whole pot would look. Do not show indentations of the profile that would be hidden by the overlap of a rim on the exterior side, but only on the cutaway side. Finally add the representation of any decoration, such as painting or incision, that may be preserved on the sherd.

Now that the pencil drawing is complete, you should trace it in ink onto vellum or mylar™ film. Conventions for pottery inking vary, but should specify the line thicknesses used for each part of the illustration and the kinds of hatching, shading, or dot pattern to represent different surface treatments and colors.

Although it is now possible to illustrate pottery on the computer, the sequence of operations would be much the same as for hand-drawn pottery illustrations.

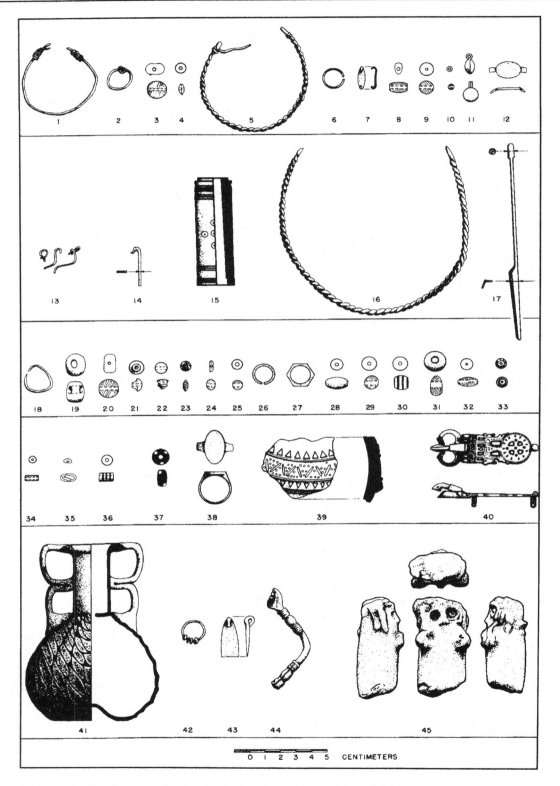

Figure 16.19. Example of a "small finds" plate from an archaeological expedition, including many small beads, metal jewellery, and a figurine (Tushingham, 1972: fig. 28).

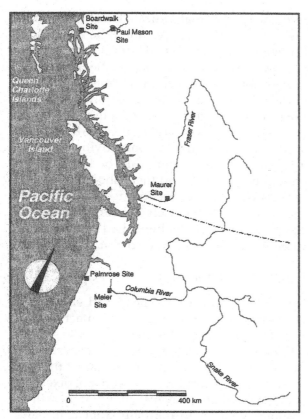

Figure 16.20. Map of the Northwest Coast of North America, showing the location of a few major sites but with only enough detail to provide orientation (Coupland and Banning, 1996).

tion, and the level of precision that is actually meaningful. Some archaeologists exert themselves to ensure that they measure their field plans with a precision of ± 1 cm, forgetting that the line thickness of a pencil at a scale of, say, 1:200 represents 20 cm! Whether or not that degree of precision will be visible on the (reduced) published plan, you should also think carefully about how meaningful it is. It is not to advocate outright sloppiness in field measurement to say that misplacing one of several dozen small stones on your map by 1 or 2 cm would be unlikely to alter your, or anyone else's, interpretation of archaeological context at the site. Consequently, you should also consider how much time you can afford to spend on ensuring extreme precision in your drawing of very small details.

Furthermore, everything that applies to graphs (chapter 2), such as ink:data ratio and chartjunk, is equally applicable to maps. Be sure your maps are not overly complicated, crowded, or misleading. A simple map that gives prominence to the information you are trying to convey (figure 16.20) is much more effective than one that crams in so many things that the point of the map is lost.

Among the things that *every* map and plan should have are the following. First and foremost, it should have a scale. It is best to make up a standard scale template on transfer paper or your computer that you can use repeatedly on maps of the same scale. Keep the scale simple and do not label more increments than is necessary to give readers a sense of magnitude. Note that it is always better to show a ruler-type scale than simply to say, for example, "1:200," because the latter will become meaningless when some printer or publisher reduces your drawing to fit a printed page. You should also have a simple, tasteful north arrow, and I would recommend orienting your drawing so that north is at least toward the top of the drawing, unless you have strong reason to do otherwise. The exception is in polar regions, where north arrows are often meaningless and lines of longitude may be much more useful for orientation. It usually helps to show where your map or plan fits into the larger picture. For the map of a small region, for example, you can show an *inset map* (or key map) of a much larger and more familiar region with a small rectangle marking the position of the territory covered on your map. In other cases, lines of latitude and longitude mark the map's position on the earth's surface. For plans of excavation areas on sites, by contrast, you should show labelled grid lines or grid corners (marked by circles or crosses) to record where the drawing fits into the overall site map, as well as the position of **benchmarks** that were used as reference points during mapping, and some levels (in meters above sea level) to position the features on the plan in their vertical dimension. Different phenomena would require different conventions for portrayal on the plans. For example, you might need conventions for different materials (stone, clay, gravel, brick), for reconstructed structure walls (perhaps dashed or greyed), for pits and postmolds, and for find-spots of individual artifacts of various kinds.

Only 15 years ago, producing a publishable map required making an original drawing on vellum or paper and then tracing it in ink onto Mylar, and the drafting room was filled with transfer sheets for lettering and applying north arrows and other devices onto the Mylar. Today you can still do maps this way, but increasingly it is better to do them on a computer. Often the first map you prepare on the computer takes even more time than drawing the map by hand with pen and ink. The great advantage is that, once you have stored a base map on your computer's disk, you can re-use it as many times as you like with variations. For example, you can modify the base map to show sites of different periods, vegetation zones, and so on. Computerized base maps are particularly convenient when you have just done a survey and would like to show a series of maps depicting site distributions at different points in time. They are also very useful for excavation maps. To copies of a base map you can add different layers or features and thus document the site's stratigraphic history or show distributions of lithics, bone, or pottery.

Stratigraphic Sections

As Harris (1979) notes, the style of stratigraphic sections varies considerably from project to project. As with maps and artifact illustrations, it is important to remember that a section drawing is an archaeologist's interpretation, in this case the interpretation of the depositional relationships represented in the section. Consequently, rather than attempting to illustrate sediments realistically, it is often better to use conventions that clearly represent the archaeologist's understanding of what is going on in the section, and to complement it with photographs and sediment samples.

No matter what conventions you use to represent interfaces and various kinds of sediments in the section drawings, there are some things that every section drawing should include. As with maps, the section drawing should include reference points that indicate where the section fits in space. First, there should be at least one horizontal line labelled with its elevation above sea level, or else a vertical scale labelled in meters above sea level. Either there should be vertical lines to mark the position of any grid lines that intersect the section, or there should be arrows and labels that relate the two ends of the section to points on an accompanying map. The vertical and horizontal scale of the drawing should be obvious, and there should be a clear label, such as "North Section" to make it easy for viewers to orient themselves. Unexcavated sediments are usually distinguished in some way, often with a "woven" type of hatching.

Computer Scanners

Today it is remarkably cheap and effective to scan drawings and even flat artifacts into a computer file that can then be edited with graphic software. The scanners and the software that accompanies them allow you to adjust the contrast, darkness, resolution (number of pixels per inch) and, where relevant, color. For most illustrations, which will normally appear in black and white, you should set the scanner on black and white or greyscale, and no more resolution than you need, to minimize the file's space on disk. Small hand-held scanners are convenient when you need to produce digitized images in the field or in a museum. Flat-bed scanners, which look like photocopiers, are much better for most work because they allow you to scan a fairly large area in one pass. For digitizing large or irregular objects you may want to capture images with a video camera connected to a computer. For maps, plans, and sections, a digitizing tablet on which you trace the image with a stylus can be very useful, and makes it unnecessary to trace the image on the screen. Most of these produce what is called a "bit-mapped" image, which consists of a matrix of numbers corresponding to the pixels on your monitor or printer. For black and white images, the numbers at each pixel position represent either 0 or 1; for greyscale and color images each pixel carries more data. Bit-mapped files are very wasteful of disk space because even white pixels must be recorded.

Computer Graphics

A "raw" scanned image will probably not be suitable for publication and, at a minimum, will have to be "cleaned up" on the computer with graphics software. Except for photographs that you would like to publish as halftones or on the internet, usually it is much better to trace the scanned image with a mouse or stylus, omitting details that are not necessary for your illustration, and then to discard the original scanned image. This results in a much cleaner-looking image that can be manipulated easily and takes up less disk space because it is no longer bit-mapped. Typically the tracing is called a vector image because a line segment is represented as the vector between two points (thus the computer only needs to record the position of two points and the thickness and color of the line that joins them). The graphic software allows you to make a wide array of line segments, polygons, rectangles, circles, arcs, and smooth, curvy lines called "bezier curves." When selecting a graphics package, you should pay attention not only to its own features but also to the various file formats that it will read and write. Otherwise you may find that your beautiful illustrations do not output properly to your publisher's page-layout software or printer.

Preparing Graphics for Publication

All illustrations, whether hand-inked or computer-generated, must be produced with the requirements of publication in mind. One of the most common mistakes archaeologists make when they produce their own illustrations is to forget what will happen to the illustration once submitted to a publisher. Most importantly, they should keep in mind that the illustrations will usually be reduced in size. Reduction can often improve the illustrations' appearance, as small defects will tend to disappear. Unfortunately, reduction will also cause thin lines to disappear or too-dense hatching to "bleed" together, so that it looks black instead of hatched. Many people who see the originals of good archaeological illustrations think they look too "blocky" because the lines are thick. In fact, heavy lines are necessary to prevent them from disappearing when reduced. The same thing applies to the point size of text in any labels on your maps and figures.

One very helpful way to avoid this problem is to make a test sheet that allows you to see the effect of various degrees of reduction. Print or ink a variety of your common symbols and conventions along with a row of line segments of varying thicknesses, and label each with a font in a different point size. Then make copies of the test graphic at several different reductions and display the result next to your drafting table or graphics computer. Keep in mind that plates illustrating several artifacts are commonly reduced to as little as 20% or 25% of the original size, while maps and section drawings are often published at 40% or 50%. The width of text columns in the journal or book series in which you intend to publish will give you some idea of the likely finished size of your graphic.

You should also pay close attention to publishers' instructions about the form and format of your illustrations. Typically publishers will ask for PMTs (photo-mechanical transfers) or black-and-white glossies of a particular size. They will also ask you to mark the back of each with a figure number or plate number, your name, and an arrow pointing to the top of the graphic. Some publishers will ask for copies of computer-generated graphics on disk. In that case you will need to know what file format they require, such as TIFF or EPS (encapsulated post-script).

Conclusions

Illustrations are an important aspect of communicating archaeological information to colleagues and the public, yet they are coded representations of our observations, and not merely artists' impressions. Illustration conventions are like the lexical conventions of digital databases. Technical drawing requires patience and basic skills rather than artistic creativity. Effective illustration also requires care to ensure that important information is obvious and clear, and not lost among unimportant detail or obliterated by size reduction during publication.

References Cited

Addington, L. R., 1986, *Lithic Illustration. Drawing Flaked Stone Artifacts for Publication*. University of Chicago Press, Chicago.

Adkins, L., and Adkins, R. A., 1989, *Archaeological Illustration*. Cambridge University Press, Cambridge.

Byrd, B. F., 1989, *The Natufian Encampment at Beidha. Late Pleistocene Adaptation in the Southern Levant*. Jutland Archaeological Society Publications 23. Aarhus University Press, Aarhus.

Cambden, W., 1806, *Britannia: Chorographical Description of the Flourishing Kingdoms of England, Scotland, and Ireland, and the Islands Adjacent from the Earliest Antiquity*, vol. 1, 2nd ed. John Stockdale, London.

Coupland, G., and Banning, E. B., eds., 1996, *People Who Lived in Big Houses: Archaeological Perspectives on Large Domestic Structures*. Prehistory Press, Madison, WI.

Harris, E. C., 1979, *Principles of Archaeological Stratigraphy*. Academic Press, London.

Hayes, J. W., 1975, *Roman and Pre-Roman Glass in the Royal Ontario Museum*. Royal Ontario Museum, Toronto.

Hoernes, M., 1892, *Die Urgeschichte des Menschen*. Vienna.

Hole, F., 1977, *Studies in the Archeological History of the Deh Luran Plain. The Excavation of Chagha Sefid*. Memoirs of the Museum of Anthropology 9. University of Michigan, Ann Arbor.

Holladay, J., 1976, A technical aid to pottery drawing. *Antiquity* 50:223-29.

Jensen, C. H., and Mason, F. H. S., 1963, *Drafting Fundamentals*. McGraw-Hill, Toronto.

Monmonier, M., 1991, *How to Lie with Maps*. University of Chicago Press, Chicago.

Newlands, D. L., and Breede, C., 1976, *An Introduction to Canadian Archaeology*. McGraw-Hill, Toronto.

Tushingham, A. D., 1972, *The Excavations at Dibon (Dhîbân) in Moab. The Third Campaign 1952-53*. American Schools of Oriental Research, Cambridge, MA.

Glossary

Absolute Pollen Frequency (APF). A pollen density measure in which pollen counts per unit volume of sediment are corrected by estimated deposition rate (depth per year) to estimated influx (counts per cm^2 per year), the same unit used for pollen "rain" in modern samples. This allows each taxon to vary independently of the others, making interpretation much easier than with percentages.

Abstract data type In database design, a class of data that does not conform to alphanumeric, numeric, boolean, text, or string types. ADTs include time fields and date fields, but could include special archaeological data types for ordinal time categories, statistical dates, stratigraphic order, and spatial context.

Accuracy Accuracy is the opposite of bias in measurement. Accuracy refers to the degree to which measured values come close to actual values. Systematic overestimate or underestimate of these values is bias.

Activity area A cluster of associated artifacts, and sometimes features, apparently associated with a single activity or group of closely related activities.

Addition rule In probability, this is the rule that, when two events are mutually exclusive, the probability that either or both of them will occur is equal to the sum of their individual probabilities: $p(A or B) = p(A) + p(B)$. For events that are not mutually exclusive, we must modify the rule to subtract the overlap between events, so that $p(A or B) = p(A) + p(B) - p(A and B)$.

Age profile Graph displaying the distribution of ages at death for a sample of animals or humans, also called a mortality profile.

Allometry A scaling of body parts in animals such that the measurement of one part is a function of the measurement of another part.

Alluvium Sediment formed by the transport of particles by water, typically with round large, rounded particles where water velocity was high, and fine particles where it water was slow-moving.

Alphanumeric In computer databases, alphanumeric is a field type that allows entry of any characters, including numerals, but will not allow any arithmetical operations on them. It will allow such operations as "contains."

Alternate retouch Retouch that occurs on the dorsal side of one edge and the ventral side of the opposite edge of a flake.

Alternating retouch Retouch that occurs on an edge of a lithic flake in such a way that it alternates between dorsal and ventral sides from one end to the other of the edge.

Amphora A Greek or Roman jar, principally used for the transport of wine, generally with a narrow neck, two handles on or just below the neck, and a wide body that tapers to a round or pointed base.

Anisotropic A mineral that causes the retardation of light waves in one axis of ocillation relative to the axis at right angles to it, as light passes through it. The two components of the light that passes through are called the fast ray and the slow ray.

Annuli (sg., annulus) Annual growth rings or increments in mollusc shell, fish vertebrae, tooth cementum, or wood.

Anterior Forward, or toward the head.

Anthropic soils Soils formed by or related to human activity.

Anthropogenic Resulting from processes in which human agency plays a large part.

Antler An outgrowth of bone with compact, bone-like outer cortex, cancellous on the interior, and somewhat fuzzy surface. Following seasonal growth, antler ossifies and is shed annually.

Appendicular Refering to the appendages, or limbs, including fore-limbs and hind-limbs.

Appliqué A ceramic finishing technique that involves joining shaped pieces of plastic body to a leather-hard surface by pressure. The applied pieces can be functional, as with handles, or decorative, as with "rope" decoration and modelled figures.

Archaeological layers Sedimentary and architectureal units that archaeologists typically define by a combination of lithological, pedological, and material cultural criteria.

Arithmetic mean This is the common "average," a measure of central tendency calculated by dividing the sum of observations by the number of observations.

Arrangement In systematics, an arrangement is a procedure that orders data into units. Classification and grouping methods create arrangements.

Arris See Dorsal ridge.

Assemblage In archaeology, this term refers to all of the artifacts, features, and other physical evidence (plant remains, animals remains, etc.) found in deposits associated with a single, continuous occupation of an archaeological site. In common usage, however, the term is sometimes treated as equivalent to "collection," extended to all the deposits from a site, or subdivided by type of material, as in "faunal assemblage."

Assertive style Style with only vague associations with social identity, such as a tendency to wear certain types of clothing or jewelry.

Attribute A characteristic of an item, such as an artifact. Examples of attributes are color, length, edge angle, and house type.

Attribute clustering Any grouping method based on associations between attributes, and including Spaulding's configurationist typology and factor analysis.

Attribute pointer In relational databases, a field in a "many" file that makes a relation with the key attribute of a "one" file. For example, the field, "Site number," could occur as an attribute pointer in a file cataloguing artifacts, and refer to the key attribute "Site number" in another file, "Sites," with a unique record for each site.

Attribute value The particular value associated with an attribute of an item. For example, "brown" could be the label for an attribute value of the attribute, color.

Autocorrelation When two variables appear to be correlated, not because of any causal relationship between them, but because they are "sub-dimensions" of some other variable.

Axial Part of a skeleton including the skull, vertebral column, ribs, and sternum.

Axis of flaking An imaginary line roughly down the middle of a lithic flake as viewed from the dorsal side, and extending from the point of percussion, that is parallel to the direction of striking, or the line of force during striking.

Backing A type of steep retouch apparently used to dull the edge of a flake, thus making it suitable for hafting or handling with bare fingers. It is common, for example, on the edge opposite the cutting edge of knives.

Bar graph A graph displaying discrete (categorical) data with bars the heights of which are proportional to the number or proportion of observations belonging to each category.

Basalt Coarse and sometimes porous volcanic rock that is not as suitable as flint or obsidian for flake production, but that can be very useful for production of grinding and pounding tools, mortars, and stone bowls.

Base The lower portion of a vessel from the lower boundary of the body to the place that would normally be in contact with the surface on which the vessel rested. In some cases, it may be a foot or tripod.

Baton A "soft" hammer used to strike flakes from a stone core, typically made of antler, bone, or wood. Also called a billet or percussor.

Baulks Strips of unexcavated sediment with vertical faces that separate excavation areas in gridded excavations and allow examination of the stratification they contain.

Bayesian analysis A probability approach that compares the uncertainty of any parameter before and after observing new data. Bayes' theorem provides the basis for combining the prior information with the data to result in a posterior statement, which also has a probability function.

Beating Also called paddling or hammer-and-anvil technique, this is a way to thin and even out the walls of coil- or slab-built vessels after they have partially hardened to "leather" hardness, to improve the bonding between coils, and, in some cases, to add surface texture. It involves holding an anvil (often just a fist) inside the vessel while the outside is struck repeatedly with a paddle, which can be wrapped with cord or fabric to add texture to the vessel surface.

Benchmark A reasonably permanent, fixed point of reference, especially a point of known position and elevation used in mapping.

Bernouli distribution A discrete probability distribution that describes situations in which there is only one trial and only two possible (and mutually exclusive) outcomes, as with dichotomous measurements. For example, the probability distribution to express the probability that a particular inhumation in a cemetery is female could be Bernoulli with an expected value of 0.5.

Bias Bias is the systematic overestimate or underestimate of a parameter or measurement, and results in inaccuracy.

Bifacial On both ventral and dorsal sides.

Bifacial retouch Retouch flaking on a lithic flake that occurs on both ventral and dorsal sides of an edge.

Billet A "soft" hammer used to strike flakes from a stone core, typically made of antler, bone or wood. Also called a baton or percussor.

Binomial distribution A discrete probability distribution that models a series of n trials with only two possible (and mutually exclusive) outcomes at each trial, as with dichotomous measurements. For example, where we have reason to expect the probability that any inhumation in a cemetery is female is 0.5, we would use the Binomial distribution to determine the probability of finding exactly two female burials and eight male burials in a set of ten.

Biostratigraphic units Divisions of the Earth's crust defined by their fossil content.

Biostratigraphy A paleontological technique for the relative chronology of deposits based on the assumption that the set of fossils found in a deposit reflects the paleoecology of a particular time and place.

Bioturbation The movement of materials in deposits by plant roots, burrowing animals, and other organisms.

Bipolar reduction Producing lithic flakes and debris by placing a core on an anvil and striking it from above with a large hammer to shatter it.

Birefringence The difference between the indices of refraction of the fast ray and slow ray as light passes through an anisotropic mineral, causing the velocities of the two light components, ocillating at right angles to one another, to differ.

Blade Conventionally, a blade is defined as any lithic flake with a length/width ratio greater than 2.0.

Blank A lithic flake ready to be retouched into a tool.

Body This term refers both to the main containing volume of a vessel (and sherds that are fragments of it) and to the prepared mixture of clay and temper used to make pottery.

Boolean In databases, a Boolean field is used to record mutually exclusive, dichotomous observations, such as "present/absent," "male/female," or "1, 0."

Box-and-dot plot A type of graph frequently used in Exploratory Data Analysis that displays the median and inter-quartile range in a box, with points to represent all the observations falling in the upper and lower quartiles.

Buccal Side towards the cheek, cheek-side. Used to orient observations on teeth.

Bulb The bulb of percussion is a raised bump that results from compaction under the force of striking a lithic core with a percussor, and is especially prominent in flakes produced by the hard-hammer technique.

Burin A tool, often thought to have been used as an engraving tool, that has a small, chisel-like and very strong working edge produced by removal of one or more spalls.

Burin spall A small, relatively thick flake removed from a flake or blade, using a snapped termination or previous burination scar as a platform.

Burnishing A finishing technique by which a surface is rubbed with a smooth stone or other tool.

Carination A reltively sudden change in the vertical profile of a vessel, typically occuring where the upper and lower parts of a restricted vessel have been joined.

Cartilage A durable, flexible animal tissue consisting of cells in a matrix of protein, carbohydrates (chondroitin), and fibres.

Carving A finishing or decorative technique that involves selective removal of material with a sharp tool, such as a knive, in a pattern.

Castellation Pronounced vertical appendage on the rim of a vessel, on analogy to the *merlon* of a castle wall.

Caudal Pertaining the the tail.

CD-ROM "Compact Disk, Read-Only Memory" is a nonmagnetic, optical storage medium in which binary data are impressed into tracks on a plastic disk as a series of pits that either do or do not reflect laser light.

Central limit theorem A theorem in statistics that assures us that, provided sample size is sufficiently large, the sampling distribution of a random sample drawn even from a rather unusual distribution is approximately normal (Gaussian) with a mean of μ and variance of σ^2/N.

Central Place Theory A spatial model for the organization of satelite sites, including smaller settlements, around a city or other site that is the focus for regional services.

Central tendency Any measure that expresses what is "typical," "average," or "common" in a group of observations, including the mode, median, and mean.

Ceramic In materials science, a ceramic is a solid made of compounds of metallic elements and nonmetallic, inorganic ones, but in archaeology the term is used to include earthenwares, terracottas, stonewares, porcelains, and other materials made of fired clay.

Ceramic ecology A framework for studying pottery from the perspective of its manufacturing steps and use, analogous in many ways to the Chaine opératoire in lithic analysis.

Chaine opératoire A perspective for studying lithic technology that emphasizes the sequence of decisions and behaviors from raw material selection and acquisition, through manufacture, use, recycling, and discard.

Chaining A problem found especially in hierarchical agglomerative clustering methods whereby items in the same group may have no attribute values in common but are still grouped together because other members of the group share attribute values with one or both of them.

Chert See Flint.

Chi-square test A nonparametric test of "goodness-of-fit" between observed and predicted values in a paradigm-like table.

China A vitrified (glassy) and nonporous ceramic fired to a temperature of 1100-1200oC.

Circle graph See Pie chart.

Class In systematics, a class is a category in a classification, that is defined by rules that are both necessary and sufficient to determine membership in the class. In Linnaean taxonomy, Class (capitalized) is the taxonomic level between Phylum and Order.

Classification A set of abstract classes (categories) defined by rules setting out the conditions that are both necessary and sufficient for membership in the class. The process of assigning items to classes. The term is often used with a less restrictive definition.

Clay This term refers both to a particular size class of particles (smaller than 0.0039 mm on the Wentworth scale) or to minerals that result from the weathering of silcate rocks containing significant amounts of alumina (Al2O3), such as feldspar. In the latter usage, it includes kaolinite, halloysite, montmorillonite, and illite.

Closed vessel A vessel with an orifice that is narrow relative to the vessel's height, also called a restricted vessel. Jars and bottles are usually closed vessels.

Cluster analysis Usually refers to a group of mathematical methods by which items are grouped by similarity coefficients or partitioned by distance in multidimensional attribute space, whether by hierarchical agglomeration, hierarchical splitting, partitioning, density searching, or clumping.

Cluster sample A sample in which the sampling elements are spaces or time periods but the analytical elements are countable observations in them.

Clustering See Grouping

Coiling A primary forming technique for producing pottery vessels, by which rope-like cylinders of the body are gradually added along the circumference of the vessel, starting at a disk-like base, to build up the vessel's shape.

Collaring That aspect of wheel-throwing a pottery vessel that involves using both hands to apply inward pressure on the rotating body to narrow it and form a neck or a closure (on a base).

Colluvium Sediment deposited by the movement of material downslope by gravity.

Combing A finishing technique in pottery manufacture whereby a tool with multiple teeth or prongs, like a fork, is dragged along the plastic or nearly leather-hard surface of the fabric to leave multiple, nearly parallel incisions, either straight or wavy.

Compensating error When errors on a sequence of measurements or on measurements subject to arithmetical operations tend to "cancel out," we say that they are compensating errors.

Compilation A set of interrelated propositions (data) describing material remains, usually through symbolic representation, that facilitates the study of ancient people. Compilations include field notebooks, artifact catalogues, and computerized archaeological databases.

Conchoidal fracture Fracture along a shock wave that radiates through a material from a point of impact in a conical fashion. Flintknapping takes advantage of this type of fracture.

Contamination This has several related meanings in archaeology. It refers to addition of unrelated (and usually later) material culture to a deposit, chemicals to a residue sample, or carbon to a radiocarbon sample. It also refers to the statistical concept of outliers (measurements or observations that do not properly belong in the study group).

Continuous In measurement theory, a continuous scale is an interval or ratio scale in which, between any two values, there is an infinity of other values.

Coprolites Fossil feces.

Core In lithic production, the core is the block of raw material from which flakes are struck. In the production of flake tools, the remnant of the core is simply a kind of debitage, or waste product. Core tools, however, are made by reducing the core by removal of flakes until it has a desirable shape and edges.

Correlation A linear relation between two interval-scale variables such that knowing the value of one allows prediction of the value of the other with a reasonably small degree of error. We can describe the relation as $y = mx + b + \varepsilon$, where m is the slope of a line, b is a constant, and ε is an error term.

Cortex The weathered surface that originally covered a lithic core, much like a rough skin, prior to flake removal. Traces of this cortex sometimes remain on parts of the core and on the outermost flakes removed from it.

Cortical flake A flake that shows even a small amount of cortex on its dorsal surface. Also called a primary flake because it would have been removed from the core early in the core-reduction sequence.

Cranial Pertaining to the skull or head.

Crossed retouch Retouch that is so steep on a lithic edge that it forms very near a 90° angle, so that it is barely visible from either dorsal or ventral sides.

Cumulative error When a sequence of measurements or arithmetic operations involves errors that are mainly or exclusively in one direction (i.e., positive or negative), we say that we have cumulative error.

Cumulative Frequency Distribution Also called an Ogive, a graph with an interval or ratio scale on the x-axis and proportion or percentage on the y-axis ranging from 0 to 1.0 or 100%. A line climbs monotonically from the origin toward the upper right corner as each observation along the x-axis is added to all the observations to its left. Commonly used to express unevenness in the distribution of wealth or in age at death.

Data dictionary Documentation of all the files, fields, relations, and processes used in a database.

Data type Determines the kind of logical operations that can be applied to the contents of a particular database field. For example, arithmetical operations, such as multiplication, can be applied to fields with the numeric data type, alphabetical sorting to fields with the alphanumeric data type, and "earlier than" to date fields and time fields.

Data-flow diagram In database management and structured systems analysis, a data-flow diagram provides a logical model of an information system, irrespective of its physical form, by depicting its logical processes and the flows of data between processes. It is made up of processes, flows, and entities (files and reports).

Database A compilation or reservoir of information that supplies its users with the data from which they make decisions, inferences, interpretations, or test hypotheses, ranging from a simple file of index cards to a computerized, relational data management system.

Date field An Abstract Data Type that records dates in m/d/y, d/m/y, or y/m/d format, and allows such operations as "earlier than" and "later than" to be performed.

Date range A date indicating years during which it is equally probable that an event took place.

Dated event The event dated by a particular chronological method, sometimes as a proxy for the target event.

Death assemblage Taphonomic term for the population of carcasses that results when members of the life assemblage die.

Debitage Archaeologists use this term inconsistently. In North American usage, it generally refers to the waste products of lithic core reduction, including the exhausted cores themselves. In Europe or in the chaîne opératoire approach, it refers to all material removed from a core, including used and unused flakes, tool blanks, and debris.

Debris Chips and chunks of lithic material removed from a core, but that do not fit the criteria for a flake or blade. Generally they have no identifiable platform and it is impossible to distinguish dorsal from ventral surfaces.

Deduction A logical form of reasoning whereby the truth of the premises entails the truth of the conclusion, and taking the form, if A is true and B is true then C must be true. In stratigraphy, for example, if layer 1 is later than layer 2, and layer 2 is later than layer 3, then layer 1 must be later than layer 3.

Dendrochronology Determining age by sequences of varying width in tree rings.

Deposited assemblage Taphonomic term for the set of carcasses or body parts that are deposited on an archaeological or paleontological site.

Descriptive statistic A numerical summary of data or estimate of a population parameter. Sample means, medians, standard deviations, and ranges are descriptive statistics.

Desert varnish A distinctive patina that occurs on lithic artifacts that have lain on desert surfaces, perhaps caused by a combination of sand-blasting during windstorms and microbial action.

Design theory The Design approach, based on the work of Pye, treats all technology as a compromise between the short-term and long-term costs, utility, and risk of failure of artifacts as they operate within a technological system.

Diatoms Microscopic algae that occur just about anywhere there is open water, siliceous valves or shells of which may be preserved in clays.

Dichotomous scale A scale of measurement in which each measurement can take one of only two values, often represented as 1 and 0, such as male and female, present and absent. See also Bernoulli distribution.

Difference-of-means test A statistical test comparing two sample means to see if a sample probably came from a given population or if two samples probably came from the same population.

Difference-of-proportions test A statistical test comparing two sample proportions to see if a sample probably came from a given population or if two samples probably came from the same population.

Differentiation rule In systematics or information languages, a set of differentiation rules deter-

mines the range and types of distinctions that can be recorded for each attribute.

Digital information language An information language that uses symbolic representation of data not only to reduce data to a conventional representation and to store it, but to facilitate data retrieval by allowing amplification of a query. Typically this is done with a computerized database management system in which conventional representations of attributes are stored in fields.

Direct measurement Any measurement for which we are able to compare an object of interest directly with a standard scale, as when we measure length by comparing an object with a distance marked on a ruler, or color by comparing the object with the color chips on a Munsell chart.

Direct retouch Retouch that occurs on an edge of a lithic flake visible only in the dorsal view.

Discrete Scales or measurements that are discontinuous, in that observations can only take certain prescribed values, and there are no values between them. For example, there can be no observations partway between two categories in a nominal scale, making nominal scales discrete. Interval and ratio scales can also be discrete when they involve counts of theoretically whole items. For example, a family can have 0, 1, 2, or 3 children, but cannot have 2.4 children, while the number of artifacts found on any square meter of a site is also discrete.

Disjunction A type of bias in a date that occurs when the dated event is older than the target event, leading to overestimate of age.

Disparity A type of bias in a date that occurs when the dated event is younger than the target event, leading to underestimate of age.

Dispersion The amount of "spread" in a set of data, a sample, or a population.

Distal At the end farthest from the body or head (in an animal), or farthest from the point of percussion and platform (in a lithic flake or blade).

Diversity A measure of variety in a set of data. A sample with high diversity could exhibit a large number of categories or taxa, a type of diversity called richness, and it may show approximately equal numbers of observations in each class (evenness), while one with low diversity may only have observations belonging to one or two classes, or may have most of the observations bunched into one class, and very few occurring in others.

Domestication Definitions vary widely, but one definition is the process by which two species become mutually dependent, the one that provides food or other resources or services depending on the other for its reproduction. In some species this leads to morphological changes, such as the loss of natural dispersion mechanisms for the seeds of domesticated cereals.

Dorsal Towards the back (of an animal), or the side of a lithic flake or blade that would have been on the outside of the core, during striking, which shows cortex or scars from previous flake removals.

Dorsal ridge The sharp ridge that marks the boundary between flake scars on the dorsal surface of a lithic flake, also called an arris.

Downdraft kiln An installation for firing pottery with a firebox, in which the fuel burns beside the chamber in which pots are fired, and separated from it by a "bagwall" so that hot gas from the fire must rise over the bagwall and then pass down through the chamber before exiting through a chimney flue on the other side. This type of kiln achieves higher temperatures and better control over atmosphere than updraft kilns.

Drawing A primary forming technique for producing pottery vessels, similar to pinching, whereby the body is pulled upward from the center of a ball of tempered clay with thumb and fingers.

Earthenware A nonvitrified and porous ceramic fired to a temperature of 900-1200°C.

Element See Sample element.

Emblematic style Stylistic variation that has a distinct symbolic referent, such as a logo. See also iconic style.

Emic Refers to statements that native (or prehistoric) informants would accept as valid or true, as opposed to **etic** categories, and based on Pike's linguistic term, phonemic (a native speaker's perception of distinct sounds).

Enamel A thin layer of glass, like a glaze, but fused to a metal surface.

Enumeration The process of counting how many objects belong in each class of a nominal scale.

Epiphysis The end of a bone, where ossification begins later than in the mid-shaft, and which fuses with the bone shaft by adulthood.

Error rate The proportion of misassignments to categories or classes of a classification. It treats the error of misclassifying one type as another type as no more serious than the error of misclassifying it as "unknown."

Estimated Number of Individuals A measure of the actual number of individuals in an unobserved population, often based on two small samples or on paired elements in fragmentary evidence (see Peterson index).

Estimated Vessel Equivalents A unit in quantifying fragmentary pottery equal to the circumferential proportion of a rim or base sherd.

Etic Refers to statements constructed by (outside) observers that can be validated analytically or scientifically. The term is based on Pike's linguistic term, phonetic (a linguist's system of distinct sounds). See emic.

Exchangeability In Bayesian analysis, if there is no *a priori* evidence to suggest that one member of the population is any different from other members with respect to the property we wish to measure, the members are said to be exchangeable, and it does not matter which ones we include in a sample.

Experimental archaeology Research in which archaeologists attempt to understand the processes that may have affected ancient material culture by conducting experiments on modern (usually replicated) artifacts and materials.

Exponential distribution A model of the falloff in frequency with distance or time appropriate, for example, to the decay of radioactive isotopes over time.

Extrinsic attribute Any attribute of an object that is not inherent in the object itself. Includes attributes of the context in time, space, function, society, and psychological state in which the object was found, made, used, seen, or discarded.

Fabric The material of an artifact. In pottery, this term describes the fired clay body and mineral inclusions (including temper) in the ceramic.

Family In the Linaean taxonomic system, Family is the taxonomic level between Order and Genus.

Fast ray The component of light passing through an anisotropic mineral with the lower index of refraction.

Feather fracture See Feather termination

Feather termination A gradual thinning of a lithic flake at the distal end to an extremely sharp point or edge.

Feldspar A crystalline mineral consisting of aluminum silicates and potassium, sodium, calcium, or barium.

Field In database design and management, a field a the space in a file dedicated to the storage of information about a particular attribute.

File In a database, a file is a logical entity for the storage of a particular class of data, containing records with identical sets of field types so that they can record the same kinds of attributes. For example, one file might record data pertaining to stratigraphy, and another data pertaining to lithic artifacts.

Finishing techniques In pottery manufacture, these are techniques to alter the surface characteristics of vessels by displacing or impressing material at the surface, applying material, or removing material.

Flake A relatively thin fragment of stone or glass removed from a core by percussion or pressure applied near the edge of a platform on the core.

Flake scar The negative relief of the ventral surface of a lithic flake that is visible on a core or the dorsal surface of another flake as the result of a previous flake removal.

Flat-file database A set of data records that are stored in a single, large table, much as in a set of file cards.

Flint Also called chert, a micro-crystalline, silicate rock formed as nodules or layers in limestone, and a common raw material for lithic reduction.

Flux Material used to lower melting temperatures of, or promote fusion between, metals or minerals, as in soldering, welding, and glass-making.

Folding In pottery manufacture, it is a kind of shaping in which the potter flares a rim outward or bends it inward, and then rolls it down to double the rim's thickness or create a complicated profile.

Foot An appendage attached along the circumference of a vessel's base to raise it above the surface on which the vessel rests.

Fossil assemblage Taphonomic term for that part of the deposited assemblage that survives in a site's or locality's deposits until discovery.

Fragments Broken parts of artifacts. In lithic analysis, fragments are parts of broken flakes and cores. Fragments of pottery are usually called sherds or shards.

Fuzzy sets Sets whose members include both certain or unambigous members and members by degree, such as individuals that are members to a degree of 60% or 50%.

Gap A source of bias in tree-ring dating (dendrochronology), representing the length of time between the formation of a dated ring and the date when the tree was cut. The gap and hiatus combined constitute a disjunction.

Gaussian distribution Also known as the normal distribution, or "bell curve," a probability density function for continuous interval data.

Genus In the Linaean taxonomic system, Genus (plural, genera) is the taxonomic level between Family and species.

Glaze A thin coating of glass fused to a ceramic surface. Most glazes used on pottery consist of silica and fluxes, such as potassium, sodium, calcium, magnesium, and lead, that bring the melting temperature down from more than 1700°C to less than 1300°C. Glazes can also contain coloring agents.

Graphical information language A set of conventions for describing entities, such as artifacts, pictorially, and in a consistent way

Grouping Systematics based on bringing together real or imaginary objects and separating them from other groups of objects, rather than on assignment to pre-defined classes. See chapter 3.

GUI General utility index, an estimate of each bone part's usefulness for meat, marrow, and grease.

Handle An appendage attached to the exterior (or rarely interior) wall of a vessel's body, neck, or rim, that facilitates the manipulation or suspension of the vessel (lifting, pouring, transport) or is a decorative feature.

Hard-hammer percussion A technique for the manufacture of stone tools that involves direct striking of a core with a hammerstone or other very hard percussor.

Harris matrix The abstract representation of unequivocal stratigraphic relationships between layers, interfaces, and features in a lattice similar to a flow diagram.

Hermeneutics An epistemological theory with roots in the study of biblical texts that understanding is based on the dialectical (back-and-forth) relationship between the whole and its parts (the hermeneutic circle). Understanding of the parts should be *coherent* with each other and the whole.

Hiatus A source of bias in tree-ring dating (dendrochronology) where a period of time intervened between the cutting of the tree and the date of interest (target event). The gap and hiatus combined constitute a disjunction.

Hinge fracture See Hinge termination.

Hinge termination A fracture at the distal end of a lithic flake somewhat like a step termination, but more curvilinear in cross-section, indicating that the shock wave of flake removal curved outwards from the core, toward the distal side of the flake.

Histogram A type of graph that depicts a frequency distribution, such that the area between any two measures on the x-axis is proportional to the number of observations in that interval.

Horn An outgrowth of epitheleal (skin) tissue, consisting of fibrous keratin, also found in hooves and claws, that is laid down in layers over proturberances of cancellous bone on the skull.

Household cluster A spatial grouping of a house, its associated features and activity areas, pits, trash middens, graves and other associated material culture around it.

HTML A computer mark-up language used to author sites on the World Wide Web.

Hypermedia Nonlinear electronic media that make links between and within documents by hypertext and electronic buttons.

Hypertext Electronic documents that include links to other documents by clicking on key words.

Hypothesis A proposition intended to explain a phenomenon.

Hypothetico-deductive method A method of scientific verification whereby hypotheses are tested by attempts to detect consequences that must occur if the hypotheses are true.

Iconic style Relatively deliberate use of style to signal group membership and other information symbolically, as opposed to isochrestic style. See also emblematic style.

Image segmentation Methods for splitting an image into areas that share some property and contrast with their neighbours. It can be used to identify regions or their edges in either spatial analysis or grouping methods.

Impressing A finishing technique in pottery manufacture whereby the potter uses a tool (including fingernails, shell edges, and so on) to displace some of the fabric near the vessel's surface while it is still plastic or nearly leather-hard.

Incision A finishing technique in pottery manufacture whereby a narrow tool cuts into the surface, displacing material to either side, and drags along to deposit more material toward the end of a linear or curvilinear trough or valley.

Indigenous remains Artifacts and ecofacts that were created only shortly before the deposit in which they were found.

Indirect measurement Measurement that does not involve direct comparison of a phenomenon with a standard scale, but is mediated by other measures thought to be correlated with the measure of interest. Indirect measures include ratios and measure of area by multiplying length and width, but also, for example, estimates of prehistoric population size by reference to site size.

Indirect percussion In lithic production, removing flakes by striking a punch that is in contact with a core.

Induction Making general inferences or conclusions on the basis of particular evidence.

Infiltrated remains Artifacts and ecofacts that were created *after* the deposit in which they were found, but worked their way into it without necessarily leaving any obvious trace of their infiltration.

Information language A language artificially created, as in databases, to ensure unambiguous communication of information.

Integer A number that is a member of the set, (-n, ..., -2, -1, 0, 1, 2, 3, ..., n).

Interface A boundary between stratified deposits, including the surface at the top of a deposit that was later buried by other deposits, or the concave surface created by cutting a pit or by erosion.

Interpretive archaeologists (Post-processual) archaeologists who use coherence of data and context in an attempt to understand the meaning of archaeological evidence, as distinct from both the more extreme relativist, post-structural archaeologists and impiricist, processual archaeologists.

Interquartile range The range of values that includes the middle 50% of a distribution.

Interval scale A measurement scale in which values not only have inherent order, but also consistent intervals between points on the scale, so that the distance between 3 and 5, for example, is identical to the distance between 6 and 8 or 7 and 9. This makes the operations of addition and subtraction possible, but not multiplication or division.

Intrinsic attribute A characteristic that is inherent in an object, such as its length or mass or chemical composition.

Intrusive Not **indigenous** to the deposit in which found, including **infiltrated remains** created *after* the deposit.

Inverse retouch Retouch that occurs on an edge of a lithic flake visible only in the ventral view.

Isochrestic style Where several alternative ways to make a tool would all satisfy its function, this kind of style (in contrast with iconic style) represents the tool-maker's particular choices among these alternatives in a particular cultural context.

Isopleth map A map that shows "contour lines" of equal density of objects that can be counted, such as artifacts.

Isotropic A mineral that does not cause retardation of light waves in one axis of ocillation relative to the other axis, as light passes through it.

Jiggering A pottery forming technique that involves use of a rotating mold that leaves its impression on either the interior or exterior surface of the vessel, which is otherwise shaped by wheel-throwing. When the clay body is placed within a concave mold, the process is sometimes known as jollying.

Joining In the manufacture of large pottery vessels, several primary components may need to be joined. Many large, globular or spherical vessels, for example, are made by joining two bowl-like pieces along their "rims," the seam between them later being removed or hidden by beating, trimming, or a finishing technique. Where the joining leaves a fairly sharp vertical angle between the two parts, the angle is called a carination.

Jollying See Jiggering.

K-means technique A clustering method whereby the multi-dimensional space of dissimilarities is partitioned into an optimal number of groups.

Kaolinite A type of clay.

Key attribute In a database, an attribute that provides unique record identifiers in a "one" file and to which an attribute pointer can link from a "many" file.

Kingdom Highest level in the Linnaean taxonomic system, as in Animal Kingdom.

Lateral Positioned away from the midline, to left or right.

Lateral view See tangential view.

Levallois A lithic technology, common in some Middle Palaeolithic assemblages, that involved preparing cores by removing flakes bifacially around the perimeter, so that the "production face" is less convex than the "platform face," and then removing blanks from the production face.

Lexical unit A term in symbolic system, such as a word in a language.

Life assemblage Taphonomic term for the living community of animals from which fossils are derived.

Lifting That aspect of wheel-throwing a pottery vessel that involves using hands or fingers to squeeze the vessel walls thinner and higher as the body rotates.

Limit The proportion of successful trials (such as "heads" or left elements) in a very large sample.

Line graph A type of graph that depicts how the value of some attribute on the y-axis varies as a function of an attribute on the x-axis. Usually the x-axis represents time, in which case the line graph can be called a time series.

Lingual Side towards the tongue, tongue-side. Used to orient observations of teeth.

Lip The part of the vessel most distant from its base as measured along the center of the vessel walls, or the portion of the vessel that would touch the surface on which the vessel rested upside-down (or orifice down).

Lithostratigraphic units Subdivisions of the earth's crust, as defined by their physical, lithologic characteristics.

Locus A spatio-stratigraphic unit describing a spatially bounded deposit, feature, or interface.

Loess Sediment accumulated by the deposition of wind-borne particles.

Mano A "handstone" or upper grinding stone, used in conjunction with a lower "metate" (quern or grinding slab) to grind materials, such as wheat, maize, and mineral pigments.

Mass Mass is a measure of the amount of material. Unlike weight, it is independent of gravity. For example, you would weigh less on the Moon than you would on Earth, but your mass would be identical in both places. Mass is measured with a balance.

MAU Minimum animal units, a measure used in zooarchaeology, similar to the Shotwell index, that it involves dividing MNE of each element by the frequency of that element in the animal's body (s).

Mean A statistical average.

Mean square error A measure of the efficiency of a possibly biased statistic or estimate, based on squared deviations from the parameter.

Measurement An observation made by reference to a standardized scale.

Medial The middle portion. Positioned close to the mid-line (of animals), or near the middle (e.g., of a blade's length).

Median The value that lies in the middle of a distribution, such that half the distribution is less than and half greater than the value.

Metate A quern or grinding slab, the lower member of a pair of grinding stones used to grind and pulverize wheat, maize, mineral pigments, or other materials as they slide back-and-forth against one another.

MGUI Modified General Utility Index, an estimate of each bone part's usefulness for meat, marrow, and grease, adjusted to account for less useful elements that may have been attached to parts of higher value.

Minimum Number of Elements MNE is the least number of whole bones or their diagnostic parts that can account for a sample of bone fragments.

Minimum Number of Individuals See MNI.

Misclassification Incorrect assignment of an observation at the nominal or ordinal scale (attributing to the wrong class or category).

MNI The least number of whole entities that can account for a sample assemblage of fragments. The frequency of the most abundant element of a taxon.

Mode The most common value in a distribution.

Model A simplified physical or conceptual representation of reality, such as a miniature wooden replica of a building or a mathematical description of a process.

Molding In pottery manufacture, a primary forming technique that involves putting clay into something that restricts its shape. In metallurgy, a technique whereby molten metal is poured into a hollow.

Monitoring Making scheduled, periodic checks on the condition of collections, recharging exhausted silica gel and taking action on deteriorated objects, where necessary.

Monotonic Having the property of either never increasing or never decreasing in one dimension as another dimension increases.

Multidimensional scaling A statistical technique that distorts multidimensional distances (dissimilarities) so that they can be portrayed on a two-dimensional "map."

Multiplication rule In probability, the multiplication rule determines the probability of the intersection of events. That is, for two events, A and B, the probability that both A and B will occur is $p(A \text{ and } B) = p(A)p(B \mid A)$. When the two events are independent, we can simplify this to $p(A \text{ and } B) = p(A)p(B)$.

Multi-stage cluster samples Cluster samples in which, rather than examine all the objects in the clusters, we only examine a sample of them. In other words, we are sampling at at least two levels, or sub-sampling.

Multivocality The concept that a single object or artifact can have quite different meanings depending on its context.

n This is the usual abbreviation for sample size, or simply "number."

Neck A restriction of a vessel's orifice, often cylindrical in shape, above the maximum diameter of the vessel's body or shoulder.

Neutron Activation A spectroscopic method (NAA) for analysing the trace elements in a material that depends on the energies of gamma rays emitted by atoms after they have been made radioactive by neutron bombardment.

New Archaeology See Processual archaeology

NISP Simple counts of specimens or fragments.

Nominal scale A scale that employs only categories, with no inherent order.

Nonparametric test A statistical test that does not assume a distribution about a parameter, such as mean or proportion.

Normal distribution See Gaussian distribution.

Numeric A data type for interval or ratio scales.

Obsidian A glass, or super-cooled fluid, formed in some volcanic eruptions.

Ogive See Cumulative Frequency Distribution.

One-sample test A statistical test of the comparison of a sample statistic with a known or hypothetical parameter value.

Open vessel A vessel with an orifice that is large relative to the vessel's height. Bowls are open vessels.

Operational definition Indirect measurement of a phenomenon that cannot be observed directly.

Optical petrography A method for identifying minerals in thin-sections with the use of a petrographic microscope and polarized light.

Optimal Foraging Theory A version of Decision Theory, borrowed from ecologists, by which foragers' decisions are assumed to be based on informed evaluation of the relative costs and benefits of alternative foraging strategies.

Order In the Linnaean taxonomic system, Order is the taxonomic level between Class and Family.

Ordinal scale A measurement scale with categories that have inherent order, so that values can be less than or greather than others.

Orientation rule A convention to ensure the consistent description of an object's features relative to one another. For example, the rule might determine which way is "up" or what is the long axis.

Orifice The "mouth" or opening, usually at the top, of a vessel.

Orthographic projection A way of depicting an object graphically, similar to a perspective view but with lines that would be parallel on the object shown parallel on paper (i.e., no foreshortening).

Ossification The process of bone formation from cartilage by the secretions of osteoblasts along canaliculi.

Otoliths "Ear stones," concretions of calcium salts in fish's inner ear.

Overshot See Plunging termination.

Oxydized A pottery fabric fired in an oxydizing atmosphere, with abundant oxygen available to form red haematite from the iron in the clay fabric or in pigments.

Paint A material applied to the surface of another material in a thin layer, to color it. Usually it is a pigment containing a coloring agent, such as metallic oxides, and sometimes organic substances, such as oils, that make it easier to brush the pigment onto the surface or to ensure that it adheres. In some people's usage, paint includes colored slips as well as pigments.

Paleoecology The reconstruction and study of ancient environments and ecologies.

Paleosol A soil profile that is buried under subsequently deposited sediment.

Palynology The study of pollen and spores.

Paleopathology The study of ancient diseases, trauma, and genetic anomalies of humans and other animals, principally through the evidence of anomalies on bone.

Paradigmatic classification A type of systematics that employs a preconceived set of classes defined by the intersection of dimensions (attributes).

Parameter A characteristic of a population, such as a mean or proportion.

Parametric test A statistical test based on comparing statistics and parameters.

Parenchymous organs Roots, tubers, rhizomes, and corms of plants.

Patina Discoloration of the surface of an artifact as a result of long exposure to the environment. In lithics patina results from hydration of the stone's outer skin. In metal artifacts it is a thin layer of corrosion products that, once stable, may prevent further damage to the artifact.

Palynologist Someone who studies pollen abundances in sediments as evidence for paleoenvironments.

Pectoral Refering to the shoulder region in animals.

Pectoral girdle The shoulder region in animals.

Pedological units Subdivisions of the Earth's crust created by alteration of its mineral and organic materials through soil-forming processes, rather than by depositional events.

Peds Aggregates of soil or sediment particles.

Pelvic Referring to the hip region in animals.

Pelvic girdle The hip region in animals.

Percussor A tool, such as a hammerstone, used to strike flakes from a core.

Peterson Index An estimate of the number of individuals that originally belonged in a (faunal) population on the basis of surviving paired elements in a sample.

Phylum Phylum (or Division) is the second-highest level in the Linnaean taxonomic system.

Phytoliths Partial records of cell shape preserved by the deposit of silica in plant cells.

PIE Pottery Information Equivalent, a unit containing as much statistical information as a single complete vessel, but based on the sum of completeness indices of sherds. PIE values yield unbiased estimates of the proportion of each pottery type in a sampled population.

Pie chart A graph that shows relative abundances by the area of wedges in a circle.

Piercing Perforating the wall of a ceramic artifact, while still plastic, by pushing a sharpened cylindrical tool, such as an awl, through it, or drilling a hole through a thin stone or fired ceramic.

Pigment An organic or inorganic coloring material.

Pinching A primary forming technique for producing cups, small bowls, and other small vessels by squeezing a ball of the body between thumb and fingers.

Platform The surface of a core where flake detachment is initiated in flint-knapping.

Platform angle The angle between the plane of the platform and the exterior (dorsal) surface of a flake or core.

Plunging termination A distinct curvature of the distal end of a lithic flake towards the center of the core, also called an overshot.

Point of percussion The point on a platform where flake detachment is initiated in flint-knapping.

Poisson distribution The probability distribution that models the frequency of items or events in space or time.

Polarized light Light whose wave vibrations are constrained (often in a single plane) rather than in all directions.

Polish A shiny surface that often occurs macroscopically or microscopically near the used edges of lithic flakes or blades as a result of use on particular materials. See also Sickle sheen.

Polythetic definition Definition of a group on the basis of a set of characteristics none of which are necessary or sufficient criteria for membership.

Polythetic sets Groups defined by polythetic definition, so that each member shares a significant number of characteristics with each other member, but we cannot predict exactly which characteristics these will be.

Population The whole entity (real or hypothetical) about which we would like to draw conclusions on the basis of a sample.

Porcelain A hard, fine, white, translucent, and extremely nonporous ceramic fired to a temperature of 1300-1450°C.

Post-processual archaeology An archaeological approach (including interpretive and post-structural archaeology) that became prominent in the 1980s, particularly in the United Kingdom, as some archaeologists became increasingly dissatisfied with processual archaeology. Varieties of this approach variously emphasize Critical Theory, Hermeneutics, historicity, multivocality, relativism, and meaning, and eschew laws, impiricism, and simple causal explanations.

Posterior Behind, or toward the tail.

Potlid fracture A crater-like pit that sometimes occurs on the surface of lithic raw material that has been heated. It appears to result from the removal of dome-shaped flakes by marked temperature differentials in the material, so freezing and thawing may also cause potlids.

Pollen Armored gametophytes. Male gametes (sperm cells) occur inside the pollen grain or pollen tube.

Pottery A collective term for ceramic containers, such as jars, bowls, and cooking pots.

Precision The degree of agreement in a set of repeated measurements.

Primary flake See Cortical flake.

Primary forming In pottery manufacture, this is the technique used to build up the overall shape of a vessel, while secondary forming techniques are used to refine this shape and thin the walls.

Principal components analysis A type of multivariate analysis for intercorrelated or covarying data that transforms data into "components" that have maximum variance subject to being uncorrelated with one another.

Probability sample A sample, such as a random sample, selected on the basis of probability theory.

Processual archaeology Also known as the "New Archaeology," a materialist archaeological approach closely associated with the work of Lewis Binford, David Clarke, Patty Jo Watson, and others that took root in the United States and United Kingdom in the 1960s and became the dominant archaeological approach in the United States in the 1970s. Its adherents attempted to model archaeology on the physical sciences, with emphasis on laws of causation, the hypothetico-deductive method, and statistical analysis, but also borrowed from the biological sciences, with emphasis on evolution and adaptationism, ecology, equilibrium, Systems Theory, and optimal foraging theory.

Proportion The ratio of the abundance of one taxon to the total of all taxa.

Proximal The end closest to the head or body (in an animal) or closest to the point of percussion and platform (in a lithic flake or blade).

Punch A tool used in pressure flaking to direct force near the edge of a core's platform in a direction that will initiate flake detachment.

Punctate decoration Impressing pottery repeatedly with the end of a stick, bone, quill, cane, or other narrow tool.

Purposive sample A sample selected on the basis of experience and judgement rather than probability theory.

Pyramidal core In lithics, a single-platform core that tapers away from the platform as a result of flake removals.

Quartz A crystalline silicate commonly used as a lithic raw material in areas where flint and obsidian are not readily available, that does not fracture conchoidally except over very short distances, because of small flaws in the crystal structure.

Quartzite A hard material not as desirable as flint or obsidian for lithic flake production, but quite suitable for production of some heavy tools, such as choppers, axes, or hoes.

Quern A grinding slab (sometimes called Metate), the lower member of a pair of grinding stones used to grind and pulverize wheat, maize, mineral pigments, or other materials as they slide back-and-forth against one another.

Radial fissures Tiny fracture lines that sometimes radiate away from the point of percussion around the bulb on the ventral surface of a lithic flake.

Radial plane The plane that radiates from the vertical axis of a pot's (radial or bilateral) symmetry or from the longitudinal axis of a tree or branch.

Radiocarbon years A unit of the abundance of radioactive 14C in a carbon sample.

Random element sample A sample selected when each element of analytical interest in the population has an equal probability of selection.

Random sample A subset of a population such that each member of the population has an equal probability of selection.

Range The difference between the lowest and highest value in a distribution.

Rank-size analysis Study of the extent to which settlement systems fit the "rank-size rule," whereby the relationship between the size of a site and its rank is log-linear.

Ratio scale An interval scale that has a real zero point, which represents the absence of some quality, so that proportionality of magnitude is preserved.

Real In database design, a data type for continuous, ratio-scale numbers.

Record In databases, the part of a file devoted to the description of a single entity, such as an artifact, through the specification of its attributes in various "fields."

Reduced A pottery fabric fired in a "reducing" atmosphere, or one in which oxygen is denied, so that iron in the fabric tends to form magnetite (black) rather than haematite (red).

Regression A mathematical relationship whereby the value of a dependent variable can be predicted from the value of the independent variable. Where the value of one is proportional to the other, we have a *linear* regression. More complicated regressions can be curvilinear or multiple regressions.

Rejuvenated core A core that has been given a new platform once it has become difficult or impossible to remove flakes or blades from the previous one.

Relational database A structured system of data files organized by controlled redundancy (key attributes and attribute pointers).

Reliability The extent to which a measure gives the same result over different situations (usually among different observers).

Residual This has two meanings in archaeology. In archaeological site formation, it is an artifact found in a layer that was created later than the time when the artifact was made, used and deposited. In statistical analysis, it is the amount of variability in a dependent variable that is not predicted by a regression (i.e., the distance a data point lies above or below the regression line).

Resist A material that a potter applies to the surface of a vessel to prevent the adhesion of slip, paint, or glaze, so that the uncoated regions will contrast with the coated ones. A wax resist burns off during firing, while other resists are mechanically removed after application of slip or paint, but before firing.

Restricted vessel See Closed vessel.

Retardation The distance by which the slow ray lags behind the fast ray, when the former exits an anisotropic crystal, as measured in wavelengths.

Retouch Modification of the edges of a lithic blank to sharpen, dull, or reshape them to make a tool.

Richness A measure of diversity equal to the number of taxa present.

Rilling The nearly horizontal grooves and ridges that are left on wheel-thrown vessels as the potter's fingers lift the body to form the rotating vessel.

Rim The portion of a vessel closest to its orifice, and generally near the top of the vessel, or a sherd from this portion.

Ripples Wave-like undulations visible on flakes that result from transmission of a shock wave through glass or chert.

Rouletting A form of impressing whereby a cylindrical tool with a raised or intaglio pattern is rolled across the plastic or nearly leather-hard surface of a ceramic fabric. The tool can be a carved stick, gear wheel, cord-wrapped stick, or carved-stone cylinder seal.

Sample A subset of a population.

Sample assemblage Tomic term for the portion of the fossil assemblage that has been excavated or collected and then analyzed.

Sample element A member of a sample, which can be a space, a time period, or a countable item.

Sample frame See sampling frame.

Sample size The number of sample elements, or observations, in a sample.

Sampling fraction The size of the sample as expressed as a proportion of the population.

Sampling frame The set of sampling elements in a population that could conceivably be included in a sample (e.g., a list of artifacts, or a set of grid squares).

Sampling strategy The plan for selecting a sample, including the type of sample element, the sampling frame, sample size, and method of selection (e.g., random or systematic).

Scars Scars are the traces of previous flake removals in lithic reduction, and reproduce, in negative, the topography of the removed flakes' ventral surfaces.

Scatterplot A two-dimensional graph with points or icons at the intersection of dimensions on an interval or ratio scale.

Scraping Thinning the walls of a pottery vessel with a tool, such as a mollusc shell or lithic flake, held almost perpendicular to the surface while the clay is nearly leather-hard. Alternatively, using a stone tool, typically with very steep retouch, to remove fat from the interior of an animal hide.

Seasonality In a settlement system, the tendency to reside at different locations at different seasons of the year. In archaeological analysis, determination of the season or seasons of occupation at an archaeological site through study of plant and animal remains and geoarchaeological evidence.

Secondary forming techniques In pottery manufacture, secondary forming techniques are used to complete or refine the shape of a vessel after primary forming either roughed out the vessel shape, or produced the vessel's components. See Joining, Beating, Scraping, Trimming, and Turning.

Segment In lithic analysis, a segment is a section of a snapped blade. Where it preserves the striking platform, it is the proximal segment, where it includes the distal end it is a distal segment, and if it lacks both ends it is a medial segment.

Segmentation rule A convention for dividing a complex entity into parts.

Self-slip A thin slurry of clay left on the surface of a pottery vessel as a result of wetting the body during the vessel's manufacture.

Sequential sampling Increasing sample size until some predetermined criterion or boundary is met in an attempt to optimize the balance between the cost of taking larger samples and the risk of poor parameter estimates.

Settlement pattern The distribution of settlements on the landscape.

Settlement system A system that includes the distribution of settlements and nonsettlement sites, the demography of their occupants, the timing of their use or occupation, the relationships between them, and the functions of nonsettlement sites.

Settlements Sites or locations that are or were habitations or aggregates of habitations.

Sexual dimorphism Patterned difference in the size, shape, or both, of males and females of the same species.

Shannon index A measure of diversity.

Shaping That aspect of wheel-throwing a pottery vessel that involves changing the vessel diameter anywhere along its profile without significantly altering its height.

Shard See Sherd.

Sherd A fragment of a broken ceramic vessel.

Shoulder The region on a vessel above the body's maximum diameter but below the neck or rim.

Sickle element One lithic component of a composite (multi-component) reaping or harvesting knife, often made from the medial and distal segments of a backed blade, or from a long, backed flake. Often it shows sickle sheen.

Sickle sheen A distinctive polish that occurs on the edge of a blade that has been used extensively to cut grasses, and thus commonly occurs on the elements of sickles used for harvesting cereals. It is thought to result from the interaction between microscopic opal minerals in the grasses and the silica in the chert, flint, or obsidian material of the flake or blade.

Significance level The probability of a type I error, or willingness to reject a true hypothesis.

Significant digits All of the certain digits in a measurement, plus the first uncertain one.

Simple Random sample A subset of a population such that each member of the population has an equal probability of selection.

Single-link clustering Adding a new member to a group on the basis of a high coefficient of similarity to only one existing member of the group.

Sintering Process that creates a coherent mass through heating, while not melting the material.

Slab-building A primary forming technique for the construction of large or rectilinear vessels from flat pieces of the body that are joined along seams.

Slip A suspension of clay particles in water. The term is most often used to describe the application of this suspension to the surface of a pottery vessel, where it leaves a thin layer of fine clay particles adhering to all or part of the surface and fired with it.

Slow ray The component of light passing through an anisotropic mineral with the higher indiex of refraction, with a velocity retarded relative to the fast ray, and with an axis of ocillation at right angles to it.

Soft-hammer percussion Removing flakes from a lithic core by striking the platform with a billet of wood, bone, or antler.

Spall See Burin spall.

Spatial autocorrelation The tendency for items found close to one another in space to be highly similar with respect to characteristics that are not independent of location.

Spatial histogram A "stepped statistical surface" or three-dimensional histogram, used to display variations in abundance over a gridded space.

Species In the Linaean taxonomic system, species is usually the lowest taxonomic level, below Genus, except where sub-species or varieties are recognized.

Spherulites Microscopic, calcareous or other crystalline particles of spherical geometry.

Spout A neck-like appendage that restricts a secondary orifice occurring to one side of a vessel's vertical axis, and typically on the vessel's upper body or shoulder.

Stamping A kind of impressing whereby a stamp, seal, or die, specially made for the purpose, is used to displace fabric near the surface of a plastic or nearly leather-hard vessel and create a pattern or design.

Stance The position that orients a vessel the way it would typically be when resting on a surface (generally with the rim horizontal).

Stance line The line representing the horizontal plane in the illustration of pottery.

Standard deviation This is simply the square root of the variance. Its only advantage over the variance as a measure of dispersion is that it has the same units as the mean.

Standard error Often abbreviated as "SE," this is the standard deviation divided by the square root of the sample size.

Statistic An estimate of a population parameter, such as mean, standard deviation, or proportion.

Steepness of retouch The angle between the flat plane of a flake and a retouched surface. A very steep retouch is fairly close to 90°.

Stem-and-leaf plot A graph used in exploratory data analysis that mimics a histogram without losing any information.

Spores Mainly airborne reproductive bodies released by nonflowering plants, such as fungi, ferns, and mosses.

Step fracture See Step termination.

Step termination A blunt fracture at the distal end of a lithic flake that appears stair-like in cross section.

Stoneware A vitrified (glassy) and not very porous ceramic fired to a temperature of 1200-1350°C.

Stratification The physical layering of deposits and interfaces in an archaeological site or geological formation.

Stratified sample The sample that results from dividing the population into subsets and sampling each.

Stratigraphy The analytical process by which an archaeologist or geologist attempts to put sets of sediments into their correct order of deposit, or to correlate sediments in different places.

Stratum This can have two meanings in archaeology. It can be a major stratigraphic layer within an archaeological site, or it can be a subpopulation in a stratified sample.

Structure chart A diagram displaying the organization, size, and data types of fields in a database file.

Style The definition of Style varies among archaeologists. It is commonly defined as any variation in an artifact that cannot be explained by variation in material, technology, or function, but some archaeologists define it as the micro-variation caused by differences in tool-makers' individual motor habits, as a symbolic component of tool design, or as learned behavior in tool production that does not affect the utility of the finished tool.

Systematic sample The sample that results from dividing the population into portions equal to the sample size and selecting one element or observation from each.

Systematic stratified unaligned sample A spatial cluster sample that results from dividing a space into equal quadrats and selecting observations in each by the intersection of random numbers along each grid axis.

Systematics The scientific definition of the entities or categories that will be units of analysis.

t-test A parametric statistical test for medium-size samples based on the t-distribution.

Tangential A view or slice that is tangent to the vertical surface of a pot or cylindrical surface of a tree or branch.

Taphonomy The study of the processes by which living animals in the biosphere are transformed and become, through fossilization, part of the earth's rock or lithosphere.

Taphonomy The study of the processes by which living organisms in the biosphere are transformed and become, through fossilization, part of the earth's rock or lithosphere.

Target event The event in which an archaeologist is interested and wishes to date.

Taxon (pl. taxa) A taxonomic category, such as a genus or species.

Taxonomy A hierarchical form of classification based on an ordered set of distinctions or oppositions.

Technical drawings Conventionally represented graphical depictions of objects intended to communicate specific information about the objects' attributes through a graphical information language, rather than to provide a "life-like" depiction. Examples are architectural plans and lithic illustrations.

Temper A filler, such as chaff, hair, or ground stone, added to clay to reduce its plasticity, prevent a clay vessel from collapsing before or during firing, to control shrinkage during drying of the vessel, to increase porosity or resistance to crack propagation, or to alter some other characteristic, such as thermal expansion coefficient, in a ceramic vessel.

Termination Refers to the cross-sectional shape of the distal end of a flake, which can be feathered, hinged, plunging, or stepped.

Terminus post quem The earliest date that could apply to a particular event. For example, a deposit that overlies an inscribed stone or coin known to date to 200 B.C. can date no earlier than 200 B.C.

Terra-cotta A very porous and relatively coarse ceramic fired to a temperature considerably less than 1000°C.

Trace elements Chemical elements that occur in a material only in very small quantities, such as a few parts per million (ppm).

Transaction time In database jargon, the time and date when a record was entered or modified.

Transformation Expressing data in different units, typically nonlinear ones like the square root or the logarithm of the measurements, to "pull in" the high values and "stretch up" the low values.

Transverse plane The plane parallel to the stance of a pot or perpendicular to the longitudinal axis in a piece of wood.

Trend surface The result of smoothing data observations over a map. It appears somewhat like a contour map.

Trimming Sometimes called fettling, this involves cutting material away from the surface of a leather-hard pottery vessel with a tool, such as a lithic flake, held at an acute angle to the vessel surface. It is commonly used to remove traces of the seam from a joined vessel.

Tripod A set of three leg-like or knob-like supports attached individually along the circumference of the base to raise it above the surface on which the vessel rests.

Turning In construction of wooden artifacts, this is a reductive forming technique using a lathe to rotate a piece of wood and a mainly stationary chisel to remove material from it, commonly used to produce wooden bowls and cups. In pottery manufacture, it is rather similar, with long curls of fabric removed from a rotating vessel by a sharp tool.

Two-sample test A statistical comparison of two sample statistics to see if the samples are likely to have come from the same population.

Type A class or category in a typology.

Type I error This is the error of inadvertently rejecting a true hypothesis.

Type II error This is the error of failing to reject a false hypothesis.

Typology As the term is used here, a classification that is explanatory or has meaning with respect to attributes that are not intrinsic to the phenomena classified.

Ubiquity The ratio of the number of cases in which at least one example of some item is observed to the total number of cases.

Uniform distribution A probability density function whereby all potential observations within a specified range have an equal probability of occurring.

Updraft kiln An installation for firing pottery or burning lime with a firebox, in which the fuel burns, below the chimney-like chamber, in which pots, for example, are fired.

Utilitarian function Archaeologists sometimes use this term for the basic cutting, beating, containing, separating, and other physical functions of artifacts, to distinguish these from symbolic or ideological functions that they may have simultaneous with the utilitarian ones.

Validity The extent to which a measure is actually measuring what is intended. Some indirect measures, for example, have low validity.

Valid time In databases, a data type for describing a date or time relevant to the item described in a record, rather than for recording a date or time when the record was created or edited (transaction time). For example, date when an artifact was excavated is a valid time, while the date and time when its description was last modified in the database is a transaction time.

Variance The sum of the squared differences between each observation and the mean.

Varves Thin silt layers deposited (annually) on the bottoms of still lakes and ponds.

Ventral Toward the stomach (in animals) or (in lithic flakes and blades) the side that was not exposed until after removal from the core.

Verification Testing a hypothesis's ability to account for new data or evaluating its probability relative to competing hypotheses.

WAE Weighted abundance of elements is a measure used in zooarchaeology in an attempt to account for the different numbers of bones in different species by counting all nonredundant examples of s types of elements and dividing by s.

Waste In lithic analysis, waste includes debris and discarded cores. In North America, it is almost a synonym for debitage.

Weight method Really the Mass method, this is a method for quantifying archaeological remains by their mass (in grams or kilograms).

Wheel-throwing In pottery manufacture, a technique using centrifugal force to help force the body upwards and outwards from the centre of a ball of tempered clay, while the potter's hands restrict the outward motion and shape the vessel.

WHMIS Workplace Hazardous Materials Information System, which specifies the health hazzards of laboratory chemicals, safety precautions, cleanup procedures, and treatments for burns or poisoning.

Windflower A graph with bars radiating outward to show magnitudes of observations in various directions.

X-Ray Diffraction A spectroscopic method for identifying the chemical compounds that make up a material, based on

X-Ray Fluorescence A spectroscopic method (XRF) for analysing the elemental composition of a material that depends on the energy signatures of electron movements within atoms as the material is bombarded with X-rays.

Z-test A parametric statistical test based on the normal or Gaussian distribution by which means or proportions can be compared.

Index

INTERDISCIPLINARY CONTRIBUTIONS TO ARCHAEOLOGY
Chronological Listing of Volumes

CHESAPEAKE PREHISTORY
Old Traditions, New Directions
Richard J Dent, Jr.

PREHISTORIC CULTURAL ECOLOGY AND EVOLUTION
Insights from Southern Jordan
Donald O. Henry

STONE TOOLS
Theoretical Insights into Human Prehistory
Edited by George H. Odell

THE ARCHAEOLOGY OF WEALTH
Consumer Behavior in English America
James G. Gibb

STATISTICS FOR ARCHAEOLOGISTS
A Commonsense Approach
Robert D. Drennan

DARWINIAN ARCHAEOLOGIES
Edited by Herbert Donald Graham Maschner

CASE STUDIES IN ENVIRONMENTAL ARCHAEOLOGY
Edited by Elizabeth J. Reitz, Lee A. Newsom, and Sylvia J. Scudder

HUMANS AT THE END OF THE ICE AGE
The Archaeology of the Pleistocene–Holocene Transition
Edited by Lawrence Guy Straus, Berit Valentin Eriksen, Jon M. Erlandson, and David R. Yesner

VILLAGERS OF THE MAROS
A Portrait of an Early Bronze Age Society
John M. O'Shea

HUNTERS BETWEEN EAST AND WEST
The Paleolithic of Moravia
Jiří Svoboda, Vojen Ložek, and Emanuel Vlček

MISSISSIPPIAN POLITICAL ECONOMY
Jon Muller

PROJECTILE TECHNOLOGY
Edited by Heidi Knecht

A HUNTER–GATHERER LANDSCAPE
Southwest Germany in the Late Paleolithic and Mesolithic
Michael A. Jochim

FAUNAL EXTINCTION IN AN ISLAND SOCIETY
Pygmy Hippopotamus Hunters of Cyprus
Alan H. Simmons and Associates

THE ARCHAEOLOGIST'S LABORATORY
The Analysis of Archaeological Data
E. B. Banning

CPSIA information can be obtained at www.ICGtesting.com
Printed in the USA
LVOW03s1445171214

419132LV00021B/268/P